LES ROUTIERS 2004

Les Routiers Guide 2004
The Road to Good Food

Les Routiers is an association of mainly owner-managed establishements. However, membership is not automatic. Many applications are refused because every establishment displaying Les Routiers' symbol must satisfy our rigourous quality criteria.
All opinions included in the Guide entries are based upon the findings of external assessors.

Published 2003 by:
Routiers Limited
190 Earl's Court Road
London SW5 9QG
Tel: 020 7370 5113
Fax: 020 7370 4528
E-mail: info@routiers.co.uk

Book trade distribution:
Portfolio Books Ltd
Unit 5, Perivale Industrial Park
Horsenden Lane South
Greenford, Middlesex
UB6 7RL

ISBN 0-900057-19-X
Copyright © 2003 Routiers Limited

Maps © Routiers Limited 2003
Great Britain Digital Database and
Greater London Digital Data
© Cosmographics Limited.
Maps designed and produced by Cosmographics.
Reproduced by kind permission of Ordnance
Survey. Crown Copyright NC/01/365".
Including mapping content © Automobile
Association Developments Limited 2001 and
© Bartholomew Digital Database.
Greater London Map based on information derived
from satellite imagery and an original ground
survey by Cosmographics. Satellite data provided
by USGS and Infoterra Ltd.

British Library Cataloguing in Publication Data.
A catalogue record for this book is available from the British Library.

Editor:
Elizabeth Carter
Production and Design Editor:
Holly Hall
Design:
Jason Regan at Sputnik
www.sputnik.uk.com

Editorial Contributors:
Hamish Anderson
Hugo Arnold
Anna Burges-Lumsden
Alex Chambers
Colin Cheyne
Denis Cotter
Martin Greaves
David Hancock

Location Photographers:
Annie Hanson
Rebecca Harris
www.britainonview.com

Maps:
Cosmographics Limited, Watford

Printed in Italy by:
London Print and Design plc,
Warwick

Digital Prepress by:
Lithocraft Limited

For Les Routiers:
Managing Director:
Nicholas Stanley
Operations Director:
Imogen Clist
Marketing Manager:
Victoria Borrows

Managing Director, Ireland:
Margaret Jeffares
Operations Manager:
Susan O'Connor

For all enquiries and information about Les Routiers establishments telephone: +44(0)20 7370 5113 and for Les Routiers establishments in Ireland telephone: +353(0) 53 58693

www.routiers.co.uk

INTRODUCTION

When, in 1936, François de Sallieu established a network of hotels and restaurants offering French long distance drivers home cooking and fairly priced accommodation, Relais Routiers was born. Quintessentially French, this was not hospitality for affluent tourists, but decent amenities for working men and regular travellers who wanted something like the comforts of home at overnight stops the length and breadth of France. But by the 1960s, the distinctive red, white and blue Les Routiers symbol had become established as a badge of quality and value for a much wider travelling public in France. Les Routiers establishments were viewed as nationwide examples of honest, good value places to eat or stay. To the British, holidaying abroad for the first time in the early 1960s, these places were a revelation.

It is this spirit of fair value, together with honest cooking and a welcoming attitude, that inspires Les Routiers in Great Britain and Ireland. Run independently of the French organisation, we have worked hard to establish our own identity since 2000, when managing director, Nicholas Stanley and a group of investors bought the English business. Routiers in Britain has picked up on all of those elements of Routiers France that exist in, or are appropriate to, Britain - individuality, rising public interest in fresh and local food - developing a well-regarded network across the length and breadth of Britain and Ireland of small, owner run hotels, restaurants, pubs, cafes, B&Bs and bistros.

Right on course for 2004.
Our key trends stand out this time around: the importance of proper food, the use of small-scale specialist producers, genuine hospitality, and affordable good value. Throughout this Guide, we have highlighted a particular group of members, the smokeries, farms and craft food producers who have been sufficiently impressed by our local food campaign to join Les Routiers.

Defying categorisation.
The number of enlightened individuals who have begun to think in terms of offering more of what people wanted, at a price they could afford, has grown as an increasing number of chefs and hoteliers take over more and more pubs and inns. This new generation has turned long-standing traditions and concepts on their heads with establishments that, refurbished and reborn and ranging from rural chic to drop-dead glamorous, have effectively blurred the line between restaurant, hotel, and pub.

Taste, flavour and value for money.
Increasingly, the public is aware that good cooks do not always need table cloths on which to present their food and that it is the overheads — the chic plates, the crystal, the linen, and the overdose of service — that put up the prices. Many chefs are far more aware of the need for sustainable agriculture and for fresh, locally sourced ingredients. Today, there is much more inventiveness in British kitchens, with ideas stimulated by the sheer wealth of local and regional produce available.

Driving forward.
Britain's world-class landscape and culture is highlighted in an interesting blend of fully illustrated and mapped Scenic Drives. These feature glorious scenery, great houses, churches and castles, as well as Les Routiers recommended places to eat, drink and stay. In addition, Just off the Motorway takes half a dozen main arterial routes and shows the fastest way to some leisurely, carefully cooked food and first-class accommodation.

I hope you will get great pleasure from visiting the establishments listed in this Guide.

Elizabeth Carter
Editor, Les Routiers UK and Ireland Guide 2004

Introduction   Page 1

How to use this Guide   Page 5

Les Routiers Awards 2003   Page 7

Features

Local Hero - food safari in Sussex   Page 11
Vino: great wine for everyday   Page 14
Farm Shops: Focus on Surrey   Page 20
French Regional Cooking at Almeida   Page 28
Bread Making at the Village Bakery   Page 85
Cooking Food Simply at the Watermill at Little Salkeld   Page 87
Wine Appreciation at the Brackenrigg Inn, Ullswater   Page 89
Destination Wine - a tour of Wickham Vineyard   Page 120
Kitchen Wisdom - from the Yorke Arms, Ramsgill   Page 236
Anyone For a Wee Dram? - on the Scottish whisky trail   Page 276
A Sense of Place - the Harbourmaster, Aberaeron   Page 288
Ireland Revisited   Page 305
The Times they are a Changing -10 years at Cork's Cafe Paradiso   Page 314

Scenic Drives

The Magic of the Mountains and Lakes - The Lake District   Page 88
The Crown of England - South Downs & The Weald   Page 205
A Sense of Space - North Norfolk   Page 148
Wild Border Country - The Scenic Route to Edinburgh   Page 283
Ironstone Country in the Heart of England - The Historic East Midlands   Page 156
Secret Shropshire -The Welsh Marches   Page 179
The Romance of Lorna Doone Country - Exmoor National Park   Page 189
A Drive in the Heart of England - The Peak District   Page 93
All Creatures Great and Small - The Yorkshire Dales   Page 225
In Search of Avalon - The Mendips   Page 186
Shimmering Lochs and Glorious Glens - Oban to Fort William Page 267
The Wonderful Welsh Borders - Abergavenny to Hay-on-Wye   Page 297
Ulster's Loughs and Limestone Hills - Belfast Circuit   Page 353
City Charms and Mountain Grandeur - Dublin Circuit   Page 323
Glorious Galway and the Hills of Connemara - Galway Circuit Page 331
Colourful Cork and the Ring of Kerry - Cork and Killarney   Page 318

Just Off the Motorway   Page 361

Maps   Page 369

A-Z Index   Page 391

Reader Report Forms   Page 399

London Page 22

Central   Page 23
East   Page 27
North, North-West   Page 29
South-East, South-West   Page 32
West   Page 37

England Page 40

Bath, Bath & NE Somerset, Berkshire, Bristol, Buckinghamshire   Page 42
Cambridgeshire, Cheshire, Co Durham, Cornwall, Cumbria   Page 51
Derbyshire, Devon, Dorset   Page 92
Essex   Page 104
Gloucestershire   Page 108
Hampshire, Herefordshire, Hertfordshire   Page 117
Isle of Man, Isle of Wight   Page 129
Kent   Page 131
Lancashire, Leicestershire, Lincolnshire   Page 139
Manchester, Greater Manchester, Merseyside   Page 145
Norfolk, Northamptonshire, Northumberland, Nottinghamshire   Page 147
Oxfordshire, Oxford   Page 165
Rutland   Page 175
Shropshire, Somerset, Staffordshire, Suffolk, Surrey   Page 177
East Sussex, West Sussex   Page 197
Warwickshire, West Midlands, Wiltshire, Worcestershire   Page 208
East Yorkshire, North Yorkshire, West Yorkshire   Page 222

Scotland Page 248

Aberdeenshire, Argyll and Bute, South Ayrshire   Page 249
Dumfries and Galloway   Page 253
Edinburgh   Page 255
Fife   Page 262
Glasgow   Page 263
Highland   Page 268
Isle of Bute, Isle of Skye   Page 274
Moray, Perth, Perth and Kinross   Page 275
Scottish Borders, Stirling, Western Isles   Page 284

Wales Page 286

Cardiff, Carmarthenshire, Ceredigion, Conwy   Page 287
Denbighshire   Page 294
Flintshire, Gwynedd   Page 295
Monmouthshire, Newport   Page 298
Pembrokeshire, Powys   Page 299
Swansea, Vale of Glamorgan, Wrexham   Page 303

Ireland Page 304

Co Carlow, Co Cavan, Co Clare, Co Cork   Page 306
Co Donegal, Co Dublin   Page 319
Co Galway, Co Kerry, Co Kilkenny   Page 330
Co Laois, Co Limerick, Co Louth   Page 339
Co Mayo, Co Meath   Page 341
Co Roscommon, Co Tipperary   Page 342
Co Waterford, Co Westmeath, Co Wexford, Co Wicklow   Page 345
Northern Ireland - Co Antrim, Co Down, Co Fermanagh, Co Tyrone   Page 351

Channel Islands Page 355

Les Routiers Guide 2004 - De bons restaurants pas chers et pour tous was originally written for truck drivers who were looking for fairly priced hotels and restaurants. It soon became popular with travelling salesmen, French and foreign tourists.

Today, the red and blue Les Routiers sign has become a cult symbol, standing alongside the Gitannes pack and the Ricard logo as the essence of French style, and the Routiers' original concept of a warm homely welcome and affordable good value is as strong today as when it was first conceived in the 1930s.

Les Routiers Guide 2004 - De bons restaurants pas chers et pour tous is a book for travellers in France, listing simple, inexpensive roadside restaurants and hotels for both truck drivers and motorists.

To obtain a copy visit:

www.routiers.com

HOW TO USE THIS GUIDE

Finding an establishment

Les Routiers Guide 2004 is sectioned into *London, England, Scotland, Wales, Channel Islands* and *Ireland*.
London is ordered alphabetically into *Central, East, North, South* and *West*.
The countries are listed alphabetically by county, listing town and then establishment name.
There are four ways to track down an establishment or establishments.

1. If you are seeking a place in a particular area, first go to the maps at the back of the book. Once you know the locality, go to the relevant section in the book to find the entry for the hotel, restaurant, pub, B&B or cafe.

2. Page borders are colour coded for each country and also have the appropriate county written down the side so you can flick through the book and find the correct area with ease.

3. Turn to the index where both establishment names and listing towns appear in alphabetical order.

4. To find a country turn to contents on page 3.

How to read a guide entry

A sample entry is set out below.
At the top of the entry you will find the establishment's name, address, and telephone number and, if it has these, an e-mail and web site address.
Also, any symbols that may apply to the establishment; an explanation of what these symbols stand for appears after the sample entry. The middle part of the entry describes accommodation, atmosphere, food, wines and so on, while the final section gives additional statistical information and the map reference number.

TOWN, COUNTY

Establishment name 🏳 ✗
Address
Telephone: +44(0)1234 222333
E-mail: info@theestablishment.co.uk
www.theestablishment.co.uk

This is where you will find descriptive information about the restaurant, hotel, pub, B&B, or cafe: décor, accommodation, cuisine, service, wine list, points of interest.
Prices: Set price lunch £12.50. Set price dinner £14.50. House wine £10.50.
Cuisine: Modern British.
Hours: 12.00-14.00. 18.00-21.00. Closed on Sunday and bank holidays.
Rooms: 22 en suite. Double rooms from £110, single from £55.
Other points: No-smoking area. Children welcome. Credit cards not accepted.
Directions: 18 miles from Oxford on the B123. (Map4, C7)

Listing Town and County:

Because many of our establishments are in the countryside, their Listing Towns may be a town several miles away. If you are unsure of the county look the town up in the index and it will refer you to the correct page.

What the symbols represent

🏳 Accommodation
✗ Food
🍺 Pub or Bar
☕ Teashop or Café
🥄 Food Shop
🍷 Choice of Wines
📋 Set Menu

Telephone: Numbers include the international code for dialling the UK from abroad. To dial from within the UK start the number with the 0 in brackets (0); from outside the UK dial all numbers *except* the 0 in brackets (0).

Photograph: These have been supplied by the establishment.

Prices: Set meals usually consist of three courses but can include more. If a set meal has fewer or more than three courses, this is stated. Where no set lunch or dinner is offered, we give the price of the cheapest main course on the menu. House wine prices are by the bottle. Prices are meant as a guideline to the cost of a meal only. All prices include Value Added Tax (VAT). In the Ireland section, prices given are in euros.

Credit cards: Very few places fail to take credit cards; those that don't are stated here.

Children: Although we indicate whether children are welcome in a restaurant, pub, or hotel, we do not list facilities for guests with babies; we advise telephoning beforehand to sort out any particular requirements.

Hours: Times given are opening times. If food serving times differ they will be stated.

Directions: These have been supplied by the proprietor of the establishment. The map reference at the end refers to the map section at the back of the Guide.

Rooms: For establishments offering overnight accommodation the number of rooms is given, along with the lowest price for a double and single room. Where this price is per person it is indicated: Double room from £65 per person. Prices usually include breakfast. 'Dinner, B&B,' indicates that the price includes bed, breakfast *and* dinner.

Miscellaneous information

Disabled: As disabilities (and needs) vary considerably, Les Routiers has taken the decision not to note whether a place is suitable for the disabled. A more satisfactory course for all concerned is to telephone the hotel or restaurant of your choice and discuss your needs with the manager or proprietor.

Vegetarians: Most restaurants now offer some vegetarian choice. Where there is greater imaginative choice, or none at all, it is mentioned in the main body of the entry.

LES ROUTIERS AWARDS 2003

Independence and breadth of choice mark out Les Routiers' highly regarded group of members, who go through a rigorous assessment process before joining. 800 establishments have made the grade, being carefully selected for their warmth of welcome and value for money. However, there are those whose levels of hospitality and cuisine surpass our entry standards, and to those we present the following National Awards (gold) and Regional Awards (silver). These are based upon recommendations by our independent assessment team. But, with such a collection of highly individual members some are hard to categorise, offering a hard-to-define extra element, be it quality, value of hospitality. To the very best of these in each, but not every region, we have awarded a Special Award (silver).

National Awards

Hotel of the Year 2003
Langar Hall
Langar, Nottinghamshire

Restaurant of the Year 2003
Let's Eat
Perth, Perth & Kinross

Inn of the Year 2003
The Star Inn
Harome, North Yorkshire

Dining Pub of the Year 2003
Trouble House Inn
Tetbury, Gloucestershire

Café of the Year 2003
Bird on the Rock Tearoom
Clungunford, Shropshire

B&B of the Year 2003
Anchorage Guest House
St Austell, Cornwall

Wine List of the Year 2003
Penhelig Arms
Aberdyfi, Gwynedd

South & South-East England

Hotel of the Year
Nineteen,
Brighton, East Sussex

Restaurant of the Year
White Star Tavern Dining Rooms
Southampton, Hampshire

Café of the Year
Claris's Tea Room
Biddenden, Kent

Inn of the Year
Five Arrows Hotel
Waddesdon, Buckinghamshire

Dining Pub of the Year
Green Man
Partridge Green, West Sussex

Wine List of the Year
Waddesdon Manor
Waddesdon, Buckinghamshire

Special Award
Pilgrims Restaurant
Battle, East Sussex
*(for committment to local produce
and support of local producers)*

South-West England

Hotel of the Year
Stoke Lodge Hotel
Dartmouth, Devon

Restaurant of the Year
Old Passage Inn
Arlingham, Gloucestershire

B&B of the Year
Anchorage House Guest Lodge
St Austell, Cornwall

Café of the Year
Lewis' Tea Room
Dulverton, Somerset

Inn of the Year
White Hart Inn
Winchcombe, Gloucestershire

Dining Pub of the Year
Trouble House Inn
Tetbury, Gloucestershire

Wine List of the Year
Corse Lawn House Hotel
Tewkesbury, Gloucestershire

East Anglia

Hotel of the Year
Hoste Arms
Burnham Market, Norfolk

Restaurant of the Year
Water Lily Patisserie & A La Carte Restaurant
Coggeshall, Essex

B&B of the Year
Bell Inn and Hill House
Horndon on the Hill, Essex

Café of the Year
Earsham Street Café
Bungay, Suffolk

Inn of the Year
White Horse
Brancaster Staithe, Norfolk

Dining Pub of the Year
The George
Cavendish, Suffolk

Wine List of the Year
Peldon Rose
Colchester, Essex

Central England

Hotel of the Year
Langar Hall
Langar, Nottinghamshire

Restaurant of the Year
Simpson's Restaurant
Kenilworth, Warwickshire

B&B of the Year
Lower Bache House,
Leominster, Herefordshire

Cafe of the Year
Bird on the Rock Tea Room
Clungunford, Shropshire

Inn of the Year
Kings Head
Bledington, Oxfordshire

Dining Pub of the Year
Olive Branch
Clipsham, Rutland

Wine List of the Year
Red Lion
Stathern, Leicestershire

North-West England

Hotel of the Year
Netherwood Hotel
Grange-over-Sands, Cumbria

Restaurant of the Year
Jumble Room
Grasmere, Cumbria

B&B of the Year
Seatoller House
Borrowdale, Cumbria

Café (take-away) of the Year
Monsieurs
Poulton-le-Fylde, Lancashire

Inn of the Year
Drunken Duck Inn
Ambleside, Cumbria

Dining Pub of the Year
Mulberry Tree
Wigan, Lancashire

Wine List of the Year
Lovelady Sheild
Alston, Cumbria

Special Award
Aynsome Manor
Cartmel, Cumbria
*(a country house hotel based on
traditional values and no pretensions)*

North-East England

Hotel of the Year
Lastingham Grange
Lastingham, North Yorkshire

Restaurant of the Year
Shibden Mill Inn
Shibden, West Yorkshire

B&B of the Year
Mallard Grange
Ripon, North Yorkshire

Café of the Year
Golden Grid Fish Restaurant
Scarborough, North Yorkshire

Inn of the Year
The Star Inn
Harome, North Yorkshire

Dining Pub of the Year
The County
Darlington, Co Durham

Wine List of the Year
Boar's Head Hotel
Harrogate, North Yorkshire

Special Award
North Beach Café
Whitby, North Yorkshire
*(courageous development - the rescue
of a derelict, art deco seaside café)*

London

Hotel of the Year
Harlingford
WC1

Restaurant of the Year
Wodka
W8

Café of the Year
Café in the Crypt
WC2

Dining Pub of the Year
The Engineer
NW1

Wine List of the Year
Whistler Restaurant, Tate Britain
SW1

Scotland

Hotel of the Year
Lodge on Loch Lomond
Luss, Argyll & Bute

Restaurant of the Year
Let's Eat
Perth, Perth & Kinross

B&B of the Year
Cosses Country House
Ballantrae, South Ayrshire

Café of the Year
Station Restaurant
Ballater, Aberdeenshire

Inn of the Year
Plockton Hotel
Plockton, Highland

Wine List of the Year
Duck's at le Marche Noir
Edinburgh

Special Award
Trigony House Hotel
Dumfries, Dumfries & Galloway
*(good value country house putting the emphasis on
authentic ingredients)*

Ireland

Hotel of the Year
Kelly's Resort Hotel
Rosslare, Co Wexford

Restaurant of the Year
Old Presbytery Restaurant
Killarney, Co Kerry

Guesthouse of the Year
Killeen House
Galway, Co Galway

Guesthouse with Restaurant of the Year
Caragh Lodge
Killorglin, Co Kerry

Café of the Year
Farmgate Café
Cork City, Co Cork

Dining Pub of the Year
McAlpin's Suir Inn
Cheekpoint, Co Waterford

Wine List of the Year
Shanahan's on the Green
Dublin City, Co Dublin

Special Award
Croom Mills
Croom, Co Limerick
*(hard to categorise - a visitors' centre
that excels at all it does)*

Wales

Hotel of the Year
Bear Hotel
Crickhowell, Powys

Restaurant of the Year
Welcome to Town Country Bistro & Bar
Llanrhidian, Swansea

B&B of the Year
Barratts Restaurant at Ty'n Rhyl
Rhyll, Denbighshire

Inn of the Year
The Harbourmaster Hotel
Aberaeron, Ceredigion

Dining Pub of the Year
Kinmel Arms
St George, Conwy

Wine List of the Year
Penhelig Arms
Aberdyfi, Gwynedd

Special Award
Dunoon Hotel
Llandudno, Conwy
*(young new owners after 25 years, yet keeping
old fashioned traditions alive in a seaside resort)*

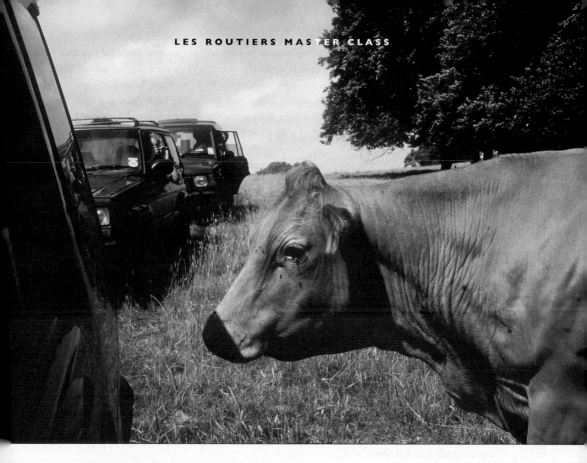

*Joining Toby Peters as he leads his first
Food Safari in deepest Sussex,
Alex Chambers discovers it is not just
about healthy food, but making the
community a nicer place for us all to live.*

LOCAL HERO

Toby Peters' enthusiasm and passion for what he does is infectious. His frustration at seeing people in supermarkets with their cookbooks open looking for food that has no bearing to that season is palpable. Time and again he stresses the importance of investing back into the local economy, towns and villages. "I believe that working with local producers is essential if we are to provide a sustainable community, environment and future for our children. It is the only route to see the spend on food go back to the farming community."

He has owned that Aladdin's cave of a deli-cum-restaurant, the Food Rooms in Battle for two and a half years, and in 2002 opened a second restaurant, the Pilgrim's Restaurant. Both establishments use food sourced from only a few miles away: naturally reared meat, poultry, fresh fish, award winning local cheeses, seasonal vegetable and fruit.

Building up a network of some 100 local producers, farmers and fishermen, has proved a painstaking process, as Toby has had to ensure that they share the same integrity and commitment, to want to "stop filling our children with additives, chemicals and food that has been unnaturally tampered with."

His idea for regular two-day Food Safaris teaching people to be brave about local, seasonal produce (one day visiting producers, the next day learning how to cook the produce) is a natural progression. Sharing this vision is Tom Kine, a chef with a CV that takes in working for Rick Stein, the River Café, and cooking for Jamie Oliver's wedding, and Ruth Edwards, who runs the nearby Cutting Edge Food and Wine School, which provides our overnight accommodation. Theirs is a journey of education and the diverse bunch that meets for this inaugural Food Safari is full of willing pupils.

It is a glorious day as we pile into two Landrovers and drive through the Sussex countryside; our first stop is Northiam Dairy, a wonderfully ramshackle farm run by fourth generation farmer Rupert Cyster. His land has been organic for five years and the herd will be certified organic by 2004.

We walk through the non-plussed Holstein cows with their full udders and are herded into the farm kitchen where the full splendour of the farm's produce is laid out: yogurts, crème fraîche, cream cheeses, drinking yogurt, and milks of varying fatness. We taste the almost sweet yoghurt, the thick, sour cream cheese, and the wonderfully creamy milk, and are unanimous in our praise. When someone mentions Philadelphia as a cream cheese it is rather like placing a Big Mac next to a fillet steak; this produce is quite unlike anything you will find in a supermarket and quite delicious.

All the while the engaging Rupert, his words spilling out, explains how it is all made. His enthusiasm, his obvious love for the countryside, and his natural disdain for supermarkets, make us eager listeners. The final act was Rupert showing us his homegrown beer, a delicious hoppy ale that was tested with some vigour that evening!

Next stop, R & J Salads in Appledore, an extraordinary place run by the larger-than-life Mrs Smith, and known to many chefs as a Mecca for salad leaves; indeed, they only sell to chefs. We are shown six tunnels full of the most diverse range of plants, truly mind boggling as we are treated to a fascinating tour of marjoram, spinach, fennel, rocket, mustard leaves, oregano, cress, thyme, coriander, mint, tarragon, sage. We taste the delicious blue borage flower, sweet romaine lettuce, mouth-burning listertian, bitter chicory, and many more – a great experience amid a realisation that our supermarket bought salads are really rather boring!

At Andy and Ann Clarke's idyllic Park Farm in Hawkhurst we are offered a deliciously simple lunch of homemade bread and Wigmore cheese, washed down with local raspberry and apple juice. This farm is a magnificent place, where integrity shines through in the production of free-range beef, lamb, pork and eggs. The meat is slaughtered and eaten locally, as they own a butcher's shop in Hawkhurst. Andy points to a neighbouring farm where the grass is a uniform dark green from the use of nitrogen and compares it to his lighter coloured grass, everywhere pockmarked with the vibrant colour of wildflowers, noting that "the wealth of natural grasses and wildflower in the diet adds to the flavour of the meat".

On to Hastings, whose beach fleet is the largest in Europe and rated as one of the most environmentally friendly in the world. But the seaside town has an air of desolation about it, extending to the beach where rusting fishing boats are pulled high up on the pebbles, sharing space with the skeletal remains of older boats. Appropriately enough, the weather takes a turn for the worst as it clouds over, the wind whipping through the rigging and sending us shivering to the building owned by Cinque Port Fisheries.

Here we find a trove of iced boxes: turbot, lemon sole, sea bass, herring, cod, plaice, monkfish, squid, lobster, all caught that day. The catch was actually relatively small as, due to the weather, most of the flat-bottomed boats couldn't get off the beach. Sadly, most of this superb fish will go abroad for, as a nation,

The cost of the two-day Food Safari costs £249 per person and includes a simple lunch at Park Farm, transport around the various locations, dinner at Pilgrims Restaurant, overnight accommodation at the Cutting Edge Cookery School, and the following day's day cookery course and lunch. For more information contact The Food Rooms, The Chapel, 53-55 Battle High Street, Battle, East Sussex. Telephone: 01424 775537

we are very unadventurous fish eaters. But a highlight of the day, for me, was discovering that Cinque Port naturally smoke local fish, be it salmon, kippers, haddock and, best of all, prawns; absolutely delicious and highly recommended.

With dusk gathering we had run out of time – the original plan to take in a cheese dairy or a fruit farm abandoned in favour of dinner at The Pilgrim's Restaurant. This classic white and black timbered building is almost unchanged since it was built in 1348 as pilgrims' lodgings. Stooping through the front door we were offered a sumptuous meal of smoked venison and locally caught monkfish. Finally, we left for Ruth Edward's house a few miles up the road to get some well-earned shuteye.

Waking up the next morning we realise the gloriousness of our situation, Ruth's splendid house is perched on a hill overlooking a stunning vineyard, a paddock of horses, and rolling hills. Decked out in our aprons, Tom Kine takes over the reigns and, using produce picked up from yesterday's visits, teaches us to cook mouth watering dishes while keeping it relatively straightforward and simple. Using these local, seasonal ingredients he delivers astonishingly original and scrumptious flavours, commenting that "six million people a year are affected by diet related illnesses".

The food we cook is fantastic. Starters of squid and prawns with capers, sage and herb vinegar served with lentil salad, mixed leaves, anchovy and rosemary sauce, and a roast beetroot salad with goats' cheese and mixed leaves, for example. Amongst main course were sea bass stuffed with summer herbs on layered potatoes and fennel with marjoram salmoriglio, and marinated butterflied leg of lamb with rosemary, lemon and garlic with salsa verde, followed by lemon cream pots with raspberries. All washed down by the wine grown a few feet from where we were eating! Absolutely blissful!

The food safari was a wonderful experience – my eyes have been opened to a new world of natural, healthy eating. What most struck me was the passion shown by everyone involved, the deep love, integrity and concern for community and jobs and a determination to see that spending on food contributes to a sustainable economy where all can live and prosper.

VINO: GREAT WINE FOR EVERYDAY

"The inspiration to write Vino stemmed not from my work within restaurants, but everyday wine drinkers - mostly thirsty friends," reveals Hamish Anderson. In this extract, he explains his philosophy behind the book.

The UK has an unrivalled selection of wine on its shelves. Unlike most major wine consuming countries we have only a fledgling national industry. We are thus happy to trawl the world in search of our bottles. The up side of this is the afore-mentioned diversity in our shops. The downside is the consumers' confusion. Go to Australia and the average wine drinker seems far more educated than the UK. However, all the thirsty local in Oz needs do is learn five or six grape varieties and a few premium-growing areas, within their country, and a lifetime of interesting drinking is assured. Wines from every important producing country on the planet confront the drinker in the UK. It is no wonder that most throw up their hands in defeat and stick to what they perceive are safe bets. This book aims to make you more confident and adventurous when selecting a bottle, whether for a dinner party or a casual drink. The information is broken down into small digestible entries, each readable in its own right. At the end of each entry are a series of links to encourage experimentation that is not just a wild stab in the dark.

Working at the Tate Gallery, whose cellar has been famous for years, I am able to indulge my passion by choosing the wines to go on the list. After helping set up the restaurants at Tate Modern, however, I soon realised that whilst people's enthusiasm for food had increased hugely, their knowledge of wine had remained fairly static. Each and every one of us is drinking more and more wine each year, yet although we are prepared to try different foods without prompting, the same is not yet true for wine. At present, there is an awful trend towards substituting the individual for the bland, as formulaic wines are made to fit a particular price bracket. Thus we now have a range of wines from around the world that all taste the same. Just as food offers you more than just the basic fuel to walk around each day, so can wine. Wine should be riding on the back of the explosion of interest in cooking. Many people are now happy to slavishly follow cookbook recipes and have heated arguments over whether Delia or Nigella has a better béarnaise sauce, and yet we still go out to eat wonderful meals and drink wines with all the character of a pre-packaged frozen dinner.

I am not trying to turn you into an underground organic wine activist or a crusader against the big wine sellers. What I really want is for you to get the most out of wine, and I believe that all you need to achieve this is a small foundation of knowledge and the confidence to experiment.

I am often asked what my top tip is when buying a wine. There is, I am afraid, no holy grail; it is simply not possible to give you ten insider points and solve all your purchasing problems. However, there is one thing I would ask you to remember above all. Grape varieties or regions do not make fine wine, wine makers and producers do. Some areas and grapes have a head start and are predisposed towards making better wine; however, it is up to man to realise this potential.

New World Label

First of all look for a grape variety; this will usually be displayed prominently. Grape variety is likely to be the defining factor in the wine's taste, so you should use this as your entry point to the book. If it is not immediately clear what grapes are being used, have a look at the back label - these are usually rammed full of information. You might also find information on whether the wine has been matured in oak barrels or not. Turning to the front label, we can discover more about the region. Use the opposite label as an example. You'll be able to look up the Napa Valley in the USA section and learn that it is California's finest region. The producer is all-important. Using the example, unfortunately, it is not enough just to remember you have enjoyed a Zinfandel from the Napa Valley. I have tasted plenty of poor Zinfandels from the region; the reason this wine is good is because of Frog's Leap.

Old World Label

Europe is altogether more complicated, I am afraid, as regional identity is the key. Europe has thousands of geographically designated areas that taste different, yet helpful information like what grape the wine is made from is not placed on the label. This is incredibly frustrating in one sense as you, the consumer, are often making a blind guess. However, spend a little time getting to know what regions you enjoy and you'll be glad of this system. The diversity of taste on offer is vast. The second spanner to throw into the works is the law that governs a wine's production. In the New World pretty much anything goes. In Europe, winemakers are restricted by a set of rules. For example, Pouilly-Fumé can only be produced from one grape and restrictions on production apply. Every country has a grading system; I will discuss each one more specifically in the country section. You need to be aware of the laws in place but generally, to my mind, they fail. Ever wondered why one Pouilly-Fumé tastes great and the next so poor? It is back to the producer I am afraid. Pouilly-Fumé is governed by France's strictest set of laws, yet much of the wine is poor; the reason the one adjacent is good is down to Domaine de Saint-Laurent-l'Abbaye, the producer.

Hamish Anderson is the sommelier at the Whistler Restaurant, Tate Britain, London SW1. His book Vino: Great Wine for Everyday Life, is published by Century.
Reprinted by permission of The Random House Group Ltd.

St Sampson, Channel Islands

THE WINE FOR FISH LOVERS

Seafood is a great restaurant choice and Muscadet Sur Lie its classic partner, yet they make a very contemporary marriage.

Certain things in life are true: fish and chips taste better eaten from newspaper; fish tastes great accompanied by a chilled glass of Muscadet Sur Lie.

OK, there is possibly an element of sentimentality in the first of those statements, but the second stands up to the cold light of logic. Why? Muscadet Sur Lie is a light wine often with a fine sparkle on the tongue. The nose is fresh and slightly salty like a sea wind in winter. The palate is crisp with lemon-style acidity and nuances of yeast and almonds. Add all this together and you have a delicate and refreshing glassful.

As for piscatorial partners, what fish doesn't enjoy a boost from a squirt of lemon and a sprinkle of salt? The affinity between fish and

yeast, be that in a beer batter or fried in breadcrumbs, has spawned a whole genre of cookery. That light spritz will also bring a little zip to cream or mayonnaise based sauces. This wine is neither too light and watery, nor too heavy and overpowering.

Muscadet Sur Lie is made from the Melon de Bourgogne grape. Although this grape originates in Burgundy, it is now grown almost exclusively in the Nantes French region where Muscadet Sur Lie is produced. Nowadays, as wine seems to be becoming increasingly homogenous, it is particularly satisfying to find a wine which remains unique.

The Sur Lie ageing process means that the wine spends more time in contact with the yeast 'lie' or lees. This is the white foamy mass of yeast particles that rise naturally to the top of fermenting wine and make the vats look like enormous bubble baths. Many producers actively stir the lees through the fermenting wine increasing its effect. Then throughout the Winter barrels are left with the lees still intact before being bottled in the Spring. This process dramatically increases the yeasty flavour and structure of the wine.

Seafood Week, 1st-8th October 2004
Muscadet Sur Lie is a keen supporter of Seafood Week as it ensures lots of opportunities for restaurants and shops to partner fish and shellfish with Muscadet Sur Lie.

Sur Lie there is no better wine for entertaining than Muscadet

As fresh and invigorating as a breath of sea air, Muscadet Sur Lie adds zest to any occasion. Matured for longer for an uplifting spritz, this maritime wine from the mouth of the Loire is perfectly entertaining, without the performance.

Muscadet Sur Lie

FEELING GOOD
WITH SEAFOOD

Seafood has a feel good factor, with special health, romantic and sexy properties that make it the ideal meal, say the Sea Fish Industry Authority (Seafish).

Fish represents the Earth's largest stock of wild food – the term 'wild' applying to all seafood except for the small, but rapidly growing proportion that are farmed. Although no one knows for sure how far back the history of seafood stretches, the appreciation and consumption of seafood certainly dates back to early times. By the Middle Ages, the demand for seafood was enormous, stimulated by the Catholic Church's insistence on meatless days.

Today, it is without doubt that fish and chips constitute one of the national dishes of Great Britain. Fried fish was an established street food in London in the 1830s, and Charles Dickens mentioned a 'fried fish warehouse' in Oliver Twist (published in installments between 1837-9) when the fish was sold with a chunk of bread.

Seafish was established in 1981 to work with all sectors of the UK seafood industry – fishermen, processors, wholesalers, importers, exporters, seafood farmers, fish friers, caterers and retailers, promoting seafood to consumers and to work with the industry to raise standards, improve efficiency and secure a sustainable future. Seafish carries out a number of activities on an annual basis, from awarding the best fish and chip shop in the UK to giving quality awards to seafood processor companies. Information about their activities can be found at their website: www.seafish.co.uk.

Seafish also actively promote the healthy qualities of seafood – one of the quickest and tastiest ways of obtaining protein, vitamins B, A and D and minerals, including calcium, and magnesium. Seafood is good for hormonal health, skin and the immune and cardiovascular systems and oil-rich fish is high in Omega 3 fatty acids that have been proved to lower blood cholesterol levels, reducing the risk of a heart attack or stroke.

The launch of Seafood Week in 2001 was seen by Seafish as a more direct means of promoting seafood and its health benefits. The now annual Seafood Week, supported in 2002 and 2003 by Les Routiers, is a chance to broaden tastes and experiment.

Yet concern about the depletion of our ocean larder as seafood becomes an increasingly important part of our diet, an issue Seafish addresses full on. This year, Seafood Week will not only be promoting the healthy properties and romantic connotations of seafood, but also encourage consumers to try different varieties of seafood. This, in turn, will encourage us to reduce the pressure on the supply of more traditional species.

www.seafish.co.uk   www.seafoodweek.co.uk
Visitors to the website will see that as well as providing suggestions for activities that the seafood industry can get involved in during Seafood Week, they can download files containing new recipes, details of the best seafood pubs, restaurants, and fish and chip shops in the UK.

Three very different Surrey farm shops reveal the diversity and commitment behind the growing farm shop movement.

FARM SHOPS:
FOCUS ON SURREY

Les Routiers believes passionately in the local food movement. It is a movement born out of widespread concern about the safety of the food we eat along with a growing consensus that locally produced food is invariably fresher, healthier and tastes better. With our promotion and accreditation of Farm Retail Association farm shops, we raise their profile in the community and encourage local trade. Our goal is simple: to play an active part in reviving local methods of food production and to encourage everyone to think once again of the men and women who produce our food as craftsmen.

On this page we focus on three Les Routiers accredited farm shops in Surrey as well as listing other farm shops across Britain, and where they can be found in this Guide

Garsons Farm

Winterdown Road, Esher, Surrey KT10 8LS
Telephone: +44 (0)1372 464778
www.garson-farm.co.uk

The old farm barn has been converted into an expansive rural shop selling real food. Although an extensive PYO operation underpins Garsons, it is backed by a philosophy of selling traditionally produced food from small independent suppliers. There's a superb range of fresh seasonal fruit and vegetables complemented by free-range eggs produced on the farm and a selection of top quality free-range meat from a local supplier. Fresh bread, handmade cakes, a selection of cow, sheep and goats' milk cheeses, ice cream from Hill Farm and Salcombe Dairies and a range of handmade soups, pies and pâtés are always available. Garsons Restaurant, situated in the Garden Centre, delivers homestyle cooking and good homemade cakes.

Other points: Garden centre. Swimming pool shop. Pet foods. Cut flowers.

Hours: Daily 09.00-18.00

Directions: A244 between Esher/Hersham, turn at Princess Alice Hospice to West End Lane. Right into Winterdown Road by Prince of Wales pub.

Priory Farm

Sandy Lane, Nutfield, Surrey RH1 4EJ
Telephone: +44(0)1737 823304
www.prioryfarm.co.uk

The Shinner family manage their farm with environmental care and they take pride in the production of quality crops. Until 1992, Priory Farm was a traditional working farm, but is now run as an extensive PYO business within a multi-site retail and leisure operation covering some 180 acres on Lower Greensand on the southern slopes of the North Downs. Three fishing lakes, a farm shop, plant centre, café with terrace and picnic area are set in a restored complex of Victorian stone buildings and barns. The shop has all the usual soft fruit and vegetables, plus meat from traceable farms including locally reared pork and lamb, free range chickens, home cured bacon, and game available in season. Freshly baked pastries, pies and quiches come from the farm kitchens and there is a range of delicatessen and grocery produce, including English farmhouse cheeses, luxury ice creams and goat and sheep milk products.

Other points: Car park. Picnic area.

Hours: 09.00-17.30 Monday-Saturday. 11.00-17.00 on Sunday.

Directions: Exit 6/M25, off A25 between Redhill and Godstone.

Secretts

Hurst Farm, Chapel Lane, Milford, Surrey
Telephone: +44 (0)1483 426543
www.secretts.co.uk

A top quality PYO operation that has pulled together a vast array of locally produced speciality foods to sell in its farm shop. Vegetables and salads are picked fresh every day, the farm range takes in strawberries, asparagus, bunched beetroot, baby courgettes (with flowers), spring onions, coriander, spinach, baby bunched carrots, broad and runner beans and sweetcorn. Other sections include a country bakery, chocolates, ice creams, groceries, delicatessen, and a cheese counter with more than 150 British and continental cheeses. Specialities extend to Halloween toffee in the autumn and whole hams, free-range turkeys and puddings at Christmas. A 1930s style teashop adjoins the shop with an inventive menu of sandwiches, country lunches, pâtés and teatime cakes. There are regular cookery demonstrations using the best of the season's produce and the southwest Surrey Farmer's Market is held at the farm on the third Sunday of every month.

Other points: Car park. Play area. Picnic area.
Flower shop. Garden centre.
Easy access/facilities for disabled.
Hours: 09.00-17.30 Monday-Saturday.
11.00-17.00 on Sunday. PYO open June-September.
For crop availability phone 01483 520556.
Directions: A3, Milford junction. At roundabout, direction Milford, at second traffic lights filter left. Look for signs on the left.

More Farm Retail Association and Les Routiers approved farmshops:

Grays, Wokingham, Berkshire	page 46
Church Farm Organics, Thurstaston, Wirral, Cheshire	page 59
Castletown Farm Shop, Rockcliffe, Cumbria	page 84
Chatsworth Farm Shop, Pilsley, Bakewell, Derbyshire	page 92
Pamphill Dairy Farm Shop, Pamphill, Wimbourne, Dorset	page 102
Over Farm Market, Over, Gloucestershire	page 112
Durleighmarsh Farm Shop, Durleighmarsh, Petersfield, Hampshire	page 119
The Barn Yard, Upchurch, Sittingbourne, Kent	page 137
Brockbushes Fruit Farm, Corbridge, Northumberland	page 162
North Acomb Farm, Stocksfield-on-Tyne, Northumberland	page 162
Millets Farm Centre, Garford, Abingdon, Oxfordshire	page 165
Rectory Farm, Staunton St John, Oxfordshire	page 173
Lashbrook Unique Country Pork, Bishopwood, Chard, Somerset	page 185
Essington Fruit Farm, Essington, Wolverhampton, Staffordshire	page 188
Hollow Trees Farm Shop, Semer, Suffolk	page 194
Tully's Farm, Turners Hill, West Sussex	page 207
The Fruit Garden, Peterston-super-Ely, Cardiff	page 287

LONDON

10 Manchester Street ★ ◈

10 Manchester Street, London W1V 4DG
Telephone: +44(0)20 7486 6669
stay@10manchesterstreet.fsnet.co.uk
www.10manchesterstreet.com

The central location, within walking distance of
Marylebone High Street, Oxford Street and Bond
Street, as well as the Wallace Collection and Madame
Tussaud's, will appeal to those looking for a stylish
hotel without having to pay through the nose. Indeed,
the aim of this boutique town house is just that: to
provide affordable accommodation with a friendly, no-
frills service. The fine, early 20th century building was
completely refurbished in the late 1990s, and the
spacious ground-floor sitting room sets the tone with
its comfortable sofas, soft lamps and laid-back air.
Double rooms are a good size and have fairly high
ceilings, fluffy bathrobes, mini-sound systems and
mini-refrigerators, satellite TV, and all the usual hotel
extras such as tea trays and trouser press. Single
bedrooms are compact but well designed, making good
use of the space available; there are also nine suites
with separate sitting rooms. Only a continental
breakfast is served, but there are plenty of cafés, bars
and restaurants within walking distance.

Prices: B&B.
Rooms: 46 en suite. Double room £120, single £95.
Other Points: No-smoking area. Children welcome.
Directions: 5 minutes walk from Baker Street tube station, off
Dorset Street. (Map 2, B5)

Cafe Bagatelle ✕

Wallace Collection, Hertford House,
Manchester Square, London W1U 3BN
Telephone: +44(0)20 7563 9505
wallace@eliance.co.uk

The bustling room couldn't be more relaxing or
evocative; the glazing over of the inner central
courtyard (formerly the sculpture garden) has created a
dramatic café-cum-brasserie filled with palms, urns and
white furniture, part of the revamp of the Wallace
Collection in 2000. Well-spaced tables are a plus, as is
an unusual wine list which brings together talented
winemakers throughout the world, with wines by the
glass starting at £3.50. Overall, there's a strong
Mediterranean feel to the food, a theme that's picked
up by the excellent fixed-price lunch menu that is quite
a bargain for central London. Start off by tucking your
napkin in and enjoying a goats' cheese and beetroot
tart with roast pepper tapénade, or a crispy duck and
watercress salad with vanilla apples. Then think about
garlic and rosemary roast rump of lamb accompanied
by sautéed potatoes and an artichoke and olive jus, or
the fillet of baby lemon sole wrapped in Bayonne ham,
and served with fennel and potato gratin. For pudding,
the coconut rice pudding brûlée with chocolate
shortbread will make you very happy.

Prices: Set lunch £17.50, £13.50 (2 courses).
Hours: 10.00-17.00. Sunday 12.00-17.00. Closed Bank Holidays.
Cuisine: Modern European.
Other Points: Totally non smoking. Children welcome.
Directions: Nearest tube: Bond Street. (Map 2, C5)

Prices: Main course from £6.75.
House wine £10.50.
Hours: Monday-Wednesday: 10.00-20.00.
Thursday-Saturday: 10.00-23.00. Sunday:
12.00-20.00. Closed 25 December and
during the day on Good Friday.
Cuisine: Traditional English.
Other Points: No-smoking area.
Children welcome. Credit cards
not accepted.
Directions: Nearest Tubes: Charing
Cross, Leicester Square. (Map 2, C7)

Café in the Crypt ★ ◈ ✕

Crypt of St Martin-in-the-Fields, Duncannon Street, London WC2N 4JJ
Telephone: +44(0)20 7839 4342
www.stmartin-in-the-fields.org

A brilliant location with Trafalgar Square and the theatre district on the
doorstep, this terrific-value café makes a great escape from the West End
crush. The crypt of the landmark church (built in 1726) is a dramatic
setting, with brick-vaulted ceilings, pillars, and gravestones on the floor.
Open from 10am until 8pm (11pm Thursday, Friday and Saturday
evenings), this is worth remembering when looking for somewhere quick
and inexpensive pre or post theatre, say, or before catching a train from
Charing Cross. The extensive buffet display seems to offer an endless
choice of pick-and-mix salads, soup, daily changing meat and fish dishes,
with avocado and tuna mayonnaise, perhaps, or papaya filled with salt
beef, peach and buffalo mozzarella salad, and stuffed peppers, among
popular choices. There's also roast leg of lamb steak with a rosemary
sauce and minted apricots, served with fresh vegetables, or wild
mushroom pasta bake with a Stilton glaze. Sandwiches include a good egg
mayonnaise with chives and corn salad, puddings take in apple and oat
crumble, and there are some lovely homemade cakes. Everything is served
in generous portions and tables are well spaced. The short, well-chosen
wine list is clearly annotated and very reasonably priced.

Ebury Wine Bar and Restaurant 🍴🍷📱✕

139 Ebury Street, London SW1W 9QU
Telephone: +44(0)20 7730 5447
nigel@eburywinebars.co.uk

One of the last remaining wine bars in London and a real classic. Two bars, both with close-packed wooden tables backed up by waiter service, with seats at the bars for eating and drinking, and lots of prints on the walls, define a look and formula that, basically, hasn't changed for years. The wine list is tremendous, and is one of the reasons for the ongoing success of the place; its globally diversified, very accessible, and there is a great house selection at keen prices with a good range by the glass. Two or three sittings per table for lunch, crowded in the early evening, is all par for the course. There's an excellent value set lunch, and bar snacks ranging from bread, houmus and roasted garlic to Thai fishcakes with soy mirin sauce and oriental dip, are available all day. The carte of contemporary brasserie fare updates some traditional comfort food: pan-fried skate with samphire and tomato salad, for example, or grilled calf's liver, cold potato and roasted pepper salad, and pork and leek sausages with pomegranate and onion jus. Enterprising puddings include assiette of lemon, and chocolate blancmange with cappuccino sauce.

Prices: Set menu £8. Main course from £9.50. House wine £12.
Hours: 12.00-14.45. 18.00-22.30. 12.00-15.00.
18.00-22.00 on Sunday. Closed Christmas-New Year.
Cuisine: Modern European.
Other Points: Children welcome.
Directions: Ten minutes walk from Victoria British Rail and Victoria tube, or Sloane Square tube. (Map 2, E5)

Food for Thought ✕

31 Neal Street, Covent Garden ,
London WC2H 9PR
Telephone: +44(0)20 7836 9072/0239

Vanessa Garrett has clocked up 24 years with Food for Thought. She continues the very high standards that have made this bustling, unpretentious vegetarian restaurant a London landmark, refusing to be 'processed, packaged, micro-waved, deep-frozen or standardized in any way'. The 18th-century listed building was once used as a banana-ripening warehouse (the hands of fruit were hung in what are now intimate seating alcoves). The basement may be cramped, the lunchtime queues legendary, but, for the price, this is still some of the best vegetarian food in town. They bake their own bread daily and hand select fresh fruit and vegetables from markets such as New Covent Garden and Borough. Flavour is everything, whether in a summer mushroom and leek soup, or a Venetian feast of roasted Mediterranean vegetables in a light tomato and basil sauce and topped with a fresh herb polenta. Long-time favourites on a menu that changes daily include vegetable stir-fry in a tamarind and ginger sauce served with brown rice, and there are wonderful cakes and puddings such as sugar-free carrot cake with apple glaze. They do takeaway from the cramped ground floor counter. Unlicensed, but you can bring your own wine and there's no corkage charge.

Prices: Set lunch and dinner £9.90. Main course from £4.
Unlicenced, BYO's welcome, no corkage charged.
Hours: 12.00-20.30, Sunday until 17.00.
Closed Easter Sunday, 24-26 December and 1 January.
Cuisine: Vegetarian.
Other Points: Totally no smoking. Children welcome.
Directions: Covent Garden tube. Head due north form exit, approximately three minutes walk down Neal Street on the left hand side. (Map 2, C7)

Fung Shing 🍴🍷✕

15 Lisle Street, London WC2H 7BE
Telephone: +44(0)20 7437 1539
www.fungshing.com

This venerable old timer is considered to be one of Chinatown's best Cantonese restaurants, widely acknowledge as one of the few places where truly authentic Cantonese food can be had. Starters might include steamed scallops in their shells with garlic and soya sauce and soft shelled crab with chilli and garlic is also worth a try. More unusual ingredients are available at a price, for example stir-fried crispy pigeon, braised double boiled shark's fin in hot pot, and braised abalone. Stewed belly pork with yam in hot pot yields yams with the required perfumed flavour and that truly soft, mushy texture that comes from long cooking, and belly pork that is as tender as could be. Other choices run to steamed eel with black bean sauce, braised chicken on the bone with clam sauce in hot pot, and pan-fried turbot with ginger and garlic sauce. Set menus offer a reassuringly familiar version of Cantonese cooking, but careful choosing amongst the chef specials will deliver a more ambitious, rewarding meal at a similar price. The wine list covers most bases, and includes a fine wine selection.

Prices: Set menu £17. Main course from £8. House wine £14.50.
Hours: 12.00-23.30. Closed 24-26 December. Open from 18.00 on Bank Holidays.
Cuisine: Traditional Cantonese.
Other Points: Children welcome. Two private rooms avaiable.
Directions: Nearest tube: Leicester Square. Behind the Empire cinema. (Map 2, C6)

Harlingford ★ ◇

61-63 Cartwright Gardens, London WC1H 9EL
Telephone: +44(0)20 7387 1551
book@harlingfordhotel.com
www.harlingfordhotel.com

Cartwright Gardens is wrapped around a residents' garden, in a crescent where all the five-floored Georgian town houses have preserved their 196-year-old character. The Harlingford is particularly noteworthy. Inside, contemporary canvasses relieve the stark look of the all-white foyer, but the lilac-themed sitting room makes use of Victorian paintings and contrasts them with modern fabrics, colours and textures. The breakfast room is dominated by an art deco illuminated stained glass mural, modern flower vases form centre pieces to each table and these splashes of colour complement the clean lines of the light white and cream design. Yet the essence of the building is here, and Regency-style drop glass chandeliers provide a reminder. There are some 43 bedrooms, smartly and stylishly revamped by designer Natalie O'Donohoe. Five different bedroom designs have been devised across a vibrant colour spectrum. Rooms are in a variety of sizes, but none are huge, in keeping with the generally intimate proportions of city-centre hotel accommodation. The rooms spread over five floors, so older or infirm guests should request ground floor accommodation. A sister hotel to the Mabledon Hotel in nearby Mabledon Court.

Prices: B&B.
Rooms: 43 en suite. Double room from £95, single from £75, family room from £105.
Other Points: No-smoking area. Children welcome. NCP car park nearby. Access to tennis courts and garden.
Directions: Few minutes walk from Kings Cross, Euston and St Pancras stations. Turn into Mabledon Place which turns into Cartwright Gardens. The hotel is at the bottom of the crescent. (Map 2, B7)

La Grande Marque 🍷 🍴 ✕

55 Leadenhall Market, London EC3V 1LT
Telephone: +44(0)20 7929 3536

Respected wine merchant Lay & Wheeler's wine bar in the city (the other is at 33 Cornhill, see following entry) occupies a former meat cellar in rejuvenated Leadenhall Market, now a smart shopping/restaurant arcade located a short walk from Fenchurch Street Station. Brick-vaulted, with a light wooden floor, wine posters, comfortable furnishings and light jazz music, it is, in essence, an upmarket sandwich bar, frequented by City suits who enjoy fine wine with their lunchtime sandwich. Accompany a generously-filled rare roast beef with horseradish, or poached salmon with dill mayonnaise sandwich, and a platter of Continental cheeses, with a bottle of vintage champagne or a Puligny-Montrachet 1er Cru from the extensive, well chosen list of wines. Blackboards list the sandwich of the week, perhaps chorizo sausage with sun-dried tomato, fine wine specials and 15 wines by the glass. Competent service from friendly staff.

Prices: Sandwiches and light lunches from £4. House wine £14.
Hours: 09.00-21.00. Closed Bank Holidays and weekends.
Food served: 11.00-20.30.
Cuisine: Sandwiches, light bites and canapes.
Other Points: Private and corporate receptions. Wine tastings. Extensive wine list.
Directions: Just off Bull's Head Passage in Leadenhall Market, very close to the Lloyds Building. (Map 1, see inset)

Lay & Wheeler on Cornhill 🍷 🍴 ✕

33 Cornhill, London EC3V 3ND
Telephone: +44(0)20 7626 0044
33cornhill@lwwinebars.com
www.lwwinebars.com

Essex-based wine merchant Lay & Wheeler's most recent wine bar venture in the City is housed in a former bank close to the Stock Exchange. Unlike La Grande Marque (see previous entry) in nearby Leadenhall Market, this conversion offers three attractive, distinctive venues for hard working City folk. In light pine and looking like the deck of a liner, with a sweeping staircase leading up to the Gallery Restaurant, the lunchtime atmosphere is busy and buisness-like with suited traders ordering fine wines to accompany delicious seafood and thick-cut sandwiches from the downstairs Seafood Bar. On display are Colchester native oysters, huge Mediterranean prawns, smoked salmon and dressed crabs and lobster. Those with more time can discuss the market over a civilised lunch upstairs, a typical meal being watercress and smoked haddock soup, confit of duck with cider jus, with lemon tart to finish. Downstairs, in the former bank vault, a boardroom is available for meetings, private lunch and dinners, and tutored wine tastings. Incidentally, the wine list draws on Lay & Wheeler's award-winning portfolio of 1,000 bins, with many offered by the glass.

Prices: Main course Gallery restaurant £9.95. Bar snacks from £4.95. House wine £11.95.
Hours: 11.00-22.00. Closed Bank Holidays and weekends.
Food served: 12.00-14.30. 17.00-20.30.
Cuisine: Modern European.
Other Points: Private and corporate receptions, lunches and dinners on the Gallery restaurant and in the exclusive board room. Wine tastings.
Directions: Bank tube station. Exit 5, Cornhill. Opposite the Royal Exchange building. 10 minutes walk from Liverpool Street station. (Map 1, see inset)

Nag's Head

🚪✗

53 Kinnerton Street, London SW1X 8ED
Telephone: +44(0)20 7235 1135
bugsmoran7@hotmail.com

Hidden away in an attractive and peaceful little mews a short stroll from Harrods, this snug little gem is probably London's smallest pub and has the feel of an old-fashioned local in a country village. Owned by the Moran family for over 30 years, it is cosy, homely and warmly traditional, with a low-ceilinged, panelled front bar and a narrow stairway that leads to a tiny back bar adorned with family memorabilia and photographs. A 1930s' What-the-butler-saw machine and a fortune-telling machine taking old pennies are popular features. The choice of piped background music is individual, perhaps folk, jazz or early show tunes. In addition to exemplary Adnams ales, pulled on attractive 19th-century handpumps, you can order a satisfying homecooked meal, perhaps chicken and ham pie, sausage, mash and beans, Mediterranean vegetable quiche, a daily roast, a range of cold meats from the salad bar, and decent sandwiches and ploughman's lunches. Please note that no credit cards are taken. Kinnerton Street runs between Motcomb Street and Wilton Place (off Knightsbridge).

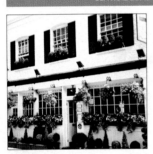

Prices: Main course bar meal £6. House wine £10.50.
Hours: 11.00-23.00. 12.00-22.30 on Sunday.
Food served: 11.30-21.30 (from 12.00 on Saturday and Sunday).
Cuisine: British.
Other Points: Children welcome over 14 years old. Credit cards not accepted.
Directions: Nearest tube: Knightsbridge. (Map 2, D5)

Swag and Tails

★🍴🍷🚪✗

10-11 Fairholt St, London SW7 1EG
Telephone: +44 (0)20 7584 6926
swag&tails@mway.com
www.swagandtails.com

Beyond the magnificent, flower-adorned façade lies a civilised yet informal bar, with original panelling, stripped wooden floors and open fires and, to the rear, a cosy, quieter dining area. Business suits, shoppers and well-heeled locals quickly fill the bar at lunchtime, attracted by the welcoming atmosphere and the modern, Mediterranean-style dishes listed on a constantly changing blackboard menu. Pop in to peruse the papers over a pint and an excellent sirloin steak sandwich, or linger longer over something more substantial. Follow warm duck liver and chorizo salad with chargrilled calf's liver, sage mash, oven-dried tomatoes, crispy pancetta and burnt butter vinaigrette, or braised leg of lamb with tomatoes, basil and pancetta. Finish with pear tatin and nutmeg ice cream, or a plate of Scottish cheeses with pear and date chutney. Good coffee and an interesting list of wines with useful tasting notes; 11 offered by the glass including decent house champagne. Note the hard-working licensees, Annemaria and Stuart Boomer-Davies, close the pub at weekends!

Prices: Main course from £10.50. Bar/snack from £7.50. House wine £11.50.
Hours: 11.00-23.00. Closed Saturday, Sunday, all Bank Holidays and 10 days over the Christmas period.
Food served: 12.00-15.00. 18.00-22.00 Monday-Friday.
Cuisine: Modern British.
Other Points: No-smoking area. Dogs welcome. Children welcome in the restaurant.
Directions: Harrods is the nearest reference point. On the opposite side of the road turn into Montpelier Street and take the first left onto Cheval Place and then the second right and first left. (Map 1, E4)

Le Truc Vert

🐦🫖

42 North Audley Street, London W1K 6ZR
Telephone: +44(0)20 7491 9988
trucvert@madasafish.com

For escaping the crowds on Oxford Street, this Mayfair version of a corner shop (with restaurant) is a perfect but intriguing refuge with food sourced from small European suppliers and producers. At the front door are stacked pestos, salsas, sun-dried tomatoes, and delicacies such as artichoke cream, as well as a range of French honeys, and top quality cheeses. Free-range organic eggs and natural yogurts are also for sale, as are pâtés, an astonishing range of fruit juices, and the vegetable display injects a good splash of colour. For a snack or lunch, you can order from the conventional menu, or make up your own selection from the goodies in the shop. Croissants, Danish pastries, quiches, savoury vegetarian pasties, muffins and cakes are all baked on the premises, and breakfast, which kicks off at 7.30 am (including Saturdays), is worth noting. By early evening the wooden tables and chairs are covered with crisp white linen, and the menu delivers the likes of seafood and sausage gumbo to start, followed by chargrilled veal escalope with roast broccoli, roast fig, watercress and blue cheese dressing, and raspberry crème brûlée to finish. You can eat well for under £20. There's a decent range of French wine.

Prices: House wine £8.
Hours: 07.30-21.00. Sunday 11.00-16.00. Closed on public holidays.
Cuisine: Modern European.
Other Points: Totally no smoking. Children welcome.
Directions: Between Oxford Street and Grosvenor Square. Nearest tube: Bond Street. (Map 2, C5)

CENTRAL LONDON

The Whistler Restaurant, Tate Britain
★ ♟ ♟ ✕

Millbank, London SW1P 4RG
Telephone: +44(0)20 7887 8825
www.tate.org.uk

Under the direction of young sommelier Hamish Anderson, the legendary Tate wine list has regained its former glory, once again offering some of the best wine value in London. It's a somewhat noisy room, open for lunch only, but white-clothed tables, and black leather banquettes and chairs create a suitably smart look. The cooking is light, modern, sophisticated, the ingredient-led dishes styled to complement the wine list. Offered on a short carte, with some seven choices per course, could be marinated smoked haddock with pickled samphire and lime, or warm Ragstone goats' cheese with tomato and red onion tart, to start. Mains take in Loch Duart salmon with cucumber, asparagus and sauce mousseline, or baked rump of Welsh lamb accompanied by salsa verde, cipolini onions and balsamic sauce. Farmhouse cheeses can be served with a glass of Quinta de la Rosa Finest Reserve.
The set lunch is good value, with smoked mackerel and Cashel blue pâté, then corn-fed chicken with peas, lemon, thyme and parsley, followed by lemon posset and shortbread biscuits. A couple of pages of sommeliers' recommendations help summarise a well annotated, in-depth list, and there is an impressive selection of half bottles. Rex Whistler's famous 1926 mural makes a fitting backdrop.
Prices: Set lunch £19.50. Main course restaurant from £10.50. House wine from £15.50.
Hours: 12.00-15.00. Sunday until 16.00.
Closed 24-27 December.
Cuisine: Modern British.
Other Points: No-smoking area. Children welcome.
Directions: Nearest tube: Pimlico. 77a bus. (Map 2, E7)

EAST LONDON

The Crown
♟ ▯ ✕

223 Grove Road, Victoria Park, London E3 5SN
Telephone: +44(0)20 8981 9998
crown@singhboulton.co.uk
www.singhboulton.co.uk

Built in 1864, the Grade II listed Crown is the second officially certified organic pub in the UK (the first is the Duke of Cambridge, see entry). It conforms with the look that distinguishes this ground-breaking group, namely shoestring decor and huge menu boards that offer totally organic food and drinks (including real ales, wines, spirits and fruit cordials). In addition, a strict fish policy means that fish is only purchased from non-depleted stocks caught by sustainable methods. The vast, open-plan bar, labyrinth of comfortable first-floor dining rooms and balconies that overlook the park, draw an eclectic mix of customers. Pop in for a late breakfast, a lunchtime snack in the bar, or relax over a three-course meal, choosing from the strongly seasonal, twice daily changing blackboard menu. Imaginative, modern cooking makes the most of the fresh ingredients, delivering simple dishes that take in, say, roast tomato soup with tapnade, then romesco fish stew with tomato, garlic, almond sauce and grilled bread. White chocolate and berry cheesecake round things off nicely, and everything is served in a relaxed and lively atmosphere that buzzes with conversation. The well-annotated wine list advises on food matching.
Prices: Main course from £8. House wine from £11.50.
Hours: 12.00-23.00. 17.00-23.00 on Monday.
10.30-22.30 on Sunday. Closed Monday lunch and 25 December.
Food Served: 12.30-16.00 Tuesday to Friday. 18.30-22.30 Monday to Saturday. 10.30-16.30 Saturday and Sunday brunch/lunch. 18.30-22.00 on Sunday.
Cuisine: Modern British/Organic.
Other Points: No-smoking area. Children welcome. Outside seating area. Licence for Civil Weddings. Opposite Victoria Park.
Directions: At the junction of Grove Road and Old Ford Road. Nearest tube: Bethnal Green, Stepney Green, Mile End, all 10 minutes walk. (Map 1, see inset)

EAST LONDON

Hanoi Café
✕

98 Kingsland Road, London E2 8DP
Telephone: +44(0)20 7729 5610
hanoicafe@hotmail.com

Situated along one of the main roads leading away from Hoxton and Shoreditch, Hai Nguyen has created a friendly neighbourhood establishment with the Hanoi Café. A relaxed laid-back atmosphere is evident, and small children are warmly welcomed, but later in the evening the place does fill with a lively crowd taking advantage of the late opening hours. This is a place that would rather concentrate on serving authentic, fresh food than impress with fancy surroundings. The interior is basic but clean, there are fresh flowers on each of the wooden tables and oriental pictures on the walls. The menu cleverly diversifies into a number of Asian cuisines, incorporating Vietnamese, Chinese, Korean, and even French. Expect the usual dishes of sweet and sour pork, sizzling beef, and spring rolls, but for the more adventurous why not try summer rolls (which you make yourself) of grilled pork belly or crispy aromatic lamb, or order a claypot dish of gingered pork, or pineapple fish; the salt and chilli spare ribs are also excellent.

Prices: Set lunch £7 and dinner £12.50.
Main course from £4.60.
House wine £8.90.
Hours: 12.00-23.30 (24.00 on Friday and Saturday). Closed 25 December and 1 January.
Cuisine: Vietnamese.
Other Points: Children welcome.
Directions: 15 minutes walk towards Shoreditch from Liverpool Street Station or a short walk from Old Street station. (Map 1, see inset)

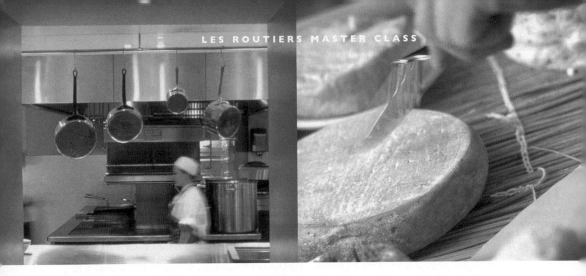

FRENCH REGIONAL
COOKING AT ALMEIDA.

Almeida, one of the smaller Conran owned and designed restaurants, looks an unlikely place for a cookery school. The cool looking restaurant complements the revamped Almeida Theatre across the road and both stand out as beacons of excellence in über-trendy Islington. The relatively young restaurant fizzes with ideas — in addition to the evolving menu of French classics, there are tapas in the bar, coffee and patisserie on the summer terrace and pre- and post-theatre menus.

The monthly cookery classes are held in the gleaming state-of-the-art steel and chrome kitchen. Here head chef Ian Wood deconstructs French regional cooking, with plenty of tricks-of-the-trade and cooking tips thrown in. The two-hour demonstration is intended to encourage interest in and enthusiasm for the different styles of regional French food and wine (regions covered in the 2003 season included Provence, Burgundy, and Languedoc-Roussillon), followed by a three course dinner in the restaurant.

Classes starts at 4.30 in the afternoon, when up to nine food enthusiasts, mostly regular customers, settle down on stools in a corner of the kitchen to watch Ian take them through a menu of simply prepared dishes, some of them Almeida menu favourites. There's no participation, but everyone enjoys seeing how dishes such as noix de coquilles St Jacques à la Provence are done in a restaurant kitchen, and the courses have been designed so that recipes are not time-consuming and can easily be recreated at home. Each participant gets a detailed information pack, complete with a brief description of the region being covered, well researched recipes with relevant historical background, and a useful list of London food shops for sourcing supplies.

After the demonstration and before dinner, there's a question and answer session with Ian in the bar over a suitably regional aperitif. Then the group moves to the restaurant where the dishes covered in the session are served, matched with wines from the area. There's no doubt about the popularity — the Burgundy class, for example, was overbooked and an extra session had to be laid on.

INFORMATION
The price per course is £75 per person, which includes the demonstration, themed on French regions, followed by a three-course dinner and wines. For more information telephone 020 7354 4777.

Almeida,, 30 Almeida Street, London N1.

Almeida Restaurant and Bar

★ ☐ ✕

30 Almeida Street, Islington, London N1 1AE
Telephone: +44(0)20 7354 4777
oliviere@conran-restaurants.co.uk
www.almeida-restaurant.co.uk

One of the smaller Conran owned and designed restaurants, Almeida incorporates a cool spaciousness with an understated French feel, in a blend of classic good looks and modern colours. The gleaming state-of-the-art steel and chrome open-plan kitchen is headed by Ian Wood whose personal take on classic French cooking is classy and assured. His brasserie menu pursues the route of French cookery honestly, builds on simplicity and is very strong as a result, as starters of boudin blanc aux pommes, and salade lyonnaise reveal. Main courses are equally appealing, with scallops provençale, steak au poivre, or pot au feu de foie gras being spot on. The trolley of charcuterie remains a great favourite, as is the extension to the idea - a fabulous trolley of tarts (from which one can choose more than one on a tasting plate). Flip over the menu and the largely French wines are listed on the reverse, offering a generous number by the glass. Simple tapas-style dishes are available in the low-slung, rich red bar. Prices throughout are not greedy, though stray away from the good value set lunch or pre-theatre menu and prices can climb - the value lies in very good quality and superb technique.

Prices: Lunch and pre-theatre set menu £17.50, £14.50 for 2 courses. Main course from £11.50. House wine £12.50.
Hours: 12.00-14.30 (15.00 on Sunday). 17.30-23.00 (18.00-22.30 on Sunday). Closed 25-26 December, 1 January and Good Friday.
Cuisine: Traditional French.
Other Points: Children welcome.
Directions: Between Angel and Highbury and Islington underground stations, off Upper Street, Islington. (Map 1, see inset)

The Drapers Arms

🍷 ▯ ✕

44, Barnsbury Street, London N1 1ER
Telephone: +44(0)20 7619 0348

It may look like a traditional London pub from the outside, but inside is a different story. The high ceilinged interior with deep-rose coloured walls, original wooden flooring, collection of stout wooden chairs and comfy sofas, is home to some fabulous cooking. Mark Emberton has breathed life into this pub and its name: the walls are filled with large contemporary 'drapery' themed photographs. Mark delivers fantastic fresh ingredients skillfully tailored into superb dishes for his ever-returning clientele. Tuck into rock oysters with shallot vinaigrette, then grilled lamb cutlets, spiced aubergine, bulgar pilaf and yogurt, and finish with a refreshing lemon tart with crème fraîche. This is a wonderful place to enjoy superb food, either relaxing on the sofas by the fire, on the solid wooden tables by the bar, or at the collection of bench seating to the left. In summer there is also a lovely paved terrace area accessed through french windows at the back. But that's not all. For a real treat, visit the dining room upstairs. In this wonderful high ceilinged room where pale blue walls contrast with deep red velvet chairs, Mark's culinary skills can be enjoyed in elegant surroundings.

Prices: Main course from £9. House wine from £11.50.
Hours: 11.00-23.00, Sunday until 22.00. Closed 25 December.
Food served: 12.00-15.00. 19.00-22.30. Sunday 12.00-16.00.
Cuisine: Modern British.
Other Points: Dogs welcome in bar. Garden. Children welcome.
Directions: Nearest tube is Highbury and Islington or Angel. (Map 1, see inset)

Duke of Cambridge

▯ ✕

30 St Peters Street, Islington, London N1 8JT
Telephone: +44(0)20 7359 3066
duke@singhboulton.co.uk
www.singhboulton.co.uk

Located in a residential street close to the centre of Islington, the Duke is an extraordinary place, combining all the trappings of a traditional Victorian pub with a low-budget modern makeover. There's a vast, high-ceilinged bar, and an intimate dining room that exudes an effortless chic through bare wood floors and a mish-mash of second-hand tables and chairs. This is the UK's first certified organic pub, so expect organic wines, spirits, organic fruit juices and infusions and, more surprisingly, five organic beers on handpump, all brewed by London's Pitfield Brewery and St Peter's Brewery in Suffolk. However, a major draw is the rustic style of cooking that draws on European influences and a wide-ranging seasonal larder of organic produce from around 60 carefully sourced suppliers. Look out for dishes such as chargrilled rib-eye steak with pan-roasted carrots, parsnips and wilted watercress, or roast cod fillet with spinach and clam broth. Starters include cauliflower and sorrel soup, and wild mushroom risotto with Pecorino cheese, while puddings run to fig tart with vanilla ice cream and apple compote with vanilla custard. Expect homemade breads and twice-daily changing chalkboard menus.

Prices: Main course from £9.50. House wine from £12.
Hours: 12.00-23.00. on Monday to Saturday. 12.00-22.30 on Sunday. Closed 25-26 December and 1 January.
Food served: 12.30-15.00 Monday to Friday. 18.30-22.30 Monday to Saturday. 12.30-15.30 Saturday and Sunday lunch. 18.30-22.00 on Sunday.
Cuisine: Modern British/Organic.
Other Points: No-smoking area. Children welcome. Courtyard.
Directions: Nearest tube: Angel. Turn right out of tube station towards Islington Green, at Green take Essex Road for about 100 yards and St Peters Street is first on the right. (Map 2, A8)

The Landseer

☐☐✕

37 Landseer Road, London N19 4JU
Telephone: +44(0)20 7263 4658

It is impossible to miss the Landseer, it's such a big pub. Within, Chris Ely has made the high-ceilinged open interior appear cosy. Perhaps it's the large wooden table by the door stacked with the day's newspapers (groaning with them at weekends). Or the filled bookshelves, comfy sofas by the fire, the pile of board games available on request behind the bar, or tempting treats on the blackboard, that make you feel you could while away a few hours here. Start with the blackboard selection of light bites and side dishes, such as delicious home made hummus with pitta bread and a variety of salads and ciabattas. Or go for the roast poussin that's basted with honey, herbs and lemon juice, roasted till crisp and juicy, and served with tarragon cream gravy. The table menus also provide useful wine tips for accompanying each dish. If by the end of it all you are still losing a long battle with Monopoly, why not treat yourself to something from the selection of home made puddings - treacle tart is sure to cheer up anyone stuck behind bars without a 'get out of jail' card.

Prices: Main course restaurant from £7. House wine £10.50.
Hours: Monday to Friday 17.00-23.00. Saturday and Sunday 12.00-23.00. Closed lunchtimes Monday to Friday.
Food served: 18.00-22.00, 22.30 Friday and Saturday. Saturday 12.30-16.30. Sunday 13.00-17.00, and 18.00-21.30.
Cuisine: Modern European.
Other Points: Outside area. Children welcome.
Directions: Archway Tube Station. (Map 1, see inset)

Crown and Goose

☐✕

100 Arlington Road, Camden, London NW1 7HP
Telephone: +44(0)20 7485 2342/8008
jlowry@ukonline.co.uk
www.crownandgoose.com

The traditional English pub has moved on, and no more so than at the Crown and Goose. Here, bohemian décor forms a great backdrop to what is a wonderful melting pot for North London's artists, writers, and media folk. Amid the cosy interior of dark green panelling, wooden shutters, sage green walls, chandeliers, the roaring fire forms a focus to a lively informal atmosphere that simply fizzes with energy. But, beware, at lunch the pub is always packed. The ever-changing menu is built around fresh ingredients, many from local suppliers. If you can find a spare corner, try a starter of crostini of butter beans, roasted peppers and pesto Parmesan, followed by the house speciality of Moroccan lamb stew, chosen from the gold-framed specials' blackboard. If the selection of homemade puddings isn't tempting enough, go for the cheeseboard - it is renowned. Jo Lowry, the Irish proprietor, makes everyone so welcome, rightly saying 'we need you, as much as you need us', an infectious enthusiasm that draws people back again and again - not only to visit the pub but also to hire the 'Chill Room' upstairs for private functions, where leather sofas and cosy corners make it the perfect place to celebrate and eat in style.

Prices: Main course restaurant meal from £8. Main course bar meal from £6.95. House wine from £10.50.
Hours: 11.00-23.00. Sunday 12.00-22.30. Closed 25-26 December.
Food served: 12.00-15.00. 18.00-22.00. 12.00-21.00 on Sunday. Closed 25-26 December.
Other Points: Totally no smoking. Dogs welcome. Children welcome over one years old.
Directions: Nearest tube: Camden Town (Map 2, A6)

The Engineer

★☐✕

65 Gloucester Avenue, Primrose Hill, London NW1 8JH
Telephone: +44(0)20 7722 0950
info@the-engineer.com
www.the-engineer.com

This old street corner pub was in on the birth of the London gastropub scene. Many pubs have since climbed on the 'gastro' bandwagon, but the Engineer, under the guidance of Karen Northcote, still tops the league. And it's great to see a pub used in the traditional sense of the word - as a welcoming open house and refreshment stop. Hospitality is taken seriously and the pub is even open for breakfast. Over buttermilk pancakes or eggs benedict it is fun to watch the early morning goings-on through the open hatch to the kitchen. The main bar has a wonderful airy feel - tall ceilings, large windows, small wooden tables with vibrant vases in acidic green and yellow displaying fresh flowers. Another dining area delivers lilac walls with a mirrored panel at dado height giving a subtle backdrop to fresh watercolour pictures. If you're staying for lunch, you can enjoy a view of the garden through french windows whilst tucking in to roast red pepper stuffed with spiced couscous and pine nuts and served with grilled haloumi cheese, followed by pan fried soft shell crab with crispy polenta, roast corn salsa and chilli jam and then perhaps by baby banana fritters with coconut ice cream.

Prices: Main course £9.75. House wine £12.50.
Hours: 09.00-23.00.
Food served: 09.00-11.30. 12.00-15.00. 19.00-22.30.
Cuisine: Modern British.
Other Points: Dogs welcome in the bar. Garden. Children welcome.
Directions: Nearest tube: Chalk Farm. (Map 1, see inset)

No 77 Wine Bar

77 Mill Lane, West Hampstead, London NW6 1NB
Telephone: +44(0)20 7435 7787

Opened in 1982, this is an archetypal wine bar with its roots firmly in that period (as far as appearances go). Sit alfresco in fine weather, or for the rest of the time squeeze around one of the small polished pine tables scattered throughout a maze of tiny quarry-tiled rooms. A good degree of intimacy is virtually guaranteed, though do beware, the atmosphere can become quite smoky unless you happen on a part devoid of puffers. What keeps this place going, however, is the simple but very wholesome and enjoyable food, and good value wines. Some dishes may appear to be rather mundane, but a beef and vegetable soup as a starter proved first class: a generous bowl of well-flavoured, rich meaty broth with finely chopped mixed vegetables - a truly homemade and deliciously warming effort. Hoisin marinated lamb shank practically fell off the bone, the meat infused with a subtle oriental flavour. The accompaniments of bok choy and plain boiled rice were in perfect balance. They also offer a proper beefburger that's virtually a signature dish; it comes with melted smoked cheese and a homemade relish of braised onions and capsicums.

Prices: Main course from £7.25. House wine £11.45.
Hours: 12.00-15.00. 19.00-23.30. Until 22.30 Sunday, Monday and Tuesday. Closed at Easter and Christmas.
Cuisine: Modern British/pan Pacific.
Other Points: Children welcome. Conservatory.
Directions: Nearest tube: West Hampstead tube. Ten minutes drive from the foot of the M1. (Map 1, see inset)

Hampstead Heath

The Salusbury

50-52 Salusbury Road, London NW6 6NN
Telephone: +44(0)20 7328 3286

At first glance you can tell this bistro style pub is run by enthusiasts (namely Rob Claasen and Nick Mash). Wooden floors, low light from glowing standard lamps, and deep red walls adorned with pictures, ooze a sophisticated yet creative atmosphere. At the open kitchen hatch a pan flash of flame and dash of olive oil adds liveliness to otherwise cool and mellow surroundings. Tuck into a modern Italian menu of cured goose breast with mushroom tartare and truffle oil, and braised venison with celeriac, olive oil and rosemary mash, and an extraordinary wine list. But it is the little details that impress - bread served on a small board accompanied by oils, salt and pepper in tiny bowls - and the general hum of contentment. But if the pub is not enough to satisfy your gastronomic curiosity - just venture a few doors down to their deli - filled with proper Italian deli aromas and goodies. These range from fresh vegetables, to lavender and spaghetti hanging from the ceiling, fresh olives, salamis and a wonderful selection of cheeses. Towards the rear is a pizza area where you can grab a fresh slice on your way to work, or sit down to enjoy on the premises.

Prices: Starter from £4.50. Main course restaurant from £9. House wine £10.
Hours: Monday 17.00-23.00. Tuesday to Saturday 12.00-23.00, Sunday until 22.30. Closed Monday lunchtime.
Food served: 12.30-15.30. 19.00-22.15. Sunday 19.00-22.00.
Cuisine: Italian.
Other Points: Children welcome until 19.00.
Directions: Nearest tube: Queens Park. (Map 1, see inset)

London - North-West

Baltic

74 Blackfriars Road, Southwark, London SE1 8HA
Telephone: +44(0)20 7928 1111
info@balticrestaurant.co.uk
www.balticrestaurant.co.uk

It may be considered a deeply cool space, the matt black floor, wonderful amber encrusted bar and neutral toned dining room creating a stylishly spare look, but it is all contained in an 18th century terraced house. The theme of the food is Eastern European - the base is certainly Polish and Russian - but mixed in with modern British ideas that embrace many influences. Starters of warm seared squid with spiced plum sauce, radish and spring onion salad, for example, or foie gras with potato pancake, and mains of pork tenderloin with apples, mustard and bacon, and braised shoulder of lamb with pomegranate, tomato and coriander, are typical examples. Puddings extend to crêpes filled with sweet cheese, nuts and raisins, and poppyseed and honey cake. Lunch is a bargain, offering cheese and potato dumplings with vegetable broth, loin of pork fried in breadcrumbs with Portobello mushrooms. There is, of course, a fabulous range of vodkas, but then Baltic is a younger sibling to Wodka, (see entry). There's also a wide ranging, high quality wine list with a decent selection by the glass.

Prices: Set lunch £13.50, set dinner £22.50. House wine £10.50.
Hours: 12.00-15.30. 18.00-23.30. Closed Saturday lunch and 25 December.
Cuisine: Eastern European.
Other Points: Children welcome. Patio.
Directions: Opposite Southwark tube and 5 minutes from Waterloo. (Map 2, D8)

The Bridge House Bar and Dining Room

218 Tower Bridge Road, London SE1 2UP
Telephone: +44(0)20 7407 5818

Adnams Brewery's sole London outpost occupies a converted former grainstore beside Tower Bridge. Not only are Suffolk ales on tap (natch), but also amazing Thames and City views, and a surprising level of stylish refurbishment. Wooden floors and Venetian blinds, and original features of metal pillars and exposed brickwork, provide a simple, yet stylish look, enhanced by vivid colours and an army of cacti. The modern British menu keeps pace, designed around fresh local ingredients, including unusual produce from Borough Market, and first-class cheeses from Neal's Yard Dairy. Chef/partner Wayne Seddon is ex L'Escargot, and offers an eclectic range of dishes. Expect starters along the lines of chicken liver and brandy parfait with roasted onion jam or wild mushroom risotto with winter herbs, cream and Parmesan, then lamb with parsley mash, butter bean, barley and vegetable broth, or rib-eye steak with fat chips and béarnaise, Broadside beer battered haddock and chips, or roast duck with lentil and basil mash and red wine gravy. Sweet ginger pudding and warm chocolate cake grace the pudding menu. Also, classy Adnams wines and warm hospitality from landlord Steve McMinn.

Prices: Set dinner £19.95. Main course restaurant from £6.75. House wine £11.50.
Hours: 11.30-23.00. Sunday 12.00-22.30. Closed 25 December and 1 January.
Food served: 12.00-15.30. 17.30-22.00. Sunday 12.00-21.30.
Cuisine: Modern British.
Other Points: Children welcome in the dining room.
Directions: 50 yards from Tower Bridge, south of the river. (Map 1, see inset)

Prices: Main course from £10. House wine £12.
Hours: 11.00-23.00. 12.00-22.30 on Sunday. Closed 25-26 December.
Food served: 12.00-16.00. 18.00-22.00. 12.00-15.30 and 18.00-22.00 on Sunday.
Cuisine: Modern British.
Directions: The Alma is opposite Wandsworth Town Railway Station, just off Wandsworth roundabout. (Map 1, see inset)

The Alma Tavern

499 Old York Road, Wandsworth, London SW18 1TF
Telephone: +44(0)20 8870 2537
drinks@thealma.co.uk
www.thealma.co.uk

Like the others in the Charles Gotto empire (the Ship and the Coopers Arms - see entries), the Alma is a distinctive, atmospheric pub. Conveniently located across from Wandsworth station and close to Young's brewery, its classic Victorian façade of bright green-tiles, adorned in summer with hanging flower baskets, immediately stands out. In the unexpectedly stylish atmosphere of the airy central room, an eclectic mix of painted pine and cast-iron tables, painted mirrors, gilded mosaics of the Crimean Battle of Alma, and a fine art deco fireplace range around a huge island bar counter. At the back, the dining room has terracotta-painted walls, a famous pale blue frieze of nymphs and a comfortable, sophisticated dining atmosphere. Using organic and rare breed meats from Gotto's Surrey farm and other carefully sourced produce, the imaginative, popular menu may offer the likes of mussels with lemongrass, tomato and coriander, guinea fowl with winter vegetables and herb lentils, or Alma steak burger with red onion relish and french fries. Sandwiches and lighter bites such as fish soup with rouille, and mushroom and chorizo frittata are available between noon and 4pm. Besides the Young's on handpump, you'll find freshly squeezed juices, excellent espresso and a superb selection of wines.

Amsterdam Hotel

7 Trebovir Road, Earls Court, London SW5 9LS
Telephone: +44(0)20 7370 2814
reservations@amsterdam-hotel.com
www.amsterdam-hotel.com

Several of the tall, white-painted buildings on this surprisingly quiet, tree-lined street just round the corner from Earls Court tube station have been converted into hotels. But the Amsterdam, with its sprucely kept porticoed entrance, railings and lights outside, and plant-filled reception within, is the pick of the bunch. This is a very cheerful, well-run hotel with charming staff who go out of their way to be helpful. The staircase and corridors are covered in bright, modern prints, and bedrooms have smartly co-ordinated furnishings; all vary in shape and size. Indeed, some are quite compact for double rooms, with prefabricated bathrooms squeezed in, but all are spotlessly maintained and very comfortable. However, family rooms are a good size, and suites have a separate lounge and kitchenette. Many rooms are no smoking. There's no restaurant as such, but downstairs in the basement a cooked breakfast is served.

Prices: B&B.
Rooms: 27 en suite. Double room from £75, single from £55.
Other Points: No-smoking area. Children welcome. Garden.
Directions: Turn left out of Earls Court tube station and take the first left into Trebovir road; the hotel is on right. (Map 1, E2)

Bull's Head and Stables Bistro ★ ♥ ▶ ✕

373 Lonsdale Road, Barnes, London SW13 9PY
Telephone: +44(0)20 8876 5241
jazz@thebullshead.com
www.thebullshead.com

The Thameside setting of this imposing 17th-century pub would be a draw in itself, but what really pulls crowds from miles around is the top-class modern jazz and blues groups that have made the Bull's Head internationally famous for over 40 years. Landlord Dan Fleming knows his jazz and attracts many American bands; nightly concerts are from 8.30-11pm (also 2-4.30pm on Sundays), held in a separate room with a genuine jazz club atmosphere; it's well worth paying the admission charge just to enter this famous room. Back in the bustling bar, alcoves open off the main area around the island servery, which dispenses Youngs cask-conditioned ales, over 80 malt whiskies and some 240 bottles of wine, 30 offered by the glass. All the food is cooked from fresh ingredients and served from noon until it's finished (they then can make sandwiches). Typical choices include soup and ciabatta, roast of the day with potatoes and three vegetables, steak and kidney pie, and treacle tart. The former Stables Bistro now houses the Nuay Thai Bistro with a Thai kitchen brigade, but you can also order at the bar in the main pub and be served there, or order authentic Thai food to takeaway.

Prices: Main course from £4.50. Thai main course from £4.75. Wine from £10.50.
Hours: 11.00-23.00
Food served: All day, Thai Bistro 18.00-22.00
Cuisine: Traditional British served at lunchtime. Thai food served in the evening.
Other Points: No-smoking area. Children welcome in daytime.
Directions: Five minutes walk along the river from Barnes Bridge station. (Map 1, see inset)

Caffé Mamma ✕

24 Hill Street, Richmond, London TW9 1TW
Telephone: +44(0)20 8940 1625
www.caffemamma.co.uk

Set on one of Richmond's main thoroughfares, Caffé Mamma continues to serve its brand of traditional Italian food, combined with a touch of theatre, some 20 years down the line. Up front, there's a bright modern feel with laminated marble café-style tables, blonde wood flooring, chairs, bar and service counter, and purple and yellow walls. At the more characterful, darker and narrower rear, trompe l'oeil décor portrays an old-time Italian street scene complete with lines of hanging washing and pavement tables and chairs. Italian staff act-up the cheery Neopolitan buzz with swift, friendly service. The laminated menu runs with traditional straightforward, no nonsense honest fare via antipasti, insalate, pasta, pizza and dolci, backed up by a small daily specials board. Soup of the day could feature asparagus, while the main course special might take in pollo cacciatore. Fine materials are evident in dishes such as tagliatelle e gamberoni (good quality pasta with king prawns and a butter and wine sauce), and trenette al pesto (egg noodles with pesto sauce made properly with fresh basil, garlic, pine nuts and pecorino). Light, cheery and not taking itself too seriously, Caffé Mamma delivers. It's a fun place to eat simple food.

Prices: Main course from £5.35. House wine £10.75.
Hours: 12.00-24.00. Sunday 12.00-23.30. Closed 25-26 December.
Cuisine: Italian/Pizza and Pasta.
Other Points: No smoking area. Children welcome.
Directions: In the centre of Richmond, heading towards Kingston and Twickenham, near river bridge. (Map 1, see inset)

Mayflower Hotel, South-West London

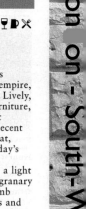

The Coopers Arms ♟ ◗ ✗

87 Flood Street, London SW3 5TB
Telephone: +44(0)20 7376 3120
drinks@thecoopers.co.uk
www.thecoopers.co.uk

Occupying a quiet corner site in Chelsea's affluent back streets, this civilised Victorian pub is part of Charles Gotto's small gastro-pub empire, which includes the Ship and the Alma in Wandsworth (see entries). Lively, light and airy with a comfortable open-plan bar filled with pine furniture, pot plants, vintage ocean liner posters and framed Mac cartoons, it attracts a well-heeled clientele in search of superior bar food and decent wines. Choose from a selection of freshly prepared dishes, with meat, game and eggs supplied by Gotto's organic Surrey farm. A typical day's menu may list roast pimento and tomato soup, and Mediterranean chicken, bacon and avocado salad with mustard vinaigrette, or, for a light snack or starter, Scottish smoked salmon and scrambled eggs with granary bread. For something more substantial choose, perhaps, braised lamb shank with roast garlic and chive mash, home-reared pork sausages and mash with onion gravy, or Aberdeen Angus rib-eye steak 'les houches' with french fries. If you have room, try the spotted dick and custard for pudding. There are tip-top Young's ales, as well as an upstairs function room that is popular for wedding celebrations; Chelsea Registry Office is just around the corner.

Prices: Main course from £8.
House wine £12.
Hours: 11.00-23.00. 12.00-22.30 Sunday.
Closed 25-26 December.
Food served: 12.30-15.00. 18.30-21.30.
12.30-15.00 on Sunday only.
Cuisine: Modern British.
Directions: Sloane Square tube station.
(Map 1, F4)

Justin James Hotel

43 Worple Road, Wimbledon, London SW19 4JZ
Telephone: +44(0)20 8947 4271
info@justinjameshotel.com
www.justinjameshotel.com

Ideal for those requiring somewhere very close to the centre of Wimbledon, this pretty, late Victorian house (it was originally built in the 1890's as a doctor's surgery) stands on a corner virtually opposite Elys Department Store. And as it is a couple of hundred yards from Wimbledon Station, travelling to central London should present no major problems. The red tile-hung exterior conveys a traditional quality, which is continued within, with visitors ringing a bell to gain admittance to what is a homely and friendly family-run set up. Very well maintained bedrooms are all en-suite, and have cable TV, tea and coffee making facilities, as well as hair dryers, phones and IT connections. There is no lounge or bar, but the neat, small ground-floor breakfast room comprises a few largish tables and offers a good traditional English breakfast. Such is the popularity of the hotel that bookings need to be made at least a month in advance. The All England Tennis Club is just over a mile away.

Rooms: 20 rooms, 19 en suite. Double room from £80, single from £45, family room from £95.
Other Points: No-smoking area. Garden. Children welcome. Car park.
Directions: Follow the A219 to Wimbledon. The hotel is a few minutes walk from Wimbledon Station. (Map 1, see inset)

The Mayflower Hotel

26-28 Trebovir Road, Earl's Court, London SW5 9NJ
Telephone: +44(0)20 7370 4934/370 0991
mayfhotel@aol.com
www.mayflower-group.co.uk

This recently renovated townhouse hotel occupies two white-stuccoed Edwardian houses that are typical of the buildings lining the leafy streets leading off Earls Court Road. The interior reveals a flair for interior design: a fusion of eastern influences with spacious modern lines. Light bedrooms with high ceilings and ceiling fans are enhanced by Indian and oriental antiques, beautiful hand-carved wardrobes and bedside tables, richly ornate beds are covered in rich, vibrant, luxurious Andrew Martin fabrics, a perfect foil to the neutral effect of pale stone and wood floors. All rooms have state-of-the-art technology with internet access, wide-screen TVs, CD players and personal safes; lighting is soft and subtle. Ensuite bathrooms are stylish and sparkling in marble and chrome with superb walk-in showers and contemporary white bowl sinks. Those on a lower floor are in an exotic dark green marble, but the fittings and general feel are the same. Breakfast is a complimentary buffet.

The fashionable shopping areas of Knightsbridge and Chelsea, and the South Kensington museums are all within easy reach and the Mayflower is perfectly located for Earl's Court Exhibition Centre. Earl's Court tube is only a minutes walk away and provides direct access to Heathrow Airport, the City and West End.

Prices: B&B
Rooms: 48 en suite.
Other Points: Children welcome.
Directions: From the Earls Court Road tube station exit left; go passed MacDonalds and take the first left into Trebovir Road. The Mayflower is 40 yards along on the left hand side. (Map 1, E2)

Murano

3 Hill Street, Richmond, London TW9 1SX
Telephone: +44(0)20 8948 8330
www.muranorestaurant.co.uk

Although a listed building and the site of the famous Maids of Honour tea shop in the 19th century, Murano offers a sleek, contemporary look. The first-floor restaurant has clean, minimalistic good looks; all blonde wood, stainless steel and plain (artex) walls, accessed via stairs or lift (stainless steel and glass, of course) from the street. The stainless steel-topped tables are tightly packed, but abundant leafy plants and fresh flowers on tables soften the hard-edged look. The seasonally changing menu reflects the décor, signals a leaning towards more serious Italian food and is dotted with a few luxury items: monkfish, sea bass, veal, and scallops all find a place. Bread comes with olive oil to dip, and a spicy spaghetti aglio e olio, followed by a generous mains of pan-fried monkfish medallions rolled in pancetta, served with sweet and sour courgettes, then panna cotta and a rich fruity coulis, all pass muster. In addition, the menu runs to sea bass fillet, braised Livornese style, with fresh tomato and saffron potatoes. Antipasti of roasted vegetables with garlic bruschetta are matched by a good torta al limone to finish. The all-Italian wine list has some good drinking under £20.

Prices: Main course from £6.45. House wine £12.15.
Hours: 12.00-15.00. 18.00-23.30. Sunday 12.00-23.30. Closed 25-26 December and 1 January.
Cuisine: Italian.
Other Points: No-smoking area. Children welcome, children's play area on Sunday.
Directions: In Richmond town centre, near Richmond Green and the river. (Map 1, see inset)

The Ship Inn

Jews Row, Wandsworth, London SW18 3TB
Telephone: +44(0)20 8870 9667
drinks@theship.co.uk
www.theship.co.uk

Approach this Victorian pub by road and you pass a bus station and a concrete works, so not the most inspiring route. Take the river walk instead, and enter the pub via the delightful, two-level terrace, complete with rose-covered rustic trellis, barbecue and summer bar; the pub really makes the most of its riverside location. Within, you'll find a light, airy conservatory bar sporting bare boards, a central wood-burning stove, a motley collection of old wooden tables and chairs, and an open-plan kitchen that produces good-quality food. Although owned by Young's, it is the flagship pub of Charles Gotto's select empire of gastro-pubs (the Alma, and the Coopers Arms; see entries). Gotto is passionate about food and sources quality produce from individual farms and producers, including Shorthorn beef, rare breed pork and lamb, and game and eggs from his own organic farm in Surrey. On the short daily changing menu you may find sardines sautéed in garlic with buttered spinach, roast cod with pesto mash, and Home Farm rack of lamb with rosemary ratatouille. Specialist cheeses are sourced from small independent producers. Naturally, the beer is good, and in addition there's freshly squeezed orange juice and a wine list of decent labels, with a choice of 10 by the glass.

Prices: Main course from £9. House wine £12.
Hours: 11.00-23.00. 12.00-22.30 on Sunday.
Food served: 12.00-22.30. 12.00-16.00 and 19.00-22.30 on Sunday.
Cuisine: Modern British.
Other Points: Garden.
Directions: Nearest train station is Wandsworth Town. From here, make your way under the railway bridge. Follow signs to Wandsworth Bridge, Jews Row is the last road on the left before the river. (Map 1, see inset)

Troubadour

265 Old Brompton Road, London SW5 9JA
Telephone: +44(0)20 7370 1434
info@troubadour.co.uk
www.troubadour.co.uk

This legendary café, the centre of London's artistic and intellectual life in the 1950s and '60s (Bob Dylan, Jimi Hendrix, Marianne Faithfull and Paul Simon all played here) celebrates its 50th anniversary in 2004. The 21st century has seen the café double in size after taking over the property next door. The original room now makes more effective use of the available space, but remains reassuringly cluttered with curios crowding walls and ceilings, small tables, wooden benches and chairs. The new extension is lighter, neater, less crowded, but manages the extraordinary feat of looking as if it has been part of the Troubadour forever. In true café style, service is relaxed, one can order coffee and cakes, tuck into a full English breakfast, or go to town on a Brompton burger done New York style with salad and fries. Pasta, served with herbs, and a splendid omelette made with free range eggs, and the ever popular bangers 'n' mash from Allen's of Mount Street, are all Troubadour classics. Wine by the glass comes in two sizes. Next door is the Troubadour delicatessen selling all manner of goodies, a boon in an area not best served by decent food shops.

Prices: Main course from £5.95. House wine £10.95.
Hours: 09.00-24.00.
Closed 26th December-1 January.
Food served: 09.00-23.00.
Cuisine: Eclectic.
Other Points: No-smoking area. Children welcome. Garden. Live entertainment. Exhibition space. Delicatessen.
Directions: Nearest tube: Earls Court/West Brompton. (Map 1, F3)

Twenty Nevern Square Hotel ★ ⟠

20 Nevern Square, Earl's Court, London SW5 9PD
Telephone: +44(0)20 7565 9555
hotel@twentynevernsquare.co.uk
www.twentynevernsquare.co.uk

Two words, individual and unique, best describe this townhouse hotel. Nowhere is this more apparent than in the 19 en suite bedrooms. Each of the luxurious rooms has been individually coordinated on an east meets west theme, with much of the furniture specially commissioned from Indonesia. Four-poster beds have been designed and carved separately, and small spaces work to maximum advantage. Unifying factors are in the use of wooden Venetian blinds and rich natural textiles - such as cotton, linen, velvet and wool. Thoughtfulness is apparent throughout the hotel, from the ornate birdcage, commissioned in Indonesia, set in a splendid 'lobby', down to the evening menu served in the little airy conservatory, Café Twenty offering a menu made up of deliciously light Mediterranean dishes made with fresh ingredients that are quick to prepare, such as Caesar salad, spaghetti carbonara, or chicken musa - fried chicken with fresh carrots and broccoli in a herb and butter sauce. In the morning, the aroma of freshly baked rolls and croissants is enough to raise any reluctant riser, filling the ground floor with wonderful smells. Continental breakfast is served in the conservatory restaurant and a full English breakfast can be ordered on request.

Prices: Set dinner £13.50. Main course from £8.50. Bar/snack from £3.95. House wine £11.70.
Hours: 16.00-23.00.
Rooms: 20 en suite. Double/twin from £110, single from £90.
Cuisine: Italian
Other Points: No-smoking area. Children welcome. Car park. 24 hour room service.
Directions: From Earls Court tube station take Warwick road exit, turn right. The second street on the right is Nevern Square. (Map 1, E2)

Adria Hotel ⟠

44 Glenthorne Road, Hammersmith, London W6 0LS
Telephone: +44(0)20 7602 6386
george@adria.demon.co.uk
www.adria-hotel.co.uk

A good-value, family run bed-and-breakfast hotel a few minutes walk from Hammersmith tube, on a road that runs parallel with the area's main shopping street - King Street. Although the building faces a nondescript, but useful, multistorey car park, the exterior is well maintained and appealing. Smart wrought-iron gates open into a tidy paved front courtyard with limited car parking, and polished stone steps lead up to an entrance porch surrounded by coloured marble tiles set into which is a video-entry intercom. The interior is neat, and up to date with brightly decorated bedrooms - some are triple bedded. Tea and coffee making facilities and TVs are provided, and compact shower rooms, entered via space-saving folding doors, are in good order. There's a south-facing basement breakfast room with dark wood tables and brown cord settees in one corner facing a TV, plus a cold drinks vending machine in the entrance hall.

Prices: B&B.
Rooms: 16 en suite. Double room from £69, single from £49.
Other Points: No-smoking area. Children welcome. Garden.
Directions: 120 yards from Hammersmith Tube, exit North. (Map 1, see inset)

Assaggi ✕

39 Chepstow Place, London W2 4TS
Telephone: +44 (0)20 7792 5501

Nino Sassu is passionate about Italian food and has worked at some of the best Italian restaurants in London. Six years ago, when he decided it was time to open his own restaurant, the space above the Chepstow pub was all he could afford. Now, his brand of carefully sourced, very fresh (he buys every day as the place has little storage) modern Italian food has the well-heeled folk of Notting Hill and beyond booking a month in advance for the 40-seater. You do not have to walk through the pub (the side-door entrance is well marked). It's a modern space filled with bright colours, vibrant with contemporary art, plain wood floor, and close wood tables. The menu is rightly recognised as one of the best modern Italians in town. Nino offers a short, seasonal list with the emphasis on the sheer quality of the raw materials. Dishes are as simple as grilled vegetables marinated with olive oil and herbs or an insalata di gamberoni, for starters, with mains taking in filetto di vitello al rosmarino and fritto misto di pesce. In between there's pasta such as tagliolini con ragu di pesce, and side dishes of potato purée or tomato, rucola and basil.

Prices: Main courses from £14.95. House wine £11.95.
Hours: 12.00-14.30. 17.30-23.00. Closed on Sundays.
Cuisine: Modern Italian.
Other Points: Children welcome.
Directions: Five minute walk from Notting Hill Gate tube, above the Chepstow pub. (Map 1, C2)

Pembridge Court Hotel

34 Pembridge Gardens, London W2 4DX
Telephone: +44(0)20 7229 9977
reservations@pemct.co.uk
www.pemct.co.uk

On the corner of Pembridge Square, a stone's throw from Portobello Road, is a pleasant, lovingly tended 19th-century town house. What makes this privately owned hotel stand out from similar places in the area is the obvious care and attention that has gone into all aspects of the hotel, whether public rooms or bedrooms. The summer of 2002 saw the total refurbishment of the lower ground floor, creating a smart, light breakfast room decorated in soft colours, an adjoining board room for small conferences, and a pretty, intimate sitting room. The ground floor sitting room is well furnished with smart cushioned sofas and armchairs, and devoted to a brilliant collection of Victorian, Edwardian and early 20th century memorabilia such as fans, gloves, hats and prints that spills out into reception, up the stairs and into the bedrooms. Churchill the cat is a welcoming presence and staff are genuinely friendly. There are 20 bedrooms, all well appointed and bang up-to-date, all totally refurbished in the last year. 14 are deluxe rooms, with satellite TV and CD players; larger rooms have sofa beds to accommodate children. Room service delivers light snacks and drinks.

Rooms: 20 en suite. Double/twin from £160-£195. Single from £160. Family room from £205.
Other Points: Dogs welcome. Children welcome. Parking available for two cars. 24 hour room service.
Directions: Two minutes walk from Notting Hill Gate tube station. (Map 1, C2)

Portobello Gold

95-97 Portobello Rd, Notting Hill,
London W11 2QB
Telephone: +44(0)20 7460 4910 or 0845 0660666
mike@portobellogold.com
www.portobellogold.com

This highly individual pub-cum-cocktail-bar-cum-restaurant has constantly evolved since Michael Bell acquired the lease in 1985. He covered the rear garden, creating a conservatory restaurant with a sliding roof, introduced large tropical plants, pioneered the 'oyster shooter' and draught wheat beer within London and, during the mid-1990s, installed computers in the bar offering free internet access, becoming one of the world's first cybercafés. Recently installed wireless internet (a "hotspot") is available free to busy business lunchers - another first. Laid back, even bohemian sums up the atmosphere. Open at 10am for coffee and homemade 'stickies', then an all-day bar menu offers Irish rock oysters, big ciabatta sandwiches, chicken Caesar salad and sausage and mash. The evening restaurant menu kicks in with an eclectic mix of seafood, perhaps Cajun prawns, sashimi, Thai moules, kippers and a wonderful seafood platter for four. Alternatives include calf's liver and bacon, and Angus ribeye steak. An impressive list of wines, real ales and Belgian Leffe on handpump are backed up by a mind-boggling array of spirits. Compact bedrooms have modem points and provide a good central base.

Prices: Set lunch £13 and dinner £19 (available 12.00-16.00 and 19.00-23.15). Main course from £6.95. House wine £10.75.
Hours: 10.00-24.00.
Food served: 12.00-24.00 (until 21.00 on Sunday).
Rooms: 7 rooms, 3 full en suite with showers. Single room from £50, double from £60. Backpackers room £45 for two.
Cuisine: Modern British.
Other Points: No-smoking. Children welcome over four years old. Garden/conservatory
Directions: Nearest tube is Notting Hill Gate. Follow the signs to Portobello Market. (Map 1, C2)

Prices: Main course restaurant from £8.95. Main course bar/snack from £3.50. House wine £10.50.
Hours: 11.00-23.00. Sunday 12.00-22.30. Closed 25 December from 15.00.
Food served: 12.00-14.30. 19.00-21.30. Until 16.00 on Sunday, no food Sunday evening.
Cuisine: Modern British.
Other Points: Dogs welcome. Garden.
Directions: From the Hanger Lane exit on the A40 take the A406 south. Turn right onto Uxbridge Road and left at Marks and Spencers. Nearest tube stations are South Ealing or Ealing Broadway. (Map 1, see inset)

Red Lion

13 St Marys Road, Ealing, London W5 5RA
Telephone: +44(0)20 8567 2541
red.lion@virgin.net

At a glance the Red Lion appears to be nothing more than a typical, traditional brass, dark wood, and smoked glass London pub, with its pumps dispensing Fuller's ales. But the glamour of film beats at its heart. The walls of Studio Six, as the pub is lovingly called by the neighbouring Ealing Studios (where they have five studios), reflect this with an array of wonderful black and white photos and colourful posters. Unusually for London, this is a real family business, run by Jonathan and Victoria Lee, with a daughter giving a helping hand in the bar and restaurant, and son Kieran cooking in the kitchen. What's more, Victoria's cousin is the main supplier for fresh wild Scottish salmon, venison, wild duck, local pheasant, and black pudding. Here you can tuck into red pepper and marinated feta cheese salad, followed by delicate rainbow trout with cherry tomatoes, red onion, roast potatoes and basil butter, with a wonderful homemade red berry crumble and ice cream to finish. On warm evenings, the walled terrace with award-winning flower displays is transformed for candlelit al fresco dining. And, you can't ignore this little pub when the most famous Guinness served at the bar was Sir Alec!

Borough Market, South-East London

WEST LONDON

Wodka ★ ♦ ✕

12 St Alban's Grove, Kensington, London W8 5PN
Telephone: +44(0)20 7937 6513

A real old favourite that wins first prize for having London's most idiosyncratic restaurant interior: part painted rough plaster, part white bathroom tiles, part wood panelling. Wodka is a fantastic eating and drinking spot - the 30-strong vodka list is heroic - and the Polish-by-inspiration menu strives hard to please. Pierogi filled with cheese, potato and spring onion remains a firm favourite, but there's also blinis topped with everything from smoked salmon and foie gras to Osietra caviar. Smoked eel with caramelised shallots, beetroot and horseradish purée, is a great example of Eastern European classics given a modern British twist. It's a theme that's picked up by main courses such as roast haunch of venison with honey-roasted pears and sour cherries. In a more traditional mode, the kitchen delivers a great dish of cabbage leaves stuffed with pork, wild rice and cranberry sauce, as well as poached salt beef with dumplings and rosol. There are some dishes in common with owner Jan Woroniecki's Baltic (see entry). Great Czech and Polish beers complement the vodkas; the wine list is a more conventional European and new world listing with prices in the main below the £20 mark.

Prices: Set lunch £13.50. Main course from £11.90. House wine £10.90.
Hours: 12.30-14.30. 19.00-23.15. Closed for lunch on Saturday and Sunday.
Cuisine: Polish.
Other Points: Children welcome. Car park.
Directions: Nearest tube: High Street Kensington, Gloucester Road. (Map 1, E3)

ENGLAND

The Hunters Rest Inn
King Lane, Clutton Hill, Bath BS39 5QL
Telephone: +44(0)1761 452303
paul@huntersrest.co.uk
www.huntersrest.co.uk

This former hunting lodge is set at the end of a winding country road. Within, a stone bar is surrounded by a number of rooms running into each other. Most are carpeted and filled with a selection of wooden and brass-topped tables and chairs, one leads into the bright conservatory with hanging baskets. Old farm paraphernalia hang from walls; dried hops are attached to the beamed ceilings along with brass plates, hunting pictures and brass horns. Food is traditional, locally sourced, and runs to a generous chicken and whole-grain mustard pie or Somerset faggots with onion gravy, both served with large jacket potato and salad with homemade coleslaw. Sea bass fillet with lemon butter sauce may appear on the specials menu. Wednesday night is family night, and kids can make use of the miniature railway in the back garden as well as a bouncy castle, plus one child eats free with every adult. Stylish bedrooms are in keeping with the cosy image of the inn. All four are individually decorated; each comes with bags of character, and a teddy bear. Victorian fittings complement the roll-top baths in two of the bathrooms. In addition, telephones come with data links and TV with video.
Prices: Set lunch £12.50 and dinner £16.50. Main course bar from £6. Main course restaurant from £10. House wine £8.50.
Hours: 11.30-15.00. 18.00-23.00. 12.00-15.00. 18.00-22.30 Sunday.
Food served: 12.00-14.00. 18.30-21.30 (22.15 Friday and Saturday).
Rooms: 4 en suite. Single room from £55, double from £75, family room from £115.
Cuisine: Traditional English.
Other Points: No-smoking area. Children welcome. Garden. Car park.
Directions: Clutton Hill lies between A39 and A37 south of Bristol, near Chelwood and Farmborough. (Map 4, B7)

Eastern Eye
8a Quite Street, Bath BA1 2JS
Telephone: +44(0)1225 422323
inf@easterneye.co.uk
www.easterneye.co.uk

Light floods into the huge, wide-open Georgian room through each of the three glass domes and the large windows set at each end. In addition, there's lovely Georgian plasterwork and mouldings, columns and fanlights: it's an extraordinary setting for an Indian restaurant specialising in the cuisine of northern India and Bengal. Start with the obligatory poppadoms and chutney tray, accompanied by cold Indian lagers (Bangla, highly recommended) while checking the menu. But be prepared to tear yourself away from the usual jalfrezi or dansak. In Bath, Eastern Eye is renowned for the quality of its food; as well as the familiar favourites, there's an interesting range of chefs' recommendations including seafood and vegetarian dishes. For example, butty kebabs (from Bengal) are small slices of delicately spiced and tender lamb cooked in a tandoori oven, a perfect partner to another Bengali dish of channa bhaji (fried chickpeas in a spicy sauce). Main courses such as Karali lamb and garlic chilli masala chicken are clearly produced with effort and pilau rice is served fresh and fluffy. The combination of freshly cooked food, reasonable prices and swift, friendly service fills the Eastern Eye; you may even have to book for a Monday night.
Prices: Main course from £7.50. House wine £11.95.
Hours: 12.00-14.30 and 18.00-23.30. Closed 25 December.
Cuisine: Indian.
Other Points: Large no smoking area. Children welcome.
Directions: Exit 18/M4. (Map 4, B7)

Prices: Set lunch £6.95 and dinner £25. House wine £12.50.
Hours: 12.00-14.30. 18.00-23.00 (until 23.30 on Friday and Saturday). Closed 25-26 December.
Cuisine: Indian.
Other Points: Totally no smoking. Children welcome.
Directions: Junction 18/M4. City centre, on Pulteney Bridge. (Map 4, B7)

Rajpoot
Rajpoot House, 4 Argyle Street, Bath BA2 4BA
Telephone: +44(0)1225 466833
www.rajpoot.com

As you descend the stairs to this basement Indian restaurant close to Pulteney Bridge, the delicious smell of spices rises to greet you. The whole place is cool and dimly lit, with each of the series of small rooms that stretch back from the bar traditionally decorated with ornate filigree lighting throwing abstract patterns on the walls. In addition, ceilings are richly painted, there's some exposed stone, doorways are arched, and tables spread with crisp white cloths. The menu is wide ranging, but majors in Bangladeshi dishes. All the favourites are there, for example, tandoori specials offer chicken tikka massala as well as the more unusual Rajpoot salmon, and there's an all encompassing tandoori thali of tandoori murg, chicken tikka, shish kebab, nan and pilau rice. Dansaks, birianys, massala and rogan josh are all on offer and there's a good range of breads. There's takeaway (natch) and the wine list includes a red and a white from India.

Tilley's Bistro

3 North Parade Passage, Bath BA1 1NX
Telephone: +44(0)1225 484200
dmott@tilleysbistro.co.uk
www.tilleysbistro.co.uk

One of the oldest houses in Bath (the refectory for the abbey) has been owned by David and Dawn Mott for the past eleven years. Their bustling bistro is spread over three floors. The main beamed dining room with an original stone fireplace at either end has a cosy wine bar atmosphere; above, up some windy stairs, is a comfortable lounge with sofas and a small bar and a private dining room. Lunch is excellent value, with substantial portions of, say, grilled mushroom stuffed with mussels and garlic and herb butter, then escalope of pork milanaise with spaghetti in a tomato sauce and melted mozzarella. In the evening, they don't differentiate between starters and main courses, simply offering a choice of medium-sized dishes of which diners should choose two or more from a range of cold, warm and hot dishes. These include smoked salmon and goats' cheese roulade, lamb kidneys in a port and cream sauce, and fillet steak au poivre. The pudding list includes Salcombe dairy ice cream as well as champagne summer fruit jelly. There's a global selection of wine, nearly all under £20, with about nine by the glass.

Prices: Set lunch £10.50 and dinner £20. Main course from £10. House wine £12.
Hours: 12.00-14.30. 18.30-23.00. Closed on Sunday.
Cuisine: French and English.
Other Points: No-smoking area. Children welcome.
Directions: M4/Junction 18. In the centre of Bath near to the Abbey. (Map 4, B7)

Court Hotel

Linch Hill, Emborough, Chilcompton, Bath BA3 4SA
Telephone: +44(0)1761 232237
reception@courthotel.co.uk
www.courthotel.co.uk

Strategically placed at the edge of the Mendip Hills with commanding views to the north, this country hotel, surrounded by three-and-a-half acres of grounds, offers peace and comfort in a relaxing atmosphere. Bedrooms in the main house are traditionally decorated, and there are further ground floor rooms in an adjacent wing. Other bedrooms are located in the lodge, which is separate from the house, and the coach house in the grounds offers the most up-to-date rooms, added in 1999. All are very well equipped with lots of extras. Traditional English sums up the cooking in the restaurant, with grilled lamb cutlets glazed with honey and rosemary, and chicken poached with a creamy Stilton sauce typical choices. The wide ranging wine list is very reasonably priced.

Prices: Sunday lunch £10.50. Main course from £12. House wine £9.25.
Hours: 12.00-14.30. 19.00-22.00. No food Bank Holidays or 25 December.
Rooms: 18 en suite. Double room from £65, single from £45.
Cuisine: Traditional English/continental.
Other Points: No-smoking area. Children welcome. Garden. Car park.
Directions: Take the A367 from Bath to Radstock, then Wells Road to Chilcompton. Take A37 from Bristol. (Map 4, C7)

Prices: Main course restaurant from £8.95. Main course bar from £5.95. House wine £10.95.
Hours: 11.00-14.30. 17.30-23.00. Saturday 11.00-23.00. Sunday 12.00-15.00. 19.00-22.30.
Food served: 12.00-14.30. 19.00-21.30, until 21.00 on Sunday.
Rooms: 8 en suite. Double/twin from £80.
Cuisine: Traditional British.
Other Points: No-smoking area. Dogs welcome. Garden. Children welcome over 10 years old. Car park.
Directions: Just off the A366 seven miles west of Trowbridge. (Map 4, B7)

The George

High Street, Norton St Philip, Bath BA2 7LH
Telephone: +44(0)1373 834224
www.thegeorgeinn-nsp.co.uk

One of the oldest inns in the country has taken on a new lease of life following a meticulous restoration: where once there were ' 35 beds and stabling for 90 horses' there are now just eight beautifully furnished bedrooms with antiques and hand-carved beds, three of them four-posters. (The Duke of Monmouth fled here in 1685 following the defeat of his rebellion at Sedgemoor; an attempt was made on his life as he stood shaving at the window.) Today's bathrooms are certainly better equipped to meet 21st-century requirements. At the heart of the pub, a huge open fire, wood floor and distinctive beams imbue the Monmouth Bar with a timeless ambience in which to enjoy Wadworths' real ales and a mighty beef sandwich, game terrine with chutney or daily specials such as pork-and-leek sausages in onion gravy. The high-pitched dining hall and original oak beamed ceiling is a spectacular setting for more formal dinners that offer wood pigeon and bacon salad, rump of lamb with redcurrant and mint sauce and a strawberry teardrop in dark chocolate casing.

The Swan Inn

Lower Inkpen, Hungerford, Berkshire RG17 9DX
Telephone: +44(0)1488 668326
enquiries@theswaninn-organics.co.uk
www.theswaninn-organics.co.uk

This restored 17th-century farmhouse pub has old beams and timbers in the rambling bar, four open fires and first-rate real ales from Butts (local) and Hook Norton breweries. It's all very traditional, but what is surprising is that owners Bernard and Mary Harris are local organic beef farmers. In addition to beef, organically reared lamb, pigs and poultry are hung and butchered on the premises and used extensively on the pub menus, as well as being on sale in the Swan's Organic Farm Shop which adjoins the pub. Typically, you can order homemade steak and ale pie, beef, leek and ale sausages with mash and onion gravy, organic beefburgers, braised lamb chops and quality steaks from the bar menu. Alternatives may include beer-battered cod and poached salmon salad. More elaborate meals are served in the Cygnet Restaurant, the changing carte perhaps listing battered tiger prawns with chilli and lime sauce, shoulder of lamb with redcurrant jus, and chocolate and hazelnut terrine with crème anglaise. Housed in a purpose-built rear extension are ten comfortable en suite bedrooms, all attractively furnished with modern pine furnishings. All enjoy peaceful rural views.

Prices: Main course restaurant meal from £12.50. Starter from £3.95. House wine £14.
Hours: 12.00-14.30. 19.00-23.00. Sunday until 22.30. Closed 25-26 December.
Food served: 12.00-14.00. 19.00-21.30. From 11.00 on Saturday, until 21.00 on Sunday.
Rooms: 10 en suite. Singles from £40, doubles from £75.
Cuisine: Modern British.
Other Points: No-smoking area. Garden. Children welcome. Car park.
Directions: From Hungerford high street follow signs to Hungerford Common; turn right signposted to Inkpen. (Map 5, C3)

The Dundas Arms

53 Station Rd, Kintbury, Berkshire RG17 0UT
Telephone: +44(0)1488 658263
info@dundasarms.co.uk
www.dundasarms.com

For more than 37 years David Dalzell-Piper has run this well-loved, reliable old-fashioned inn, which thrives in its position on a narrow strip of land between the River Kennet and the restored Kennet and Avon Canal. With passing narrowboats it is no wonder that tables on the riverside patio are very popular on warm summer days. Local ingredients are prepared with skill, confidence, and a notable lack of fuss. These talents show up well in traditional country dishes like roast breast of Quantock duck with cider and apple sauce, and calf's liver with bacon and onion gravy. Game from local dealers feature on the winter blackboards that hang in the civilised bar, alongside lighter dishes, perhaps home-potted shrimps, duck liver pâté, and baked cod with decent chips. For pudding there may be bread and butter pudding or iced coffee and praline mousse. Alternatively, round off with a plate of British and Irish cheeses, and a glass of vintage port. The inn is famous for its serious 200-strong wine list; house wines are excellent, too. Comfortable en suite bedrooms are in a converted livery and stable block, with sliding picture windows opening on to a quiet and private riverside terrace.

Prices: Main course restaurant from £13. House wine from £13.50.
Hours: 11.00-15.00. 18.00-22.30. Open until 14.30 on Sunday. Closed Sunday evening, Christmas and New Year.
Food served: 12.00-14.00. 19.00-21.00. No food all Sunday and Monday evening.
Rooms: 5 en suite. Doubles/twin room from £70.
Cuisine: Modern British.
Other Points: No-smoking area. Patio. Children over two welcome. Car park.
Directions: Exit13/14/M4. Take the A4; halfway between Newbury and Hungerford, one mile south by the canal. (Map 5, C3)

The Red House

Marsh Benham, Newbury, Berkshire RG20 8LY
Telephone: +44(0)1635 582017

An18th-century pub lies tucked away in a pretty hamlet off the A4 between Newbury and Hungerford. New owners took over in 2000 and set about seriously restyling the pub interior and menus. Stripped wood floors, warmly painted walls and comfortable furnishings is the result in the bar-cum-bistro, while bookcases and huge paintings characterise the more formal front restaurant. The introduction of an imaginative modern British menu (with a Gallic twist from Yves Girard) has proved a great success, drawing visitors back to this long-established Kennet Valley favourite. A typical meal from the carte might comprise pan-fried scallops on fresh linguine with saffron velouté and mussels, followed by cod fillet on beetroot risotto with a white wine and herb velouté, or beef fillet with fondant potatoes, baby vegetables and morel sauce, and warm chocolate tart with berry coulis. The daily changing set menu offers a good choice and exceptional value. There's a select list of wines with six favourably priced house wines by the glass, impeccable service from Xavier le Bellego and his team, and splendid alfresco terrace with upmarket teak furniture overlooking sloping lawns and peaceful water meadows.

Prices: Set lunch and dinner £16.95. Main course restaurant from £14.25. Main course bar £9.75.
Hours: 12.00-15.00. 18.00-23.00. Closed Sunday and Monday evening, 25-26 December and 1 January.
Food served: 12.00-14.00. 19.00-22.00.
Cuisine: Modern European.
Other Points: No-smoking area. Garden. Car park.
Directions: Exit 13/14 M4. Just off the A4 three miles west of Newbury and five miles east of Hungerford. (Map 5, C3)

Prices: Main course restaurant meal from £9.95. House wine £11.90.
Hours: 11.00-24.00. 11.00-23.00 on Sunday. Closed 25-26 December evening and 1 January evening.
Food served: 12.00-14.30 (until 15.00 at the week-end). 18.30-22.00 (until 21.30 on Sunday).
Rooms: 6 en suite. Double room from £75, single from £60.
Cuisine: Traditional and Modern British.
Other Points: No-smoking area. Children welcome. Garden. Car park.
Directions: Curridge is signposted off B4009 (Goring road) 3 miles north of Newbury. Junction 13/M4. (Map 5, C3)

The Bunk Inn
Curridge, Newbury, Berkshire RG18 9DS
Telephone: +44(0)1635 200400
www.thebunkinn.co.uk

The Liquorish family pub empire around Newbury continues to go from strength to strength. Mickey and father Jack expanded the well established Bunk Inn by opening six executive-style bedrooms in early 2003. All are kitted out with quality fabrics and fittings, smart en suite facilities, and a host of added extras that ensure a comfortable stay. The accommodation should appeal to those looking for a bustling and informal pub rather than the faceless Chieveley Travel Inn. The present food set up should not disappoint, as sound traditional favourites rub shoulders with modern pub dishes on the daily chalkboard menu and weekly changing carte. Take comfort in bangers and mash or a 'Bunk' long loaf snack. Or head for the attractive conservatory dining room for crab cakes with sweet chilli dressing, slow-roasted lamb shoulder with port and redcurrant gravy. Both the apple tarte tatin and vanilla panna cotta with winter berry compote come highly recommended. Altogether, the welcoming beamed bar, stone-floored restaurant with local paintings and fresh flowers, and a splendid flower festooned terrace, create a civilised atmosphere.

The Ridgeway, Streatley

Windsor Castle

London Street Brasserie 📖✗

2-4 London Street, Riverside, Reading,
Berkshire RG1 4SE
Telephone: +44(0)1189 505036
www.londonstbrasserie.co.uk

The bright, clean and modern restaurant certainly draws the crowd with its contemporary good looks of white walls, polished-wood floors, wood tables, high-backed mauve-dressed chairs and colourful pictures (for sale). Sliding doors to one side of the ground-floor dining room open onto a small decked area. Subtle background jazz music catches the mood. The carte hits a modern European note with nods to the Mediterranean, Orient and Asia within its ambitious repertoire. Spoil yourself with Sevruga caviar, six smoked salmon blinis and a miniature frozen Smirnoff, or cruise straight into the main starters of, say, seared peppered tuna loin with oriental pickled vegetables, lemon oil, sesame soy and oyster dressing and crispy wonton. Classic brasserie dishes such as entrecote with béarnaise sauce and chipped potatoes, sit side by side with more distinctly modern combinations of pink-roasted venison fillet, McSween's haggis, figs, baby spinach, port, redcurrant and juniper sauce. Bread is from Degustibus, there are excellent local cheeses, and puddings can be as richly indulgent as hot chocolate fondant with Baileys ice cream. The 40-bin globetrotting wine list offers eight by the glass. Under the same ownership as the Crooked Billet, Stoke Row (see entry).

Prices: Set lunch £12.95 (2 course, 12.00-19.00 everyday). Main course from £11.00. House wine £13.50.
Hours: 12.00-22.30 (23.00 on Friday and Saturday). Closed 25-26 December and 1 January.
Cuisine: Modern British.
Other Points: Riverside terrace (heated).
Directions: Exit 10 or 11/M4. Follow signs to 'Oracle' park in 'Oracle' multi-storey car park. (Map 5, C4)

The Star Inn 📖✗

Broadmoor Road, Waltham-St-Lawrence, Reading,
Berkshire RG10 0HY
Telephone: +44(0)1189 343486
james@thestar-inn.co.uk
www.thestar-inn.co.uk

Situated in pretty Waltham St Lawrence, midway between Reading and Maidenhead, the spick-and-span Star Inn is an unassuming village local run by Wadworth tenants, James Barrons-Ruth and Jayne Barrington-Groves. Sound investment by both the brewery and tenants over the past three years has resulted in the refurbishment of the traditional pub interior (new carpet and upholstered benches and stools), and the addition of a smart gravelled patio area with pot-plants and picnic tables. Although the lunchtime menu offers pub favourites for speed and convenience, James refuses to serve chips or any deep-fried foods, preferring to prepare everything on the premises. Typically, chicken Caesar salad and freshly made soups will accompany the giant filled baps (roast beef and horseradish), and excellent home-baked pizzas (pesto and black olive) on the lunchtime board. Expect a touch more imagination in the evening, with James's seasonally changing menu and daily specials choice offering whole sea bass on pimentoes with garlic, sherry and oyster sauce, and roast shoulder of lamb with port, garlic and rosemary. Tip-top Wadworth ales as well as interesting bin-end wine specials.

Prices: Main course restaurant from £10.95. Main course bar/snack from £5.75. House wine £9.95.
Hours: 11.30-14.30, until 15.00 at weekends. 18.00-23.00. Closed Christmas Day evening and Boxing Day.
Food served: 12.00-14.00. 19.00-21.30. Sunday 12.00-14.00.
Cuisine: Modern pub food.
Other Points: No-smoking area. Garden. Children welcome over 12 years old. Car park.
Directions: Exit 8 or 9/M4, to White Waltham heading west through Cox Green on Broadmoor Road for two miles to Waltham-St-Lawrence. (Map 5, C4)

The Harrow 📖✗

West Ilsley, Newbury, Berkshire RG20 7AR
Telephone: +44(0)1635 281260

The handsome, 600-year-old building is in an idyllic setting overlooking the village cricket field, pond, and beyond, across rolling downland. Morland founded their brewery in the village in 1711 before moving to nearby Abingdon, but their excellent Original Ale can still be found at the Harrow, Morland's first ale house. It's a real local. There's plenty of space within the smartly rustic bar with its antiques, country settles, old paintings and a relaxing, unpretentious atmosphere. The front terrace delivers summer drinking and eating, backed up by serene village views. Superior pub food ranges from good lunchtime baguettes or homemade 8oz beefburger topped with Stilton, to imaginative dishes offered on both the lunchtime blackboard and daily evening menus. Here you may find carrot and parsley soup, or rabbit confit with vanilla risotto and raspberry vinaigrette as a starter, then rib-eye steak with béarnaise sauce and green beans, or sea bass with chorizo, deep-fried anchovies with tomato and herb sauce. Puddings are good, look out for warm caramelised fruit tart and vanilla ice cream. There's a good list of wines with eight offered by the glass.

Prices: Main course bar from £6. Main course restaurant from £10. House wine £10.
Hours: 11.00-15.00. 18.00-23.00. Check for seasonal changes in opening hours.
Food served: 12.00-14.00 18.00-22.00.
Cuisine: Modern British and French.
Other Points: No-smoking area. Well behaved dogs welcome. Children welcome. Garden. Car park.
Directions: Village signposted off the A34, approximately seven miles north of M4 and A34 junction. (Map 5, C3)

Gray Of Wokingham

Heathlands Road, Wokingham, Berkshire RG40 3AN
Telephone: +44(0)1189 785386
bethruach@hotmail.com

This straightforward, down-to-earth family run PYO farm has 65 acres under cultivation and offers a long list of freshly picked homegrown produce for sale in their farm shop. Soft fruits such as gooseberries, strawberries, raspberries, red and black currants, as well as new potatoes, broad and runner beans, cabbage, cauliflower, carrots, beetroot, peas, courgettes, rhubarb, red and white onions, and cabbage all come from the farm. Crops are grown with care for the environment under the LEAF scheme and the shop is open from late May to mid October. It's an interesting place to take children, a lot less commercialized than some farm shops, but there's a play area and a picnic area.

Hours: Late May-mid October: Monday-Saturday 09.00-18.00. Closed Sunday.
Other points: Parking. Children's play area. Picnic area. Easy access for disabled.
Directions: Leave Peach Street Wokingham by Easthampstead Road. At White Horse PH turn right into Heathlands Road. Farm is 0.3m on the right. Or leave Nine Mile Ride B3430, opposite Ravenswood Centre. Farm 1 mile on the left. (Map 5, C4)

Ganges

368 Gloucester Road, Bristol BS7 8TP
Telephone: +44(0)117 9245234

The menu at this vividly decorated, long-standing Indian restaurant tries to follow the course of the sacred River Ganges, and offers dishes from the three main regions through which the river flows (rising in Tibet, flowing through India and reaching the sea at its destination in Bangladesh). However, the major influence comes from North India. Thus, familiar curries range from a mild lamb pasanda to a fiery vindaloo king prawn, alongside biryanis and a good choice of reasonably priced set menus. From a variety of tandoori dishes, there's an all encompassing thali of tandoori murg, lamb tikka, shish kebab, nan, pilau rice, and chicken tikka. Vegetarian dishes (including a vegetarian thali) are a strength; all vegetables used are fresh. Wines stay well below the £20 mark, many are under £15, and there's a choice of bottled and draught beers.

Prices: Set lunch and dinner from £14.50. House wine £8.95.
Hours: 12.00-14.30. 18.00-23.30. Closed 25-26 December.
Cuisine: Indian and Bangladeshi.
Other Points: No-smoking area. Children welcome.
Directions: On the A38 Gloucester Road. (Map 4, B6)

San Carlo Restaurant

44 Corn Street, Bristol BS1 1HQ
Telephone: +44(0)117 9226586

The tall Victorian building stands in an attractive pedestrianised area in the city centre. Within, it is one long, relatively narrow room with the back slightly elevated, creating an area that would be suitable for private parties. There's a strong Mediterranean feel to the place, a theme common to all three restaurants in this small, stylish group that's adopted a fairly uniform look of mirrored walls, white-tiled floor, and colour in the form of potted plants and trees of different shapes and sizes. It aims for a busy, buzzy atmosphere, delivering old favourites at reasonable prices; indeed the cooking is a cut above the norm for a city-centre eaterie majoring in pizzas and pastas. The lengthy menu lists familiar trattoria dishes: fritto misto; buffalo mozzarella with tomato, basil and avocado; saltimboca all romana; piccata al limone; and suprema di pollo genovese. Blackboard specials extend the choice with a range of seafood that could include dressed crab, grilled Dover sole and mixed grill of fish. There's a selection of well-priced Italian wines, with a good selection by the glass and France and the new world bringing up the rear.

Prices: Main course from £11. House wine £11.20.
Hours: 12.00-23.00.
Cuisine: Italian.
Other Points: Children welcome.
Directions: In Bristol city centre.
(Map 4, B6)

The Chequers Inn

Kiln Lane, Wooburn Common,
Buckinghamshire HP10 0JQ
Telephone: +44(0)1628 529575
info@chequers-inn.com
www.chequers-inn.com

The charming 17th century inn lies midway between the M4 and M40, perched on the rolling Chiltern Hills and has been carefully and lovingly developed over the last 25 years by Peter Roehrig. You can either stop for a pint of Ruddles and a snack in the convivial bar, with its beamed ceiling, oak posts, flagstoned floor and warming winter fire, or head for the elegantly designed restaurant for a some imaginative cooking that utilizes fresh local ingredients. A meal in August could open with roast pepper stuffed with feta, marinated olives and sun-dried tomatoes, then pan-fried John Dory fillets on a nage of seafood and baby vegetables, then and finish with peach Melba. The carte delivers the likes of white asparagus and black truffle soup, and mignon of pork fillet, scallops and marinated fennel with caper and lemon oil jus. Cottagey bedrooms have views over the surrounding countryside from leaded windows and every room exudes real country character through the use of stripped pine and heavy quality fabrics. Each comes with every modern amenity, and there is one room with a huge four poster bed that's popular as a bridal suite.

Prices: Set lunch £17.95. Set dinner £26.95. Main course restaurant from £15.95. Bar sandwiches from £4. House wine £9.50.
Food served: 12.00-14.30. 19.00-21.30. Saturday 12.00-22.00 and Sunday 12.00-21.30.
Rooms: 17 en suite. Rooms between £77.50 - £107.50.
Cuisine: British and French.
Other Points: No-smoking area. Dogs welcome in some areas. Garden. Children welcome. Car park.
Directions: Exit2/M40. Follow the signs to Beaconsfield, join A40 towards High Wycombe and turn left into Broad Lane in 2 miles. (Map 5, B4)

The Ivy House

London Road, Chalfont St Giles,
Buckinghamshire HP8 4RS
Telephone: +44(0)1494 872184
www.theivyhouse-bucks.co.uk

17th-century brick-and-flint free house set in the heart of the Chiltern Hills with views across the Misbourne Valley. The wood and slate-floored bar, with its old beams, cosy armchairs, wood-burning fires and fine old pictures offers four changing real ales, an extensive range of malt whiskies and a select list of wines (20 by the glass). A menu of modern British dishes prepared by chef/proprietor Jane Mears and her team reveals a happpiness to experiment with ingredients to produce unusual dishes - look to the blackboard for the day's creations. Beyond a commendable 'slimline menu' for diners on diets, choices range from homemade soups, to baked field mushrooms with wild mushrooms, cream and garlic among starters. Main courses extend to loin of lamb with redcurrent and mint sauce, seared tuna with ginger, lime and herb butter, or chargrilled sirloin steak with creamy peppercorn and brandy sauce, plus winter casseroles, summer salads, Thai curries, pasta meals and homemade puddings, perhaps classic bread and butter pudding.

Prices: Main course from £8.95. House wine £9.95.
Hours: 12.00-15.00. 18.00-23.00. Weekends 12.00-23.00. Closed Christmas Day.
Food served: 12.00-14.30. 18.30-21.30. Weekends 12.00-21.30.
Rooms: 5 new luxury rooms from December 2003.
Cuisine: Modern British/global.
Other Points: No-smoking area. Dogs welcome. Children welcome. Garden and courtyard. Car park.
Directions: Exit2/M40. Situated directly between Amersham and Gerrards Cross on the A413. (Map 5, B4)

The White Hart Inn

Three Households, Chalfont St Giles, Buckinghamshire HP8 4LP
Telephone: +44(0)1494 872441
chef.around@btopenworld.com
www.white-hart-inn.com

There is a comfortable contemporary feel throughout this 100-year-old inn situated on the edge of Chalfont St Giles in the heart of the Chiltern Hills. Inside, expect to find a light bar with tiled floors, relaxing armchairs and sofas with scatter cushions, fresh flowers, a log burning fire, and a long wooden bar serving Greene King ales and ten wines by the glass. Imaginative menus combine the best of traditional and modern pub cooking, and make good use of the finest quality local ingredients. Pop in for a lunchtime snack and you will find chicken Caesar salad, smoked haddock risotto with poached egg, and marinated chicken and roasted vegetable sandwich, served with homecooked crisps, on the bar menu. For something more substantial look to the restaurant where perennial pub favourites are given a welcome modern twist. Follow wild mushroom and tarragon risotto, with beer battered cod and chips, or rack of lamb with rosemary and thyme reduction. Modern bedrooms are housed in two detached buildings behind the inn, one a converted stable block, the other a purpose-built lodge. All rooms are clean and tidy, and well appointed with TV and en suite bathrooms.

Prices: Main course from £9.50. House wine £9.95.
Hours: 11.30-14.30, until 15.00 weekends. 18.00-23.00, 19.00-22.30 Sunday. Closed 26 and 27 December.
Food served: 12.00-14.00 and 18.30-21.30 Monday to Saturday. 12.00-14.30 and 19.00-21.00 on Sunday.
Rooms: 11 en suite. Double room from £97, single from £77.50. Family room £107.
Cuisine: Modern and traditional pub food.
Other Points: No-smoking area. Children welcome. Garden. Car park.
Directions: Situated between Amersham and Gerrards Cross. (Map 5, B4)

The Swan Inn

Village Road, Denham, Buckinghamshire UB9 5BH
Telephone: +44(0)1895 832085

In search of a third pub to expand their highly successful dining pub empire (see Alford Arms, Berkhamsted, and Royal Oak, Marlow), David and Becky Salisbury couldn't resist buying the Swan Inn. Perfectly situated a few minutes from the M25 and M40, it stands in an upmarket village filled with fine houses and brick and timber cottages. Like its stylish siblings, the Swan's single bar and informal dining area has been tastefully refurbished and features a rug-strewn floor, a comfortable mix of sturdy tables and cushioned settles, large prints, and a splendid open log fire. Food follows the tried and tested formula of a chalkboard and regularly changing printed carte delivering modern pub food. 'Small plates' range from rustic breads with roast garlic for an appetiser, to starters/light meals such as Thai-scented mussels with coconut and coriander or french onion and gruyère tart with rocket. More substantial offerings include baked whole sea bass on hazelnut couscous with bok choi and coriander and cumin broth, rib-eye steak with handcut chips and horseradish and parsley butter, or calf's liver with garlic mash, roast baby beetroot and tarragon jus. The best motorway pit-stop for miles.

Prices: Main course from £9.25. House wine £10.75.
Hours: 11.00-23.00. Sunday 12.00-22.30. Closed 25-26 and 31 December, 1 January in the evening.
Food served: 12.00-14.30, Sunday until 15.00. 19.00-22.00.
Cuisine: Modern British.
Other Points: Dogs welcome. Garden. Children welcome. Car park.
Directions: Exit1/M40 and exit17/M25. From M40 take the A412 Uxbridge to Rickmansworth Road and turn left in 200 yards for Denham. (Map 5, C4)

Green Dragon

8 Churchway, Haddenham, Aylesbury, Buckinghamshire HP17 8AA
Telephone: +44(0)1844 291403
paul@eatatthedragon.co.uk
www.eatatthedragon.co.uk

This very civilised dining pub was once the 17th century manorial court of Buckinghamshire, where the last man to be hanged in the country was tried. Decorated in warm olive green and antique rose, with tasteful prints and watercolours, an eclectic mix of attractive tables and chairs, and an open log fire, it offers a relaxed atmosphere, an excellent pint of village-brewed Notley Ale from Vale Brewery, and Paul Berry's imaginative modern cooking. Begin, perhaps, with hot sweet and sour tiger prawn broth, or crisp confit of duck with pineapple chutney. Mains bring coriander-crusted cod fillet with spinach linguine, chilli and tomato jam, rump of English lamb on olive mash with MacSween black pudding, or homemade steak and kidney suet pudding. Fish dishes run to a full flavoured dish of monkfish wrapped in Cumbrian ham on crushed sweet potato and chorizo with fresh pea sauce. Leave room for Tuscany orange cake with mascarpone cream or lemon and lime tart with raspberry sorbet. Alternatively, finish with a plate of British and Irish organic cheeses. Excellent value set-price dinner Tuesday and Thursdays, and lunchtime sandwiches. Good list of wine with several offered by the glass. Summer seating in a sheltered rear courtyard.

Prices: Set 2-course menu Tuesday & Thursday £10.95. Main course from £9.95. House wine £11.50.
Hours: 12.00-14.00. 19.00-21.30. Sunday until 21.00
Cuisine: Traditional and Modern British.
Other Points: No-smoking area. Children welcome over seven years. Garden. Car park.
Directions: Village signed off A418 between Thame and Aylesbury, 3 miles north of Thame. (Map 5, B4)

The Royal Oak

Frieth Road, Bovingdon Green, Marlow,
Buckinghamshire SL7 2JF
Telephone: +44(0)1628 488611

Part of David and Becky Salisbury's flourishing little
pub empire, which includes the estimable Alford Arms
at Frithsden and the Swan at Denham (see entries), the
Royal Oak stands on the edge of Marlow Common.
Fronted by a gravel terrace edged with rosemary, with
bay trees in pots either side of the door, this lovely
cream-painted cottage has been refurbished with style.
Beyond a cosy snug (open fire, rug-strewn boards,
terracotta walls, an array of scrubbed oak tables,
chairs and cushioned pews), piped jazz, and a buzzy
atmosphere characterise the beamed and open-plan bar
and dining areas. Informality is the key here, eat
anywhere with the choice extending to both the rear
terrace and the landscaped garden in summer. Both
chalkboards and printed menus deliver food that
reveals a lot of imagination at work in the kitchen.
'Small plates' range from seared salmon with pea and
mint guacamole, to substantial dishes such as duck leg
confit on bok choi with hoi sin jus, or roast cod on
saffron braised fennel and tomato stew. Try the rustic
breads with roast garlic and olive oil for dipping, there
are freshly-cut lunchtime sandwiches, and good
puddings. Short list of well chosen wines with most
offered by the glass.

Prices: Main course from £9.50. House wine £10.75.
Hours: 11.00-23.00. 12.00-22.30 on Sunday.
Closed 25-26 December.
Food served: 12.00-14.30 (until 15.00 on Sunday). 19.00-22.00.
Cuisine: Modern British.
Other Points: Children welcome. Garden. Car park.
Directions: In Marlow take the A4155 towards Henley-on-Thames
and turn right in 300 yards signposted Bovingdon Green.
Junction 4/9/M40. (Map 5, C4)

The Stag

The Green, Mentmore, Buckinghamshire LU7 0QS
Telephone: +44(0)1296 668423
reservations@thestagmentmore.com
www.thestagmentmore.com

When Mike Tuckwood moved to this quiet
Buckinghamshire backwater his aim was to revive the
flagging fortunes of The Stag. Four years on, his fresh
modern approach to running a traditional country pub
has paid dividends. The classic bar is the place to
sample Charles Wells ales and some good bar food:
sandwiches and salads, for example, and one-dish
meals of local sausages with mash and onion gravy, or
tagliatelle with spinach, pine nuts and cream.
Imaginative, seasonally-changing evening menus are
served in the stylishly modernised two-tiered
restaurant, which has direct access to a charming
garden. A plate of buffalo mozzarella (from a local
buffalo herd) with balsamic and black pepper
strawberries makes an unusual starter, with fresh local
asparagus with butter and carpaccio of English beef
with red onion and black pepper typical of other
choices. Thoughtful attention to inherent flavours
produces main courses such as calf's liver with bacon,
spring onion mash and balsamic tomatoes, and red
snapper with aubergine chutney and mussel-infused
rice. An alternative to a dessert of bread and butter
pudding is a plate of British cheeses.

Prices: Set lunch and dinner £25.00. Main course from £15.
Traditional Sunday lunch. House wine £13.40.
Hours: 12.00-15.00. 18.00-23.00. All day at weekends.
Food served: 12.00-14.00. 19.00-21.00. 19.00-20.30 Sunday.
Restaurant closed Monday all day. No bar food Monday evening.
Cuisine: Modern British.
Other Points: No-smoking area. Dogs welcome. Children welcome
at lunch and over 12 years old in the evening. Garden.
Limited car park.
Directions: Five miles north east of Aylesbury off A418 towards
Leighton Buzzard. (Map 9, E4)

The Crooked Billet

2 Westbrook End, Newton Longville, Milton Keynes,
Buckinghamshire MK17 0DF
Telephone: +44(0)1908 373936
john@thebillet.co.uk
www.thebillet.co.uk

John Gilchrist and chef/partner Emma Sexton. have not looked back since
taking on the lease of this pretty 18th-century thatched pub. The rambling
and tastefully refurbished interior comprises two intimate wine-themed
dining rooms, with red walls, terracotta tiled floors and lightwood tables,
while original oak beams, open log fires and simple pine tables
characterise the informal bar area. Here sandwiches such as open smoked
salmon, prawn and rocket, and, salads of medium rare fillet steak, or
chicken Caesar, are served at lunchtimes only, alongside a short carte.
Balanced weekly changing evening menus make good use of first-rate local
produce, including herbs and chutneys from 'Captain Tom' and meat from
Pollards, the village butcher, and Isle of Man hand-dived scallops. A
typical meal may begin with pan-fried boudin blanc, potato purée, pan-
fried foie gras and port reduction. For main course, choose roasted bream
fillet, olive oil crushed potatoes, artichoke heart, salsify and 20 year old
balsamic reduction. Finish with roasted purple fig and almond tart with
honey date and late-bottled port ice cream or cheeses from Neal's Yard
Dairy. An impeccable list of 300 wines featuring all the French classics
and a good showing from the new world, all available by the glass.

Prices: Main course bar meal £7.50. Main
course restaurant £11. House wine £13.
Hours: Tuesday-Friday 12.00-14.30. 17.30-
23.00. 12.00-23.00 on Saturday. 12.00-
16.00. 19.00-22.30 on Sunday. Closed first
two weeks January, 25-26 December.
Food served: 12.00-14.00. Sunday 12.00-
15.00 only. Tuesday-Thursday 19.00-21.30.
Friday and Saturday until 22.00.
Cuisine: Modern and Classic British.
Other Points: No-smoking area. No dogs.
Children over five. Garden. Car park.
Directions: Village signposted off A421
Buckingham road, 3 miles west of Milton
Keynes. J13/M1. (Map 5, B4)

Five Arrows Hotel ★ ▯ ✗ ⌀

High Street, Waddesdon, Aylesbury,
Buckinghamshire HP18 0JE
Telephone: +44 (0)1296 651727
bookings@thefivearrowshotel.fsnet.co.uk
www.waddesdon.org.uk

A delightful Victorian confection built by the
Rothschilds' in 1887 as part of Baron Ferdinand's plan
for a 'model village' to surround his French-style
chateau, Waddesdon Manor (see following entry). Now
a stylish small hotel-cum-inn run by Julian Alexander-
Worster, you enter straight into the bar, from which
open several civilised dining rooms with rug-strewn
wood or stone floors, antique tables, and pictures from
Lord Rothschild's collection. Locally sourced
ingredients plus garden herbs influence the menu,
crayfish tail salad with dill mayonnaise, for example,
or salmon fishcakes with coriander jam. Thai
marinated red mullet on soy noodles comes as a starter
or main course, or there could be fillet steak with red
shallot butter. To finish, choose between the cheese
table or brioche bread and butter pudding and
homemade honeycomb ice cream. There are also
blackboard specials and lighter lunchtime meals. The
good wine list majors on the various Rothschild wine
interests with eleven by the glass. Eleven good-sized en
suite bedrooms are individually decorated and boast
extra large beds along with all modern comforts. Two
suites in the converted Courtyard Stables.

Prices: Main course from £13.50. House wine £12.50.
Hours: 11.30-15.00. 17.30-23.00. 12.00-15.00. 19.00-22.30 on
Sunday. Closed 25-26, 31 December and 1 January.
Food served: 12.00-14.30. 19.00-21.30. 12.30-14.00.
19.30-21.00 Sunday.
Rooms: 11 en suite. Double room from £90, single from £70.
Cuisine: Modern British/Continental.
Other Points: No-smoking area. Children welcome over 12
years old. Garden. Car park.
Directions: Six miles north west of Aylesbury beside the A41 in
Waddesdon. (Map 5, B4)

Manor Restaurant ★ ▯ ♥ ✗

Waddesdon Manor, Waddesdon, Aylesbury,
Buckinghamshire HP18 0JH
Telephone: +44(0)1296 653242

One of the great 19th century Rothschild houses in
Europe is shielded from the realities of 21st century
existence by mature trees and acres of parkland. Now
run by the National Trust (seasonal entrance fee),
Waddesdon Manor ranks as one of the finest houses in
Britain. And in the relaxed surroundings of the
ground-floor servants' hall you will find one of the
most original restaurants in England. With its core
clientele firmly in mind, the kitchen mixes National
Trust tearoom classics with a lunch menu that is an
inspired juxtaposition of traditional dishes from the
Rothschild menu books and up-to-date cooking. Simple
menu descriptions translate into equally
straightforward dishes such as smoked haddock
chowder with curry oil, or braised ham hock with
mustard mash, braising juice and vegetables with
parsley. The kindly priced wine list, with its full range
of Rothschild family wines from around the world, will
appeal to serious oenophiles, and the advice of the
young sommelier should be heeded. In the grounds is
the Stables Restaurant with a casual air and gingham
tablecloths indicating a choice of simpler dishes such
as soups, sandwiches, filled jacket potatoes, popular
cakes and pastries. Also in the grounds, in a delightful
setting, is the old Victorian Dairy, elegantly restored
and fully equipped for weddings and private dinners.

Prices: Set lunch £20. Main course restaurant from £9.50.
House wine £11.50.
Hours: 12.00-15.00. Closed Monday and Tuesday and Christmas to
the end of February.
Cuisine: Modern European.
Other Points: No smoking. Garden. Children welcome. Car park.
Directions: Off the A41 between Bicester and Aylesbury.
(Map 5, B4)

The Green Man ▯ ▯ ✗

Thriplow, Royston, Cambridgeshire SG8 7RJ
Telephone: +44(0)1763 208855
www.greenmantriplow.co.uk

In the heart of a small Cambridgeshire village stands this traditional
looking village local - cream painted with attractive window boxes. Décor
within is traditional with red patterned carpet, deep red walls and
matching curtains, open fire in a black metal grate, and a comfortable
dining area with leather sofas in one corner. The menus read well, offer
excellent value and evident passion in both compilation and cooking. The
set price menu delivers layered terrine of game infused with port, brandy
and Madeira, poached fillet of brill on rösti potatoes with buttered

Prices: Set lunch £13.95. Set dinner £24.
Main course restaurant from £15.50. Main
course bar/snack from £4.50.
House wine £10.50.
Hours: 12.00-15.00. 18.00-23.00.
Closed Sunday evening and all day Monday.
Food served: 12.00-14.00. 18.00-21.30.
Cuisine: Modern British.
Other Points: No-smoking area.
Children welcome. Garden. Car park.
Directions: Exit10/M11. Three miles
south of junction off B1368. (Map 10, D5)

spinach and a poaching liquor sauce with mushrooms, shallots, tomato
concasse and chives. Drop scones in toffee sauce served with caramelised
bananas in rum syrup and spiced honey ice cream bring up the rear. Carte
options could include millefeuille of buttered crab, and braised shoulder
of lamb with foie gras. Every two months there's a gourmet evening with
matching wine list, and there's a separate lunch menu offering fresh pasta,
sandwiches and there's a Sunday lunch menu. The short global wine list
reflects the menu and is changed regularly. Beers change continually, with
the emphasis on small breweries, so expect Bateman's 12 Bore, Adnams
Broadside and Milton's Morselium.

The Anchor Inn

Sutton Gault, Sutton, Ely, Cambridgeshire CB6 2BD
Telephone: +44(0)1353 778537
AnchorInnSG@aol.com
www.anchor-inn-restaurant.co.uk

Robin and Heather Moore's marshland oasis is protected from the New Bedford River by a veritable rampart of earthworks. Descend, then pass a riverside patio into the low, brick-built 16th-century pub. Beer jugs hanging from hooks, scrubbed pine tables, and gas-lights, enhance the cosy atmosphere in the low-beamed bars. The innovative, daily changing menus reflect the changing seasons and rely on fresh local produce, including market-fresh fish, and duck from the marshes. Typically, start with Mediterranean fish soup or duck confit terrine with blackberry and apple compote, and progress to seared pigeon breasts with sweet potato mash, lentils, chorizo and roast chicory, or baked gilt-head bream with vanilla and vermouth sauce. Home-made puddings are served with homemade ice cream and might include Arabian orange cake. A medley of unusual British cheeses with warm bread is another option. Lighter lunchtime snacks range from ploughman's platters, to saffron risotto with creamy leek, and hot smoked salmon salad. there's a classy list of wines. Booking is advisable at weekends. Two comfortable en suite bedrooms consist of a spacious suite and a charming twin-bedded room.

Prices: Main course restaurant from £10.50. House wine £12.50.
Hours: 12.00-15.00. 19.00-23.00. Closed 26 December.
Food served: 12.00-14.00. 19.00-21.00. Until 14.30 on Sunday and from 18.00-21.30 Saturday evening.
Rooms: 2 en suite. £75 per room.
Cuisine: Modern British.
Other Points: No-smoking area. Garden. Children welcome. Car park.
Directions: Exit M11 at Cambridge. Follow A14 to Bar Hill; take the B1050 to Earith, then at junction on River Ouse take the B1381 to Sutton. (Map 10, D5)

Cock Pub and Restaurant

47 High Street, Hemingford Grey, Cambridgeshire PE28 9BJ
Telephone: +44(0)1480 463609
oliver.thain@condorpubs.com

The Cock is no longer an ordinary village local. Oliver Thain and chef Richard Bradley have revamped the interior, giving a contemporary look to the bar and restaurant through bare boards and a pale yellow and sage green décor. The cooking is modern British with the occasional foray further afield. Fresh local produce is used in preparing the short, imaginative carte, while daily deliveries of fresh fish dictate the chalkboard menu choice. Choose from game pâté with chutney, or baked duck parcel with sweet and sour cucumber to start, then follow with Angus T-bone steak with mustard roasted onions, braised lamb shank with date sauce or try their homemade beef and porter sausages with flavoured mash. Round off with sticky toffee pudding or a plate of unusual British and Irish cheeses. The set light lunch lunch menu is amazing value for money; alternatively order a bacon, mushroom and tomato sandwich, served with sautéed potatoes. Excellent ales from East Anglian breweries; 8 wines by the glass, and peaceful views across the willow-bordered Great Ouse river

Prices: Set lunch from £9.95. Main course restaurant from £8.95. House wine £8.95.
Hours: 11.30-15.00. 18.00-23.00. Sunday 12.00-16.00. 18.30-22.30.
Food served: 12.00-14.30. 19.00-21.30. Sunday 12.00-15.00.
Cuisine: Traditional British and Modern European.
Other Points: No-smoking area. Dogs welcome. Garden. Children welcome over eight years old. Car park.
Directions: Village signposted from southbound carriageway on A14, 4 miles west of Huntingdon. (Map 10, D5)

The King William IV

Chishill Road, Heydon, Cambridgeshire SG8 8PN
Telephone: +44(0)1763 838773
www.kingwilliv.freeuk.com

Unremarkable from the outside, but an Aladdin's Cave within, overflowing with agricultural oddities, giant bellows, cast iron cauldrons, wrought-iron lamps, casks, decorative plates, heavy beams, tiled floors and rustic tables, some of them suspended by chains from the ceiling. Beyond this jumble of artefacts is the decorative stone bar counter that dispenses Adnams, Fuller's and Greene King real ales. Vegetarians will love this place, with over a dozen unusual dishes that have won awards for the licensee, Elizabeth Nicholls (who, on her arrival six years ago, set the trend for more vegetarian cooking in pubs). Choices include chestnut and leek cottage pie, spinach and spring onion cakes with Dijon mustard sauce, and Mediterranean vegetable moussaka with Greek salad. Meat lovers can order braised lamb shank with roasted garlic and red wine jus, or aromatic chicken and pistachio korma. A chalkboard lists lunchtime baguettes and local produce is used wherever possible on the menu. It may be very atmospheric on a winter's evening, but escape the dark interior on fine summer evenings and enjoy a drink on the decking terrace, complete with teak furnishings and outdoor heaters.

Prices: Main course from £7.95. House wine £12.25.
Hours: 12.00-2.30. 18.00-23.00
Food served: 12.00-14.00. 18.30-22.00. 12.00-14.30 and 19.00-21.30 on Sundays.
Cuisine: Modern European.
Other Points: No-smoking area. Children welcome. Garden. Car park.
Directions: Three miles east of Royston off B1039. Two miles from Exit 9 and 10 of the M11. (Map 10, E5)

Waddesdon Manor, home of Manor Restaurant and Stables Restaurant, Waddesdon, Buckinghamshire

Old Bridge Hotel ★ 🏠 ✕ ✿
1 High Street, Huntingdon, Cambridgeshire PE29 3TQ
Telephone: +44(0)1480 424300
oldbridge@huntsbridge.co.uk
www.huntsbridge.com

The epitome of a town-house hotel for the 21st-century, with elegant 18th-century architecture brought up to date with a contemporary design that mixes tartans with waxed pastel colours, wood with wicker, and sea grass with rich classic colours of reds, greens and browns. The 24 bedrooms make up an eclectic range of individual rooms, some quite traditional, making the best of the elegant town-house architecture. Others are striking design statements. The main dining room is all about restrained elegance: light panelled walls, lots of white linen, red high-back chairs. But the terrace restaurant is boldly designed, dominated by huge Julia Rushbury murals and big windows, giving a real orangery feel. Chef/patron Martin Lee interprets the Huntsbridge Group philosophy of well-sourced materials prepared in imaginative yet restrained dishes with a modern country-house menu. Ideas range from salad of caramelised rhubarb, Roquefort and purple basil, to Cornish lamb sweetbreads with braised vegetables, oregano, Parmesan. The range of outstanding wines is a top-class, wonderful selection - the classics are the best of their kind - and very good value, with a brilliant selection by the glass.
Prices: Set lunch £15.50. Main course from £12.75.
House wine £12.
Hours: 12.00-14.30. 18.00-22.00.
Rooms: 24 en suite. Double room from £120, single from £80.
Cuisine: Modern British.
Other Points: No-smoking area. Children welcome. Garden. Car park.
Directions: At the intersection of the A1 (north-south) and the A14 (east-west). (Map 10, D5)

Pheasant Inn 🏠 🍷 ✕
Keyston, Huntingdon, Cambridgeshire PE18 0RE
Telephone: +44(0)1832 710241
pheasant.keyston@btopenworld.com

At the heart of the village, beneath a huge sycamore tree, sits the Pheasant, formed from classic 16th-century English cottages, with dark thatch, a mass of floral planters and tubs and alfresco tables and chairs out front make you a temporary part of this picture-postcard scene. Within, it is quintessentially 'olde England': leather upholstery, the odd stuffed bird, hunting and shooting prints, old horse-drawn implements suspended from the ceiling, a mass of blackened beams, brick inglenooks, flagstone floor and stripped boards. There's nothing 'olde worlde' about the cooking, however. Garden pea soup with pancetta, Cornish crab with caviar, chilli, and lime on cucumber jelly, new season's lamb's liver, fresh pasta with spring vegetables, and cherry and chocolate cake for pudding show modern food cooked with skill and assurance, and based on prime raw materials. The delights of the wine list are a joy to behold, with some 40 of the 100 well-chosen bins priced at 20 or under. The higher-priced bottles benefit from a straight cash mark-up that means this is the place to experiment - sheer hedonism at a very fair price and really good value.
Prices: Set price lunch £14.95.
House wine £11.50.
Hours: Food served: 12.00-14.00. 18.30-21.30 (19.00-21.00 Sunday).
Cuisine: Modern British.
Other Points: No-smoking areas. Dogs welcome daytime only. Children welcome. Car park.
Directions: Village signed off A14 west of Huntingdon. (Map 9, D4)

Prices: Main course bar meal from £9.50.
House wine £11.50.
Hours: 11.30-15.00. 18.00-23.00. Sunday from 12.00.
Food served: 12.00-14.00. 18.30-21.30. 12.00-14.30 on Sunday.
Cuisine: Modern British.
Other Points: No-smoking area. Restaurant non smoking. Children welcome. Garden. Car park.
Directions: Two miles west of Cambridge. From London leave the M11 at the A1303 exit. From the north take the A14 then A1307. (Map 10, D5)

Three Horseshoes ★ 🍷 ✕
High Street, Madingley, Cambridge, Cambridgeshire CB3 8AB
Telephone: +44(0)1954 210221

Within this picturesque thatched inn, the quintessentially rural look gives way to country chic and a lively cosmopolitan atmosphere. The Victorian orangery look does justice to the original architecture, mixing a light Mediterranean feel with period elegance through pastel-coloured waxed wood, stripped boards, old-style foodie prints, brick fireplaces, lots of light wood, leather-topped bar stools and banquettes. Moving through to the conservatory restaurant, though similar in design and with an identical menu to the bar area, white linen, wicker chairs, lots of shrubs and indoor plants growing up trellis create a relaxed mood. Richard Stokes's confident cooking is a sound interpretation of the Huntsbridge Group's policy of seasonal food using prime raw materials. Thus, a typical spring meal could bring lovely fresh salads of crab or asparagus, pan-fried halibut, or squab pigeon with olive oil braised leeks, peas, trompette mushrooms, liver crostini, dauphinoise potato and red wine, and chargrilled rump of lamb with peppers, summer chard, 'faggots and mushy peas', and caper, lentil and mint salsa. As with all Huntsbridge places, there is a superb choice of wines, offering the great and godly as well as the unusual, with 34 halves listed.

Sheene Mill Restaurant with Rooms

39 Station Road, Melbourn, Cambridge,
Cambridgeshire SG8 6DX
Telephone: +44(0)1763 261393
info@sheenemill.co.uk
www.sheenemill.co.uk

Celebrity TV chef, designer bedrooms, beautiful setting, good food, quaffable wines, what more could you want? The lovely 16th century watermill, with 18th century additions, sits on the outskirts of the sleepy town of Melbourn. The restaurant is a rich palette of powder blue, dark ochres and yellows, slate (floor) and dark blue (high-backed chairs). Here, Steven Saunder's cooking is effusive and exuberant; in other words, lots of unrestrained gutsy flavours reflected in a contemporary style that jumps around the globe. From a lunch menu comes organic asparagus soup with pesto, confit belly pork, creamed cabbage, fondant potatoes and mustard jus, with baked nectarines and franzipan and vanilla ice cream nicely rounding things off. At dinner there could be salad of wood pigeon, roasted aubergine salad and sweet corn relish, then Asian spiced salmon, stir-fried vegetables, crispy noodles and coriander salsa. Menus change daily, dependant on what local, organic or seasonal produce is available. The wine list has some lovely wines from around the world and is usefully divided into food-friendly groups. Bedrooms have been designed by the likes of David Emmanuel and Anna Ryder-Richardson; bathrooms range from minimalism to the out-and-out luxurious.

Prices: Main course dinner from £17. Main course lunch from £8.50. House wine £14.
Hours: 12.00-14.00. 19.00-22.00. 12.00-14.30 on Sunday. No food on Sunday evening. Closed 26 December and 1 January.
Rooms: 9 en suite. Double rooms from £90, single from £75.
Cuisine: Eclectic.
Other Points: Totally no smoking. Children welcome. Garden. Car park. Licence for Civil Weddings.
Directions: Off A10, 10 miles south of Cambridge. (Map 10, E5)

The Jolly Abbot

High Green, Abbotsley, St Neots,
Cambridgeshire PE19 6UL
Telephone: +44(0)1767 677747
jolly.abbot@virgin.net
www.thejollyabbot.co.uk

James Noble's traditional village pub is the only one in the area recognised by the Vegetarian Society. Not only does James produce an inventive vegetarian menu, but he strives to be 100% organic. That philosophy extends beyond the food: all the furniture and knick-knacks are reclaimed - tables and chairs, for example, have been purchased second hand, and the wine rack is made from terracotta drainpipes. The Jolly Abbot is an appealing place with bags of character in the restaurant. Those here for the vegetarian menu could start with hot herb mushroom and samphire salad, and go on to Thai vegetable curry with sweet potato chips. But meat and fish eaters are not neglected, and have their own comprehensive menu that runs to griddled calf's liver with juniper sauce and parsley mash, or poached or sautéed salmon. Come on a Sunday night and James has a clear-out. For £3.95 to £5.95, he will cook whatever is left in his fridge - it's called Sunday surplus. The detailed wine list is well annotated and offers a nice cross-section of choice and price. Regular beers include Fuller's London Pride and Greene King IPA, and the guest ale is often Woodforde's Wherry.

Prices: Main course restaurant from £11.25. Light snacks from £3.95.
Hours: 12.00-15.00. 17.30-23.00. Closed Monday.
Food served: 17.30-23.00.
Cuisine: Modern Pub Food specialising in Vegetarian.
Other Points: No-smoking area. Dogs welcome. Children welcome over 14 years old. Car park.
Directions: A1 to St Neots then A428 and B1046. (Map 10, D5)

Cherry House Restaurant

125 Church Street, Werrington, Peterborough, Cambridgeshire PE4 6QF
Telephone: +44(0)1733 571721

On the main road running through a village suburb on the outskirts of Peterborough, the Cherry Tree occupies a quaint 16th-century thatched cottage with a manicured lawn and a pond. Within, the décor takes a traditional line in the beamy, exposed-stone, open-fireplace dining room, and the time-honoured style follows through to the kitchen, where regional ingredients figure and cream and butter sauces are popular. French-trained Andrew Corrick is passionate about his food and over some eight years has created a loyal following for his cooking, both the set-price lunch and dinner menus. His is a lively mix of ideas, ranging from the classic - venison terrine and chicken liver parfait with red onion marmalade - to the Mediterranean-inspired: grilled fillet of salmon, black olive tapénade and provençal vegetables. Or there could be medallions of Grasmere Farm pork fillet topped with a prune and coriander soufflé and a creamy Marsala sauce, or supreme of chicken in a cream and sherry sauce with artichokes, mushrooms and fresh herbs. For simpler tastes, and at a supplement to the menu, there is a selection of grilled steaks. The wine list, helpfully organised by style, offers a fairly comprehensive selection that aims mostly for everyday drinking at reasonable prices.

Prices: Three course set menu £19.95. House wine £9.50.
Food served: 12.00-14.00 and 19.00-21.30 Tuesday to Friday. 19.00-22.30 on Saturday and 12.00-14.30 on Sunday. Closed on Monday.
Cuisine: Modern British with French influence.
Other Points: No smoking area. Garden. Children welcome. Car park.
Directions: North of Peterborough, The Cherry House is signposted off the A15. (Map 9, C2)

Tickell Arms

Whittlesford, Cambridge, Cambridgeshire CB2 4NZ
Telephone: +44(0)1223 833128

Over the years this beautiful blue and white Gothic villa has been cherished both for its eccentricity and its exquisite garden. The original owner Kim Tickell, died some years ago, but his name lives on and this inn still preserves Tickell's air of flamboyance. Country house chic prevails: elegant fireplaces, terracotta walls, and a magnificent collection of objet d'arts in the main bar, to the plant-filled conservatory dining room beyond Chippendale french-arched doors. In September 2001 ex-Quo Vadis head chef Spencer Patrick, bought the pub and the style and quality of the food changed dramatically. But don't expect to order a ploughman's lunch to accompany your pint of local Milton ale, as Spencer only offers set two or three-course lunch and dinner menus. Lunch is very good value, the limited choice daily menu listing, say, terrine of smoked pork knuckle and foie gras with red onion compote, followed by a well executed main course of steamed dorade with herb risotto and spiced mussels. Evening additions may include a panaché of sea scallops, cauliflower purée and sauce Perigord, duck with foie gras, morels and lime jus, and vanilla cream with candied rhubarb. Excellent wines are laid out on the bar, and there's piped classical music.

Prices: Set lunch £15.50. Set dinner £30.50. House wine £15.50.
Hours: 12.00-14.30. 19.00-23.00. Closed Monday.
Food served: 12.00-14.30. 19.00-21.00. No food on Sunday evening.
Cuisine: Modern British.
Other Points: No-smoking area in restaurant. Garden. Children welcome over 10 years old. Car park.
Directions: Exit10/M11. Take the Whittlesford turn off A505 and then North Road into the village. (Map 10, E5)

Brasserie 10/16

Brookdale Place, Chester, Cheshire CH1 3DY
Telephone: +44(0)1244 322288
www.brasserie1016.com

At the south end, close to Chesters ring road (easily accessible from all directions), Neal Bates and Mark Jones Brasserie 10/16 has gone down well with a broad spectrum of Chester folk who crowd in for the stylish sofa-strewn bar, the modern good looks of the restaurant, buzzy atmosphere, and the good food. Indeed, you can't miss the large, glass-fronted building with its name written large. And, once inside, sitting comfortably in the window, you can see the rest of Chester flying by. The food is gutsy with enough in the way of salsas, pancetta, mozzarella, truffle oil and the like to confirm a wide-ranging interest: like the prawn, chilli and corriander salsa salad with sour cream that began one meal. More straightforward dishes take in old favourites such as fillet of beef with creamed leeks and mustard crumble with bacon mash and Cabernet Sauvignon sauce. Lunch delivers good value, and banana parfait with rum and raisin sauce, and pecan pie with toffee sauce make great puddings. Service hits just the right spot between efficiency and general friendliness. The short wine list has the same global appeal as the food, and theres a good selection of house wines by the glass or bottle.

Prices: Set lunch £4.90 and dinner £8.80 (both 2 courses). Main course from £6.95. House wine £9.95.
Hours: 12.00-14.30. 17.30-22.00. 12.00-22.00 on Sunday.
Cuisine: Modern British with Mediterranean.
Other Points: No-smoking area. Children welcome. Pay and Display Car park.
Directions: Junction 12/M53. Follow signs for the A56 until the end of the road, where you come to a large roundabout - 10/16 is between the first and second exits, opposite the Gorse Stacks car park. (Map 8, B5)

The Pheasant Inn

Higher Burwardsley, Tattenhall, Chester, Cheshire CH3 9PF
Telephone: +44(0)1829 770434
reception@thepheasant-burwardsley.com
www.thepheasant-burwardsley.com

It's plain to see that this rambling place was once a farm, and the more surprising, therefore, to find that there has been an ale-house here since the 17th century. The oldest part, the half-timbered sandstone farmhouse, is the setting for the beautifully refurbished wood-floored bar, which has a bright, modern feel and claims to house the largest log fire in Cheshire. A tasteful contemporary style extends to the imposing, stone-flagged conservatory restaurant that looks over a tiered patio and, beyond, across the Cheshire plain towards North Wales. Butternut squash and chilli soup, or scallop and lobster terrine could be followed by local pork and apple sausages with blue cheese creamed potatoes and a rich port wine jus. In addition, there are interesting daily specials and good puddings include prune tart with vanilla anglaise and honey and poppy seed ice cream. The old barn has been skillfully converted into eight very comfortable bedrooms, including two suites and spotless bathrooms. Two further bedrooms, housed in the pub proper, boast original beams and brighter bathrooms.

Prices: Set lunch £12 and dinner £17. Main course from £6.50.
Hours: 11.00-23.00 (until 22.30 on Sunday).
Food served: 12.00-14.30. 18.30-21.30. 12.00-17.30. 18.30-20.30 on Sunday.
Rooms: 10 en suite. Singles from £55, doubles from £70. Family room from £100, suite from £80.
Cuisine: Modern British.
Other Points: No-smoking area. Children welcome. No dogs. Garden. Car park.
Directions: A41 south of Chester; 1 mile after Flatlow Heath turn left signposted to Burwardsley. Turn right in Tattenhall then take immediate left. At post office in Burwardsley, bear left up Higher Burwardsley Road to the inn. (Map 8, B5)

England - Cheshire

The Cholmondeley Arms

Bickley Moss, Cholmondeley, Malpas, Cheshire SY14 8HN
Telephone: +44(0)1829 720300
guy@cholmondeleyarms.co.uk
www.cholmondeleyarms.co.uk

The former Victorian schoolhouse has retained a schoolroom atmosphere through its high-roofed halls, large windows, and huge radiators; steep, white-painted gables and the octagonal bell tower aid the illusion. However, pastel painted walls are covered with tasteful pictures and prints, there are open fires, stripped pine tables topped with church candles and fresh flowers, and the old blackboards are put to good use, listing the daily changing specials and a selection of eight house wines (all available by the glass). Starters include chargrilled scallops salad with prawns and baby spinach. Rib-eye steak lightly peppered and cooked rare, follows, with its counterpart of fillets of sea bass on buttered samphire with a light velouté sauce. Sandwiches, Cheshire cheese and pickles, and the 'headmaster' lunch of rib-eye steak baguette with mustard mayonnaise, make an appearance at lunchtime Classic puddings run to spotted dick and custard, and meringues and cream, and there's Adnams, Bank's Bitter, Marstons Pedigree and a monthly changing guest on draught. Comfortable overnight accommodation is situated across the car park in what was the head teacher's house. All six bedrooms are bright and cottagey with garden views and en suite bath or shower rooms.

Prices: Set lunch/dinner £16. Main course from £9.95. Main course (bar/snack) £6. House wine £10.50.
Hours: 11.00-15.00. 18.30-23.00. Closed 25 December.
Food served: 12.00-14.15. 18.30-22.00.
Rooms: 6 en suite. Double room from £60, single from £45.
Cuisine: Modern British.
Other Points: Children welcome. Garden. Car park.
Directions: On A49 two miles south of A534 Wrexham to Nantwich road. (Map 8, B5)

Plough at Eaton

Macclesfield Road, Eaton, Cheshire CW12 2NH
Telephone: +44(0)1260 280207
theploughateaton@computerpost.net
www.comedinewithus.co.uk

There is a Dr Who touch to this 17th century redbrick inn: from the red telephone box at the front, to the 400-year-old, galleried Welsh Barn, transported in pieces and reassembled in situ like a jigsaw. It's the perfect setting for a small country wedding, especially as the Plough now has its own civil licence plus stable block converted into eight luxurious bedrooms. The pub itself is plushly comfortable with attentive service, open-hearth fires and an extensive range of freshly prepared food. Portions are vast; delicious homemade chicken liver p t with salad, and baguette could feed two. Other dishes include traditional sausage and mash and chicken chasseur, as well as more adventurous choices such as barramundi fish steak. Steaks arrive piled with real chips and onion rings. At weekends, the Barn offers a more refined choice of dishes such as peppered duck breast with burnt orange sauce.

Prices: Set lunch £10.95 and dinner £14.95. Main course from £7.95. House wine £9.75.
Hours: 11.30-23.30. Closed 25-26 December evening and 1 January.
Food served: 12.00-14.30. 17.30-21.30. 12.00-20.30 on Sunday.
Rooms: 8 en suite. Single room from £50, double from £60.
Cuisine: Modern British.
Other Points: No-smoking area. Children welcome. 'Secret' bar garden.
Directions: On the A536 between Macclesfield and Congleton. (Map 8, B6)

Dimitris

149 Ashley Road, Hale, Altrincham, Cheshire WA14 2UW
Telephone: +44(0)161 9264670
hale@dimitris.co.uk
www.dimitris.co.uk

In order to concentrate on his simple, straightforward formula of Mediterranean inspired restaurants (see entries for Dimitris in Leeds and Manchester), Dimitri Griliopoulos has sold his delis and coffee shop in Manchester, replacing them with a restaurant in the Cheshire town of Hale - the menu, and the incredibly cheerful, willing staff, remain common to all. The keenly priced, daily changing lunch special is designed to lure folk in during the day with the likes of vegetable soup with feta followed, perhaps, by prawn tagliatelle. There's also a well thought out Sunday brunch menu that extends choice beyond the full English to a Mediterranean breakfast of bowls of marinated feta, olives and capers to spread on hot bread. This is all served against a backdrop of a downstairs tapas-style bar filled with plain wood tables, big windows and shelving (allowing people to stand and nibble over drinks) and an upstairs dining room designed with a strong Italian feel that comes into its own in the evenings. The pick of the good-value wine list is a Navarra Chardonnay (placed third best in the world at the International Gastonomy Summit in 2002, and first in the world for value), at £12 a bottle it has to be tried.

Prices: Set lunch, 2 course, £7.25. Set dinner £15.35. Main course restaurant from £8.35. Main course bar from £5.45. House wine £10.95.
Hours: Open all day 11.00-midnight.
Cuisine: Mediterranean.
Other Points: No-smoking area.
Directions: M56. Between the Altrincham and Hale turn offs. (Map 8, A5)

Sutton Hall

Bullocks Lane, Sutton, near Macclesfield,
Cheshire SK11 0HE
Telephone: +44(0)1260 253211

An impressive building standing at the end of a long
drive in lush parkland, which began life as an
endowment to a monastery in the 11th century, before
becoming a baronial residence in the 16th century and,
in the more recent past, a nunnery (until some 30 years
ago). Proprietor Robert Bradshaw has, for the past 20
years, described Sutton Hall as a pub, restaurant and
hotel, in that order. The hall is full of old-world
atmosphere, with black oak beams, flagstones, huge
log-burning fireplaces, leaded windows, splendid pieces
of furniture and suits of armour characterising the bar
and day rooms. Beyond the traditional bar menu
featuring homemade soup, steak, kidney and oyster pie
and the usual sandwiches, daily specials may include
crab and chilli mousse, grilled tuna with lime juice and
black pepper, and venison steak with cream, brandy
and peppercorn sauce. There are good value set-price
lunch and dinner restaurant menus. A handsome
staircase leads to spacious, characterful bedrooms, all
with four-poster beds, Gothic windows, and compact
modern bathrooms.

Prices: Set lunch £13.95 (4 course) and dinner £23.95 (5 course).
Sunday lunch £15.95 (4 course). House wine £10.95.
Hours: 11.00-24.00. 11.00-22.30 on Sunday.
Food served: 12.00-14.30 (until 14.00 on Sunday). 19.00-22.00.
Rooms: 9 en suite. Double room (all 4-poster beds) from £90,
single from £75.
Cuisine: Traditional English and Continental.
Other Points: Children welcome in restaurant only. Garden.
Car park. Licence for Civil Weddings.
Directions: South of Macclesfield via the A523, left at Byrons Lane,
right at Bullocks Lane. (Map 8, A6)

Romper

Ridge End, Marple, Stockport, Cheshire SK6 7ET
Telephone: +44 (0)161 4271354
marple-uk.com/pubguide/romper.htm

Follow The Ridge signposts to reach this beautifully
located dining pub, set high above the Peak Forest
Canal with super views across the Goyt Valley from its
sunny patio. Inside, low oak beams and subtle lighting
create a cosy atmosphere throughout the four
interconnecting rooms, two of which are neatly laid
with deep red tablecloths. Traditional bar food ranges
from ploughman's platters, filled rustic rolls (bacon
and mushroom), and fresh haddock in beer batter at
lunchtime, to pasta meals, marinated lamb with mint
and redcurrant sauce, and daily blackboard specials.
Range of malt whiskies and Theakston Bitter on tap.

Prices: Main course bar from £4.95. Main course restaurant from
£7.50. House wine £9.95.
Hours: 11.30-15.00. 17.30-23.00. 12.00-22.30 on Sunday.
Food served: 12.00-14.30. 18.00-21.30. 12.00-21.30.on Sunday.
Cuisine: Traditional British and Continental.
Other Points: No-smoking area. Children welcome. Terrace.
Car park.
Directions: Take the A6 from Stockport. In High Lane, before
Disley turn left towards Marple Ridge. (Map 12, F5)

The Oddfellows Arms

73 Moor End Road, Mellor, Stockport, Cheshire SK6 5PT
Telephone: +44(0)161 4497826

Built in 1700, the pub catered for the refreshment needs of mill workers
from the many nearby mills that have long since been demolished. In
1860, the Oddfellows Society (a forerunner of the modern day trade union
movement) required a meeting room and approached the landlord and
over the years the name stuck. Within, it's rather like walking into
someone's home. White walls and a brick fireplace with brass surrounds
add warmth to the bar room, there's a mix of flag and carpeted floors, old
prints on the walls and a magnificent kitchen range set bang in the
middle. This is the place to settle with a jar of Adnams or Marstons
Pedigree, but most people are here for the food, whether bar snacks of
chargrilled rib-eye steak marinated in red wine and garlic on french bread,
or a full-blown three course meal. The restaurant is upstairs. Seafood is a
speciality, say, lobster Thermidor, whole plaice grilled on the bone with
tartare sauce, or fillet of cod in ale batter, with chips and mushy peas.
Meat dishes can include slow-braised and honey-glazed ham shank with a
white wine and whole-grain mustard cream sauce. The global wine list is
fairly priced.

Prices: Sunday lunch £11.45. Set lunch £14
and dinner £20. Main course from £10.
House wine £8.45.
Hours: 12.00-15.00 Tuesday-Sunday. 17.30-
23.00 Tuesday-Saturday. 19.00-22.30 on
Sunday. Closed Monday. Closed 25-26 and
31 December, 1 January; 3 weeks summer.
Food served: 12.00-14.30 18.30-21.30.
12.00-14.00 only on Sunday.
Cuisine: International.
Other Points: No-smoking area. Children
welcome. Small patio. Car park.
Directions: J1/M60. From Stockport
follow the A626 to Marple and then follow
signs to Mellor. (Map 9, B2)

Plough and Flail

Paddock Hill Lane, Mobberley, Cheshire WA16 7DB
Telephone: +44(0)1565 873537

Award-winning hanging baskets provide a riot of colour at this 19th-century town-meets-country pub, formerly a pair of quaint stone cottages, set in the heart of affluent North Cheshire. A series of interlinking rooms allows the smartly furnished inn to cater for large numbers without losing a sense of intimacy. Brasses and memorabilia add to the atmosphere, while handwritten seasonal menus attempt to be humourous in describing a broad range of traditional pub food. Choices range from homemade soups, beer-battered cod with chips and mushy peas and sea bass with Thai broth to lamb shank on bubble and squeak, and the ultimate steak 'stack' special. 'Butties, wraps and baps' are also available as is the daily hot roast carvery.

Prices: Main course bar meal £7.50. House wine £10.50.
Hours: 12.00-14.30. 18.00-21.00 (21.30 Friday and Saturday). 12.00-20.00 on Sunday.
Cuisine: Traditional English.
Other Points: No-smoking area. Children welcome. Garden. Car park.
Directions: Off B5085 between Knutsford and Wilmslow. In Mobberley to turn left into Moss Lane (just past Bird in Hand), bear off right into Paddock Hill, then left at phone box. (Map 8, A6)

Dog Inn

Well Bank Lane, near Knutsford,
Cheshire WA16 8UP
Telephone: +44(0)1625 861421
dog-inn@paddock-innsfsnet.co.uk

A quiet setting deep in the Cheshire countryside is one of the captivating features of this pretty, flower-adorned, 18th-century inn. Within easy driving distance of three major motorways, it is well worth seeking out for good quality homecooked food, prepared from local produce and home-grown herbs, and comfortable overnight accommodation in six en suite rooms. Served throughout the two dining rooms, each featuring fresh flowers and open fires, the daily changing blackboard menu may list steak and mushroom pie, poached salmon with cucumber jus, haddock and prawn gratin, fresh beer-battered cod with hand-cut chips, and rack of lamb with apricot and ginger sauce. Served with a mind-boggling selection of well cooked vegetables, portions are not for the faint-hearted, so arrive hungry and ready for a satisfying feast. There is also a range of traditional roasts and a good choice of sandwiches, as well as ploughman's lunches and salads. Puddings are picked from a trolley: At the bar, expect to find tip-top local ales from Hydes and Weetwood Breweries, a sound choice of wines (five by the glass), and a wide selection of malt whiskies. Bedrooms are of a very high quality and are extremely well maintained and presented.

Prices: Main course bar meal from £10. House wine £9.95.
Hours: 11.30-15.00. 17.00-23.00. Open all day Sunday.
Food served: 12.00-14.30. 19.00-21.30. 12.00-20.30 on Sunday.
Rooms: 6 en suite. Double room from £75, single from £55.
Cuisine: Traditional English.
Other Points: No-smoking area. Children welcome. Garden. Car park.
Directions: Two miles north of Knutsford off the A50. Turn left at the Whipping Stocks pub and continue for two miles. (Map 8, A6)

Prices: Set lunch £12. Main course from £8.95. House wine £9.95.
Hours: 12.00-15.00. 17.30-23.00. 12.00-23.00 on Saturday. 12.00-22.30 on Sunday. Closed 25 December.
Food served: 12.00-14.30. 18.30-21.30. From 18.00 Saturday and Sunday. Until 21.00 on Sunday.
Cuisine: Modern pub food.
Other Points: No-smoking area. Children welcome. No dogs. Garden. Car park.
Directions: On the main A49, adjacent to Oulton Park race circuit, on the Warrington side of Tarporley. (Map 8, B5)

The Fox and Barrel

Forest Road, Cotebrook, Tarporley, Cheshire CW6 9DZ
Telephone: +44(0)1829 760529
info@thefoxandbarrel.com
www.thefoxandbarrel.com

Head north from Tarporley along the A49 to locate this civilised dining pub set in unspoilt Cheshire countryside. Step into the neatly refurbished bar and get a warm welcome from licensees Martin and Peterene Cocking, who have successfully created a thriving food pub that also welcomes drinkers. Beyond the snug bar, with its huge log fire, china ornaments and jugs, mix of tables and chairs, and daily newspapers, the half-panelled dining area sports a rug-strewn wood floor and rustic farmhouse tables topped with church candles. Seasonally-changing menus list 'lite bites' such as salmon and dill fishcakes with lemon mayonnaise, a bowl of mussels, and roast ham ploughman's, all served with a basket of own-baked bread,. More inventive restaurant meals take in shellfish terrine with a tomato and mixed herb dressing, and braised shank of lamb steak served with a leek, celeriac and potato mash with pan-fried shallots and a red wine sauce. Puddings include candied lemon cheesecake with Chantilly cream, and spiced raisin and ginger pudding with local Snugbury's ice cream. There's a good choice of wines with a dozen by the glass, malt whiskies, a secluded summer patio for al fresco imbibing, and live New Orleans jazz every Monday.

Church Farm Organics

Church Lane, Thurstaston, Wirral, Cheshire CH61 0HW
Telephone: +44(0)151 6487838
www.churchfarm.org.uk

This family run organic 70-acre farm is situated within a conservation area with superb views over the River Dee and in an area well known for walking and horse riding. The farm is Soil Association certified organic, and grows a wide range of produce including vegetables and salads, and takes in the short asparagus season that starts in May and ends the third week in June. The organic asparagus is cut and bagged fresh every day and is so popular it is often in short supply. PYO and ready picked strawberries start from mid June until the end of August - the only organic strawberries on the Wirral. A lavender maze opens towards the end of the strawberry season and you have the choice of solving the maze or just relaxing and picking your own bunch of lavender. At the end of October there are a number of events such as pumpkin carving competitions and haunted hay rides, with Christmas bringing turkeys and Christmas trees. There's a popular box scheme, a coffee shop, and B&B at the farmhouse.

Hours: 10.00-17.00 Monday and Tuesday. 09.00-17.00 Wednesday-Saturday. Sunday 11.00-17.00
Other points: Coffee shop. Parking. Plants and shrubs for sale.
Directions: Exit 4/M53 Clattacadge. Take the A540 Chester to Heswall. Continue until you reach Thurstaston, then follow the brown tourist signs to the farm. (Map 8, A5)

The Chetwode Arms

Street Lane, Lower Whitley, Warrington, Cheshire WA4 8EN
Telephone: +44(0)1925 730203
gfidler6@aol.co.uk

Named after Sir John Chetwode, this 400-year-old pub oozes old-world charm and character. Intimate nooks and crannies abound within the rambling low-beamed interior, with its mix of bare board, stone-flagged and carpeted floors, farmhouse tables, cushioned pews, collections of memorabilia, and five open log fires. There's a good summer garden in which to relax with a pint of Cains Bitter or one of 12 wines available by the glass. Blackboards list the imaginative range of modern pub food that attracts supporters from miles around. Dishes are prepared to order from quality produce, much of it sourced from local suppliers, including fruit and vegetables from Manchester market, although prime Welsh Black beef comes from Graig Farm Organics in Powys. Begin an enjoyable meal with scallop and lobster chowder with aïoli, or black pudding with red wine gravy and spiced apple chutney. Braised leg of lamb on confit garlic mash with ratatouille and red wine sauce, steak, kidney and root vegetable pie, or roast and smoked salmon fishcakes with sour cream and chive dip make satisfying main courses. Lighter bites include salad platters with chunky homemade chips, beer- and marmalade-glazed ham and pickles, and generous sandwich platters.

Prices: Set lunch and dinner £13/£30. Main course from £8.95. Main course (bar/snack) from £4.25. House wine £10.95.
Hours: 12.00-23.00. Sunday 12.00-22.30. Closed 1 January.
Food served: 12.00-15.00. 18.00-21.00.
Cuisine: Modern and Traditional British.
Other Points: Smoking throughout. Children welcome. Car park. Garden.
Directions: On the A49 two and a half miles south of J10/M56. (Map 11, F4)

The Dusty Miller

Wrenbury, Nantwich, Cheshire CW5 8HG
Telephone: +44(0)1270 780537
admin@dustymill-wrenbury.co.uk
www.dustymiller-wrenbury.co.uk

The position of this handsomely converted 19th-century watermill is lovely, beside the Llangollen branch of the Shropshire Union Canal and next to a striking counter-weighted drawbridge. The River Weaver also flows through the pub garden and picnic tables among rose bushes on a raised gravel terrace are popular with locals and narrowboat owners enjoying pints of Robinsons Ales and summer hog roasts. The comfortably modern interior has tall arched windows facing the water, hunting prints on terracotta walls and an eclectic mix of tables and seating. Good bar food is built around quality local ingredients and ranges from starters of Clewlow's black pudding with smoked bacon and tomato relish, to mains of chargrilled Lakeland lamb steak marinated in coconut and lime with red onion and mint salsa, or Cheshire beef braised in Old Tom ale with smoked bacon and mushrooms. A chalkboard lists fresh fish from Fleetwood, perhaps smoked haddock with prawns baked in mustard and cider sauce. The unusual raspberry Pavlova ice cream (made at Drumlan Hall Farm, Tattenhall) served with lemon cream sauce and shortbread comes highly recommended. Alternatively, order a plate of cheese from a menu that lists individual makers.

Prices: Main course from £9.95. House wine £12.75.
Hours: 11.30-15.00 Tuesday-Saturday. 18.30-23.00 Monday-Saturday. 12.00-15.00. 19.00-22.30 on Sunday. Closed Monday lunchtime.
Food served: 12.00-14.00 Tuesday-Sunday. 18.30-21.30 Tuesday to Saturday. 18.30-20.30 on Monday. 19.00-21.00 on Sunday.
Cuisine: Traditional and Modern British.
Other Points: No-smoking area. Children welcome. Garden. Car park.
Directions: Signposted from the A530 Nantwich to Whitchurch Road. (Map 8, B5)

England - Cheshire

Number 34

★ ⌁

34 The Bank, Barnard Castle, Durham, Co Durham DL12 8PN
Telephone: +44(0)1833 631304
evasreid@aol.com
www.number34.com

A hat maker's shop until the owner went bankrupt and ended up in jail, a pub and, until recently, an antique shop, Number 34 has had a bit of a chequered history. Eva and Ian Reid have, quite frankly, transformed the place into a charming guesthouse. As is the case with many B&Bs nowadays, it offers the comforts and luxury of a smart hotel, while remaining small, intimate and very relaxing. The sitting room is crammed with books, and the dark terracotta walls, sofas and a log fire show it has been put together with style and comfort in mind. The dining room is in keeping with the period of the house, with dark antique furniture contrasting with vivid yellow walls. Here, breakfast is served, with ingredients sourced locally and organically where possible. Upstairs, the Georgian drawing room is now a huge twin-bedded room, but still retains the original window seats and has an adjoining sparkling white bathroom with an interesting odd-shaped bath. Then there's the beamed blue room with an en suite bathroom and, at the back of the house, a small but pretty room with adjacent bathroom. Decanters of sherry, TVs, thick towels and lovely bath goodies are all provided.

Rooms: 3 rooms, 1 en suite, 2 with private bathroom. Double/twin from £50. Single from £35.
Other Points: Totally no smoking. Garden. Children welcome over 12 years old.
Directions: A1 or M6 take the A66 to Barnard Castle. Number 34 is on the main street just below the Butter Market. (Map 12, D5)

Clow Beck House

✗ ⌁

Croft-on-Tees, Darlington, Co Durham DL2 2SW
Telephone: +44(0)1325 721075
reservations@clowbeckhouse.co.uk
www.clowbeckhouse.co.uk

David and Heather Armstrong's Clow Beck has won nearly every award going (including Les Routiers in 2001) and it's not difficult to see why. Approached via a long drive, the immaculately kept garden catches the eye. The farmhouse has a large barn-style restaurant and a resident's lounge, which is lavishly decorated in period style. A couple of bedrooms are in the main house with the remainder in two buildings to the side of the house. Purpose built, the bedrooms are spacious, well designed, with each decorated in a different style. Most are classical in design but one room has an oriental theme, for instance, and there is a strikingly decorated room in black and white with animal prints. The usual trouser press and hairdryer are surpassed by all sorts of thoughtful additions from a TV guide, cafetière, and Radox, to CD player, sweeties, and dressing gown; little extras that make the place stand out. The dinner menu is built around local supplies, perhaps a spiral of locally made cumberland sausage with a tangy tomato relish, then rack of Yorkshire lamb, roasted with a honey, mustard and apricot glaze, with sticky toffee pudding to finish. There's a separate vegetarian menu and breakfast is faultless.

Prices: Main course from £11. House wine £11.
Hours: Dinner served 19.00-20.30.
Closed 25 December and 1 January.
Rooms: 13 en suite. Double room from £90, single from £60. Family room from £105.
Cuisine: Modern British.
Other Points: No-smoking area. Children welcome. Garden. Car park.
Directions: Exit A1 to Darlington A66. Take the A167 from Darlington for 4 miles to Croft-on-Tees. Follow brown highway signs to Clow Beck House. (Map 12, D6)

The County

★ ▯ ✗

13 The Green, Aycliffe, Darlington,
Co Durham DL5 6LX
Telephone: +44(0)1325 312273
www.the-county.co.uk

Andrew Brown won Raymond Blanc's first scholarship in 1995 and part of the prize was to work in the kitchens at Le Manoir aux Quat'Saisons. This was followed by stints with Gary Rhodes at the Greenhouse in London. In 1998, Andrew headed north to try his hand at a village pub near Darlington. The County is a stylishly modernised pub overlooking Aycliffe's pretty village green. The light, airy bar and bistro have adopted a rustic-chic look, the pared-back decor featuring chunky tables and padded pine chairs on wooden or tiled floors. In the main, the place offers first-class modern British cooking in an informal but civilized pub setting, but drinkers are made very welcome and real ale enthusiasts will find four brews on tap. Open sandwiches, freshly-battered haddock, and sausages and black pudding mash may appear on the bar menu. In the bistro, materials run to smoked haddock, leek and saffron chowder, and crispy duck with stir-fried vegetables, noodles and an orange maltaise sauce, while sympathetic treatment of fish has included dressed crab with lobster gratin. Leave room for an excellent pudding, perhaps rich chocolate torte with Grand Marnier crème anglaise. A global list of wines represents value for money.

Prices: Main course from £10.75. Main course bar meal from £7.50. House wine £11.45.
Hours: 12.00-14.00 (until 15.00 on Sunday). 17.30-23.00. 18.45-23.00 on Saturday. Closed Sunday evening, 25-26 December and 1 January.
Food served: 12.00-14.00. 18.00-21.15. 18.45-21.15 on Saturday.
Cuisine: Modern British.
Other Points: No-smoking area. Children welcome. Car park.
Directions: Exit59/M1. Towards Aycliffe village on the A167, turn right into the village and then right immediately on to The Green. (Map 12, D6)

The Rose and Crown at Romaldkirk

Romaldkirk, Barnard Castle, Co Durham DL12 9EB
Telephone: +44(0)1833 650213
hotel@rose-and-crown.co.uk
www.rose-and-crown.co.uk

In their 14 year tenure at this exemplary Teesdale retreat, Christopher and Alison Davy's tireless enthusiasm and dedication to providing high standards of hospitality, service and cooking has created one of the finest all-round inns in the country. Much of this success can be attributed to consistent cooking that is inspired by the seasons and backed by first-class local produce (served in the cosy lounge bar, and in the smart bistro-style Crown Room). Lunchtime filled baps (ham and mustard mayonnaise) are well presented and traditional favourites such as beef, kidney and mushroom pie are always cooked with flair. Weekly changing menus may also list pan-fried pigeon with onion confit and juniper sauce, and confit of lamb of haricot bean cassoulet and mint pesto. Exemplary puddings are typified by baked chocolate cheesecake with marmalade ice cream, but there's perfectly-selected local cheeses. Four-course dinners are served at elegantly clothed tables in the part-panelled restaurant. In the en suite bedrooms (two superb suites and five equally impressive courtyard bedrooms), creaking floorboards, beams, stripped stone walls, are matched by well-chosen antique furniture, stylish contemporary fabrics, and a host of cosseting extras.

Prices: Set lunch £14.95 and dinner £26. Main course bar meal from £7.95. House wine £12.95.
Hours: 11.30-15.00. 17.30-23.00. 19.00-22.30 on Sunday. Closed 24-26 December
Food served: 12.00-13.30. 18.30-21.30. 19.00-21.00 on Sunday.
Rooms: 12 en suite. Double/twin room from £96.
Cuisine: Modern British.
Other Points: No-smoking area. Children welcome. Car park.
Directions: Six miles north west of Barnard Castle on the B6277 towards Middleton-in-Teesdale. (Map 12, C5)

Durham Cathedral

The Manor House Hotel and Country Club

The Green, West Auckland, Co Durham DL14 9HW
Telephone: +44(0)1388 834834
enquiries@manorhousehotel.com
www.manorhousehotel.net

This quintessential English manor house is built on foundations that date back to the 12th century. Restoration has been sympathetic and the casual, rug-strewn reception sets the tone. The Beehive Bar has great character, helped by an immense stone fireplace incorporating the original beehive oven. The Juniper Brasserie delivers a popular battered cod fillet with fresh pea purée and homemade chunky chips, as well as a popular two course lunch menu that does not compromise on quality. There's a medieval swagger to the Juniper Restaurant that is not reflected in the upbeat and wide ranging modern menu that offers up to date ingredients and ideas. Grilled fillet of turbot comes with Jersey Royals, buttered asparagus and raw tomato butter sauce, for example, as well as a rump of lamb roasted with a sweet potato purée, honey-glazed parsnips and rosemary jus. Good value seems to be the priority, not least on a wine list that offers plenty by the glass. Individually decorated bedrooms take in four-posters, splendid inlaid wooden beds, and lovely period furnishings and details; many of the ensuite bathrooms are quite spacious, in keeping with the style of the rooms, and there is an ongoing programme of upgrading to enhance appearance and practicality.

Prices: Sunday lunch £12. Set dinner £19.95. Main course bar from £7. Main course restaurant from £12. House wine £11.50.
Hours: 12.00-14.00. 19.00-21.30.
Rooms: 35 en suite. Single from £38.50, double from £77. Family room from £87.
Cuisine: Eclectic.
Other Points: No-smoking area. Children welcome. Garden. Car park.
Directions: Exit 58 off the A1 (M). Take the A68 and follow it to West Auckland. (Map 12, C6)

Bay Hotel

Helston, Coverack, Cornwall TR12 6TF
Telephone: +44(0)1326 280464
enquiries@thebayhotel.co.uk
www.thebayhotel.co.uk

The Lizard Peninsula is an area of outstanding natural beauty and its position, on England's most southerly point, ensures a mild climate. It is the ideal spot for a traditional seaside hotel, and the Bay complies with ample supplies of friendliness, peace and beautiful scenery. The location is idyllic, surrounded by gardens and fields sweeping down to the beach. The Goldsworthy family have honed and sharpened their hospitality skills over they years, and offer something for everyone. Splendid sea views are to be had from most rooms with day rooms exuding a comfortable, old-fashioned feel. Crisply maintained bedrooms have pretty bed linen and all the expected amenities such as tea and coffee making facilities, TVs and hairdryers. The hotel is not suitable for children under 16 years.

Prices: Set dinner £21.50 (5 courses). House wine £7.95.
Hours: 18.30-21.30. Closed from November-Christmas, and mid January-March
Rooms: 14 rooms, 13 en suite. From £51.50 per person for dinner, bed and breakfast.
Cuisine: Traditional English/global.
Other Points: No-smoking area. No children under 16. Garden. Car park.
Directions: From Helston, take B3292 to St Keverne; Coverack is signed. (Map 3, E3)

Barbara Hepworth Museum, St Ives, Cornwall

Prices: Set dinner £18.
Hours: Dinner by prior arrangment.
Rooms: 2 rooms, 1 en suite. Double room from £35, single from £18.
Cuisine: English home-cooking.
Other Points: Totally no smoking. Garden. Children welcome. Car park.
Directions: Exit A30 at Launceston. Follow the signs for the B3254 to South Petherwin. One mile after the village turn left signed to Drinnick. The house is 200 yards on the left. (Map 3, D4)

Hornacott

South Petherwin, Launceston, Cornwall PL15 7LH
Telephone: +44(0)1566 782461
otwayruthven@btinternet.com

Jos and Mary Anne Otway-Ruthven's 300-year-old former farm house, with extraordinary rambling gardens sloping down to a stream, offers quite unique bed-and-breakfast accommodation. The building used to store grain for the still intact (and listed) mill, and visitors sleep in the converted grain loft. There is just one double bedroom, but with the privacy of own self-contained rooms. A private entrance leads into a sitting room with magazines, CD player, and double doors giving on to the wooded valley; there's the pretty bedroom with fresh flowers, TV and tea tray; and a tasteful modern bathroom with robes and toiletries. All the décor, lighting and furniture is in harmony with the age of the house. Breakfast looks to local suppliers in the shape of butchers sausages and free-range eggs, and is served in the dining room at a polished oak table. The garden is unusual (and popular with keen gardeners) in that it ranges from plants typical of Cornwall and the West Country to examples from other countries, all blended into the natural landscape. This is a peaceful, quiet spot, run with charm and dedication.

The Springer Spaniel

Treburley, Launceston, Cornwall PL15 9NS
Telephone: +44(0)1579 370424
wagtail.inns@virgin.net

The Springer Spaniel may look like any other unassuming roadside pub, but venture inside this 18th-century building and it is immediately evident that this is no ordinary hostelry. The main bar has a high-backed settle and two farmhouse-style chairs fronting a wood-burning stove, comfortable wall benches, rustic tables and a relaxing, chatty atmosphere - no intrusive music or games here (and there's a separate beamed dining-room where booking is essential at weekends). It is obvious that food is taken seriously here. Emphasis in the kitchen is on the use of fresh local ingredients. For a light snack choose the pan-seared scallops with hog's pudding and white wine sauce, or smoked duck salad with melon and raspberry dressing. More substantial fare, listed on the main menu and daily changing chalkboards (also served in the bar), may include the likes of fillets of sea bass with a roast pepper butter, and rack of lamb with a mustard and herb crust, redcurrant and mint dressing and parsnip mash. Quality of food is matched with good service, a well-chosen list of wines (seven by the glass), and tip-top West Country ales Sharps Doom Bar, Cornish Coaster and Springer Ale - on handpump.

Prices: Main course restaurant meal from £8.95. Main course bar meal from £4.95. House wine £9.95.
Hours: 12.00-15.00. 17.00-23.00.
Food served: 12.00-14.00. 18.30-21.00.
Cuisine: Traditional and Modern British.
Other Points: No-smoking area. Children welcome. Garden. Car park.
Directions: Beside A388 midway between Launceston and Callington. (Map 3, D4)

Royal Oak

Duke Street, Lostwithiel, Cornwall PL22 1AG
Telephone: +44(0)1208 872552
mghine@aol.com

In addition to being some 700 years old, this unassuming, stone-built, town-centre pub has the romantic cachet of being reputedly linked to nearby Restormel Castle by a smuggling or escape tunnel. The lively, slate-flagstoned public bar is genuinely local, attracting a good loyal following who seek out the choice of real ales, including Sharp's Own Bitter from Cornwall, and the interesting range of bottled beers and lagers. By contrast, the comfortably furnished and carpeted lounge bar is very much geared to a dining clientele. Close inspection of a fairly standard, and lengthy, printed menu (and of the additional blackboard selection) will reveal some good homecooked dishes, for which Eileen Hine is justly renowned, served in very generous portions. Her excellent 'cow pie' (steak and kidney marinated and cooked in real ale) is legendary, but look out for ragout of beef, and medallions of pork with a wild mushroom sauce, accompanied by fresh local vegetables. Puddings include a delicious homemade treacle tart or apple pie served with thick clotted cream. Upstairs bedrooms continue to be upgraded (two new rooms have been added since the last Guide entry), all are spacious, well decorated, and furnished with a mix of period and pine furniture.

Prices: Main course from £8.25. Main course bar meal from £5.95. House wine £9.95.
Hours: 11.00-23.00. sunday 12.00-22.30.
Food served: 12.00-14.00. 18.30-21.15.
Rooms: 8 en suite. Double room from £75, single from £43.
Cuisine: Traditional English.
Other Points: No-smoking area. Children welcome. Garden. Car park.
Directions: Just off A390 in town centre. (Map 3, E3)

Trewithen Restaurant

3 Fore Street, Lostwithiel, Cornwall PL22 0BP
Telephone: +44(0)1208 872373
brianrolls1@supanet.com
www.trewithenrestaurant.supanet.com

'Although we are occasionally influenced by fashion we have never been followers of fashion', writes Brian Rolls, who has been at the helm of this well-respected restaurant for 23 years, his co-chef Kathryn Rowe for 21 years. They have more than stood the test of time, backed by loyal supporters and a sourcing policy that is in total harmony with the local farming and fishing communities. The restaurant is part of Cornish heritage too: the original walls date from the 17th-century, when it was part of the Duchy Palace complex; the Duchy Palace next door (now a Masonic lodge) was the seat of the Cornish Parliament in the 13th-century. West Country specialities are strongly represented with locally reared meats such as venison served with a juniper berry sauce and smoked bacon and mushrooms, or pork from Tywardreath accompanied by a mushroom and porcini sauce. The daily catch could include sea bass crumbed in oats and served with citrus and caper sauce, or, from the short lobster menu (available between June and September), look out for a classic lobster Newburg. Ice creams are made on the premises, as are the chocolates served with coffee. Booking in advance is recommended.

Prices: Set dinner £26. Main course from £15. House wine £11.25.
Hours: 19.00-21.30. Closed Sunday and Monday except for Bank Holidays weekends and Mondays during the Summer.
Cuisine: Modern British with International influences.
Other Points: No-smoking area. Children welcome. Garden.
Directions: A390, halfway between Liskeard and St Austell, 5 miles south Bodmin (A30) and five miles east of the Eden.Project (Map 3, E3)

England - Cornwall

The Plume of Feathers

Mitchell, Truro, Cornwall TR8 5AX
Telephone: +44(0)1872 510387
theplume.mitchell@virgin.net

The former run-down 16th-century coaching inn has been transformed into a stylish pub-restaurant with rooms. With a bright new approach chef/patron Martyn Warner has refurbished the bar and dining area, installed pine tables topped with candles and fresh flowers, painted half-boarded walls, stripped old beams and added modern art. An interesting range of modern European dishes mixed with British classics, run to tapas with chargrilled bread, handmade Cornish pasty with fries, Caesar salad and green Thai chicken with coconut cream. Dinner is a tad more serious, offering the likes of lamb shank with chorizo, chick pea, butter bean salsa and rosemary oil, or duck confit on mash with braised red cabbage and red wine jus. In addition, there are daily specials, perhaps seared tuna on roasted vegetables with red pepper juice and basil oil. Typical puddings include warm Bakewell tart and banana sticky toffee pudding. Expect Sharp's and Skinner's ales on tap, freshly squeezed orange juice and nine wines by the glass. Careful conversion of barns has created five extremely comfortable bedrooms, all kitted out with handmade pine furniture, iron or brass beds, large-screen TVs, modern art, and well-equipped en suite bathrooms.

Prices: Main course from £8.50.
House wine £9.75.
Hours: 10.30-23.00.
Closed 25 December evening.
Food served: 12.00-22.00.
Rooms: 5 en suite. Double room from £55, single from £41.25.
Cuisine: Modern European/British.
Other Points: No-smoking area. Dogs welcome in the bar. Children welcome. Garden. Car park.
Directions: At the junction of A3076 and A30, seven miles from Newquay.
(Map 3, E3)

Great Western Hotel

Cliff Road, Newquay, Cornwall TR7 2PT
Telephone: +44(0)1637 872010
bookings@great-western.fsnet.co.uk
www.chycor.co.uk/greatwestern/

'Nothing stands between the hotel and the magnificent Atlantic Ocean except our own private lawn' boasts the hotel's brochure. Indeed, the panoramic views over Great Western Beach (named after the hotel) are magnificent, and public rooms and bedrooms make the most of it all. Built in 1875 as a superior boarding house in anticipation of the coming of the railway in 1876, the hotel has grown considerably in stature and standing over the years, with a now imposing façade and everything thoroughly up to date within. Light and airy en suite bedrooms are very well maintained and equipped, there's a splendid indoor swimming pool with a jacuzzi, and there's a choice of eating places and bars. And the hotel seems to have thought of all possible requirements to make a family holiday successful regardless of weather conditions, including a ten-hole mini golf course, pool table and Sky TV in the bar, as well as a children's area in the Belle Bar.

Prices: Set dinner £16. Main course (bar/snack) from £4.
House wine £7.85.
Hours: 11.00-23.00.
Rooms: 72 rooms, 70 en suite. Double room from £43 per person, single from £48 (dinner, bed & breakfast).
Cuisine: Modern British.
Other Points: No-smoking area. All bedrooms are non-smoking. Children welcome. Garden. Car park. Indoor heated pool.
Directions: From Indian Queens (A30) to Quintrell Downs, right at roundabout to seafront. Hotel on right. (Map 3, E3)

Molesworth Manor

Little Petherick, Wadebridge, Padstow,
Cornwall PL27 7QT
Telephone: +44(0)1841 540292
molesworthmanor@aol.com
www.molesworthmanor.co.uk

The lovely Grade II former rectory dates from the 17th century and stands in the centre of the village of Little Petherick, two miles south-east of Padstow. Jessica Clarke has taken over the running of this unconventional country guesthouse from her parents, together with her partner, Geoff French. This is a genteel house, with spacious hallways, sitting rooms with antique furniture, open fires, rugs on the floors; the décor is completely in keeping with the age of the house. Eleven bedrooms present varying degrees of grandness and carry names evocative of the house in its heyday: Her Ladyship's and His Lordship's Rooms on the first floor, for example, and the Cook's Room and the Butler's Room on the second. Open fireplaces, wrought-iron or brass bedsteads, and good Victorian furniture complement the house style. Six bedrooms have en suite bathrooms; the rest have their own private facilities. Breakfast is a splendid cold buffet served in the conservatory. No dinner is served, but there are plenty of pubs, restaurants and bistros in the vicinity, including many highly rated places in nearby Padstow. Note that no credit cards are taken.

Hours: Closed November-January.
Rooms: 11 rooms, 9 en suite and 2 with private facilities. Double room from £32-£42 per person, single from £30.
Other Points: No-smoking area. Garden. Children welcome. Car park.
Directions: Situated off the A389 from Wadebridge to Padstow in village of Little Petherick. The manor is signposted and halfway up/down the hill. (Map 3, D3)

Penzance Arts Club ✗ 🗐

Chapel House, Chapel Street, Penzance,
Cornwall TR18 4AQ
Telephone: +44(0)1736 363761
reception@penzanceartsclub.co.uk
www.penzanceartsclub.co.uk

When Belinda Rushworth-Lund set up the Penzance
Arts Club in a splendid Grade II Georgian house
dating from 1781, she was reflecting the fact that West
Cornwall has the greatest concentration of working
artists outside the East End of London. The house
stands high above the sweep of Mount's Bay and mixes
shabby chic with lots of artists' work. Period features
are to be seen in an entrance hall (which serves as a
gallery space) marble fireplaces, sweeping staircase,
and tall french windows leading to a balcony and small
walled garden. The lounge bar oozes a convivial,
clubby atmosphere, and art courses, jazz, and poetry
readings are offered. Accommodation in seven
bedrooms is provided for members, but temporary
membership at a nominal premium is available.
Needless to say, the bohemian nature of the place is
not for everyone, but many first-time visitors go on to
enroll full-time to enjoy the on-going benefits. The
seven bedrooms are spacious, strikingly, colourfully
designed with fabulous views across to St Michael's
Mount – not all are en suite. Food in the relaxed,
informal bistro is good, with largely organic raw
materials sourced locally, perhaps fish from Newlyn or
local organic meat. The style is eclectic and the menu
daily changing.

Prices: Main course restaurant from £9. House wine £9.
Hours: 09.30-23.00. Saturday 12.00-23.00, Sunday 17.00-23.00.
Food served: 18.30-21.30 Tuesday-Saturday.
Rooms: 7. Double/twin from £60. Single from £45.
Cuisine: Modern British.
Other Points: No-smoking area. Garden and Patio.
Children welcome.
Directions: Follow Harbour and Ferry signs. Cross bridge, turn
right into Quay Street. Chapel Street is on the right. (Map 3, E2)

Cottage Restaurant ✗ 🗐

The Coombes, Polperro, Cornwall PL13 2RQ
Telephone: +44(0)1503 272217

The typical fisherman's cottage has been carefully
extended to provide a cosy, tiny bar leading into a
beamed restaurant that's covered in watercolours,
plates, and pretty knick-knacks, with polished tables
laid with lace doilies and coasters. Dave and Pam
Foster have built up a loyal following, drawn as much
by the warm, homely atmosphere as by the cooking,
especially the very fresh fish on offer. Blackboard
menus give the catch of the day from local trawlers,
brill with tomato and dill sauce, maybe John Dory
with prawn and lemon butter, all served with a choice
of potatoes and fresh vegetables. The printed menu
brings a rich seafood and lobster chowder to start,
with main courses extending to prime west country
fillet and sirloin steaks, roast rack of lamb and
Cornish chicken. Portions are generous, and puddings
run to raspberry crème brûlée with clotted cream, or a
traditional spotted dick. Bedrooms are charming,
continuing the cottage theme with pretty bed linen,
good pine furniture, and plenty of hanging space.
Rooms above the restaurant have views onto the street,
but at the back, across a striking garden, are two very
comfortable garden rooms. All rooms are en suite with
gleaming modern bathrooms.

Prices: Main course from £11.50. House wine £9.95.
Hours: 19.00-21.00. Closed from end Oct to beginning of April
Rooms: 5 en suite. Double room from £57.
Cuisine: Seafood/traditional English.
Other Points: No smoking. Children welcome. Garden.
Free parking for bed and breakfast.
Directions: A38 from Plymouth to A387 (Looe). Follow signs to
Polperro. Restaurant 300 metres from the roundabout into the
village. (Map 3, E3)

Nelsons Restaurant ✗

Big Green, Saxon Bridge, Polperro, Cornwall PL13 2QT
Telephone: +44(0)1503 272366
nelsons@polperro.co.uk
www.polperro.co.uk

The striking, ivy-covered house fits the 'little fishing village' image that
Polperro likes to promote, with its brass portholes and nautical theme;
although it is a long walk from the public car park in bad weather. Peter
Nelson has been here for 30 years, but time has in no way dimmed his
enthusiasm: 'fresh fish and shellfish in abundance' he enthuses, when
asked to describe his menu. Regulars and tourists are drawn by his sound
cooking, and by the friendly service in the intimate, rich red and green
ornate interior. Daily fish specials are chalked up on a board, but those
who hanker after the old classic dishes will find the likes of baked
Polperro crab Mornay, lobster Thermidor, and fillet of sole caprice on the
printed menu. It is not all seafood, however. A selection of beef dishes

Prices: Main course from £11.95.
Set menu £12.75 (2 courses).
Hours: 11.00-14.00 Thursday, Friday and
Sunday. 18.45-21.45. Closed on Monday.
Cuisine: Seafood/French.
Other Points: Children welcome.
Directions: 25 miles from Plymouth (A38)
and five miles from Looe (A387). On the
Saxon Bridge in Polperro. (Map 3, E3)

takes in plain grilled steaks, tournedos Rossini, and entrecote chasseur, or
Gressingham duck with orange and Cointreau. Downstairs, there's
Captain Nemo's bar-brasserie offering a simpler, more informal menu of
crab salad, garlic mussels, seafood pancake filled with Polperro crab and
prawns, steak and kidney pudding, and seafood linguine with seafood and
Parmesan sauce.

Plantation 🍵 ✕

The Coombes, Polperro, Cornwall PL13 2RG
Telephone: +44(0)1503 272223
linda@cox4.fsbusiness.co.uk

Built by an enterprising local lad who returned with a
fortune made on the North American plantations, this
black and white house on the main street is now a
classic tearoom. Beams, plates, figurines, creamers, a
fireplace surrounded by lots of brass knick knacks and
topped by a huge copper hood, create a traditional,
cosy look. Friendly, comfortable service delivers
excellent cakes (lemon meringue, chocolate fudge cake,
cherry and almond cake and lovely fruit cake), or there
are Cornish cream teas, and speciality leaf teas are
properly served with tea strainer, extra hot water, and
the choice of lemon or milk (so rare these days). Daily
specials are prepared each day, perhaps cottage pie or
braised steak, and popular choices can soon run out. A
printed menu supplements the specials with the likes of
sandwiches and salads. Outside is a large, attractive,
leafy terrace with palm trees and lots of tables and
chairs. It is quite a sheltered spot, beside the tiny River
Pol which runs through the village into the narrow
harbour.

Prices: Main course from £6.15. House wine £8.95.
Hours: 10.00-22.00. Restaurant 17.30-21.30. Closed Saturday
except on Bank Holiday week-ends, and October to Easter (open
for two weeks over Christmas).
Cuisine: Traditional British/vegetarian/mediterranean
and seafood.
Other Points: Children welcome. Tropical riverside tea garden.
Directions: Take the A38 from Exeter to Plymouth, the A387 to
Looe, main road from East Looe to Polperro. (Map 3, E3)

Port Gaverne Hotel 🛏 🍴 ✕ ◈

Port Gaverne, Port Isaac, Cornwall PL29 3SQ
Telephone: +44(0)1208 880244. Freephone 0500 657867
www.portgavernehotel.co.uk

In new ownership since early 2002, this famous
Cornish coastal inn has seen a seamless changeover.
Graham and Annabelle Sylvester have retained many
long-standing staff, including chef of 20 years, Ian
Brodey, while ensuring that upgrading and
refurbishment keeps abreast of today's expectations.
There are 15 very good value bedrooms with a fresh,
comfortable look and gleaming modern bathrooms, a
charming, traditional beamed bar with log fire,
matched by an equally beamed and pleasant restaurant
resplendent with fresh flowers and a wonderful lack of
formality. Noted for very fresh fish and a commitment
to local produce, Port Gaverne succeeds admirably in
balancing good food and hospitality to all comers with
a wholly acceptable degree of Cornish idiosyncracy.
Dinner could produce gratin of local smoked haddock
in a parsley and cream sauce, whole grilled Torbay sole
with buttered prawns and mushrooms, and a selection
of regional cheeses as an alternative to pudding. A
short, user-friendly wine list delivers some two dozen
wines and offers a decent cross-section of styles and
good value.

Prices: Set dinner £22. Sunday lunch £10.95. Main course bar/snack
from £4.95. House wine £9.95.
Hours: 11.00-23.00, Sunday 12.00-22.30.
Closed 1-14 February.
Food served: 12.00-14.00. 18.30-21.30.
Rooms: 15 en suite. Double/twin from £70. Single from £35,
family from £70.
Cuisine: Traditional and Modern British.
Other Points: No-smoking area. Dogs welcome. Garden. Children
welcome. Car park.
Directions: Signposted from the A30 north of Camelford and the
A389 from Wadebridge via the B3314. Follow the signs to Port
Isaac. (Map 3, E3)

Prices: 4 course dinner by prior
arrangement from £29.
Hours: Closed December-mid February
Rooms: 3 en suite. Double room from £39
per person, single from £65.
Other Points: No-smoking area. Garden.
Car park. Jacuzzi and outdoor pool.
Directions: A30/A391. Two miles east of
St Austell on the A390; take the turning for
Tregrehan across from the St Austell
Garden Centre. Then immediately turn left
into the driveway leading into the
courtyard of the lodge. (Map 3, E3)

Anchorage House Guest Lodge ★ ◈

Nettles Corner, Boscundle, Tregrehan Mills, St Austell, Cornwall PL25 3RH
Telephone: +44(0)1726 814071
stay@anchoragehouse.co.uk
www.anchoragehouse.co.uk

The immaculately kept and extended Georgian-style lodge is set in stylish
landscaped gardens that contain a 15 metre lap pool. Within, all is
decorated with verve, passion and comfort. The lounge is spacious and
comfortable, with abundant reading matter and complimentary tray of
sherries, leading to the grand but informal plant-filled conservatory where
breakfast and dinner is served on a polished mahogany table (dinner
Wednesday, Friday and Sunday; other days by arrangement). Jane and
Steve Epperson are genuinely welcoming, and refreshingly laid back.
They've spent over ten years constantly improving the property and their
personal hospitality to deluxe standards. It is the bedrooms that are the
star turn. There are only three, but each is elegant, individual (including a
two-storey loft suite), spotlessly maintained with every luxury one could
wish for: chocolates, biscuits, fresh flowers, a turn down service, king and
super king-size beds. Magnificent bathrooms have large baths and
separate power showers, lots of lotions and potions. There's also a jacuzzi
and bathrobes are provided for those wishing to use it.

Auberge Asterisk

Mount Pleasant, Roche, St Austell, Cornwall PL26 8LH
Telephone: +44(0)1726 890863
ferzan@l'auberge.freeserve.co.uk

Viewed from the A30 this cream coloured, squarely solid old house looks like a rural French Relais Routiers with its large, slightly faded sign prominently displayed on high. This is a very simple restaurant with rooms, run with dedicated enthusiasm by Ferzan Zola, almost as a one-man operation. Food is the thing here with fresh produce delivered daily and translated into an eclectic menu that delights as much in old classics as in interpretations of modern ideas. Expect fish terrine served with saffron or mustard sauce, or a fresh, clean tasting seafood salad of prawns, baby octopus and shellfish. Main courses run to fillet of local beef with ginger and black beans, venison steak with Calvados and cream, or monkfish with a saffron sauce. Puddings are a speciality, with meringue roulade, Grand Marnier soufflé, profiteroles and even a homemade Black Forest gateau. The wine list is short but wide ranging and prices are, well, a steal. Upstairs are five en suite bedrooms, neat, well-maintained rooms with pretty views, offering very good value in an area that is becoming increasingly short of bed space with the runaway success of the Eden Project; it is necessary to book for both rooms and restaurant.

Prices: Main course from £12. House wine £8.
Hours: 19.00-21.00 Wednesday-Saturday for non-residents.
Rooms: 3 en suite. Double room from £49.50, single from £34.75.
Cuisine: Modern European.
Other Points: Children welcome. Garden. Car park.
Directions: On the A30. 2 miles west after Innisdown roundabout (Bodmin By-Pass). (Map 3, E5)

Bodrugan Barton

Mevagissey, St Austell, Cornwall PL26 6PT
Telephone: +44(0)1726 842094
bodruganbarton@ukonline.co.uk

Named after Sir Henry de Bodrugan who lived here some 500 years ago, Bodrugan Barton offers an outstanding level of farmhouse accommodation. Tim and Sally Kendall's farmhouse, with matching barn cottages and huge courtyard, includes a heated indoor swimming pool, badminton and table tennis. Within the solid stone walls of the farmhouse, family portraits and paintings old and new line deep-coral-coloured walls. The enormous breakfast-cum-sitting room has deeply comfortable sofas and a wood-burning stove in the arched stone fireplace, and the large hall and stairway lead to three comfortable bedrooms with views overlooking the grounds and beyond. Breakfast is hearty, with most items home-produced, especially the bread. All this is set in an Area of Outstanding Natural Beauty, with the secluded Colona Bay nearby. This makes a wonderful base for walking holidays. Note that no credit cards are taken.

Hours: Closed 12 December to 12 January.
Rooms: 3 rooms, 1 with shower, 1 with private bathroom, 1 with private shower.
Other Points: Totally no smoking. Garden. Children welcome over 12 years old. Car park.
Directions: Drive through Mevagissey and past Portmellon, up the steep hill and the entrance is on the left. (Map 3, E3)

The Old Inn

Churchtown, St Breward, Bodmin Moor, Cornwall PL30 4PP
Telephone: +44(0)1208 850711
darren@theoldinn.fsnet.co.uk
www.theoldinnandrestaurant.co.uk

The highest pub in Cornwall stands at 700 feet on the edge of Bodmin Moor, and is a low white-painted cottage with a bar that dates back 1,000 years (when it was the alehouse for the builders of the adjacent church). The weathered carved stone cross set in the front lawn is said to be of Saxon origin. Beyond the deep entrance porch, the strongly traditional interior exudes charm and atmosphere, with slate floors, part-exposed walls, thick beams, oak settles and a roaring winter log fire in the huge granite fireplace. Tools, traps, brasses and banknotes enhance the inn's rural character. Food at the Old Inn is wholesome, unpretentious and not for the faint-hearted - portions are very generous! Walkers, locals and moorland trippers tuck into hearty pub favourites like ploughman's, homemade pies and curries and Charlie Harris's garlic sausages and chips, all washed down with a tip-top pint of Sharps local ale - try the excellent Doom Bar. Locally reared beef provide the excellent steaks, and fresh fish, notably the huge cod (deep-fried in beer batter), is landed at nearby harbours along the north Cornish coast.

Prices: Main course from £5.95. House wine £9.95.
Hours: 11.00-23.00. Sunday 12.00-22.30.
Food Served: 12.00-14.30. 18.00-21.00.
Cuisine: Modern British and homemade Cornish dishes.
Other Points: No-smoking area. Garden. Children welcome. Car park. 140 seat restaurant available for functions.
Directions: Follow the signposts for St Breward from A30. The Old Inn is adjacent to the village church. (Map 3, D3)

Mevagissey Harbour, Cornwall

The Gurnards Head Hotel

Treen, Zennor, St Ives, Cornwall TR26 3DE
Telephone: +44(0)1736 796928
enquiries@gurnardshead.free-online.co.uk
www.gurnardshead.fsnet.co.uk

On the rugged north-west edge of Cornwall, with the sea on one side and the moors on the other, stands this sturdy, white-painted traditional-looking Cornish pub. The bar is beamed and has a great screened-concrete floor with fireplaces at each end, prints and pictures cover the walls, and there's a very good choice of real ales. The warmth of the décor makes a suitable backdrop for a menu lighter than the Cornish norm. Regular menus are in modern country-pub mode with 3,000 miles of nearby ocean dictating an emphasis on first-rate local seafood; the cooking does not compromise the quality. Lunch is a simple affair, with soups, sandwiches and blackboard specials, but Cornish seafood broth, made with cider, crab, cockles, mussels, prawns, scallops, white fish, vegetables and herbs, is as popular at lunch as in the evening. The evening menu brings whole megrim sole, perhaps, or pan-fried John Dory, lemon sole and monkfish with nut-brown butter, pickled marsh samphire and lemon rondelle. Meat eaters are not neglected with the likes of confit of duck, or Aberdeen Angus sirloin. The six bedrooms are warm and comfortable, decorated in country fashion with pine furniture, and bathrooms with modern shower units.

Prices: Main course from £10.50 House wine £12.60 litre.
Hours: 12.00-14.15. 18.30-21.15. 12.00-14.15 and 19.00-21.15 on Sundays.
Rooms: 6 en suite. Double rooms from £55. Single occupancy £5. or £10. supplement.
Cuisine: Seafood/eclectic.
Other Points: No smoking area. Garden. Children welcome. Car park.
Directions: 5 miles from St Ives on the St Ives to Lands End Road, B3306. (Map 3, E2)

The Old Count House

Trenwith Square, St Ives, Cornwall TR26 1DQ
Telephone: +44(0)1736 795369
counthouse@connexions.co.uk
www.connexions.co.uk/counthosue/index.htm

The Old Count House, built from local granite, dates from 1825 and was so named because it was from here that the wages were counted out and paid to the tin miners of Wheal Trenwith. Now run as a seaside B&B, a reminder of those days can be seen on the walls in the small bar-cum-dining room, where the boards used for the daily tally of the production to each shaft still hang. Other rooms take in a small sitting room with open fire, TV, lots of magazines, books, comfy sofas and chairs, and nine small, cosy bedrooms. Eight are en suite, with the ninth a single room with private bathroom. All are well kept, come with tea trays, most have TV, are individually decorated (one four-poster and one canopied bed) and have modern bathrooms – mostly with showers. There's a Finnish sauna in the conservatory, and robes are provided for guests' use. Breakfast is a hearty full English, with dinner by arrangement. This is a modestly priced, good-value B&B, close to St Ives town centre, beaches and Tate Gallery, with the Lost Gardens of Heligan and the Eden Project one hour's drive away.

Prices: B&B. Set dinner on request £15. House wine £7.95.
Rooms: 9 rooms, 8 en suite, 1 with private bathroom. Double room from £60, single from £35.
Cuisine: Traditional English.
Other Points: No-smoking. Garden. Car park.
Directions: Exit A30 Hayle bypass at roundabout for St Ives. At second mini roundabout turn left and follow the signs for day visitors to St Ives via Halsetown, B3311. At junction with B306 turn right to St Ives; after approximately half a mile follow the signs to St Ives leisure centre. Trenwith Square is on the right after the school. (Map 3, E2)

The Garrack Hotel and Restaurant

Burthallan Lane, St Ives, Cornwall TR26 3AA
Telephone: +44(0)1736 796199
garrack@accuk.co.uk
www.garrack.com

The creeper-clad Garrack Hotel has been run by the Kilby family for 36 years and details remain constant and reassuring: the welcome is warm, there's a special homely feel, and the food is always good. Surrounded by two acres of garden and overlooking Porthmeor Beach, sea views are to be had from all aspects of the public rooms, and from many of the bedrooms. In the main house these are decorated in an unfussy country fashion, but rooms in the sea-facing lower-ground-floor wing are in a more modern style and some rooms have four-poster or half-tester beds and spa baths. A big attraction is the small, stand-alone leisure centre, with its indoor pool. The restaurant is a well-matched addition to the main building. Here, Phil Thomas adopts a classic modern English approach. Seasonal materials are a strength, the roll call taking in a starter of pan-fried south coast scallops with smoked paprika, oyster mushrooms and a lime and coriander oil, followed by pan-fried Cornish monkfish with courgettes and red onions roasted in pumpkin oil with a poppy seed cream. The wine list is carefully selected from various suppliers to achieve global choice. Fair wine prices are achieved by applying fixed mark-ups, rather than the traditional percentage.

Prices: Set dinner £25.50 (four courses). House wine £9.05.
Hours: 19.00-21.00.
Rooms: 18 en suite. Doubles from £114, single from £68.
Cuisine: Modern English.
Other Points: No smoking area. Garden. Children welcome. Car park.
Directions: Leave the A30 and follow the signposts to St Ives, A3074. At the second mini roundabout take the first left, B3311, signposted St Ives. In St Ives at the first mini roundabout take the first left and follow the signs for the Garrack Hotel. (Map 3, E2)

The White Hart Hotel

The Square, St Keverne, Helston,
Cornwall TR12 6ND
Telephone: +44(0)1326 280325
whitehart@easynet.co.uk
www.white-hart-hotel.co.uk

Overlooking the square and church in the heart of this pretty village on the Lizard Peninsula, the Travis family's 18th-century inn serves as a thriving community local and as a dining pub where seafood is taken very seriously. Divers, walkers and tourists mingle with locals in the welcoming, wood floor bar as this popular pub is close to Flambards Theme Park and an easy stroll from the coast path and one of the best diving sites in the country. Head for the neatly refurbished dining room, where exposed beams, sea-grass matting and local art are the backdrop for fresh fish and seafood landed at nearby Coverack and Helford: oven roasted monkfish with mixed peppers; whole grilled John Dory or lemon sole; seared scallops with bacon and garlic and parsley sauce; whole hot baked local crab with chips and dips. Alternative choices run to prime fillet steak served on a bed of garlic mussels, pasta and vegetarian dishes and more traditional pub meals. Don't forgo the excellent crab sandwiches if you are here at lunchtime - or the indulgent, weekend-long Crab Festival in mid-July. There's comfortable cottagey accommodation in two en suite bedrooms.

Prices: Main course restaurant from £7.95. House wine £7.95.
Hours: 11.00-14.30. 18.00-23.00 (18.00-22.30 Sunday).
Closed 25 December evening.
Food served: 12.00-14.00. 18.30-21.00.
Half an hour later from April to October.
Rooms: 2 en suite. Double room from £50, single from £35.
Cuisine: Traditonal, Seafood and Modern European.
Other Points: No-smoking area. Children welcome. Garden. Car park.
Directions: Village on B3293 11 miles south east of A3083 and Helston. (Map 3, E3)

St Mawes Hotel

The Seafront, St Mawes, Truro, Cornwall TR2 5DW
Telephone: +44(0)1326 270266
burrowsemma@msn.com
www.stmaweshotel.co.uk

In a splendid setting, right on the sea front, this pretty cream—painted hotel is a popular destination for both residents and passers-by. This is especially true of the Fountain Bar, which opens out on to the street in summer. Here a casual Mediterranean look, with vibrant colours, wood floor, even sofas, keeps the atmosphere informal. It's the Mediterranean that inspires the menu in the bright, modern brasserie too. Local smoked seafood platter (salmon, mackerel, mussels, prawns) may head a list of starters that could also run to local crab bisque, and fresh local smoked duck breast with apple and walnut salad and raspberry dressing. A main course of pan-fried wild sea bass is served with mashed potatoes, sauce vierge and vegetables, while chargrilled tuna steak comes with Niçoise salad and quails' eggs. The wine list complements the food, with Australia, Chile and South Africa supplying house wines by the glass, and a short, well-annotated selection by the bottle at very reasonable prices. Five simple but stylish bedrooms include three with stunning sea views. Walls are painted white to absorb the magnificent sea light, have fresh flowers, TV and tea trays, and modern bathrooms are all en suite.

Prices: Main courses from £9.95.
House wine £9.95.
Hours: 12.00-14.30. 18.00-21.30.
Rooms: 5 en suite. Singles from £25, doubles from £60.
Other Points: No-smoking.
Children welcome.
Directions: From St Austell take the A390 to Truro and follow the signs to St Mawes on the A3078. (Map 3, E3)

Cadgwith Cove Inn

Cadgwith, Ruan Minor, Helston,
Cornwall TR12 7JX
Telephone: +44(0)1326 290513
enquiries@cadgwithcoveinn.com
www.cadgwithcoveinn.com

An unspoilt fishing hamlet of thatched cottages on the rugged Lizard coastline is the appealing setting for this 300-year-old pub, formerly the haunt of smugglers. In front of the plain, whitewashed building a sunny patio affords drinkers views across the old pilchard cellar to the cove. A few steps down the lane is the shingle beach and the colourful fishing vessels that provide the inn with freshly-caught red and grey mullet, sea bass, gurnard, and the best crab and lobster. Furnished simply and decked with mementos of bygone seafaring days, the two bars, both with open fires to warm those stormy winter nights, serve five real ales, notably Sharp's superb Doom Bar Bitter. Although much of the printed menu lists traditional homemade pub food, note and try the delicious white crab meat sandwiches or the famous Cadgwith crab soup served with thick crusty bread. Fish fanciers should look no further than the blackboard, which lists the daily catch, or plump for the ever-popular beer-battered haddock and chips. Alternatives include a proper Cornish pasty and a real Cornish cheese lunch, and hearty nursery puddings. Seven homely and simply equipped bedrooms; only two en suite.

Prices: Set lunch from £10. Set dinner from £13. Main course restaurant from £5.95. House wine £8.95.
Hours: 12.00-15.00. 19.00-23.00. Monday to Thursday. Until 17.00 Thursday and all day at weekends. Winter variations.
Food served: 12.00-15.00. 19.00-21.30.
Rooms: 7 rooms, 2 en suite. From £19.75 B&B.
Cuisine: Seafood and Traditional European.
Other Points: Dogs welcome. Garden and patio.
Children welcome.
Directions: Village signposted off A3083 9 miles south of Helston. (Map 3, F2)

Smugglers Cottage of Tolverne

Tolverne, Philleigh, Truro, Cornwall TR2 5NG
Telephone: +44(0)1872 580309
tolverne@btconnect.com
www.tolverneriverfal.co.uk

The Newman family has been running this thatched 15th century cottage on the banks of the River Fal (arrive by boat or car) since 1934 and have gained quite a reputation for hospitality and good home cooking. It's a truly unique place, full of history with nautical memorabilia crowding the interior (the Americans used the cottage and slipway as an embarkation point for the D-Day landings, and General Eisenhower visited the troops here), and one of the dining rooms is devoted entirely to the SS Uganda. Commitment to good food includes four different varieties of proper Cornish pasties (considered something of a speciality), and excellent chicken and ham pie, fish pie, or filled baguettes and ciabatta, with good puddings and cakes (cream teas are excellent). There are non-smoking dining rooms and the bar has a collection of over 100 malt whiskies.

Prices: Main course from £5. House wine £9.
Hours: 10.30-17.30. In high season to 20.30.
Closed from November-May.
Cuisine: Modern British.
Other Points: No-smoking area. Children welcome. Garden. Car park
Directions: Near the King Harry Car Ferry, on the Roseland Peninsula, on the banks of the river Fal. (Map 3, E3)

Charlotte's Tea House

Coinage Hall, 1 Boscawen Street, Truro, Cornwall TR1 2QV
Telephone: +44(0)1872 263706

Coinage Hall stands on an ancient site, possibly dating from 1302 and the halcyon days of Cornish tin mining, although the present Grade II listed building dates from 1848. Now carefully restored, the tearoom is set on the first floor. You ascend a big wooden staircase lined with antiques, mirrors, and pictures, to a Victorian-styled room filled with antiques and hung with beautiful chandeliers, with staff in traditional uniform; it's a glorious step back in time. Local produce is used where possible, especially eggs and vegetables that are delivered from a nearby farm. All cakes and scones are made on the premises, with cream teas and Charlotte's high tea (one of the highlights of a visit here) served all day. There's also a champagne breakfast for two, light lunches of local crab open sandwiches, omelettes and eggs every which way, quiches, soups, jacket potatoes, and locally made luxury ice cream (with clotted cream), which is delicious. Daily specials are listed on the blackboard and there's a very good selection of leaf teas.

Prices: Main course from £5.
House wine £7.95.
Hours: 10.00-17.00. Closed Sunday, 25-26 December and Bank Holidays.
Cuisine: Modern British.
Other Points: Totally no smoking.
Children welcome. Credit cards
not accepted.
Directions: Take the A30 to Truro centre.
(Map 3, E3)

Royal Cornwall Museum Café

River Street, Truro, Cornwall TR1 2SJ
Telephone: +44(0)1872 272205
enquiry@royal-cornwall-museum.freeserve.co.uk
www.royalcornwallmuseum.org.uk

It's a real find. This café-cum-art gallery in what used to be until fairly recently a Baptist chapel, is a spacious mid-Victorian building with a high ceiling and a lovely maple wood floor. Situated next to the Royal Cornwall Museum, visitors are surrounded by local artists' work, which changes each month. The café is welcoming for children too, helped by the south facing sheltered courtyard – perfect for the summer months (and with large outdoor heaters, possible for the more hardy to brave the elements all year round). The café is well laid out for wheelchairs, with easy access everywhere, including a lift to the upstairs seating and air conditioning is a bonus for everyone. There is a wide range of pastries, sandwiches, salads, and light lunches are available, with locally caught crab taking a starring role. Roast chicken with salad and new potatoes, and scampi and chips, are favourites while Thai fish salad and grilled goat's cheese served with cider apple chutney are typical of imaginative specials.

Prices: Main course from £4.25. Wine, by the glass, £1.50.
Hours: 10.00-16.30. Closed on Sunday.
Cuisine: Traditional English.
Other Points: No-smoking area. Children welcome. Courtyard garden.
Directions: Follow the A390 to Truro, left down Station Hill towards town centre. (Map 3, E3)

Buskers

Polmorla Mews, Wadebridge, Cornwall PL27 7LR
Telephone: +44(0)1208 814332
www.buskers-wadebridge.com

The L-shaped former stables and courtyard is full of character with marble tables and pretty metal chairs filling a courtyard that's almost totally enclosed by stone walls. This small cobbled area is where locals and visitors take coffee, brunch or dinner beneath heavy hanging baskets cascading with beautiful blooms. From the courtyard the restaurant's front door leads into an attractive interior. Rough plastered mustard walls downstairs and the deep aubergine walls upstairs are covered with guitars, accordions, drumkits and wonderful music posters covering all eras, reminders of Mike Holloway's passion for music. By day, expect anything from brunch of bacon, egg, sausage and chips, soup and homemade bread, and filled baguettes. With evening candles the mood changes, the cooking delivering seared scallops with Proscuitto and sun-blushed tomatoes, for example, or homecured salmon with dill mustard sauce. Mains take in Hungarian fish stew, and ever changing specials boards courtesy of Maggie Holloway who runs the kitchens. The kitchen promotes Cornish produce wherever possible, a member of the Campaign for Real Food: scallops from Looe, mussels from Fowey, Cornish cheese and wine, and Roskilly's homemade ice cream, as an alternative to house offerings of apricot and almond tart, or pineapple and ginger roulade.

Prices: Main course from £10. House wine £9.95.
Hours: 10.30-15.00. Evenings from 18.30 till late. Winter opening hours Tuesday to Saturday; Summer opening hours Monday to Saturday. Closed Sunday.
Cuisine: Eclectic, specialising in fresh fish and shellfish.
Other Points: No-smoking area. Chidlren welcome. Courtyard.
Directions: In the centre of Wadebridge off Polmorla Road and Polmorla Walk. (Map 3, D3)

Lovelady Shield

Alston, Cumbria CA9 3LF
Telephone: +44(0)1434 381203
enquiries@lovelady.co.uk
www.lovelady.co.uk

Built on the site of the 14th century Love of Our Lady convent and approached by a tree-lined drive, the classical Georgian house stands in a wonderfully secluded spot by the river. The interior exudes an air of soothing relaxation, aided admirably by Peter Haynes who is a natural and experienced host and runs everything with total enthusiasm. Smart bedrooms each have their own distinctive character, but are all charming and softly decorated in creams and white, with CD players and Scrabble in every one. Dinner is well worth the asking price and after 15 years at the stove, there is agreement that the formula of a four-course, short choice dinner has not stifled Barrie Garton's sense of adventure. He produces classic country house-style dishes with a few modern touches. Thus a June dinner could deliver warmed fresh asparagus spears with a fine herb butter sauce, followed by spicy parsnip and creamy apple soup, then a tournedos 'en croute' of prime Aberdeen Angus beef fillet, cooked in a light puff pastry parcel with red wine and wild mushroom sauce. Fresh peaches, flamed in brandy and honey and served with banana ice cream make a great finale. A seriously thoughtful list of over 100 bins should inspire wine lovers.

Prices: Set price dinner £32.50 (4 courses). House wine £12.95.
Hours: Open for dinner 19.00-21.00. Sunday lunch on first Sunday of every month.
Rooms: 10 en suite. Rooms from £60 per person including dinner and breakfast.
Cuisine: Modern British.
Other Points: No-smoking area. Children welcome over 7 years old. Garden. Car park. Licence for Civil Weddings.
Directions: On the Durham Road (A689) just outside Alston. (Map 11, C4)

Drunken Duck Inn ★ 🏠 ✗ ✍

Barngates, Ambleside, Cumbria LA22 ONG
Telephone: +44(0)15394 36347
info@drunkenduckinn.co.uk
www.drunkenduckinn.co.uk

There are fabulous views towards Lake Windermere from this 17th-century inn which stands in splendid isolation. However, the inn is extremely popular and has its own fishing tarn, micro-brewery (Barngates), modern cooking and stylish accommodation. Beyond the traditional bar, three adjoining rooms feature original beams, open fires, stripped settles, antiques and a wealth of landscape and sporting prints; the residents lounge is particularly elegant and comfortable. Justifiably popular food makes good use of fresh local produce, the simpler lunchtime menu offering Holker Hall venison and red wine pie, and fresh plaice grilled with Flookburgh shrimps. More elaborate evening dishes may open with duck and spring onion confit with chilli jam and coriander dressing with Cumbrian beef fillet with roast mushroom fritter, asparagus and red wine jus, among the main course options. Melting dark chocolate tart with pistachio ice cream may appear on the list of homemade puddings. As well as Cracker Ale, Tag Lag, Chesters Strong and Ugley brewed behind the inn, you will find 20 wines by the glass. Overnight guests are housed in stylish, individually designed bedrooms, all with modern creature comforts, including TV, video, and impeccable bathrooms.

Prices: Main course from £8.95. House wine £9.50.
Hours: 11.30-23.00 (12.00-22.30 Sunday).
Food served: 12.00-21.00 daily
Rooms: 16 en suite. Double room from £85, single from £63.75.
Cuisine: Modern British.
Other Points: Car park. Garden. Children welcome. Fly Fishing. Dogs welcome in public areas only.
Directions: Exit 36/M6. Take the A592 from Kendal to Ambleside, then follow signs to Hawkshead on the B5286 an turn right in two and a half miles (inn sign). (Map 11, D4)

The Old Dungeon Ghyll 🏠 🏠 ✗ ✍

Great Langdale, Ambleside, Cumbria LA22 9JY
Telephone: +44(0)15394 37272
www.odg.co.uk

The Old Dungeon Ghyll is special because of its location (at the head of the Great Langdale Valley, at the foot of some of Englands steepest passes), and links to the walking and climbing community; it is the perfect climbers' hotel. Three hundred years ago it was a farm, but the traditional hotel has been added to over the years and now has 14 bedrooms. Run for almost two decades by Neil and Jane Walmsley, it has a terrific atmosphere. The Hikers Bar has flagged floors, wooden pew seating, and a huge range at one end. Food is good, substantial stuff, nothing too fancy, just homemade lasagne, curries and pies. Beer includes Jennings, Theakston and the local Yates. The simply-styled hotel is clean and comfortable. Only four of the fourteen rooms are en suite; there's no telly (as there's no reception), but each room is prettily furnished in cottage style with patchwork quilts and pine furniture. The dining room is the venue for homemade bread and marmalades at breakfast, and an evening meal that may consist of leek and potato soup, braised beef or salmon with hollandaise, and fresh fruit Pavlova, chosen from two or three choices at each course.

Prices: Set dinner £18 (4 courses). Main course from £7.95. House wine £8.95.
Hours: 12.00-14.00. 18.00-21.00. Closed over Christmas for four days.
Food served: Dinner from 19.30, one sitting only.
Rooms: 14 rooms, 4 en suite. Double/twin room from £79.
Cuisine: Traditonal British.
Other Points: No-smoking area. Garden. Children welcome. Car park.
Directions: Exit 36/M6 towards Ambleside on the A591, then take A593 towards Coniston and the B5343 to Great Langdale. The hotel is at the top of the valley. (Map 11, D4)

Tufton Arms Hotel 🏠 🏠 ✗ ✍

Market Square, Appleby-in-Westmorland, Cumbria CA16 6XA
Telephone: +44(0)17683 51593
info@tuftonarmshotel.co.uk
www.tuftonarmshotel.co.uk

This former Victorian coaching inn was comprehensively renovated 13 years ago by the Milsom family to reflect the ambience of that period: attractive wallpapers, lots of prints in heavy frames, heavy drapes, old fireplaces and large porcelain table lamps. The heavily-balustraded main staircase is a magnificent feature. Bedrooms vary from suites with period fireplaces, antique furnishings and large old-style bathrooms, to more conventional well-equipped en suite rooms with good proportions, but there are some compact and simply-furnished rooms to the rear. Light lunch and supper menus are served in the bar, with a more formal choice available in the stylish restaurant with its conservatory extension. Cooking is of a high standard, be it rack of Cumbrian fell-bred lamb, or game from the local Dalemain Estate, where Nigel Milsom regularly arranges shooting parties (along with fishing, a major attraction for many guests). Fish is delivered from Fleetwood, to create, perhaps, paupiette of lemon sole stuffed with smoked salmon with a dill white wine sauce. There is a French accent to the carefully selected, well-annotated wine list. Prices are very reasonable, with many bottles priced under £20.

Prices: Set dinner £23. Main course restaurant from £8. Main course bar from £6.85. House wine £9.50.
Hours: 11.00-23.00, Sunday 12.00-22.30.
Food served: 12.00-14.00. 18.30-21.00.
Rooms: 21 en suite. Double/twin from £95.
Cuisine: Traditional English and French.
Other Points: No-smoking area. Dogs welcome. Children welcome. Car park.
Directions: Exit38/M6. Take the B6260 to Appleby via Orton. (Map 11, D4)

The Dukes Head ▯✕⌽

Armathwaite, Carlisle, Cumbria CA4 9PB
Telephone: +44(0)1697 472226
hh@hlynch51.freeserve.com
www.dukesheadhotel.co.uk

First licensed when the Carlisle to Settle railway was
being built, this homely whitewashed inn stands in the
heart of a tiny village in the beautiful Eden Valley.
Long a favourite among ramblers, bird-watchers and
fishing folk (who come in search of the finest trout and
salmon in the North of England), the inn remains
firmly traditional throughout. Beyond the civilised
lounge bar, with its stone walls, open fires, sturdy oak
settle and tables, and antique country prints, you will
find a locals' bar, a neat dining room, and a glorious
garden that borders the River Eden. One menu
operates throughout, and offers a wide range of
promising dishes that make excellent use of fresh local
ingredients, including hot potted Solway shrimps, game
in season, and cumberland sausage made by a local
butcher. There's a good choice of salads, omelettes and
sandwiches. A typical meal may begin with pork,
venison and apricot terrine with cumberland sauce,
followed by trout with lemon and chervil stuffing or
sirloin steak with peppercorn sauce, with ginger,
sultana and walnut sponge to finish. The half-dozen
bedrooms are simply and traditionally furnished, the
most popular being the three with en suite bathrooms.
Prices: Main courses from £6.45. Sunday lunch set menu £12.95.
House wine £12.00.
Hours: 11.00-15.00. 17.00-23.00. Closed Christmas Day.
Food served: 12.00-13.45. 18.15-21.00.
Rooms: 5 rooms, 3 en suite. Double room from £52.50,
single from £32.50.
Cuisine: Traditional British.
Other Points: Restaurant no-smoking. Children welcome. Dogs
welcome. Garden. Car park.
Directions: Armathwaite is located off the A6 Penrith to Carlisle
road, 7 miles south of Carlisle. (Map 11, C4)

Leathes Head Hotel ▯✕⌽

Borrowdale, Keswick, Cumbria CA12 5UY
Telephone: +44(0)17687 77247
email@leatheshead.co.uk
www.leatheshead.co.uk

Janice and Roy Smith have created an elegant,
comfortable country hotel out of this Edwardian
Lakeland slate house set in three acres of garden. An
open hallway leads to several lounges, one non-
smoking, and a lovely sun lounge with wicker furniture
and spectacular views; log fires burn in cooler months.
Of the eleven en suite bedrooms, standard rooms are
small but prettily designed, superior rooms are larger
with sitting areas; best rooms are the two with double
aspects. The restaurant is only open to non-residents if
they can be accommodated. David Jackson is a
talented chef who has been running the kitchen since
1994, working single handedly with an ancient Aga, he
produces excellent modern British food that keeps its
feet firmly on the ground. The emphasis is on local
produce, and the daily changing five-course dinner
menu may offer slow-baked terrine of bacon, cornfed
chicken livers and turkey, baked Finnan haddock
mornay as an intermediate course, followed by pan-
seared escalope of beef with a tomato and pesto cream
sauce. The reasonably priced wine list is an unshowy
but thoughtful range encompassing a good variety of
grapes and styles.
Prices: Set price dinner £22.95 (4 courses + coffee). House wine
£9.75. Lunch by prior arrangement.
Hours: 19.30-20.15. Closed from mid-November to mid-February,
but open Christmas and New Year.
Rooms: 11 en suite. Double room from £67.95 per person, single
from £77.95. Includes dinner, bed and breakfast.
Cuisine: Modern British.
Other Points: Smoking in the bar only. Children welcome over 9
years old. Garden. Car park.
Directions: Exit 40/M6. Take A66 towards Keswick. Left at second
roundabout, signed Borrowdale, then left at T junction. Hotel on
B5289, 3.75 miles out of Keswick. (Map 11, D3)

Seatoller House ★▯✕⌽

Borrowdale, Keswick, Cumbria CA12 5XN
Telephone: +44(0)17687 77218
seatollerhouse@btconnect.com
www.seatollerhouse.co.uk

This traditional Lakeland building has a fascinating history. It is famed
for the location of the lake hunts - an historic, unique (invite only)
manhunt over the surrounding high craggy terrain - that takes place twice
a year and dates from 1898. The house has been a guesthouse for over a
century; its visitors' books dates back to the 19th century. This is an
informal and relaxed place, where friendliness, camaraderie and
tranquillity are the main appeal. Rooms are prettily decorated in a cottage
style and named after local wildlife and are TV-free zones. All have
stunning views of either the garden or surrounding fells. Dinner is a
communal affair with everyone sitting down, house party style, around
two large tables. Food is local and seasonal with ideas ranging from
Marguerite Patten to Paul Heathcote and produce taking in organic flour
from the Watermill at Little Salkeld for homebaked bread (see entry),
Cumberland organic mustard and locally brewed Jennings ale. A typical
dinner menu might include honey and mustard baked Waberthwaite ham
served with Cumberland mustard mash, steamed broccoli and roasted
butternut squash, and local cheeses. The short wine list is outstandingly
good value, with Australian house wines at £7.95.

Prices: Set dinner £14. House wine £8.50.
Hours: Dinner served at 19.00.
Closed December-February.
Rooms: 10 rooms, 4 en suite. Double
room from £51, single from £27.50, family
room from £63.
Cuisine: Modern British.
Other Points: No-smoking area. Children
welcome. Garden. Car park.
Directions: Junction 40/M6. Seatoller is
eight miles from Keswick along the B5289
past the shores of Derwent Water.
(Map 11, D3)

England - Cumbria

The Blacksmiths Arms

Talkin Village, Brampton, Cumbria CA8 1LE
Telephone: +44(0)169773452
info@blacksmithstalkin.co.uk
www.blacksmithstalkin.co.uk

The Blacksmiths Arms is all you would expect of a traditional inn: whitewashed walls without, low beamed ceilings and plain wooden tables within. The menu is simple but tasty, hearty and very good value. It may be standard fare along the lines of deep-fried mushrooms, chicken and mushroom pie, and bacon roulade, but all produce is locally sourced, where possible. Trout, for example, comes from the farm down the road, the famous cumberland sausage is made locally, all meat and vegetable supplies are from local farmers, and the ice cream is made in Cumbria. Just the one menu is available, but you can choose where to eat, either in the bar area, the garden room with its lovely views on to a small, enclosed garden, or the more formal restaurant with dark wood panelling. Of the five en suite bedrooms, each with its own individual colour scheme of plain painted walls and matching patterned fabrics and the usual tea and telly facilities, only one room has a bath; the rest have showers. The best rooms are in the older part of the building and have sloping ceilings and beams.

Prices: Main course in the restaurant from £5.95. Main course (bar/snack) from £3. House wine £7.95.
Hours: 12.00-15.00. 18.00-23.00 (until 22.30 on Sunday). Closed 25 December.
Food served: 12.00-14.00. 18.00-21.00.
Rooms: 8 en suite. Double room from £25.00 per person, single from £35.
Cuisine: Modern British.
Other Points: No-smoking in the bedrooms. Garden. Car park.
Directions: South of Brampton off B6413. At the crossroads turn right over the level crossing and take the second left signposted to Talkin. Exit 43/M6. (Map 11, C4)

Tarn End House Hotel

Talkin Tarn, Brampton, Cumbria CA8 1LS
Telephone: +44(0)1697 72340
www.tarnendhouse.co.uk

The location beside Talkin Tarn is a delight, with views over peaceful countryside to the fells, and gardens with mature trees and lawns running down to the water's edge. What distinguishes this hotel, however, is David and Vivienne Ball's solid, old fashioned take on running a hotel - evident in the décor whose well-worn feel projects a relaxed homely ambience. The old fashioned style extends to bedrooms (all en suite, mostly with baths), which are comfortable and very traditionally furnished. In addition, the food quality and value is exceptional. David Ball does all the cooking, making everything from soups and pâtés to desserts - they still use a trolley, not over-loaded with flash desserts, but with examples of what is available. Flavours are not overstated, meats and vegetables are cooked with skill and care, for example, a breast of chicken with a subtle taste of lemon, garlic and ginger jus. The wine list is pretty comprehensive without including vintages and offers particularly good value. It is the authenticity and honesty of approach that makes you appreciate what the Balls are doing. The place will not appeal to all - too staid, maybe old fashioned - but they are friendly people doing what they believe in; it is their home and their style.

Prices: Set lunch £13.75 and dinner £18.95. Main course restaurant from £9.75. House wine £8.95.
Hours: 12.00-13.45. 19.00-20.30. Monday open to residents only. Closed 27-29 December and the month of January.
Rooms: 6 en suite. Double/twin from £55.
Cuisine: Modern English.
Other Points: No-smoking in bedrooms and the restaurant. Garden. Children welcome. Car park.
Directions: Exit43/M6. Go to Brampton on A69, then take B6413 south towards Castle Carrock taking second left after crossing railway lines. (Map 11, C4)

The Blacksmiths Arms

Broughton Mills, Broughton in Furness, Cumbria LA2 6AX
Telephone: +44(0)1229 716824
blacksmitharms@aol.com
www.theblacksmitharms.com

Set in the wonderfully named Lickle Valley, the 16th century Blacksmiths Arms is a picture-postcard pretty country pub, its whitewashed exterior festooned with colourful hanging baskets and window boxes. Roses and flowerbeds border the sheltered front patio filled with rustic tables and chairs. Formerly a farmhouse with a little shop in the back and, in those days, open as an inn in the evening only, it is said that Coleridge stopped here for a rum butter sandwich on his way through the fells to visit Wordsworth. The interior has a country cottage feel with uneven stone-flagged floors and higgledy-piggledy rooms awash with memorabilia and old prints. The vast majority of visitors come for the food. Locally reared and slaughtered beef is used for the sizzling steak platters, and the lamb Henry, which is slow cooked and served with minted gravy is equally a very popular dish. Alternatives include starters like battered Lancashire cheese with cumberland sauce, pan-fried black pudding with apple sauce, with Herdwick lamb chops, beef Wellington and fresh beer battered haddock among the main courses, washed down with an excellent pint of Jennings Cumberland Ale or farmhouse cider. Sweets are homemade and could include banana pudding.

Prices: Main course from £6. House wine £7.95.
Hours: Winter hours 12.00-14.30 Tuesday-Friday. 17.00-23.00 Monday-Friday. 12.00-23.00 on Saturday. 12.00-22.30 on Sunday. Summer hours open all day, everyday. Closed Monday lunch and 25 December.
Food served: 12.00-14.00. 18.00-21.00.
Cuisine: Modern pub food.
Other Points: No-smoking area. Children welcome. Patio. Car park.
Directions: In Boughton take A593 towards Coniston and take minor road to Broughton Mills in two miles. (Map 11, D3)

Bridge Hotel

Buttermere, Cockermouth, Cumbria CA13 9UZ
Telephone: +44(0)1768 770252
enquiries@bridge-hotel.com
www.bridge-hotel.com

The building dates from 1735 and its evolution from old coaching inn to elegant Lakeland hotel has been very successful. Approached by the main entrance, one enters a lobby with the lounge to one side: beautiful cream sofas and an open fire that welcomes and warms. On the other side, the dining room has starched white linen and is decorated in creams and pale yellows. It offers a five-course set dinner menu that could include goose on balsamic, pear Roquefort salad, and pork on sautéed broccoli with tomato salsa. Individually designed bedrooms are designated superior, featuring bold, contrasting colours, or four-poster (perhaps decorated in antique style with matching cream and burgundy drapes, canopy and wallpaper). Expect telephones, but no TVs or radios due to the bad reception in the area. Most of the rear-facing bedrooms have their own wooden balconies. This all contrasts well with the popular, homely bar and its traditional Lakeland character: two large, beamy rooms filled with copper-topped tables, comfy chairs and wooden pews. The menu is pretty familiar, hotpot of lamb, vegetables and black pudding with a few interesting additions such as smoked salmon pâté and homemade bread.

Prices: Set dinner £25 (5 courses). House wine £9.95.
Hours: 10.30-23.00.
Food served: Bar meals 12.00-21.30. Supper 19.00-20.30.
Rooms: 21 en suite bedrooms plus 6 self-catering apartments and a luxury farm cottage. Bedrooms from £58 per person.
Cuisine: Traditional English/European.
Other Points: No-smoking area. Children welcome. Garden/patio. Car park.
Directions: A66 past Keswick for Cockermouth. Turn left into Braithwaite and first left onto Newlands Pass for Buttermere. (Map 11, D3)

Aynsome Manor Hotel

Cartmel, Grange-over-Sands, Cumbria LA11 6HH
Telephone: +44(0)15395 36653
info@aynsomemanorhotel.co.uk
www.aynsomemanorhotel.co.uk

Cartmel and the surrounding South Lakes area is rural, tranquil and, by dint of being close to Morecambe Bay, has a very mild climate. For centuries this has been a favoured area – Cartmel Priory dates from 1188 – and Aynsome Manor expresses this feeling of peace and tranquillity well. Now the home of the Varley family, it conveys the genuine feeling of a lived in, and loved, country house. It's a delight: the entrance hall-cum-small lounge has an open fire and comfy seating, there's a small separate bar, and the dining room has polished tables, a magnificent ornate ceiling, cut glass, linen, candles, and old pictures. En suite bedrooms are spacious and tastefully appointed with craftsman-fitted furniture and fabrics and wall coverings adding light and colour. In the kitchen care is taken in sourcing local suppliers as much as possible for the generally contemporary dishes on offer. Three options per course appear on the set dinner menu, warm salad of black pudding, potato, asparagus and soft poached egg with balsamic dressing, perhaps, followed by cream of celery and Stilton soup. Mains could be roast saddle of Holker Estate venison with cocoa nibs, baby vegetables with juniper mash and redcurrant infusion. Service is charming and the wine list is well chosen.

Prices: Set lunch £15.50. Set dinner £20. House wine £12.50.
Hours: 19.00-20.30. Open for lunch and dinner on Sunday for residents only. Closed first three weeks in January.
Rooms: 12 en suite. Double/twin room from £58, single from £68. Prices include dinner and breakfast.
Cuisine: Modern British.
Other Points: No-smoking area. Dogs welcome. Garden. Children welcome over five years old. Car park.
Directions: Exit36/M6. Follow the A590 to Barrow. At the top of Lindale Hill turn left and follow the signs to Cartmel. (Map 11, D4)

Howbarrow Organic Farm

Howbarrow Farm, Cartmel, Grange-over-Sands, Cumbria LA11 7SS
Telephone: +44(0)15395 36330
enquiries@howbarroworganic.demon.co.uk
www.howbarroworganic.demon.co.uk

Paul Hughes and Julia Sayburn have owned their ancient, idyllic farm since 1984 and have built up a totally organic smallholding that is certified by the Soil Association. Their shop, the only organic outlet in the area (and voted UK Organic Farm Shop of the Year, 2002), sells a whole range of own produce: bread, preserves, pickles, vegetables and eggs, poultry, bacon and gammon (from rare or traditional breeds), as well as herbal tinctures, dry goods and other locally produced organic food. Shopping can be combined with a 30-minute farm trail, which takes in the livestock-holding pens. Three attractive bedrooms, not en suite, come with panoramic views and a superb organic breakfast served at a huge wooden table in a kitchen that oozes atmosphere. This is a real farm-cum-family experience, a 16th-century farmhouse with open fires, oak beams and slate-flag floors which is wonderfully authentic and relaxing (but if the thought of kittens trying to sit on your head is offputting, this is probably not the place for you). There's a TV room, but reception can be terrible and don't expect your mobile to work.

Prices: Set dinner £17.50.
Hours: 10.00-17.00. Shop open Wednesday - Saturday.
Rooms: 3 rooms not en suite. Double room from £50, single from £25.
Cuisine: Organic Modern British.
Other Points: Totally no smoking. Garden. Children welcome. Car park. Soil Association approved. Credit cards not accepted.
Directions: Exit 36/M6 take the A590 and follow the signs to Cartmel. From the village square go past the race course. Quarter of a mile, take the left hand turning signposted cul-de-sac after the old grammar school; the farm is at the end of the lane, approximately one mile. (Map 11, D4)

The Pheasant

Bassenthwaite Lake, Cockermouth, Cumbria CA13 9YE
Telephone: +44(0)17687 76234
info@the-pheasant.co.uk
www.the-pheasant.co.uk

The long white-washed inn, now quietly bypassed by the A66, stands on the old road on the edge of Wythop Forest. Now more of a county house with the cosiness of an old inn, it is the ambience of the Pheasant that is memorable. The characterful old building delivers a great red-painted bar, a very civilized and gracious drawing room (where traditional hot and cold bar snacks are served), a dining room, open fires, and highly polished period furniture. Lunch or dinner in the low-ceilinged dning room offers plenty of choice. Modern British in outlook, the kitchen produces seared cannon of fell-bred lamb with wild mushroom risotto, crisp pancetta and port jus, or escalope of pork fillet with roast stuffed apple and mustard cream sauce. Smoked salmon with warm Puy lentil salad, and lime and lemon posset with homemade shortbread, top and tail main course choices. Many of the wines on an eclectic list are priced under £20. Bedrooms have been refurbished and offer comfortable accommodation with fixtures, fittings, and fabrics of high quality with some of the furniture made by a local joiner/cabinet maker. Rooms have good space and are well-appointed with extras, but TVs are on request.

Prices: Set lunch £19.95. Set dinner £26.95. House wine £12.95.
Hours: 07.30-22.30.
Closed Christmas day.
Food served: 12.00-14.00. 19.00-21.00.
Rooms: 13 en suite. Double/twin from £130.
Cuisine: Traditional British and French.
Other Points: No-smoking area. Garden. Children welcome over eight years old.
Directions: Located midway between Keswick and Cockermouth and signposted from the A66. Exit 40/M6. (Map 11, C3)

Quince and Medlar

13 Castlegate, Cockermouth, Cumbria CA13 9EU
Telephone: +44(0)1900 823579

Think vegetarian restaurant and what do you conjure up? Hessian tablecloths and copious amounts of mung beans? Think again. At the Quince and Medlar you may order mung beans, but they will arrive stuffed into mangetout with ginger cheese and dressed leaves. And the dark, heavy floral wallpaper, deep-blue window dressings and lacy tablecloths lend an air of informal elegance to the two small, intimate dining rooms and sitting room. Colin and Louisa Le Voi have owned this landmark vegetarian restaurant for 15 years, winning many awards from the Vegetarian Society for their innovative take on meatless cooking. Menus centre on appetising combinations. A starter of herb millet muffins comes with a perfect sun-dried tomato tapnade, while beetroot and horseradish fill a sweet potato tuile. Mains of red onion tart, wild mushrooms, feta cheese, pine nuts and Madeira sauce, or Wensleydale cheese mousse, french beans, cashew nuts and tomato relish, testify to the imagination at work here and local produce is firmly to the fore. The wine list is totally organic, has a French focus, but offers up interest from elsewhere too, including a clutch of English country wines.

Prices: Main course from £11.50. House wine £10.75.
Hours: Tuesday to Saturday 19.00-21.30. Closed Sundays and Mondays, 24-26 December and one week in mid January.
Cuisine: Vegetarian.
Other Points: Totally no smoking. Children welcome over 5 years old.
Directions: Exit 40/M6, take the A66 to Cockermouth. Once in town the restaurant is next to Cockermouth Castle, opposite Castlegate Art Gallery. (Map 11, C3)

Winder Hall Country House

Low Lorton, Cockermouth, Cumbria CA13 9UP
Telephone: +44(0)1900 85107
stay@winderhall.co.uk
www.winderhall.co.uk

This historic manor house dates from the 15th century and is set in a quite Lakeland village surrounded by half an acre of secluded gardens. Although billed as a guest house, Winder Hall resembles a small country house hotel, furnished in a period style. Since taking over the Hall in September 2002, Nick and Ann Lawler have carried out some refurbishment, to maintain and gently improve the quality and ambience. There's a small lounge with comfy sofas, an open fire and an honesty bar, lovely bedrooms are individually decorated with tasteful colours and fabrics, and are spacious enough to include armchairs and splendid old pieces of furniture, and there's a striking oak panelled restaurant, again with an open fire. The emphasis is on personal service, and the interest in the source of food and wine supplies is also evident. Open to residents only, the cooking makes good use of local produce. Choice is confined to starters and puddings, with, perhaps, crab and ricotta tartlet with yogurt mayonnaise, then glazed duck breast with an apple and sage chutney, sticky toffee pudding with hot toffee sauce, with local Cumberland cheeses to finish. The annotated wine list focuses on value and character.

Prices: Set dinner £20 (4 courses). House wine £9.95.
Hours: Set dinner served at 19.30.
Rooms: 6 en suite. Double room from £45, single room from £60.
Cuisine: Modern British.
Other Points: Totally no smoking. Children welcome. Garden. Car park. Fishing rights.
Directions: Exit 40/M6. From Keswick take the A66 west to Braithwaite, then the B5292 Whinlatter Pass to Lorton. Take a sharp left at the B5289 signed to Low Lorton. (Map 11, C3)

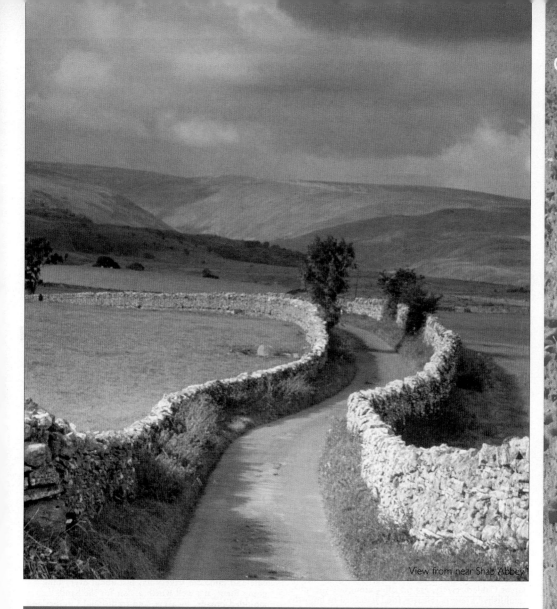

View from near Shap Abbey

CONISTON, CUMBRIA

Prices: Main course from £7.25.
House wine £10.
Hours: 12.00-23.00.
Food Served: 12.00-21.00
Rooms: 16 en suite. Rooms from £37.50
per person.
Cuisine: Modern British.
Other Points: No-smoking area. Garden.
Children welcome. Car park.
Directions: On A593 eight miles south of
Ambleside. J36/M6. (Map 11, D4)

The Black Bull

1 Yewdale Road, Coniston, Cumbria LA21 8DU
Telephone: +44(0)1539 441668
i.s.bradley@btinternet.com
www.conistonbrewery.com

Both Turner the artist, and the poet Coleridge enjoyed the hospitality of
this 400-year-old coaching inn in the shadow of Coniston's 'Old Man'.
Donald Campbell stayed here when attempting his ill-fated water speed
records on Coniston Water, an event commemorated in the name of the
inn's Bluebird Bitter (Champion Beer of Britain in 1998) which is brewed
in the micro-brewery adjacent to the pub. Enjoy an award-winning pint in
the traditionally furnished bar, with its exposed beams, open fires and
Campbell memorabilia, or relax on the beck-side terrace to the rear of the
pub. The wide-ranging bar menu caters for all tastes, from sandwiches,
ploughman's and salads to freshly-battered haddock and chips, local
Esthwaite smoked trout, half shoulder of local lamb, generous Cumbrian
grills, and a selection of locally-made vegetarian dishes. Or, there is a
separate evening restaurant menu featuring such classic dishes as trout
with almonds and steak Diane. Wherever you choose to dine, round off
with a classic sticky toffee pudding or the Black Bull's speciality plum
pudding. Lakeland explorers will find the en suite accommodation homely
and traditional, the 17 clean and comfortable bedrooms being split
between the main inn and the converted coach house, the latter featuring
modern pine-furnished rooms.

The Shepherd's Arms Hotel

Ennerdale Bridge, Lake District National Park, Cumbria CA23 3AR
Telephone: +44(0)1946 861249
enquiries@shepherdsarmhotel.co.uk
www.shepherdsarmhotel.co.uk

The entrance to Val and Steve Madden's soft cream-washed country hotel is welcoming and homely. It's popular with walkers as this is Stop No. 2 on Wainwright's Coat to Coast Walk. Proceed through into the bar, and you will find a pleasant sitting area with bookcase and open fire, as well as the bar area proper. There is also a rear conservatory with french doors leading out to gardens, which border a lovely, fast flowing stream. The decorative theme is high Victorian, particularly in the restaurant. Although the demand is not for fancy food, Steve insists that all ingredients are authentic and local: blackboards and a specials' list feature local game and meats. The bar menu may offer steak and real ale pie, as well as soups, sandwiches and salads. In the restaurant, expect leek and potato soup, half-shoulder of Herdwick lamb with garlic and mint gravy, and chocolate and orange sponge with fudge sauce. The wine list is very reasonably priced, with a good global spread and comes with helpful notes on the partnership of wine and food. Real ales include Coniston Brewery's Bluebird and Timothy Taylor's Landlord. Pleasant en suite bedrooms have views, homely touches and period furnishings.

Prices: Set dinner £15.50. Main course restaurant and bar from £5.95. House wine £8.95.
Hours: 11.00-23.00. Sunday 12.00-22.30.
Food served: 12.15-14.00. 18.30-21.00.
Rooms: 8 rooms, 6 en suite, 2 with private facilities. Double/twin from £59. Single occupancy from £32.
Cuisine: Modern British.
Other Points: No-smoking in dining room and conservatory. Tables outside. Children and dogs welcome. Car park.
Directions: Village signposted off A5086 Egremont to Cockermouth road. (Map 11, D3)

The Burnmoor Inn

Boot, Eskdale, Cumbria CA19 1TG
Telephone: +44(0)1946 723224
enquiries@burnmoor.co.uk
www.burnmoor.co.uk

The route to the Burnmoor via the coast or, for the more adventurous, over the terrifying Hardknott Pass (the steepest mountain pass in England) may not be the most accessible, but it is well worth the detour; the Eskdale Valley is a beautiful, lush and unspoilt part of western Cumbria. Originally built as a farm in 1578, the typical Lakeland inn was converted in 1764 and has a homely bar, open fire and walls crammed with local adverts. Local ales, including new ones from the Great Gable Brewery, are on offer alongside the more established brewers. Hearty food is served in both the bar and cosy, cottagey restaurant, with dishes ranging from sandwiches and jacket potatoes, to a Cumberland tatie pot of lamb, beef and black pudding. A specials' board could list the likes of a casserole of Isle of Jura venison, and own-grown herbs, summer vegetables and salads are a feature. Much of the menu is homemade, but if not, that fact is honestly stated. The nine bedrooms are simply furnished in a bright, rural style. Colourful walls, crisp white floral duvets, amusing animal prints and views over the surrounding fells provide a comfortable base. Poor reception dictates the peace of a TV-free environment; all rooms have radios.

Prices: Set lunch £12 and dinner £16. Main course from £7.50. Main course (bar/snack) from £7. House wine £10.
Hours: 9.00-23.00. From 19.00 on 25 December.
Food served: 11.00-17.00. 18.00-21.00. No food 25 December.
Rooms: 9 en suite. Rooms from £30 per person. Double room four nights for price of three all year, and three nights for two Nov-Mar.
Cuisine: Traditional English.
Other Points: No smoking area. Garden. Children welcome. Car park.
Directions: From the south, exit 36/M6. Head to Newbridge, Greenodd and the Broughton-in-Furness; then head towards Ulpha, drop down into Eskdale and the turn right into Boot. (Map 11, D3)

The Hazelmere Café and Bakery

1 Yewbarrow Terrace, Grange-over-Sands, Cumbria LA11 6ED
Telephone: +44(0)15395 32972
hazelmeregrange@yahoo.co.uk

Grange-over-Sands is an oft forgotten pretty seaside town on the northern edge of Morecambe Bay. Ian and Dorothy Stubley's long-established peaches-and-cream café and fantastic bakery has just about everything going for it. It's well worth a visit for the hand-moulded breads, focaccia, and traditional Cumberland rum nicky alone. There are even homemade frozen ready meals (such as butter bean and rosemary casserole) to take away. The popular café has a traditional, gentle feel, but the Stubleys have managed to put together an eclectic menu that puts the emphasis on local produce where possible. Thus, you will find Penrith goats' cheese and salmon smoked in Cartmel among the usual tuna sandwiches and homemade scones, although the unusual extends to aubergine tagine and Stilton, pear and cinnamon toasted sandwiches. Children are very welcome and have their own sensible menu. The real treat of the Hazelmere, however, is the tea selection. The tea menu has a list of instructions about the correct serving and drinking of tea, and it even boasts tea from Argentina. Dorothy imports her teas herself (as well as making research trips abroad) and is passionate about tea drinking being established as a serious and wonderful ritual.

Prices: Main course from £6.95. Set lunch £6.25. House wine £1.85 for a glass.
Hours: Summer 10.00-17.00. Winter 10.00-16.30. Closed 25 December and 1 January.
Cuisine: Traditional English.
Other Points: No smoking area. Children welcome.
Directions: Exit 36/M6 take the A590 then the B5277, signposted Grange-over-Sands. Pass Grange Station and at the mini roundabout take the first exit, 25 yards on the right. (Map 11, D4)

Netherwood Hotel ★ ⛶ ♣ ▶ ✕ ✿
Lindale Road, Grange-over-Sands
Cumbria LA11 6ET
Telephone: +44(0)15395 32552
blawith@aol.com
www.netherwood-hotel.co.uk

This stately looking mansion has impressive mullioned windows and occupies an elevated position, set back from the main road with a woodland backdrop and terraced garden to the front (with a great display of topiary), and sweeping views of the famous sands of Morecambe Bay. The place has the feeling of a family country house with a relaxed atmosphere, yet it provides excellent facilities for meetings and functions, in addition to a very well equipped gym and pool. Great pride is taken in the fact that this is a family run establishment, and it shows in the high level of service. The Fallowfield brothers are constantly working to make improvements to the hotel and its facilities. The comfort in lounges has been enhanced, there is much new carpeting and bedrooms are being refurbished continuously, offering space, subtle warm tones, elegant quality furniture and immaculate bathrooms. Magnificent views over the gardens to Morecambe Bay complement set-course dinners of, say, sliced duck breast with sweet pineapple and cumberland sauce, Caribbean guinea fowl, sweet potato cake, banana croquette, tomato and chilli salsa, and cherry, almond tart frangipane with crème anglaise and peach sorbet.

Prices: Set lunch £16 and dinner £27. House wine £13.
Hours: 12.30-14.00. 19.00-20.30.
Rooms: 28 en suite. Rooms from £70 per person, family room from £150.
Cuisine: Global.
Other Points: No-smoking area. Children welcome. Garden. Car park. Licence for civil weddings.
Directions: Exit 36/M6, then A590 for Barrow-in-Furness. Left at the roundabout onto the B5277, then left again at Lindale roundabout; hotel on the right before the train station.
(Map 11, D4)

The Jumble Room ★ ♠ ✕
Langdale Road, Grasmere, Cumbria LA22 9SU
Telephone: +44(0)15394 35188
thejumbleroom@which.net
www.thejumbleroom.co.uk

The Jumble Room has been in Andy and Chrissy Hill's family for more than 50 years. It started life at the beginning of the 18th century as Grasmere's first shop where, among other things, Grasmere Rushbearing Gingerbread was made. Yet today, the small and colourful café-cum-restaurant is a wonderful contemporary find in traditional Lakeland. During the day the café serves a whole range of snacks, sandwiches and light meals with the emphasis firmly on local and organic produce. All show flair, imagination and could include smoked salmon and dill tartlets, or home-cured bacon with brie on organic toast. It is the evening, however, when the Jumble Room really comes into its own: vinyl tablecloths replaced with crisp linen, the handmade velvet cushions plumped, and out come the candles. The menu has influences from Troutbeck to Thailand, with starters of Morrocan spiced lamb kofta made with Herdwick lamb, fresh coriander, cumin, preserved lemons, tarragon, or muscat chicken served with buttered, minted new potatoes and organic greens. Jumble Room fish and chips is always available and delicious puddings change so often they are difficult to list. The good-value wine list is an eclectic mix from around the world with six European organics.

Prices: Main course from £9. Main course bar/snack from £5. House wine £9.95.
Hours: 10.30-16.30. 18.00-22.30. Closed all day Monday and Tuesday, 23-27 December, and lunch in winter.
Cuisine: Global.
Other Points: Totally no smoking. Children welcome.
Directions: From Ambleside take the A590 and turn left into Grasmere. Turn left again at the church and take the first right opposite the tourist information. The Jumble Room is 200 yards along on the right hand side. (Map 11, D4)

Sarah Nelson's Grasmere Gingerbread Shop ✿
Church Cottage, Grasmere, Cumbria LA22 9SW
Telephone: +44(0)15394 35428
sarahnelson@grasmeregingerbread.co.uk
www.grasmeregingerbread.co.uk

Tucked away in the picturesque village of Grasmere (famed for its connection with Wordsworth), this tiny shop is a wonderful find. The business has been in the family for 150 years, and the little girl pictured with her grandmother in the photo on the shop wall is Joanne, who runs the shop today. Many have tried to copy the world-famous secret gingerbread recipe, which is not the usual sticky, spongy variety, but more of an intensely flavoured biscuit (and is sold traditionally wrapped in a classically designed blue and white paper). The gingerbread is baked daily in the little kitchen at the back of the shop; intense, spicy smells greet you as you enter. You can also purchase locally made fudge, sticky toffee sauce and the award-winning Cumberland rum butter. There is a world-wide mail order service. Please note that no credit cards are taken in the shop, only with mail order.

Hours: 09.15-17.30 (from 12.30 on Sunday). Seasonal opening hours. Closed 24-26 December and Good Friday.
Cuisine: Traditional English.
Other Points: Totally no smoking. Children welcome. No credit cards.
Directions: From the south take exit 36/M6, then the A590 north on to the A591 through Windermere and Ambleside into Grasmere. (Map 11, D4)

Queen's Head Hotel

Main Street, Hawkshead, Ambleside,
Cumbria LA22 0NS
Telephone: +44(0)15394 36271/+44(0)800 137263
enquiries@queensheadhotel.co.uk
www.queensheadhotel.co.uk

The black-and-white painted frontage of this 16th-century inn-cum-hotel hides an interior full of period character: traditional beamed bars with open fires, and ales dispensed by bow-tied barmen, perhaps Hartleys XB and Robinsons Bitter. Fifteen small, prettily decorated bedrooms are charming, in a smart rural-chic style, taking in coordinating floral fabrics and colours, and brass, canopied and four-poster beds. Rooms at the front have the best views over the village. The inn may be traditional in its look, but the food on offer ranges far and wide. The salad bar brings Cumbrian roast beef with watercress, chilli, radish and soy sauce, or the separate Herdwick lamb menu could include Herdwick sausage set on a savoury cabbage with a rich red wine sauce Otherwise, a meal could open with hot broad bean and crispy pancetta crostini with a radicchio and mint dressing, and go on to marinated pork fillet roasted on rhubarb and served on a potato and sage rösti. There's a real vegetarian menu. Look out for the famous Cirt Clog (20 inches in length) displayed in the bar, it was made in 1820 for a local man who contracted elephantiasis.

Prices: Main course lunch from £6.75. House wine £9.95.
Hours: 11.00-23.00 (until 22.30 on Sunday)
Food served: 12.00-14.30. 18.15-21.30.
Rooms: 14 rooms, 12 en suite, two with private bathroom. 2 four-poster beds and 2 family rooms. Double room from £30 per person, single from £41.
Cuisine: Modern British.
Other Points: No-smoking area. No dogs. Children welcome.
Directions: Exit 36/M6 and follow the A590 to Newby Bridge. Take the second right and follow the road for eight miles into the centre of Hawkshead. (Map 11, D4)

The Punch Bowl Inn

Crosthwaite, Kendal, Cumbria LA8 8HR
Telephone: +44(0)15395 68237
enquiries@thepunchbowl.fsnet.co.uk
www.thepunchbowl.fsnet.co.uk

On entering the old Lakeland stone building you are immediately struck by the old country pub feel that the exposed stone, beams, warm carpeting and old furniture brings. An archway leads beyond the bar to the low-ceilinged dining room, which is surprisingly spacious, with different interconnecting areas instilling a feeling of intimacy. Open fires add to the warm feel, aided by polished tables and walls are crammed with framed menus, accolades and memorabilia from Stephen Doherty's glittering past with the Roux Brothers. A short menu, based around local, simple or regional notions of food delivers dishes that are very simple and very, very good. A meal here could be as light as a two-course lunch of flaked tuna and crab salad niçoise with pickled anchovies, with interesting English regional cheeses to follow. Or, from the carte, grilled goats' cheese on filo with roast beetroot, crumbled Roquefort and a walnut oil dressing, with a mains of boned, rolled stuffed saddle of rabbit, celeriac mash, buttered spinach and a tarragon velouté. Real ales include Black Sheep Bitter and Coniston Brewery's Bluebird, and there's a short but excellent global wine list. The three en suite bedrooms are full of character and quite individual.

Prices: Main course restaurant and bar from £7.95. House wine £11.75.
Hours: 11.00-23.00. Sunday 11.00-15.00. Closed Sunday evening, last week November, first week December and one week January.
Food served: 12.00-14.00. 18.00-21.00. No food on Monday.
Rooms: 3 en suite. Double/twin from £60.
Cuisine: Modern British.
Other Points: No-smoking area. Terrace. Children welcome. Car park.
Directions: Crosthwaite is signposted off A5074 south east of Windermere. Pub next to church. (Map 11, D4)

Prices: Set dinner £19 (4 courses). House wine £10.75. Dinner for residents only.
Hours: Closed mid-November until mid-March.
Rooms: 14 en suite. Room from £38 per person.
Cuisine: Traditional British/Continental.
Other Points: Totally no smoking. Children welcome over five years old. Garden. Car park.
Directions: From the M6/exit 40 take the A66 to the roundabout with the A591. Turn left at the roundabout then take the first right into Vicarage Hill, the hotel is two hundred yards on the right. (Map 11, C4)

Lairbeck Hotel

Vicarage Hill, Keswick, Cumbria CA12 5QB
Telephone: +44(0)1768 773373
routiers@lairbeckhotel-keswick.co.uk
www.lairbeckhotel-keswick.co.uk

Built in 1875 for a local dignitary, this grand Victorian house retains much of its original character, including a barley-twist staircase and ornate, tiled fireplace set, unusually, under a window. Ivy-clad and secluded, with grounds filled with mature plantings, a feeling of peace and tranquillity prevails, yet the centre of Keswick is but a ten-minute walk. The bedrooms retain the names given by the original owners: School Room, for example, or the Housekeepers Room. The Drawing Room is a favourite with pink floral décor, tasteful antique furniture and a balcony from which to enjoy fine views. All rooms are en suite, individually designed with views over the garden or of the surrounding fells; single rooms are a refreshingly decent size. Floral wallpapers and traditional style dominates, but there are a few modern twists such as funky lights in some bathrooms. Dinner, served to residents only, is in full English country house mode, but with contemporary touches. A typical meal would take in starters of leek and potato soup, then roast leg of local lamb, or lightly fried sea bass with butter, parsley and lemon, and special sticky toffee pudding with hot butterscotch sauce and cream to finish.

The Fat Lamb Country Inn

Crossbank, Ravenstonedale, Kirkby Stephen, Cumbria CA17 4LL
Telephone: +44(0)15396 23242
fatlamb@cumbria.com
www.fatlamb.co.uk

The former farmhouse, a rambling 17th-century Pennine limestone building, is set in magnificent open country mid way between the Lake District and the Yorkshire Dales National Park. Resplendent with summer flowers without, it is pleasantly old fashioned within. Nothing fancy, just a pleasant lived-in feel, with a bar warmed by an old range, a lounge that looks over the garden, and leads into a residents' lounge and coffee area, and an attractive restaurant that has exposed stone walls and low beams. Paul Bonsall has been at the helm since the late 1970s, and has built up a sound reputation for food, hospitality, and peace - there are no pool tables, jukebox, or video games. Indeed, en suite bedrooms provide solid comfort, are well equipped with good furniture, and have a pleasant cottagey look that seems appropriate for the location. Fresh local produce appears on menus and blackboards where the emphasis is on providing sound ingredients cooked to satisfy a fairly traditional clientele, but with plenty of added flair and interest.

Prices: Set lunch £11.50. Set dinner £20 (4 courses). Main course restaurant £7.80. Main course bar £6.20. House wine £10.
Hours: 12.00-15.00. 18.00-23.00, Sunday until 22.30.
Food served: 12.00-14.00. 18.00-21.00. Saturday and Sunday 12.00-21.00.
Rooms: 12 en suite. Double from £76.
Cuisine: Modern British.
Other Points: No-smoking area. Garden. Children welcome. Car park.
Directions: Exit38/M6. Head east towards Brough on A685. Turn right into Ravenstonedale and pass through village on minor road south to A683. (Map 12, D5)

Shepherds Inn

Melmerby, Penrith, Cumbria CA10 1HF
Telephone: +44(0)1768 881217
theshepherdsinn@btopenworld.com

Set in a lovely Eden Valley village, this traditional inn has made its name by offering an astonishing selection of good food. Indeed, such is the fame of this 18th century inn that brown tourist signs show the way from as far as Penrith. Martin and Christine Baucutt, who created this dining pub of repute in 1979, have now moved on but Garry and Marcia Parkin have maintained the successful formula as they worked for the Baucutts in the past. The Cumberland sandstone building dates from 1780 and is 100 metres from another Melmerby landmark, the Village Bakery (see following entry). Meat, fruit and vegetables are local and bread is homemade. Although it gets very busy, standards in the kitchen never falter, putting an imaginative twist on classic pub favourites. Lunchtime snacks take in hot ciabatta filled, perhaps, with freshly grilled sardines and olives, they do a great cumberland sausage, egg and chips, and there's a good vegetarian selection. Some 50 malt whiskies, English fruit wines, and a range of European bottled beers complement the very good real ales on offer. Wines (with eight by the glass) have been chosen with a keen eye for value, bolstered by some impressive bin ends.

Prices: Main course from £5.50. House wine £7.65.
Hours: 10.30-15.00. 18.00-23.00. 12.00-15.00 and 19.00-22.30 on Sunday.
Closed 25 December and 26 December day.
Food served: 11.30-14.30. 18.00-21.45. 12.00-14.30 and 19.00-21.30 on Sunday. Until 21.00 Monday-Thursday during winter.
Cuisine: British.
Other Points: No-smoking area. Children welcome. Car park.
Directions: Exit 40/M6. Nine miles east of Penrith on A686 towards Alston. (Map 11, C4)

Village Bakery

Melmerby, Penrith, Cumbria CA10 1HE
Telephone: +44(0)1768 881811
guide@village-bakery.com
www.village-bakery.com

As an organisation, the Village Bakery requires little introduction, its name almost synonymous with the word organic: under founder, Andrew Whitley, it has been committed to producing organic food for the last 25 years. But changes are afoot. Bells of Lazonby, a long established local commercial bakery, has taken over the business with the intention of providing greater production capacity for Village Bakery products. However, Andrew Whitley will continue to run the popular bread making courses. The renowned café remains the same, opening with breakfast of raspberry porridge, oak-smoked Inverawe kippers, or a classic fry up with free-range egg, home-cured bacon, and cumberland sausage. All-day snacks take in sandwiches filled with roast ham and Cumberland mustard, or smoked chicken and avocado salad. Lunch could be a hearty bowl of mixed vegetable soup, pork tenderloin with mushroom sauce, and fruit pie with cream or yogurt, to finish. High quality organic produce is used throughout: if you order a ham sandwich, the bread will have been freshly baked and the ham will have been cooked on the premises. Salads and eggs come from the Bakery's own small holding. There's a take away service, perfect for walkers, and a shop selling their own and other organic produce.

Prices: Lunch from £3.10. Special set menu dinners from £25. House wine £8.50.
Hours: 08.30-17.00. Sunday from 09.30. Open Saturday evening once every two months - this may increase during the year.
Cuisine: Organic Modern British.
Other Points: Totally no smoking. Children welcome. Garden. Car park.
Directions: Exit 40/M6, then follow A66, A686 to Melmerby (nine miles from the motorway). (Map 11, C4)

The Wheatsheaf Hotel

Beetham, near Milnthorpe, Cumbria LA7 7AL
Telephone: +44(0)15395 62123
wheatsheaf@beetham.plus.com
www.wheatsheafbeetham.com

The atmospheric old coaching inn is distinguished by dark, heavy wood panelling and moulding with the small bar counter screened from the lounge, which features lots of polished wood. It's a place that appeals to those looking for a restful atmosphere. Bar food runs to the likes of soup, sandwiches and salads, as well as beef and ale pie, and fillet steak with traditional accompaniments. The main restaurant is on the first floor. Here, seasonal menus are built around local produce, starters such as filo parcels of melting Cumbrian cheese with tomato chutney, or seared scallops with confit new potatoes and a ginger and honey soy reduction. The Wheatsheaf's own-recipe sausages are served with cumberland gravy, or there could be slow-braised lamb shank with creamy mash and a redcurrant and red wine reduction, or roasted tenderloin of pork stuffed with apricots and served with savoy cabbage, bacon and black pudding. Finish with sticky toffee pudding and caramel sauce, or local and regional cheeses. Good-sized bedrooms are attractively and individually decorated with flair.

Prices: Main course restaurant from £6.95. Bar/snack from £2.95. House wine £10.95.
Hours: 12.00-15.00. 17.30-23.00. Sunday 18.30-22.30.
Food served: 12.00-14.00. 18.00-21.00. Sunday 12.00-14.15. 18.30-20.30.
Rooms: 6 en suite. Doubles/twins from £65. Winter breaks available from £40 per night per room.
Cuisine: Modern and Traditional British.
Other Points: No-smoking dining-rooms. Garden. Children welcome. Car park.
Directions: One mile south of Milnthorpe off A6. J35/M6. (Map 11, D4)

New Village Tea Rooms

Orton, Penrith, Cumbria CA10 3RH
Telephone: +44(0)1539 624886

Christine Evans has run this traditional tearoom for 10 years. It's a homely place and worth knowing about as the pretty village of Orton is very close to junction 38 of the M6; indeed, Christine has built up a regular clientele who break long journeys with her, rather than use the impersonal motorway services. The tearooms are small and in Lakeland style, with cream walls, open fire, wooden tables with dark green and lace cloths, a dresser stocked with homemade cakes and biscuits and an open-plan kitchen. There are six tables downstairs and five up, plus seating in the small garden. Homemade scones, sandwiches, toasties, jacket potatoes and Lakeland ice cream dominate the printed menu, with a chalkboard detailing the day's specials. These run to soups of lentil and bacon, or carrot and lemon, bakes such as chicken and broccoli, or potato, courgette and tomato, and sticky toffee pudding or chocolate and orange crumble for pudding. All are homemade. Cakes are available, wrapped, to take away, plus a large selection of specials to take away, frozen, as ready meals.

Prices: Lunchtime special from £5.50.
Hours: Winter 10.30-16.30. Summer 10.00-17.00. Closed Sunday before 25 December to 2 January.
Cuisine: Tea Room.
Other Points: All no smoking. Garden. Car park. No credit cards accepted. No licence.
Directions: Exit 38/M6 take the road signposted to Appleby. In Orton take the Shap Road in front of the George Hotel. New Village Tea Room located straight ahead opposite the post office. (Map 11, D4)

The Highland Drove Inn

Great Salkeld, Penrith, Cumbria CA11 9NA
Telephone: +44(0)1768 898349
highlanddroveinnn@btinternet.com
www.highland-drove.co.uk

Donald Newton is proud of the fact that he is creating a good all-round country inn renowned for its food and conviviality. Set close to the rear of the church in a picturesque Eden Valley village, this archetypal village inn resembles a white-washed old farmhouse with its old wooden porch and abundance of flowers. Within, there's an attractive brick and timber bar, old tables and settles in the main bar area, a separate games room, and a lounge area with a fire, dark wood furniture and tartan fabrics. Food, however, is nearly always served in the restaurant upstairs, which was newly-built three years ago. The restaurant is unique with its hunting lodge feel and is the core of the business, but the bar is still very much a locals' bar and an important part of the community - the balance is well kept. The kitchen produes satisfying country cooking that takes in fish soup with smoked sausage, beans, rouille and garlic croutons, then mains of smoked haddock and queen scallops with a lightly curried coconut cream sauce, or Cranston's pork and leek sausages with chive mash, onion marmalade and red wine gravy, with chocolate orange pots to finish. Beers are well looked after and care is taken with wines by the glass. Bedrooms are small but nicely decorated and very well equipped for a country inn.

Prices: Set lunch £12.95. Set dinner £18.50. Main course restaurant from £8.95. Bar snack from £4.95. House wine £9.95.
Hours: 12.00-15.00. 18.00-23.00. Open all Sat. Closed Mon lunch.
Food served: 12.00-14.00. 18.30-21.00, until 20.30 Sunday.
Rooms: 3 en suite, soon to be 5. Double/twin from £50.
Cuisine: Eclectic Bistro.
Other Points: No-smoking area. Dogs welcome. Garden. Children welcome. Car park.
Directions: Exit40/M6. Take A66 eastbound, then A686 towards Alston. In four miles left B6412 for Great Salkeld. (Map 11, C4)

The Old Smokehouse and Truffles

Brougham Hall, Brougham, Penrith, Cumbria CA10 2DE
Telephone: +44(0)1768 867772
sales@the-old-smokehouse.co.uk
www.the-old-smokehouse.co.uk

Brougham Hall was once known as the Windsor of the north – a historic hall dating from the 14th-century – which the current owner has spent 15 years rebuilding the outer walls. The smokery is run from two tiny rooms with a traditional smoker and best-quality oak chips. It is all done by hand and much depends on the time of the year and the temperature, as only the best ingredients are used. They smoke their own-made sausages (delicious added to soups and stews), as well as offering hot-smoked venison, pork and Mansergh lamb, and wild Scottish salmon. Wild char is listed among more unusual smokings that include Parmesan and Stilton. Handmade chocolate truffles are made next door. No machinery is used and chocolates are rolled by hand in a process that takes three days, creating wonderfully smooth centres and flavours such as apricot and Cointreau, black Russian, and orange brandy. If you can't make the trip to Cumbria to visit Brougham Hall, smokery produce and chocolates are available by mail order.

Hours: 10.00-17.00 April-October. 10.00-16.30 and closed at weekends October-March. Closed during parts of January and February.
Other Points: Children welcome. Car park.
Directions: On the B6262, just off the A6, one mile south of Penrith. (Map 11, C4)

Saddleback Foods and Smokerie

Scarfoot, Plumpton, Penrith, Cumbria CA11 9PF
Telephone: +44(0)1768 885599
enquiries@saddlebackfoods.co.uk
www.saddlebackfoods.co.uk

These days smoking is more about combining wonderful smoky aromas without overpowering the natural taste of the food, as opposed to the traditional preservation of valuable food supplies to see us though the winter. This is understood well by Jane Farkins and Mark Atkinson, their elusive mix combining brine, smoke, and natural flavour, is a revelation. In 2003 Saddleback Foods moved from Mark's family farm into custom built premises, enabling expansion from smoked produce to ready meals, quiches, roast and cured meats, pâtés and fresh meat, under the name Eden Valley Farmed Meats They seek to use only local produce wherever possible. Meat from the family farm is killed in a local abattoir and returned to Saddleback Foods for hanging before being packed and distributed; in effect, controlling every step from field to plate. Beef and lamb come from the family farm, but pork is sourced from nearby farms, although the plan is to establish their own pigs – Saddlebacks, of course. Their shop, Wine and Dine in Penrith, sells own produce alongside Cumbrian specialities – ales, preserves, pies, ice cream, damson gin and much more. A mail order service is available.

Prices: From £2.95 for a smoked chicken breast to £19.95 per kilogram for smoked salmon.
Hours: Mail order available.
Cuisine: Smoked and roasted meats, game, poultry and fish.
Directions: (Map 11, C4)

Prices: Main course lunch from £4.
Hours: 10.30-17.00. Closed 25 December-2 January.
Cuisine: Organic.
Other Points: Totally no smoking. Children welcome. Car park.
Directions: Six miles from exit 40/M6. Take the A686 for five miles to Langwathby, left at the village green, then two miles to the mill. (Map 11, C4)

Watermill

Little Salkeld, Penrith, Cumbria CA10 1NN
Telephone: +44(0)1768 881523
organicflour@aol.com
www.organicmill.co.uk

One of the few water-powered corn mills in the country, set in breathtaking scenery off the Alston road, the pink-painted buildings are tucked away at the bottom of the village beside Sunnygill Beck whose water is channeled down the mill race to turn the wheels. As well as the flour mill, there's a tea room with a small shop and gallery, and Anna Jones's own smallholding with goats. Of the two ancient wheels, one is covered in moss, the other, making the most incredible racket, produces flour from grain grown to bio-dynamic organic standards by English farmers, and sold to local shops and used for the breads and cakes on offer in the tearoom. You can pay to have a guided tour of the mill and attend bread-making courses. The teashop offers a whole range of juices, soft drinks and light snacks, all organic and vegetarian (in February 2002, a Soil Association licence was granted). A late breakfast brings porridge with maple syrup and toast with Watermill marmalade, tea produces scone with homemade jam, and in between, theres a miller's lunch of Loch Arthur cheese and homemade chutney, and quiche with a variety of salads.

Hours: 09.30-17.00 Monday to Saturday.
10.00-16.00 on Sunday.
Other points: Ample parking. Tea-room.
Directions: Junction 44/M6. Keep going
on to the A74, then turn left at
Floriston/Rockcliffe exit and take the first
right in to the car park. Look out for the
straw bale sign. (Map 11, C4)

Castletown Farm Shop

Floriston Rigg, Rockliffe, Carlisle, Cumbria CA6 4HN
Telephone: +44(0)1228 674400
info@castletownfarmshop.co.uk
www.castletownfarmshop.co.uk

An array of organic and conventionally grown vegetables and fruit and
soft fruits is displayed at this well-run farm shop, but most impressive is
the range of home-reared meats. All the fresh meat and game, where not
supplied by the Estate, is locally produced. The animals, taken directly to
the local abattoir, are not stressed by herding and travelling long
distances, and are then hung and cut by the farm's own butcher. This
ensures complete traceability from producer to consumer. The result is
healthy meat with old-fashioned flavour and texture. The cheese counter
is very extensive, with cheeses sourced from creameries and farms
throughout the British Isles and Ireland and offering a wide range from
traditional flavours to more unusual cheeses. From the Castletown
Kitchen comes a range of frozen ready meals, prepared with own
ingredients where possible.

Dalesman Country Inn

Main Street, Sedbergh, Cumbria LA10 5BN
Telephone: +44(0)15396 21183
info@thedalesman.co.uk
www.thedalesman.co.uk

A popular and comfortably modernised 16th-century
coaching inn situated in an old market town and close
to scenic walks along the River Dee or up on the
Howgill Fells. Stripped stone and beams, cushioned
farmhouse chairs and stools around copper-topped
tables, gundog pictures, and log-effect gas fires set the
scene in the rambling, open-plan bar and dining room
where you can enjoy good homemade food prepared
from local produce. Arrive early for the excellent value
lunchtime menu that features soup and crusty bread,
lasagne, homemade pies, and Dalesman Club
sandwiches. Influenced by the seasons and changing
fortnightly, the evening menu may extend the choice to
duck leg confit with spiced red cabbage and orange
sauce, noisettes of lamb with roast plums and basil
mash, baked monkfish wrapped in bacon with a
creamy mustard sauce, and game in season from
Cartmel. For pudding choose steamed ginger pudding,
or Wensleydale cheese with biscuits and cranberry
sauce. Booking is essential for the popular Sunday
roasts. The five spacious and comfortably furnished
bedrooms are cottagey in style with pine furnishings,
and spruce en-suite bathrooms.

Prices: Set lunch £10 and dinner £18. Main course from £8.
House wine £8.
Hours: 11.00-23.00. 12.00-22.30 on Sunday.
Food served: 12.00-14.00. 18.00-21.00 Monday-Friday. 12.00-14.30.
18.00-21.30 Friday and Saturday. Lunch until 14.30 on Sunday
Rooms: 7 en suite. Rooms £30 per person.
Cuisine: Modern British and traditional pub food.
Other Points: No-smoking area. Children welcome. Car park.
Directions: On A684 in village centre; 11 miles east of Kendal;
5 miles from Junction 36/M6. (Map 11, D4)

The Hermitage

Shap, Penrith, Cumbria CA10 3LX
Telephone: +44(0)1931 716671
jeanjackson_hermitage@btopenworld.com

This is the most picturesque rustic house you could
imagine: an ancient tumbling cottage that has been
owned by Jean Jackson for many years. The
whitewashed front, with a small drive, wonderful
gardens to the front and rear, gives way to a beautiful
stained-glass door in the entrance hall, and a dark,
tastefully furnished lounge with antiques and period
furniture. Spacious bedrooms are individually and
tastefully furnished, with a heavy emphasis on floral
design: wallpapers match the bed covers, but one
bathroom has been painted deep red to give it a more
'macho' feel. The whole place is immaculate and has a
charming, old, lived-in feel.

Rooms: 3 en suite. Double rooms from £23, single from £20.
Other Points: No-smoking area. Children welcome. Garden.
Directions: Three miles from exit 39/M6, at north end of village.
(Map 11, D4)

BREAD MAKING
AT THE VILLAGE BAKERY

Village Bakery founder and passionate bread maker, Andrew Whitley, runs a dozen courses a year set over a weekend with no more than 12 people attending each course. The cost of £295 includes refreshments and meals, with a full dinner provided on the Saturday evening in the Village Bakery restaurant. But the cost does not cover accommodation and you need to arrange that yourself in the area

The courses take place in the original bakery with its wood fired ovens and includes quite a diverse mix of people drawn from all over the UK and as far away as Japan and the USA – most will have little or no experience of bread making. As the cost suggests, the course tends to be taken up by those seeing it as a recreational rather than totally practical learning experience. That does not mean that the course content is any less thorough. Andrew takes everyone through all aspects of bread making, from the very rudiments and history up to the variety of products seen today. He also discusses the influence of yeast and how to make breads naturally without the addition of yeast. All in all, this is a very hands-on experience and you genuinely learn a lot about bread and the making of it.

Considerable reference to the Village Bakery in the food media, especially the BBC, means that the year's courses are usually filled by March. In addition, ad hoc five-day master classes are arranged as and when demand and feasibility permit.

INFORMATION
Weekend courses cost £295 and include refreshment and meals but not accommodation.
For more information telephone Andrew Whiteley, Bread Matters Ltd, 01768 881899

The Village Bakery, Melmerby, Penrith, Cumbria

The Eagle & Child

Kendal Road, Staveley, Kendal, Cumbria LA8 9LP
Telephone: +44(0)1539 821320
eaglechildinn@btinternet.com
www.eaglechildinn.co.uk

This handsome 18th-century village pub has been transformed by owners Richard and Denise Coleman. A modern feel has been given to the beamed bar, the smart burgundy carpet, polished slate floor and comfortable banquette seating blending well with a lovely old stone fireplace and collections of tankards, truncheons and fishing memorabilia. The deep burgundy and cream décor extends upstairs to five tastefully decorated bedrooms, all sporting attractive patchwork quilts and spotless en suite bathrooms. Served throughout the bar and restaurant is a seasonally changing menu of traditional pub food given a modern twist. Emphasis is on quality local produce, including fresh bread and meat from village suppliers and fish and game from nearby Cartmel and Hawkshead. From lunchtime filled ciabattas and creamy smoked mackerel pâté with redcurrant and raisin confit, the menu extends to Kentmere lamb shank on mustard mash with minted sherry jus, and sea bass with Oriental tossed salad and a honey and citrus dressing. Good puddings include traditional sticky toffee pudding. On the blackboard list of real ales you will find Cumbrian brews from Coniston, Jennings and Dent, alongside Black Sheep, and eight wines by the glass.

Prices: Set lunch and dinner £9.95. Main course from £7.95. House wine £7.95.
Hours: 11.00-23.00.
Food served: 12.00-15.00. 18.00-21.00.
Rooms: 5 en suite. Double room from £55.
Cuisine: Modern British.
Other Points: No-smoking area. Children welcome. Riverside garden. Car park.
Directions: On A592 nine miles south of Windermere. Exit 36/M6. (Map 11, D4)

Brackenrigg Inn

Watermillock, Lake Ullswater, Penrith,
Cumbria CA11 0LP
Telephone: +44(0)17684 86206
enquiries@brackenrigginn.co.uk
www.brackenrigginn.co.uk

The long, white-washed inn dates from the 18th century and its position overlooking Ullswater is beyond compare. An appealing homely feel is retained, thanks in part to the attractive panelled bar with polished floor boards, open fire and view over the surrounding countryside, and the carpeted lounge-cum-family dining room with its polished mahogany furniture. The separate restaurant is also traditionally appointed and has splendid views. A sound local reputation for well executed, contemporary food has been built up over the years. So, what to expect? Well, certainly a menu that is available in the bar, lounge, terrace (weather permitting) as well as the restaurant. Chicken confit with Bury black pudding, perhaps, followed by roast rump of lamb with a warm new potato and red pepper salad infused with basil and served with balsamic roasted tomatoes and Madeira jus, all washed down by locally-brewed beers or wine from a very reasonably priced list. All the en suite bedrooms are decorated and furnished in similar style, with fine views, but although some are smallish, the good-sized windows stop them from feeling cramped.

Prices: Set Sunday lunch £9.95. Set dinner £17.95. Main course restaurant from £10.50. Main course bar from £7.95. House wine £10.95.
Hours: 11.00-23.00.
Food served: 12.00-14.30. 18.30-21.00.
Rooms: 17 en suite. Double/twin from £27. Single from £32. Family suites and cottages from £24.50.
Cuisine: Modern British.
Other Points: No-smoking area. Dogs welcome. Garden. Children welcome. Car park.
Directions: On A592 south west of Penrith; 6 miles from Exit40/M6. (Map 11, C4)

Prices: Bar meals from £6. Set dinner (4 courses) £22. House wine £11.90.
Hours: 11.00-23.00.
Food served: Bar food 11.00-21.00. Restaurant 19.00-21.00.
Rooms: 14 en suite. Rooms from £49 per person.
Cuisine: Traditional British.
Other Points: No smoking area. Children welcome. Dogs welcome.
Directions: Wasdale Head is signed off A595 between Egremont and Ravenglass. (Map 11, D3)

Wasdale Head Inn

Wasdale, Gosforth, Cumbria CA20 1EX
Telephone: +44(0)19467 26229
wasdaleheadinn@msn.com
www.wasdale.com

Wasdale is one of the quietest, most unspoilt valleys in the northern lakes, famed for its deepest lake, tallest mountain, smallest church and biggest liar. The whitewashed inn, set right at the top of the valley at the foot of Great Gable, is popular with serious walkers and ramblers, a theme picked up in the large, functional public bar with its climbing memorabilia and stunning photos of the surrounding fells. Expect homebrewed Wasdale and Great Gable beers in addition to Cumbrian micro-brewery ales, and substantial food, served from a hot store. By contrast, the residents-only part of the building is imposing. The bar has large Tudoresque furniture and the lounge is elegantly furnished. The restaurant (open to non residents) offers a four-course, traditional British dinner along the lines of air-dried Cumbrian ham, parsnip soup, fillet steak with mushroom sauce and baked raspberry custard. The pick of the 14 bedrooms is the garden room, with its muslin-draped four-poster. Four suites in a separate building have kitchen units, and dinner can be served for you to reheat. The Christmas package is legendary. No turkey or telly? Then the Baa Humbug! Stuff the Bloody Turkey! break is for you.

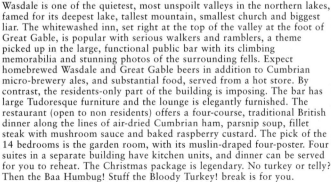

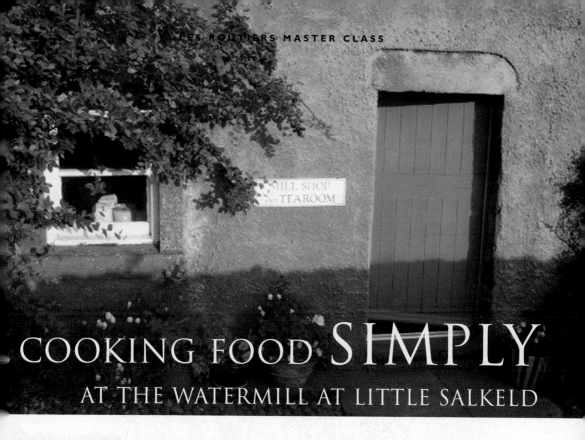

COOKING FOOD SIMPLY
AT THE WATERMILL AT LITTLE SALKELD

Worthy of a visit just for the lovely rural setting and delightful old farm building and watermill with its historical atmosphere, Ana Jones's bread making and cookery courses are a revelation. Ana has been at the Watermill for 25 years and her passion for the quality and origin of raw food is undiminished. Such is the commitment, she sources her wheat for her bread from two organic farms which produce biodynamically. Biodynamics was introduced in the 1920s by Rudolf Steiner to address the then concerns about the trend towards mass production. It goes beyond an organic approach, taking a holistic view that embraces the welfare of livestock and the land.

It is this philosophy that underpins the Watermill's one-day courses. Ana takes no more than eight people on each, exploring not only bread making, but also soup making, vegetarian cooking, salads, dressings and pastry making. All the courses aim to encourage people to discover and appreciate real ingredients and how to make good food simply. For example, in the bread making course, you learn as much about the importance of basic flours and the milling process as you do about bread making itself.
Ana's enthusiasm is infectious, she is a natural teacher, and her ability to make people feel confident in making bread, combined with her dynamic philosophy, has changed attitudes to food and how it is perceived. Each course encourages participants to find out for themselves what enjoyment and benefits can be gained from working with quality raw ingredients. Ana inspires people through her passion for what she does and through her desire for us all to understand better the fundamentals of food and the pleasure it can give.

INFORMATION
One day courses cost £40 per person, to include refreshments and a wholefood lunch.
All sorts of people come and they have usually found out about the courses by word of mouth or through knowing the Watermill. A newsletter and website - www.organicmill.co.uk - also keep people informed. For more information telephone 01768 881523.

Watermill, Little Salkeld, Penrith, Cumbria

THE MAGIC OF MOUNTAINS AND LAKES

The beauty and grandeur of this enchanting corner of the country is well known.
Many of Lakeland's most famous and best-loved landmarks crop up on this drive.
Drive length: 73 miles

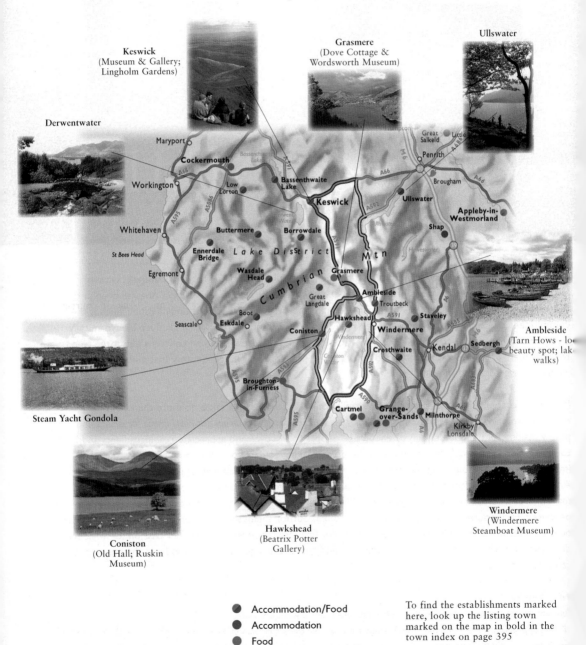

Keswick
(Museum & Gallery;
Lingholm Gardens)

Grasmere
(Dove Cottage &
Wordsworth Museum)

Ullswater

Derwentwater

Steam Yacht Gondola

Ambleside
(Tarn Hows - lo
beauty spot; lak
walks)

Coniston
(Old Hall; Ruskin
Museum)

Hawkshead
(Beatrix Potter
Gallery)

Windermere
(Windermere
Steamboat Museum)

● Accommodation/Food

● Accommodation

○ Food

🍃 Food Shop

To find the establishments marked
here, look up the listing town
marked on the map in bold in the
town index on page 395

WINE APPRECIATION
AT THE BRACKENRIGG INN, ULLSWATER

Two or three courses per year are run as residential weekend courses for 10-16 people, hosted by Peter Edwards who tutors wine appreciation courses all over the north west of England. Each course covers grape varieties, growing areas and, of course, sampling wines to demonstrate the characteristics of each – based around five modular sessions. People come from all over the UK and enjoy the mixture of learning about wine plus the free time on Saturday afternoon along with the social/house party atmosphere.

The courses are educational, but with a strong recreational bias. They are advertised through the national press, the inn's own website and specialist magazines such as English Country Inns and Woman & Home which sometimes bring guests who have bought their partner the weekend as a present.

INFORMATION

Price per course is £189 per head and covers accommodation on Friday and Saturday nights, a buffet meal on Friday evening, picnic Saturday lunch, gala dinner on Saturday night, and Sunday lunch. For more information telephone 01768 486206 or email: enquiries@brackenrigginn.co.uk

Brackenrigg Inn, Watermillock, Lake Ullswater, Penrith Cumbria

Queens Head

Townhead, Troutbeck, Windermere
Cumbria LA23 1PW
Telephone: +44(0)1539 432174
enquiries@queensheadhotel.com
www.queensheadhotel.com

Built to accommodate travellers on the Windermere to Penrith coaching route, this atmospheric inn continues to provide first-class hospitality to 21st century tourists. Tradition reigns supreme in the bustling bar, distinguished by its extraordinary bar counter fashioned from a genuine Elizabethan four-poster bed, by antique beams, settles and wooden furniture, and a rambling interior thats a maze of cosy alcoves and little rooms. Food is up to date with an excellent-value set menu and an ambitious evening menu offering modern British dishes. Starters run to crab, salmon and coriander cakes, and decent soups served with homemade bread. After mains of, say, red bream with mixed bean and saffron risotto and chive cream, there could be classic sticky toffee pudding. At lunch there are sandwiches, warm salads and one-dish specials such as steak, ale and mushroom cobbler. Tip-top ales on handpump favour Cumbrian micro-brewery beers from Jennings, Coniston and Barngates. The short list of affordable wines offers useful tasting notes and eight house wines by the glass. Period features and modern comforts characterise the stylish, individually decorated bedrooms. Some have four-poster beds and all offer en suite facilities and memorable valley views.

Prices: Set lunch and dinner £15.50. House wine £10.
Hours: 11.00-23.00. 12.00-22.30.
Closed 25 December.
Food served: 12.00-14.00. 18.30-21.00.
Rooms: 14 en suite. Double room from £75, single from £60.
Cuisine: Modern British.
Other Points: No-smoking area.
Directions: J36/M6. Take the A590/591 to Windermere and then take A592 towards Ullswater. (Map 11, D4)

Why go to...The Lake District
Squeezed within an area some 30 miles across are 16 major ribbon lakes in glacial valleys with England's highest mountains rising in between. Stunning scenery that has drawn high-profile residents over the centuries, from Lakeland poets Wordsworth and Coleridge, and Victorian art and literary critic John Ruskin, to the famous children's authors Arthur Ransome and Beatrix Potter; each has spawned a major tourist attraction. However, the one single influence on the region's hotel scene was the opening in 1949 of Sharrow Bay Hotel - the first country house hotel in the country. With every highly polished surface lovingly covered with knick-knacks, objects d'art, pictures, chintz, brocade and doilies, a standard was set for Lakeland hotel décor that has yet to be challenged.

The Red Lion Inn

Main Street, Hognaston, Ashbourne,
Derbyshire DE6 1PR
Telephone: +44(0)1335 370396
lionrouge@msn.com
www.lionrouge.com

An unpretentious 17th-century inn with beamed and
quarry-tiled L-shaped bar sporting colourful rugs,
three open log fires, an eclectic mix of old farmhouse
tables, sturdy pews and chairs, magazines, and piped
classical music. Local drinkers fill the bar early and
late in the evening; at other times food is the emphasis
in the candlelit room and the intimate back room -
ideal for families or parties. Blackboards list the
imaginative choice of modern pub food. Soundly
cooked dishes, carefully prepared from fresh local
produce and served on enormous white plates, range
from a starter of duck leg confit with cumberland
sauce, to mains of braised shank of lamb with mash
and mint gravy. Lighter meals include pork and
tarragon sausages and lamb moussaka, and there's
comforting homemade nursery puddings. Expect a
warm welcome, friendly service and, if staying
overnight, excellent accommodation in three very
comfortable and tastefully decorated bedrooms. Book
the Yellow Room, with its huge pine bed, quality
armchairs, cast-iron fireplace and village views; all
rooms have well-equipped en suite bathrooms.
Prices: Main course from £7.95. House wine £10.95.
Hours: 12.00-15.00 18.00-23.00 Tuesday to Saturday.
(19.00-22.30 Sunday). Closed Monday lunch and the 25 December.
Food served: 12.00-14.00 Tuesday to Saturday (12.00-14.15
Sunday) 18.30-21.00 Tuesday-Saturday.
Rooms: 3 en suite. Double room from £80, single from £50.
Cuisine: Modern and Traditional British
Other Points: No smoking area. Children welcome over 10 years.
Car park. No Dogs.
Directions: J25/M1. From Ashbourne take the Wirksworth Road
(B5035). After four miles turn right for Hognaston. (Map 9, C3)

The Devonshire Arms

Beeley, Matlock, Derbyshire DE4 2NR
Telephone: +44(0)1629 733259
jagrosvenor@devonshirearmsbeeley.co.uk
www.devonshirearmsbeeley.co.uk

The handsome 18th-century village inn is surrounded
by classic Peak District scenery and situated between
Haddon Hall and magnificent Chatsworth House.
Converted from three stone cottages in 1747, it soon
became a thriving coaching inn serving the route
between Bakewell and Matlock. The comfortably
civilised interior comprises three attractive beamed
rooms, with stone-flagged floors, roaring log fires,
cushioned antique settles, farmhouse tables, and
tasteful prints, and a separate taproom where walkers
with muddy boots are welcome. Traditional
homecooked bar food is available all day and ranges
from freshly made soups with crusty bread, Devonshire
ploughman's with four cheeses and homemade
piccalilli, to chicken and leek suet pudding, braised
lamb knuckle with rosemary sauce, and smoked
haddock rarebit. Friday is fresh fish night, so arrive
early to sample beer-battered cod and chips, grilled
halibut with orange and lemon butter and a mammoth
seafood platter. On Sunday note the special Victorian
breakfast (booking essential), complete with Bucks Fizz
and newspapers. Excellent Black Sheep and Theakston
ales on draught, a good-value list of wines, and
numerous malt whiskies.
Prices: Main course from £6.75. House wine £9.75.
Hours: 12.00-23.00 (until 22.30 on Sunday).
Closed 25 December.
Food served: 12.00-21.30
Cuisine: Traditional and Modern British.
Other Points: No-smoking area. Garden. Children welcome.
Car park.
Directions: Junction 28/M1. Take the A6 and then on to the B6012
to Beeley and Chatsworth. (Map 8, B7)

Biggin Hall Country House Hotel

Biggin-by-Hartington, Buxton, Derbyshire SK17 0DH
Telephone: +44(0)1298 84451
enquiries@bigginhall.co.uk
www.bigginhall.co.uk

Biggin-by-Hartington is a beautifully located village some 12 miles from
Buxton, surrounded by glorious open countryside in the Peak District
National Park. Biggin Hall, a Grade II star listed building, is the home of
James Moffett, and has been completely renovated to draw out the
original character of the building and is now run as a proper, but not
intimidating, country house hotel. Public rooms are a tour de force of
tradition and comfort: the rug-strewn lounge with its massive log filled
fireplace and a mish mash of furniture and styles, or the unpretentious
book lined library - throughout there's a wonderful get-away-from-it-all
atmosphere. The dining room is the setting for some good country
cooking with a menu built around local lines of supply. Homemade cream
of mushroom soup, then fillet of haddock with lemon and parsley butter
sauce, followed by queen of puddings could be a typical evening meal.
The short wine list is modestly priced. Bedrooms are spacious enough to
absorb antique wardrobes, sofas or armchairs and show them off to good
advantage. Decorated in soft pastel shades, the rooms offer lots of extras
and equally spacious bathrooms with quality toiletries.

Prices: Set dinner £15.50. House wine £9.
Hours: Dinner served at 19.00.
Rooms: 20 en suite. Double room from
£64, single from £57, family room £86.
Cuisine: Traditional English.
Other Points: No-smoking area. Children
welcome over 12 years old. Garden.
Car park.
Directions: Just off the A515, half way
between Ashbourne and Buxton in the
village of Biggin-by-Hartington. (Map 9, B2)

England - Derbyshire

The Nags Head Inn
Hill Top, Castle Donington, Derbyshire DE74 2PR
Telephone: +44(0)1332 850652
idavisonc.@aol.com

The rather ordinary-looking 19th-century pub positively bustles with activity due to its close proximity to East Midlands Airport, Castle Donington motor racing circuit, and the M1 (junction 24). The well-established landlord/chef, Ian Davison, offers a good selection of modern pub dishes in the traditionally furnished bar, with its open winter fires, and well-decorated dining areas. Blackboards offer a range of interesting sandwiches such as tomato, mozzarella and pesto on warm ciabatta, and light dishes such as beef stir-fry with rice, and pasta with salmon and dill cream sauce. For a full meal try bacon and poached egg salad, or grilled goats' cheese with cranberry dressing for starters, moving on to sliced fillet of beef with Cajun spices and tzatziki dressing, or duck breast with stir-fried 'pacsoi' and curry oil, or aubergine, black olive and polenta layer with sun-dried tomato dressing. Finish with homemade bread and butter pudding or treacle oat tart. Beers are limited to Banks Mild, Marston's Pedigree and Mansfield Bitter, while the fairly priced list of wines offers six house wines by the glass.

Prices: Main course restaurant £12.95. Bar meal from £4.95. House wine £11.95.
Hours: 12.00-14.30. 17.30-23.00. 19.00-22.30 Sunday. Closed 26th Dec to 2nd Jan.
Food served: 12.00-14.00. 18.30-21.15. No food on Sunday
Cuisine: Modern British.
Other Points: No-smoking area. Garden. Car park.
Directions: J23A/J24. Head for East Midlands Airport, go past entrance and up to traffic lights at Donington Park. Turn right, past park entrance and follow road around airport. Nags Head on right before descent into Castle Donington. (Map 9, C3)

Hardwick Inn
Hardwick Park, Chesterfield, Derbyshire S44 5QJ
Telephone: +44(0)1246 850245
batty@hardwickinn.co.uk
www.hardwickinn.co.uk

Dating from around 1600 and built of locally quarried sandstone, this striking building was once the lodge for Hardwick Hall and stands at the south gate of Hardwick Park. The hall is owned by the National Trust, so the inn draws much of its trade from visitors exploring the magnificent park and lovely Elizabethan hall; it can be very busy at weekends. The inn, owned by the Batty family for three generations, has a rambling interior that features good period details such as stone-mullioned windows, oak ceiling beams and large stone fireplaces with open fires. Simple furnishings include upholstered wall settles and mahogany tables, while one room has a fine 18th-century carved settle. Traditional food takes in ploughmans lunches, and a whole range of steaks, jacket potatoes and sandwiches, with blackboard daily specials offering hearty homemade pies, and a feature of the pub, fresh fish delivered daily from Scarborough. Look out for beer battered cod or haddock, and crab or lobster salads, or opt for one of the daily carvery roasts, usually with topside of beef and local lamb, served with roast and boiled potatoes, Yorkshire pudding and three vegetables. Theakston ales are on handpump.

Prices: Set lunch £11.80 and dinner £12.85. Main course from £6. Main course(bar/snack) £5. House wine £7.75.
Hours: 11.30-23.00. 12.00-22.30 on Sunday.
Rood Served: 11.30-21.30. 12.00-21.00 on Sunday.
Cuisine: Traditional British.
Other Points: No-smoking area. Children welcome. No dogs. Garden. Car park.
Directions: Two and a quarter miles from Exit29/M1. Take the A6175, then in quarter of a mile turn left and follow the tourist board signs to the pub. (Map 9, B3)

Chatsworth Farm Shop
Stud Farm, Pilsley, Bakewell, Derbyshire DE45 1UF
Telephone: +44(0)1246 583392
farmshop@chatsworth.org
www.chatsworth-estate.org

Chatsworth Farm Shop was established in 1977 to sell beef and lamb from the Duke and Duchess of Devonshire's farms and venison from the park direct to local customers. It has grown to become one of the leaders in its field and is one of the best-known farm shops in the country. The butchery made the shop's reputation from the beginning, using, for example, traditionally farmed and hung beef, which gives a fuller flavour and tenderness. They also offer 16 varieties of sausages and a good selection of seasonal game. The kitchen was added in 1984. A team of chefs and bakers make bread and delicatessen foods, including a wide variety of cakes and farmhouse pâtés. The cheese counter offers a choice of 120 cheeses, including Harrington Stilton made in Derbyshire, there's a selection of locally grown fruits and vegetables, a range of marmalades, preserves, and chutneys, and a thriving mail order business.
Hours: Monday-Saturday: 09.00-17.00.
Other points: Delivery service by courier.
Directions: 1.75 miles from Chatsworth House. Follow brown Stately Home signs from most directions & exit 29/M1. (Map 9. B3)

THE HEART OF ENGLAND

At the centre of England's vast industrial heartland you'll discover a haven of green dales and high moorland offering a constantly changing backdrop of spectacular scenery and distant horizons.
Drive length 78 miles

Eyam
(plague village; museum)

Chatsworth
(house and parkland)

Peveril Castle

Stockport

Mellor

Marple

Sheffield

Peak

Prestbury

Buxton

Macclesfield

Pilsley

Chesterfield

Haddon Hall

Bakewell

Beeley

Eaton

Arbor Low Stone Circle

Leek

District

Biggin

Matlock

Riber Castle
Wildlife Park

Stanshope

Hognaston

Dovedale

Market House, Winster

● Accommodation/Food

● Accommodation

● Food

🥄 Food Shop

To find the establishments marked here, look up the listing town marked on the map in bold in the town index on page 395

Stanshope Hall

Stanshope, Ashbourne, Derbyshire DE6 2AD
Telephone: +44(0)1335 310278
naomi@stanshope.demon.co.uk
www.stanshope.net

Stanshope Hall is an impressive building, the cellar
dates from the 16th century but the Grade II listed
house was rebuilt in the 17th century. Public rooms
have something of a theatrical feel to them. Points of
interest include trompe l'oeil chandeliers made from
cereal boxes, and door frames throughout that, if not
informed, one would believe to be marble. The veneer
on the antique tables in the dining room reflects
evening candles and firelight, and magazines and books
are in abundance in the drawing room. Imposing
bedrooms are individually styled and painted. Among
the usual tea and telly facilities (good choice of teas),
there is a basket of fruit and locally made biscuits.
Naomi Chambers cooking adds some modern twists to
an otherwise largely traditional style. The limited
choice, three-course menu includes vegetables from the
garden and puts the emphasis on local and seasonal
produce such as game and local trout. A starter of red
pepper and aubergine soup could be followed by
venison casserole, with warm pear and almon tart for
pudding. Albeit a three-table, three-bedroom property,
there are still some eight whites and eight reds to
choose from, with half bottles available. Selections are
global and reasonably priced.

Prices: Set dinner £22. House wine £9.75.
Hours: 19.00-20.00. Closed 25-26 December.
Rooms: 3 en suite. Double room from £60, single from £30,
family room from £80.
Cuisine: Modern British.
Other Points: No-smoking area. Garden. Children welcome.
Car park.
Directions: Junction 24/M1. From Ashbourne take A515 towards
Buxton. Take turning signposted Thorpe, Ilam and Dovedale. Go
through Thorpe to Ilam village and turn right at memorial.
Stanshope is 3 miles along a windy, hilly road. (Map 9, B2)

Waterman's Arms

Bow Bridge, Ashprington, Totnes, Devon TQ9 7EG
Telephone: +44(0)1803 732214

Situated on the banks of the River Harbourne at the
top of Bow Creek, the Waterman's is a popular
summer spot with resident ducks and, if you are lucky,
kingfishers to keep you company. Bow Bridge is
recorded in the Domesday Book and the inn has been
in other lives a smithy, brewery, and a prison during
the Napoleonic Wars. Tardis-like inside, a series of
neatly furnished rooms radiate away from the central
servery, all filled with a mix of rustic furniture, old
photographs, brass artefacts and other memorabilia.
Food ranges from light snacks of filled baguettes, crab
sandwiches, Caesar salad and mussels cooked in white
wine, cream and onion sauce, to more hearty dishes
such as half shoulder of lamb, steak, mushroom and
stout pie and steaks from the grill. The inn has fifteen
comfortable bedrooms, including five rooms in a side
extension overlooking the flower-filled garden, each
neat with floral, cottagey fabrics and co-ordinating
friezes, attractive dark-stained modern furniture and
good en suite facilities. Direct-dial telephones and TVs
are standard throughout. A peaceful base from which
to explore the South Hams and Dartmoor.

Prices: Main course from £7.95. Bar meal from £4.95.
House wine £8.95.
Hours: 11.00-23.00. 12.00-22.30 on Sunday. Restaurant open
19.00-21.30.
Rooms: 15 en suite. Single room from £54, double room from
£69, family room from £79.
Cuisine: Traditional English.
Other Points: No-smoking area. Children welcome. Garden.
Car park.
Directions: Follow A381 out of Totnes towards Kingsbridge.
Halfway up the hill, turn left at the sign for Ashprington and the
Waterman's Arms. (Map 4, E5)

Prices: Set lunch £10 (2 courses), set
dinner £12 (2 courses). Main course from
£8. House wine £10.
Hours: 12.00-14.00, 18.00-21.30.
Rooms: 15 en suite. Double room from
£75, single from £50.
Cuisine: Specialises in local seafood.
Other Points: No-smoking area. Children
welcome. Garden. Car park.
Directions: J27/M5. One mile north of
Bideford on the A386, Limers Lane is on
the right. (Map 3, C4)

Riversford Hotel

Limers Lane, Northam, Bideford, Devon EX39 2RG
Telephone: +44(0)1237 474239
riversford@aol.com
www.riversford.co.uk

The Jarrard family run their hotel with style and simplicity, drawing on
strong, loyal support (built up over the last 30 years), who appreciate the
enviable value. All 15 bedrooms are en suite, are very well maintained and
individually decorated in light, relaxing colours; best rooms have four-
poster beds. Pleasant public rooms include the light, airy restaurant with
lovely garden views to the water beyond. Nigel Jarrard presides over the
kitchen and is to be praised for his efforts to buy locally. Game comes
from local shoots, Somerset and Dorset cheeses are from Hawkridge
Farms, vegetables are locally grown, meat supplied by a local butcher.
Tradition has its way with items such as tournedos Rossini, and Devon
lamb chops with mustard and brown sugar, but there are modern touches.
Fish is a speciality, and local sea bass could be teamed with dill and
orange sauce or king scallops sautéed in garlic, ginger and Thai spices and
served with a lemon and tarragon sauce. The short selection of wines
continues the theme of fair value.

Masons Arms

★ 🍴 🅿 ✗ ✍

Branscombe, Seaton, Devon EX12 3DJ
Telephone: +44(0)1297 680300
reception@masonsarms.co.uk
www.masonsarms.co.uk

Tucked down long twisting lanes in an unspoilt Devon village stands this delightful 14th-century, creeper-clad inn, just a 12-minute stroll through fields to the sea. There's period charm aplenty in stone walls, slate floors, open fires and the oak beams that were once the timbers of smugglers' boats. The enormous central fireplace is used in winter to cook beef or lamb spit-roasts. Good food, served throughout the rambling bar and split-level dining areas, features locally grown produce, especially excellent fresh fish and crab landed on Branscombe beach. From ploughman's lunches and sandwiches, the choice extends to crab bisque and confit of duck pancakes. Main-course options include the likes of whole sea bass with caper and nut brown butter, and roast haunch of venison. The fixed-price menu in the newly appointed Waterfall Restaurant may also offer roast duck with bitter orange sauce, and scallops and king prawns with spring onion and ginger. Drink local Otter ales, farm cider or choose from 14 wines by the glass. Quaint, compact bedrooms are in the inn or there are converted thatched cottages, where pretty rooms offer a mix of reproduction, antique and cane furnishings. The most luxurious (and spacious) have splendid four-poster beds, and deep sofas.

Prices: Set meal £25 and £20 (2 courses). House wine £11.
Hours: 11.00-15.00 Monday-Friday. 11.00-23.00 Saturday and 12.00-22.30 Sunday.
Food served: 12.00-14.00 Monday-Friday 12.00-14.15 Saturday and Sunday. 19.00-21.00 Monday to Sunday.
Rooms: 24 rooms, 22 en suite. Rooms from £50-£150.
Cuisine: Modern/traditional British.
Other Points: No smoking area. Garden - Terrace and Patio. Children welcome. Car park.
Directions: Village signposted off A3052 between Sidmouth and Seaton. (Map 4, D6)

The Floating Bridge Inn

🍴 🅿 ✗

Coombe Road, Dartmouth, Devon TQ6 9PQ
Telephone: +44(0)1803 832354

Fuelled with enthusiasm, Jim and Gay Brent arrived in Dartmouth in July 2002 to take on this 17th-century riverside pub. Perfectly located, overlooking the River Dart where the town's Higher 'floating bridge' Ferry docks, and below the Britannia Naval College, this former ferry keeper's cottage was in need of some refurbishment. Without spoiling the traditional atmosphere, the Brents have smartened up the pine-panelled bar, filled with Naval College memorabilia, and popular with visiting yachtsmen, and completely refurbished the dining room. River views, evening candlelight and a warm welcome now draw folk in for Jim's food, in particular the chalkboard list of locally-caught fish, crab and lobster. Freshly-prepared dishes from the main menu range from firm pub favourites such as garlic prawns, seafood mornay and prime English steaks to paella and rack of lamb with red wine and rosemary sauce. In the bar, tuck into a decent sandwich filled with fresh local crab, or choose the homemade steak and kidney pie, liver and bacon casserole, or large battered fresh cod served with chips and peas.

Prices: Set lunch and dinner £15. Main course restaurant from £12. Bar snack from £2.50, bar meals from £4.95. House wine £8.
Hours: 12.00-23.00, until 22.30 Sunday.
Food served: 12.00-14.00. 18.00-22.00. Bar food served from 12.00-22.00 everyday. Check for seasonal variations.
Cuisine: Traditional pub food. Restaurant specialises in fish.
Other Points: No-smoking area. Dogs welcome. Roof terrace. Children welcome.
Directions: The pub is adjacent to the Higher Ferry slipway in Dartmouth. (Map 4, E5)

Stoke Lodge Hotel

★ 🍴 ✗ ✍

Cinders Lane, Stoke Fleming, Dartmouth, Devon TQ6 0RA
Telephone: +44(0)1803 770523
mail@stokelodge.co.uk
www.stokelodge.co.uk

Tucked alongside a steep, narrow winding village street high above Start Bay is this charming country house hotel. Visitors are not only taken by the comfortable country house décor in the lounge-cum-bar and restaurant, but also by the relaxed ambience and friendly welcome that goes with it. The sympathetically extended south-facing building (the core is 17th century with an 18th century façade), has much to offer: lawns, terraces, tennis court and outdoor swimming pool make the most of one of the best climates in Britain, backed up by an indoor swimming pool, sauna, spa bath, and snooker. Bedrooms are bang up to date, with individual décor and several four-poster beds. Cooking takes note of local supply lines. The daily changing set menu offers a good choice of dishes that are best described as traditional, but there's nothing wrong with that when they include smoked eel with horseradish sauce, cream of leek soup, and grilled lamb cutlets with cumberland sauce. Old favourites appear on the dessert menu, notably bread and butter pudding with custard, and sherry trifle. Stephen Mayer runs his hotel well, with plenty of hands-on commitment; it makes a tremendous holiday base (with lots to offer children).

Prices: Set lunch £13.95 and dinner £18.95. Main course from £11.95. House wine £9.95.
Hours: 12.00-13.45. 19.00-21.00.
Rooms: 25 en suite. Double room from £85, single from £51.
Cuisine: Modern British.
Other Points: No-smoking area. Children welcome. Garden. Car park. Indoor and outdoor swimming pools.
Directions: From M5 at Exeter, take A38 towards Plymouth. Turn off at Buckfastleigh and follow signs to Totnes and then Dartmouth (A381 or A3122). Turn right to Stoke Fleming. (Map 4, E5)

Carved Angel Cafe

21A Cathedral Yard, Exeter, Devon
Telephone: +44(0)1392 210303
enquiries@thecarvedangel.com
www.thecarvedangel.com

Run under the direction supervision of Peter Gorton, owner of the legendary West Country restaurants, the Carved Angel and Horn of Plenty, the Carved Angel Café offers quality food at all levels, be it coffee and croissant, tea and cake, small bites, or daily lunch and early evening specials. Raw materials are fresh, seasonal and locally sourced, and the informal setting with its buzz and continental attitude makes it one of the best foody café-cum-bistros in the south west. Crab cakes, chicken parfait with warm brioche, or sweet garlic and mascarpone risotto press all the right buttons while conveying a sense that this is more than just ordinary café food. Factor in an assured combination of medallions of pork with apple compote and a sweetcorn and sage pancake, matched by grilled bream on a Thai noodle broth, and you have an imaginative kitchen at work. Alongside caramelised passion fruit cream with tropical fruit compote and toffee wafers, there's chocolate Jaffa mousse cake with orange caramel sauce, and local cheeses with apple chutney. Afternoon cakes are made on the premises, as are the scones for cream teas.

Prices: Main course restaurant from £6.95. Main course snack from £4.95. House wine £10.50.
Hours: 09.00-17.00. 19.00-21.30. Sunday 10.00-16.00. Closed Sunday evening.
Cuisine: Modern British.
Other Points: Totally no smoking. Children welcome.
Directions: Exit31/M5. Follow the signs to Cathedral and Quayside. (Map 4, D5)

Blagdon Manor

Ashwater, Beaworthy, Holsworthy,
Devon EX21 5DF
Telephone: +44(0)1409 211224
stay@blagdon.com
www.blagdon.com

It's fitting that on their return to their native rural Devon, Steve and Elizabeth Morey should get it so right. This is just the way a small restaurant with luxury bedrooms should be run: welcoming, inviting, relaxing. The Grade II listed building was built in two parts, one dating from the 16th century, the other from the 17th, and is cleverly bought together with a bar/lounge and library in the oldest part reached through a covered cobbled courtyard. The seven bedrooms are all charming, individually decorated and supremely comfortably appointed, with views over gardens and beyond. The dining room leads to the newly built conservatory and is the setting for cooking that mixes innovation with sound workable combinations of ingredients and flavours. The starting point is prime raw materials ranging from Devon beef, via new season's lamb, to regional cheeses. These are assembled into short three course menus that might offer warm salad of ham hock with lentils, shallot and English mustard vinaigrette, and confit of Gressingham duck with wild mushrooms and balsamic vinegar jus. Fish dishes are enticing, perhaps a mains of pan-fried fillet of cod with king prawns and a tomato and pepper dressing. Desserts may include an intense, delicate lemon posset with pistachio tuile biscuit.

Prices: Set lunch £14. Set dinner £25. House wine £9.50.
Hours: 12.00-14.00. 19.00-21.00. Closed Mon/Tues lunch and Sun/Mon dinner to non-residents; two weeks end Jan and early Nov.
Rooms: 7 rooms en suite. Double/twin from £90. Single from £72.
Cuisine: Modern British.
Other Points: No-smoking area. Dogs welcome. Children welcome over 12 years old. Garden. Car park. Private dining.
Directions: Signed from A388 at Blagdon Cross, One mile north of Launceston. (Map 3, D4)

Dèdés Hotel and Wheel Inn

1-4 The Promenade, Ilfracombe, Devon EX34 9BD
Telephone: +44(0)1271 862545
jackie@dedes.fsbusiness.co.uk
www.clayshooting-dedes.co.uk

The setting, right on Ilfracombe's front, overlooking Wildersmouth Beach, offers wonderful views across the sea and coastal hills. Built at the turn of the 19th century, and owned by the same family since 1946, Dèdés has built up a reputation for sporting breaks. The hotel's championship clay-pigeon shooting ground is suitable for novices and improvers, instruction is first class, and game and rough shooting for small parties can be arranged. Flexibility of meals is another plus; through a combination of the Wheel Inn and Wheel Room restaurant, most times and bases are covered. Local fish is an obvious strength, with lobster and crab, platters of mixed seafood, grilled whole plaice or Exmoor trout, offered with some good steaks, game in season, and meaty mixed grills.

Those who lament the passing of the traditional seaside hotel would be very happy here. Plenty of opportunities for shore-based pastimes, magnificent views from well maintained, traditionally-styled bedrooms, and the kind of service that only a family-run hotel can guarantee.

Prices: Set dinner £10. House wine £9.80.
Hours: 12.00-14.00. 18.00-21.00 (20.30 in winter). Closed 25-26 December.
Rooms: 17 rooms, 12 en suite. Double room from £18.50 per person, single from £19.50.
Cuisine: Traditional English.
Other Points: No-smoking in restaurant. Children welcome. Car park.
Directions: Exit 27/M5, then A361 to Barnstaple and Ilfracombe, then follow signs to Sea Front. (Map 3, C4)

The Staghunters Hotel

Brendon, Lynton, Devon EX35 6PS
Telephone: +44(0)1598 741222
enquiries@staghunters.fsnet.co.uk
www.staghunters.com

An historic inn on the site of an old abbey (the chapel has been incorporated into the lounge) and set beside the East Lyn River deep in Doone Valley. This is a friendly family run hotel that makes a great base for exploring Exmoor and Lorna Doone country. Homely, simply furnished bars offer a short menu of good country cooking, say soup, grilled sardines, or cottage pie with garlic bread and salad, washed down with a pint of Exmoor Gold. In the restaurant (lovely garden views) there could be local trout poached in white wine with bay, or large pork chop pan-fried with sage, apple and cider and finished in cream. All are served with good, fresh vegetables, and the menu is extended by a daily specials board. Pretty, cottagey bedrooms are comfortably appointed, all are en suite, one has a four-poster bed; residents have their own sitting room. In addition, trout and salmon fishing can be arranged on six miles of river at Water Authority rates, pets are welcome, there's stabling for visiting horses, and golf can be arranged at nearby Saunton Golf Club.

Prices: Set dinner £16.95. House wine £8.50.
Hours: 07.00-14.30. 17.00-23.00.
Food served: In the bar 19.30-21.30. In the restaurant 19.30-20.30.
Rooms: 12 en suite. Single from £40, double from £60. Family room from £70.
Cuisine: Traditional British.
Other Points: No-smoking area. Children welcome. Garden. Car park.
Directions: Follow the A39 from Lynton towards Porlock, the Staghunters Hotel is signposted to the right approximately five miles from Lynton. (Map 3, C5)

The Jack in the Green Inn

London Road, Rockbeare, Exeter, Devon EX5 2EE
Telephone: +44(0)1404 822240
info@jackinthegreen.uk.com
www.jackinthegreen.uk.com

A welcome peace has descended on this unassuming, white-painted roadside pub since the new stretch of the A30 opened between Exeter and Honiton. Although cars in numbers have stopped whizzing past, the pub continues to be busy, thanks to a well-deserved reputation locally for upmarket, modern pub food. Within, you will find a neatly refurbished open-plan bar and dining area featuring dark wood furnishings, church pews, a carved oak dresser and warming open fire, plus deep sofas for those intending to eat in the main dining area (where a set menu is offered). Matthew Mason offers a wide range of dishes on several blackboards. For a hearty snack look to the impressive ploughman's board (Capricorn goats' cheese, local ham, Cashel Irish Blue), or to the main board for steak and kidney pie, salmon fishcakes with pepper mayonnaise, or local bangers and mash. Making good use of local raw materials, monthly set menus may list Devon beef fillet with oxtail risotto and red wine jus, red mullet with ratatouille and tapenade sauce, and homemade puddings to finish. In addition, expect an impressive range of local cheeses, carefully chosen wines (a dozen by the glass), and West Country real ales.

Prices: Set lunch and dinner £21.25. Main course bar meal from £7.50. Main course restaurant meal from £9.50. House wine from £9.50.
Hours: 11.00-14.00. 17.30-23.00. Open all day Sunday. Closed 24 December-3 January.
Food served: 11.00-1400. 17.30-21.30. Sunday from 12.00-21.30.
Cuisine: Modern British.
Other Points: No-smoking area. Garden. Car park.
Directions: Five miles along the old A30 from junction 29 off the M5 towards Honiton. (Map 4, C5)

Clocktower Tearooms

Connaught Gardens, Sidmouth, Devon EX10 8RZ
Telephone: +44(0)1395 515319

The sight of the Clocktower Tearooms is astonishing: the building (former lime kilns) has been lovingly renovated to a very high standard (wood carvings by local craftsmen are outstanding), and is perched right on the edge of a cliff, giving breathtaking views over Jacob's Ladder Beach. Situated in Connaught Gardens, on the west side of Sidmouth's sea front, the building is reached from a walled rose garden, which is only a small part of these award-winning gardens. The addition of a conservatory gives extra seating to a very popular operation (note that it is open only during the day). Scones and cakes are made on the premises - the smell on entering is wonderful - and in addition to cakes, toasted teacakes and scones with clotted cream, there are light meals of smoked haddock fishcakes, home-crumbed plaice, or cod in beer batter. Crabs (in season) are handpicked and delivered daily, chickens are free-range, and the local butcher supplies meat for the likes of steak and ale pie and cottage pie; all dishes are made on the premises. Staff make you feel welcome, and owners June and Stewart Fraser are always on hand to make sure things run smoothly.

Prices: Main course from £7.50. House wine £7.95.
Hours: 10.00-14.30. Closed 25 December.
Cuisine: Traditional English.
Other Points: Totally no smoking. Dogs welcome. Children welcome. Garden. Car park.
Directions: Exit30/M6 - A3052 to Sidmouth. At sea front turn right, pass the Victoria Hotel and then go into Peak Hill Road. (Map 4, D6)

The Tower Inn
Church Road, Slapton, Kingsbridge, Devon TQ7 2PN
Telephone: +44(0)1548 580216
towerinn@slapton.org
www.thetowerinn.com

Tucked away behind the church and standing beside the dramatic, ivy-clad ruins of the chantry tower, the 14th-century Tower Inn is a truly atmospheric village pub. It was built to accommodate the artisans working on the monastic collegiate next door and later became the college's guesthouse where alms and hospitality were dispensed. Six hundred years on and guests continue to be warmly welcomed, refreshed with local ales such as Dartmoor IPA and wolfing down an eclectic range of modern pub food. Expect hearty lunchtime sandwiches (try the delicious fresh crab), alongside a platter of locally smoked fish, fishcakes with warm citrus and cream dressing, and local pork sausages with grain mustard mash and onion gravy. Evening specials could include Brixham fish, perhaps baked sea bass on braised fennel with orange and fennel butter and rack of lamb on mint and cherry risotto with chilli tomato dressing. Round off with white chocolate and orange terrine. Stone walls, open fires, low beams, scrubbed oak tables and flagstone floors characterise the welcoming interior, the atmosphere enhanced at night with candlelit tables. Accommodation is provided in three cottage-style en suite bedrooms, all comfortably furnished and equipped with modern facilities.

Prices: Main course from £9. House wine from £10.
Hours: 12.00-14.30 (until 15.00 on Sundays) and 19.00-23.00 daily. Closed 25-26 December evening.
Food served: 12.00-14.15 (until 14.30 on Sunday). 19.00-21.30.
Rooms: 2 en suite. Room from £50.
Cuisine: Modern British.
Other Points: No smoking area. Garden and courtyard. Children welcome. Car park.
Directions: Off A379 between Dartmouth and Kingsbridge, or off A381 between Totnes and Kingsbridge. (Map 4, E5)

The Millbrook Inn
South Pool, Kingsbridge, Devon TQ7 2RP
Telephone: +44(0)1548 531581
www.millbrookinn.co.uk

Customers arrive at this small pub close to the Salcombe estuary by boat when the tide is high, and the Millbrook stream flows past the sunny rear terrace. White painted under its natural stone roof, the 400-year-old Millbrook has two cosy beamed bars with open fires and displays of clay pipes, horse brasses and attractive drawings and paintings, plus a welcome new dining area. Local farm cider and decent ale provide accompaniments to good, homemade bar meals, notably fresh local fish and prime Scottish beef. Lunchtime favourites include traditional ploughman's (try the rare roast beef), an excellent wholemeal sandwich generously filled with fresh crab, and splendid summer salads with local seafood, smoked salmon or homebaked ham. For something more substantial order the steak pasty, fisherman's pie, tagliatelle pesto, or look to the blackboard for roasted cod, homemade crab cakes, rack of lamb or fillet steak. Expect hearty puddings like sticky toffee pudding and apple cider cake (both served with Devon clotted cream), or opt for one of the Salcombe Dairy ice creams. Short, select list of wines; eight by the glass.

Prices: Main course from £4.95. House wine £9.95.
Hours: 12.00-14.30 (until 15.00 on Sunday). 18.00-23.00 Monday-Saturday. 19.00-22.30 Sunday. Summer variations.
Food served: 12.00-14.00 and 19.00-21.00 daily. Check for seasonal variations.
Cuisine: Traditional English.
Other Points: No-smoking area. Children welcome in family room. Garden. Credit cards not accepted.
Directions: Village signposted off A379 at Frogmore, east of Kingsbridge. (Map 4, E5)

The Osborne Hotel
Hesketh Crescent, Meadfoot, Devon TQ1 2LL
Telephone: +44(0)1803 213311
enq@osborne-torquay.co.uk
www.osborne-torquay.co.uk

Situated in an impressive Regency crescent with a magnificent view over the bay below, the Osborne is a haven of tranquillity. The hotel is made up of 29 bedrooms, Langtry's Restaurant and the more laid-back brasserie – a large high-ceilinged, modern looking room with a black and white tiled floor, which serves food, cocktails, and coffees all day. It leads to a decked sun terrace, the perfect location for soaking up a few rays, watching the tennis below, or the magnificent sea view beyond, and eating smoked mackerel with salad and chips. The restaurant offers more serious dining. The ingredient-led menu describes a confident style that's strong on fresh, clear flavours. The set lunch is excellent value. Dinner could bring mains of slow-roast venison with truffle potato, braised leeks and port balsamic jus, with Pavlova minestrone of fruits, candied fennel and basil to finish. Bedrooms at the very top of the house are a good size, have panoramic views, and large en-suite bathrooms, some with separate bath and shower. On lower floors, the rooms get larger and the first floor rooms have a balcony. The leisure facilities are good too, ideal for a short-break or family holiday. There's a small well-equipped gym, indoor and outdoor swimming pools, sauna and outdoor tennis court.

Prices: Set dinner £22.95. House wine £13.75. Brasserie from £5.25.
Hours: Restaurant 19.00-21.30. Brasserie 12.00-15.00. 18.00-23.00
Rooms: 29 en suite. Rooms from £55. Supplement charged for sea view, single occupancy.
Cuisine: Langtry's: modern British.
Other Points: Non smoking area. Restaurant is all non smoking. Garden. Children welcome. Car park.
Directions: In Meadfoot located on the seafront. (Map 4, D5)

The Sea Trout Inn

Staverton, Totnes, Devon TQ9 6PA
Telephone: +44(0)1803 762274
www.seatroutinn.com

The peaceful Dart Valley, a few miles upstream from the historic town of Totnes, is the setting for this attractive 15th-century inn. A fishing theme runs through the pub, some specimens mounted in showcases, others depicted in paintings or on plates. Bar areas are traditional in character, the neat, rambling lounge bar sporting pine furnishings, open fires and a wide-ranging bar menu (booking advisable). Typical choices range from starters of smoked salmon platter and avocado and bacon salad, to homemade steak and ale pie, or ham, egg and chips, chicken with tarragon sauce, whole Brixham plaice and, naturally, local trout with lemon butter sauce. More imaginative restaurant food is served in the neatly appointed, conservatory dining room which overlooks the sheltered patio-style garden. Here you may find fresh Brixham fish and locally sourced meats. There's also a separate beamed public bar with adjoining pool room - a popular retreat for locals - and a well-stocked bar offering Palmers ales and nine wines by the glass. Upstairs, 10 bedrooms are decorated in cottage style with co-ordinating fabrics, darkwood furniture and bathrooms (three with shower only) featuring an attractive fish tiles and good toiletries.

Prices: Set Sunday lunch £13.95. Set dinner £21.50. Main course from £8.95. House wine £8.95.
Hours: 11.00-15.00. 18.00-23.00.
Food served: 12.00-14.00 (14.30 on Sundays) and 19.00-21.00 (21.30 Friday and Saturday).
Rooms: 10 en suite. Single room from £39.50, double room from £50.
Cuisine: Modern British.
Other Points: No-smoking area. Garden. Children welcome. Car park.
Directions: Staverton is signed off A384 between Totnes and the A38 at Buckfastleigh. (Map 4, D5)

Cridford Inn

Trusham, Newton Abbot, Devon TQ13 0NR
Telephone: +44(0)1626 853694
cridford@eclipse.co.uk

Hidden in the Teign Valley between Exeter and Dartmoor, this thatched inn (dating from 1081) is the oldest domestic dwelling in Devon. Carefully restored in 1993, the ancient longhouse has a charming interior, the two interconnecting bars displaying original and huge beams, rustic stone fireplaces and floors, and the earliest example of a domestic window in Britain. In the separate dining room you can see a mosaic date stone in the preserved Saxon stone floor, fine oak pillars and small stained-glass windows. In general, the food on offer is traditional pub fare ranging from sandwich platters, tagliatelle carbonara, scampi and chips and the generous Cridford brunch at lunchtime, to tiger prawns with chilli dip, crusty bread and rocket salad, beer-battered cod and chips, smoked haddock florentine and rump steak in the evening. Additional evening specials may include salmon with cider, cream and tarragon sauce, sea bass with lemon grass and ginger, and Malaysian-born Jasmin's very authentic curries, perhaps beef rendang with rice and coriander or Thai chicken curry. Upstairs, three simple, yet comfortably furnished bedrooms are all individually decorated with pretty, co-ordinating floral fabrics and all have well-equipped en suite bathrooms.

Prices: Set lunch £10 (2 course). Set dinner £15. Main course from £6.50. House wine £10.50.
Hours: 11.30-15.00. 19.00-23.30. Check seasonal variations. Closed 25 December evening and 8-28 January.
Food served: 12.00-15.00. 19.00-21.30.
Rooms: 4 en suite. Single room from £50. Double room £60.
Cuisine: Traditional pub food and South-East Asian.
Other Points: No-smoking area. Small garden. Dogs welcome in bar and accommodation. Children welcome. Car park.
Directions: From the A38 take the B3193 Teign Valley Road. Take a right at the first T junction over the river and follow the single track road to Trusham. (Map 4, D5)

Mortehoe Brasserie

2 The Crescent, Mortehoe, Devon EX34 7DX
Telephone: +44(0)1271 870610
Stevedlawn@aol.com
www.mortehoebrasserie.com

The views from the ancient clifftop village of Mortehoe are stunning and long scenic walks are part of the charm, a lure for visitors in the summer; at all other times the sense of peace is tangible. Steve and Sue Lawn's brasserie fits the charm of the village exactly as the 200-year-old building has plenty of character. Within, the open-plan room is contemporary in style: lots of pine, bare floor boards, tiling, and modern artwork on the walls. Menus are built around sensibly sourced materials and with long opening times, have a something for everyone appeal: locally made sausages with a creamy mash, or slow braised haunch of Exmoor venison with an intense cranberry and port jus. Even relatively humble items get a look in, generally jazzed up as in sliced field mushrooms served on toasted ciabatta with Parmesan flakes and basil pesto. Fish is well judged, breakfast is served all day, and there are afternoon teas, lunchtime sandwiches and locally made burgers. The fairly even global wine list offers a good value selection with nothing over £18. Three fresh, colour coordinated double en suite rooms (shower only) offer very good value for money. Two have access to the balcony, the third looks out over lovely National Trust land.

Prices: Main course restaurant from £10.95. Snacks from £2.75. House wine £10.45.
Hours: 09.00-17.30. 19.30-23.30.
Rooms: 3 en suite. Double/Twin from £20 per person.
Cuisine: Modern British with Mediterranean influences.
Other Points: No-smoking area. Dogs welcome in the B&B only. Children welcome during the day.
Directions: Exit27/M5. From Ilfracombe or Barnstaple, head for the Mullacott Cross and turn west at the Mullacott roundabout. Mortehoe is approximately two miles on the top of the hill leading to Woolacombe bay. (Map 3, C4)

England - Devon

Shave Cross Inn

Shave Cross, Marshwood Vale, Bridport, Dorset DT6 6HW
Telephone: +44(0)1308 868358
roy.warburton@virgin.net
www.theshavecrossinn.co.uk

Situated in a remote and peaceful spot in the beautiful Marshwood Vale, this charming 14th-century thatched cob-and-flint inn was once a resting place for pilgrims on their way to the shrine of St Witta at Whitchurch Canonicorum. A stone floor, inglenook fireplace, beamed ceiling, and rustic furnishings testify to the age and there's a delightful flower-filled sun-trap garden. Fresh from three years in Tobago, Marshwood-born Roy Warburton returned to his roots in April 2003 to restore the fortunes of this cracking country pub - in decline after months of closure and uncertainty. With him came a Caribbean chef who has really spiced up the menu, noteworthy in an area renowned for traditional pub food. Look to the imaginative carte for such exotic offerings as jerk chicken salad with plantain, bacon and aïoli, and roast Creole duck with cherry compote. Traditional tastes are well catered for, both the good value set and bar menus list freshly battered haddock and chips and rump steak, the latter also featuring decent ploughman's lunches (very local Denhay cheddar), and fresh crab sandwiches. Other than plantain, all produce is sourced from Dorset and Somerset, with tip-top ales from the local Branscombe Vale and Quay Breweries.

Prices: Table d'hote £14.95. Main course restaurant from £13.95. Main course bar from £6.95. House wine £8.
Hours: 10.30-15.00. 17.00-23.00. 12.00-22.30 on Sunday. Closed Monday except Bank Holidays.
Food served: 11.00-15.00. 17.00-21.30, Sunday 18.00-20.00.
Cuisine: Traditional British and Caribbean.
Other Points: No-smoking area. Dogs/Children welcome. Garden. Car park.
Directions: From Bridport take B3162 north for two miles and turn left signposted Broadoak. Pub in 3 miles. (Map 4, D6)

The Royal Oak

★ 🍴 🅳 ✕

23 Long Street, Cerne Abbas, Dorchester, Dorset DT2 7JG
Telephone: +44(0)1300 341797
royaloak@cerneabbas.fsnet.co.uk

The eye-catching building with its thatched roof and creeper-clad walls dates from the 16th century. In its time it has been a blacksmiths shop and a popular coaching stop. Now a thriving village local with a traditional interior featuring flagstone floors, open log fires, beams and bric-à-brac, it not only attracts hungry walkers and tourists on the Hardy Trail but local diners in search of hearty and genuinely homecooked food that utilises first-class produce from local suppliers. Regular menus range from pub favourites such as ham, egg and chips, to specialities of steak and Blue Vinney pie with shortcrust pastry, perhaps, and local game pie. Additive- and hormone-free steaks are sourced from accredited herds and served with a choice of sauces. Daily dishes on the handwritten menu extend the choice and may include rare breed pork, apple and cider casserole, and fresh local seafood, perhaps steamed whole seabass with cream and basil sauce. Round off with apple and blackberry crumble from the blackboard list of homemade desserts. Five real ales on handpump, 13 wines by the glass and an enclosed rear garden with decking and heaters for summer use.

Prices: Starters from £3.50. Main course from £6.75. Snack/walkers favourites from £3.50. House wine £9.95.
Hours: 11.30-15.00. 18.00-23.00. 12.00-15.00 and 19.00-22.30 on Sunday.
Food served: 12.00-14.00. 19.00-21.30 (21.00 on Sundays). Open later in the Summer.
Cuisine: Traditional English/Modern British.
Other Points: No-smoking area. Courtyard garden and decking. Children welcome.
Directions: Village signed off A352 Dorchester to Sherborne road, 6 miles north of Dorchester. (Map 4, D7)

The Fox Inn

🅳 ✕ 🍴

Corscombe, Dorchester, Dorset DT2 0NS
Telephone: +44(0)1935 891330
dine@fox-inn.co.uk
www.fox-inn.co.uk

Built as a cider house in 1620 on an old droving route to Yeovil, the pretty, rose-adorned thatched pub of stone and cob is located down a corkscrew of narrow lanes deep in unspoilt Dorset countryside. It's everybody's idea of the perfect country pub with two charming beamed bars, one with a huge inglenook fireplace and real log fire, stone-flagged floors and gingham-clothed tables, the other filled with old pine furniture and chatty locals. Country pub cooking at its best, with all dishes freshly prepared from quality Somerset and Dorset produce, includes local estate venison with red wine and cranberry, and rack of Dorset lamb with rosemary gravy, and the blackboard features fresh fish from West Bay. Other dishes that have impressed include mussel and bacon chowder, and local braised rabbit with olives, lemon and thyme. Puddings range from sticky toffee pudding to vanilla cream terrine with redcurrant coulis. Accompany a first-class meal with a pint of Exmoor Ale drawn from the cask, decent wines (six by the glass), or perhaps a glass of homemade elderflower cordial. Tucked under the heavy thatch with rural views are four cottagey en suite bedrooms, all tastefully decorated and furnished with antique beds.

Prices: Main course from £8.50. House wine £10.50.
Hours: 12.00-15.00. 19.00-23.00. Closed 25 December.
Food served: 12.00-14.00. 19.00-21.00 (until 21.30 at week-end).
Rooms: 4 en suite. Double room from £75, single from £55.
Cuisine: Modern British.
Other Points: No-smoking area. Garden/conservatory. Well-behaved children welcome. Car park.
Directions: From Yeovil, take the A37 towards Dorchester. After one mile turn right towards Corscombe and follow the lane for five and a half miles. Alternatively, take the A356 from Crewkerne to Maiden Newton for five miles. (Map 4, C6)

England - Dorset

The Museum Inn ★ 𝕯 ✕ ✍
Farnham, Blandford Forum, Dorset DT11 8DE
Telephone: +44(0)1725 516261
themuseuminn@supanet.co.uk
www.museuminn.co.uk

Vicky Eliot and Mark Stephenson restored and re-opened the inn in May 2001. Throughout the three civilised, beamed rooms around the bar, yellow-washed walls, flagstone floors, open fires and scrubbed tables set the scene for some superlative bar food. Mark Treasure, who earned a Michelin star at the Feathers Hotel in Woodstock (see entry), takes sourcing prime local produce very seriously. Only traditionally-reared traceable meats feature on the daily menus, with free-range poultry, game from neighbouring estates, and local organic herbs and vegetables. Dishes in the bar may include roast shoulder of lamb with black olives and basil jus, or rib-eye steak with mash, bacon and root vegetables, and posh lunchtime sandwiches. In The Shed restaurant (booking essential), there may be roast scallops with parsnip purée, chorizo sausage and white truffle oil, and pot-roasted guinea fowl with smoked bacon and savoy cabbage. The cooking is backed up by an excellent list of wines, with eight by the glass, and handpulled ales from small independent breweries such as Ringwood, and Hop Back. Style and attention to detail extends to eight en suite bedrooms. All are individually decorated with warm colours and quality fabrics, and furnished with easy chairs and comfortable beds; stable rooms are more compact.

Prices: Main course from £9.50. House wine £10.95.
Hours: 11.00-15.00. 18.00-23.00 (until 22.30 on Sunday).
Food served: 12.00-14.00 (until 15.00 on Sunday). 19.00-21.30.
Rooms: 8 en suite. Double room from £75.
Cuisine: Modern European.
Other Points: Terrace. Car park.
Directions: Village signposted off the A354 Salisbury to Blandford road. (Map 4, C7)

Pamphill Dairy Farm Shop, Restaurant and Butchery
Pamphill, Wimborne, Dorset BH21 4ED
Telephone: +44(0)1202 880618
info@pamphilldairy.com
www.pamphilldairy.com

In 1983, the Richardsons had to stop milking their 100 cows at Pamphill, due in part to the introduction of milk quotas. So they converted the old farm buildings into a farm shop to give employment to their cowman and his staff. The shop houses an extensive range of produce, some of which is grown on the farm, and much of it is produced locally. Expect to find orchard and soft fruits, vegetables, eggs, homemade cakes and jams, dairy produce, locally baked bread and honey. A butchery sells fresh meats, homemade sausages and pies, and is also the main outlet for beef from the Ruby Red North Devons of Kingston Lacy Park. Plants from a local nurseryman are on sale at very good prices, there's a pet food department, and a tea room situated in the former milking parlour for morning coffee, cream teas and light lunches - using local produce where possible.

Hours: Daily 08.30-17.30.
Other points: Ample parking. Children's play area. Scenic walks. Picnic area. Garden centre. Easy access and facilities for disabled.
Directions: From Wimborne take the B3082. Left at Pamphill Post Office and look for signs.)(Map 4, D7)

The Old Forge
Compton Abbas, Shaftesbury, Dorset SP7 0NQ
Telephone: +44(0)1747 811881
theoldforge@hotmail.com
www.SmoothHound.co.uk/hotels.oldforge

The small car-restoration garage, complete with vintage cars, an ancient hand fuel pump and walls covered with old enamel signs is a great draw for guests at this country cottage offering accommodation with breakfast, and owner Tim Kerridge is very happy to show visitors around. The garage is part of a 17th-century thatched building that was once a forge, and the original forge is still preserved alongside massive bellows and other artefacts. The sitting room, where breakfast is served, has white-painted stone walls, a large wood-burning stove, flagged floors, antique furniture, hanging rugs and a forest of beams. With soft light from table lamps, it has a cosy, comfortable look. Both bedrooms have beamed ceilings under the eaves and a welcoming, very attractive old-fashioned cottage look mixed in with present-day comforts such as tea trays and private bathrooms (one en suite).

Rooms: 3 rooms, 1 en suite, 1 private bathroom. Singles from £40, doubles from £45.
Other Points: No smoking area. Garden. Children welcome. Car park.
Directions: Off the A350 Shaftesbury to Blandford Forum road, signposted to Compton Abbas. (Map 4, C7)

Manor House

Beach Road, Studland Bay, Dorset BH19 3AU
Telephone: +44(0)1929 450288
themanorhousehotel@lineone.net
www.themanorhousehotel.com

The early 18th-century Gothic manor house is set in 20 acres of secluded grounds with delightful views over Studland Bay. It's a comfortable, charming hotel still retaining the old-world charm of a one-time seaside residence. The baronial-feel, oak-panelled dining room with fireplace and dark-wood furniture, together with its adjoining bright conservatory, look out over the lawn to the sea, as does the comfortable, country-style lounge. Bedrooms are charming, light, spacious, individual, with period furnishings and atmosphere to match. All are en suite with every convenience and many with sea or garden views. There's also a bar, plus outdoor tennis courts to work off dinner. This is a meal to look forward too, with many raw materials locally sourced. Venison, for example, is shot and butchered locally, shellfish is delivered from Weymouth, and regional cheeses run to Dorset Blue Vinney, Stinking Bishop and Somerset brie. The repertoire runs to deep-fried lemon sole goujons with lemon and garlic mayonnaise, then steamed fillet of cod with a saffron sauce. Around 40 affordable wines are bolstered by a few specials. English breakfasts are of the kind to set you up for the day.

Prices: Set dinner £30 (4 courses). Lunchtime bar meals. House wine £12.
Hours: 12.00-14.00. 19.00-21.00. Closed for three weeks in January.
Rooms: 21 en suite. Double room from £65 per person, including dinner, single £85.
Cuisine: Modern British/European.
Other Points: No-smoking area. No children under 5 years. Garden. Car park.
Directions: 3 miles from Swanage, 3 miles from Sandbanks Ferry. (Map 4, D8)

Lovells Court

Burton Street, Marnhull, Sturminster Newton, Dorset DT10 1JJ
Telephone: +44(0)1258 820652
maryann@lovellscourt.co.uk

Mary-Ann Newson-Smith's Edwardian house is set in attractive gardens and makes a comfortable base for visitors wishing to explore Hardy Country. Pass through the heavy oak front door and you enter a spacious, elegant country house (in style and decoration) with far reaching views over the garden and countryside. Period details are spot on: there's a magnificent open stairway, big cast-iron radiators, brass chandeliers, and dark oak furniture in the hallway. The burgundy and cream breakfast room has three tables (for those with a horror of sharing a table at breakfast), a large fireplace in an arched alcove and good views; breakfast is based on local supplies and includes homemade preserves. Two of the three bedrooms are en suite; the third has its own private bathroom. All the rooms are spacious, one is twin-bedded, and are well equipped with TVs, and tea trays, comfortable chairs and antique pine furniture. Please note that no credit cards are taken.

Rooms: 3 rooms, 2 en suite, 1 with private bathroom. Singles from £30, doubles from £50.
Other Points: Totally non-smoking area. Garden. Children welcome over 12 years old. Car park.
Directions: From the A30 at East Stour take the B3092 signposted Marnhull. After three miles, turn right down Church Hill and follow for three quarters of a mile. Lovells Court is on the left hand side, just beyond the village shops but before Blackmore Vale Inn. (Map 4, C7)

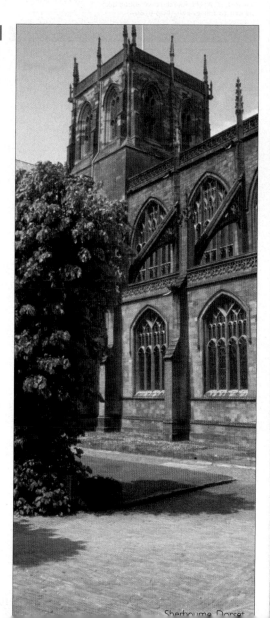

Sherbourne, Dorset

Green Dragon

🍴 ▯ ✗

Upper London Road, Youngs End, Braintree, Essex CM77 8QN
Telephone: +44(0)1245 361030
green.dragon@virgin.net
www.greendragonbrasserie.co.uk

Hard beside the A131 close to the Essex County Showground, this classic 18th-century inn was formerly a private house and stables, the latter housing the recently converted Barn and Hayloft (non-smoking) restaurants, with their stripped brick walls and fine old beams. Within, the lounge and Parlour bars done in yellows and browns with lots of original beams, red carpets, banquettes and traditional pub furnishings, provide a cosy atmosphere in which to relax with a pint of Greene King IPA or Abbot Ale, or a decent glass of wine. The same blackboard and extensive printed menus are served throughout, but the range of light snacks to proper dishes offers great flexibility. Traditional pub staples are made from scratch with good ingredients, so tuck into calf's liver and bacon with onion mash, beef and Abbot Ale pie, daily curry and pasta dishes, and homecooked ham, egg and chips. There's more ambitious offerings from the Duke of Buccleuch's estate beef (rib-eye with garlic butter) and shoulder of lamb with wine, herbs and garlic, as well as speciality seafood dishes like hot potted shrimps, whole Scottish langoustines, seared scallops with smoked bacon, and cod fillet deep-fried in beer batter

Prices: Set lunch £12 and dinner £16.50. Main course from £7.50. House wine £9.
Hours: 12.00-15.00. 17.30-23.00. 12.00-22.30 on Sunday.
Food served: 12.00-14.00. 18.00-21.00 (until 22.00 on Friday and Saturday). 12.00-20.00 on Sunday.
Cuisine: Traditional British.
Other Points: No-smoking area. No dogs. Children welcome over eight years old. Garden. Car park.
Directions: M11 Stansted exit. Take the A120 to Braintree then the A131 towards Chelmsford. At the fourth roundabout take the exit to Youngs End. (Map 6, B6)

The Cricketers

▯ ✗ ♨

Clavering, Saffron Walden, Essex CB11 4QT
Telephone: +44(0)1799 550442
info@thecricketers.co.uk
www.thecricketers.co.uk

The large, neatly maintained, white-painted 16th century inn is located at the Newport end of the village and is the family home of Jamie Oliver - it was in this kitchen that the young Jamie first discovered his passion for cooking. Within, are highly polished wood tables, gleaming brass knick-knacks and glasses, a log fire, and the place has a pleasant, well cared for atmosphere. Light floods in due to the modern open-plan layout: standing timbers that once formed walls dividing the place into small rooms now act as partial dividers. From quite an extensive bar menu there could be pigeon breasts sautéed pink with apple, celeriac and hazelnut dressing, or chargrilled rib-eye steak with artichoke and garlic pesto, with blackboard specials changing everyday. Fish features in a big way with perhaps fillet of sea bass with pizzoccheri and fennel and dill olive oil, or whole plaice, grilled on the bone, served with lemon, sea salt and thyme. The restaurant offers an imaginative set dinner menu with plenty of choice at each course and a blackboard lists a great selection of wines by the glass. The adjacent Pavilion has eight en suite bedrooms, decorated to a very high standard with quality oak furniture and stylish fabrics.

Prices: Set lunch from £20. Set dinner from £26. Main course bar/snack from £6.50. House wine £9.50.
Hours: 10.30-23.00. Closed 25-26 December.
Food served: 12.00-14.00. 19.00-22.00.
Rooms: 14 en suite. Double/twin from £100, singles from £70.
Cuisine: Modern European.
Other Points: No-smoking area in restaurant. Garden. Children welcome. Car park.
Directions: Exit8/M11. Take the A120 west; turn right onto the B1383 to Newport; turn left along B1038 for Clavering. (Map 6, B5)

Water Lily Patisserie & Restaurant

★ ▯ ✗

3A Church Street, Coggeshall, Colchester, Essex CO6 1TU
Telephone: +44(0)1376 564464
paulfarmer5@aol.com
www.thewaterlily.co.uk

It's a real joy to eat at Paul Farmer's charming restaurant set in the heart of a small historic village where antique shops blend with the 16th and 17th century buildings. Simple décor with lots of dark wood, some beams and panelling produces a restful atmosphere. Front of house benefits enormously from the presence of Joanne Farmer. Friendly and smiling, she is just the sort of person to encourage a loyal following of local regulars. Paul was formerly head of banqueting at London's Grosvenor House, and has worked at the Ivy with Mark Hix. All this makes for a cooking style that takes its influences mainly from France and Italy backed up by a lot of confidence and expertise. Much of the repertoire has a cosmopolitan feel to it, be it an intense wild mushroom cappuccino, or halibut provençale lightly seared on the griddle and served with savoy cabbage, fried vegetables and provençale sauce. Desserts are a highlight, showing real skill at pastry work and taking in a passion and white chocolate delice, triple chocolate brownies and tarte aux fraises. Set menus are good value, and a compact, well-chosen, helpfully priced wine list comes by the glass or bottle.

Prices: Set lunch from £10.95. Set dinner £14.50. Main course restaurant from £16.95. Main course bar/snack from £4.50. House wine £13.75.
Hours: 12.00-16.00 (until 14.00 on Sunday). 19.00-23.00. Patisserie open until 19.00 daily. Closed Monday and throughout January.
Food served: 12.00-14.00. 19.00-22.00.
Cuisine: French fusion.
Other Points: No-smoking area. Garden. Children welcome.
Directions: From the M25 take the A12 exit for Kelvedon. Follow the signs to Coggeshall, approximately five miles from the Kelvedon turn off. (Map 6, B6)

The Peldon Rose Inn ★ ▯ ✕

Mersea Road, Peldon, Colchester, Essex CO5 7QJ
Telephone: +44(0)1206 735248
peldon@lwwinebars.com

The fortunes of this historic 600-year-old timbered pub were restored in 2001 when Colchester-based wine merchant Lay & Wheeler decided to rescue it from sad decay. Now, after some careful refurbishment, this locally famous old smugglers inn is back on track, offering good quality pub food and comfortable accommodation. Old-world charm abounds in the ancient bar (standing timbers, 'skull-shattering' beams, antique mahogany tables, huge log fires and leaded-light windows), and in the adjacent dining area (wonky timbered walls, tiled floor and upholstered chairs), contrasting with the light, comfortably stylish rear conservatory. Bar food utilises locally sourced produce, notably Mersea Island fish and oysters. Follow pork and game terrine with red onion marmalade with, say, simply grilled Dover, whole local plaice or cod with decent chips and salad, or braised venison with smoked bacon and field mushrooms. Good sandwich choice, pasta meals and ploughman's lunches, while homemade puddings include chocolate pecan nut tart and steamed apple pudding. Not surprisingly, the short wine list is of superior quality, offering good tasting notes and close to 20 by the glass. Stylishly simple en suite bedrooms sport contemporary colours and furnishings and are well equipped.

Prices: Main course from £6.75. House wine £9.95.
Hours: 11.00-23.00, Sunday until 22.30. Closed 25 December.
Food served: 12.00-14.15. 18.30-21.00, Friday and Saturday until 21.30. Summer until 21.30 every night.
Rooms: 3 en suite. Double/twin room from £60.
Cuisine: Modern and Traditional British.
Other Points: No-smoking area. Garden. Children welcome. Car park.
Directions: On the B1025 south of Colchester, close to the causeway to Mersea Island. (Map 6, B7)

The Whalebone ▯ ▯ ✕

Chapel Road, Fingringhoe, Colchester,
Essex CO5 7BG
Telephone: +44(0)1206 729307

The 250-year-old inn is well worth tracking down for the peaceful valley views from the glorious garden, or for the convivial atmosphere, crackling log fires, and a first-class pint of Ridley's Rumpus. In the light and airy, tastefully decorated interior expect scrubbed pine tables on bare boards and local watercolours on yellow washed walls. Vivien Steed's inventive food is detailed on changing blackboard menus that make sound use of fresh produce, notably West Mersea seafood, game from local shoots, and homebaked breads. Typically, a meal may commence with Mersea mussels in a white wine, garlic, cream and parsley broth, with steak and kidney pudding, lamb's liver and bacon with mash and Madeira sauce, or rack of lamb with parsnip purée and port sauce for main course. Good desserts include rice pudding with apricot compote, and triple chocolate brownie with homemade vanilla ice cream. The short list of wines offers a global choice and good tasting notes; five available by the glass. Open from 10am all week for hearty breakfasts and decent coffee.
Occasional summer music and Shakespearean plays in the garden.

Prices: Main course from £7.95-£12.95. House wine £10.95.
Hours: 10.00-15.00 (until 16.00 at weekends). 17.30-23.00
Food served: 12.00-14.30. 18.00-21.30.
Cuisine: Modern British.
Other Points: No-smoking area. Dogs welcome. Children welcome. Car park.
Directions: Leaving the A12 take the A133 to West Way and turn right. Take third exit at Balkerne Hill roundabout into Southway and then follow the B1025 to Haye Lane. Turn left and left again; the pub is on the crossroads. (Map 6, B7)

Prices: Set lunch £9.95. Main course restaurant from £10.95. House wine £9.95.
Hours: 11.30-15.00. 18.30-23.00.
Food served: 12.00-14.00. 19.00-21.00 weekdays (until 21.30 on Friday and Saturday). Sunday 12.00-15.00 and 19.00-21.00.
Cuisine: Modern European.
Other Points: No-smoking area. Garden. Children welcome. Car park.
Directions: Exit7/M11. Follow the A1124 towards Halstead and follow the signs to Earls Colne. (Map 6, B6)

The Carved Angel ▯ ✕

Upper Holt Street, Earls Colne, Colchester, Essex CO6 2PG
Telephone: +44(0)1787 222330
enquiries@carvedangel.com
www.carvedangel.com

Melissa and Michael Deckers changed this fine 15th-century building from an ailing village boozer to a contemporary gastropub three years ago. Refurbished with style and panache, expect a relaxing, bright and airy conservatory area with deep fireside sofas, and a separate dining area furnished with pine tables and quirky paintings. However, conscious not to be perceived as solely a restaurant, the Deckers have preserved the traditions of a country village pub, namely real ales, log fires, comfortable seating and a convivial, informal atmosphere. Food is taken seriously, and the evolving blackboard menus list an imaginative range of modern British dishes, with odd forays abroad for inspiration. Speciality breads dipped in olive oil and balsamic vinegar pots left on the table preceed pan-fried snapper on crushed potatoes with Asian dressing. Move on to beef fillet with sesame bok choi and Thai-flavoured jus, or chargrilled monkfish with wilted spinach, garlic mash and herb butter sauce. Leave room for chocolate tart with orange syrup. Good-value set lunch menu and regular theme nights that celebrate regional cuisines. Excellent wines include Michael's special selection; 14 by the glass. Super decked terrace for al fresco dining.

Southend-on-Sea, Essex

Prices: Set lunch £15.95. Main course from £12. House wine £10.50.
Hours: 11.00-14.30. 17.30-23.00. 12.00-16.00. 19.00-22.30 on Sundays.
Food served: 12.00-13.45. 18.45-21.45. Sunday 12.00-14.15. 19.00-21.45.
No food served Bank Holiday Mondays.
Rooms: 15 en suite. Rooms from £50. Suites from £75.
Cuisine: Modern British.
Other Points: No-smoking area. Children welcome. Courtyard. Car park.
Directions: Exit30/31 of M25. Follow A13 for Tilbury and Grays and then A128; follow tourist signs. (Map 6, C6)

Bell Inn & Hill House ★❑◗✕◈

High Road, Horndon-on-the-Hill, Essex SS17 8LD
Telephone: +44(0)1375 642463

Family-run for some 60 years, with John and Christine Vereker currently at the helm, this medieval inn is renowned by dint of its culinary ambition, but it is definitely still a pub. Beams, old photographs, flagstone floors, panelled bars, testify to the simple pubby appearance, as do five changing micro-brewery real ales. There's a trick to eating here. Either book in the restaurant or take first come, first served in the bar where, if no table is vacant, they take your name and you wait, propping up the bar in true pub fashion, until one is free. The menu, chalked up on several boards, is lengthy and lively. It reflects a contemporary understanding of modern ideas and imaginative pairings, say, pancetta roasted cod brandade with black pudding dim sum, or rib-eye steak with caramelised onion and gremolata sauce. The selection of British cheeses should gladden the hearts of wine lovers who want to continue exploring the Bells' outstanding wine list, but puddings such as lemon and cardamom tart, are backed up by an impressive dessert wine list. It is worth noting that there are stylish bedrooms divided between the inn and Hill House, next door.

Lion and Lamb

Stortford Road, Little Canfield, Great Dunmow, Essex CM6 1SR
Telephone: +44(0)1279 870257
info@lionandlambtakeley.co.uk
www.lionandlambtakeley.co.uk

On the A120 between Takeley and Great Dunmow and overlooking farmland yet easily accessible from the M11 (with Stanstead Airport a few miles away), this popular family dining pub is 200 years old in parts. Both the character bar and modern dining room extensions feature open brickwork, log fires, exposed pine, oak beams and a wealth of decorative memorabilia. Outside is a large garden, with a children's Wendy house making it a popular spot for families at weekends. The varied menu is a cut above the norm, with traditional favourites done well - Sunday lunch rare roast rib of beef with Yorkshire pudding, for example - and plenty of modern touches such as local handmade Dunmow sausages with mash and onion gravy, roasted salmon with coriander and chilli crust, Thai chicken, and chargrilled tuna with mango, pineapple and sweet chilli salsa. Fish comes directly from Billingsgate. For a light snack try the gruyère and dry-cured ham panini or a hearty cheese ploughman's lunch. The small family owned Ridleys Brewery in Essex provide beers that are worth sampling; six wines are offered by the glass.

Prices: Sunday set lunch £16. Main course restaurant meal from £8.50. Main course bar meal from £5. House wine £10.75.
Hours: 11.00-23.00. 12.00-22.30 Sunday.
Food served: 12.00-22.00. 12.00-21.00 on Sunday.
Cuisine: Traditional/Modern British.
Other Points: No-smoking area. Children welcome. Garden. Car park.
Directions: Exit 8/M11, and take the B1256 east to Takeley and Dunmow. Pub on the left just after entering Little Canfield. (Map 6, B6)

The Stour Bay Café

39-43 High Street, Manningtree, Essex CO11 1AH
Telephone: +44(0)1206 396687
jaynewarner@ukonline.co.uk

Together with Fordwich in Kent, Manningtree claims to be the smallest town in the UK, so finding this fine-looking, green-painted Suffolk town house should not be difficult. Within, among the beams, wood flooring, exposed brickwork and bright orange-painted walls covered with paintings and candle holders, new owners Jayne and Andrew Warner are proving that lightning can strike in the same location more than once – they have turned this landmark little restaurant into their own proud legacy. The Bay in question is an inlet on the River Stour, and the style of food reflects the location with a strong emphasis on fish. The uncomplicated modern menu delivers eight or so dishes per course, including salad of smoked eel, kipfler potato and sweet-cured bacon, as well as roast turbot on the bone with cockle and herb butter, and meaty dishes such as duck liver and foie gras terrine with macerated prunes and oranges, and pork steaks on crushed black olive potatoes. The set lunch is quite a bargain. The atmosphere is helped by informal and friendly service that sets a busy pace without making people feel rushed. The global wine list is very reasonably priced and offers six red and six white by the glass.

Prices: Set lunch £11.50. Set Sunday lunch £14.50. House wine £12.50.
Hours: 12.00-14.00. 19.00-21.30 (Sunday 12.00-14.30 only). Closed Monday, Saturday lunch, Sunday evening and first two weeks January.
Cuisine: Modern British.
Other Points: No smoking. Children welcome.
Directions: A137 from Colchester to Manningtree. Stour Bay Café is situated on the High Street. (Map 6, B7)

Black Buoy Inn

Black Buoy Hill, Wivenhoe, Colchester, Essex CO7 9BS
Telephone: +44(0)1206 822425
enquiries@blackbuoy.com
www.blackbuoy.com

A great location on winding narrow streets less than 100 yards from the River Colne and its bustling quay is one of the reasons for tracking down this 16th-century riverside pub, formerly three fisherman's cottages and now Wivenhoe's oldest trading inn. Beams, nooks and crannies and a real old fashioned atmosphere combined with decent Suffolk ales and popular bar food prepared from fresh ingredients are further reasons for visiting this friendly local. Old favourites include lunchtime rolls, jacket potatoes, ploughman's lunches and a hearty 'late' breakfast, as well as liver and bacon, lamb steak with garlic and rosemary and chargrilled rump steak with hand-cut chips. Look to the chalkboard for the day's fresh fish, local game in season and, perhaps, lobster from the local fishermen. If you have room try one of the good British nursery puddings. There's a sound wine selection and, most importantly, parking hidden away to the rear. Still in existence, although not in use, is an 18th-century smuggler's tunnel that ran from the quay to the inn's cellar and St Mary's Church.

Prices: Main course from £7.25. House wine £7.50.
Hours: 11.30-15.00. 18.30-23.00. 12.00-16.00 and 19.00-22.30 on Sunday. Closed 1 January evening.
Food served: 12.00-14.00. 19.00-21.00 (21.30 on Friday, Saturday and Sunday). 12.00-15.00 Sunday lunch.
Cuisine: Traditional English.
Other Points: No-smoking area. Children welcome. Car park.
Directions: From Colchester take the A133 towards Clacton, then the B1027 and B1028. In Wivenhoe turn left into East Street (after the church). (Map 6, B7)

The Old Passage Inn ★ ◗ ✕ ✍

Passage Road, Arlingham, Gloucestershire GL2 7JR
Telephone: +44(0)1452 740547
oldpassageinn@ukonline.co.uk
www.fishattheoldpassageinn.co.uk

On the banks of the River Severn, with wide views across to the village of Newnham, this formerly no frills ferry inn has morphed nicely into a stylish restaurant with rooms. Jo Moore, daughter of hotelier and restaurateur Somerset Moore, has created a relaxed look, one that's bright, airy and modern, with the restaurant getting the best out of the river views and leading out to a summer patio. The emphasis on fish is clear from the shellfish tank on display in the entrance. Upstairs are three upscale bedrooms complete with modem points, sound systems and good bathrooms. As a place to eat, or to take a short break, the Old Passage has proven immensely popular with booking essential. Patrick Le Mesurier runs the kitchen, building his menus around West Country produce. Shellfish platters, lobsters and oysters feature, but a knack of using first class ingredients to best advantage is seen in harmonious dishes such as smoked eel with a carrot salad dressed with coriander oil and creamed horseradish, and steamed turbot (at the peak of freshness), with dilled cucumber and fresh citrus segment dressing contributing an extra dimension. A few meat dishes run to organic lamb sausages, or Severn Vale Aberdeen Angus fillet steak.

Prices: Main course from £10.50. House wine £10.50.
Hours: 12.00-14.00. 19.00-21.00 (until 21.30 on Friday and Saturday). Closed all day Monday, Sunday evening and 24-31 December.
Rooms: 3 en suite. Double room from £80, single from £50.
Cuisine: Seafood.
Other Points: No-smoking area. Children welcome over one year old. Dogs welcome. Garden. Car park.
Directions: Exit13/M5. Follow the A38; go through Frampton to the River Severn on the B4170. (Map 4, A7)

Hotel on the Park ◗ ✕ ✍

38 Evesham Road, Cheltenham, Gloucestershire GL52 2AH
Telephone: +44(0)1242 518898
stay@hotelonthepark.co.uk
www.hotelonthepark.co.uk

The Grade II house, built in 1830, has been renovated with a lavish touch by Darryl Gregory, using lots of bold colours and personal touches such as the collector's edition Scrabble and Monopoly sets in the small, intimate library, and teddy bears tucked into corners. Regency house details are picked up in dramatic black and cream striped wallpaper on the stairs and landing, and in highly individual bedrooms that run to chinoiserie and dramatic use of greens, reds and golds. All bedrooms are different, filled with antiques, sofas (some rooms have separate dressing/sitting areas), and a sense of comfort is uppermost. The teddy bear motif runs throughout, and every room contains dressing gowns, and CD players. The drawing room is dramatic: high ceilings, lots of black, plenty of cushions, a long bar for drinks. Across the corridor is the Bacchanalian Restaurant, a lovely room with soaring columns and a black and white tiled floor. Produce comes from the Vale of Evesham and delivered on a set price menu (with supplements). Risotto of goats' cheese and rocket with thyme marinated tomatoes, to start perhaps, with mains including roasted Gressingham duck breast on Savoy cabbage and beetroot dauphinoise, and pudding of creamed vanilla rice with raspberry sorbet.

Prices: Set lunch £17.95. Set dinner £22.50. House wine £12.45.
Hours: 12.30-13.45. 19.00-21.00, until 21.30 Saturday and Sunday from 19.30-21.00
Rooms: 12 en suite. Double/twin from £104.50. Single from £82.50.
Cuisine: Modern British.
Other Points: No-smoking area. Dogs welcome by prior arrangement. Children welcome over eight years old. Car park.
Directions: On the A435 Evesham Road, five minutes on foot from the centre of town. (Map 4, A7)

The Red Lion ◗ ✕ ✍

Lower High Street, Chipping Campden, Gloucestershire GL55 6AS
Telephone: +44(0)1386 840760
theredlioninn@btopenworld.com

Former wine merchant, Roger Lee has taken over this 16th century (and earlier) Cotswold stone inn on the High Street. The framework was already there, an evocative interior of bare stone walls, leaded-light windows, polished flagstone floors, convivial bar and cosy dining alcoves, but Roger has taken the place by its scruff, cleaned it up, improved the décor (menus likewise, under Jean Lee's supervision), and revamped the rear patio. There are still minor things to do in the five quiet, quaint bedrooms across the courtyard in converted former stables, with new showers planned, and telephones to be installed. The buying policy in the kitchen extends to well-sourced local produce with the menu highlighting "Flavours of the Three Counties" where prominence is given to Gloucestershire, Worcestershire, and Herefordshire produce, with named suppliers. Summer lunches have brought fresh tuna, anchovies, olives and egg, as well as chicken, wild mushroom and coriander pancakes. In the evenings, there could be seared scallops with potato purée, crisp bacon and herb oil, and Gloucester Old Spot chop, sun-dried tomato, basil and grain mustard mash. The 30-bin wine list is classified by style, is strong on the new world, kind on price, and has six wines by the glass.

Prices: Main course from £10.50. Main course bar/snack from £5. House wine £11.50.
Hours: Monday 17.00-23.00. Tuesday-Sunday: 10.00-23.00.
Food served: 12.00-14.30. 18.00-21.00. Closed Monday lunch.
Rooms: 5 en suite. Double/twin from £70. Four poster £80. Single from £55.
Cuisine: Traditional British.
Other Points: No-smoking area. Children welcome. Garden. Car park.
Directions: In the centre of Chipping Campden. (Map 4, A8)

Hotel on the Park, Cheltenham, Gloucestershire

The Bell at Sapperton

Sapperton, Cirencester, Gloucestershire GL7 6LE
Telephone: +44(0)1285 760298
thebell@sapperton66.freeserve.co.uk
www.foodatthebell.co.uk

Restored and refurbished with style in 2000 by Paul Davidson and Pat Le-Jeune, the 300-year-old Bell continues to go from strength to strength. Civilised in every way, exposed stone walls, polished flagstones, bare boards, open log fires and individual tables and chairs set the style; added touches include tasteful wine prints, daily newspapers and fresh flowers. Use of fresh produce is the key to the popularity of the seasonally-changing menu and includes homemade bread, fish from Cornwall and local organic and rare breed meats, notable beef from the Cirencester Park herd. Follow warm Cerney goats' cheese on saffron and fruit couscous, or lobster risotto, with confit shoulder of lamb on roast garlic mash, and chargrilled thyme chicken with garlic risotto and wild mushrooms. Fishy options from the daily blackboard menus extend the choice to include, perhaps, seared king scallops with pancetta and stir-fried greens. Good walkers' snack menu lists a hearty three-cheese ploughman's. Three real ales, including the excellent local Uley brews, and the wine list has 14 by the glass and is strong on single-supplier wines. There's a secluded rear courtyard and landscaped front garden for summer imbibing.

Prices: Main courses from £9.75. Main course (bar/snack) from £6. House wine £12.50.
Hours: 11.00-14.30. 18.30-23.00. 12.00-15.00. 19.00-22.30 Sunday. Closed the evening of 25 December, 31 December and 1 January.
Food served: 12.00-14.00. 19.00-21.30.
Cuisine: Modern British.
Other Points: No smoking area. Garden. Children welcome over ten years (before 18.30). Car park. Tethering rail for horses.
Directions: J15/M4, J11A/M5. Midway between Stroud and Cirencester. Follow signs off the A419 to Sapperton village. (Map 4, A7)

The Organic Farm Shop Café

Abbey Home Farm, Burford Road, Cirencester, Gloucestershire GL7 5HF
Telephone: +44(0)1285 640441
info@theorganicfarmshop.co.uk
www.theorganicfarmshop.co.uk

One of no more than a dozen Soil Association Certified organic cafés in the country, Hilary Chester-Master's expanding business is located on her organic farm north of Cirencester. The recently enlarged café, set adjacent to her well stocked organic shop and education centre – the Green Room (where seminars and cooking demonstrations are held) - offers a vegetarian menu inspired by the seasonal produce from the farm. Here, one can expect delicious fresh salads (broad bean, feta and mint), homemade soups, quiches and pasties, alongside a good range of cakes and generously filled rolls and sandwiches; there's also a take-away menu. Hilary opened her Organic Farm Shop at Abbey Home Farm in June 1999. Her objective was to establish a market garden and to offer fresh local organic produce, including eggs, beef, lamb and pork from Abbey Home Farm, direct to the local community. The highly labour intensive 15 acre vegetable growing area which surrounds the shop produces over 230 varieties of vegetable, herbs, soft fruit and cut flowers for the shop and café.

Prices: Main course £6.75.
Hours: 09.00-16.00. Saturday till 15.30.
Cuisine: Vegetarian and vegan/special diets.
Other Points: No-smoking area. Children welcome. Terrace. Car park.
Directions: Two miles north of Cirencester just off the A417. (Map 4, A7)

Prices: Main course from £6.95. House wine £9.95.
Hours: 08.00-23.00. 09.00-22.30 on Sunday. Closed 25 December evening.
Food served: 12.00-14.00 (14.30 on Sunday). 18.45-22.00 (21.30 on Sunday).
Rooms: 11 en suite. Double room from £80, single from £60.
Cuisine: Modern British.
Other Points: Children welcome. Garden. Car park.
Directions: Junction 15 or 17/M4. From Cirencester, take the A429 towards Malmesbury. On reaching Kemble turn left to Ewen. (Map 4, B7)

Wild Duck Inn

Ewen, Cirencester, Gloucestershire GL7 6BY
Telephone: +44(0)1285 770310
wduckinn@aol.com
www.thewildduckinn.co.uk

The Cotswold-stone Elizabethan inn is well worth seeking out. Creeper-clad, with well-tended gardens and lawns, and a lavender-lined entrance path, the building creates a favourable first impression. The bar brims with character, atmosphere and appeal, with rich burgundy walls festooned with old portraits and hunting trophies. The restaurant's labyrinth of small rooms offer dining space amid dark beams, more burgundy walls and wooden tables and chairs; the same printed menu is available throughout, along with daily changing blackboard specials. The lively repertoire draws the crowds with its modern edge and realistic pricing, perhaps a one-course lunch of Wild Duck burger with bacon, cheese, and chips, or pan-fried Cajun chicken with wild rocket salad, spicy fries and lemon mayonnaise. Dinner could run to game terrine with port wine and raspberry jelly, and fillet of red bream poached in a seafood laska with prawns, mussels, spring onion, and lime. The compact, globetrotting wine list offers some 26 by the glass, and the bar has six real ales. And, for those wishing to uncork a few bottles without driving home, 11 en suite bedrooms offer traditional comforts, two in the oldest part of the building have four-posters and overlook the garden.

The Wyndham Arms Hotel

Clearwell, The Royal Forest of Dean,
Gloucestershire GL16 8JT
Telephone: +44(0)1594 833666
nigel@thewyndhamhotel.co.uk
www.thewyndhamhotel.co.uk

A historic, traditional inn that is over 600 years old and set in the heart of the 27,000 acre Forest of Dean. It is filled with oak beams, flagstones, exposed original red brick and has ancient Clearwell Castle (now a wedding/function venue) literally next door. Bedrooms, however, are much more recent (1990s) and in an adjacent building. They are spacious and well equipped with well-lit tiled and modern en suite bathrooms.

New owners Nigel and Pauline Stanley, and chef Ewan Jones are very hot on local foodstuffs. These can include seasonal game from Lydney Park Estate, single herd meats, Gloucester Old Spot pork products, Brooks local ice cream, and real ales from Freewinners in the forest and Orchard Ciders from Brockweir in the Wye Valley. They are also active in the community cooperative for supplies of vegetables, salads and herbs, and local farmhouse cheeses. Translated on the menu, this brings ham hock and pork terrine with spiced pear chutney, pan-fried venison with parsnip rösti and a juniper berry sauce, or monkfish tail with mash, ratatouille and tomato cream sauce, and lemon tart with a warm fruit coulis, or lemon sorbet to finish.

Prices: Main course from £8.95. House wine £10.95.
Hours: 11.00-23.00. Sunday 12.00-22.30. Closed the first week of January.
Food served: 12.00-14.00. 19.00-21.30. Sunday 12.00-14.30 and 19.00-21.00.
Rooms: 18 en suite. Single from £45, double from £85.
Cuisine: Modern British.
Other Points: No-smoking in the restaurant. Dogs welcome. Garden. Children welcome. Car park.
Directions: Exit2/M48. Via A48 and B4228 signed Forest of Dean, 12 miles from Chepstow. (Map 4, A6)

New Inn At Coln

Coln St-Aldwyns, Cirencester,
Gloucestershire GL7 5AN
Telephone: +44(0)1285 750651
stay@new-inn.co.uk
www.new-inn.co.uk

The handsome Elizabethan-coaching inn, considered one of England's finest inns, was rescued from near-dereliction by Brian and Sandra-Anne Evans in 1992. Tastefully-furnished rooms within include the Courtyard Bar with its hop-adorned old beams, flagstone floors, stone walls and open fires. Here an ambitious modern bar menu is offered, built around notably fresh, quality materials. Choice ranges from updated classics, such as local game pie, and smoked bacon and roast baby onions with new potatoes, to modern British combinations of black pudding and cheddar cheese hash browns, apple purée and Meaux mustard,. You will also find with a decent pint of Butcombe or Hook Norton and eight wines by the glass. Dinner in the candlelit dining room sees Sarah Payton's more adventurous fixed-price menu deliver a starter of warm goats' cheese and potato terrine with tomato and mustard seed chutney, and a main course of Parma ham-wrapped roast pork fillet with potato and leek dauphinoise, black pudding and sweet onions. Self-styled as 'a private castle of comfort', smart overnight accommodation is in 14 beautifully furnished en suite bedrooms that boast some fine antiques.

Prices: Set lunch £25 and dinner £31. Main course bar meal from £8.50. House wine £12.50.
Hours: 11.00-23.00. 12.00-22.30 on Sunday.
Food served: 12.00-14.00 (until 14.30 on Sunday). 19.00-21.00 (until 21.30 on Friday and Saturday).
Rooms: 14 en suite. Double room from £115, single from £85.
Cuisine: Modern British.
Other Points: No-smoking area. Children welcome over 10 years old. Terrace. Car park.
Directions: Village signed off B4425 Cirencester to Bibury road or A417 Cirencester to Fairford road. J15/M4. (Map 4, A8)

The Hare and Hounds

Fosse Cross, Chedworth,
Gloucestershire GL54 4NN
Telephone: +44(0)1285 720288

The refurbished country pub's 14th-century charms are apparent in its bare stone walls, flagstones, sturdy oak beams, ancient staircases, and small nooks and crannies, while urns, brass kettles and bed warmers around the fireplaces maintain pub-style traditions. The three huge stone fireplaces, including one with a working bread oven, are lit in the morning, keeping the place cosy all day. There's also a modern conservatory that holds two tables and allows a lot of light to filter through. The regularly changing menu picks up on Mediterranean and Eastern influences but doesn't neglect traditional favourites. Local produce features venison, pheasant, pigeon, veal, and steak, as well as an award-winning goats' cheese from North Cerney. Terrine of pigeon and spiced pickle wrapped in Parma ham and served with a mustard and thyme vinaigrette, and fillet of beef coated in fines herbes, with wild mushrooms and a port wine sauce, typify the style. The wine list is short and well priced, with nine by the glass.

Prices: Bar main course from £5.50. Restaurant main course from £8.95. House wine £9.95.
Hours: 11.00-15.00. 18.00-23.00.
Food served: 12.00-14.30. 19.00-21.30.
Cuisine: International.
Other Points: No-smoking area. Garden. Children welcome. Car park.
Directions: A429 north of Cirencester going towards Stow. 10 minutes from Cirencester, 20 minutes from Stow-on-the Wold and Bourton-on-the-Water. (Map 4, A8)

White Horse

Cirencester Road, Frampton Mansell, Gloucestershire GL6 8HZ
Telephone: +44(0)1285 760960
www.cotswoldwhitehorse.com

Looks can be deceiving. Many driving past this unprepossessing stone pub, set hard beside the A419 between Stroud and Cirencester, would not give it a second glance. But step inside, and you will find a stylishly-refurbished, individual interior with brightly-painted walls adorned with unusual modern art, sisal carpeted floors, chunky tables and colourful cushioned chairs. Shaun and Emma Davies transformed the fortunes of this once ordinary pub. Modern menus are built around fresh produce from quality local suppliers: meat comes from Chesterton Farm butchers near Cirencester who specialise in rare and traceable breeds, and fish is delivered twice-weekly from Looe in Cornwall. Top-quality vegetables are used creatively, for example, carrot purée carries a hint of cumin; in addition, chips are handcut and bread is baked daily on the premises. Typical dishes include duck leg confit with chorizo sausage and balsamic, and black bream with braised fennel and a caper and chive cream. White and dark chocolate mousse may appear on the pudding menu. Sourcing everything locally extends to real ale, so expect interesting brews from Hook Norton, Uley and Arkells breweries. The global selection of wines focuses on smaller growers with six by the glass or 50cl pot.

Prices: Set lunch and dinner £20. Main course from £8.95. Main course bar meal from £4.95. House wine £10.75.
Hours: 11.00-15.00. 18.00-23.00. 12.00-16.00 on Sunday. Closed Sunday evening and 24-25 December.
Food served: 12.00-14.30. 19.00-21.45. 12.00-15.00 on Sunday.
Cuisine: Modern British.
Other Points: Children welcome. Garden. Car park.
Directions: J15/M4. J13//M5. Between Cirencester and Stroud on the A419. On the main road, not in the village of Frampton Mansell itself. (Map 4, A7)

Over Farm Market

Over, Gloucester, Gloucestershire GL2 8DB
Telephone: +44(0)1452 521014
www.over-farm-market.co.uk

Another extensive PYO business that has developed its farm shop into an extensive business not only selling own-grown produce, but also those of local and regional producers. The farm enjoys a long growing season. It gets underway in spring with asparagus and runs through the summer with broad beans, squashes, pumpkins (with the majority sold at the October Pumpkin festival for Halloween), brussel sprouts and onions. Potatoes, however, are the main crop with six varieties grown. A butchery is a recent addition selling locally grown and slaughtered meat. The beef comes from the farm's own herd that grazes along the banks of the River Severn on pasture that is free from sprays and fertilizers, pork comes from Gloucester Old Spots reared near Newent, and the lamb is locally produced. Sausages and burgers are made on the premises. There is also an extensive cheese counter, bakery goods and jams, pickles and mustards.

Hours: 09.00-18.00 Monday-Saturday. 10.00-17.00 on Sunday. PYO 09.00-19.00.
Other points: Parking. Farm animals including water buffalo, ostriches and goats.
Directions: Exit 11/M5. One mile west of Gloucester on north side of A40 dual carriageway. (Map 4, A7)

The Plough at Kelmscott

Kelmscott, Lechlade, Gloucestershire GL7 3HG
Telephone: +44(0)1367 253543

This pretty 17th century inn lies tucked away down single-track roads in a peaceful and totally unspoilt village. It has long been a favourite among Thames path walkers and the boating fraternity. However, new owners have completely refurbished the interior, giving it a stylish, contemporary rustic look, mixing original flagstones and plenty of exposed brick and timbers with a semi-circle pine bar, modern wooden chairs and tables (with quality cutlery and glassware). Matching the surroundings is an imaginative modern British menu. Lunchtime dishes such as stir-fried squid with rice and sweet chilli sauce, grilled gilt head bream with anchovy and parsley butter, and salad niçoise may be taken in small or large portions, while alternatives include speciality platters (assorted charcuterie with chutneys), thick-cut sandwiches, and grilled whole lemon sole. Evening dishes produce pan-fried chorizo, tiger bay prawns, garlic butter and smoked paprika, and beef fillet on swede and carrot purée, colcannon, sweet roasted beetroot and a mustard and tarragon sauce. Puddings run to baked Alaska and hot toffee pudding. Last to be refurbished were the eight en suite bedrooms. One sports an Indian theme and another is decorated in William Morris style.

Prices: Main course bar from £7.50. Main course restaurant from £9.50. House wine £10.50.
Hours: 11.00-15.00 (Sunday 12.00-15.00). 18.00-23.00. Closed Monday and 6-20 January.
Food served: 12.00-14.30. 19.00-21.00.
Rooms: 8 en suite. Single from £45, double from £75. Family room from £85.
Cuisine: Modern British.
Other Points: Children welcome. Garden. Car park.
Directions: Take A416 from Lechlade towards Faringdon; then follow signs to Kelmscott. 20 minutes from Junction 15/M5. (Map 4, A8)

The Fox Inn

Lower Oddington, Stow-on-the-Wold,
Gloucestershire GL56 OUR
Telephone: +44(0)1451 870555
info@foxinn.net
www.foxinn.net

The Fox attracts people from far and wide, drawn by its informal atmosphere and quality cooking - no bookings are taken, so arrive early, as the place fills rapidly. Behind the yellow-stone facade lies a first-class interior. The balance between country brasserie and village pub has been carefully thought out in a succession of rooms that have attractive colour schemes, comfortable, old pine tables on polished slate floors, fresh flowers, background classical music and evening candlelight. Choose from the regularly changing hand-written menu and begin perhaps with courgette and Stilton risotto, or warm salad of chicken livers and cranberries. Follow with grilled organic sausages with celeriac and potato purée and Cumberland sauce, or homemade beefsteak and brown ale pie. There's a Sunday sirloin beef roast (served rare) and simpler lunchtime snacks like toasted ciabatta with ham, tomato and cheese. Homemade puddings may include apple and almond bake with crème anglaise, and treacle tart. Super overnight accommodation in three individually furnished bedrooms, each kitted out with antique wooden beds, quality fabrics and spotless, well-equipped bathrooms. Walled cottage garden and patio.

Prices: Main course from £7.95. House wine £11.25.
Hours: 12.00-15.00. 18.00-23.00. 19.00-22.30 on Sunday. Open all day Saturday and Sunday in summer. Closed 25 December.
Food served: 12.00-15.00. 18.30-22.00. 12.30-15.00 and 19.00-21.30 on Sunday.
Rooms: 3 rooms, 2 en suite. Double/twin room from £58.
Cuisine: Traditional and Modern British.
Other Points: Children welcome. Garden. Car park.
Directions: Off the A436, three miles from Stow-on-the-Wold towards Chipping Norton. (Map 9, E3)

The Wheatsheaf Inn

West End, Northleach,
Gloucestershire GL54 3EZ
Telephone: +44(0)1451 860244
caspar@wheatsheafatnorthleach.com
www.wheatsheafatnorthleach.com

The setting of this stone-built former coaching inn is apparently everything anyone could wish for, with an outlook on to the broad main street of a historic Cotswold wool town, flagstone floors, beams, log fires and lots of old wood. The bar deals in cask-conditioned ales from small local breweries and a blackboard menu, and the classy, understated dining room is marginally more formal. Modern British favourites are inspired by what is available locally, warm pigeon salad with summer berries, and Gloucester Old Spot pork chop with apple mash, for example, or cod in beer batter and chips. Lemon posset, or Eton mess are classic desserts, with local cheeses making a savoury alternative. Small blackboards list special wines of the moment, and the well-annotated list offers some impeccable choices on a globally inspired list; 20 are offered by the glass. As a weekend retreat the Wheatsheaf can hardly be faulted, offering some of the best value in the area. Eight en suite bedrooms are available, and though they currently lack the effortless rustic chic of the downstairs bar and restaurant, size, character and comfortable furnishings are ample compensation.

Prices: Main course from £7. Main course bar/snack from £4. House wine £10.50.
Hours: 12.00-23.00. Sunday until 22.30.
Food served: 12.00-15.00 (Saturday 12.00-18.00). 19.00-22.00, Sunday until 21.00.
Rooms: 8 en suite. Double/twin from £55, single £45, family £65.
Cuisine: Modern British.
Other Points: Garden. Dogs welcome in bar only. Children welcome. Car park.
Directions: Village just off A429 between Stow-on-the-Wold and Cirencester. Exit 15/M4. (Map 4, A8)

Butchers Arms

Sheepscombe, Painswick, Gloucestershire GL6 7RH
Telephone: +44(0)1452 812113
bleninns@clara.net
www.cotswoldinns.co.uk

Set in the heart of *Cider with Rosie* country, with glorious views over the rolling Stroud Valley, this mellow-stone pub dates from 1620 and was originally a butchery for deer hunted in Henry VIII's deer park. The pub sign showing a butcher supping a pint of ale with a pig tied to his leg is famous. As part of Jonny Johnston's small Blenheim Inns group of pubs, it dispenses a good range of beers - Hook Norton, Wye Valley Dorothy Goodbody's Golden Ale and local guest brews, perhaps Uley Old Spot - and offers an interesting choice of traditional and modern pub food. The homely, rustic bar and adjoining beamed dining room are the setting for cooking that relies on locally sourced raw materials such as handmade sausages from Jessie Smith in Dursley, smoked fish from Severn and Wye Smokery, and fresh fish and game from Cooks in nearby Minsterworth. Also on the menu there could be lunchtime snacks like homemade soups, filled rolls, Caesar salad and a decent ploughman's lunch. Evening additions include local trout, prime steaks and daily specials such as lamb shank braised in honey and garlic with mash.

Prices: Main course from £7.50. Bar snack from £4. House wine £8.95.
Hours: 11.30-14.30 (until 15.00 on Saturday). 18.30-23.00 (from 18.00 on Friday and Saturday). 12.00-15.30 and 19.00-22.30 on Sunday. Closed 25 December evening.
Food served: 12.00-14.30 (until 15.00 on Sunday). 19.00-21.30.
Cuisine: Modern and Traditional British.
Other Points: No-smoking area. Children welcome. Garden. Car park.
Directions: Junction 11a/M5. Just off the A46 between Cheltenham and Stroud, near Painswick. (Map 4, A7)

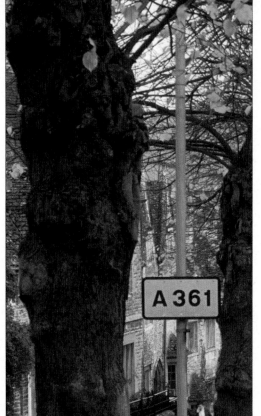

Autumn Cotswolds, Gloucestershire

A 361

The Falcon Inn

New Street, Painswick, Gloucestershire GL6 6UN
Telephone: +44(0)1452 814222
bleninns@clara.net
www.falconinn.com

Built of mellow Cotswold stone in 1554, this handsome coaching inn and former courthouse stands opposite the church with views across a rolling Cotswold scene. The inn's colourful history takes in staging cockfights and, in 1794, was the site of the first Masonic ceremony in Gloucestershire; it's also the setting of the world's oldest bowling green. Interconnecting bar and dining areas are full of traditional character, the scene set by stone, tiled or carpeted floors, wood panelling, open log fires, and a mix of wooden benches and more formal furnishings. The food is reliant on local produce, notably local shoots, butchers meats and specialist vegetable suppliers. Regularly changing blackboards list the likes of organic pork loin with cider, honey and apple sauce, or braised venison with root vegetables and bramble jus, and fish dishes such as whole lemon sole with lemon and black pepper. Twelve en suite bedrooms are split between the main building and the converted coach house. All are individually decorated, with four-poster rooms in the inn and more up-to-date colours, fabrics and furnishings in the coach house accommodation. Televisions, tea trays, telephones, hair dryers and clock-radios are standard throughout.

Prices: Set lunch £12 and dinner £16. Main course £7.50. Bar snack from £4. House wine £8.95.
Hours: 11.00-23.00. 12.00-22.30 on Sunday. Closed 25 Dec evening.
Food served: 12.00-14.30 (until 15.00 on Sunday). 19.00-21.30 (until 22.00 on Saturday).
Rooms: 12 en suite. Double room from £65, single room from £45.
Cuisine: Modern and Traditional British and European.
Other Points: No-smoking area. Children welcome. Garden. Car park.
Directions: Junction 11a/M5. Painswick is on the A46 between Cheltenham and Stroud. (Map 4, A7)

Prices: Main course restaurant from £6.95. Main course bar from £5.95. House wine £9.95.
Hours: 11.00-15.00. 18.00-23.00. Sunday 12.00-15.30.
Food served: 12.00-14.00. 18.45-22.00. Sunday 12.00-14.30. 18.45-21.45.
Cuisine: Modern British/Oriental and Thai.
Other Points: Dogs welcome. Garden. Children welcome. Car park.
Directions: Exit17/M4. Village signposted off A419 between Swindon and Cirencester at Cerney Wick (B4696). (Map 4, B7)

The Bakers Arms

Somerford Keynes, Cirencester, Gloucestershire GL7 6DN
Telephone: +44(0)1285 861298
wduckinn@aol.com

Set in the heart of a pretty Cotswold village, this sizeable pub dates from the 15th century, and comes with an attractive garden and courtyard under a vine-covered arched trellis with summer tables and chairs. There's a lovely traditional feel to the bar, from the large open fireplace to the dark red plaster walls and the low beamed ceiling. Yet it is a comfortable, charming room brightened up with oil paintings, hops hanging over windows, and a large framed mirror, An extension offers diners their own room, overlooking the courtyard and garden. Meat and vegetables are locally produced and appear on chalkboards that list a choice of mainly traditional pub food, say soup, lasagne, hot chilli with rice and soured cream, beer-battered fish and chips, and steak and kidney pie. However, more contemporary dishes run to grilled goats' cheese with Mediterranean vegetables and salsa, deep-fried squid rings with salad and lemon mayonnaise, or salmon steak with herb crust and tagliatelle. The short wine list is very well annotated, offers excellent value with most wines under £15; two wines are available by the glass and there are a couple of half bottles. Wadworth 6X, Bakers Dozen and Bombadier are on tap.

Eagle and Child

Digbeth Street, Stow-on-the-Wold, Gloucestershire GL54 1BN
Telephone: +44(0)1451 830670
ihfo@theroyalisthotel.co.uk
www.theroyalisthotel.co.uk

Alan and Georgina Thompson have transformed Stow-on-the-Wold's the Royalist - reputed to be the oldest inn in England - keeping an eye for metropolitan sophistication and producing a country hotel noted for good taste and urbane comfort. The attached pub, the Eagle and Child, is the social hub, delivering pub food that manages to be both rustic and seriously accomplished, served in modest, unassuming surroundings. Informality and flexibility go hand in hand with flagstone floors, beams, simple furnishings; the light flooded conservatory offering a striking contrast to dark wood. There's a range of pub classics, but the sausages with onion gravy are local, the fish freshly beer battered and the chips exemplary. And the menu stretches further, delivering marinated venison with bubble and squeak, and sea bass with aubergine caviar, sun-dried tomato and pea risotto. This is satisfying food, based on unfussy descriptions and straightforward ideas. Success is founded on prime raw materials and sound technique. Farmhouse cheeses are kept in good condition and puddings run to sticky toffee pudding with vanilla ice cream and banana fritters with toffee sauce. Hook Norton Best Bitter and Timothy Taylor Landlord are on handpump and wines offer fair drinking at fair prices.

Prices: Set lunch and dinner £14. House wine £12.50.
Hours: 12.00-23.00 (until 22.30 on Sunday).
Food served: 12.00-14.30. 18.00-22.00. 12.00-15.00. 18.00-21.00 on Sunday.
Rooms: 8 en suite. Single room from £50, twin from £70 and double from £90.
Cuisine: Modern British.
Other Points: No-smoking area. Children welcome. Car park for residents only.
Directions: 20 miles south of Exit15/M40 on A429. On entering Stow-in-the-Wold turn into Sheep Street. (Map 5, B3)

The Trouble House

Cirencester Road, Tetbury,
Gloucestershire GL8 8SG
Telephone: +44(0)1666 502206
enquiries@troublehouse.co.uk
www.troublehouse.co.uk

Michael and Sarah Bedford run this refurbished Wadworth pub in rural Gloucestershire, with great enthusiasm. The setting may be rustic, with scrubbed tables, wooden floors, hop-adorned beams, open fires and pastel-painted walls, but Michael's inspired modern cooking continues to please, drawing restaurant tourists prepared to travel across the Cotswolds for a table - do book, as trade is brisk. Sound ideas and techniques, attention to detail and use of first-class ingredients results in honest, full flavoured and robust cooking, notably lamb broth with new potatoes and peas, or braised ox cheek with horseradish mash and roasted swedes. A deft touch is also evident with mushroom tart with soft poached egg, and poached pink sea bream with herb risotto. Round off with chocolate tart or a plate of fine farmhouse cheeses. In addition to Wadworth 6X and Henry's IPA on handpump, expect a short, sensibly priced list of wines with eight by the glass. The Trouble House is uniquely named after a series of unfortunate events at the pub, namely agricultural riots, two suicides and a disastrous fire. And amongst the various ghosts reported to haunt the place, there's a lady in blue who is only visible to women.

Prices: Main course from £12. House wine £11.
Hours: 11.00-15.00. 18.30-23.00. 12.00-15.00 and 19.00-22.30 on Sunday. Closed 25 December-4 January.
Food served: 12.00-14.00. 19.00-21.30. No food on Monday.
Cuisine: Modern British and French.
Other Points: No-smoking area. Children welcome over 14 years old. Garden. Car park.
Directions: One and a half miles from Tetbury along the A433 towards Cirencester. (Map 9, F2)

Corse Lawn House Hotel

Corse Lawn, Tewkesbury,
Gloucestershire GL19 4LZ
Telephone: +44(0)1452 780771
enquiries@corselawn.com
www.corselawn.com

The Hines' elegant Queen Anne country hotel is like no other: a laid-back retreat that exudes the charm and imitation (with English nobs on) of a French auberge. There are no bold design, striking colours or fabrics here, just quiet country good taste as seen in soft tones, standard lamps and country prints. Bedrooms are spacious. Even in the newer parts, where it is very hard to see the join, large beds, sofas, fresh fruit, mini fridges with fresh milk, are standard in every room. A big plus is the heated swimming pool in a see through dome in the garden. Baba Hine's kitchen matches the setting with admirable aplomb, skimping neither on quality nor finesse in both the bistro and the restaurant. In the latter, a set meal could take in cream of cauliflower soup with truffle oil and croutons, roast best end of lamb with Provençale mash and aubergine crisps, and lemon tart with lemon ice cream. There's an extensive carte, say terrine of game with chicory and pear salad and blackberry salsa, and roast whole dab on the bone with tartare sauce. The peerless choice of wines by the glass is what one would expect of the descendants of one of France's noblest wine houses.

Prices: Set lunch £18.50. Set dinner £27.50. Main course restaurant meal from £15. House wine £11.50.
Hours: 11.00-23.00. 12.00-22.30 on Sunday. Closed 24-26 December.
Food served: 12.00-14.00. 19.00-21.30 restaurant and brasserie.
Rooms: 19 en suite. Single room from £85, double from £130.
Cuisine: Anglo-French.
Other Points: No-smoking area. Garden. Children welcome. Car park.
Directions: Exit1/2/M50. Five miles south-west of Tewkesbury on the B4211. (Map 4, A7)

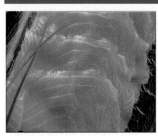

Severn & Wye Smokery

Chaxhill, Westbury on Severn, Gloucester, Gloucestershire GI14 1QW
Telephone: +44(0)1452 760190
info@severnandwye.co.uk
www.severnandwye.co.uk

The reputation for quality has been maintained for some 30 years at this stone-fronted smokery on the A48 south of Gloucester. The whole process, from filleting to slicing, is still done by hand using time-honoured skills. As the smokery is situated on the edge of the Forest of Dean, between two of England's most celebrated salmon rivers (the Severn and the Wye), they are able to call on local fishermen who still use all the traditional fishing methods (long and lave nets, puchin weirs to stopping boats), to provide supplies of the very best wild salmon; the fish is available both fresh in season, and smoked all year round. Such is the quality of all the smokery produce that they deliver to the food halls at Harvey Nichols, Selfridges, and to a number of top chefs. Mail order expands the business, and smoked wild salmon, as well as smoked Scottish salmon, mackerel, halibut, kippers, trout and eel fillets, chicken, and duck, are all available.

Cuisine: Smokery/fishery`
Other Points: Welcome children. Car park.
Directions: J11/M5. Go west on the A40 and turn onto the A48 to Chepstow, the smokery is on the right after approximately nine miles. (Map 4, A7)

The White Hart Inn ★ ◗ ✕ ◔

High Street, Winchcombe, Cheltenham,
Gloucestershire GL54 5LJ
Telephone: +44(0)1242 602359
enquiries@the-white-hart-inn.com
www.the-white-hart-inn.com

For a taste of Swedish hospitality head for this 16th-century former coaching inn, refurbished with impeccable taste by Nicole and David Burr. Nicole is from Stockholm and a Scandinavian influence runs through the cool elegance of the minimalist dining room, as well as the opulent Victorian restaurant, extending to the eight stylishly decorated bedrooms. It also influences the contemporary menus - even the chefs and front of house staff are Swedish. In the traditional pubby front bar, order pints of local Stanney Bitter, and team it with a bar meal of a trio of Gloucester pork sausages with wholegrain mustard mash and onion gravy. But there's also salmon fishcakes served with dill mayonnaise, Swedish meatballs, or a trio of Scandinavian open sandwiches – freshwater prawns, homemade pickled herrings, and gravad lax. In the restaurant, order something more traditional, perhaps rack of English lamb (served pink) with ratatouille. Beef and lamb come from the Sudeley Castle Estate, and other supplies are sourced as locally as possible. Individually designed and decorated bedrooms offer a high level of comfort, with modern facilities and luxury en suite bathrooms.

Prices: Set lunch £12.95 and dinner £17.95. Main course restaurant meal from £11.95. Main course bar meal from £5.95. House wine £10.95.
Hours: 08.00-22.00. Closed 25 December.
Rooms: 8 en suite. Single room from £55, double from £70.
Cuisine: Modern British with Scandinavian specialities.
Other Points: No-smoking area. Children welcome. Patio. Car park. Meeting facilities.
Directions: Exit 9/M5. In the centre of Winchcombe on the B4362 Cheltenham to Stratford road. (Map 5, B2)

The Hampshire Arms ◗ ✕

Pankridge Street, Crondall, Farnham,
Hampshire GU10 5QU
Telephone: +44(0)1252 850418
paulychef@hantsarms.freeserve.co.uk
www.thehampshirearms.co.uk

Behind the Hampshire Arms unpretentious pub exterior, chef-proprietor Paul Morgan is a dynamo of energy and culinary dedication. His passion for fresh food and quality ingredients extends to making everything on the premises, including breads, ice creams and chocolate petit fours. Presently, Pauls stage of a conventional carpeted pub bar, popular with local drinkers, a traditional lounge with open log fire and hop bines and simple, unpretentious rear dining room, fail to compliment the style and quality of his food. However, come the autumn of 2003, this will all change as Paul has major refurbishment plans. Seasonally changing menus offer an intelligent and well balanced range of modern dishes. This might translate as game terrine with fruit chutney and walnut loaf, or scallops wrapped in bacon with bubble and squeak and a leek and chive sauce to start. Brill with green pea risotto, and sautéed crayfish tails and clams in garlic could follow, or slow-roasted lamb shank with butter bean and pesto mash and vine tomatoes. Finish with winter berry crumble or choose from an impressive cheese board. Filled baguettes and lighter dishes are also available at lunchtime.

Prices: Main course from £14.50. House wine £9.95.
Hours: 11.00-15.00. 17.30-23.00.
Closed one week over Christmas.
Food served: 12.00-14.00. 19.00-21.30.
No food Sunday evening.
Cuisine: Modern British.
Other Points: No-smoking in the restaurant. Garden. Children welcome. Dogs welcome in bar area.
Directions: Exit 5/M3. Take the A287 for Farnham, turn off at Crondall. (Map 5, C4)

The Golden Pot ⓓ ✕
Reading Road, Eversley, Hampshire RG27 0NB
Telephone: +44(0)118 973 2104
jcalder@golden-pot.co.uk
www.golden-pot.co.uk

John Calder took over this 18th-century, creeper-clad brick pub in February 2003. It was a natural progression: the long-standing licensees were friends and John is committed to maintaining the pub's reputation as a foodie destination in north Hampshire. Although there have been subtle changes to the menu, the famous rösti remains a regular. With John came chef Lewy, who, with admirable dexterity, prepares an extensive menu from fresh ingredients in his small kitchen. Typical starters include roasted scallops wrapped in smoked salmon and served with celeriac puree, or wild mushrooms with basil-infused ciabatta. Among the main courses, creamed spinach and Madeira sauce accompanies roasted wing chop of veal, and basil mousse with a tarragon and red wine sauce come with a trio of lamb cutlets. Lighter meals and interesting daily blackboard specials, say Cajun chicken with Caesar salad or hot smoked salmon and prawn salad, are served throughout the two civilised and relaxing bar areas and the more formal restaurant. Sunday lunches are very popular, so are the puddings such as lemon torte and summer pudding. A sound list of wines (ten by the glass) is complemented by Greene King ales on handpump.

Prices: Main course restaurant from £10. Main course bar from £6.50. House wine £12.50.
Hours: 11.00-15.00. 17.30-23.00. Sunday 12.00-15.00. Closed Sunday evening during the winter.
Food served: 12.00-14.15. 19.00-21.15. Sunday 12.00-14.00. Bar food served from 18.00.
Cuisine: Modern British.
Other Points: No-smoking area. Dogs welcome on a lead. Garden. Children welcome. Car park.
Directions: Exit4/M3 and Exit11/M4. Eversley Cross is on B3272 north of Yateley, south of Finchampstead. (Map 5, C4)

Rose and Thistle ⓓ ✕
Rockbourne, Fordingbridge, Hampshire SP6 3NL
Telephone: +44(0)1725 518236
enquiries@roseandthistle.co.uk
www.roseandthistle.co.uk

Originally two 17th-century thatched cottages, this delightful, long, low whitewashed pub has a tranquil setting in a picturesque downland village. The low-beamed interior is unspoilt, tastefully furnished with polished oak tables and chairs, carved benches and cushioned settles, and features two huge fireplaces with winter log fires. Country-style fabrics, dried flowers, and magazines add to the civilised atmosphere. Quality pub food, served in the civilised, music-free lounge-cum-dining area, is up to date, and sensibly light and simple at lunchtimes. Note daily homemade soup, 'elegant' Welsh rarebit, local sausages and mash, and ploughman's (rare roast beef with horseradish sauce). Evening dishes are more elaborate, featured on a monthly-changing menu and daily specials' board. Typical dishes include roast rack of lamb, beef medallions with Stilton and port sauce, and fresh fish (also available lunchtimes), such as mackerel fillets with creamy mustard sauce, roast cod with lemon and black pepper crust, and John Dory stuffed with lime and coriander butter. Traditional bread and butter pudding, seasonal game from local shoots, Sunday roasts (booking advised), good ales and wines.

Prices: Main course bar from £7.45. Main course restaurant from £10. House wine £9.95.
Hours: 11.00-15.00. 18.00-23.00. 12.00-22.30 on Sunday. Closes at 20.00 on Sunday from October to March.
Food served: 12.00-14.30. 19.00-21.30. No food Sunday evenings in winter.
Cuisine: Modern British.
Other Points: No-smoking area. Children welcome. Garden. Car park.
Directions: From Salisbury take the A354, turn off at the signpost to Rockbourne. From Fordingbridge take the Sandleheath road and at the crossroads turn right to Rockbourne. (Map 4, C8)

Prices: Main course restaurant meal from £10.50. House wine £10.25.
Hours: 11.00-15.00. 19.00-23.00. Closed Sunday evening, all day Monday, 25 December and 1 January.
Food served: 12.00-15.00. 19.00-23.00.
Rooms: 2 en suite. Double room from £62.75.
Cuisine: Modern British and European.
Other Points: No-smoking area. Children welcome. Garden. Car park. Credit cards not accepted.
Directions: A303/M3. Signed left for Longstock, one mile north of Stockbridge, off the A3057. (Map 5, D3)

Peat Spade Inn ⓓ ✕
Longstock, Stockbridge, Hampshire SO20 6DR
Telephone: +44(0)1264 810612
peat.spade@virgin.net

Unusual paned windows overlook the peaceful village lane and idyllic heavily thatched cottages at this striking, redbrick and gabled Victorian pub in the heart of the Test Valley, only 100 yards from the famous trout stream. Walkers hiking the Test Way long-distance path will find the pub a convenient lunchtime pit stop (good downland walks to Danebury Hillfort). Although you will find decent Hampshire ales on handpump, the place feels more like a restaurant, and this is backed up by some serious pub food which is served throughout the uncluttered and neatly furnished bar and the elegant, pine-furnished dining areas. Chef/proprietor Bernie Startup uses local and organic produce where possible, including game from Leckford Estate and vegetables from Warborne Organics in the New Forest, in a sound repertoire of dishes that offers some rewarding modern cooking. Menus change every three weeks and may offer squash and almond soup, Hereford beef and red wine casserole, duck and chorizo tagliatelle with paprika cream, and baked lemon cheescake. Lighter lunchtime dishes include warm salads and decent sandwiches. Two comfortable bedrooms are very good value and make a good base for trout fisherman and visitors exploring the beautiful Test Valley.

The Bush Inn

Ovington, Alresford, Hampshire SO24 ORE
Telephone: +44(0)1962 732764
thebushinn@wadworth.co.uk
www.wadworth.co.uk

Located just off the A31 on a peaceful lane, this
unspoilt 17th-century rose-covered cottage enjoys an
idyllic village setting, just yards from one of
Hampshire's famous chalk trout streams. Inside, the
rambling series of softly-lit bars boast dark-painted
walls, an assortment of sturdy tables, chairs and high-
backed settles, and a wealth of old artefacts and old
hunting prints. On cold winter days the place to sit
with a pint of excellent Wadworth ale is in front of the
roaring log fire, while perusing the blackboard menu
above the fireplace. Chef/landlord Nick Young uses
quality ingredients, notably Angus beef, Loch Fyne
seafood, and local game, in preparing his daily
changing range of dishes. Begin, perhaps, with smoked
trout mousse or freshly-made leek and potato soup,
and follow with duck leg confit with sweet potato
chips and dressed leaves; chargrilled fillet steak with
Roquefort cheese and balsamic roasted cherry
tomatoes; grilled whole bass with mushroom sauce, or
peppered venison on spiced red cabbage with whisky
and sherry vinegar sauce. The pudding board may
highlight rum and banana crumble with banana ice
cream. Those desiring a lighter snack will find decent
sandwiches and ploughman's lunches.

Prices: Main course from £8. House wine £10.
Hours: 11.00-15.00. 18.00-23.00. 12.00-15.00 and 19.00-22.30 on
Sunday. Closed 25 December.
Food served: 12.00-14.00. 19.00-21.00. Sunday 12.00-14.00 only.
Cuisine: Modern British.
Other Points: No-smoking area. Dogs welcome. Garden. Car park.
Directions: Junction 10/M3. Village is signposted off the A31
between Winchester and Alresford. (Map 5, D3)

Ship Inn

White Hill, Owslebury, Winchester,
Hampshire SO21 1LT
Telephone: +44(0)1962 777358
theshipinn@freeuk.com

Set beside a quiet country lane of the edge of the
village, its tile-hung façade brightened by flower-
festooned tubs and baskets, this 300-year-old pub,
originally called the Britannia, has a splendid garden
and lovely views across Winchester and the Solent. The
knocked-through main bar is packed with oak beams,
standing timbers (from an 17th-century ship), a large
open fire and sporting and naval mementoes - all the
trappings of a traditional country inn. However, the
restaurant opens into a bistro-style extension, which
matches the ambitious food. Dishes such as Thai
crabcakes with hot chilli dip, smoked haddock rarebit
with spinach mash, roasted vegetables and white wine
sauce, braised lamb shank with roasted vegetables and
red wine sauce, and rib-eye steak with pepper sauce,
set the pace. Daily specials may take in locally made
wild boar sausages and award-winning faggots, with
snacks running to toasted ciabattas and homebaked
ham, egg and chips, in addition to Sunday roasts and a
summer garden menu. At the bar, expect to find
Greene King ales alongside excellent Pots Ale from the
local award-winning Cheriton Brewhouse, and a
blackboard list of twelve wines by the glass.

Prices: Main course from £6.95. House wine £10.
Hours: 11.00-15.00. 18.00-23.00. 11.00-23.00 on Saturday.
12.00-22.30 on Sunday.
Food served: 12.00-14.00. 18.30-21.30. 12.00-21.30 on Saturday.
12.00-21.00 on Sunday.
Cuisine: Modern British/traditional English.
Other Points: No-smoking in the restaurant. Children welcome.
Dogs welcome in the old bar. Garden and patio. Car park.
Directions: J11/M3. Follow B3335 and signs to Marwell Zoo. The
Ship Inn is two miles north, past the entrance. (Map 5, D3)

Durleighmarsh Farm Shop
Rogate Road, Petersfield, Hampshire GU31 5AX
Telephone: +44(0)1730 821626

The scenic PYO and farm shop is surrounded by 350 acres of farmland and the family run barn of a shop offers a good selection of PYO and ready picked fruit and vegetables. They kick off the season with asparagus (for which Durleighmarsh is famous), and go on to new potatoes, soft fruits including red and white currants, gooseberries, tayberries, cherries, plums, strawberries, and broad beans, sweetcorn and spinach. You can pick your own bunches of culinary herbs and everything, both in the fields and in the shop, is well labelled so you can tell whether it is own grown or bought in. They stock a good range of local produce ranging from bacon and cheese to ice cream, cakes jams and chutneys.

Hours: From Oct to March: 09.00-17.00 Monday to Saturday, Sundays 09.00-13.00. Then April, May and September 09.00-17.30 and June-August 09.00-19.00.
Other points: Parking. Picnic area. Cottage garden plants and herbs including dried flowers.
Directions: 5 minutes from Petersfield on the A272 Rogate Road. 1mile west of Rogate, signposted. (Map 5, D4)

The Selborne Arms
High Street, Selborne, Alton, Hampshire GU34 3JR
Telephone: +44(0)1420 511247
info@selbornearms.co.uk
www.selbornearms.co.uk

Selborne was made famous over 200 years ago by the writings of the clergyman and pioneer naturalist Gilbert White, who lived at The Wakes, a large house (open) overlooking the green and church. Just along the road is the Selborne Arms, a traditional and simply furnished village local, which provides welcome refreshment to the many walkers and tourists that throng to this village. Food is a cut above the norm, everything being freshly prepared by chef/landlord Nick Carter, and served in the two homely bars which sport hop-strewn beams, wooden floors, and a huge fireplace with a roaring winter log fire. Weary walkers can tuck into the good-value lunchtime buffet (soup, cold meats, cheese, salads and fresh crusty bread), or order one of Nick's speciality sandwiches, perhaps the 'Selborne Feast' filled with pastrami, roast beef, salt beef and Swiss cheese. In addition to more traditional choices: homemade curry; ploughman's lunches; steak and kidney pie, the daily changing chalkboard menu may list rich salmon tagliatelle, half-roast peppered duck with orange, elderflower and coriander sauce, lamb shank on celeriac purée with lamb gravy, and venison steak with confit shallots, roast artichoke and red wine sauce. Handpumped ales include brews from local micro-breweries; eight wines by the glass.

Prices: Main course restaurant from £6.95. Main course bar from £4.95. House wine £8.95.
Hours: 11.00-15.00. 18.00-23.00. Sunday 12.00-22.30. Open all day Saturdays during the summer.
Food served: 12.00-14.00. 19.00-21.00.
Cuisine: Modern International.
Other Points: Garden with childrens play area. Children welcome. Car park.
Directions: Village on B3006 between Alton and A3 near Liss, 4 miles south of Alton. (Map 5, D4)

The Restaurant at Wickham Vineyard
Botley Road, Shedfield, Hampshire SO32 2HL
Telephone: +44(0)1329 832985
erica@wickhamvineyard.co.uk
www.wickhamvineyard.co.uk

Tucked away behind the vineyard shop and buildings, the restaurant looks out across acres of vine groves, and, on a warm summer day, one might almost believe this were Bordeaux. Within, a light, clean, contemporary look blends harmoniously with the vinous surroundings. Modern paintings, sculptures, and glasswork continue the theme. French doors open on to a patio, and, along with a full-length picture window, provide a perfect vista across the vineyard. The cooking takes its lead from the décor and strikes the same contemporary note, with modern, well-constructed dishes at set prices for two or three courses (lunch is particularly good value), with a lengthier repertoire offered in the evening. Dish descriptions are mercifully light on adjectives, perhaps oxtail or maybe pumpkin soup with chives and plentiful froth, or terrine of slow-roast pigeon and foie gras. Mains might take in roast cod with spiced lentils and celery choucroute, or braised shank of lamb with Lyonnaise potatoes and rosemary jus. Desserts, perhaps a chocolate délice with raspberry sorbet help to round off a good showing. Wickham wines, available by the glass or bottle, open the list, backed up by a further house selection with a global slant that is echoed throughout the main list.

Prices: Set lunch £17.50. Set dinner £31. House wine from £11.
Hours: 12.00-14.00. 19.00-21.30. Closed all day Monday and Tuesday, three weeks at Christmas and the week over August Bank Holiday.
Cuisine: Modern British.
Other Points: Totally non smoking. Children welcome. Terrace, garden and vineyards. Car park.
Directions: Halfway between Botley and Wickham on the A334, exit 7 or 10/M27. (Map 5, D4)

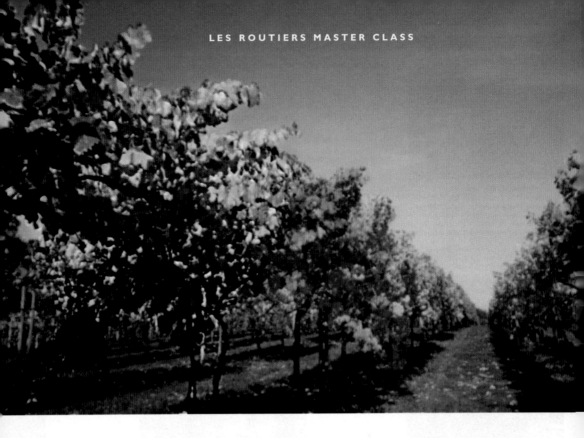

Why go all the way to Burgundy or Bordeaux, wonders David Hancock as he takes a tour around Wickham Vineyard in Hampshire.

The resurgence of English vineyards has been remarkable. Pioneered by Sir Guy Salisbury-Jones, who planted the first commercial vineyard at Hambledon in Hampshire in 1952, small vineyards now abound in southern England. The best sweep from Norfolk in the east to Wiltshire in the west, but most are found in the counties of Kent, Sussex and Hampshire.

Although the main hazard for the English grower is still the weather, milder winters and warmer summers, combined with modern wineries and expert advice from successful American and Australian vignerons, has seen wine production in Britain grow to a sizeable industry. Over four hundred vineyards, both large and small, cultivate over two thousand acres of land dedicated to wine-production throughout England, Wales and the Channel Islands, proving beyond doubt that wine can be produced successfully and to a high quality in this country.

For those with experience of visiting vineyards, particularly those of famous French châteaux, a tour of an English vineyard will strike a very different chord. The whole affair is more relaxed and informal than in France, particularly for the novice or mildly interested party, and you will not find locked gates, frosty welcomes or staged and often over-elaborate presentations.

This is particularly true if you visit the vineyard and winery at the beautiful Wickham Estate in Hampshire. Situated on the gentle south-facing slopes of the Meon Valley, a mile from the Hamble estuary, the vineyard was established in 1984 and now covers 18 acres of the 40-acre estate, with further planting being planned Gordon and Angela Channon were new to the complex business of wine making when they took over the estate in 1999, the necessary and very steep learning curve from wine drinkers to experienced vignerons

DESTINATION WINE

assisted by a globe-roaming Australian consultant. Currently the vineyard produces between 40,000 and 50,000 bottles per year and offers a good choice of wine styles from dry white through to oaked red and traditional method sparkling wine.

Arranged around a courtyard of stylishly converted barns, the modern estate complex comprises a high-tech winery filled with gleaming steel fermenting vessels and oak barrels, a tasting room and shop, storage facilities, and a first-class restaurant with picture windows and vineyard views.

The art of wine making conquered, the Channon's set about re-invigorating the marketing side of the business, producing a new brochure advertising their improved vineyard tour and wine tastings. Then, in 2001, chef James Graham took charge of the restaurant. Passionate about local produce, he offers contemporary modern menus to match the excellent Wickham wines and the serene setting. The perfect finale, following a fascinating tour of the estate.

To take a tour of the vineyard with Angela as guide and experience her passion and knowledge for wine and the day-to-day running of the vineyard first hand, you will have to be part of a group (minimum 15, maximum 45). However, individuals can stroll among the vines and listen to Angela through a highly acclaimed audio tour, which covers the same ground in equal depth.

After a brief history of wine making in England, from the introduction of vines in AD280 by the Romans to its current revival in the mid-20th century, Angela details the development of the vineyard since 1984. Moving from the newer vines (5 years old) to the original vines (18 years old), you learn that the grape

varieties grown on the estate originate from Germany or Alsace. Schonburger, Seyval and Faber grapes were chosen for their traditional white wines, a blend of Bacchus and Reichensteiner grapes for the distinctive white fumé that is fermented in French oak barrels, and the robust Pinot Noir and Rondo grapes for the only red wine produced. Unlike most French and southern European vines, these hardy varieties suit the English clay soil and unpredictable climate.

Angela explains that as these vines grow higher above the ground, the delicate flowers that form in late March to early April generally avoid damage from late winter frosts. However, an alarm rings outside her bedroom window if the temperature falls below minus four degrees centigrade. It is then that you realise the challenges that English viticulturists face, that running a vineyard in England is an expensive and time-consuming business, requiring dedication and a scientific approach. Angela details the seasonal work required. As the soil is not ideally suited to vine growing, pruning is essential in January for the vines' energy to be channelled into producing good-quality grapes rather than unnecessary foliage, which can encourage disease. Soil core tests are sent away for analysis and advice is given on whether to add more phosphate or nitrogen for improving the yield. Too much rain during the growing season will encourage fungal diseases so sulphur is liberally applied to the vine to keep mildew at bay, but the balance is delicate, as some rain is required to help the fruit develop. All this culminates in the excitement of the day-by-day monitoring of the sweetness and acidity of the grapes during September, prior to the vendage in late September and early October.

Wickham has one of the most modern and best equipped wineries to be found in England, based on Australian technology and including state-of-the-art Italian steel fermenting vessels and traditional French oak barrels. Every item of the wine making equipment is explained to you, as is the wine making process, from the crushing and pressing of the grapes and the fermentation of the must, to the clarification, filtering and bottling of the wines themselves. Audio-tour visitors have accompanying sounds and music to bring the whole experience in the winery to life. To experience the harvest in full swing, time your visit for October; to view the bottling of the previous vintage ensure you visit during April.

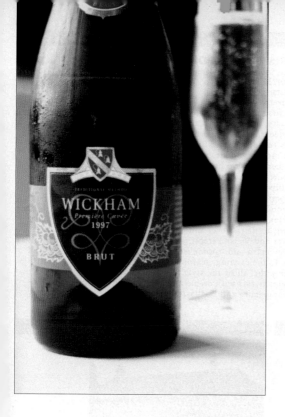

After an hour among the vines and vessels and, hopefully, enlightened and enthused about wine making in Hampshire, it is now time to sample the fruits of the Channons' labours. Group visitors will be treated to a tutored tasting of the Wickham wines, shown exactly how to hold the glass, identify the 'nose' of the wine, how to oxygenate the wine in your mouth to release the flavour, and how to identify between tannins and acidity in the wine. Audio-tour visitors will miss out on this invaluable advice, but can taste the wines in the Tasting Room, where individual bottles, cases of wine and wine accessories, together with local produce and gifts are for sale.

At Wickham Vineyards, Angela and Gordon Channon have succeeded in devising an educational two-hour tour that captivates the visitor. Extend the visit to take in lunch, or, during the summer months, dinner in the restaurant. This showcases Wickham's fine wines and James Graham's inventive cooking in a contemporary, stylishly decorated dining room that looks out across the vines, and, on a warm summer day, one might almost believe this were Bordeaux.

INFORMATION
Vineyard & Shop Open: 10.30-17.30; Sunday 11.30-17.00.
Audio Tours: daily February to December £2.75; £1 children; £2 senior citizens
Group Tours: Monday to Friday (weekends by arrangement) early April to mid October.
Minimum 15, maximum 45 people. £4 per person
For more information telephone 01329 834042
e-mail: angela@wickhamvineyard.co.uk; website: www.wickhamvineyard.co.uk)

Wickham Vineyards, Botley Road, Shedfield, Southampton, Hampshire

The White Star Tavern & Dining Rooms
★ 🍷 ✗

28 Oxford Street, Southampton, Hampshire SO14 3DJ
Telephone: +44(0)2380 821990
manager@whitestartavern.co.uk
www.whitestartavern.co.uk

Southampton's first and long awaited gastropub opened in May 2002 in the old part of city, just minutes from Ocean Village and West Quay. Two young entrepreneurs, Mark Dodd and Matthew Boyle, realised the huge potential of this run-down Irish bar in the city's up-and-coming 'restaurant row' and set about creating a stylish bar and restaurant in what was a former shipping hotel in the days of the Titanic. Smart front lounge areas sport modern brown leather banquettes and cream walls adorned with shipping photographs, yet retain the original flagstone floors and the period open fireplaces. Beyond the large wooden bar, lies the spacious, wood-floored and panelled dining rooms. Good use of fresh produce from Hampshire suppliers can be seen in a snack menu offering hot open sandwiches (roast beef and creamed horseradish), chorizo and rocket bruschetta and Welsh rarebit, and in the lunchtime carte with calf's liver with parsley mash and caramelised onions, and saffron, tomato and spinach risotto. In the evening, seafood chowder, and whole bass stuffed with fennel and garlic, show the style. Homemade breads and puddings (pear and frangipane tart with crème anglaise). There's an impressive list of cocktails, champagnes and vodkas; eight wines by the glass.

Prices: Main course restaurant evening meal from £8.50, lunch from £6.95. House wine £11.50.
Hours: 12.00-15.00. 17.30-23.00. Friday to Sunday open all day. April-October open all day every day. Closed 25-26 December and 1 January.
Food served: 12.00-15.00. 18.00-21.30 (22.00 Friday/Saturday). 12.00-21.00 Sunday.
Cuisine: Modern British.
Other Points: No-smoking area. Children welcome weekend days.
Directions: Exit 14/M3. Take A33 to Southampton and head towards Ocean Village and Marina. (Map 5, D3)

Fox Inn
🍷 ✗

Tangley, Andover, Hampshire SP11 0RY
Telephone: +44(0)1264 730276
thefoxinn@tangley-fsbusiness.co.uk

Well worth the diversion off the A343 north of Andover, the Fox is a remote, 300-year-old white-painted brick and flint cottage that has been dispensing ales since 1830. Located at a fork of tiny lanes and enjoying unspoilt rural views from its front terrace, it offers a welcoming atmosphere within its tiny, rustic bars and homely restaurant. Reliably good food from the blackboard menu, served throughout the pub, includes value-for-money lunchtime snacks and imaginative evening dishes, perhaps crab, salmon and coriander fishcakes, chicken and avocado salad, beef stroganoff, pork steak with lemon and herb butter, supreme of chicken with Boursin, and grilled whole sea bass. Good baguettes are served at lunchtimes only.

Prices: Main course £8. House wine £9.95.
Hours: 11.30-15.00. 18.00-23.00.
Food served: 12.00-14.30. 18.00-21.30.
Cuisine: Traditional English.
Other Points: No-smoking area. Children welcome. Patio. Car park.
Directions: Off the A343, north of Andover. (Map 5, C3)

White Lion
🍷 ✗ 🛏

Fullerton Road, Wherwell, Hampshire SP11 7JF
Telephone: +44(0)1264 860317

Right in the centre of one of Hampshire's prettiest villages, just a stone's throw from the River Test, this 17th-century coaching inn is a thriving community local with a loyal trade. It is also popular lunchtime destination among walkers exploring the beautiful Test Valley. Legend has it that shots fired at Wherwell Priory from Oliver Cromwell's cannons fell short, and one cannon ball fell down the chimney of the inn instead - where it can be seen to this day. The recently re-thatched old coach house to the rear was once a courthouse and mortuary. Traditional English pub food cooked on the premises from carefully sourced fresh ingredients is the key to the popularity of the food here. Eat in the beamed bar where a warming log fire burns in winter, or in the homely dining room. Sample smoked trout from the Chilbolton Estate, handmade sausages and cooked meats from the renowned John Robinson butchers in Stockbridge, or homecooked specials like minted lamb casserole, or pork and cider casserole. There are good salad platters, ploughman's lunches with locally baked bread, and decent baked ham, egg and thick-cut chips. Overnight accommodation is in three homely bedrooms.

Prices: Main course restaurant from £7.50. Main course bar meal from £5.50. House wine £9.75.
Hours: 10.00-14.30 Monday-Friday. 10.00-15.00 Saturday and Sunday. 19.00-23.00 Monday and Tuesday. 18.00-23.00 Wednesday-Saturday. 19.00-22.30 Sunday.
Closed in the evening on the 25-26 December and 1 January.
Food served: 12.00-14.00. 19.00-21.30 (20.30 on Sunday).
Rooms: 3. Double room from £45, single from £32.50.
Cuisine: Traditional English.
Other Points: No-smoking area. Garden. Children welcome over 12 years old. Car park. Folk club.
Directions: A303/M3. Take the A2057 from Andover turning left, on the B3048 to Wherwell. From Stockbridge turn right off the A2057 at Testcombe/Fullerton. (Map 5, D3)

The Red House Inn

21 London Street, Whitchurch, Hampshire RG28 7LH
Telephone: +44(0)1256 895558

Just a short walk from the famous working Silk Mill and the River Test in the heart of Whitchurch, the Red House is a plain, white-painted, 16th-century pub offering decidedly good modern cooking. Using the best local produce available, chef/patron Shannon Wells takes great pride in carefully preparing the imaginative selection of dishes that are listed on the short, seasonally-changing menu and daily specials' boards. With local drinkers using the separate and quite rustic public bar, diners can relax in the tastefully decorated lounge-cum-dining-room (booking advisable), with its fine beech floor, potted plants and huge wall mirrors. Sample chicken, artichoke and feta ravioli with cep sauce, or smoked halibut and red onion tart with red pepper coulis and quails' eggs for starters. Follow with chump of lamb with Parmesan and rosemary polenta and Madeira jus, Cajun salmon on baby spinach with gnocchi and sun-dried tomato butter, or excellent chargrilled steaks. Round off with double chocolate pie, butterscotch sauce and mint cream, or lemon tart with strawberry and rum coulis. Dishes are well presented and service friendly and efficient. Lighter bites include interesting pasta dishes and generously filled baguettes with decent chips and salad. Note the excellent value set menus, tip-top ales from local micro-breweries (try a pint of Pots Ale), and the terraced patio garden beyond the car park for summer al fresco dining.

Prices: Set lunch £16.20. Set dinner £20.25. Main course restaurant from £9.95. Bar snack from £6.95. House wine £10.95.
Hours: 11.30-15.00. 18.00-23.00. Sunday 12.00-15.00. 19.00-22.30.
Cuisine: Modern.
Other Points: No-smoking area. Dogs welcome. Garden. Children welcome. Car park.
Directions: Between Newbury and Winchester off the A34. (Map 5, C3)

The Wykeham Arms

75 Kingsgate Street, Winchester, Hampshire SO23 9PE
Telephone: +44(0)1962 853834

A fine 250-year-old building located in the oldest part of the city near the Cathedral Close has long been regarded as one of the best all-round inns in the country. The rambling series of bars and eating areas are furnished with old pine tables and old-fashioned school-room desks, have four winter fires and quite a collection of hats, tankards, pictures, and military memorabilia. Modern pub food, alongside more adventurous evening choices, attracts food lovers from far and wide. Lunch could be raised chicken pie with apple and stem ginger chutney, goats' cheese risotto with chilli oil and Parmesan, or an upmarket sandwich. In the evening there's an imaginative repertoire of dishes built around fresh ingredients. Begin with winter vegetable soup, move on to seared tuna with coriander couscous and chilli jam, or duck breast with a rich Cassis sauce. Satisfying puddings range from lemon tart to elderflower jelly with strawberry compote. A well-chosen list of wines, complete with personal and informative tasting notes, favours Burgundy and there are 18 by the glass. Stylishly decorated and thoughtfully equipped bedrooms are split between the inn and Saint George, a 16th-century annexe across the street.

Prices: Sunday lunch £14.50 (2 courses) and £18.50. Main course restaurant from £13.95. Main course bar from £6. House wine £11.45.
Hours: 11.00-23.00. Sunday 12.00-22.30. Closed Christmas Day.
Food served: 12.00-14.30. 18.30-20.45. Sunday 12.00-13.45.
Rooms: 14 en suite. Doubles/twin room from £90, single from £50. Suite £135 and four-poster £120.
Cuisine: Modern British.
Other Points: No-smoking area in restaurant. Dogs welcome in bar. Garden. Car park.
Directions: Close to Winchester College and the Cathedral. (Map 5, D3)

The Stagg Inn & Restaurant

Titley, Kington, Herefordshire HR5 3L
Telephone: +44(0)1544 230221
reservations@thestagg.co.uk
www.thestagg.co.uk

The domain of local boy and Roux-trained chef Steve Reynolds, whose passion for food has put this rural local on the culinary map. Steve delves deep into the fine raw materials that the Welsh Borders has to offer, notably fruit and vegetables from local organic farms, and producing seasonally influenced menus that are simply described. He makes just about everything on the premises, including bread and preserves. With his assured, yet restrained touch, exemplary dishes include pan-fried foie gras teamed with Pembridge apple jelly. Interesting flavour combinations include jasmin scented sauce and sultanas partnering Trelough duck, and tomato and ginger sauce with organic salmon fillet. Puddings bring a white chocolate and lemon cheesecake and the first-class selection of twenty Welsh and Herefordshire unpasteurised cheeses, all with excellent tasting notes, are very good value. Or, in the suitably informal surroundings in the homely pine furnished bar, wash down excellent organic local pork sausages with Gregg Pitt's Perry, Ralph's Radnorshire cider or one of ten wines by the glass. Then retire to one of the two en suite bedrooms, with brass beds, antique furniture and thoughtful extras such as fresh flowers, bottled water and cafetière coffee.

Prices: Main course restaurant from £11.50. Main course bar meal from £7.50. House wine £11.90.
Hours: 12.00-14.00. 18.30-22.00 Tue-Sat. 12.00-14.00. 19.00-21.00 Sun. Closed Mon, first two weeks of Nov, 25-26 Dec, 1st Jan, Tue after Bank Holiday and May Day.
Rooms: 2 en suite. Double room from £70, single from £40.
Cuisine: Modern British.
Other Points: No-smoking in dining rooms. Children welcome. Garden. Car park.
Directions: On the B4322 between Kington and Presteigne. (Map 5, A1)

The Verzons

Trumpet, Ledbury, Herefordshire HR8 2PZ
Telephone: +44(0)1531 670381
info@theverzons.co.uk
www.theverzons.co.uk

You get what you see at David Barnett-Roberts' exemplary country inn: tranquil rural surroundings, great views. Indeed, relaxation is the key at this extended Georgian farmhouse that shows its origins throughout with tiled flooring, exposed brickwork and beams, and log-burning stoves. A stylish central staircase leads to quiet, inviting bedrooms with views across to the Malvern Hills. The carefully updated rooms offer all the modern accoutrements (satellite TV, modem points) without detracting from a period style that picks up on the antiques and classic furnishings of the public rooms below. The traditional drift of the menu is the same throughout, whether eating in the bar or dining room, offering reliable country cooking backed up by careful sourcing of local ingredients. Thus, a typical meal could open with trio of game bird terrine with redcurrant and ginger, and go on to pan-fried tenderloin of pork, sautéed greens, chestnuts and warm apple sauce. Blackboards list daily specials, say, smoked haddock fillet with egg pasta and creamed leek sauce. The generously priced house wine selection reveals care in purchasing across a broad spectrum, backed up by such real ales as Hook Norton and Shepherd Neame's Spitfire.

Prices: Main course restaurant from £9.50. Main course bar/snack from £5.50. House wine £9.75.
Hours: 11.00-23.00. Sunday 12.00-22.30. Closed 26 December.
Food served: 12.00-14.00. 19.00-21.30.
Rooms: 8 en suite. Double room from £78, single from £45. Family room from £88.
Cuisine: Traditional and Modern British.
Other Points: No-smoking area. Dogs welcome. Garden. Children welcome. Car park.
Directions: Exit 2/M50. Via A417 Ledbury to A438 Hereford. 12 miles east of Hereford. (Map 5, B1)

Lower Bache House

Kimbolton, Leominster, Herefordshire HR6 0ER
Telephone: +44(0)1568 750304
leslie.wiles@care4free.net
www.smoothhound.co.uk/hotels/lowerbache.htmls

Set in a tiny hamlet, down a narrow country lane, Rose and Leslie Wiles homely, comfortable 17th-century farmhouse is exactly what many are looking for in a B&B. Set in 14 acres of gardens and nature reserve, it used to be a cider mill, and this is incorporated into the lovely, old-style dining-cum-sitting room, with its high vaulted ceiling, stone walls and flagstone floor. The two main house bedrooms are the pick - large suites, with oak beams, separate sitting room and (nice touch) fresh milk with the hot drinks tray. There is also a cottage suite, which is a charming three-room complex. Local farm produce appears on a breakfast menu that spoils with its choice not just bacon and eggs combinations, but the likes of kedgeree as well. Dinner is by arrangement with a small but good selection of wines. Raw materials are, as much as possible, organic and local, and often from their own kitchen garden. Start, perhaps, with home-smoked salmon with caviar, go on to lamb chops with courgette and garlic, sautéed potatoes and vegetables, and finish with classic tarte au pomme. Both Rose and Leslie are delightful, and work hard to make Lower Bache a memorable experience.

Rooms: 3 en suite. Singles £43.50, doubles £33.50 per person.
Other Points: Totally no smoking. Garden. Children welcome over 8 years old. Car park.
Directions: Kimbolton village is two miles north of Leominster (which is off the A49). Lower Bache is signposted at the top of the hill on the Leysters road (A4112). Look out for the white butterfly sign. (Map 5, A1)

Prices: Main course from £9.95.
House wine £8.85.
Hours: 12.00-15.00. 18.30-23.00.
19.00-22.30 on Sunday.
Food served: 12.00-14.00. 18.30-21.30.
19.00-21.00 on Sunday.
Other Points: No-smoking area. Children welcome. Patio. Car park.
Directions: From Ross-on-Wye follow the signs to M50, junction 4 and take the B4221 to Upton Bishop, approximately two miles. (Map 8, E5)

Moody Cow

Upton Bishop, Ross-on-Wye, Herefordshire HR9 7TT
Telephone: +44(0)1989 780470
www.moodycow.co.uk

The older sibling of the Moody Cow at Sibford Gower, Oxfordshire (see entry) and run on the same lines by James Lloyd. The well established original, created in 1993, continues to offer fresh, well-cooked food at good value prices (given the generous portions). An informal atmosphere infuses the pub and country bistro (hop-strewn beams, stripped floorboards and stonework, an eclectic mix of country furnishings), and a rustic restaurant housed in a converted barn. Food is a mix of traditional English and European with a few exotic ideas creeping in for good measure. Although the seasonally changing menu is extensive, everything is freshly prepared on the premises using local meat, fruit and vegetables, and herbs from a farm in the village. Fish and chips is served in newspaper (on request), game is pot-roasted or casseroled, and pork fillet may be marinated in honey, thyme and wine. Snacks and starters include salmon fishcakes with horseradish crème fraîche, and ciabatta open sandwiches. Look to the chalkboard for fresh fish and chef's daily specials, while the pudding menu may highlight hot chocolate pudding. Drink Wye Valley Butty Bach or opt for the very drinkable house wines.

The Pheasant at Ross ★ 🛏 🍷 ✕

52 Edde Cross Street, Ross-on-Wye, Herefordshire HR9 7BZ
Telephone: +44(0)1989 565751
info@pheasants-at-ross.co.uk
www.pheasants-at-ross.co.uk

Eileen Brunnarius cooks like a dream with an eye for detail and flavours that are often inspirational. Her in-depth knowledge of food history, her sourcing of ingredients to accompany the best available produce from Herefordshire and the Welsh Borders, results in a style loosely defined as English, ancient and modern. She adapts many old recipes from a former age when the cooking of today's rare breed meats was commonplace, accompanied by traditional varieties of vegetables, fruits and herbs. Mace butter with crab tart, or roasted pepper sauce with goats' cheese fritters, might be followed by caraway, dates and apple with braised Old Spot pork or black pudding and cider brandy sauce with Ross Cobb chicken breast. Adrian Wells backs this up with his own idiosyncratic views on wine, many of them from the Malvern Fine Wine Company, offering unusual and rare flavours that demonstrate the best of the by-ways of the wine world. As a result, and because The Pheasant holds regular food/wine evenings for private clients, it is usually open for dinner bookings only on Thursday, Friday and Saturday evenings. There is only one sitting and an intimate atmosphere is created in which neither the cook nor the guests are unusually hurried.

Prices: Set dinner £25. House wine £12.50. Open Sunday-Wednesday for groups if booked in advance.
Hours: 19.00-21.30. Thursday - Saturday. Closed Sunday, Monday, Tuesday, Wednesday, first week of June and 22 December-2 January.
Cuisine: Modern British.
Other Points: Totally no-smoking. Children welcome.
Directions: Two minutes from the centre of Ross-in-Wye. (Map 8, E5)

Allt-yr-Ynys Hotel 🛏 ✕ ⬦

Walterstone, Abergavenny, Herefordshire HR2 0DU
Telephone: +44(0)1873 890307
allthotel@compuserve.com
www.allthotel.co.uk

Many original features remain in this beautifully preserved 16th-century manor house which was once owned by William Cecil, chief minister to Elizabeth 1. Note the fine moulded ceiling and oak panelling in the sitting room (a comfortable, classically furnished room) and the Jacobean suite still retains its original oak panelling and 16th-century four poster bed. All in all, there are 19 en suite bedrooms, split between the main house and converted old stables and outbuildings, most with views over the mountains and woodlands. Strikingly decorated, some with canopied beds, tasteful fabrics and furnishings, these offer every modern convenience. This extends to a heated indoor swimming pool and spa pool. The kitchen is loyal to regional and local produce, offering Welsh lamb, beef and cheeses in starters such as braised Brecon faggots on herb mash with a Guinness and honey gravy. Mains could take in best end of Welsh spring lamb baked on a lyonnaise potato and rosemary gateau and served with Madiera gravy, of baked delice of River Wye salmon on a carrot, lemon and herb compote with parsley and cognac cream. Equally appealing are puddings such as mixed berry and vanilla panna cotta with a pear and cinnamon purée.

Prices: Set lunch £16.95 and dinner £25. Main course from £11. House wine £14.75.
Hours: 12.00-15.00. 18.00-22.00.
Food served: 12.00-15.00. 19.00-21.30.
Rooms: 21 en suite. Double room from £85, single from £65.
Cuisine: Modern British.
Other Points: No-smoking area. Children welcome. Garden. Car park. Licence for Civil Weddings. Swimming pool, spa and sauna.
Directions: A465 Abergavenny to Hereford road. Turn off five miles north of Abergavenny at Old Pandy Inn; 400 metres, turn right at Green Barn. (Map 8, E5)

Bell Inn 🛏 ✕

4 Town Lane, Benington, Stevenage, Hertfordshire SG2 7LA
Telephone: +44(0)1438 869270
d&b@bellbenington.co.uk
www.bellbenington.co.uk

Set in a picturesque village close to Benington Lordship Gardens and excellent walking country, the Bell is a well-run 15th-century hostelry that oozes old-world charm. Rug-strewn polished floorboards, wood-burning fires, low beams, sloping walls, and an unusual faded stag-hunt mural set the evocative scene in which to enjoy well-kept Greene King ales and generous homecooked food. Follow a winter country stroll with a hearty meal by the warming wood-burning stove, starting perhaps with a bowl of mussels with tomato, onion and garlic sauce, or a smoked salmon and dill platter. Home-made hamburger with salad and chips, chicken, gammon and leek pie, beef Stroganoff, Angus T-bone steak, and steak and kidney pie cooked in Guinness are popular main courses. Look to the chalkboard for the daily curry and pasta dish alongside, perhaps, calf's liver, lamb shank and pork in Calvados. Pleasant rear garden with rural views for summer drinking.

Prices: Main course from £7.95. House wine £8.95.
Hours: 12.00-15.00. 18.30-23.00 (22.30 on Sunday).
Food served: 12.00-14.00. 19.00-21.30.
Cuisine: Modern British/traditional English.
Other Points: No smoking in dining room. Children welcome over 4 years. Garden. Large carpark.
Directions: Follow brown tourists signs for Benington Lordship from A602 Stevenage to Hertford, or A507 Baldock/Buntingford. (Map 6, B5)

Alford Arms

Frithsden, Berkhamstead, Hemel Hempstead, Hertfordshire HP1 3DD
Telephone: +44(0)1442 864480

Follow the brown signs for Frithsden Vineyard (which is located right behind the pub), to find David and Becky Salisbury's pretty, cream-painted pub tucked away in a tiny hamlet surrounded by unspoilt National Trust land. Styled 'country pub and eating' on the menu, it is just that, offering an informal atmosphere that welcomes both drinkers and diners. Generally, the stylishly modernised interior, with its tiled and wooden floors, old scrubbed pine tables and attractive prints, bustles with folk enjoying imaginative modern British cooking that relies on quality local, free-range and organic produce. Listed on the carte or daily changing chalkboard are 'small plates' of, say, grilled goats' cheese with pan-fried pears, and tomato dressing, or oak-smoked bacon on bubble and squeak with hollandaise sauce and poached egg. Eclectic main courses range from braised lamb shank on spiced Puy lentils with roasting juices, or confit duck leg on risotto cake with damson jus, to twice-cooked chicken breast with bacon, sage, and confit potato cake. Warm treacle tart, spiced apple and blackberry crumble, or warm chocolate brownie, are typical desserts. Great care is taken in presentation of dishes and flavours shine through. Marstons Pedigree, Brakspear and Tetleys are on handpump and a short, sensibly priced list of wines offers 13 by the glass. On warm days tables spill out onto the sun-trap front terrace.

Prices: Main course from £9. House wine £10.75.
Hours: 11.00-23.00. 12.00-22.30 on Sunday. Closed 25-26 December.
Food served: 12.00-14.30 (until 15.00 on Sunday). 19.00-22.00.
Cuisine: Modern British.
Other Points: Children welcome. Garden/terrace. Car park.
Directions: From Berkhamsted High Street, follow signs for Potten End and then Frithsden (Map 5, B4)

The Cabinet

High Street, Reed, Hertfordshire SG8 8AH
Telephone: +44(0)1763 848366
thecabinet@btopenworld.com
www.thecabinetinn.co.uk

The pretty, white clapboard building has been an inn since the 16th century and many original features are still retained, such as low beams, and cottagey windows. TV chef Paul Bloxham has done a superb job, transforming a tired boozer into a contemporary rural gastropub that incorporates locals at the bar drinking Nethergate's Suffolk County, Old Growler, and Adnams Broadside, a 'snug' smoking room with high-backed tobacco-coloured leather dining chairs, and a smart dining room with soft colours, crisp table linen, gleaming glass ware, and fresh flowers. An enthusiastic menu is built around local ingredients such as vegetables from an organic nursery and rare breeds such as Tamworth pigs. The bar lunch menu is a simplified version of what's available in the restaurant - perhaps pan-fried scallops with sun-blushed tomatoes and red pepper vinaigrette, or roasted quail with local mixed greens and lemon garlic dressing. Dinner in the dining room brings carrot and Moroccan preserved lemon soup, duo of Tamworth pork with baby leeks and celeriac puree, and apple tart with lavender ice cream. Outside, a spacious outdoor dining room has been created, with heaters extending the season and an open kitchen with wood-burning rotisserie for cooking Tamworths and free-range chickens.

Prices: Set lunch £15 and dinner £25. Main course restaurant from £13. Main course bar from £5. House wine £12.
Hours: 12.00-15.00. 18.00-23.00. Closed Monday.
Food served: 12.00-14.30. 18.00-22.30. Sunday 12.00-16.00.
Cuisine: Modern French and British.
Other Points: No-smoking area. Dogs welcome in the bar. Garden and terrace. Children welcome. Car park.
Directions: Off A10 betwen Buntingford and Royston. (Map 10, E5)

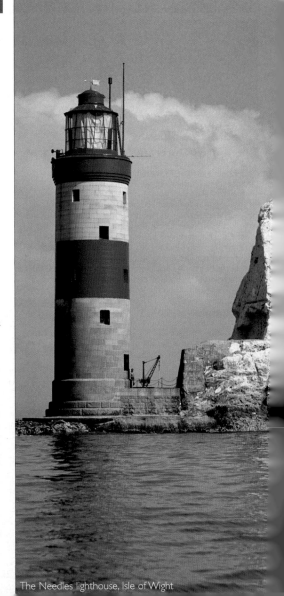

The Needles lighthouse, Isle of Wight

George and the Dragon

High Street, Watton-at-Stone,
Hertfordshire SG14 3TA
Telephone: +44(0)1920 830285
georgeanddragon@virgin.net
www.georgeanddragon-watton.co.uk

First licensed in 1603, this lovely old village pub is difficult to miss as it dominates the village centre with its exterior of pink-painted pebbledash. Inside homely bars, there are exposed beams, open log fires, yellow stained walls hung with paintings, attractive old scrubbed tables, and welcome touches like fresh flowers and the day's newspapers. Despite the rather gentrified trappings, this is still a real pub, offering local gossip, good drinking with tip-top Greene King ales, and a guest beer on handpump. The ambitious choice of starters ranges from Corsican fish soup, tomato, and red onion and pesto tart, to homemade gravadlax with dill, mustard and crème fraîche. Lamb shank braised in red wine, John Dory with chilli and spring onion butter, roast duck breast with red onion marmalade, and prime Aberdeen Angus steaks from the chargrill are typical main courses. Millionaire's bun, which is fillet steak in a toasted roll with salad garnish, is popular, as are lighter options like smoked salmon sandwiches, fishcakes with lime and coriander sauce, and creamy tagliatelle with fresh Parmesan.

Prices: Main course from £7.85. House wine £13.85 a litre.
Hours: 11.00-15.00. 18.00-23.00. Open all day on Saturday.
Food served: 12.00-14.00. 19.15-22.00.
No food on Sunday evening.
Cuisine: Modern pub food.
Other Points: No-smoking in dining area. Children welcome until 21.00. Garden. Car park.
Directions: In the centre of the village on the A602 between Hertford and Stevenage. (Map 6, B5)

Waterfall Hotel

Shore Road, Glen Maye, Peel, Isle of Man IM5 3BG
Telephone: +44(0)1624 844310
jim@breadner.co.uk

The former smugglers' haunt stands at the head of one of the loveliest glens on the island, Glen Maye, and the name relates to its spectacular waterfall. The beach is a short stroll away. This is a family run pub, with three generations currently involved, and the emphasis is on a warm welcome and unpretentious, good quality food at reasonable prices, served all day. All meat served is Manx (steaks are a speciality), queenies are caught locally, as are fresh crab and fish, and spices for the daily curry are imported directly from Goa. If the famous fish and chips or the aforementioned curries do not appeal then a choice for a typical supper could be pan-fried local scallops with a lime and chilli butter, or perhaps lamb cutlets in garlic and rosemary or mint marinade. Whether sitting in the cosy beamed bar and dining area, preferably by the roaring fire in the winter months, or enjoying the warmth on the sun patio in the summer months, this charming pub has a comforting and relaxing atmosphere which is enhanced by its glorious setting.

Prices: Main course from £6.95. House wine £8.25.
Hours: 11.00-23.00.12.00-14.30 and 19.30-22.30 on Sunday. Closed 25 December.
Food served: 12.00-21.30 Monday-Saturday.
12.00-14.00 and 19.30-21.30 on Sunday.
Cuisine: Traditional English/International.
Other Points: No-smoking area. Children welcome. Garden. Car park.
Directions: Three miles south of Peel on the coast road. (Map 11, D1)

The Crab & Lobster Inn

32 Forelands Field Road, Bembridge, Isle of Wight PO35 5TR
Telephone: +44(0)1983 872244
allancrab@aol.com
www.crabandlobsterinn.co.uk

Tricky to locate but well worth the effort, this well established clifftop inn stands above Bembridge Ledge and affords magnificent views across the Solent and English Channel, particularly from the flower-adorned summer terrace. A popular watering hole for coast path walkers, it also attracts locals and visitors for the fresh locally-caught seafood listed on daily changing blackboards. Arrive early for a table as the nautically themed and traditionally furnished bar and dining areas fill quickly, especially during summer months. True to its name, house specialities are the crabs and lobsters that are caught on Bembridge Ledge all year round and served every which way - crab sandwiches and salads, and magnificent crab and lobster platters for two. Meaty alternatives on the straightforward bar menu include homemade lasagne, ham, egg, and chips, and chargrilled sirloin steak with mushrooms and fries. From the restaurant carte, choose from a page of lobster specials (whole with garlic or lemon; as thermidor; or half topped with crab). Otherwise, opt for whole Dover sole, glazed duck with plum sauce or pork fillet with fennel, rosemary and mustard sauce. En suite bedrooms are a recent addition, all are light and airy, kitted out with modern comforts, and enjoy stunning sea views.

Prices: Main course restaurant from £8.25. Main course bar from £5.95. House wine £8.50.
Hours: 11.00-15.00. 18.00-23.00. Open all day Saturday and Sunday 12.00-22.30.
Food served: 12.00-14.30. 18.00-21.30.
Rooms: 5 en suite. £35 per person per night including breakfast.
Cuisine: Modern European.
Other Points: No-smoking area. Dogs welcome. Children welcome. Car park.
Directions: Centre of Bembridge. (Map 5, E4)

The New Inn ⚑✕
Mill Lane, Shalfleet, Isle of Wight PO30 4NS
Telephone: +44(0)1983 531314
martin@thenew-inn.co.uk
www.thenew-inn.co.uk

Built in 1743 on the site of an old 'Church House', this lovely cream-painted former fishermen's pub oozes historic charm, and the original flagstone floors and inglenook fireplaces are thought to be from the original house. Conveniently located on the route of the 65-mile coast path trail and a short stroll from Newtown Creek and Nature Reserve, the pub is a popular watering-hole among the walking and yachting fraternities. The beamed bars also quickly fill with diners, as the New Inn has long been famous for its fresh fish and seafood, with crab and lobster landed at Newtown Quay. Chalkboard menus list the market-fresh choice, perhaps up to 16 types and including local sea bass and mackerel, cod with prawn and peppercorn sauce, sardines with garlic and black pepper butter, and their mammoth seafood platter for two. Carnivores are not forgotten, the menu does extend to prime steaks (with all the trimmings), pork fillet with apple and cider sauce, sausages, mash and onion gravy, and game in winter. More traditional pub meals on printed menus include freshly-cut sandwiches (try the excellent crab), filled baguettes and ploughman's lunches. Wash a satisfying meal down with a first-class pint of Ventnor Golden, which is brewed on the island.

Prices: Set lunch and dinner from £18-£25. Main course restaurant from £12. Main course bar from £8. House wine £9.95.
Hours: 12.00-15.00. 18.00-23.00 (until 22.30 on Sunday).
Food served: 12.00-14.30. 18.00-21.30.
Cuisine: Seafood.
Other Points: No-smoking area. Dogs welcome. Garden. Children welcome. Car park.
Directions: On the main Newport to Yarmouth road (A3054), by the traffic lights in Shalfleet. (Map 5, E3)

The Tiger Inn ⚑✕
Stowting, Ashford, Kent T25 6BA
Telephone: +44(0)1303 862130
willettiger@aol.com
www.tigerinn.co.uk

The Tiger dates from 1676 when Amos Whittell was granted a licence to serve home-brewed ales and cider. A bit of its history is preserved on the exterior - embossed into the rendering are the words Mackeson Hythe Ales. The single front bar is rustic, unpretentious and full of rural charm, with stripped-oak floors, two warming wood-burning stoves, old cushioned church pews, comfortable worn sofas, and sturdy scrubbed tables topped with candles, with a separate restaurant/function room to the rear. Generally filled with locals, the bar is relaxed and informal, and the homecooked food hearty. Chalked up on the blackboard, daily changing dishes range from tiger prawns in garlic with lime and coriander, and baked sea bass with chickpeas and tomato and ginger sauce, to calf's liver with paprika, wild mushrooms and sour cream, and honey-glazed duck with parsnip mash and cumberland sauce. Alongside Everard's Tiger, naturally, tip-top ales include a micro-brewery guest ale. Don't miss the summer barbecues on the front patio, the annual beer festival, and traditional live jazz every Monday evening.

Prices: Main course from £10. House wine £10.30.
Hours: 12.00-15.00. 18.30-23.00. 12.00-22.30 on Sunday. Closed Monday lunch.
Food served: 12.00-14.00. 18.30-21.00.
Cuisine: Global.
Other Points: No smoking area. Dogs welcome. Children welcome. Garden. Car park.
Directions: Exit 11/M20 Go towards Canterbury on the B2068 for three miles then turn left to Stowting. (Map 6, C7)

Prices: Cream tea from £3.85.
Hours: 10.30-17.20. Closed for around three weeks in January.
Cuisine: Traditional tea shop.
Other Points: Totally no smoking. Children welcome. Garden. Car park. Credit cards not accepted.
Directions: Exit 8/M20, and take the B2163 to Sutton Valence, then the A274 to Biddenden. Or, exit 9/M20, then A28 towards Tenterden, then A262 to Biddenden. (Map 6, D6)

Claris's Tea Room ★ ☕
1/3 High Street, Biddenden, Kent TN27 8AL
Telephone: +44(0)1580 291025
info@collectablegifts.net
www.collectablegifts.net.

Claris's has been here for ever: the present owners for 19 years, and the menu virtually unchanged for all that time. It's housed in one of the lovely 15th century half-timbered and brick buildings that make up the high street, and is old fashioned in looks and concept: a small room, with low beams, pretty white lace table cloths and everything served on white crockery. Simplicity is what it's all about here. Sandwiches of Scotch smoked salmon, cheese or ham on brown or white bread, home made tomato soup served with thick slices of hot-buttered toast, creamed mushrooms, poached egg, or baked beans on toast - that's it really. And lovely homebaked cakes: cream laden meringues, chocolate cake, fruit cake, lemon Madeira, Victoria sponge. A lot of custom is just for the cakes and Claris's cream tea is a treat: two homemade scones with a choice of Tiptree jams and fresh cream, and a pot of Indian and China tea (there's also some good herbal and fruit varieties). Unlicensed.

Froggies at the Timber Batts
School Lane, Bodsham, Wye, Kent TN25 5JQ
Telephone: +44(0)1233 750237

Fans of Joel Gross, dismayed by the closure of Froggies in the centre of Wye, are beating a path to the Timber Batts, a 15th-century pub (built in the reign of Henry VII), set in a hamlet deep in the Kent countryside. The place has suddenly gone from being just another rural pub popular with the walking fraternity, to one with an authentic French restaurant attached that is now attracting a broader customer base. The beamed and timbered bar has an inglenook fireplace the size of a small room and, on a lower level, a reception bar that also boasts an open fire, plus a sofa and comfortable seating. The restaurant has its own huge fireplace, more beams, plus old pine tables (some with low back settles), and candles. Favourites from Froggies of Wye days – superb stuffed mussels, a classic duck confit salad, perfect rack of lamb with herbs, or prime fillet of beef with Roquefort sauce – are staples of the printed menu. Profiteroles, tarte tatin or crème brûlée are classic puddings and there's a blackboard listing daily specials and bar snacks. Sourcing is impeccable: game from local shoots, locally-grown vegetables, but cheeses are as French as the wine list, which includes the house wine grown and produced by Joel's cousin in the Loire Valley.

Prices: Set Sunday lunch £18. Set dinner £25. Main course from £12. Main course bar from £6. House wine £12.
Hours: Normal pub hours. Closed Monday and Tuesday following a Bank holiday.
Food served: 12.00-14.30. 19.00-21.30. No food Sunday evening.
Cuisine: Traditional French.
Other Points: No-smoking area. Dogs/children welcome. Garden. Car park.
Directions: Exit 9/M20. Follow signs to Ashford. Take A28 to Canterbury and follow signs to Wye. Carry on and go through Hastingleigh; in half a mile down the hill turn left. (Map 6, C7)

Flying Horse Inn
The Lees, Boughton Aluph, Ashford, Kent TN25 4HH
Telephone: +44(0)1233 620914

Reputed to be the oldest pub in Kent (crystal clear water from a restored well inside the pub was used for brewing in the 15th century), the Flying Horse is benefiting from a fresh look from new landlord Simon Chicken. The four upstairs bedrooms are being renovated, but the 'olde worlde' look of the central bar and restaurant has been retained. There are roaring log fires, inglenooks, lots of beams, and plenty of bric-a-brac. On the lunch and dinner blackboard menus there could be chicken livers with leaves and raspberry dressing to start, garlic mushrooms, or roasted tomato and basil soup. Main courses take in local beef fillet with a mustard and mushroom sauce, salmon fillet wrapped in prosciutto with lentils, spinach and yogurt, and pork chop topped with apple purée and cheddar cheese, and the traditional Sunday roast lunch is very popular. Real ales include IPA, London Pride, and Courage Best, and there is a back bar for private parties. It's covered with climbing wisteria at the front and looks out over the cricket pitch (outside tables mean you can watch a match during the season) and there's a very large garden to rear; there's also plenty of parking space.

Prices: Set lunch £12. Set dinner £16. Main course restaurant from £8. Main course bar from £3.50. House wine £9.50.
Hours: 12.00-23.00, Sunday 12.00-22.30.
Food served: 12.00-15.00, 18.00-21.00. Sunday 12.00-16.00. Closed Sunday evening.
Rooms: 4. Doubles from £40.
Cuisine: Traditional and Bistro.
Other Points: No-smoking area. Dogs welcome. Garden. Car park.
Directions: Exit 9/M20. (Map 6, C7)

The White Horse Inn
53 High Street, Bridge, Canterbury, Kent CT4 5LA
Telephone: +44(0)1227 830249
thewaltons_thewhitehorse@hotmail.com

The white-painted 16th cnetury building wears its age well, looking very pretty in summer with an abundance of flowers in hanging baskets. Two entrances can cause momentary confusion, one leads into the restaurant, the other straight into the traditional looking central bar, which has a magnificent log burning inglenook, wood panelling, and beamed ceiling. This comfortable room dispenses Shepherd Neame's Masterbrew, very good wines from a well-annotated list, and some excellent bar food. Ben Walton spent some time with Michelin-starred chef Samuel Gicqueau at the late Sandgate Hotel near Folkestone, and brings a touch of class to the kitchen. His good-value brasserie menu delivers a satisfying pork and pistachio terrine with a salad of green beans and chutney, herb sausage and leek casserole with garlic and herb mash. Move into the small, stylish restaurant and the cooking impresses with its technique and flair. Start with caramelised calf's sweetbreads and a fricassee of asparagus and morel mushrooms, perhaps, followed by roasted troncon of turbot on a bed of braised Jerusalem artichokes with a champagne sauce. And the hot chocolate fondant with banana ice cream and warm caramel sauce is worth a detour on its own.

Prices: Set lunch and dinner £22.50. Main course from £13.50. Bar snack from £3.75. House wine £11.50.
Hours: 11.00-15.00. 18.00-23.00. Sunday 12.00-16.00. Closed Sunday evenings, 26 December and 1 January.
Food served: 12.00-14.30. 19.00-21.30.
Cuisine: Modern English.
Other Points: No-smoking area. Dogs welcome. Garden. Children welcome. Car park.
Directions: Three miles south of Canterbury off A2 in the centre of Bridge. (Map 6, C7)

The Duke William

The Street, Ickham, Canterbury, Kent CT3 1QP
Telephone: +44(0)1227 721308
carol@thedukewilliam.co.uk

Etched-glass windows overlooking the main village street give the summer flower-adorned Duke William a 19th-century feel, although the pub was in fact built in the early 17th century. There is just one bar, a slightly chintzy room where the brick inglenook fireplace and beamed ceiling hint at the building's real age. Beyond lies the dining area, decorated with collections of old rifles and farming implements, and the conservatory restaurant with its light-wood tables and cane chairs. The separate public bar has a pool table and a vocal, Guinness-loving parrot. Expect a long bar menu, one that runs the whole gamut of popular snacks from baguettes, curries, pizzas and pasta to steak and kidney pie and paella. The equally extensive restaurant menu features meat and fish cooked every which way and highlights additional game dishes in season. Larger-than-life landlord, Alistair McNeill (Mac), and his family have been at the helm for some 20 years now.

Prices: Set menu £15.95, £16.95 at week-ends. Main course from £6.50. House wine £10.20.
Hours: 11.00-15.00 and 18.00-22.00 Tuesday to Saturday. 18.00-22.00 on Monday and 12.00-17.00 on Sunday only.
Cuisine: French and English.
Other Points: No smoking area. Garden. Children welcome. Car park.
Directions: Take the A257 from Canterbury and turn left in Littlebourne, signposted Ickham. (Map 6, C7)

Grove Ferry Inn

Upstreet, Canterbury, Kent CT3 4BP
Telephone: +44(0)1227 860302
groveferry@shepherdneame.co.uk
www.shepherdneame.co.uk

The makeover of the Grove Ferry Inn by the Shepherd Neame Brewery is impressive. Gone is the chips-with-everything image, in comes a contemporary makeover that makes the most of this solid, creeper-clad inn next door to the Stodmarsh Bird Sanctuary. In the spacious bar slate floors give way to carpeted areas, there are sofas and armchairs, log fires, modern paintings. In the restaurant, big windows looking out onto the River Stour take in the magnificent deck with outdoor heaters, the big riverside garden, and views of boats moored on either side of the river. A blackboard lists dishes of the day, and there's a printed menu. Warm goats' cheese on a garlic crouton with chilli butter, or Whitstable Bay organic sausages with chive, spring onion mash and rich gravy shows a kitchen trying hard. Bar snacks offer more familiar farmhouse ched-dar and chutney sandwiches, and homecooked gammon with chips and fried egg. Bedrooms are eye-catching - simple, modern and very good value. Polished floor-boards, a large rug, a massive mirror catching the light, natural colours, crisp white duvet cover and linen, stone-coloured throws. Two rooms have small balconies overlooking the river, all but one room has internet access; bathrooms are neat and modern, with slate floors.

Prices: Set lunch £10. Set dinner £16. Main course restaurant from £7.50. Main course bar from £6. House wine £10.50.
Hours: 11.00-23.00.
Food served: 12.00-21.00.
Rooms: 6 en suite. Double/twin from £75.
Cuisine: Modern British.
Other Points: No-smoking area. Dogs welcome. Garden. Children welcome. Car park.
Directions: Just off the A28 between Canterbury and Margate between the village of Upstreet and Grove. (Map 6, C7)

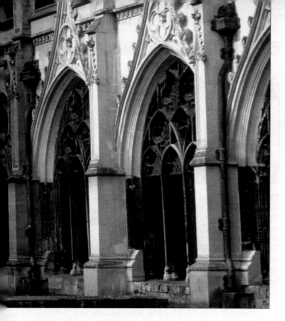

Sylvan Cottage

Nackington Road, Canterbury, Kent CT4 7AY
Telephone: +44(0)1227 765307
jac@sylvan5.fsnet.co.uk

Built in the 1650s as two cottages, the aptly named Sylvan Cottage is set in a semi-rural location, yet is a gentle, 20-minute walk to the medieval city centre. Great if you want a break from the car as well, as Jac is happy to pick up guests from the train or bus stations in Canterbury. Cricket fans will enjoy the proximity to Kent County Cricket Ground some ten minutes walk away, and the fact that Jac and Chris Bray's two sons are both county cricket players. Also, Sylvan Cottage is an ideal overnight stop for Dover and Le Shuttle. The configuration of the house means that there are two entrance halls, two inglenooks in the main sitting room and guest bedrooms are in their own wing, ensuring real privacy. The three bedrooms are very comfortably furnished with ribbon-trimmed duvet covers and floral borders; each room has its own bathroom and comes with bathrobes and hair dryers. In addition, guests are welcome to use the kitchen to make tea and coffee. And you get a good breakfast, prepared by Chris from locally bought ingredients that are organic as far as possible; dinner is available by arrangement.

Prices: Bed and Breakfast. Dinner by arrangement.
Hours: Ring to check annual closures.
Rooms: 3 en suite. Double room from £45, single from £35.
Cuisine: Modern British
Other Points: Totally no smoking. Garden. Children welcome. Car park.
Directions: Exit 11/M20 take the B2068 signposted to Canterbury. Cross the A2 and Sylvan Cottage is 100 yards down on the right hand side. Look for the post box in the wall of the white house. If travelling from the A2, head for the County Cricket ground and take the B2068 to Hythe. (Map 6, C7)

Why go to...East Kent
Sandwich is one of the best preserved medieval towns in Britain, separated from the sandy beaches of Sandwich Bay by the Royal St George golf course, the venue for the 2003 British Open. The course inspired Ian Fleming to include the scene in Goldfinger where James Bond takes on the villain over the links for a bar of gold. Walletts Court, near Dover, set in an area of outstanding beauty and Les Routiers Hotel of the Year for South-East England, 2002, was where many of the major players stayed. Or there's trendy Whitstable, Canterbury and its two world heritage sites - the cathedral and St Augustine's Abbey - the Roman Richborough Castle, the nature reserves of Stodmarsh and Gazen Salts, and Pfizer, which manufactures Viagra.

The White Hart

Worthgate Place, Canterbury, Kent CT1 2QX
Telephone: +44(0)1227 765091

Tucked within the city walls, backing on to Dane John, the White Hart is a pretty little pub with a popular walled garden seating 60, and a pleasing modernised interior with wood floors, pine furniture and walls painted with a mural depicting Kent County cricket ground. This is an extremely well-run, hospitable pub; manager Mark Copestake's father runs the Griffins Head at Chillenden (see following entry), so the business is in the blood. Lunchtime menus are divided between a blackboard and a printed list, and detail straightforward, homemade fare at very reasonable prices. This translates as steak and ale pie, liver and bacon with onion sauce, shepherd's pie, as well as sandwiches, jacket potatoes and omelettes, and traditional Sunday roasts which always include rare roast beef. No food is available in the evenings. As well as good cask ales from Shepherds Neame, there's a wide selection of regularly changing wines, offering a good choice of countries and regions, with some 20 available by the glass and dispensed by knowledgeable bar staff.

Prices: Set lunch £12.15 and dinner £16.95. Main course from £6.25. Main course bar meal from £2.90. House wine £11.
Hours: 11.00-23.30. 12.00-15.00 Sunday. Closed Sunday evening, 25-26 December and 1 January.
Food served: 12.00-14.30 (until 16.00 Saturday and 15.00 Sunday). 18.00-20.30.
Cuisine: Traditional and Modern English.
Other Points: Large garden. No dogs.
Directions: Within City walls of Canterbury, just off The Windcheap roundabout and Castle Street. (Map 6, C7)

Griffins Head

Chillenden, near Canterbury, Kent CT3 1PS
Telephone: +44(0)1304 840325

The impressive black-and-white, half-timbered Wealden hall house was originally built in 1286 as a farmhouse to serve the local estate. Although ale and cider were brewed on the premises for the workers, it was only granted a licence in 1753 so that the rector could hold tithe suppers in the buildings. The present Tudor structure is built around the original wattle and daub walls, remains of which can be viewed in one of the three unspoilt rooms, which also feature flagstone floors, exposed brick walls and beams, old scrubbed pine tables and church pews. Here, the full complement of cask-conditioned Shepherd Neame ales and a good list of wines, including interesting bin ends and a splendid choice of champagnes, are served. Chalkboard menus list a good range of hearty dishes, including local estate game (roast partridge with red wine sauce) and asparagus in season, steak and kidney pie, lambs' liver and bacon, Barnsley chops, lasagne, mature Cheddar ploughman's lunches, homemade soups, and various fishy options. Finish with a good nursery pudding, perhaps treacle sponge and custard, or a plate of cheese and a glass of port. Rambling roses and clematis fill the attractive garden popular in summer for weekend barbeques.

Prices: Main course bar meal £6. House wine £10.
Hours: 11.00-23.00. 11.00-18.00 on Sunday.
Closed on Sunday evening.
Food served: 12.00-14.00. 19.00-21.30
Cuisine: Traditional and Modern British.
Other Points: Garden. Car park.
Directions: Take the A2 from Canterbury, then left on the B2068 towards Wingham. Follow signs to Nonnington; the pub is 1 mile past Nonnington. (Map 6, C7)

Dunkerley's of Deal Restaurant

19 Beach Street, Deal, Kent CT14 7AH
Telephone: +44(0)1304 375016
dunkerleysofdeal@btinternet.com
www.dunkerleys.co.uk

This popular seafront hotel makes the best of its position by the pier on the sea front. Of the 16 bedrooms, six have views over the English Channel, and all are very comfortably designed with solid, quality furniture and furnishings. A favourite spot is the pub-style bar-cum-bistro, which draws a good mix of customers with its pleasant atmosphere and Edwardian look that runs to frosted glass and brass divisions for people dining, as well as ceiling fans and crystal chandeliers. The more formal restaurant continues the Edwardian theme with its burgundy and white colour scheme, upholstered chairs, and ceiling fans. The repertoire is strong on fish, but not exclusively, and is built around good materials well treated and particularly well timed, with sea bass teamed with saffron mash and red pepper fondue, for example, or Barbary duck breast with thyme roasted vegetables, cranberry and orange. Some dishes are simple, Dover sole with lemon butter and fried potatoes, for example. Puddings range from cinnamon brûlée with sultana and apple compote to dark chocolate tart with lemongrass ice cream and kumquat syrup. The well-annotated wine list lingers longest in France and is notable for its selection of half bottles and for very reasonable prices.

Prices: Set lunch £11.95 and dinner £24. Main course from £14.95. House wine £8.95.
Hours: 12.00-14.30. 19.00-21.30. 18.00-22.00 on Saturday.
Rooms: 16 en suite. Double room from £100, single from £60.
Cuisine: Modern British.
Other Points: No-smoking area. Children welcome.
Directions: From M25 follow signs for M26. At Dover take A258 to Deal. Dunkerley's is on the seafront (Map 6, C7)

Wallett's Court Country House Hotel and Spa

Westcliffe, St Margaret's-at-Cliffe, Dover, Kent CT15 6EW
Telephone: +44(0)1304 852424
stay@wallettscourt.com
www.wallettscourt.com

A country house hotel that has grown, almost organically, since that day, a quarter of a century ago, when the Oakley family purchased what was a rundown Jacobean farmhouse. The house retains many period features, but there's a total lack of pretension, the sitting room is filled with odd sofas, armchairs, coffee tables and candles, and service is relaxed, but professional. Main house bedrooms range from small but comfortable standard rooms to vaulted beamed ceilings and antique four-poster beds. Other cosy rooms are in conversions in the grounds. Additional farm outbuildings now house a state-of-the-art gym, indoor swimming pool, sauna, mineral steam room, and hydrotherapy spa and there's an all-weather tennis court. Stephen Harvey delivers food with a broadly English character, derived in large part from carefully sourced materials: many are local and therefore seasonal. Brochettes of Rye Bay scallops and medallions of monkfish with a truffled balsamic reduction, and delicate fillets of Dover sole, poached in lime butter, Kentish asparagus and broad beans could make up a typical summer meal. Generous portions may put a stop on pudding for some, but a light finish is to be had with a timbale of summer fruits set in champagne jelly with fruit liqueur.

Prices: Set price lunch £17.50. Set price dinner £35. House wine £14.95.
Hours: 12.00-14.00. 19.00-21.00. Closed Monday and Saturday lunch and 24-26 December.
Rooms: 16 en suite. Double room from £90, single from £75.
Cuisine: Modern British.
Other Points: No-smoking area. Children welcome. Garden. Car park.
Directions: From Dover, follow the signs for A258 Deal. Once on the road, take the first right to St Margaret's at Cliffe; hotel is one mile on the right. (Map 6, C7)

The Swan at the Vineyard 🍴✕

The Down, Lamberhurst, Kent TN3 8ER
Telephone: +44(0)1892 890170
varnett@ukonline.co.uk
www.newwavewines.com/shop/home/vineyards/lamberhurst.htm

Situated within the Lamberhurst Vineyard in the heart of the Kent countryside, this pretty-in-pink country pub draws attention with its colourful overhanging flower baskets and large outdoor drinking and eating area. Walk through the low wooden door and you are in a classic English pub: wooden beams, old fashioned, simple furniture and traditional ornaments. The well-worn carpets and huge fireplace in one half of the pub lend a comforting air and cosy drinking; the other half is a dining area with wooden floors and tasteful pictures. Sean and Vanessa Arnett have given the Swan a suitably rustic feel. Gone is the loud music, standard pub grub and flashing fruit machines (just one is tucked away in the corner of the bar) replaced by a relaxed atmosphere and some extraordinary food. Simple dishes run to grilled lemon-scented sardines on honey and dill leaves and a trio of dips, or prime sirloin minute steak served with potato chips. From the carte comes saladette of smoked goose breast, white grape and spring onion with a compote of fresh green fig, and confit of lamb loin chop and roasted rack with mint sherbet on a cracked pepper potato crush and redcurrant jus. Wine from the vineyard adds interest to the short, well-annotated wine list.

Prices: Main course restaurant from £10. Main course bar/snack from £6. House wine £9.50.
Hours: 12.00-14.30. 18.00-23.00. 12.00-18.30 Sunday. Summer all day Thursday to Sunday. Closed 1 January.
Food served: 12.00-14.00. 18.30-21.00. Sunday 12.00-15.00. (Summer hours).
Cuisine: Modern British.
Other Points: No-smoking area. Dogs welcome. Garden. Children welcome. Car park. Function room. Vineyard and shop.
Directions: Take B2100 off A21 in Lamberhurst, signed Wadhurst. At cross roads, turn right for pub. (Map 6, D6)

The Soufflé 🍴✕

31 The Green, Bearsted, Maidstone, Kent ME14 4DN
Telephone: +44(0)1622 737065

The pretty Grade II 16th-century house is heavily beamed with standing timbers, sloping floors and old fireplaces. It creates a traditionally English, low-key look thats based on soft colours, white linen tablecloths, high-backed padded chairs, cut-glass wineglasses, and fresh flowers and is a real success story for Nick and Karen Evenden. A tasteful invention runs through menus that nod to Nicks smart hotel background, has gentle inflections of time spent with Marco Pierre White, but shrewdly relies on a sound, unpretentious style that takes note of the seasons. Dishes are simple in concept with an underlying richness. Just look at these: a signature pan-fried Rye Bay scallops with black pudding, parsley sauce, olive oil hollandaise and creamed potatoes; fillet of halibut with a chowder sauce, smoked bacon, baby clams and sweetcorn; or pan-fried calf's liver with a confit of limes and caramelised onions. Some desserts are so popular they are rarely off the menu - notably a classic lemon tart with créme fraîche ice cream and raspberry coulis - but theres also panna cotta set in a fresh raspberry jelly. The French-led wine list acknowledges other wine-growing countries, and prices in general are below £20.

Prices: Set lunch £16.50. Set dinner £22.50. House wine £12.50.
Hours: 12.00-14.00. 19.00-21.30. No food all day Monday, Saturday lunch and Sunday dinner.
Cuisine: Modern European.
Other Points: No-smoking area. Garden. Children welcome over seven years old. Car park.
Directions: Exit 7/M20, turn left at the roundabout and follow the Bearsted Road into the village. Soufflé is on the left. (Map 6, C6)

Stone Court Hotel and Chambers Restaurant 🍴✕🛏

28 Lower Stone Street, Maidstone, Kent ME15 6LX
Telephone: +44(0)1622 769769
www.stonecourthotel.com

The house dates from 1716, initially used as a residence for Crown Court judges, and has been saved from dereliction by restaurateur and hotelier, Musa Kivrak. He has taken the judges theme, naming bedrooms after them, for instance, and using judges' gavels as key holders. What is interesting is that this new town centre hotel is not part of a chain, is clearly run by a dedicated owner, and it fizzes with activity, with small function rooms, private dining rooms, a keenly priced Sunday carvery, and afternoon teas. The bar is lovely with original panelling, large inglenook and is very intimate. The 16 bedrooms range in shape and size, the best being quite spacious with four poster beds, solid furniture, muted colours and modern marble tiled bathrooms. Each room is different but all are well appointed. Dinner in Chambers Restaurant, an elegant, tastefully decorated room in pale yellow and rich deep blue with well-spaced tables and white cloths, is a formal affair. The food doesn't aim to break any moulds, offering carefully prepared tuna tartare with wasabi emulsion and somen noodle salad, followed by duck breast with wild cranberry and peach cream sauce with rösti potatoes, and passion fruit crème brûlée with vanilla ice cream to finish.

Prices: Set lunch £17.50. Set dinner £24.50. Main course restaurant from £18.50. Main course bar from £4.50. House wine £15.50.
Hours: 12.00-14.30. 18.30-21.30.
Rooms: 16 en suite. Double/twin from £95. Single from £75. Family room from £135.
Cuisine: Modern British and French.
Other Points: No-smoking area. Children welcome. Car park. Licenced for Civil Weddings.
Directions: Exit6/M20. Take the A229 Hastings Road to Palace Avenue. The entrance to the car park is on the right hand side of the road after the police station. (Map 6, C6)

England - Kent

Spotted Dog

Smarts Hill, Penshurst, Tonbridge, Kent TN11 8EE
Telephone: +44(0)1892 870253
www.thespotteddog.net

Ben Naude and Kirsten Price, together with chef Nathan Ali, worked together at the Museum Inn, Farnham, Dorset (see entry). Together they bring talent, ambition and sheer enthusiasm to this atmospheric clapboard inn. Panelling, low-slung beams, open fires (one in a great inglenook), nooks and crannies are as you would expect of a pub made up of several early 16th century cottages. There's the usual pubbier look to the series of rooms, but good taste keeps it simple: hop garlands, a few horse brasses, old photographs, various spotted dog motifs. Blackboards list daily specials, there are light lunch bites of soups, a classic club sandwich and goats' cheese baguette with basil oil, and a menu that reflects a contemporary understanding of modern ideas, definitely raising the food stakes above the norm for this part of the county. Pork leek and herb sausages are teamed with sweet potato and celeriac mash and onion gravy, and braised shank of lamb is served with Puy lentils and basil jus. Yet the kitchen never loses sight of the fact that this is a pub - presentation is stylish not pretentious and portions generous without being overwhelming.

Prices: Main course bar meal from £8.95. House wine £10.50.
Hours: 11.00-15.00. 18.00-23.00 (11.00-23.00 Thursday-Saturday in summer). Sunday 12.00-15.00. 18.00-22.30.
Food served: 12.00-14.30. 18.00-21.30. 14.30-18.00 limited menu served on Friday and Saturday. 12.00-20.00 on Sunday.
Cuisine: Modern pub food.
Other Points: No-smoking area. Dogs welcome. No children under ten years old after 19.00 inside. Terrace.
Directions: B2176 and B2110, through Penshurst village, third turning on the right. (Map 6, C6)

The Dering Arms

Station Road, Pluckley, Ashford, Kent TN27 0RR
Telephone: +44(0)1233 840371
info@deringarms.com
www.deringarms.com

Built in 1840 as a hunting lodge for the Dering family, this handsome building boasts curving Dutch gables, rounded triple lancet 'Dering' windows, and a rather spooky grandeur. The interior is all flagstone and board floors, open log fires, light oak panelling and stripped pine. First-class pub food reflects James Buss's passion for fresh fish and seafood and quality local produce. Herbs come from the pub garden and bread is baked on the premises. Fresh fish from Hythe dominates the restaurant menu and daily chalkboard specials: sea bass with minted leeks and red wine sauce, red mullet with couscous and saffron sauce, or monkfish wrapped in bacon with orange and cream sauce. Otherwise, you might find confit of duck with bubble and squeak and wild mushroom sauce and whole crab salad. In the bar, all-day breakfasts, pasta and ploughman's are mainstays, and puddings include tarte tatin and lemon posset. There's good local Goachers ales on handpump, Kentish farm cider, homemade lemonade, and an interesting list of 170 wines that favours France, notably some fine clarets. Homely bedrooms are simply furnished and good value but lack en suite facilities.

Prices: Main course from £14. House wine £10.
Hours: 11.30-15.00. 18.00-23.00. Sundays from 12.00 and 19.00. Closed 26 and 27 December.
Food served: 12.00-14.00. 19.00-21.30.
Rooms: 3. Double room from £40, single from £30, family room from £50.
Cuisine: Seafood.
Other Points: Children/dogs welcome. Garden. Car park.
Directions: From Ashford take the A20 north and follow the signposts to Pluckley for two miles. Turn left into the village square and continue for two miles; the pub is just before the railway station. (Map 6, C6)

Chequers Inn

The Street, Smarden, Ashford, Kent TN27 8QA
Telephone: +44(0)1233 770217
www.thechequerssmarden.co.uk

Although the quaint, weatherboarded hostelry is very olde worlde in looks, refurbishment has left it all in superb condition, with flagstone floors, heavy timbers, open fires, lots of paintings and evening candles creating a model country inn. The restaurant has been carefully thought out, with oak tables and chairs, beams galore and an enormous fireplace; another dining area has attractive French pine furniture. The food will not disappoint either; indeed, it draws an appreciative crowd. The repertoire is built around a modern menu that is as adept at contemporary combinations of smoked haddock with chorizo and a mild curry sauce, as it is with English classics of steak and kidney pie with shortcrust pastry. In addition, there is a separate bar menu that uses fresh produce to good effect. The wine list is good value, and there are eight by the glass. Should you wish to stay the night, you have the choice of four en suite bedrooms, all decorated in a cosy country style with oak furniture; one has an old four-poster bed. Brave hearts can ask for the room haunted, reputedly, by the ghost of a 19th-century French soldier (supposedly murdered for his money), who paces up and down.

Prices: Set lunch £15 and dinner £20. Main courses from £10. Main course bar meal from £7. House wine £9.95.
Hours: 11.00-23.00.
Food served: 11.30-14.30. (12.00-15.00 on Sunday.) 18.00-21.30 (until 22.00 on Saturday).
Rooms: 4 en suite. Double/twin room from £70, single from £40.
Cuisine: Modern British.
Other Points: No-smoking area. Garden. Children welcome. Car park.
Directions: Junction 8/M20. Follow signs to Leeds Castle then Sutton Valence, then Headcorn. Go through Headcorn village, follow the sign for Smarden on your left, go to the end of that road, turn left and then right into the inn next to the church. (Map 6, D6)

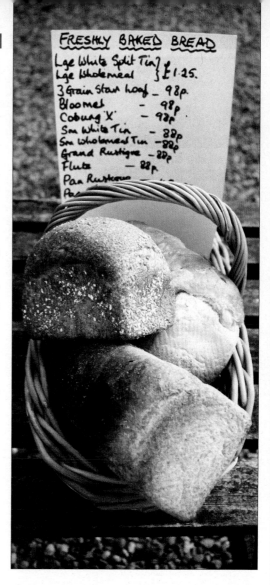

FRESHLY BAKED BREAD
Lge White Split Tin ⎱ £1·25.
Lge Wholemeal ⎰
3 Grain Star loaf - 98p
Bloomer - 98p
Coburg 'X' - 98p
Sm White Tin - 88p
Sm Wholemeal Tin - 88p
Grand Rustique - 88p
Flute - 88p
Pan Rustique

Red Lion
⭐ 🄳 ✗ ⌘

The Street, Stodmarsh, Canterbury, Kent CT3 4AZ
Telephone: +44(0)1227 721339
tiptop@talk21.com

Folk come from miles around to eat and drink in Robert Wigan's quirky 15th century pub. Five miles from Canterbury, it's set in a rural village adjoining the famous Stodmarsh Nature Reserve . Within, low ceilings, stone and wood floors, hop garlands, fresh flowers, candles on plain wood tables, an open log fire, all add to the rustic charm of the tiny rooms. Beer is tapped direct from hop sack-covered barrels behind the bar, and the food is outstanding. A blackboard by the entrance displays a versatile, ingredient led menu, a mix of contemporary ideas and good country cooking that extends to proper buttery pastry for pies and delicious puddings. Local, free range and organic ingredients make their way into the kitchen with game from local shoots, seasonal fruit and vegetable from nearby farms, and locally smoked ham all playing there part. A huge success is the pub's damned good breakfast, a weekend treat for families, but worth considering during the week - it's a cracking pick-me-up! Tuck into local butcher sausages, bacon, own eggs, mushrooms, grilled tomatoes, even kidneys and T-bone steaks (from a local beef farm), toast, marmalade, washed down with strong tea, good coffee, a pint of Shepherd Neame's finest, or champagne.

Prices: Main course bar meal from £9.95. House wine £10.95.
Hours: 10.30-23.00. 11.00-22.30 Sunday.
Food Served: 12.00-14.00. 19.00-21.30.
Rooms: 3, not en suite. Double room from £40.
Cuisine: Traditional British using local produce.
Other Points: Children welcome. Garden. Car park. Summer BBQ.
Directions: A257 from Canterbury, follow signs to Stodmarsh.
(Map 6, C7)

Hours: 10.00-17.00 daily. Closed Mondays September-May.
Other points: Wild flower walks. Picnic area.
Directions: Leave M2 at exit 4 or 5 and cross A2. Farm is 0.25 miles north of the A2, between Rainham and Newington; turn north opposite Rainham Little Chef, in the direction of Upchurch. (Map 6, C6)

The Barn Yard
🐖

Gore Farm, Upchurch, Sittingbourne, Kent ME9 7BE
Telephone: +44(0)1634 235059
mikeblee@the-barnyard.co.uk
www.the-barnyard.co.uk

A collection of 17th century barns has been rebuilt to provide an extensive farm shop complex that endeavours to buy locally first then British wherever possible. Local produce includes a wide range of apple juices and honey, and there is frozen Kent game. The dairy sells more than 100 British cheeses from all over the British Isles, as well as Kentish ice creams and cooked meats, there's a pantry filled with preserves, mustards, freshly baked breads and cakes, and the farm shop itself is stocked with seasonal fruits and vegetables from Gore Farm and other local growers. Apples, plums, strawberries, pumpkins, runner beans and sweetcorn are typical of the produce sold, and there is a vast pick-your-own from March to September, plus walking in 150 acres of fruit farm. There's also a coffee shop for lunches and morning and afternoon cakes, and a maize maze to solve.

Swan on the Green

West Peckham, Tonbridge, Kent ME18 5JW
Telephone: +44(0)1622 812271
bookings@swan-on-the-green.co.uk
www.swan-on-the-green.co.uk

The row of tiny cottages that make up this pretty pub was built in 1526 and a licence granted in the 17th century. Within, Gordan Milligan has renovated and decorated with restraint and good taste. The whole place is open plan with bare boards, beams, exposed brick contrasting with plain cream plastered walls, contemporary art, log fires, fresh flowers and chunky evening candles creating a surprisingly modern, light look that sits well with the age of the building. In addition, there are pale wood pews, wood tables, and kitchen chairs and a gleaming espresso machine. The simple lunch and adventurous evening menus change daily, with the former offering ploughman's of English cheeses, ciabatta filled 'flutes' of, say, ham and honey mustard, and more substantial strips of chicken marinated in citrus, wok-fried and mixed with cardamom infused couscous. For dinner expect individual baked tartlet with a filling of Roquefort cheese and creamed leeks, then chargrilled duck breast kebabs marinaded in Seville oranges and kumquats and served with minted noodles, or fresh crabmeat and shrimp fishcakes with a lime and caperberry crème fraîche and sweet basil couscous. The microbrewery behind the pub provides an astonishing range of own-brewed beers on handpump.

Prices: Main course from £9.95. House wine £11.
Hours: 11.00-15.00, (Saturday until 16.00). 18.00-23.00. Sunday 12.00-16.00. 19.00-22.30. Closed 25 December.
Food served: 12.00-14.00. 19.30-21.30.
Cuisine: Modern Pub Food.
Other Points: Dogs welcome on a lead. Children welcome. Car park.
Directions: West Peckham is off the B2016, half a mile north of the junction of A26/A228, north east of Tonbridge. (Map 6, C6)

Wheelers Oyster Bar

8 High Street, Whitstable, Kent CT5 1BQ
Telephone: +44(0)1227 273311
www.whitstable-shellfish.co.uk

A Whitstable landmark, the striking pink and blue Victorian facade still a remarkable sight on the increasingly gentrified High Street. Originally a simple oyster bar, Wheelers has been in the same family since it was established in 1856 and has no connection with the London Wheelers. When Mark Stubbs arrived in 1997, word spread quickly that here was a chef who could cook seafood. But such was the strain put on the three (yes, three) tables in the back restaurant, it is now necessary to book weeks in advance in season. What strikes most is the freshness and intensity of flavour. Dishes work because they have been carefully considered, as in pan-fried langoustine with roasted ceps, baby artichokes, herb salad and barrigole sauce. Classic combinations get an inventive twist, as can be seen in a savoury Caesar salad with a whole warm Whitstable lobster and finished with a Caesar dressing, aged Parmesan and deep-fried anchovies. A cold menu (to eat in or take away) is offered in the diminutive Victorian front oyster bar (four stools): delicate tarts of crab, prawns and butter sauce, hot smoked salmon fillets, crab sandwiches, oysters, eels, mussels, and octopus. There's no licence, but no corkage charge.

Prices: Main course from £10.00. Unlicenced.
Hours: 13.00-19.30. Closed on Wednesday, and the last two weeks of January.
Cuisine: Seafood.
Other Points: Children welcome. Credit cards not accepted.
Directions: Exit 7/M2. Turn off the Thanet Way at the roundabout to Whitstable and follow road through town. Restaurant at the end of the high street. (Map 6, C7)

Prices: Main course from £4.95. Starters and sweets from £1.50.
Hours: 11.00-18.00.
Rooms: 17 en suite. Prices from £24 per person.
Cuisine: Traditional and Modern British.
Other Points: No-smoking area. Children welcome. Car park.
Directions: Take the M55 towards Blackpool and follow the red signs for central car park. Leave the car park for the one-way system, Central Drive. Then turn left and Hornby Road will be the first immediate right. (Map 11, E4)

Raffles Hotel and Tea Rooms

73-77 Hornby Road, Blackpool, Lancashire FY1 4QJ
Telephone: +44(0)1253 294713
enquiries@raffleshotelblackpool.fsworld.co.uk
www.raffleshotelblackpool.co.uk

The reception is small and informal, setting the relaxed tone of the house, and there's a comfortable lounge and bar. In addition, there are two bedrooms on the ground floor for guests who are not so nimble on their feet. All bedrooms are compact, but not small, and meticulously decorated. For example, fancy staying in a fabulous, oriental-themed room with Thai furniture, Chinese bedspread, and butterflies, scorpions and one large spider decorating the walls? Or rooms inspired by north Africa, Egypt and India? Graham Poole and Ian Balmforth, the owners of this exceptional B&B-cum-hotel in the heart of Blackpool (minutes from the Tower), have a real passion for their spick-and-span little gem. The standard of décor is high, housekeeping is exemplary, and attention to detail spot on. On arrival you will be served freshly brewed tea or coffee in your room, despite the fact that do-it-yourself tea trays are standard issue in bedrooms, alongside the TV and quality towels. For a traditional seaside break, Raffles is really very good value for money. And, it is worth noting that the recently acquired premises next door have been converted into a tea room where meals as well as cakes and scones are served.

Why go to...Blackpool
It's brash, bold, and in your face, but behind the superb white knuckle rides of the Pleasure Beach and the relentless beat of the Golden Mile's amusement arcades, fish and chip shops, candyfloss, novelty rock, and pubs galore, there's a savvy town employing sophisticated marketing techniques to get its message over. This is a fun town, shrewdly giving 16 million visitors a year exactly what they want, aided by seven miles of beach, trams and two piers. When other resorts close up for the winter, Blackpool's season is just beginning, as over half a million light bulbs create the illuminations which decorate the Golden Mile from the beginning of September to early November.

Assheton Arms

Downham, Clitheroe, Lancashire BB7 4BJ
Telephone: +44(0)1200 441227
asshetonarms@aol.com
www.assheton-arms.co.uk

Very little has changed in this lovely old village situated at the base of Pendle Hill since it was bought by the Assheton family in 1558. Devoid of TV aerials, dormer windows, and street signs, Downham is often used by film and television companies for period village scenes. The Assheton Arms retains a cheerfully-warm traditional air and enjoys pretty pastoral views from comfortable window seats, and from picnic tables on the front terrace. A single, beamed bar and the rambling adjoining rooms house an array of solid oak farmhouse tables and wing-back settees, a huge central stone fireplace with the date 1765 carved into it, and a large blackboard that lists a good-value choice of honest, homecooked dishes. Using fresh local produce where possible, a typical menu may offer potted Morecambe Bay shrimps, Loch Fyne oysters, ham and vegetable broth, or a ploughman's lunch with Chris Sandham's creamy Lancashire cheese. For something more substantial opt for the steak and kidney pie, casserole of venison, bacon and cranberry, cumberland sausage and mash, or whole lemon sole with parsley butter and tartare sauce. Arrive early as the pub regularly bustles with local drinkers quaffing tip-top Castle Eden Ale.

Prices: Main course from £9.50. House wine £10.75 a litre.
Hours: 12.00-15.00. 19.00-23.00 (22.30 on Sunday) Closed first full week in January.
Food served: 12.00-14.00. 19.00-22.00.
Cuisine: Traditional British.
Other Points: No-smoking area. Children welcome. Car park.
Directions: Off the A59, 3 miles north-east of Clitheroe. (Map 12, E5)

The Villa Country House Hotel

Moss Side Lane, Wrea Green, Kirkham, Preston,
Lancashire PR4 2PE
Telephone: +44(0)1772 684347
thevilla@mercuryinns.com
www.villahotel-wreagreen.co.uk

Just minutes from the M55 (junction 3), and a world away from the traffic of nearby Preston and Blackpool, stands this mid-19th century building at the end of a drive across open fields. Now a stylish hotel-cum-pub, it offers 25 bedrooms in a recently and tastefully built new wing. These rooms are well fitted with all the extras, even air conditioning. The hotel caters for local business trade as well as those seeking a comfortable and more peaceful base from which to visit Lytham's famous golf links or, perhaps, Blackpool. Smart public areas include an attractive pubby bar with comfy seating areas (with two Jennings ales and a guest on hand pump) and a restaurant made up of three areas with panelling, heavy stonework, an open fireplace and french windows opening onto the gardens. The tables and furnishings add to the period and character. Menus are up-to-date, the bar snack menu listing speciality sandwiches (rump steak with roasted onions) and good salads. Freshly prepared dishes from the carte may include seared red mullet with asparagus and smoked salmon with dill and vermouth sauce, or braised shoulder of lamb with onion mash and red wine jus. Excellent value set-price lunch or early evening menu.

Prices: Set lunch and dinner (18.00-20.00 Monday-Friday) £15.95. Main course from £9.50. House wine £10.95.
Hours: 11.00-23.00. 12.00-22.30 on Sunday.
Food served: All day. Reduced hot menu 14.00-18.00.
Rooms: 25 en suite. Single room from £80, double £90, family room from £90.
Other Points: No-smoking area. Children welcome. Garden. Car park.
Directions: Junction 3, Kirkham, just off the M55. (Map 11, E4)

Corporation Arms

Lower Road, Longridge, Preston,
Lancashire PR3 2YJ
Telephone: +44(0)1772 782644
info@corporationarms-longridge.co.uk
www.corporationarms-longridge.co.uk

Take the B6243 out of Preston, or exit the M6 (junction 31A), to locate this country pub-restaurant set in picturesque countryside south of Longridge and the Bowland Forest. En suite bedrooms make this roadside pub a peaceful overnight alternative to the Forton Services Travel Inn. Comfortable, old-world beamed bar and restaurant with winter log fires, stone and carpeted floors, plain wooden tables topped with church candles, and a wealth of paraphernalia adorning walls and shelves. Menus feature local Cumberland sausages and Bury black pudding on leek mash with caramelised onions and red wine gravy, and Ribble Valley lamb shoulder with rosemary and red wine sauce, alongside dill and lemon battered haddock with hand-cut chips, and grilled steaks with all the trimmings. Lovely rear garden in which to enjoy a pint of Jennings Bitter.

Prices: Set menu £12.95 Monday-Friday. Main course bar meal from £5.95. Main course restaurant meal from £8.95. House wine from £10.25.
Hours: Open: 11.00-23.00. 11.00-22.30 on Sunday.
Food served: 12.00-14.30. 18.00-21.30. 12.00-20.00 on Sunday.
Rooms: 5 en suite. Rooms from £40.
Cuisine: Modern British.
Other Points: No-smoking area. Children welcome. Garden. Car park. Air-conditioned rooms.
Directions: Junction 32/M6. Follow the signs for Broughton. Get to the crossroads and turn right, follow this road for about seven miles until you get to Longridge Stone Bridge roundabout. Continue straight on for one mile. The pub is just outside Longridge on the left hand side. (Map 11, E4)

Red Lion

New Street, Mawdesley, Lancashire L40 2QP
Telephone: +44(0)1704 822208/999
redlion@cybase.co.uk

Edward Newton is enthusiastic about his 19th-century whitewashed village inn and is keen to pursue excellence. Of the two very well kept bars, one is a locals' bar, the other a lounge leading into the restaurant. The furnishings and atmosphere are typical of a popular pub, with a feature made of the fireplace, and there are flowers, pictures and ornaments contributing to this, as well as real ales from Webster, Theakston and Black Sheep breweries. An attractive conservatory extension added to the rear has provided a spacious and airy restaurant Food is good, reliant on local supplies and runs to own-grown herbs in the summer. Bar snacks, served at lunch on Wednesday to Saturday only, take in soup, triple-decker sandwiches, and deep-fried breaded cod goujons with chips and peas. A set two- or three-course lunch and 'early doors' menu could include Thai fishcake with sweet chilli sauce, or baked salmon with white wine cream, and lemon syrup sponge with lemon sauce. A carte extends choice, running to boiled Bury black pudding with bacon risotto, peppercorn and thyme jus, and pot-roasted lamb shank with tarragon and red wine gravy. A compact wine list with good choice under £15, offers four by the glass.

Prices: Set lunch £12 and dinner £13. Main course restaurant meal from £7.50. Snack from £2.50. House wine £11.
Hours: 12.00-23.00.
Food served: 12.00-14.00. 18.00-21.00. 12.00-20.00 on Sunday. No food served Monday and Tuesday.
Cuisine: Modern British.
Other Points: No-smoking area. Garden. Children welcome. Car park.
Directions: Junction 27/M6. Heading north on the B5246 from Parbold, turn left into Malt Kiln Lane and continue for one and a half miles into Mawdesley. (Map 11, F4)

Kicking Donkey ▯✕
Narrow Moss Lane, Ormskirk, Lancashire L40 8HY
Telephone: +44(0)1695 572657

An attractive country pub with wooden beams and two roaring coal fires within, the Kicking Donkey is for those looking for an old fashioned, traditional pub. The white and black exterior with it's hanging baskets and window boxes overflowing with flowers and a pretty beer garden means that whatever the weather, a visit here is a pleasant experience. The pub attracts a good local following, drawn by the excellent selection of beers (Tetley Best Bitter and Marstons Pedigree plus a monthly changing guest ale) at reasonable prices. Most of the bar food is standard pub fare. You can expect their own steak and kidney pie, grilled lamb cutlets and Lancashire black pudding backed up by very good chips as well as blackboard specials. Also available are spicy taco goujons and on Saturday nights there is a famous Oriental carvery. For the traditionalists there is a popular British carvery on Wednesday nights and all day Sunday.

Prices: Main course from £4.95. House wine £6.95.
Hours: 12.00-14.00. 17.30-21.30. Sunday 12.00-20.00. Closed 25 December evening.
Cuisine: Pub food.
Other Points: No-smoking area. Children welcome. Garden. Car park.
Directions: From the signs from Ormskirk for Southport, go through the traffic lights at Fiveways and then take the first right down Grimshaw Lane. This leads on to Narrow Moss Lane. (Map 11, F4)

Monsieurs ★ ✕
12d Blackpool Old Road, Poulton-le-Fylde, Lancashire FY6 7DH
Telephone: +44(0)1253 896400

Monsieurs offers the residents of Poulton-le-Fylde a respite from cooking their own dinners. The spick-and-span take-away, run for the last ten years by Guy and Anita Jenkinson, is right in the centre of town, opposite the library. Although only a takeaway, the entrance has the atmosphere of a Mediterranean cafe, but with a servery counter (with kitchen fully visible behind) and a couple of comfortable chairs and some magazines provided while you wait for your order to be prepared. Daytime demand dictates that the choice is simple, with breakfast, available from 10am to 2pm, running to bacon and egg sandwiches and plates of scrambled egg on toast, while lunch takes in sandwiches, homemade soups and baked potatoes. However, the evening offering is impressive. French-style cooking with coq au vin, chicken à la crème, navarin of lamb and beef bourguignon always available, as well as side dishes of ratatouille, Vichy carrots and garlic sautéed potatoes, and lasagne, spaghetti bolognaise, and spicy chicken curry expanding the range. Puddings are available too: good British offerings of fruit crumbles, sticky toffee and bread and butter puddings.

Prices: Main course from £8. Snack from £5.
Hours: 10.00-14.00 (breakfast and lunch). 17.00-21.00. Friday and Saturday until 22.00. Closed Sunday and Monday, last two weeks of July and first week of August.
Cuisine: Traditional French and English/takeaway.
Other Points: No smoking area. Children welcome. Car park. Credit cards not accepted.
Directions: Exit 3/M55, thenA585 to Fleetwood. Left at first traffic lights, then left at the second lights onto the A586, and into Poulton one-way system. Situated opposite the library. (Map 11, E4)

Campions Dining Rooms and Bar ▯▯▯✕
Cuerdale Lane, Samlesbury, Preston, Lancashire PR5 0UY
Telephone: +44(0)1772 877641
campions@mercuryinns.com
www.campions-samlesbury.co.uk

Open all day and just a stone's throw from the M6 (junction 31), this elegant old hall with its gothic-style bar and restaurant is the perfect retreat. Sink into deep leather sofas or armchairs and relax with a drink in the wood-panelled bar, or dine well in the informal restaurant, where deep yellow walls, wooden floors and solid tables topped with church candles succeed in creating a cosy ambience. Food is imaginative and freshly prepared from good ingredients. Starters of Thai spiced mussels with sweet potato broth and goats' cheese parfait with aubergines and baby leeks and a sweet pepper fondue, alongside main courses of roast cod on crayfish mash, breast of Longridge duck with star anise jus, and chargrilled Angus beef fillet with wild mushroom sauce and hand-cut chips show the modern style. Alternatively, choose from the bar menu. Short global list of wines (13 by the glass, including champagne) and Jennings ales on tap.

Prices: Set dinner £14.95, 2 courses for £11.95 (Tuesday-Friday). Sunday set lunch £9.95. Main course from £9.50. House wine from £9.95.
Food Served: 12.00-14.00. 18.00-21.00 (until 21.30 on Friday and Saturday). 12.00-21.00 on Sunday. Closed Monday.
Cuisine: Modern British.
Other Points: No-smoking in restaurant. Children welcome. Car park.
Directions: On the Preston to Blackburn road, A59. (Map 11, E4)

England - Lancashire

Inn at Whitewell

Forest of Bowland, Whitewell, Clitheroe,
Lancashire BB7 3AT
Telephone: +44(0)1200 448222

Richard Bowman and his staff imbue this ancient stone
inn with warmth, personality, and a pleasing
quirkiness. It's set amid the wild beauty of north
Lancashire, overlooking the River Hodder, yet despite
its splendid isolation there is much to enjoy: eight
miles of fishing rights, a wine merchants, an art
gallery, a shop selling homemade food products, and
17 individually decorated bedrooms. It's relaxed, laid
back, even mildly eccentric, with a haphazard
arrangement of furnishings, bric-à-brac, open log fires,
heavy ceiling beams and colourful rugs throughout the
stone-floored taproom, rambling dining areas and
library. The bar supper choice may include fish pie,
and beer-battered haddock and chips, with salads and
substantial sandwiches appearing at lunchtime. Local
produce features on the evening carte, perhaps cannon
of Bowland lamb with mushroom and spinach farce
and tarragon jus, or local estate venison with walnut
and thyme rösti, baked figs and sloe gin sauce. It's
worth saving space for pudding as well as specialist,
prime-condition British and Irish cheeses. A superlative
wine list completes the picture. Individual bedrooms
are furbished with antique furniture, peat fires and
Victorian baths. Brilliant extras include video recorders
and stereo systems; the best and largest rooms
overlook the river and the country beyond.

Prices: Main course restaurant from £12. Main course bar
from £7.50. House wine £9.50.
Hours: 11.00-15.00 (from 12.00 on Sunday). 18.00-23.00.
Food served: 12.00-14.00. 19.30-21.30.
Rooms: 17 en suite. Double/twin room from £92.
Cuisine: Modern British.
Other Points: Children welcome. Garden. Car park. Licence for
Civil Weddings. Fishing.
Directions: Exit 32/M6 to Longridge. Centre of Longridge follow
signs to Whitewell. (Map 11, E4)

The Mulberry Tree

9 Wrightington Bar, Wrightington, Wigan,
Lancashire WN6 9SE
Telephone: +44(0)1257 451400

The Mulberry Tree stands out as a versatile, well run
pub-cum-restaurant. Mark Prescott trained under the
Roux brothers, and he brings a high level of
sophistication to this versatile operation. As you enter,
there is a separate dining room to the left, an open-
plan dining area to the right, with the lounge and bar
straight ahead. Subtle lighting, pale eggshell walls, and
a warm red carpet, matched with light wood tables and
chairs, creates an uncluttered, modern look. Young,
hardworking staff brings a professional but not stuffy
approach to service, delivering lunchtime sandwiches,
salads, and starters such as chicken liver parfait and fig
chutney, and mains of slow roast belly pork with
pancetta, ribollita and Parmesan crisp, in the bar. The
dining room carte is where more luxurious ingredients
come into play with seared scallops, Avruga caviar and
white truffle oil partnering cream of cauliflower soup,
and whole lobster teamed with cream champagne and
herb sauce, but there are simpler dishes like roast lamb
rump with crushed new potatoes and sauce choron.
The list of some 50 wines covers a lot of territory, is
well annotated, and provides great deal of choice for
under £20. The connoisseurs list is worth exploring.

Prices: Main course restaurant from £9.95. Main course bar
from £8.50. House wine £13.50.
Hours: 12.00-15.00. 17.00-23.00.
Closed 26 December and 1 January.
Food served: 12.00-14.00 (until 15.00 on Sunday). 18.00-21.30
(until 22.00 on Friday and Saturday).
Cuisine: Classical French and Modern British.
Other Points: No-smoking area. Totally no smoking in restaurant.
Children welcome. Car park.
Directions: Exit27/M6. Four miles from Wigan. Take the road
towards Parbold and the immediate right after the motorway exit
by the garage in to Mossy Lea Road for 2 miles. (Map 11, F4)

The Bell Inn

East Langton, Market Harborough, Leicestershire LE16 7TW
Telephone: +44(0)1858 545278
www.thebellinn.co.uk

Alistair Chapman's creeper-clad village inn continues to go from strength
to strength, the latest addition to this thriving business being a micro-
brewery (Langton Brewery) which produces the popular Caudle and
Bowler beers for the pub and local free houses. The Bell dates from the
16th century and features a welcoming stone-walled bar with sturdy pine
tables, a blazing winter log fire fronted by deep sofas, and some seriously
low ceiling beams. In addition to a cracking pint of ale, you will find a
traditional menu of homely pub food. From lunchtime sandwiches,
baguettes and filled jacket potatoes, the main menu lists pheasant and
port pâté, wild mushroom pancake, chicken au poivre, boeuf
bourguignon, and fish pie. Weekly-changing specials include speciality
sausages from the local butcher, or even oven-baked trout (caught by a
customer) in tarragon butter. Excellent handcut chips accompany sirloin
and fillet steaks. Upstairs, two neat en suite bedrooms are well decorated
and equipped with modern comforts. Expect friendly and efficient service
from the enthusiastic owners. There is a pleasant front walled garden for
summer al fresco dining and the pub is within easy reach of Rutland
Water and canal towpath walking at Foxton Locks.

Prices: Main course from £8.95. Snack
from £2.75. House wine £9.75.
Hours: 11.30-14.30 Mon-Sat. 19.00-23.00
Mon to Thur. 18.30-23.00 Sat. 12.00-15.00
and 19.00-22.30 Sunday.
Closed 25 December.
Food served: 12.00-14.00 (until 15.00 on
Sun). 19.00-21.00 (until 22.00 Fri and Sat).
Rooms: 2 en suite. Single from £39.50,
double from £55.
Cuisine: Traditional British.
Other Points: No-smoking area. Children
welcome. Garden. Car park.
Directions: Two miles north west of
Market Harborough off A6. (Map 9, D4)

England - Lancashire

The Black Boy Inn
Main Street, Hungarton, Leicestershire LE7 9JR
Telephone: +44(0)116 259 5410
markandrachel@theblackboyinn.fsbusiness.co.uk

Mark and Rachel Thompson took over this former scampi-and-chips village pub in late 2001. A total overhaul of the menu, redecoration of the premises, and a lot of imagination (the outside decking for summer dining is a nice touch), has turned the place around. It's a relatively new building, so don't expect a lot of character, just a simple open-plan look with traditional pub-style tables and chairs and an open fire, plus a very friendly atmosphere. Menus offer a modern British take with everything made from scratch (except the ice cream), all listed on a chalkboard that delivers a nice balanced selection and very good value for money. The menu changes every six weeks, with grilled goats' cheese and red onion marmalade a typical starter. Main courses could take in pork loin, red cabbage and cider sauce, as well as traditional pub stalwarts such as beef, ale and mushroom pie. Pecan pie with clotted cream, or orange and Cointreau crème brûlée make a great finish. A limited wine list offers excellent value with four house wines from France and Australia priced at £9. Tiger is the regular cask ale, with Wadworth 6X and St Austell HSD popular guests.

Prices: Main course restaurant from £6.95. Bar snack from £3.50. House wine £9.
Hours: 12.00-15.00. 18.00-23.00. Closed Sunday evening and all day Monday.
Food served: 12.00-14.00. 18.00-21.00, until 21.30 Friday and Saturday.
Cuisine: Traditional and Modern British.
Other Points: No-smoking area. Garden. Children welcome. Car park.
Directions: Seven miles east of Leicester off A47. (Map 9, C4)

San Carlo Restaurant
38 - 40 Granby Street, Leicester, Leicestershire LE1 1DE
Telephone: +44(0)116 251 9332

This small chain of city-centre eateries (see Birmingham and Bristol) majoring in pizza and pasta is a cut above the norm, delivering a uniform contemporary look, simple, clean cooking, and fair prices. Mirrors lining the walls and white-tiled floors define a sleek Mediterranean look that's softened by lots of potted plants and trees. This branch, ranging over three floors, has a great atmosphere. The look may be modern but the food is traditional, with an extensive range of pizza and pasta, and classic trattoria dishes such as pollo sorpresa and saltimbocca alla romana. Seafood is delivered once, sometimes twice daily, and the seafood specials board is updated accordingly. Sardines, dressed crab, lobster tagliolini, grilled Dover sole, and king prawn and monkfish kebab, are typical examples. The wine list covers an extensive selection of Italian and French wines, with just a couple from the new world, and a dozen are served by the glass.

Prices: Main course from £9. House wine £11.20.
Hours: 12.00-23.00.
Cuisine: Italian.
Other Points: No-smoking area. Children welcome.
Directions: Situated in Leicester city centre just outside the busy shopping area. (Map 9, C3)

The Red House
23 Main Street, Nether Broughton, Melton Mowbray, Leicestershire LE14 3HB
Telephone: +44(0)1664 822429

This early Victorian house, now a modern restaurant with rooms, combines a relaxed atmosphere with extensive menus and is fast becoming a local hit. The bar has a traditional feel (lots of dark wood furniture) where chalkboards offer the day's bar menu, which includes a pasta, soup of the day, fish and chips with mushy peas, or Caesar salad. But contemporary styling distinguishes the restaurant with, for example, a bar that consists of a pine wood frame filled with old books. Or, for a change of scene, step through an arched walkway to the adjoining dining room that's filled with light from patio doors that look on fo the back lawn. Here you can choose the likes of grilled black pudding with onion rösti, poached egg and mustard hollandaise, slow-roast belly pork with apple sauce and sage and onion stuffing, and apple and rhubarb crumble with cinnamon ice cream, from a seasonally-inspired menu. Match this with a wine list that is expansive in style and global in outlook, but very keenly priced. Eight en suite bedrooms are imaginatively designed. As well as DVDs, there are goodies such as olives, pistachio nuts, mineral water, and freshly-baked cookies.

Prices: Main course restaurant from £8.95. Bar snacks from £5. House wine £11.50.
Hours: 11.00-15.00. 17.00-23.00. Closed 25 December and 2 January.
Food served: 12.00-15.00. 17.00-23.00. Sunday 12.00-17.00 restaurant and 12.00-20.00 bar.
Rooms: 8 en suite. Doubles/twin room from £50 per person.
Cuisine: Modern British.
Other Points: No-smoking area. Dogs welcome in public bar. Children welcome. Garden. Outside garden bar and open kitchen.
Directions: Exit 21 and 22/M1. Situated on the A606 between Nottingham and Melton Mowbray, five miles north of Melton. (Map 9, C4)

England - Leicestershire

The Red Lion Inn

★ ▯ ▯ ▯ ✕

Red Lion Street, Stathern, Leicestershire LE14 4HS
Telephone: +44(0)1949 860868
redlion@work.gb.com
www.theredlioninn.co.uk

Fresh from earning a coveted Michelin star at their successful first pub venture, the Olive Branch at Clipsham, Rutland (see entry), Ben Jones, Marcus Welford and Sean Hope have moved across the border into the Vale of Belvoir to revitalise this 16th century pub. Informality, real ales, fine wines and good quality innovative and traditional food using local produce sum up the philosophy, so, expect rural chic throughout (chunky tables and chairs, deep sofas). The converted skittle alley dining room comes with low beams, terracotta walls and wood-burning stove. As the back of the menu indicates, there's a passion for quality suppliers: Brewster's Bitter on handpump is brewed in the village, game comes from the Belvoir estate, cheese, sausages and fruits are sourced from local farms and dairies, and bread is baked in neighbouring Rearsby. There's something for everyone on the daily changing menu, including salad of duck confit with orange and beetroot, Gloucester Old Spot sausages with buttered spinach and onion gravy, and chargrilled beef fillet with rösti and red wine sauce. Lunchtime additions include excellent sandwiches (spicy chicken burger in naan). Homely puddings like apple and sultana round off proceedings. Three en suite bedrooms were about to be added as we went to press.

Prices: Set lunch £11. Main course restaurant from £8.50. Main course bar from £3.95. House wine £10.50.
Hours: 12.00-15.00. 18.00-23.00, Friday from 17.30. Saturday 12.00-23.00. Sunday 12.00-17.30. Closed 26 Dec and 1 Jan.
Food served: 12.00-14.00. 19.00-21.30. Sunday 12.00-15.00.
Cuisine: Modern Pub Food.
Other Points: No-smoking area. Dogs/children welcome. Garden. Car park.
Directions: From A1 follow A52 towards Nottingham. Turn left towards Belvoir Castle for three miles; Stathern is signposted left. (Map 9, C4)

The Bakers Arms

▯ ✕

Main Street, Thorpe Langton, Market Harborough, Leicestershire LE16 7TS
Telephone: +44(0)1858 545201

First-class, modern pub food, period charm and a relaxed, informal atmosphere are among the attractions at Kate Hubbard's civilised 16th-century thatched pub. Spick and span inside with its ancient walls, low-beamed ceilings and cosy dining areas, tastefully kitted out with pine tables, antique pews, terracotta walls, open fires and rug-strewn floors, it attracts a well-heeled local clientele. Although more restaurant than pub in terms of style of operation it maintains a distinct pub atmosphere, although it's not the sort of place one would pop in for a pint. Emphasis is on good food prepared from fresh ingredients. The balanced menu is chalked up on boards and may list chicken liver pâté with red onion marmalade or pan-fried scallops with butter bean mash and honey and mustard dressing for starters. Main course options range from confit of lamb with onion sauce and pea purée, to sea bass with saffron potatoes and mussels, and cod fillet with Welsh rarebit crust and pesto mash. For pudding, try the hot chocolate fudge cake with vanilla ice cream or the white chocolate and raspberry trifle. Good global list of wines; four by the glass.

Prices: Main course from £8.95. House wine £9.95.
Food served: 18.30-21.30 Tuesday to Saturday and 12.00-14.00 Saturday and Sunday. Closed all Monday and Tuesday, Tuesday to Friday lunch.
Cuisine: Modern British.
Other Points: No-smoking area. Garden. Children welcome over 12 years old. Car park.
Directions: Take B6047 north of A6 two miles north of Market Harborough. Turn right at first crossroads for Thorpe Langton. (Map 9, D4)

Canal, Manchester

The Lea Gate Inn

Leagate Road, Coningsby, Lincolnshire LN4 4RS
Telephone: +44(0)1526 342370
theleagateinn@hotmail.com
www.theleagateinn.co.uk

The last of the once numerous Fen Guide Houses, places of safety on the treacherous eastern marshes before they were drained, it would have had a blazing beacon attached to the gable wall on dark winter nights to guide travellers on their way. Dating from 1542, it is Lincolnshire's oldest licensed premises and today provides overnight refuge for modern-day travellers in eight very comfortable en suite bedrooms. Housed in a new annex that's linked to the modernised inn, these rooms are tastefully decorated and well appointed with TV, radio, beverage trays and hairdryers. The spacious Millennium Suite boasts a jacuzzi bath, bathrobes and CD player. Traditional features such as brick and beams and open fires can be found in the cosy bar, and there's a separate carpeted restaurant. Daily chalkboard specials such as duck leg confit with cumberland sauce enhance the extensive printed menus that list Lea Gate favourites, namely grilled Grimsby haddock, local sausages and mash, steak and kidney pie, traditional grills, lunchtime ploughman's, sandwiches and toasted panninis.

Prices: Set lunch £10.95. Set dinner £16. Main course from £4.95 at lunch and £6.95 at dinner. House wine £7.50.
Hours: 11.30-14.30. 18.30-22.30. Closed evening of 25th and 26th December and 1st January day.
Food served: 11.30-14.00 (Sunday from 12.00). 18.30-21.00 (Friday, Saturday and Sunday from 18.00).
Rooms: 8 en suite. Double room from £65, single from £49.50, family room from £75.
Cuisine: Traditional.
Other Points: No-smoking area. Children welcome. Garden. Car park.
Directions: On main A153 or B1192, between Horncastle and Sleaford, close to RAF Coningsby. (Map 10, B5)

Hillcrest Hotel

15 Lindum Terrace, Lincoln, Lincolnshire LN2 5RT
Telephone: +44(0)1522 510182
reservations@hillcrest-hotel.com
www.hillcrest-hotel.com

A really lovely town-house hotel, an old rectory set on a secluded leafy avenue close to the cathedral and arboretum. Jennifer Bennett is a personable, chatty host and her team really put effort into making you feel at home. Indeed, it is the homely warm ambience that really makes Hillcrest so appealing; it is rather cosy and cosseting. The décor mixes some bold old-fashioned touches with rich patterns and colours, which suit the ornate plasterwork and high ceilings. It's a lovely mélange of thoughtful furnishings and personal touches. The food matches the house: hearty, soundly prepared fare, no surprises, just good home cooking. A generous starter of smoked salmon roulade, for example, followed by loin of lamb with a special lime and cointreau glaze and lots of fresh vegetables, which barely leaves room for a rich pudding selection that includes locally made ice cream. A short list of mainly new world wines provides good drinking at reasonable prices. There are 15 bedrooms, spread over four floors and all are individual; the best is a spacious yet cosy four-poster with solid pine furniture, lace and floral dressed wooden bed, and a small bathroom.

Prices: Set dinner £18. Main course from £12.75. House wine £11.50.
Hours: 12.00-14.00. 19.15-20.30. No food all day Sunday and Saturday lunch. Closed from 21 December to 6 January.
Rooms: 14 en suite. Double room from £83, single from £61.
Cuisine: Modern European.
Other Points: No-smoking area. Children welcome. Garden. Car park. Internet.
Directions: From Wragby Road/Lindum Hill (A15), take very small road - Upper Lindum Street. Go to the bottom of the road, then turn left into Lindum Terrace; the hotel is 200 metres on right. (Map 9, B4)

Prices: Set lunch from £9.95, set dinner from £13.95. House wine £10.95.
Hours: 11.00-24.00. Closed 25-26 December and 1 January.
Cuisine: Mediterranean.
Other Points: Children welcome. Heated arcade. Street parking.
Directions: At the end of Deansgate, near GMEX and Castlefield just off the main road in the arcade. (Map 12, F5)

Dimitris Tapas Bar and Taverna

Campfield Arcade, Tonman Street, Deansgate, Manchester M3 4FN
Telephone: +44(0)161 839 3319
manchester@dimitris.co.uk
www.dimitris.co.uk

Set meals at good prices are what the growing Dimitris chain is famous for. It all started at this Manchester site (now celebrating its 13th year), where the laid-back atmosphere and relaxed look of wood floors and red and white checked cloths set off the honest-to-goodness Mediterranean cooking. The mix of outside heated dining area, large interior restaurant, separate bar and cellar bar has a something-for-everyone appeal, which is matched by a menu that mixes Greek taverna favourites such as hummus and taramasalata with guacamole and tapenade. In the mains section, Loukanika pork sausages made with wine and served with tsatsiki, or octopus slowly cooked with onions in red wine, vie for attention with salt and pepper spare ribs and chorizo sausage and salsa, and so on through salads, vegetables, pasta and couscous. What sets the cooking apart is the policy of offering good food at affordable prices. Popular dishes such as the Kalamata platas and the mega mezzes are set menus for two or more people and are exceptional value, as is the Manchester soup and sandwich lunch deal at £2.95. The wine list takes a popular global view and includes a few well-priced Greek wines.

Ramsons ★ ▯ ♟ ✕

16-18 Market Place, Ramsbottom, Bury,
Greater Manchester BL0 9HT
Telephone: +44(0)1706 825070
chris@ramsons.org.uk

Ramsons is a perfect little restaurant. Inside, three small ground-floor rooms are decorated in a stylish yet timeless manner and Chris Johnson's Italian influenced menu is a model of flexibility. It opens, say, with an Italian breakfast or brunch, going on to tremendously good value lunches or early dinners of wild boar salami with rocket and Parmesan shavings, and steamed fillet of salmon with roast fennel and champagne sauce. He builds his dishes around prime raw materials, impeccably sourced and simply cooked to retain flavours, as can be seen in a classic roast sirloin of beef with baby potatoes and red wine sauce served for Sunday lunch. Seasonality oozes from the impressive repertoire, and flavours work well, whether it's a starter of wild nettle soup with basil infusion, or pudding of rhubarb crumble and Jersey cream. The wine list is concise but inspiring, and is accompanied by excellent tasting notes. A retail discount for those wanting to take some home is a novel touch. You are also invited to check the cellar for the many wines that are stocked but not on the list. The basement café is modelled on an Italian enoteca and has a good menu of light dishes.

Prices: Set lunch and dinner £14.50. Main course from £13.50. House wine £10.
Hours: 12.00-14.30. 18.00-22.00. 13.00-15.30 on Sunday. Closed all day Monday and Sunday evening.
Cuisine: Italian Influenced.
Other Points: Totally no smoking. Well-behaved children welcome (no special children menus).
Directions: From the M66 take exit 1 northbound. Turn right at the lights and left at the next lights. Take a right at the third lights, Ramsons is on the right hand side. (Map 9, A2)

Rams Head Inn ▯♟D✕

Denshaw, Oldham, Greater Manchester, OL3 5UN
Telephone: +44(0)1457 874802
ramshead-denshaw@btconnect.com
www.country-inns-co.uk

The former 400-year-old stone farmhouse and coaching inn stands 1,212 feet above sea level and has panoramic views across Saddleworth Moor. Renowned for being snowbound on wild winter days, warming log fires are a welcome feature within the four comfortably modest rooms, each sporting low oak beams, old wood panelling, early Victorian church pews, and a wealth of fascinating memorabilia. Chalkboards list the impressive range of food on offer, notably speciality seafood and winter game dishes, with the emphasis firmly on fresh seasonal produce. In addition to hearty sandwiches (roast beef and horseradish) and starters like game terrine with cumberland sauce, substantial main courses may include venison haunch with red wine and juniper sauce, baked haddock on chive mash with rich cheese sauce, or roast suckling pig stuffed with garlic and herbs. Also, expect handcut chips with your whole lemon sole, and freshly baked bread rolls with your starter. Finish with their famous sticky toffee pudding, served with hot toffee sauce, or the chocolate pecan tart. There's a good global list of wines with useful tasting notes (eight by the glass), and sound northern ales - Tetley, Black Sheep, Timothy Taylor - on handpump.

Prices: Main course from £10. House wine £9.95.
Food Served: 12.00-14.00. 18.00-22.00. (12.00-14.30 and 18.00-20.30 Monday) 12.00-20.30 Sunday. Closed 25 December.
Cuisine: Modern British. Seafood and Game Specialities.
Other Points: No-smoking area. Car park. No Dogs.
Directions: From Oldham take A672 Halifax road from Mumps roundabout. Exit22/M62. (Map 12, F5)

Prices: Set 2 course lunch and dinner £8.95. (Dinner between 18.00-19.15). Main course from £6.95. House wine £9.25.
Hours: 12.00-23.00, Sunday until 22.30. Closed first week of January.
Food served: 12.00-14.00. 18.00-21.30. Sunday 12.00-20.00.
Cuisine: Modern British.
Other Points: No-smoking area. Outside area. Children welcome over five years old. Car park.
Directions: Exit23/M6. Take A580/A570 and follow signs to Crank. (Map 11, F4)

The Red Cat ▯♟D✕

8 Red Cat Lane, Crank, St Helens, Merseyside WA11 8RU
Telephone: +44(0)1744 882422
redcat@amserve.net

This traditional-looking Lancashire red-brick pub is easily missed, and that would be a great shame. On entering, the place looks like any other local until you venture into the lounge bar and you see the blackboard - someone here knows proper food. Ian Martin has cooked at several well-known country house hotels and his approach is spot on, but he has had to battle against an inherited reputation for fairly basic pub staples. He is succeeding with a fresh, modern menu that delivers seared king scallops with asparagus and rocket, corn-fed Goosnargh chicken with Burgos black pudding, girolle mushrooms and cream sauce, and wild Lune salmon with poached samphire and sorrel sauce. Then there is the amazing wine list. You will be hard pressed to find another list anywhere that offers such a selection of classic wines and vintages - and at very reasonable prices. Ian Martin's knowledge of what he has is detailed, and he is keen that visitors should have the opportunity to drink really good vintages without having to accept a high mark-up. If there is one complaint, it is that there is no accommodation. Having to drive could spoil the enjoyment of sampling some great wines.

Kings Head   🅳✕

Harts Lane, Bawburgh, Norwich, Norfolk NR9 3LS
Telephone: +44(0)1603 744977
anton@kingshead-bawburgh.co.uk
www.kingshead-bawburgh.co.uk

A bustling atmosphere, sunny yellow walls, thick beams and standing timbers, interlinked rooms with a mix of open fires and a couple of wood burning stoves (one in an impressive inglenook), give this 17th-century building oodles of charm. Uncomplicated dishes such as assiette of seafood: marinated anchovies, fresh oysters, prawns and smoked mackerel pâté, or pan-fried chicken breast with black pudding and pork stuffing, accompanied by braised cabbage, celeriac and potato rösti and a lemon and thyme sauce, represent a forgotten English cuisine, one that celebrates traditional country cooking with a fresh look and seasonal ingredients. Local produce plays a big part in the imaginative menu with the likes of Cromer crab and crayfish pâté, and rare-breed pork with cranberry, pistachio and pork stuffing, bacon mash and whole grain mustard sauce. However, there's a willingness to move with the times since Thai curry with scallops, cashew nuts, baby corn and jasmine rice, and pan-fried sea bass with pappardelle pasta, roast red peppers, oven-dried tomatoes and sauce verde, share equal billing. The short, global selection of wines are reasonably priced with some 15 available by the glass; Woodfordes Wherry is the most popular ale.

Prices: Main course from £6.95.
House wine £9.95.
Food Served: 12.00-14.00. 18.30-21.30.
12.30-14.30 on Sunday. Closed 25
December evening.
Cuisine: Traditional/fusion.
Other Points: No-smoking area. Children welcome. Garden. Car park.
Directions: Take A47 west of Norwich, then B1108; pub signposted down Harts Lane off B1108 in Bawburgh. (Map 10, C7)

White Horse   ★🍷🅳✕🛏

Main Road, Brancaster Staithe, King's Lynn,
Norfolk PE31 8BY
Telephone: +44(0)1485 210262
reception@whitehorsebrancaster.co.uk
www.whitehorsebrancaster.co.uk

The neat, white-painted pub frontage gives nothing away. Even in the bar with the counter propped up by locals sinking pints, you remain unaware. It is as you head towards the conservatory dining room that you notice the huge windows framing one of the best views in this part of Norfolk, straight over the tidal marshes to Scolt Head Island. Reflecting the view, colours are muted, natural, with found objects from the beach complementing contemporary artwork. Original bedrooms are in an extension facing the marsh, designed in a wave to give every spacious room a piece of terrace. The roof is famously grassed over, overlooked by a cool, modern terrace. New bedrooms upstairs feature handsome modern furniture, simple clean lines, and soft colours. The two-tiered Room at the Top is the pick, with fantastic marsh views and a telescope. Evening candles on well-spaced tables create a soft look for dinner, and the emphasis is on fresh fish, say a timbale of local crab with aïoli, herb leaf salad and vintage balsamic. Mains run to baked fillet of plaice, spiced lentil dahl and crème fraîche. Beers come from East Anglian brewers and the wine list is good value with 11 by the glass.

Prices: Main course from £8.95. House wine £10.50.
Hours: 11.00-23.00 Monday to Saturday (11.00-22.30 Sunday)
Food served: 12.00-14.00. 18.45-21.00.
Rooms: 15 en suite. Double room from £76.00. Single supplement £20 per night.
Cuisine: Modern British.
Other Points: No-smoking area. Children welcome. Car park. Sun Deck Terrace. Conservatory Dining Room.
Directions: Midway between Hunstanton and Wells-next-Sea on the A149. (Map 10, C6)

The Hoste Arms   ★🍷🅳✕🛏

The Green, Burnham Market, Norfolk PE31 8HD
Telephone: +44(0)1328 738777
reception@hostearms.co.uk
www.hostearms.co.uk

The handsome, pale yellow-painted 17th-century inn, has been transformed into a rare combination of stylish pub, restaurant and upmarket hotel by Paul Whittome. The rustic, unpretentious bar (no food served here) has an impressive range of East Anglian ales; adjoining, panelled dining areas require advance booking. The extensive menu focuses on fresh Norfolk produce with a policy of sourcing ingredients from a 20-mile radius. Daily-changing menus may list Burnham Creek oysters with red wine and shallot vinegar or seared scallops with hazelnut and coriander butter among the starters or snacks. Mains range from chargrilled rump steak with chips, to sea bass with steamed asparagus and pink grapefuit dressing. For pudding there may be warm treacle tart, or a savoury like Welsh rarebit with Serano ham and poached egg. The well chosen list of wines includes quality French offerings, plenty of new world bottles and some dozen by the glass. Strong colours, tasteful fabrics, four-poster beds and handsome bathrooms characterise the comfortable, individually designed and very well equipped bedrooms that are split between the inn and converted buildings to the rear.

Prices: Main course from £9.25. House wine £10.95.
Hours: 11.00-23.00. Sunday 12.00-22.30.
Closed New Years Eve to non-residents.
Food served: 12.00-14.00. 19.00-21.00.
Rooms: 36 en suite. Double/twin from £102. Single from £74. Children £20.
Cuisine: Modern British with Pacific Rim influences.
Other Points: No-smoking area. Dogs welcome. Children welcome. Garden. Car park.
Directions: Signposted off the B1155, five miles west of Wells-next-the-Sea. By the green in the village centre. (Map 10, C6)

A SENSE OF SPACE

North Norfolk's desolate coastline of expansive salt marshes and sand dunes stretching into the distance has been described as a remote corner of England. Away from the sea the county's rural hinterland is dotted with sleepy villages, small towns and historic houses.
Drive length: 82 miles

Cley-next-the-Sea
(smokery;
birdwatching)

Blakeney
(seal trips)

Brancaster

Burnham Market
(shopping)

Sandringham

Houghton Hall

Holt
(shopping;
Baconsthorpe Castle)

Sheringham
(Sheringham Park (N
North Norfolk Railw
Muckleburgh Collect

● Accommodation/Food

● Accommodation

● Food

🌶 Food Shop

To find the establishments marked
here, look up the listing town
marked on the map in bold in the
town index on page 395

Ratcatchers Inn

Easton Way, Eastgate, Cawston, Norwich, Norfolk NR10 4HA
Telephone: +44(0)1603 871430
www.the-ratcatchers.co.uk

A pleasantly old-fashioned pub, dating from 1861, and unusually named after the local ratcatcher who used to do his business with the council representatives outside the house (receiving a penny a tail, for the rats he caught). It stands in a rural spot just off the B1149 one mile south of Cawston, and folk come from miles around, packing the neatly furnished bar and restaurant areas which are both laid up for diners, for food is very much the thing here. This instills confidence in the kitchen, and it's advisable to book. There's real enthusiasm for food here, in particular a passion for using fresh local produce. In fact, all ingredients are sourced within a forty mile radius of the pub, including fish from Kings Lynn, first-class meat and game from Clarks butchers along the road, and homegrown herbs. This is clearly evident in the likes of pork sausages served with creamy mashed potatoes, onion and red wine gravy, and daily fish specials such as Norfolk coast shellfish. There's also a good range of naturally aged steaks, popular curries and, of course, the Ratcatchers award-winning steak and kidney pie. Portions are generous. A wide-ranging wine list offers good value drinking.

Prices: Set lunch £18 and dinner £25. Main course from £7.95. House wine £9.50.
Hours: 12.00-14.00. 18.00-22.00. Saturday and Sunday 12.00-22.00.
Cuisine: Traditional British and Continental.
Other Points: No-smoking area. Children welcome. Garden. Car park.
Directions: Eastgate is signed off B1149 Norwich to Holt road, 10 miles north of Norwich. (Map 10, C7)

thecafe at Whalebone House

High Street, Cley-next-the-Sea, Norfolk NR25 7RN
Telephone: +44(0)1263 740336
whalebone.house@virgin.net
www.thecafe.org.uk

Kalba Meadows and John Curtis are strongly committed to using produce from local, sustainable and organic sources and list all their suppliers on the menu. Their contemporary vegetarian cooking reflects this total dedication - around 60% of all produce used is organic, including all wines and they aim to be 80% organic in the next two years. In 2003, their environment and sustainability policies achieved runner-up in the North Norfolk Environment Award. Blackboards offer a daily changing menu with influences coming from all around the Mediterranean. Saturday and Sunday lunch dishes, say, of roasted red peppers and red onions, then a salad of Ardrahan cheese with warm Jersey Royals tossed in toasted walnut oil and home-grown mesclun. The four-course set dinner brings caponata with a rosemary farinata to start, mains of couscous and chickpea pilaff with roasted roots, chermoula and a sweet-spicy tomato confit, with regional British, French, Irish and Italian cheeses and salad followed by home-grown peaches poached in brandy with lavender shortbread. Two good value double rooms are available (minimum stay two nights). Bathrobes, slippers, binoculars, books, CD player, cafetière, and hot waterbottles are part of the extras in rooms with North African or oriental styling.

Prices: Set lunch £14.50 and dinner £22.50. House wine £13.
Hours: 13.00 lunch served on Sunday only. Dinner 19.30 for 20.00 Tuesday-Saturday. Booking essential. Closed December and January.
Rooms: 2 en suite. Single nights not accepted. Two nights for two people from £200 for dinner, bed and breakfast.
Cuisine: Modern British Vegetarian.
Other Points: Totally no smoking. Credit cards not accepted.
Directions: On the A149 coast road midway between Cromer and Wells-next-the-Sea. (Map 10, C7)

The Kings Head

26 Wroxham Road, Coltishall, Norwich, Norfolk NR12 7EA
Telephone: +44(0)1603 737426
kevin.gardner@tiscali.co.uk

The 17th-century King's Head is one of several inns that once served a thriving quayside community in the days when Wherry boats traded goods along the Broads. A fishy theme dominates the menus, and. Kevin Gardner is diligent in sourcing the best quality shellfish and fish. In addition, Kevin uses Norfolk marsh samphire, locally picked wild mushrooms and fresh asparagus in season from Grange Farm along the road. Typical seafood dishes include crab rösti with avocado and sweetcorn salsa, roast turbot with red wine dressing and a rocket and watercress salad, and pan-fried sea bass with smoked bacon wrapped scallops and buttered tagliatelle. Meat-eaters will find chicken and pork terrine, rack of lamb with roast shallots and Madeira sauce, gruyère-glazed pork fillet with tomato fondue, tagliatelle and red wine sauce, and excellent local estate game on the menu. Good puddings include vanilla crème brûlée, or try a plate of first-class cheeses. More traditional pub fare can be found on the lunchtime and early evening bar menu, perhaps homemade filled baps, sausage and mash, and deep-fried lemon sole with chips and tartare sauce. Four homely upstairs bedrooms; two en suite.

Prices: Set lunch £8.95. Main course from £10.25. Main course (bar/snack) £6.95. House wine £11.75.
Hours: 11.00-15.00. 18.00-23.00. 11.00-22.30 on Sunday.
Food served: 12.00-14.00. 19.00-21.00.
Rooms: 4 rooms, 2 en suite. Rooms from £25 per person.
Cuisine: Modern British.
Other Points: No-smoking area. Children welcome. Car park.
Directions: On B1354 between Aylsham and Wroxham, north of Norwich. (Map 10, C7)

England - Norfolk

Prices: Fishmongers.
Hours: 08.00-17.30.
Other Points: Car park.
Directions: In the town centre of
Cromer. (Map 10, C7)

Richard and Julie Davies

7 Garden Street, Cromer, Norfolk NR27 9HN
Telephone: +44(0)1263 512727

Cromer is a Norfolk seaside resort, noted for its local seafood catch, and
from the outside, this small, glass-fronted retail unit looks like any
fishmongers. But Richard and Julie Davies are the most famous retailer
and wholesaler in these parts - a prominent seafaring family going back
eight generations (the fish shop was opened 30 years ago). Although they
sell an abundance of wet fish (from Lowestoft) and shellfish (notably
King's Lynn shrimps), within the neat, white shop the counter display is
dominated by dressed Cromer crab - their speciality. Cromer crabs are
smaller than those from other parts of the country, but far sweeter and
meatier. Richard Davies uses the most up to date equipment, including the
use of catamarans (for speed) to work his 700 crab pots; once landed,
crabs are sorted, washed and boiled in 25 minutes, ensuring that they are
sold in the best condition. They also catch their own lobsters.

The Victoria at Holkham, Norfolk

Lower Farm

Harpley, Kings Lynn, Norfolk PE31 6TU
Telephone: +44(0)1485 520240

The elegant, chalk-coloured Victorian manor house, surrounded by a beautiful, spacious garden, has been owned by the Cases for 60 years. It's full of charm and elegance, with period furniture, lovely paintings, fresh flowers, knick-knacks and ornaments creating a homely feel. Rooms such as the dining room are given character by old mahogany furniture and a long, highly-polished dining table, the venue for a really comprehensive breakfast with lots of fruit, and all ingredients, acquired from local suppliers. Three spacious bedrooms have a fresh, clean feel, with facilities running to a mini-fridge, large TV and bathrobes; only one room is not en suite, but has an adjoining bathroom. No evening meal is served, but Harpley is just 20 minutes drive to the coast and there are many restaurants and country pubs on the way. Stables are on site, so horse riders are welcome. Note that credit cards are not accepted.

Rooms: 3 rooms, 2 en suite and 1 with private bathroom. Double room from £25 per person, single from £30.
Other Points: No-smoking area. Children welcome over 12 years old. Garden. Car park. Credit cards not accepted.
Directions: Just off the A148, seven miles south west of Fakenham. (Map 10, C6)

The Hare and Hounds

Baconsthorpe Road, Hempstead, Holt,
Norfolk NR25 6LD
Telephone: +44(0)1263 712329

An attractive, unspoilt, Norfolk flint-and-brick pub, dating from the 17th century, enjoying a delightful setting in the depths of the country between Hempstead and Baconsthorpe. The nice old-fashioned interior has tiled floors, a variety of rustic furnishings, cottage windows with deep sills, and a woodburning stove. With a relaxing atmosphere undisturbed by music or games, it serves as a popular meeting place for locals in search of Adnams and Woodforde's ales and traditional homecooked pub food. Chalkboards above the huge fireplace list the day's choice, ranging from good pub staples like decent pies (beef and Adnams ale, sausage and herb), ham, egg and chips, fisherman's pie, and freshly cooked lamb's liver with bacon and onions to various 'Hounds' specials, perhaps wild salmon fishcakes served with new potatoes and salad, and venison steak cooked in garlic butter. Good fishy options include fresh sardines and huge cod and lemon sole, simply grilled in lemon and butter and served with decent chips. Peaceful tiered garden with fish pond for summer days, Close to ruined Baconsthorpe Castle and an easy drive from Blakeney and other coastal hot spots.

Prices: Main course from £8.95. House wine from £8.
Hours: 11.00-15.30 (Sunday from 12.00). 18.00-23.00.
Food served: 12.00-14.30. 18.30-21.30.
Rooms: 3 en suite. £25 per person per night. Children over six half price.
Other Points: No-smoking area. Garden. Children welcome. Car park.
Directions: Village signed off A148 east of Holt; pub located between Hempstead and Baconsthorpe. (Map 10, C7)

Marsham Arms Inn

Holt Road, Hevingham, Norwich, Norfolk NR10 5NP
Telephone: +44(0)1603 754268
nigelbradley@marshamarms.co.uk
www.marshamarms.co.uk

Local landowner Robert Marsham built this roadside hostelry during the 18th century as a staging post for drovers travelling to Norwich market. Set back from the B1149, with an attractive creeper-clad facade, the wood beams and large open fireplace in the entrance are original features.
It is now a traditional country inn offering comfortable accommodation in ten en suite bedrooms housed in a purpose-built block to the rear of the pub. Clean and tidy, and well equipped with TV, hot drinks' tray, telephone, and clock radio, they make a good base from which to explore Norwich. Those on business, in particular, may find the location and informality of the inn more suitable than staying in a city-centre hotel; note the newly equipped conference suite. Traditional homecooked bar food relies on local lines of supply and includes sound pub favourites, notably grilled bacon or hot sausage baguettes, garlic mushrooms, ploughman's lunches, seafood Mornay, and steak and kidney pie with shortcrust topping. Steaks come from the local butcher, who also provides the meat for an excellent mixed grill; there's a popular help-yourself salad bar, and daily fish dishes on the chalkboard. Local Adnams and Woodfordes ales are on handpump.

Prices: Lunch main course from £7.50. House wine £9.50.
Hours: Wednesday-Sunday: 09.00-23.00, Monday and Tuesday closed between 15.00-17.00.
Food served: 12.00-15.00. 18.00-21.30.
Rooms: 10 en suite. Single room from £48, double from £70.
Cuisine: Modern and Classic British with ethnic influences.
Other Points: No-smoking area. Children welcome. Garden. Car park.
Directions: Four miles north of Norwich airport on the B1149 and two miles north of Horsford. (Map 10, C7)

The Old Laundry

Heydon Hall, Heydon, Norwich, Norfolk NR11 6RE
Telephone: +44(0)1263 587343

With just 100 inhabitants, Heydon is one of less than a dozen privately owned villages in Britain. The road ends at the impressive gates of Heydon Hall. Now many people could be fooled into thinking that they were about to stay in the Hall itself (we were), but the Old Laundry is a self-contained annexe, albeit Georgian and originally the servants quarters. Sarah Bulwer Long (whose ancestors built the Hall) has had this renovated and modernised for bed and breakfast guests. A simply furnished reception area leads into a stone-floored sitting room strewn with rugs and decorated in a cosy, traditional manner with good soft furnishings. Breakfast is served here, so two round wooden dining tables are set each morning, with evening meals on request. Eggs, vegetables and fruit are all home grown and fish comes from Burnham Market. Both bedrooms have a fresh clean look, with fresh flowers, one has a large en suite bathroom with the bath set magnificently in the middle of the room, the other is adjacent. For the price, the Old Laundry is a bargain, especially when you consider the 15 acres of beautiful parkland, and the small swimming pool available to guests.

Rooms: 2 rooms, 1 en suite. Rooms between £40 and £60.
Other Points: No-smoking area. Children welcome by prior arrangement. Garden. Car park.
Directions: Between Norwich and Cromer, 12 miles north of Norwich. (Map 10, E5)

The Victoria at Holkham

Park Road, Holkham, Wells-next-the-Sea,
Norfolk NR23 1RG
Telephone: +44(0)1328 711008
victoria@holkham.co.uk
www.victoriaatholkham.co.uk

The imposing building situated at an entrance to Holkham Hall, and just a short stroll from Holkham's magnificent sandy beach, was built in the early 1800s to house the entourage of gentry visiting the hall. It was re-opened in July 2001 after extensive refurbishment by Viscount Coke, and offers overnight accommodation in eleven individually decorated, en suite bedrooms. Most have memorable marsh views across Holkham Nature Reserve, all are beautifully furnished with unique furnishings sourced from Rajasthan, alongside huge beds, and luxurious bathrooms with rolltop baths and classy toiletries. The colonial theme extends to the informal bar and brasserie: carved wood furniture, huge sofas, tables with fat candles and bowls of fruit, and a wealth of Indian artefacts. Menus focus on fresh, local produce, notably beef and seasonal estate game, as well as fish and seafood from the Norfolk coast, with lunch bringing smoked haddock fishcake with buttered spinach, roasted tomatoes and herb oil. Equally accomplished dinners might include chilled crab mayonnaise with linguine, crème fraîche and Avruga caviar, and saddle of venison with roasted root vegetables, figs and red wine sauce. First-class ales are on tap and decent wines with a dozen by the glass.

Prices: Main course restaurant from £6. House wine £11.50.
Hours: 08.00-23.00.
Food served: 12.00-14.30. 19.00-21.30. Fri/ Sat until 22.00.
Rooms: 11 en suite. Low season £55 and high season £85.
Cuisine: Modern British.
Other Points: No smoking in restaurant. Dogs welcome in the bar. Car park.
Directions: On A149 3 miles west of Wells-next-the-Sea. (Map 10, C6)

Prices: Main course from £9. Main course bar meal from £5. House wine from £9.95.
Hours: 12.00-15.00. 18.00-23.00. Closed 25 December evening.
Food served: 12.00-14.00. 19.00-21.30. 12.30-15.00 on Sunday.
Cuisine: Modern British.
Other Points: No-smoking area. Children welcome. Garden. Car park.
Directions: Off A140 Norwich to Cromer Road. Go through Aylsham, past Blickling Hall, then take next right turn. (Map 10, C7)

Walpole Arms

The Common, Itteringham, Aylsham, Norfolk NR11 7AR
Telephone: +44(0)1263 587258
goodfood@thewalpolearms.co.uk
www.thewalpolearms.co.uk

BBC's Masterchef producer Richard Bryan and Norfolk wine merchant Keith Reeves combined their respective talents to buy this unspoilt brick and timber cottage in 2001. The result, with the help of chef Andy Parle, formerly at Adlard's in Norwich, is an exceptional pub-restaurant offering first-class modern British and Mediterranean-inspired food. Daily menus reflect the passion for fresh local produce, notably Morston mussels, Cromer crab, lamb from the Walpole estate, organic beef from the National Trust's Felbrigg estate, venison from nearby Gunton Hall, and local farm fruit and vegetables. Typically, starters range from white bean, sage and chorizo broth, to Norfolk game terrine with prune and walnut salad. Mains include a well-presented summer stew of lamb with potatoes, peas, lettuce and mint, and salmon and smoked haddock fishcakes with lemon and herb mayonnaise. Round off with lemon posset with lemon polenta shortbread. There's the choice of dining in the rustic and informal opened-up bar, which retains plenty of original character, or book a table in the more formal dining room. Excellent East Anglian ales from Woodfordes and Adnams breweries and, as one would expect, a top-notch list of wines.

Beechwood Hotel ★ ▯ ✕ ✎

Cromer Road, North Walsham, Norfolk NR28 0HD
Telephone: +44(0)1692 403231
enquiries@beechwood-hotel.co.uk
www.beechwood-hotel.co.uk

Don Birch and Lindsay Spalding have created a peaceful hotel and you get a feel of days gone by in the classic, traditional decor and the myriad of personal touches about the place. But the words classic and traditional do not mean old fashioned or dowdy. The architecture and history of this elegant, ivy-clad red brick manor house are respected, but there is real flair for decoration shown within. The bar and lounge has squashy leather sofas and tub chairs, and the sitting room, well supplied with books and magazines. Well-equipped bedrooms are a lovely mix of shape and individually styled with a warm yet restrained informal country house look. All the rooms are non-smoking, as is most of the ground floor except the bar and terrace. The blues and creams of the partitioned dining room create an intimate space to enjoy Steven Norgate's cooking which features the best of traditional recipes combined with local ingredients and a contemporary touch. Dressed Cromer crab with spring onion and capsicum dressing, say, or medallions of pork on celeriac and sage purée with crackling, butterscotch apples and calvados jus. This Guide's Hotel of the Year for 2002 award has been followed by VisitBritain's award of Hotel of the Year for 2003.

Prices: Set lunch £17 and dinner £32. House wine £16.
Hours: 19.00-21.00. 12.00-14.00 Sunday.
Rooms: 11 en suite. Double room from £90, single from £65.
Cuisine: Modern British.
Other Points: No-smoking area. Dogs welcome. Children welcome over ten years old. Garden. Car park.
Directions: Leave Norwich on B1150. In North Walsham turn left at first set of traffic lights and right at next set. (Map 10, C7)

The Last Wine Bar and Restaurant ▯ ▯ ✕

70-76 St George's Street, Norwich, Norfolk NR3 1AB
Telephone: +44(0)1603 626626
email@lastwinebar.fsnet.co.uk

Called 'The Last' because of its location in a Victorian shoe factory, this wine bar in an intriguing old building is set in the oldest quarter of Norwich. The space yields several dining areas and a lively upstairs bar. It has a distincitve atmosphere with an eclectic mix of customers - a cross section of young and old. The kitchen explores various Mediterranean styles, with the bar delivering good value dishes that run to charmoula chicken with roasted red onion salad, rib-eye steak and frites, or salmon fishcake with french beans and dill sauce, and bread and butter pudding for £13.60 for three courses. In the restaurant expect a weekly changing menu that could open with Mediterranean fish soup or fresh Cromer crab with avocado and lemon dressing, go on to pan-fried duck breast marinated in tamarind, and finish with vanilla cheesecake with caramel sauce. Some interesting specials include char-grilled squid with mussel and pepper salad and Serrano ham with Manchego cheese and pequillo peppers. The wine list is globally ranging with a good selection of wines by the glass.

Prices: Main course from £9.90. Main course bar/snack from £6.90. House wine £10.90.
Hours: 12.00-14.30 18.00-23.30. Closed Sunday, Bank Holiday Mondays, 25-26 December.
Cuisine: Modern British with Moroccan attitude!
Other Points: No-smoking area. Children welcome over 12 years old.
Directions: Locate St Andrews Hall at the top of St George's Street. Go over the bridge and past the Playhouse; on the left at the junction with Colegate. (Map 10, C7)

The Merchant House ★ ▯ ✕

10 St. Andrews Hill, Norwich, Norfolk NR2 1AD
Telephone: +44(0)1603 767321

Tucked down St Andrews Hill, on the site that was formerly occupied by Brasted's, is a new restaurant that is meeting with approval for the understated elegance of light, space, clean lines, and an understanding of the real cosset factor. Andy Rudd heads the kitchen, a young chef with a passionate approach to food. His strength is an intelligent interpretation of ideas that can result in some dazzling dishes. Ingredients of the highest quality are handled with skill. Note an extraordinarily good value set lunch of impeccably timed seared organic salmon served with a fresh tasting cucumber salad dressed with tomato vinaigrette, followed by chump of lamb with roasted Mediterranean vegetables, and bitter chocolate tart with crème fraîche to finish. The lunch carte keeps value to the fore, often offering simplified versions of dishes on the more expensive evening menu: seared foie gras, for example with braised lentils and peach chutney, or beef fillet with fondant potato and wild mushrooms à la crème. Front of house is headed by Michael Lane who presides over service that is wonderfully lacking in pretension.

Prices: Set lunch from £13.95. Set dinner £23.95. Main course meal from £16.95. House wine £13.95.
Hours: 12.00-14.00. 19.00-21.30. Closed Sunday, Monday and two weeks in February, August and all Bank Holidays.
Cuisine: Modern British.
Other Points: No smoking in the restaurant.
Directions: In the centre of Norwich. (Map 10, C7)

Broom Hall Country Hotel

Richmond Road, Saham Toney, Thetford, Norfolk IP25 7EX
Telephone: +44(0)1953 882125
enquiries@broomhallhotel.co.uk
www.broomhallhotel.co.uk/ad/lr/

The Rowlings lovely Victorian house, set in 13 acres of parkland and two acres of traditional English country garden, has homely old fashioned touches to the décor, such as the family photos on the wall in the sitting room. Here, a lovely melange of antique-style furniture, open winter fire and warm rich décor, contrasts with a bright and airy blue-tiled conservatory, used for snack lunches and sunny breakfasts all year, in addition to meals offered in the traditional Swallowtails restaurant next door (named after a rare Norfolk butterfly). A heated indoor swimming pool is a bonus, and there is outside seating for informal eating on the patio. The ten bedrooms are all individually furnished with marble fireplaces and period-style furniture; both the four poster bed and the half tester rooms stand out, complete with corner baths. On the top floor, the cheaper eaves rooms have all the character that sloping roofs bring. Set price dinners are good value with the likes of homemade asparagus soup to start, then roast cod fillet topped with crispy leeks or grilled breast of Norfolk duck glazed with a honey and rosemary infused sauce (offered as a supplement). The short wine list offers very good value.

Prices: Set price dinner £16.50. House wine £8.
Hours: 12.00-14.00. 19.00-20.30. 12.30-14.00 and 19.00 on Sunday.
Rooms: 10 en suite. Double rooms from £70, single from £45.
Cuisine: Modern British.
Other Points: Totally no smoking except for the bar. No smoking area. Children welcome. Garden. Car park. Licence for Civil Weddings.
Directions: One mile from Watton, on the B1077 to Saham Toney and Ashill. (Map 10, D6)

The Rose and Crown

Old Church Road, Snettisham, King's Lynn, Norfolk PE31 7LX
Telephone: +44(0)1485 541382
info@roseandcrownsnettisham.co.uk
www.roseandcrownsnettisham.co.uk

Tucked away just off the main road that runs through the village centre, the white-painted 14th century inn was originally built to house craftsmen working on the church. Within, there's a warren of bars, with heavy oak beams, uneven red-tiled floors, huge inglenook fireplaces and comfortable settles, a small informal dining room, and to the rear, a modern extension that caters admirably for families who flock here in season. Anthony and Jeanette Goodrich use the best seasonal and local produce, notably Cromer crab, Brancaster lobsters, oysters and mussels, Sandringham Estate beef and locally grown asparagus and soft fruits. At lunchtime expect decent sandwiches, pigeon breast and chorizo salad, citrus roasted sea bass with Mexican spiced potatoes, and fresh tagliatelle with pistou and chargrilled aubergines. Evening additions may include salmon, cranberry and ginger fishcakes with aïoli and chilli jam, and pheasant with beetroot and pearl barley risotto. For pudding try the warm rhubarb and molasses tart with pecan nut ice cream. Five real ales complement the food, and the well chosen list of wines offers twenty by the glass. Stylishly modern en suite bedrooms are individually decorated in bold colours with matching soft furnishings and thoughtful extras.

Prices: Main course from £8. House wine £11.
Hours: 11.00-23.00. sunday 12.00-22.30.
Food served: 12.00-14.00 (until 14.30 on Saturday and Sunday). 18.30-21.00 (untill 21.30 on Saturday and Sunday).
Rooms: 11 en suite. Double/twin room from £45, single from £55.
Cuisine: Modern British.
Other Points: No-smoking area. Children welcome. Garden. Car park.
Directions: Village signed off A149 between King's Lynn and Hunstanton, ten miles north of King's Lynn. (Map 10, C6)

The Lifeboat Inn

Ship Lane, Thornham, Hunstanton, Norfolk PE36 6LT
Telephone: +44(0)1485 512236
reception@lifeboatinn.co.uk
www.lifeboatinn.co.uk

The rambling, 16th-century smuggler's inn is characterised by low-beamed ceilings, tiled floors, carved oak tables, five log-burning fires, ships' lamps, and nautical and farming bric-à-brac. The splendid conservatory features an ancient vine (that thrives on Abbot Ale) and leads to the sun-trap walled patio garden. Bar food is consistently good, traditional country cooking that is designed to offer the best of local produce, whether fish or game. A perennial favourite is a steaming bowl of Brancaster mussels, harvested daily in season. Alternatives include chargrilled steaks, pan-fried liver and smoked bacon on olive mash with red wine jus, and interesting blackboard specials, perhaps oven-baked sea bass and winter game casserole, and there are good traditional snacks like soup, open sandwiches and ploughman's lunches. In the evening restaurant, a good value set menu offers dishes such as dressed Cromer crab with lemon and dill mayonnaise, and local pheasant casseroled in Guinness with cranberries, mushrooms, shallots and parsley mash. Expect well-kept East Anglian ales, a dozen wines by the glass, and comfortable, pine-furnished en suite bedrooms in the adjoining converted barn. All are individually decorated and well equipped.

Prices: Set dinner £25. Main course bar meal from £8.50. House wine £10.50
Hours: 11.00-23.00 (12.00-22.30 Sunday).
Food served: 12.00-14.30. 18.30-21.30.
Rooms: 14 en suite. Double Room from £72.
Cuisine: Traditional & Modern British.
Other Points: Children/dogs welcome. Garden. Car park.
Directions: Inn signposted off A149 coast road, six miles east of Hunstanton. (Map 10, C6)

Three Horseshoes 🚪✕🛏

Bridge Street, Warham, Wells-next-the-Sea,
Norfolk NR23 1NL
Telephone: +44(0)1328 710547

An alehouse since 1725, an old-fashioned atmosphere
still infuses the timeless, three-roomed interior. Gas
lighting, stone floors, scrubbed tables, Victorian
fireplaces and time-honoured pub games, including a
rare example of Norfolk 'twister', a fascinating red
and green dial for playing village roulette, and a 1930s
one-arm bandit converted to take modern coins, will
all fascinate. The well stocked bar dispenses tip-top
East Anglian ales (Woodforde's, Buffy's, Greene King)
tapped from the cask, homemade lemonade, and local
Whin Hill cider (in summer). Hearty country cooking
is the order of the day here, with traditional Norfolk
dishes based on local ingredients, including fish and
game, highlighting both the unpretentious printed
menu and interesting choice of daily specials. Typical
choices range from Wareham mussel soup, soused local
sprats, grilled local herrings, to pot-roast pigeon,
chicken and leek pudding, and braised pheasant, with
good accompanying vegetables, but no chips. Round
off with a homemade nursery pudding such as golden
syrup sponge or toffee apple crumble. They don't take
bookings so arrive early for a table if eating. Homely
bed and breakfast is offered in four simple bedrooms
(one with en suite facilities) in the adjoining Old Post
Office Cottage.

Prices: Main course from £6.50. House wine £7.95.
Hours: 11.30-14.30 (from 12.00 on Sunday). 18.00-23.00
(until 22.30 on Sunday). Closed 25-26 December.
Food served: 12.00-13.45. 18.00-20.30.
Rooms: 3 rooms, 1 en suite. Rooms from £24.
Cuisine: Traditional English.
Other Points: No-smoking area. Children welcome. Garden.
Credit cards not accepted.
Directions: Small turning off A149 between Wells-next-the-Sea and
Stiffkey. (Map 4, D7)

Fisherman's Return 🚪✕🛏

The Lane, Winterton-on-Sea, Norfolk NR29 4BN
Telephone: +44(0)1493 393305
fisherman_return@btopenworld.com
www.fishermans-return.com

Traditional 17th century brick and flint pub, formerly
a row of fisherman's cottages, set in the heart of a
popular holiday village and just a few minutes from
vast open beaches and nature reserves. After a long
bracing walk across the dunes, or a day's exploration
of the nearby Broads, the friendly and unpretentious
bars, complete with warming wood-burners and local
photographs and prints, are a welcome retreat in which
to find good East Anglian ales (Woodfordes, Adnams,
Mauldons) and some hearty home-cooked food. A
good summer family room (Tinho) in a timbered rear
extension has pool table and games, and there's a
lovely enclosed garden with a pets' corner and an
adventure playground. The printed menu sticks to the
traditional, but look to the blackboard for interesting
daily specials such as hearty homemade soups and
casseroles, local crab, mussels and mackerel, winter
game dishes, and fresh fish like oven baked sea bass
with tomato, anchovies and roasted red peppers, and
hot Winterton smoked salmon. A tiny, flint-lined spiral
staircase leads up under the eaves to three clean and
modestly comfortable bedrooms of varying sizes, all
with en suite bath or shower rooms.

Prices: Main course from £7.75. House wine £9.75.
Hours: 11.00-14.30. 18.30-23.00. 11.00-23.00 on Saturday.
12.00-22.30 on Sunday.
Food served: 12.00-14.00. 18.30-21.00.
Rooms: 3 en suite. Single room from £45, double from £70.
Cuisine: Traditional English and Continental.
Other Points: No-smoking area. Children welcome. Garden.
Car park.
Directions: Eight miles north of Great Yarmouth off the B1149.
(Map 10, C8)

The Windmill at Badby 🚪✕🛏

Main Street, Badby, Daventry, Northamptonshire NN11 3AN
Telephone: +44(0)1327 702363
www.windmillinn.co.uk

The very essence of an English country inn - a 17th-century date, honey-
coloured stone trimmed with thatch, and pretty village location - that
works hard to maintain standards. In the two beamy, flagstoned bars (one
with a huge inglenook fireplace and both sporting cricketing and rugby
pictures), Flowers Original, Bass, Boddingtons and Wadworth 6X are
drawn from the cask, and the restaurant menu aims straight for the heart
of traditional British cooking with some snappy updating. Roast
Gressingham duck breast, for example, comes with ginger, mango, lime
and honey glaze, and burgers are made with venison and served with a
creamy peppercorn sauce. Owners John Freestone and Carol Sutton are
passionate about food and makes the effort to source raw materials
locally. Wines appeal to both fans of old and new world, styles are varied
and prices ungreedy. In a pleasant, modern extension at the back are eight
en suite bedrooms that are traditionally styled to be in keeping with the
older building. Rooms are very well maintained and offer a high standard
of comfort; all have satellite TV as well as the usual tea trays, trouser
press and hair dryer.

Prices: Main course from £8.25.
House wine £9.50.
Hours: 11.30-15.30. 17.30-23.00.
Food served: 12.00-14.00 and 19.00-21.30
Monday to Saturday. 12.00-14.00 and
19.00-21.00 on Sunday.
Rooms: 10 en suite. Double room from
£69.50, single from £57.50.
Cuisine: Global.
Other Points: No smoking area. Garden.
Children welcome. Car park.
Directions: Exit 16/M1. Three miles south
of Daventry on A361; ten minutes from
M1. (Map 9, D8)

IRONSTONE COUNTRY IN THE HEART OF ENGLAND

An undiscovered corner of central England, dotted with villages and
sleepy market towns built from the unique local red-brown ironstone.
Drive length: 53 miles

Rutland Water

Stamford
(museum;
Burghley House)

Oakham
(castle; museum)

Bourne

Melton Mowbray

Clipsham

Stretton

Oakham

A606

Rutland
Water

A47

Stamford

Werrington

Peterborough

Elton Hall

Uppingham

Lyddington

Harringworth

Fotheringhay

East Langton

Thorpe
Langton

Bulwick

Fotheringhay
(church; castle)

Oundle

Market
Harborough

Corby

Sawtry

Kettering

Uppingham

Bede House, Lyddington

● Accommodation/Food

● Accommodation

● Food

🦪 Food Shop

To find the establishments marked
here, look up the listing town
marked on the map in bold in the
town index on page 395

Queen's Head
Main Street, Bulwick, Northamptonshire NN17 3DY
Telephone: +44(0)1780 450272

Situated in the heart of a pretty village opposite the church, this quaint old country pub has bags of character. From the front door you enter a tiny drinking bar warmed by an open fire and dominated by plenty of timber joints and beams, with those wonky, uneven walls which indicate great age. Guest ales are changed regularly, but you should find Shepherd Neame Spitfire or Nethergate.

Food is served in three small adjoining rooms, each strewn with rugs and furnished with classic wood furniture and knick-knacks. One room, with just a large dining table, can be used for private bookings. By contrast, the chalkboard menu takes a more modern approach with starters of goats' cheese, red pepper and pesto tartlet, or warm salad of chorizo, black pudding and potatoes. Main courses run to roasted chicken breast filled with chestnut, bacon and mash, red wine and thyme jus, or pan-fried venison steak with fresh cranberry and claret sauce and accompanied by rosemary mash. Overall, this is a village pub with lots of rustic charm. It's a great stop off if you are travelling on the A43.

Prices: Main course from £9.95. Main course bar from £6.50. House wine £9.95.
Hours: 12.00-14.30. 18.00-23.00 (22.30 Sunday). Closed Monday.
Food served: 12.00-14.00. 18.00-21.00 (22.00 Friday and Saturday evening). Lunch only on Sunday.
Cuisine: Modern British with Mediterannean influences.
Other Points: Totally no smoking in restaurant. Dogs welcome in bar only. Garden. Children welcome. Car park.
Directions: Just off A43 between Stamford and Corby.
(Map 10, D5)

The White Swan
Seaton Road, Harringworth,
Northamptonshire NN17 3AF
Telephone: +44(0)1572 747543
thewhiteswan@fsmail.net
www.thewhite-swan.com

The 16th century pub comprises two adjoining rooms and a separate restaurant, with six neatly decorated en suite bedrooms offering comfortable accommodation. The bar is cosy, with part deep-red plaster walls, part-exposed brick, and many ancient, wood-cutting instruments. A huge fireplace links the bar with the equally cosy restaurant. Food is a strength: Paul Brennan, as chef, delivers sound contemporary cooking from an imaginative, ingredient-led menu that takes in sauté of wild English mushrooms with Madeira, cream, truffle and toasted sun-dried tomato bread as a starter, and crisped duck breast, pommes fondant, creamed leeks, roast honey and lime parsnips and juniper jus as a main course. A specials' board over the fireplace lists the likes of pan-fried fillet of sea bass with sautéed potatoes, wild mushrooms and french beans, capers, lemon oil and balsamic reduction. Wines are reasonably priced and have a global reach, while regular cask ales run to Timothy Taylor's Landlord, with a guest such as Old Speckled Hen.

Prices: Main course restaurant £12. Main course bar/snack £8. House wine £10.95.
Hours: 11.45-14.30. 18.30-23.00. Sunday until 15.00 and 22.30.
Food served: 12.00-14.00. 19.00-21.30
Rooms: 6 en suite. Double room from £65, single from £45.
Cuisine: Modern pub food.
Other Points: No-smoking area in main restaurant. Garden. Children welcome. Car park.
Directions: Two miles from A47 between Leicester and Peterborough; four miles from A43 between Stamford and Corby. (Map 9, D4)

The Blue Plate Cafe
The Old Bakery, The Ridings, Northampton,
Northamptonshire NN1 2BP
Telephone: +44(0)1604 620020

The converted bakery still has the original ovens on show but the makeover is decidedly modern, with strong use of the colour blue. Overall, this is an ideal town-centre eatery, great during the day for shoppers or office workers, and bringing out the candles in the evening; however, for strangers to town it may be a bit hard to find at the back of a small shopping arcade. The menu is updated monthly and runs on innovative modern lines that incorporate American themes with popular modern British ideas. Brunch brings American breakfasts of bacon, french toast, eggs, potato hash, and maple syrup, as well as a classic English full monty, but also takes in lunch dishes such as Caesar salad, eggs florentine, and omelette Arnold Bennett. Good pre- and post-theatre menus top and tail a flexible dinner carte that is as happy to serve sandwiches, say grilled chicken with prosciutto, baby spinach, tomato and mozzarella, as well as more substantial steaks, chargrilled calf's liver and bacon, and beer-battered fish and chips. Prices are reasonable and the service relaxed and efficient. There is an even mix of global wines for under £20, with a number under £15.

Prices: Set lunch £8.50 (2 courses). Main course from £10. House wine £10.95.
Hours: 12.00-14.30. 17.30-22.30. Monday to Thursday. Open until 23.00 Fridays. 12.00-23.00 Saturdays. Closed Sundays, Bank Holidays and 25 December.
Cuisine: Global.
Other Points: No-smoking area. Children welcome. Car park close by.
Directions: Exit15/M1. Follow the signs to the town centre. 'The Ridings' is betwen St Giles and Abington Street. (Map 9, D4)

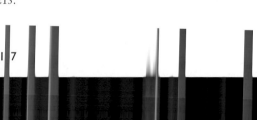

Falcon Inn ★♟♟🏠✗
Fotheringhay, Oundle, Northamptonshire PE8 5HZ
Telephone: +44(0)1832 226254

For a small village it packs a lot of history: Richard III's birthplace, and Mary Queen of Scots place of execution. The Falcon stands in the middle of all this, run by Ray Smikle and John Hoskins of the Huntsbridge Group. Candles, fresh flowers, Windsor chairs, high-backed tapestry-covered chairs, some exposed stone, and discreet soft colours define the bar. The double conservatory dining room looks towards the church, providing a slightly more formal setting, with a mix of green director and Lloyd Loom chairs complementing the pale-green hand-painted walls. There's a snack menu chalked up on a board, but the printed, monthly-changing menu is offered in the bar as well as the dining room. This fits the bill nicely, aware of the rural location and tastes, but managing to be thoroughly modern. Thus, a December meal could open with a rich game terrine with plum jam and toasted brioche. Venison casserole with mashed potato, fried celeriac and carrot crisps, could follow, with vanilla rice pudding with poached winter fruit salad, making a great finish. There are few wine lists of 100 bins that could be so indulgent, and with such an eclectic, esoteric and stimulating selection.

Prices: Set lunch £14.75. Main course restaurant from £9.75. Main course bar from £8.95. House wine £11.50.
Hours: .12.00-15.00. 18.00-23.00. Sunday 12.00-15.00. 19.00-22.30.
Food Served: 12.00-14.15. 18.30-21.30.
Cuisine: International.
Other Points: No smoking area. Children welcome. Garden. Car park.
Directions: Village signposted off A605 between Oundle and Peterborough, one mile north of Oundle. (Map 9, D4)

Cottage Inn ♟🏠✗◇
Dunstan, Craster, Alnwick,
Northumberland NE66 3SZ
Telephone: +44(0)1665 576658
enquiries@cottageinnhotel.co.uk
www.cottageinnhotel.co.uk

Purchased as a row of derelict cottages in 1975, the Cottage Inn was, briefly, a modest guesthouse before finally opening as a pub in 1988. The beamed bar, with ancient exposed brick, dark wood panelling, and a substantial brick fireplace, is an atmospheric room, one where drinkers and diners mingle easily. There's a relaxed approach to eating: the same menu is available throughout, either in the bar, the plant-filled conservatory, or the medieval-styled Harry Hotspur restaurant. The smokery, Robsons of Craster, supply the Craster kippers served at breakfast, and as the lunch and dinner menus first course of kippers 'n' custard. There's also Craster smoked salmon, and a ramekin of pigeon pie to start, with mains running to breast of pheasant, or local game and steak pie, and shoulder of lamb hotpot. Snacks and simpler dishes are also available. Local ales (Wylam Bitter, Cottage Inn Ale) are complemented by a decent choice of reasonably priced wines with ten by the glass. At the back, overlooking the pub's eight-acre wooded garden, is a wing of peaceful ground-floor bedrooms. The 10 en suite rooms are fully equipped, comfortable and good value.

Prices: Set dinner £14. Main course from £6.45. Main course (bar/snack) £6.95. House wine £8.55.
Hours: 11.00-24.00.
Food served: 12.00-14.30. 18.00-21.30.
Rooms: 10 en suite. Double room from £63, single from £35. October-April special break offers.
Cuisine: Traditional English and Scottish.
Other Points: No-smoking area. Children welcome. Garden. Car park. Adventure playground.
Directions: From A1 at Alnwick take B1340 towards Seahouses and follow Craster signs right. (Map 12, A6)

The Ship Inn 🏠✗◇
The Square, Low Newton on Sea, Alnwick, Northumberland NE66 3EL
Telephone: +44(0)1665 576262
forsythchristine@hotmail.com
www.theshipinnnewtonbythesea.co.uk

The aptly named Ship is an unprepossessing, very traditional coastal inn, in a National Trust preserved village, featuring simple features such as tongue and groove boarding and flooring, settles and plain scrubbed wood tables and a solid fuel stove. Christine Forsyth runs her business with great enthusiasm. A great champion of local and regional produce, you may find on her printed and blackboard menus Boulmer crab sandwiches, ploughman's made with unpasteurised cheddar from Doddington Dairy, Craster kippers with new potatoes, lobsters from Newton Bay (50 yards from the pub), meat from nearby farms and fish from Amble day boats. Lunch brings a good value mix of sandwiches, stotties (a kind of bread roll), soup and salads. The evening carte is equally good value, noted for sound country cooking that ranges from lemon sole with lemon butter and parsley, served with new potatoes and stir-fried vegetables, to lamb cutlets with redcurrant and port sauce. A 'serious' chocolate cake served with a rich dark chocolate and rum sauce making an irresistible dessert. Regional beers include Premium, Black Sheep, Gold, Tankards and Landlord's Choice, and there are just two wines available by the glass.

Prices: Main course restaurant from £7.95. Main course bar from £3.50. House wine £8.95.
Hours: 11.00-23.00. Sunday 12.00-22.30.
Food served: 12.00-14.30 Monday to Sunday. 19.00-20.00 Tuesday to Saturday.
Rooms: Self catering accommodation sleeps 4. £55 per night. Weekly from £250.
Cuisine: Modern Pub Food.
Other Points: Totally no smoking during food serving hours. Dogs welcome. Garden. Children welcome.
Directions: From A1 at Alnwick take the B1340 (Seahouses). At crossroads with B1339 follow Ship Inn signs. (Map 12, A6)

Hadrian's Wall, Northumberland

The Victoria Hotel

Front Street, Bamburgh, Northumberland NE69 7BT
Telephone: +44(0)1668 214431
enquiries@victoriahotel.net
www.victoriahotel.net

This Victorian stone-built affair, complete with pointed roof, coat of arms and gables, exudes a sense of well being. Within, open fires burn in the sitting room and bar, there are fresh flowers, rugs strewn on bare boards, a sense of quiet good taste in the decor. The inviting bar mixes marble and wood tables, covers the walls in mirrors and offers a blackboard selection of bar food such as local cod and chips and mushy peas, Bamburgh bangers, mash and onion gravy, and game casserole with herb scones and mash. The split-level restaurant contrasts peach walls and a black and white tiled floor and tartan-style carpet with light panelled walls. An evening brasserie menu delivers tian of Seahouses smokie, fresh asparagus and Jersey Royal potato salad, tower of pork and black pudding with wholegrain mustard and crispy chives, and glazed lemon tart with fresh raspberries. Superior rooms are the business: spacious, with sofa, writing desk, four-poster bed, robes, fresh fruit and mineral water, large modern bathrooms; standard rooms are smaller with a range of good amenities, but some smaller bathrooms are shower only.

Prices: Bar main £6. Main course restaurant £10. House wine £10.65.
Hours: 11.00-23.00, until 24.00 weekends.
Food served: 08.00-21.00 (22.00 in the summer). Brasserie open in the evenings and Sunday lunch.
Rooms: 30 en suite. Double room from £84, single from £47.
Cuisine: Eclectic.
Other Points: No-smoking area. Dogs welcome. Children welcome. Terrace.
Directions: A1 12 miles north of Alnwick take B1341 east to Bamburgh. (Map 12, A6)

Riverdale Hall Hotel

Bellingham, Northumberland NE48 2JT
Telephone: +44(0)1434 220254
iben@riverdalehall.demon.co.uk
www.riverdalehall.demon.co.uk

Run by the Cocker family for 25 years, this country house hotel is also a popular local with a good reputation for food. The atmosphere is lively, service friendly and faultless, and the cricket field in the grounds explains much of the décor (and some of the sporty clientele): trophies and cricketing photos adorn many of the walls, clashing merrily with the rural-chic stencilling. The popular bar menu changes daily and includes sandwiches, jacket potatoes and steaks. There is also an extremely good-value set menu. We eschewed slow-cooked lamb on root mash with wine gravy and Cajun-spiced sea bass, for an excellent simply cooked fillet steak with chips, followed by garden-fresh rhubarb crumble and some local Northumbrian cheeses. Moving into the restaurant, locally made pork and leek sausage served with red onion and pepper chutney and garlic-parsnip mash makes a generous starter on the good-value set dinner menu, especially when it is followed by a middle course of french onion soup. Local venison is next, served with lentils, green vegetables and a redcurrant and tarragon jus. If you have room, a selection of local cheeses is an alternative to white chocolate panna cotta. Twenty-two simply furnished bedrooms, a heated indoor swimming pool and sauna complete the picture.

Prices: Set lunch £11.95, set dinner £18.95. House wine £9.40.
Hours: 12.00-14.30. 18.00-21.30.
Rooms: 22 en suite. Double room from £78, single from £44. 4 self-catering properties available.
Cuisine: Traditional English.
Other Points: No-smoking area. Children welcome. Garden. Car park. Indoor swimming pool.
Directions: From the A69 take the B6320 to Bellingham. After the bridge in Bellingham, turn left. The hotel is 150 yards on the left. (Map 12, B5)

Tuggal Hall

Chathill, Alnwick, Northumberland NE67 5EW
Telephone: +44(0)1665 589229
ccbucknall@lineone.net

Mrs Barratt's substantial manor house, set in its own grounds, is impressively classic and elegant in style, but it is very much a family home. It is imperative to book, as no signs are apparent outside and people will not be taken on spec. A large entrance hall with huge flower arrangements and lemon and burgundy tones sets the style. The sitting room has a TV (there are none in bedrooms), deep white comfy sofas, and plenty of local literature and magazines The dining room has wonderful wallpaper covered with birds and trees, and highly polished furniture gleams. Both bedrooms have private bathroom and are styled in a classic country-house manner with antiques and patterned wallpaper. There is also a single room (for those travelling in parties of three). Locally sourced raw materials, often home-grown, dictate the content of the dinner menus, and the style is classic country-house cooking. Tomato and mint soup may be followed by poached lemon sole in white wine with a beurre blanc sauce, garden spinach and carrots, with blackcurrant fool for dessert, and local cheeses. There is no licence, but guests can bring their own wine. Breakfast features eggs from Tuggle Hall hens.

Prices: B&B. Dinner by prior arrangement, £27.50 (5 courses). BYO wine.
Hours: Closed over Christmas and New Year.
Rooms: 2 with private bathrooms. Prices from £40 per person.
Cuisine: Modern British.
Other Points: Totally no smoking. Children welcome over 12 years old. Garden. Car park.
Directions: Leave Alnwick bypass (A1) at the turn for Denwick/Seahouses B1340. Tuggall Hall is eight miles north on the left. (Map 12, A6)

The Pheasant Inn

Stannersburn, Kielder Water, Hexham,
Northumberland NE48 1DD
Telephone: +44(0)1434 240382
enquiries@thepheasantinn.com
www.thepheasantinn.com

The former staging post for the Royal Mail is a very
well-maintained building, with attention to detail
evident inside and out. The decor is cottagey and
entirely appropriate to the style of the building and
area; indeed, the inn wears its comfortable look well.
Polished wood tables and chairs add to the country
look of the low-ceilinged dining room. This is not a
grand room, being more in the style of the comfortable
farmhouse it once was. The menu delivers sound,
traditional country cooking, with the most popular
dish being roasted Northumberland lamb with a
rosemary and redcurrant jus. Lamb, beef and game
come from a local butcher, fresh fish is from South
Shields, and Northumberland farmhouse cheeses are
from Blagdon. Eight bedrooms provide an excellent
standard of accommodation. All the light, prettily
decorated rooms are well proportioned with good en
suite bathrooms and have the usual tea and telly
facilities. Timothy Taylor's Landlord, Black Sheep
Bitter and Old Speckled Hen are on tap, and the short
wine list offers good choice under £15.

Prices: Evening main course from £9.25, lunch main course from
£6.75. House wine £9.95.
Hours: 11.30-15.00. 18.00-23.00. Sunday 12.00-15.00. 19.00-22.30.
Closed Monday and Tuesdays November - March.
Food served: 12.00-14.30. 19.00-21.00.
Rooms: 8 en suite. Double/twin from £65. Single from £35 and
family from £75.
Cuisine: Traditional Pub Food.
Other Points: No-smoking area. Dogs welcome. Garden. Children
welcome. Car park.
Directions: Follow signs to Kielder Water from B6320 at
Bellingham, 17 miles north of Hexham. (Map 11, B4)

Langley Castle Hotel

Langley-on-Tyne, Hexham,
Northumberland NE47 5LU
Telephone: +44(0)1434 688888
manager@langleycastle.com
www.langleycastle.com

Built in 1350, this is one of the few medieval fortified
castle hotels in England. With castellated towers,
mullioned windows and seven-foot-thick stone walls, it
is hard not to be drawn back in time. The medieval
feel has been captured well in huge public rooms and
bedrooms. In the latter, in particular the named rooms,
deep-set windows are draped and canopied and four-
poster beds are swagged and tasselled, and luxurious
bathrooms take on a touch of glamour with swaths of
cloth framing baths. And there can be few more
evocative settings for a meal. The Josephine
Restaurant, with its exposed stone and arched
doorways, forms the backdrop to Andrew Smith's
classic Anglo-French cooking. The set-price menus use
locally and regionally sourced raw materials, and are
complemented by a separate menu offering dishes at a
supplement. From the main menu there could be ham
hock and vegetable terrine with homemade apricot-
scented pease pudding, loin of Langley lamb rolled
with a venison and rosemary farce and served with
port wine jus and parisienne of vegetables, and a tangy
lemon cream tart with orange and lemon syrup and a
lime sorbet. The wine list is well annotated with good
choice both inside and outside France.

Prices: Set lunch £18.50. Set dinner £29.50. Main course restaurant
from £12.50. Main course bar/snack from £7.50.
House wine £12.75.
Hours: 12.00-14.00. 19.00-21.00.
Rooms: 18 en suite. Double rooms from £115, single from £99.50.
Cuisine: Modern British.
Other Points: No-smoking area. Children welcome. Garden. Car
park. Licence for Civil Weddings.
Directions: M6. Situated between Newcastle and Carlisle, two
miles south on the A686 from Haydon Bridge. (Map 12, C5)

Prices: Set Sunday lunch £7.90 and dinner
£15. Main course from £6.95.
House wine £10.50 (litre).
Hours: 11.30-15.00. 18.00-23.00 Monday-
Friday. 11.30-23.00 on Saturday.
12.00-23.00 on Sunday.
Food served: 12.00-14.00. 18.00-21.00.
Rooms: 4 en suite. Double room from £29
per person, single from £38.
Cuisine: Modern British.
Other Points: No-smoking area. Children
welcome. Car park.
Directions: A1 south of Berwick, take
B6525 (Wooler) for six miles, then B6353
left to Lowick. (Map 12, A5)

Black Bull Inn

2-4 Main Street, Lowick, Berwick-upon-Tweed,
Northumberland TD15 2UA
Telephone: +44(0)1289 388228

Nigel and Margaret Lambert have taken over this pleasant country inn
that dates from the 17th century. A popular local, it enjoys a quiet edge-
of-village location and, as a convenient off-the-A1 stopping point, is hard
to beat. For those staying in one of the comfortable en suite bedrooms, it
is well placed for visiting Wooler and the Cheviot Hills, with Yetholm and
Kelso beyond, or for exploring Holy Island and the magnificent
Northumberland coast. The bustling bars have bags of charm with
original beams still visible in the snug. The large back dining room draws
locals for traditional pub food with staples running to homemade soups,
locally-smoked salmon, pies of steak and kidney or chicken and
mushroom, as well as gammon and pineapple, deep-fried haddock and
chips, and homemade lasagne. In addition, there could be grilled local
Tweed salmon, evening steaks with classic accompaniments of onions and
mushrooms, red wine and cream sauce or peppered sauce. A great pub
breakfast will set you up for a day's walking or sightseeing. A two-
bedroomed self-contained cottage is also available.

Brocksbushes Fruit Farm

Stocksfield, Corbridge, Northumberland NE43 7UB
Telephone: +44(0)1434 633400
wjd@brockbushes.co.uk
www.brockbushes.co.uk

When Caroline Dickinson started her farm shop, her intention was to create a shop that was as near to a fresh produce stall at a village fête as possible. Attractively laid out, there is a wide range of freshly picked fruit and vegetables, backed up by an extensive PYO operation out in the fields. Caroline also cooks hams, pies, scone, tarts and cakes, including a four-month matured fruit cake with alcohol added for Christmas. Soups and fresh and frozen ready meals are also made on the premises.

Hours: Monday-Sunday: 09.30-19.00.
Other points: Ample parking. Children's play area. Picnic area. Facilities for the disabled.
Directions: 16m west of Newcastle-upon-Tyne. North side of Styford roundabout (junction of A68/A69) 2 miles east of Corbridge. (Map 12, C5)

North Acomb Farm

North Acomb, Stocksfield, Northumberland
Telephone: +44(0)1661 843181
www.northacombfarmshop.co.uk

Robin and Caroline Baty have run their family farm situated in the heart of the beautiful Tyne Valley for 25 years. Most of the produce on sale in their farm shop is either own grown or own made, though they specialize in Aberdeen Angus beef imported from Scotland. However, in addition to selling own lamb and pork, ham and bacon is cured on the premises and own-recipe sausages, renowned for their texture and flavour, are popular staples. They also sell milk, own-made butter and cream from their Friesian herd. In the farmhouse kitchen, Caroline oversees the making of homemade cakes and ready prepared frozen meals, including Lancashire hot pot and pasties. For Christmas, they rear turkeys and geese.

Hours: 09.00-17.00 Tuesday-Thursday. 09.30-17.30 Friday. 09.30-17.00 Saturday. 09.30-13.00 Sunday.
Directions: 15 miles west of Newcastle, 5 miles east of Corbridge. From A69, take B6309 direction Bywell/Stocksfield. Signposted.

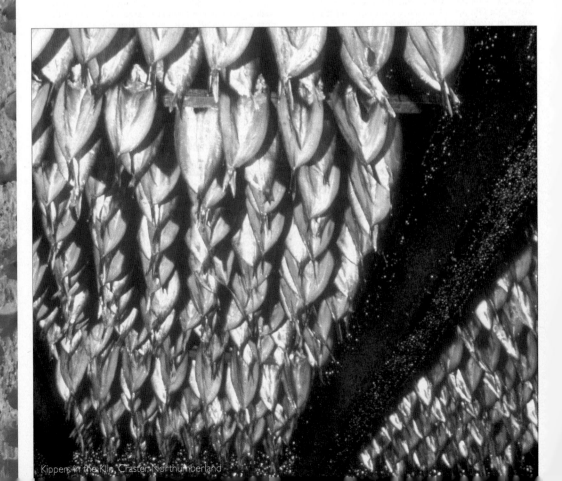

Kippers in the Kiln, Craster, Northumberland

Jackdaw Restaurant

34 Castle Street, Warkworth, Northumberland NE65 0UN
Telephone: +44(0)1665 711488

The family restaurant-cum-craft shop chimes well with the picturesque Northumbrian village. The semi-detached stone house dates from 1717, stands on a steep hill leading to the castle, and is a small-scale operation run in a relaxed manner by husband and wife team Rupert and Gillian Bell: she cooks, he runs front-of-house. In cool weather there's a roaring fire, and polished antique tables set the scene for a menu that blends traditional British styles with a slight modern twist and makes good use of local ingredients. Meat, for example, is from the butcher, R Turnbull, who buys from local farms and owns one of the last remaining small slaughterhouses in Northumberland. Main courses at lunch have a satisfying traditional ring, say, sausages with colcannon and rich onion gravy. But in the evening there could be braised beef olives with black pudding, button onions and mushrooms. Starters take in smoked Tweed salmon, or fresh asparagus with hollandaise sauce, puddings of brown sugar meringues with raspberry purée, and rhubarb crème brûlée or a selection of Northumbrian cheeses. The wine list is a short, thoughtful, well-annotated global trip. Jackdaws is open in the afternoon for tea of homemade scones, fresh lemon sponge, or ham or cheese sandwiches.

Prices: Sunday set lunch £12.25.
Main course from £7.95.
House wine £9.95-£11.95.
Hours: 12.30-14.00. 19.00-21.00. Closed Sunday and Thursday evening, all day Monday and January to mid February.
Cuisine: Traditional English.
Other Points: Totally no smoking. Children welcome.
Directions: 7 miles south of Alnwick on the A1068 coast road. (Map 12, B6)

Martins Arms Inn

School Lane, Colston Bassett,
Nottingham NG12 3FD
Telephone: +44(0)1949 81361

Colston Bassett is a remarkable village, relatively unspoilt by 20th-century developers, and giving a vivid lesson in 17th-century English history with its Civil War connections. Right at the heart of the village stands the Martins Arms, an Elizabethan farmhouse that became first a beer house then an inn in 1844. Beautifully furnished with tasteful window drapes, scatter cushions on sofas and settles and with splendid open fires and a fine collection of hunting prints, it exudes country-house charm. Good bar snacks range from speciality sandwiches (steak with anchovy mayonnaise, sun-blushed tomatoes and rocket), ploughman's lunches featuring, of course, Colston Bassett Stilton, to interesting light meals or starters such as warm Stilton and red onion tart with caramelised pears. Inventive main courses take in cumin-roasted loin of lamb, sweet potato sauté and aubergine confit with game in season from nearby Park Farm Estate. Round off with an excellent homemade pudding, perhaps raspberry and mascarpone shortbread with stem ginger, or a plate of local cheeses served with homemade compote and biscuits. A fairly priced list of wines from Lay and Wheeler includes six by the glass, and Adams and Timothy Taylor are amongst an impressive range of real ales.

Prices: Set lunch £15-18 and dinner £25. Main course restaurant from £13.95. Main course bar meal from £9.50. House wine £12.75.
Hours: 12.00-15.00. 18.00-23.00 (until 22.30 on Sunday). Closed 25 December evening.
Food served: 12.00-14.00. 18.00-22.00. 12.00-14.30 and 18.30-21.00 on Sunday.
Cuisine: Modern British.
Other Points: No-smoking area. Children welcome. Garden. Car park. Antique shop.
Directions: Village signposted off A46 east of Nottingham, 20 miles north of Leicester. (Map 9, C4)

The Robin Hood Inn

High Street, Elkesley, Nottinghamshire DN22 8AJ
Telephone: +44(0)1777 838259

Elkesley is worth noting as you travel on the A1, and the Robin Hood, an unassuming village local with good bar food, is worth going those extra few miles beyond the Little Chef. Pull off the A1 into the pub car park and settle in the homely, comfortable lounge bar or the tiny dining room. For 19 years Alan Draper has been offering weary travellers sustenance in the form of well-presented favourites like filled baguettes, ploughmans lunches, decent ham, egg and chips, and freshly-battered haddock and chips. Or look to the main menu and the specials board for more ambitious alternatives, perhaps potted crab with herb salad and gazpacho dressing, Thai chicken and noodle soup with tomato and red chilli, lamb leg confit with mint pesto, garlic and thyme sauce, smoked haddock fishcake on steamed spinach and mustard cream sauce, and fillet steak with balsamic shallots and red wine sauce. Sweet-toothed diners can round off with caramelised lemon tart with pistachio ice cream or syrup sponge and custard. The varied and excellent-value mid-week menu could entice you to go for four courses.

Prices: Main course from £8. House wine £9.50. Set lunch and dinner from £12.
Hours: 11.30-14.30 (12.00-15.00 Sunday). 18.30-23.00 (19.00-22.30 Sunday).
Food served: 12.00-14.00 Monday to Sunday lunch 18.30-21.00 (Monday to Saturday) No food Sunday evening.
Cuisine: Modern British.
Other Points: No-smoking area. Children welcome. Garden. Car park.
Directions: Two and a half miles south of Worksop, just off A1. (Map 8, A8)

Langar Hall

★ ❚ ✕ ◈

Langar, Nottingham, Nottinghamshire NG13 9HG
Telephone: +44(0)1949 860559
langarhall-hotel@ndirect.co.uk

Thanks to the efforts of Imogen Skirving, the 170-year-old house has the feel of a family home and as such is crammed full of antiques and personal artefacts. Large ancestral portraits line the wide stone staircase in the entrance hall, which displays an informality (sale of local honey, for example) that is continued throughout the hotel. Public rooms have a relaxed lived-in style, full of books, plump sofas, open fires and fantastic country views. Bedrooms in the main house vary in size, but come with all sorts of extras such as big towels, and dressing gowns. Courtyard rooms, known as the Church Wing, are more up-to-date, but equal the main house in their appeal. With bottle-green marble pillars and a huge fireplace topped with a large antique mirror, the restaurant occupies what was an inner hall. Silver candelabra, fine crystal and fresh flowers decorate tables, which are large and well spaced. Toby Garratt, who has been at Langar since the early 90s, follows local supply lines with his predominantly traditional menus, which feature the likes of seared scallops and cider beurre blanc, organic free-range guinea fowl with citrus sauce, and panna cotta with rhubarb soup. The wine list is particularly good value.

Prices: Set lunch from £15. Set dinner from £30.
Hours: 12.00 - 14.30. 19.00 - 21.30.
Rooms: 11 en suite. Double rooms from £130, single from £65.
Cuisine: English.
Other Points: No-smoking area. Children welcome. Car park. Licenced for civil weddings. Garden.
Directions: 15 miles from Nottingham on the A52. (Map 8, B8)

World Service

❚ ✕

Newdigate House, Castle Gate, Nottingham, Nottinghamshire NG1 6AE
Telephone: +44(0)115 8475587
enquiries@worldservicerestaurant.com
www.worldservicerestaurant.com

The elegant exterior of Newdigate House, the 17th-century Georgian building housing World Service, is difficult to fully appreciate as it is located in a fairly narrow lane that leads up to the castle. A high boundary wall creates a delightful private courtyard, oriental style garden and a pleasant, south-facing terrace with canvas parasols. The Marshall Room is part of a modern addition comprising a cosy panelled bar, a lighter, airy part overlooking the garden, and the dining area set in a raised rear section. World fusion describes the décor: walls are lined with rectangular framed mirrors, from the ceiling hang horizontal panels of oriental patterned fabrics, and colours are shades of brown and cream, all mixed in with stone buddahs, vases, masks, and statues. Dishes, however, are in a more modern British vein, pointing out flavours by the use of bright relishes and accompaniments such as orange salad and beetroot caper salsa with fillet of halibut and spiced rice. The very good value, short choice set lunch continues the theme with a straightforward crab bisque, then braised lamb shank with new potatoes and sugar snap peas, followed by an outstanding warm chocolate fondant. Voted Nottingham Restaurant of the Year for 2002 by Nottingham's restaurant-going public.

Prices: Set lunch £14. House wine £10.90.
Hours: 12.00-14.15. 19.00-22.00 Monday to Saturday. 12.00-15.00. 19.00-21.00 Sundays. Closed 1-8 January.
Cuisine: Modern European.
Other Points: No-smoking area. Children welcome.
Directions: Park at the top of the town in the NCP car park. Turn right up the side of Broad Marsh shopping centre. Continue up Castle Gate and cross the main road. World Service is in the first large house on the right. (Map 9, C3)

Mussel and Crab

🍷 ❚ ✕

Sibthorpe Hill, Tuxford, Newark, Nottinghamshire NG22 0PJ
Telephone: +44(0)1777 870491
musselandcrab1@hotmail.com
www.musselandcrab.com

Just a short drive from the A1, this busy, energetic country pub is clearly popular. It offers various eating areas, a couple of bars with welcoming log fires, a mass of specials blackboards, and has all the wine list out on display. Then there are two distinct restaurant areas, one offering the period surroundings of a traditional oak beamed dining room; the other sheer vibrant Mediterranean, with terracotta and ochre hues. There's a light snack menu and a carte, as well as the wealth of choice on the specials boards. Naturally, considering the name, the emphasis is on fish, and Bruce Elliot-Bateman and chef Philip Wright firmly set out their stall when they aim to provide the freshest fish, whether native or exotic, with much of it delivered daily from Brixham. Choose from starters of crab bisque, smoked fish platter, or butterflied sardines dusted with Parmesan and deep fried. Main courses might be swordfish on a bed of sliced red onions and tomato mixed with pesto, or baked sea bass with roasted Mediterranean vegetables and Provençale sauce. Meat options range from seasonal game from local shoots, to pork Wellington and a huge mixed grill.

Prices: Main course from £11. House wine £9.95.
Hours: 11.00-14.30 Monday-Saturday. 11.00-15.00 Sunday. 18.00-23.00 Monday-Saturday. 18.00-22.30 Sunday.
Food served: 12.00-14.30 Monday-Saturday (12.00-14.45 Sunday). 18.00-22.00 Monday-Saturday (18.00-21.00 Sunday).
Cuisine: Modern British.
Other Points: Car park. Totally non-smoking.
Directions: From junction A57/A1 (Markham Moor), take B1164 to Ollerton/Tuxford; pub 800 yards on right. (Map 9, B4)

England - Oxfordshire

The Fish   🍷🍷🛏✕✗
4 Appleford Road, Sutton Courtenay, Abingdon,
Oxfordshire OX14 4NQ
Telephone: +44(0)1235 848242
mike@thefish.uk.com
www.thefish.uk.com

An unassuming, late 19th-century brick-built pub set
in a pretty Thames-side village, famous as the final
resting place of George Orwell. Run by Mike and
Jenny Gaffney since 1995, the Fish is a well-established
and comfortable pub-restaurant offering a high
standard of modern British cooking, notably innovative
seafood dishes using fresh fish from Brixham and
Penzance. Table mats, linen napkins, quality cutlery
and candles grace polished mahogany tables in the
Victorian-style restaurant; french doors lead out to a
peaceful patio and garden. At lunchtime, opt for the
excellent value set menu or order Cornish scallops with
garlic wrapped in ham, or crispy duck confit with fruit
compote, from the light lunch menu. Fish choices from
the carte extends to sea bass with red pepper coulis,
herb oil, aubergine and potato caviar, or hake fillet
and asparagus with chilli and lime hollandaise, with a
delicious rack of English lamb with roasted garlic and
tarragon sauce a well endorsed meat option. There's a
decent list of wines and Greene King IPA on
handpump. Overnight accommodation is in four neatly
appointed upstairs bedrooms.
Prices: Set lunch £15.95. Set dinner £21.95. Bar meal from £6.95.
House wine £12.
Hours: 12.00-15.30. 18.00-23.30.
Closed 25 December - 1 January (not all days - ring to check).
Food served: 12.00-14.00. 19.00-21.00.
Rooms: 2 rooms. Single room from £36, double from £45.
Cuisine: Modern British.
Other Points: No-smoking area. Children welcome.
Dogs welcome. Garden. Car park.
Directions: Village signposted off A415 2 miles south east of
Abingdon. (Map 5, B3)

Millets Farm Centre
Garford, Abingdon, Oxfordshire OX13 5PD
Telephone: +44(0)1865 391555
www.milletsfarmcentre.com

From May to October Millets Farm has over 50 acres
of crops exclusively for pick-your-own harvesting. A
choice of over 30 different fruits and vegetables can be
picked throughout the warmer months - with many
new varieties of certain crops extending the season.
But the extensive farmshop offers the same produce,
picked fresh daily, for those who lack the time or
inclination for PYO. Alongside is a bakery selling
breads and cakes made from locally grown and milled
wheat, a delicatessen with a good cheese counter, a
butcher selling locally reared meats, and a wet fish
shop. There's also an in store wine department.
Hours: Daily 09.00-17.00. PYO available June-September.
Other points: Parking. Play area. Children's farm. Garden centre.
Picnic area. PYO fruit and veg. Easy access disabled.
Directions: 4 miles west of Abingdon on A415 (follow brown
tourism signs). (Map 5, B3)

The Kings Head Inn   ★🍷🍷🛏✕✗
The Green, Bledington, Kingham, Oxfordshire OX7 6XQ
Telephone: +44(0)1608 658365
kingshead@orr-ewing.com
www.kingsheadinn.net

The quintessential Cotswold village pub on the Oxfordshire border is a
delightful 15th-century stone building in a gloriously unspoilt spot hard
by a green complete with a brook. The original bar is charming (low
ceilings, a huge stone fireplace, ancient settles and flagstone floors), while
the separate dining area is an informal setting for some imaginative pub
food. Fresh local produce, notably free-range and organic ingredients, and
fish delivered direct from Cornwall feature on the ever-changing menus.
Modern influences on traditional English dishes can be seen in such
starter choices as home-potted shrimps. Main courses include shank of
English lamb, thyme and root vegetable casserole and grated horseradish.
Good homemade puddings run to apple and plum crumble with custard,
or there could be some unusual British and Irish regional cheeses. Lighter
lunchtime choices are listed on the blackboard. Try one of the four ales on
handpump, or a bottle of wine from the interesting global list that offers
six by the glass and informative tasting notes. High standard, en suite
bedrooms are split between the main building and the converted barn
across the courtyard. All are well appointed.

Prices: Set lunch from £15 and dinner
from £20. Main course from £8.50.
House wine £10.25.
Hours: 11.00-15.00 18.00-23.00 (18.30-
22.30 Sunday). Closed 25-26 December.
Food served: 12.00-14.00. 19.00-21.30.
(19.00-21.00 Sunday).
Rooms: 12 en suite. Double from £65.
Cuisine: Traditional/modern British.
Other Points: No smoking area. Garden.
Children welcome. Car park.
Dogs Welcome.
Directions: On the B4450 between
Chipping Norton and Stow-on-the-Wold.
(Map 9, E3)

Blenheim Palace, Oxfordshire

The Angel Brasserie

14 Witney Street, Burford, Oxfordshire OX18 4SN
Telephone: +44(0)1993 822714
jo@theangel-uk.com
www.theangel-uk.com

Jonathan and Josephine Lewis are justly proud of their beautifully restored 16th century coaching inn, situated a short stroll from Burford's historic high street. Colourful window boxes and decorative signs cover the mellow Cotswold stone façade and within there's an informal brasserie that occupies two beamed rooms, each filled out with sturdy pine tables and chairs and winged armchairs front the log fire in the bar. Jonathan's robust modern European dishes are proving very popular locally, with visitors returning to sample fresh ravioli of crayfish with shellfish sauce, or roast cod with seafood paella, guinea fowl with lemon grass sauce, and pan-fried rib-eye steak with girolle mushrooms. Puddings may include warm prune and frangipane tart with homemade coffee and cardamom ice cream. Both the sheltered sun trap courtyard and walled garden make ideal spots for summer meals. Refurbishment extends upstairs to three themed bedrooms, each styled with an Indian, French and or Italian look and antique furnishings. Decorated and equipped to a high standard with modern en suite bathrooms and added extras like bathrobes, television and video, there's also a lovely residents' lounge. It is a super place to stay in the heart of the Cotswolds.

Prices: Main course from £11.50. House wine £13.75.
Hours: 12.00-14.00 Tuesday-Sunday. 19.00-21.30 Tuesday to Sunday. Closed Monday.
Rooms: 3 en suite. Double room from £85, single from £70.
Cuisine: Modern British.
Other Points: No-smoking area. Garden. Children welcome over 9 years old.
Directions: Witney street is halfway down the main street in Burford. (Map 9, F3)

The Inn for All Seasons

The Barringtons, Burford, Oxfordshire OX18 4TN
Telephone: +44(0)1451 844324
sharp@innforallseasons.com
www.innforallseasons.com

The atmospheric, creeper-clad inn has been sympathetically restored and maintained by the Sharp family, yet retains much 17th century charm. Period furniture, ancient oak beams, original fireplaces with blazing log fires characterise the flagstone bar, which is also full of sporting and flying memorabilia. Fresh fish up from Brixham makes up the specials' board: whole grilled lemon sole with lemon and parsley butter, for example. Shellfish, such as Irish rock oysters from Co Louth, whole grilled lobster or whole cock crabs with garlic mayonnaise and a glass of Chablis (summer only), are a great draw. Locally supplied meat stars in dishes such as roast rack of Cotswold lamb, served pink with a leek and spring onion mash, and thyme and red wine sauce, or grilled Hereford sirloin steak accompanied by a green peppercorn sauce and chunky chips. Seasonal game also features, as do good lunchtime sandwiches, soups, honey roasted Gloucester ham, and hand-raised pork pies. Puddings run to steamed syrup sponge. Real ales include tip-top Wychwood Bitter, Wadworth 6X and Shires, there's a dozen decent wines by the glass and up to 60 malt whiskies. Ten bedrooms are all well equipped with neatly kept en suite bathrooms.

Prices: Set menu from £15-£25. Main course meal from £9.95. House wine £10.95.
Hours: 11.30-14.30. 18.00-22.00, until 21.30 on Sunday.
Rooms: 10 en suite. Four poster from £59.50 per person. Double room from £75.
Cuisine: Modern British and European.
Other Points: Children welcome. Garden. Car park.
Directions: Three miles west of Burford on the A40 towards Cheltenham. (Map 9, F3)

England - Oxfordshire

The Lamb Inn

Sheep Street, Burford, Oxfordshire OX18 4LR
Telephone: +44(0)1993 823155
info@lambinn-burford.co.uk
www.lambinn-burford.co.uk

The 14th century Lamb Inn is every inch a classic Cotswold inn: tucked down a quiet market town side street town with honeysuckle and rose entwined in the golden stonework. Within, centuries of history are etched in the beams, mullioned windows, worn flagstones and antique settles that characterise the rustic bar and beautifully furnished lounges. New owners Bruno and Rachel Cappuccini arrived here in December 2002 and have begun refreshing the decor throughout the fifteen en suite bedrooms and have completed the simple, stylish refurbishment of the restaurant. Bar meals, served throughout the ground floor, run from various sandwiches and starter or main course size Caesar salad or salmon and smoked haddock fishcakes, to more substantial offerings like rib-eye steak with roasted garlic mash and red wine jus. Cooking moves up a gear for dinner in the restaurant, say lobster, monkfish and scallop ravioli with a bouillabaisse beurre blanc, then grilled dorade with sweet chilli vegetables and a lime coriander butter sauce, and chocolate and blueberry terrine to finish. Bedrooms vary in size and ooze cottagey appeal; all have antique furniture, pretty fabrics and many also have old beams and timbers in evidence.

Prices: Sunday lunch £22.50. Main course restaurant from £10. House wine £13.50.
Hours: 12.00-14.30. 19.00-21.30, until 22.00 Friday and Saturday.
Closed 28-29 December.
Rooms: 15 en suite. Double/twin from £125. Single from £80.
Cuisine: Modern British.
Other Points: No-smoking area. Dogs welcome. Garden. Children welcome.
Directions: Exit8/M40. Take the A40 towards Cheltenham and Burford is signposted off this road. Turn right down the high street and first left, the hotel is at the end. (Map 9, F3)

Red Lion Inn

High Street, Chalgrove, Watlington,
Oxfordshire OX44 7SS
Telephone: +44(0)1865 890625

Some of the timbers date from the 11th century, although the earliest record of it being a pub is 1637. Unusually, the Red Lion has always been owned by the parish church and once provided free dining facilities for the church wardens. Nowadays this cream and red painted village inn draws visitors from well beyond the parish for its very good food. The atmosphere inside is decidedly relaxed and unpretentious. The range of modern dishes is chalked up daily on the blackboard in the bar, the choice often featuring bouillabaisse with aïoli, and chargrilled haggis with whisky and shallot cream sauce among the starters. For mains try the calf's liver on garlic mash with excellent braised red cabbage and shallot jus, locally shot pheasant with Stilton and onion sauce, or the beer battered haddock and decent chips. Lunchtime favourites include filled ciabatta rolls and old Oxford sausages with spicy red cabbage and mash. Puddings include the traditional steamed treacle pudding with custard, or a choice of homemade ice creams. New owners took over the Red Lion as we went press so menus and opening/food times may well change.

Prices: Main course from £6.95. House wine £9.95.
Hours: 12.00-15.00. 18.00-23.00.
(19.00-22.30 Sunday evenings)
Closed 24 December to 1st January.
Food served: 12.00-14.00 (12.00-14.30 Sundays). Limited menu Monday and Tuesdays. 19.00-21.00 No food Sunday evening and May Day.
Cuisine: Traditional British.
Other Points: No-smoking area. Children welcome. Garden. Car park.
Directions: On B480 between Watlington and Stadhampton, 10 miles south east of Oxford. (Map 5, B4)

The Bull Inn

Sheep Street, Charlbury, Oxfordshire OX7 3RR
Telephone: +44(0)1608 810689

Overlooking the main street of this handsome, small Cotswold town, the civilised Bull Inn dates from the 16th century. Roy and Suzanne Flynn have over the past eight years created an appealing inn, drawing folk from all around for good old-fashioned hospitality and imaginative, freshly-prepared food. Behind the mellow stone exterior lies a relaxed, tastefully furnished lounge and dining room. The equally welcoming bar area features wooden floors, heavy beams, and loyal locals quaffing pints of Hook Norton and Greene King ales. A snack in the bar will deliver hot jumbo baguettes and a range of daily specials on a short blackboard menu. Also available in the bar, but best enjoyed in the comfortable dining room, are the more adventurous dishes listed on a further blackboard. A typical meal here may begin with a warm salad of chicken livers and bacon, or mussels in white wine with garlic and cream, followed, perhaps, by Mediterranean-style fish stew, rack of local lamb with red wine, thyme and juniper sauce, or game from nearby Cornbury Park. Round off with bread and butter pudding with prunes and armagnac, or a plate of Oxford Blue cheese. Attractive vine-covered side terrace and overnight accommodation in three en suite bedrooms.

Prices: Sunday lunch £20. Main course from £10. House wine from £10.95.
Hours: 12.00-15.00. 19.00-23.00. Sunday 12.00-16.00.
Closed Sunday evening, all day Monday,. Bank Holidays, 25, 26, 31 December and 1 January.
Food served: 12.00-14.00. 19.00-21.00. Until 21.30 Friday and Saturday. 12.00-15.00 Sunday.
Rooms: 3 en suite. Double/twins from £77.
Cuisine: Modern British.
Other Points: No-smoking area. Garden. Children welcome over five years old if eating. Car park.
Directions: Village signposted off A40 along B4437 two miles north of Woodstock. (Map 5, B3)

England - Oxfordshire

The Chequers ⬛ ▯ ✕

Goddards Lane, Chipping Norton, Oxfordshire OX7 5NP
Telephone: +44(0)1608 644717
enquiries@chequers-pub.co.uk
www.chequers-pub.co.uk

Josh and Kay Reid gave up their lives as, respectively, a transport manager and teacher some dozen years ago to enter the pub game, running a smaller pub nearby as a trial for a year, before tenanting the Chequers, which is a Fullers pub. The 16th-century building, has a strongly traditional look, with low ceilings, open fires and rugs on flagstone floors giving a very cosy feel, and the location, in the middle of a bustling market town, certainly draws some appreciative customers.

The restaurant was originally an open courtyard, but it has been glassed over and is now conservatory-style with a high sloping glass roof. Here, a popular menu with global appeal is served. Start with leek parcels filled with smoked cheddar, mushrooms and onion and served with a sweet balsamic dressing, or grilled goats' cheese on olive and garlic crostini. Continue with fillets of sea bass on roasted Mediterranean vegetables with basil pesto, or strips of chicken breast and cashew nuts stir-fried with sweet peppers, onions and beansprouts. Blackboard specials and lunchtime sandwiches, ploughman's and salads extend the choice. The global wine list details some 20 bottles, with ten available by the glass.

Prices: Set lunch £12 and dinner £16. Main course restaurant from £7. Main course bar meal from £5. House wine £9.50.
Hours: 11.00-23.00. 12.00-22.30 on Sunday. Closed 25 December.
Food served: 12.00-14.30. 18.00-21.30. 12.00-17.00 on Sunday.
Cuisine: British with global influences.
Other Points: No-smoking in the restaurant. Children welcome over 14 years old.
Directions: On the A44 between Oxford and Evesham and Oxford and Stratford. (Map 5, B3)

The Fox and Hounds ▯ ✕

Christmas Common, Watlington, Oxfordshire OX49 5HL
Telephone: +44(0)1491 612599

'Come here for a totally organic experience' states the blackboard menu at this classic 15th-century pub. Brakspears brewery and tenant Judith Bishop sympathetically refurbished and extended this brick and flint cottage two years ago, successfully transforming it from a rural local (that had once seen life as the village shop and off-licence) to a modern dining pub, without losing any of its character. Beyond the timeless bar (red and black tiled floor, low-beamed ceiling, simple wooden benches and huge inglenook fireplace), is a dining room, replete with wooden floors, high rafters, and eclectic mix of furnishings, and french doors leading to the garden. Judith's passion for everything organic ranges from locally grown fruit and vegetables, game from Stonor Park and local shoots, to farm reared meats, unusual cheeses, and organic ciders, ales and wines. Lunch in the bar includes doorstep sandwiches of, say, ham and mustard, Welsh rarebit, and ham hock caramelised with brown sugar and thyme with crusty bread or potatoes. Served from an open-to-view kitchen, food in the dining room is more imaginative. Start, perhaps with chicken and pea risotto, followed by medallions of pork with pear, apple and mustard herb mash and a rich red wine sauce.

Prices: Main course from £10. Bar meal from £4.50. House wine £10.
Hours: 11.30-15.00. 18.00-23.00 Monday-Thursday. 11.30-23.00 Friday and Saturday. 12.00-22.30 on Sunday. December 25 open for drinks only 12.00-14.00. Open all day Easter-September.
Food served: 12.00-14.30 (until 15.00 on Sunday). 19.00-21.30.
Cuisine: Modern British.
Other Points: No-smoking area. Garden. Children welcome over ten years old. Car park.
Directions: Exit 5/M40. Take A40 towards Stokenchurch, then in two miles take right turn, signed Christmas Common. (Map 9, F4)

Plough at Clanfield ⬛ 🍷 ▯ ✕ 🛏

Bourton Road, Clanfield, Oxfordshire OX18 2RB
Telephone: +44(0)1367 810222
ploughatclanfield@hotmail.com
www.theplough.tablesir.com

Wisteria and roses clinging to the Cotswold-stone walls of this Elizabethan manor create an idiosyncratic English image that goes down well with American tourists. Within, there is a comfortable bar-cum-lounge with heavy beams, a stone fireplace at one end, a large inglenook at the other. A recent extension has doubled the number of rooms to 12. Each room is individually styled in striking country house-chic, ranging from smart four-posters to cottagey rooms with sloping ceilings under the eaves. In the Shires Restaurant, quality fresh ingredients, many of them locally sourced, and skilful presentation are high points of a contemporary repertoire enlivened with Mediterranean influences. A starter of baked aubergine and goats' cheese tower comes with basil oil dressing, and a terrine of duck livers with wild mushrooms and chilli jam. Mains might include roast rack of lamb, ratatouille and Marsala jus, or seared fillets of Scottish salmon with asparagus and hollandaise sauce. Desserts run the gamut from a trio of homemade chocolate and Ovaltine ice cream in a brandy snap basket, to glazed lemon tart with passion fruit ice cream. The wine list strikes a good balance between regions and offers some varied drinking for under £20.

Prices: Set lunch £17.50 and dinner £23.50. House wine £11.75.
Hours: 12.00-14.00. 19.00-21.00 (20.00 on Sunday). Closed all day Monday, Tuesday lunch and 24th December-7th January.
Rooms: 12 en suite. Double room from £95, single from £82.25.
Cuisine: Modern British.
Other Points: No-smoking area. Garden. Children welcome over 12 years. Car park.
Directions: M40/ Junction 8. Located at junction of A4095 and B4020 between Witney and Faringdon. 16 miles west of Oxford. (Map 5, B3)

The Shepherd's Crook

The Green, Crowell, Chinnor, Oxfordshire OX39 4RR
Telephone: +44(0)1844 351431
scrook@supanet.com

Daily deliveries of fresh fish are the highlight of the ever-changing blackboard menus at this honest, rural local by the village green, beneath the wooded escarpment of the Chiltern Hills. In fact, landlord Steven Scowen is passionate about the quality of the food he offers, sourcing meat and game from local farms and butchers, and using homegrown herbs and vegetables to accompany his wife's freshly-cooked dishes. Dine in the refurbished bar, with its tasteful mix of stripped brick, flagstones, oak beams and open fire, or at oak tables in the raftered dining room. Expect black pudding topped with pancetta, cheese ploughman's with homemade pickles and thick-cut sandwiches (salt beef, bacon and avocado) at lunchtime. The menu extends to king prawns with garlic and chilli, Oxford sausages with mustard mash and onion gravy, and steak and kidney pie in the evening. Suitable fishy options may be Cromer crab salad, and wild sea bass fillet with spring onion, ginger and garlic. Also of note are the well-kept handpumped ales (Steven's other passion), namely Bathams Best, Hook Norton Best, Timothy Taylor Landlord and guest brews, and an unusual list of wines that includes French wine from a private vineyard and a choice of Lebanese bottles.

Prices: Main course bar meal from £5. Main course restaurant from £10. House wine £11.95.
Hours: Monday-Friday 11.30-15.00. 17.00-23.00. Saturday 11.00-23.00.
Food served: 12.00-14.30. 19.00-21.30 (Sunday 19.00-21.00)
Cuisine: Modern British/seafood.
Other Points: No-smoking area. Children welcome. Garden. Car park.
Directions: On the B4009 between Chinnor and Junction 6/M40 (Map 5, B4)

The Snooty Fox Inn

Littleworth, Faringdon, Oxfordshire SN7 8PW
Telephone: +44(0)1367 240549

Initially, you walk into a large, mainly open-plan room with plenty of space, a few private dining areas with lots of oak beams, and wooden tiled flooring to the rear. Walking further into the pub, you come across the modern looking bar, a huge wine rack beside it, and lots of comfy sofas opposite. Here, Greene King IPA, Adnams and Tetley Imperial are dispensed. The main part of the restaurant is more open, has real wood flooring and a big brick fireplace with an open fire (blazing in cooler months), while overhead the ceiling gets higher, exposing lots more timber beams. Chalkboards offer a wide-ranging list of reasonably priced wines, and a specials' board delivers the likes of grilled lamb cutlets with pan-fried crushed potatoes and a light mustard grain sauce, or a warm goats' cheese salad with crispy Parmesan. In addition, an extensive printed menu delivers lamb kidneys' turbigo, and goes on to slow-roasted half-shoulder of lamb glazed with honey with a mushroom and rosemary sauce. Sandwiches, filled baguettes and a popular 'light eating' section of, say, home-cooked ham, egg and chips, or traditional bangers and mash with onion gravy are also available.

Prices: Main course restaurant from £9.95. Bar snack from £7.95. House wine £11.
Hours: 12.00-15.00. 18.00-23.00.
Open all day during the summer.
Food served: 12.00-14.30. 18.30-21.30 (until 22.00 on Friday and Saturday). 12.00-21.30 on Sunday.
Cuisine: Modern Brasserie Food.
Other Points: No-smoking area. Dogs welcome. Garden. Children welcome. Car park.
Directions: Exit 16/M4. On A420 Swindon to Oxford road, two miles east of Faringdon. (Map 5, B3)

White Lion

Goring Road, Goring Heath, Crays Pond, Oxfordshire RG8 7SH
Telephone: +44(0)1491 680471
reservation@innastew.com
www.innastew.com

The unassuming 300-year-old building is set back from a rural crossroads in the hamlet of Crays Pond, close to the Oxfordshire/Berkshire border. Stuart and Caroline Pierrepont bought the lease to this very untypical Greene King pub in 2002 and, following extensive refurbishment, have created a stylish, popular country pub-restaurant. There may be an emphasis on dining, but there's a laid back, local feel to the homely, simply furnished bar. It is open all day (from 8.30am) for breakfast, morning coffee, lunch and afternoon teas and is a great place to relax with a pint and the daily papers. However, the serious action takes place in the dining room and plant-filled conservatory. Rug-strewn wood floors, deep red walls lined with unusual prints, chunky candles and simple furnishings set the scene for the daily changing menu with its emphasis on fish (delivered twice-weekly from Cornwall). The kitchen successfully combines traditional favourites with modern ideas, say, carpaccio of tuna with salad niçoise, or chicken liver pâté with onion marmalade. Calf's liver and bacon with salsa verde, or roast sea bream with homemade pasta and fresh asparagus, could follow. Round off with bread and butter pudding with banana ice cream.

Prices: Set lunch £18. Set dinner £25. Main course restaurant from £7.50. House wine £11.95.
Hours: 08.30-23.00. Saturday from 11.00 and Sunday from 12.00. Closed Monday.
Food served: 12.00-14.00. 18.00-21.30. Sunday 12.00-15.00.
Cuisine: Modern British.
Other Points: No-smoking area. Dogs welcome. Garden. Children welcome. Car park.
Directions: Exit 12/M4. Follow the signs to Pangbourne and then to Whitchurch. Go over the toll bridge and two miles along to Crays Pond. (Map 5, C4)

The Leatherne Bottel

The Bridleway, Goring-on-Thames, Oxfordshire RG8 0HS
Telephone: +44(0)1491 872667
leathernebottel@aol.com
www.leathernebottel.co.uk

The setting of Annie Bonnet's restaurant wows visitors with its location right on the banks of the Thames (in summer tables are set right on the banks of the river under a pagoda-style structure). You couldn't find a more unique location, or, given its rural seclusion, a more energetic place. The former coaching inn now wears the air of a country house: a small intimate bar leading into a sequence of low ceilinged rooms, all elegantly decorated. The kitchen is passionate about using the best produce with salad leaves and herbs grown on the premises and featuring in dishes such as scallop ceviche, pickled salad vegetable, tomato and basil broth. There's an abundance of fish and shellfish in summer, say, pan-fried pink bream accompanied by steamed spinach, Puy lentils, and saffron infused mussel sauce, with seasonal game bringing oven-roasted venison, plum-millet risotto, mole and cashew nut sauce. Combinations are intelligent, and different food cultures live happily side by side. The monthly changing set lunch and dinner menus are excellent. The homemade bread is irrisistible - it can be ordered in advance to take home and bake yourself. The wide-ranging wine list is high on quality, although outside the selected house wines there is little below £20.

Prices: Set dinner £23.50. Main course from £17.95.
House wine £14.75.
Hours: 12.00-14.00. (14.30 on Saturday, 15.30 on Sunday).
18.30-21.00 (21.30 on Saturday and Sunday).
Closed Sunday evening.
Cuisine: Modern British.
Other Points: Children welcome over 10 years old. Garden.
Car park.
Directions: Exit 12/M4 or Exit 6/M40. Off the B4009 Goring to Wallingford road. (Map 5, C4)

Falkland Arms

Great Tew, Chipping Norton, Oxfordshire OX7 4DB
Telephone: +44(0)1608 683653
sjcourage@btconnect.com
www.falklandarms.org.uk

Dating back to the 16th century, the creeper-clad, honey-stoned Falkland Arms, set opposite the church, must be close to everybody's ideal country pub, with high-backed settles, a flagstone floor, huge log fire, a prized collection of hundreds of jugs and mugs hanging from old beams. Now owned by Wadworth Brewery and well run by chef/manager Paul Barlow-Heal, it offers good, homecooked food, as well as character and charm in spades. Lunchtime food, served in the bar and garden, is listed on a short blackboard menu and may feature steak and kidney pie and freshly made salmon fishcakes alongside traditional snacks (soup, filled baguettes, ploughman's). The small dining room has more adventurous evening meals (booking advisable), the daily changing menu perhaps offering potato, garlic and thyme soup, braised lamb shank with mash and rosemary gravy, and apple tart with caramel ice cream. Six cottagey en suite bedrooms, two with four-posters, are furnished with antiques and decorated with pretty, co-ordinating fabrics.

Prices: Main course restaurant from £7.25. Bar snack from £3.95.
House wine £7.95.
Hours: 11.30-14.30. 18.00-23.00. Sunday open until 15.00 and 19.00-22.30. Closed 25-26 December and 1 January evenings.
Food served: 12.00-14.00. 19.00-20.00. Sunday 12.00-14.00.
Rooms: 6 en suite. Doubles from £65, singles from £40.
Cuisine: Modern British.
Other Points: No-smoking area. Dogs welcome in bar. Garden.
Children welcome over 14 years old.
Directions: Exit11/M40. Take A361 towards Chipping Norton, then in seven miles turn left to the Tews and turn left left again for Great Tew. (Map 5, B3)

Prices: Set lunch (2 course) £10. Main course restaurant from £14. Main course bar from £6.95. House wine £12.95.
Hours: 11.00-23.00, Sunday until 22.30.
Food served: 12.00-14.30. 19.00-21.00, until 21.30 Saturday. Sunday 12.00-15.00.
Cuisine: Modern Pub Food.
Other Points: No-smoking area in restaurant. Dogs welcome. Garden. Children welcome. Car park.
Directions: On B481 between Reading and Nettlebed, just north of Sonning Common. Exit11/M4. (Map 5, C4)

The Greyhound

Gallowstree Road, Rotherfield Peppard, Henley-on-Thames, Oxfordshire RG9 5HT
Telephone: +44(0)1189 722227

Set back from the road in the charmingly named village of Rotherfield Peppard, the Greyhound looks every part the quintessential country pub, pretty as a picture with an ancient brick and timber façade, wonky tiled roof and an attractive front garden equipped teak tables and cotton parasols in summer. Step inside and you won't be disappointed with the woodblock floor and the open brick fireplace in the classic beamed bar, or the range of ales on handpump. Up a few steps and located in a converted pitch-roofed old barn is the main dining area, replete with rug-strewn wooden floors, hop-strewn rafters, and a real eclectic mix of furnishings. Chef/patron Kevin Whitehouse took over in July 2002 and introduced a varied bar menu, highlighting traditional favourites (steak and kidney pudding, lamb stew in Guinness with dumplings), alongside pasta with pesto, roasted vegetables and mozzarella, filled ciabatta sandwiches, and salmon on mussel and prawn stir-fry. 'Dinner at the Greyhound' is a tad more elaborate, a typical meal featuring courgette and Stilton soup, sautéed king prawns with scallop risotto and green herb dressing or fillet steak on garlic rösti with brandy cream, with warm date sponge with toffee sauce to finish.

The Stonor Hotel and Restaurant

Stonor, Henley-on-Thames, Oxfordshire RG9 6HE
Telephone: +44(0)1491 638866
info@mystonor.com
www.mystonor.co.uk

Viewed from the road, surrounded by open countryside, the Stonor Arms appears much like a well-maintained country pub. The interior, however, is more upmarket. This is, in reality, a smart country house hotel with a walled garden and elegant rooms. The original 18th century building has been carefully extended to house 11 smartly furnished en suite bedrooms and a lovely conservatory, which spans the garden side of the building, and is home to the restaurant. Good food ranges from simple soup and sandwiches, washed down with a pint of Brakspears or a choice of one of five wines by the glass, to some quite sophisticated cooking. An ingredient led menu offers imaginative combinations, say, seared scallops, shredded duck, pickled pear, crème fraîche and soy dressing with crispy pancetta. Mains follow this theme with rump of lamb served with warm Middle Eastern chickpeas, griddled vegetables and barberry and harissa salad with chermoula, but there's also the safety net of a classically inspired Scottish sirloin steak, glazed wild mushroom and peppercorn butter, slow cooked tomato and hand cut chips, for the less adventurous. Wines, divided in France, Rest of Europe and Rest of the World, are a well-chosen good value selection.

Prices: Set lunch £20. Set dinner £30. Main course restaurant from £18.50. Main course bar from £15.50. House wine £14.50.
Hours: 11.00-23.00, Sunday 12.00-22.30.
Food served: 12.00-14.30. 19.00-22.00.
Rooms: 11 en suite. Double/twin £150.
Cuisine: Modern British.
Other Points: No smoking in restaurant. Dogs welcome in bar and rooms. Garden. Children welcome. Car park.
Directions: On B480 towards Watlington, 5 miles north of Henley-on-Thames. Exit6/M40 (Map 5, C4)

The Three Tuns Foodhouse

5 Market Place, Henley-on-Thames, Oxfordshire RG9 2AA
Telephone: +44(0)1491 573260
thefoodhouse@aol.com/info@thefoodhouse.co.uk
www.thefoodhouse.co.uk

Situated in the market place in the heart of Henley, wedged between shops and banks, this tiny, early 16th century pub is easily missed. Although small inside, good use has been made of the available space. This is a fashionable foody pub with antiques on display everywhere. In fact, everything you see is for sale and you can ask to see the antiques price list alongside the food menu. Keiron Daniels is passionate about food, proudly buying about 50% of his produce locally, and delivering an elegant menu with an express choice at lunchtime that could run to olive and goats' cheese soufflé on a bed of leaves. The evening menu brings white bean and chestnut mushroom to start, with mains along the lines of confit duck leg served with sautéed potatoes, green beans and red wine sauce. It's also possible to buy goodies such as pickled green figs, Spanish mountain honey and French chocolate walnuts to take home. The wine list offers a good selection of mainly French wines with at least one option for most of the other wine producing countries. And as this is a Brakspear pub, expect to see their seasonal ales, and Mild and Bitter on tap.

Prices: Express lunch £5 including wine Monday-Saturday. Set dinner £15 Monday-Thursday. Main course lunch around £6. House wine £13.
Hours: 10.00-15.00. 17.00-23.00. Open all day Friday and Saturday. Closed Sunday evenings and Christmas Day.
Food served: 12.00-15.00. 17.30-22.00. Saturday and Sunday breakfast 09.00-23.00.
Cuisine: Modern British.
Other Points: No-smoking area. Garden. Children welcome. Car park.
Directions: In the centre of Henley-on-Thames. (Map 5, C4)

The Lodge

Horton Hill, Horton-cum-Studley, Oxford, Oxfordshire OX33 1AY
Telephone: +44(0)1865 351235
res@studleylodge.com
www.studleylodge.com

Reading the opening lines in the Lodge's quirky purple and orange Lyrics brochure: 'For eating, meeting, drinks and forty winks, the Lodge is the tops', it is immediately clear that this younger sibling of Studley Priory Hotel is not your average village inn. Jeremy Parke's bold refurbishment of the pub has proved a resounding success, attracting visitors for Simon Crannage's modern British cooking, and the contemporary accommodation. The orange theme runs through the minimalist decor within the spacious modern bar, airy dining areas and the adjoining, well-equipped conference room. 'Lodgings' are available in 16, stylishly simple en suite bedrooms, each with satellite TV, and modem points. 'Lashings' of freshly made food, including homemade breads and ice creams, and dishes run from haddock and leek chowder, to main course shoulder of lamb with smoked bacon and black pudding mash, or silver bream with shellfish stew. 'Lubrication and laughs' can be found in Hook Norton cask ales, a short, global list of wines; six by the glass, and monthly celebration dinners.

Prices: Main course restaurant from £10.50. Main course bar/snack from £3.95. House wine £13.75.
Hours: 12.00-14.00, until 15.00 Saturday and Sunday. 19.00-21.30, until 22.00 Friday and Saturday, 21.00 on Sunday.
Rooms: 16 en suite. Double/twin from £70. Single from £60.
Cuisine: Modern British.
Other Points: No-smoking area. Garden. Children welcome. Car park.
Directions: Exit8/M40. Signposted Oxford, dual carriageway to Headington roundabout. Last exit, singed Crematorium, for Horton-cum-Studley down Bayswater road. Go over the staggered crossroads into the village, the Lodge is on your right hand side. (Map 5, B3)

England - Oxfordshire

Cotswold Lodge Hotel

66A Banbury Road, Oxford, Oxfordshire, OX2 6JP
Telephone: +44(0)1865 512121
cotswoldlodge@netscapeonline.co.uk
www.cotswoldlodgehotel.co.uk

The setting, a few minutes drive from the town centre on the way to monied North Oxford, gives the best of both worlds: accessibility to the centre of Oxford, as well as a tranquillity you would be hard pressed to find in other more corporate hotels. Public rooms and the maze-like layout of the bedrooms lend an air of intimacy. From the moment you step into the entrance hall with the elegant drawing room to the left, and the clubby bar to the right, you can see the attention to detail that has been put into the building. The comfortable bedrooms come in all shapes and sizes. If you want to splash out, the richly coloured Merton suite right under the eaves (one of ten highly individual suites) is recommended. Cheaper, but very desirable alternatives are the light but cosy rooms overlooking the sun-trap of a courtyard, with balconies on the upper floor. The restaurant delivers a broadly based set-price menu (complemented by a more extensive carte). Fresh ingredients are part of the appeal of dishes such as warm chicken liver salad with herb oil and balsamic vinegar, and mignons of beef with a red wine and shallot sauce.

Prices: Set lunch and dinner £22.85.
House wine £15.75.
Hours: 12.00-14.30. 18.30-22.00.
Rooms: 49 en suite. Double room from £175, single from £125.
Cuisine: Modern British.
Other Points: No-smoking area. Children welcome. Car park.
Directions: Half a mile north of the city centre. (Map 9, F3)

Radcliffe Camera, Oxford

The White House

2 Botley Road, Oxford, Oxfordshire, OX2 0AB
Telephone: +44(0)1865 242823
thewhitehouseoxford@BTinternet.com
www.thewhitehouseoxford.co.uk

The painted brick and flint building just eight minutes walk from the city centre with a perfectly maintained back garden (one of only two such in Oxford), is quite a find, and worth knowing about. Inside, wood tiled floors, white plaster walls and an exposed brick fireplace with a black stove make up the look of the modern-style restaurant. Walking through to the dining extension brings you into a lovely bright area with the patio doors running the length of the room and looking out onto the garden and large patio, which can accommodate 60 in warm weather. There's also a more traditional bar area serving a bar and lounge menu devoted to soups, sandwiches and salads, or classic hot dishes of grilled sausage, mash and onion gravy. The restaurant menu delivers contemporary pairings such as crispy duck leg pancakes, spring onions, cucumber and hoisin sauce, alongside more popular dishes of calf's liver and bacon with a shallot sauce. The wine list is a good value, evenly global selection with plenty of choice, especially by the glass where some seven are offered, or for beer drinkers there's Greene King Abbot Ale and Wadworth 6X on draught, with a guest such as Hook Norton.

Prices: Main course bar meal from £4.50. Main course restaurant £9.95. House wine £10.
Hours: 11.00-23.00. Sunday 12.00-22.30.
Food served: 12.00-14.30. 18.00-21.00. Sunday from 19.00.
Cuisine: Eclectic.
Other Points: Dogs welcome. Garden. Car park.
Directions: Eight minutes walk from the centre of Oxford. (Map 9, F3)

The Perch & Pike Inn

South Stoke, Goring, Oxfordshire RG8 0JS
Telephone: +44(0)1491 872415
edwinjtpope@aol.com
www.perchandpike.com

Back on track thanks to the style and vision of Edwin Pope and chef Tim Sykes, this is a much talked-about dining destination. Add four individually designed en suite bedrooms in a magnificent barn conversion and you have the perfect country retreat. Inside, the spick-and-span bar, complete with low-beamed ceilings, red-tiled and brick floors and open fires, offers a cosy, traditional atmosphere in which to quaff a pint of Brakspear ale. In contrast, the ambience and decor in the 50-seater barn restaurant is up-to-the-minute, with modern artwork on the walls and stylish tables and chairs on a light wood floor. The attraction is the imaginative, monthly-changing dinner menu that utilises fresh local produce. Typically, begin with confit of duck on rocket with truffle oil dressing, then follow, perhaps, with marinated roast rump of lamb with pesto mash, roasted shallots and artichokes. Finish with locally made ice creams, or pear and red wine tart. Expect equally enticing lighter lunch and sandwich menus. Flower-filled window boxes and tubs give a splash of colour to the gravelled entrance with its upmarket benches and brollies.

Prices: Set lunch £15. Set dinner £25. Main course restaurant from £12.95. Main course bar/snack from £7.50. House wine £10.
Hours: 11.00-15.00. 18.00-12.00. Sunday 12.00-17.00. Closed Sunday evening.
Food served: 12.00-14.30, until 15.30 on Sunday. 19.00-21.30 Tuesday to Saturday.
Rooms: 4 en suite. Double/twin room from £55.
Cuisine: Modern British.
Other Points: No-smoking area. Dogs welcome. Garden. Children welcome. Car park.
Directions: Exit12/M4. Follow the signs to Pangbourne and then to Streatley. Turn right through Goring to the T junction. Turn left into South Stoke, left again will take you to the Inn. (Map 5, C4)

Rectory Farm

Stanton St John, Oxford, Oxfordshire OX33 1HF
Telephone: +44(0)1865 351677
richardstanley@farmline.com

Pick-your-own asparagus is the thing at Rectory Farm. To pick, they recommend you hold the asparagus spear (shoot) about six inches from the tip and snap it off. If it's the sharper more acidulated French-style white asparagus (the same variety just grown in trenches or banked soil to exclude light), you are after, all you do when you see a tip breaking through the soil, is to burrow down with a long knife and cut it off a few inches underground. The season opens around the end of April and goes on to mid-June, but they sell freshly picked asparagus in the farm shop. Later on they have strawberries, raspberries, broad beans, sugar snap peas as well as pumpkins and potatoes. There is also a mail order service.

Hours: Daily 09.30-19.00.
Other points: Parking. Children's play area. Picnic area. Easy access for disabled.
Directions: Off B4027 Islip/Wheatley road on outskirts of Stanton St John. From Oxford A40 Headington roundabout, take north direction signed Stanton St John. Follow farm signs after three quarters of a mile. (Map 5, B3)

Prices: Set lunch £14.95. House wine £12.
Food Served: 12.00-14.30 and 19.00-22.00. 12.00-22.00 on Sunday.
Cuisine: Modern British.
Other Points: Garden. Car park.
Directions: Exit 8/9/M4 and follow signs for Henley, then A4130 to Nettlebed. Turn left and follow signs to Stoke Row. (Map 9, F4)

The Crooked Billet

Newlands Lane, Stoke Row, Henley-on-Thames, Oxfordshire RG9 5PU
Telephone: +44(0)1491 681048
www.crookedbillet.co.uk

Do ask for directions when making that very essential booking, or you'll be running all over the place trying to find this well-hidden little gem - a typically quaint village pub that has morphed into a restaurant. However, the interior retains all the usual ancient pub trappings of small, intimate rooms with low, heavy-beamed ceilings, part quarry-tiled and woodblock floors, and well-used rustic wood furniture. There's a mish-mash of old pictures and artefacts on the walls and around the inglenook fireplace, and the accumulated character of smoke-stained paint work also adds to the charm. The menu choice is extensive, with a long carte and set lunch of two or three courses, say fresh tomato soup with rocket pesto and slow-roast cherry tomatoes, accompanied by a pannier of crusty bread and marinated olives. After mains of pan-fried halibut fillet served on a bed of stir-fried Provence summer vegetables with a chive and anchovy dressing, there could be an exemplar summer pudding, with summer berry coulis, fresh strawberries and clotted cream. An enthusiastic wine list roams the wine growing regions of the world. Under the same ownership as London Street Brasserie, Reading (see entry).

The Fleece

11 Church Green, Witney, Oxfordshire OX28 4AZ
Telephone: +44(0)1993 892270
fleece@peachpubs.com
www.peachpubs.com

Victoria Moon and Lee Cash have seen their fledgling Peach Pub Company grow from one pub to three over the summer of 2003. Immediately after buying the One Elm in Stratford-upon-Avon (see entry) they were offered the lease on the Fleece, a stylish 11-bedroomed inn overlooking the church green in upmarket Witney, and just couldn't let it go. Late summer refurbishment to the bar and dining areas has seen the successful Peach Pub Company formula replicated here. The trademark leather sofas around low tables, individual mirrors and modern artwork on warm, earthy coloured walls, a laid-back atmosphere, and a Continental-style opening time of 8am for coffee and breakfast sandwiches appears to have found favour among Witney residents. Equally popular is the all-day sandwich, salad and deli-board menu, the latter offering starters or nibbles with drinks of charcuterie, cheese, fish and unusual antipasti. Modern main menu dishes range from spicy smoked chicken tagliatelle, to whole sea bass with sun-dried tomato, artichoke and crushed potatoes, and confit pork belly with creamed horseradish and cabbage. Winter refurbishment of the already stylish en suite bedrooms will see the current decor and furnishings replaced with warm, vibrant colours, funky/chic mirrors, fabrics and furnishings.

Prices: Main course restaurant from £7.50. Main course bar/snack from £1.35. House wine £10.50.
Hours: 08.30-23.00. Sunday 08.00-22.30.
Rooms: 10 en suite. Double/twin from £75. Single from £65 and family from £85.
Cuisine: Modern European.
Other Points: Dogs welcome. Garden. Children welcome. Car park.
Directions: Town centre. Whitney is just off A40 Oxford to cheltenham road. (Map 5, B3)

Greens Restaurant

Witney Lakes Resort, Downs Road, Witney,
Oxfordshire OX29 0SY
Telephone: +44(0)1993 893000
resort@witney-lakes.co.uk
www.witney-lakes.co.uk

To find Greens Restaurant follow signs to the Witney Lakes Resort on the western edge of the town. This combines an 18-hole golf course and a Scandinavian chalet-style building housing a private health club and business conference centre, and restaurant. The latter comes with a peaceful lakeside setting with views across neat fairways to the 18th hole. Light and airy with a central bar area and a splendid summer dining terrace, it offers, unusually for such a location, good quality brasserie-style cooking. Sean Parker is passionate about local produce, sourcing all meats, free range eggs and soft fruits from local farms as well as using quality small suppliers associated with the Oxfordshire Food Group. Commendably, everything is freshly made on the premises, including bread made from flour milled at nearby Shipton. A typical menu might offer full flavoured salmon and smoked haddock fishcakes with homemade tartare sauce, or pan-fried chorizo, bacon, new potatoes and garlic with dressed leaves as a simple starter, or main course. Other dishes include pork fillet with port and redcurrant sauce, dark and white chocolate mousse, and handmade British farmhouse cheeses.

Prices: Main course restaurant from £9.50. Main course bar/snack from £6. House wine £10.95.
Hours: 12.00-15.00. 19.00-22.00.
Closed Saturday lunch and Sunday evening.
Cuisine: Modern British.
Other Points: Totally no smoking. Garden and Terrace. Children welcome. Car park. Private dining. Golf course.
Directions: Exit9/M40. From Oxford A40 take the second turning for Witney and turn right at the roundabout following the signs to Witney Lakes Resort. From Cheltenham or Burford take the A40 follow the signs to Oxford and then as above. (Map 5, B3)

Ricci's On the Green

Goring Road, Woodcote, Oxfordshire RG8 0SD
Telephone: +44(0)1491 680775
www.chezricci.co.uk

This country restaurant with two en suite bedrooms is part of a large, timber-framed house with climbing plants of various sorts winding their way up the front. In keeping with its position overlooking the village green, there's a rustic feel to the open-plan dining room, all wooden beams, low ceilings, slate-framed windows and wood floor, with plants and old farm wheelbarrows scattered around. Owner Michel Ricci is a pleasant host, with a real passion for food. A meal, which might consist of tian of fresh Cornish crab bound in a lemon and coriander mayonnaise topped with a rouille sauce, then braised rabbit accompanied by a cassoulet of beans, smoked bacon, rosemary, garlic and chorizo, with a rich red wine sauce, and a classic lemon tart and Chantilly cream to finish, reveals a restrained yet correct style from a kitchen that is reliant on decent materials and careful techniques. In winter, the business lunch menu of one, two or three courses with a glass of wine is a special bargain. The enthusiasm brought to bear by Michel is just as apparent in his short wine list. The prices are fair, the choices sensible and interesting, and you are urged on the menu to ask about bin ends.

Prices: Set lunch £10.50 (2 courses). Set dinner £17.50 (2 courses), includes half carafe wine. House wine £9.50.
Hours: 19.00-22.00 Wednesday-Saturday. 19.00-21.00 on Sunday. Closed Monday and Tuesday.
Rooms: 2 en suite. Double/twin from £50.
Cuisine: French.
Other Points: Garden. Children welcome. Car park.
Directions: Exit12/M4. Turn right at Pangbourne mini roundabout and left at George Hotel. Turn right at Crays Pond crossroads and immediately left to Woodcote. (Map 5, C4)

Feathers Hotel

★ ❑ 🍷 ▯ ✗ ✿

Market Street, Woodstock, Oxfordshire OX20 1SX
Telephone: +44(0)1993 812291
enquiries@feathers.co.uk
www.feathers.co.uk

It took four 17th century buildings to produce this gem of an inn, which explains the warren of rooms and passages, fireplaces and flagstone floors. Tucked away at the back is an atmospheric yet elegant bar where drinks and bar meals are dispensed, with customers spilling out into a stylish, parasol-shaded courtyard in summer. Rustic chic dictates contemporary colours, deep sofas, leather armchairs, soft lamplight and lots of flowers throughout, especially in the sitting rooms and intimate corners. The restaurant has a lighter feel and the contemporary look is matched by ambitious modern cooking of, say, chicken and foie gras terrine with fig chutney, and roast rump of lamb with sweet potato sauté, aubergine confit and spiced lamb jus, chosen from a market menu that is priced at two or three courses. The extensive wine list has a good global spread, an excellent selection of wines by the glass, plus a good section on French country wines, and some big names from Burgundy and Bordeaux to appeal to the serious oenophile. Bedrooms are well laid out with the emphasis on comfort, achieved through modern fittings and bold fabrics and designs. Each is individual with antique pieces adding character to even the smallest room.

Prices: Set lunch £19.50. Set dinner £28.50. Main course restaurant from £20. Main course bar from £6.95. House wine from £13.50.
Hours: 12.00-23.00.
Food served: 12.00-14.30. 18.30-21.30.
Rooms: 20 en suite. Double/twin £135-£225. Single occupancy £89.
Cuisine: Traditional with modern influences.
Other Points: No-smoking area in restaurant. Dogs welcome. Garden and courtyard. Children welcome.
Directions: Just off A44 in centre of Woodstock. Exit8/9 M40. (Map 9, E3)

Olive Branch

★ ❑ 🍷 ▯ ✗

Main Street, Clipsham, Oakham,
Rutland LE15 7SH
Telephone: +44(0)1780 410355
olive@work.gb.com
www.theolivebranchpub.com

Whilst retaining all of its pub qualities - space for just having a drink, a casual relaxed style which takes in both decor and service - Sean Hope, Ben Jones and Marcus Welford are to be congratulated for putting flesh on a brilliant gastropub vision, and for pulling in industry gongs. With vaguely open-plan rooms within, styled in a pleasing eclectic manner, a pleasant sheltered paved area with tables and chairs without, this is a boon for travellers on the A1. Wine is obviously a passion, and blackboards almost cover the bar area detailing various choices such as keenly-priced house specials, mixing classics with up and coming producers from around the world. Chalkboards list lunchtime sandwiches and the very good-value set lunch. Otherwise, you are offered a printed menu, which is served anywhere in the pub. Grab a menu and a table and someone comes and takes your order, appears to be the style. Staff are all young and enthusiastic. There could be game terrine with Cumberland sauce, and sweet pepper and chorizo soup to start. Then pan-fried skate with parsley mash and nut brown butter, with chocolate roulade with black cherry compote or a plate of local and regional cheeses to finish.

Prices: Set lunch £11.50. Main course restaurant meal from £8.95. Main course bar meal from £6.75. House wine £10.50.
Hours: 12.00-15.00. 18.00-24.00. 12.00-17.00 on Sunday. Closed Sunday evening, 26 December and 1 January.
Food served: 12.00-14.00. 19.00-21.30. 12.00-15.00 on Sunday.
Cuisine: Modern pub food.
Other Points: No-smoking area. Children welcome. Garden. Car park.
Directions: Two miles off the A1 at the B668 junction north of Stamford. (Map 9, C4)

Ram Jam Inn

▯ ✗ ✿

Great North Road, Stretton, Oakham,
Rutland LE15 7QX
Telephone: +44(0)1780 410776
rji@rutnet.co.uk

When the Ram Jam Inn (on the A1) opened in 1987 it was keeping up a long-standing tradition - the Great North Road is lined with pubs. This modern coaching inn is the business: petrol, a snack or meal, real ales, a decent wine list, and a bed for the night. It may be small in scope but it is upscale in attitude, the very antidote to motorway service stations. Inside, the stylish, open-plan café -bar sports comfortable sofas, tiled floors and terracotta walls, and there are daily papers to peruse while waiting for your food. Breakfast is the business, served from 7-11.30am, with local sausages, exemplary bacon, and brilliant hash browns, or there's grilled kipper fillets and freshly-squeezed orange juice. Light meals and snacks, available all day, range from Rutland black pudding with warm shallot, apple and pickled walnut compote to chargrilled minute steak. Those with more time can relax and order from the bistro menu, perhaps marinated venison with mash, braised red cabbage and red wine jus. Smart and comfortable en suite bedrooms overlook the garden and they are surprisingly quiet considering the proximity to the road.

Prices: Main course restaurant meal from £8.25. Main course bar meal from £6.95. House wine £11.
Hours: 07.00-21.30. Closed 25 December.
Rooms: 7 en suite. Double room from £57, single from £47.
Cuisine: Modern British.
Other Points: No-smoking area. Children welcome. Garden. Car park.
Directions: A1 north bound, travel six miles to the junction for Oakham (B668), through the Texaco forecourt. (Map 9, C4)

The Old White Hart Inn

51 Main Street, Lyddington, Rutland LE15 9LR
Telephone: +44(0)1572 821703

Truly a traditional local, this honey-coloured 17th century stone pub stands by the village green with its pretty cottages and backdrop of the picturesque Welland Valley. Popular in summer for its charming walled garden and twelve floodlit pétanque pitches, it is a useful stop for visitors to nearby Bede House and Rutland Water. Good bar food and more elaborate restaurant dishes are available within the traditionally furnished bar and dining areas. At lunchtime, relax in the cosy beamed bar with its splendid log fire and order, perhaps, mussels in white wine and garlic, or deep-fried Grimsby haddock from the specials board. Lighter bites include a good selection of sandwiches. In the evening the seasonally changing menu may list duck liver parfait with tomato chutney, and pheasant on crushed parsnip cake with thyme jus, with daily fresh fish specials listed on the blackboard. Stuart East sources quality produce locally, in addition to shooting his own game, and making his own sausages. A select global list of wines includes 6 by the glass. Five welcoming and well-appointed bedrooms are bright, clean and comfortable, one has a character timbered ceiling and open fireplace, and a huge bathroom with jacuzzi and separate large shower.

Prices: Set lunch and dinner £12.95, two courses for £9.95 (order before 19.30). Main course from £8.95. House wine £11.
Hours: 12.00-14.00. 18.30-23.00. 19.00-22.30 on Sunday.
Food served: 12.00-14.00. 18.30-21.00. 12.00-14.30 Sunday.
Rooms: 5 en suite. Single room from £50, double from £75. Jacuzzi double room £80.
Cuisine: Traditional British.
Other Points: No-smoking area (totally no smoking in restaurant). Children welcome. Garden. Car park.
Directions: One and a half miles south of Uppingham off A6003. (Map 9, D4)

The Burlton Inn

Burlton, Shrewsbury, Shropshire SY4 5TB
Telephone: +44(0)1939 270284
reservations@burltoninn.co.uk
www.burltoninn.co.uk

Since acquiring this former coaching inn on the historic London to Holyhead route six years ago, Gerry and Ann Bean have transformed the 200-year-old whitewashed stone building. The place is lovely in summer, with colourful hanging baskets and tubs adorning the exterior, and a cosy haven in winter within, when bar and restaurant are warmed by log fires. Décor and furnishings are traditional, while candles, fresh flowers, daily newspapers and magazines create a relaxed and welcoming atmosphere. Food is well presented and all meat and game are locally sourced. Those seeking a lunchtime snack can order open sandwiches or ciabatta bread filled with roasted red pepper and goats' cheese, or tuck into a local cheese ploughman's. Alternatively, begin a full-blown meal with duck, pheasant and pistachio terrine with orange butter, then venison casserole with sweet potato mash, and finish with a homemade pudding or a plate of cheese. The latest addition to this successful pub is six individually designed en suite bedrooms, housed in a separate block. All are decorated to a high standard with a light, contemporary feel, and well equipped with plenty of extras.

Prices: Main course from £7.50. House wine £11.
Hours: 12.00-14.00 and 18.30-21.45 from Monday to Saturday. 12.00-14.00 and 19.00-21.30 on Sundays. Closed 26 December, 1 January and Bank Holiday lunch.
Rooms: 5 en suite. Singles from £45. Doubles from £70.
Cuisine: Modern British.
Other Points: Car park. Garden. Children welcome.
Directions: From Shrewsbury, go north towards Ellesmere on the A525. (Map 8, B5)

Bird on the Rock Tearoom

Abcott, Clungunford, Shropshire SY7 OPX
Telephone: +44(0)1588 660631

Mrs Beeton-meets-the-1930s-in-the-21st century, just about sums up this classic tearoom, a 17th century magpie-timbered country cottage, run by a couple of enthusiasts who have brought their design and stage skills to an ever-growing, appreciative public. Started nearly five years ago, Douglas and Annabel Hawkes came from the movie industry (Annabel's finest hour being a couturier to Madonna's Evita). Everything is in period, from Douglas's black and white waiters uniform with ankle-length apron to the Spode-Italian design china and the cotton doilies that cover the sugar. Bread, cakes, homemade chutney, herb scones and the like are from Mrs Beeton's original recipes and they are perfect; the Victoria sponge is a must. From the Gamekeepers lunch with cheese and homemade chutney, progress to Classic Cream Tea, or Poirots Sleuths Tea, with The Complete Jeeves served on a silver cake stand (£9.99 and advance booking only) as a special treat. All produce is sourced from the best possible suppliers: single herd cream from a Herefordshire farm, for instance, organic smoked salmon and their own smoked tea (accredited by the Tea Council) from a smokery in nearby Clunbury.

Prices: Lunch from £4.50. Afternoon teas from £4.50. Menu varies with seasons.
Hours: 10.00-18.00 Wednesday to Sunday during the Summer and 10.00-17.00 during the Winter. Closed Monday and Tuesday. Hours vary with seasons.
Cuisine: Specialises in Teas. Traditional English.
Other Points: Totally no smoking. Children welcome. Garden. Car park.
Directions: Eight miles north west of Ludlow on the B4367 to Knighton (Map 8, C5)

England - Shropshire

The Crown at Hopton

Hopton Wafers, Cleobury Mortimer,
Shropshire DY14 0NB
Telephone: +44(0)1299 270372
www.crownathopton.co.uk

The creeper-clad Crown is set in gardens sloping down
to one of the many streams that flow down to the
Teme Valley. Inside, the Rent Room, where once local
villagers came to pay their rents, preserves its rural
character with an atmospheric bar furnished with
black settles, pews, cushioned seats and old paintings,
and featuring several large fireplaces. Promising
blackboard menus in the smartly appointed Poacher
Restaurant emphasise fish such as seafood medley on
pesto and sun-dried tomato beurre blanc. In addition,
there's local game in season and dishes such as chicken
liver and brandy parfait with cumberland sauce, and
lamb noisettes with redcurrant, port and rosemary
jus. Enhanced by daily specials, seasonal menus in
the bar list sound pub favourites alongside venison
sausages with mustard mash, half shoulder of lamb,
and desserts like Bakewell tart and crème brûlée.
A good range of real ales includes Woods Shropshire
Lad and a fair list of wines with ten half bottles and a
dozen by the glass. Exposed rafters and timbers,
sloping corridors and creaky floorboards characterise
the seven en suite bedrooms, where guests are assured
a high degree of comfort.

Prices: Main course bar meal from £7.25. Main course restaurant
meal from £10. House wine £11.75.
Hours: In the bar 12.00-15.00. 18.00-23.00. 12.00-22.30 on Sunday.
Food served: 12.00-14.30. 19.00-21.30. 18.30-22.00 on Saturday.
18.30-21.00 on Sunday.
Rooms: 7 en suite. Single from £47.50, double from £75.
Cuisine: Traditional and Modern British.
Other Points: No-smoking area. Children welcome. Garden.
Car park.
Directions: Two and a half miles west of Cleobury Mortimer on
A4117 between Kidderminster and Ludlow. (Map 8, D5)

Cookhouse

Bromfield, Ludlow, Shropshire SY8 2JR
Telephone: +44(0)1584 856565
info@thecookhouse.org.uk
www.thecookhouse.org.uk

Formerly a farmhouse, the Cookhouse was once
occupied by Clive of India (his original coat of arms
now hangs in the Lounge Bar). There's a rather curious
blend of traditional and contemporary looks, the
façade is classic Georgian, but within, the Lounge Bar
sums it up neatly. It dates from the 17th century and is
a hugely atmospheric beamed room, yet is approached
via a surprising, functionally modern bar serving local
ales such as Hobsons Bitter and Town Crier, and eight
wines by the glass. Next door, an unpretentious,
simply-designed Café Bar provides casual lunches of
bangers and mash, or battered cod and chips, or
perhaps a more ambitious toasted goats' cheese with
red pepper dressing, and darne of salmon with caper
crust, served with mixed leaves and new potatoes,
making a keenly-priced set two-course meal at lunch or
dinner. More sophisticated, and pricier, cooking in the
next door modern restaurant delivers bright modern
British dishes along the lines of pastilla of duck and
cherries with a cinnamon sauce, and roast fillet of
lamb in a chicken and herb mousse with spinach and
rosemary jus. The wine list is selected to offer a
reasonably wide selection at good prices.

Prices: Set lunch £15.45. Restaurant main course from £12.95.
Cafe/bar main course from £6.95. House wine from £9.75.
Hours: 11.00-23.00. 12.00-22.30 on Sunday.
Food served: 12.00-15.00 and 18.00-22.00. Saturday 11.00-22.00.
Sunday 12.00-21.00.
Rooms: 15 en suite rooms new for late Summer 2004.
Cuisine: Modern British.
Other Points: No smoking area. Children welcome. Garden.
Car park.
Directions: Two miles north of Ludlow on the A49. (Map 8, C5)

De Greys

5-6 Broad Street, Ludlow, Shropshire SY8 1NG
Telephone: +44(0)1584 872764
degreys@btopenworld.com
www.degreys.co.uk

De Greys, situated in a classic black and white timbered building in the
centre of town, is a Ludlow institution, a classic tearoom now run by
French chef Jean Bourdeau. The tearoom-cum-restaurant is at the back,
behind the shop, a dark room heavy with beams and timbers, some lovely
stained-glass windows, and traditionally styled with red carpets,
tablecloths and curtains. Waitresses (and there are lots of them running
around) wear black dresses with white collars, cuffs and frilly aprons. De
Greys is open all day serving tearoom traditionals such as morning
breakfasts, Welsh rarebit, toasted teacakes, pastries and afternoon teas,
and by 10am the place is bustling with mid-morning shoppers. In
addition, there is a printed menu that takes popular dishes and gives them
a twist: prime Herefordshire rump steak with thyme jus, for example, or
roasted confit of duck leg with sautéed garlic potatoes, button mushrooms
and a rich herb sauce. From 7pm to 9pm, this menu continues, backed up
by a specials board that majors in fresh fish. The set evening menu is
great value, the wine list a well annotated, keenly priced global selection.

Prices: Set dinner £15.95-£20. Main course
from £8.95. Main course (bar/snack) from
£5.95. House wine £8.50.
Hours: 09.00-17.00 Monday-Thursday and
Sunday. 09.00-17.30. 19.00-21.00 Friday and
Saturday. Closed 1 January.
Cuisine: Modern British and
traditional French.
Other Points: No-smoking area. Garden.
Children welcome. Bakery shop.
Directions: Take the A49 to Ludlow. De
Greys is found in the centre of Ludlow, just
below the Buttercross clock tower.
(Map 8, C5)

The Feathers Hotel ★ ⬛ 🍷 ✕ ✎

Bull Ring, Ludlow, Shropshire SY8 1AA
Telephone: +44(0)1584 875261
feathers.ludlow@btconnect.com
www.feathersatludlow.co.uk

Ludlow's best known and most photographed building is finally shaking off its corporate identity. The stunning 17th-century black and white building, described as 'that prodigy of timber framed houses and the most handsome inn in the world' by the New York Times, is now owned and run by people who care. Immediate improvements mean that rooms are looking and feeling more welcoming. The 40 bedrooms are divided into standard and four poster rooms with a luxury four-poster suite. Stuart Leggett runs the kitchens utilising raw materials that are sourced locally and offering dishes that can be modernised traditional, such as pan-roast Clun Valley lamb, petit ratatouille, minted new potatoes, garlic confit and red wine sauce, or based on clear modern thinking, say, peppered Gressingham duck, spiced de Puy lentils, celeriac fondant, roast pickled pear and walnut jus. The sensibly short dinner menu is set for two or three courses and brings, say, pan-fried wild turbot, horseradish gnocchi, purple sprouting broccoli and béarnaise sauce, with Valrhona chocolate fondant, almond milk ice and chilled Irish coffee to finish. An astute selection of wines offers good drinking from around the world.

Prices: Set lunch £16.50 and dinner £25. Main course from £12. House wine £12.
Hours: 12.00-14.30. 18.30-21.30 (22.00 on Friday and Saturday).
Rooms: 40 en suite. Double room from £80, single from £60, suite from £115.
Cuisine: Modern British.
Other Points: No-smoking area. Children welcome. Car park. Licence for Civil Weddings.
Directions: From Hereford take the A49 towards Leominster and on to Ludlow. (Map 8, C5)

The Roebuck Inn ⬛ ✕ ✎

Brimfield, Ludlow, Shropshire SY8 4NE
Telephone: +44(0)1584 711230
peter@theroebuckinn.fsnet.co.uk
www.theroebuckinn.com

Acquisition by Peter and June Jenkins at the beginning of 2003 has seen few changes in format, and this civilised village inn continues to fly the flag for country pubs with locals quaffing pints of Woods Parish Bitter. However, eye-catching improvements include a colourful new dining room décor, new fabrics in the three delightful bedrooms, which are maintained to a very high standard, and a cleaned up rear courtyard sporting cheerful summer baskets. Chef of twelve years, Jonathan Waters, has been retained. Everything is made on the premises, from bread to petit fours, with the focus on local ingredients. Pan-seared scallops may appear as a starter, accompanied by butterbean purée, smoked paprika butter sauce and crispy bacon lardons. Main course portions are generous: the inn's famous fish pie, for instance, representing down to earth rather than fanciful cooking. The kitchen also produces excellent game or fish specials, perhaps grilled fillets of sea bass with fish paella and a chorizo oil dressing. Finish with plum and almond pie. The well-organised list of wines offers good French and new world selections. Upstairs in the en suite bedrooms you'll find plenty of extras such as homemade cake, cafetière coffee, and magazines.

Prices: Main course restaurant from £8.95. Main course bar/snack from £4.50. House wine £11.
Hours: 11.30-15.00. 18.30-23.00. 12.00-15.00. 19.00-22.30 on Sunday.
Food served: 12.00-14.30. 18.45-21.30. 19.00-21.00 on Sunday.
Rooms: 3 en suite. Double room from £70, single from £45.
Cuisine: Modern British.
Other Points: No-smoking in the restaurant. Courtyard. Children welcome. Car park.
Directions: Just off the A49, four miles south of Ludlow near the A456 junction. (Map 8, C5)

Prices: Set lunch £13.50 and dinner £15. House wine £7.75.
Hours: 12.00-14.00 Wednesday-Friday. 18.00-21.00 (from 17.00 on Friday). Open all day Saturday, Sunday and Bank Holidays. Closed all day Monday and Tuesday lunch.
Food served: 12.00-14.00 (until 15.00 on Sunday). 19.00-21.00.
Cuisine: Traditional English/International.
Other Points: No smoking area. Children welcome. Garden. Car park.
Directions: North of Bewdley on B4194 to Kinlet, right along B4363 and then follow signs left to Stottesdon. Exit6/M5. (Map 8, C5)

The Fighting Cocks ⬛ ✕

1 High Street, Stottesdon, Cleobury Mortimer, Shropshire DY14 8TZ
Telephone: +44(0)1746 718270

Tiny Stottesdon lies hidden in the rural heart of Shropshire and the Fighting Cocks is the true hub of the community. It is an unspoilt, unassuming gem of a local that dates from 1830, and is well worth the drive down winding lanes for the first-class Hobsons real ales, and Sandra Jefferies's homecooked food. With quality meat butchered and hung by a local farmer, seasonal vegetables, and fruit sourced from a nearby organic farm, Sandra takes pride in preparing good traditional pub meals, and has won the British Meat Steak Pie of the Year Award (which comes accompanied by fresh vegetables, perhaps parsnips with ginger and crème fraîche, lemon cabbage and dauphinoise potatoes). Choose lemon and pepper chicken, venison casserole, aromatic lamb, Vietnamese beef stew, and popular curries from the blackboard, or freshly-made sandwiches and hot filled baguettes from the laminated list. Puddings may include fruit pies and chocolate and rum pot. Traditional Sunday lunches and fish and chips to take away on Fridays. Prices are amazingly good value and the service is warm and friendly. Enjoy lunch or supper in one of the three homely low-beamed rooms, each sporting open fires (one fronted by a leather sofa) and interesting paintings and old photographs.

SECRET SHROPSHIRE

The Welsh Marches were once a bitterly contested land of lush pastures, wooded valleys and rolling hills, with ancient castles and classic towns forming an integral part of the landscape.
Drive length: 68 miles

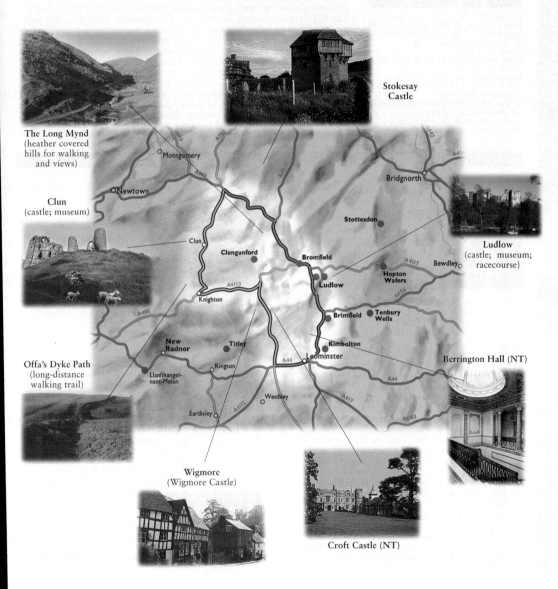

Stokesay Castle

The Long Mynd (heather covered hills for walking and views)

Clun (castle; museum)

Ludlow (castle; museum; racecourse)

Offa's Dyke Path (long-distance walking trail)

Berrington Hall (NT)

Wigmore (Wigmore Castle)

Croft Castle (NT)

● Accommodation/Food

● Accommodation

● Food

🌶 Food Shop

To find the establishments marked here, look up the listing town marked on the map in bold in the town index on page 395

The Hundred House Hotel

Bridgnorth Road, Norton, Shifnal, Telford, Shropshire TF11 9EE
Telephone: +44(0)1952 730353/+44(0)845 6446 100
hundredhouse@lineone.net
www.hundredhouse.co.uk

The mellow, creeper-clad red brick inn is a jumble of ages and styles and has a 14th century half-timbered, thatched barn in the car park. The main building is of Georgian origin and has quarry-tiled floors, exposed brickwork, beamed ceilings and oak panelling. The personality of the inn gains from the inimitable input from the Phillips family over the past 17 years. This enthusiasm extends to the excellent food on offer. Stuart Phillips sources top-notch local produce and cooks both a brasserie-style and full restaurant menu, enhanced by daily specials. He gives a distinctly modern touch to such dishes as confit of duck leg with rocket and chorizo salad and white bean purée. Delicious homemade puddings may include caramelised apple tarte tatin. Lighter dishes of local pork sausages with mash and onion gravy, and chargrilled Cajun chicken with sweet red pepper coulis, are also on offer. Still very much the village local, however, expect to find five real ales on handpump and a well-chosen list of wines. Both names and colour schemes in the ten enchanting en suite bedrooms reflect the magnificent herb and flower garden, incorporating pastel shades, brass bedsteads with patchwork covers, rocking chairs and even padded swing seats suspended from the rafters.

Prices: Main course restaurant from £10. Main course bar, £7.95. House wine £12.50.
Hours: 12.00-15.00. 18.00-23.00. 19.00-22.30 on Sunday. Closed 25-26 December evening.
Food served: 12.00-14.30. 18.00-22.00. (19.00-21.00 Sunday).
Rooms: 10 en suite. Single room from £75, double from £99, family room £125.
Cuisine: Modern British.
Other Points: No-smoking area. Children welcome. Garden. Car park.
Directions: Beside the A442 midway between Bridgnorth and Telford. Exit4/M54. (Map 8, C6)

The Three Horseshoes

Batcombe, Shepton Mallet, Somerset BA4 6HA
Telephone: +44(0)1749 850359

Despite its rural location, this lovely old stone pub with its secluded garden and patio is within easy reach of Bruton, Shepton Mallet and Frome. Inside, the long and low-beamed main bar has exposed stripped beams and is tastefully decorated - terracotta sponged walls with ivy-leaf stencilling are hung with various paintings. Scrubbed pine tables, cushioned window seats and a huge stone inglenook with open log fire enhance the relaxing, cottagey atmosphere and there is an adjoining, less intimate stone walled restaurant extension. Expect modern cooking with an inventive carte listing starters such as tian of Cornish crab and prawns with dill crème fraîche. Among the main courses, calf's liver and bacon is served with red wine gravy, pan-fried chicken is accompanied by gratin potatoes and a lemongrass and thyme jus, and chargrilled beef fillet may come with roasted cherry tomatoes and burgundy jus. Look to the blackboards for daily fresh fish dishes and lighter lunchtime meals. For pudding try the galliano and brioche bread-and-butter pudding, or a plate of west country cheeses. In addition you will find good local ales and at least ten wines by the glass.

Prices: Main course bar meal from £6. Main course restaurant meal from £9. House wine £10.95.
Hours: 12.00-15.00. 18.30-23.00.
Food served: 12.00-14.00 (until 14.30 at weekends). 19.00-21.30 (21.00 on Sunday).
Cuisine: Modern British.
Other Points: No-smoking area. Dogs welcome. Children welcome. Garden. Car park.
Directions: Village signposted off A359 Frome road north of Bruton. (Map 4, C7)

Blackmore Farm

Blackmore Lane, Cannington, Bridgwater, Somerset TA5 2NE
Telephone: +44(0)1278 653442
dyerfarm@aol.com
www.dyerfarm.co.uk

This fabulous old manor house attached to a working farm dates from the 14th century, one of the very few to have preserved its original state including the oak front door, stone archways, garderobes, and chapel; the latter serving as a museum showing ancient artefacts. Ann Dyer keeps an immaculate house true to its 14th century origins. It is decorated in medieval Tudor style with an architectural or historical surprise at every turn. The Great Hall has a striking fireplace, the lintel constructed from a single piece of local sandstone. A long English oak table, made by local craftsmen - the perfect place to enjoy a breakfast of farm bacon and eggs - dominates the room. A spiral staircase leads to bedrooms of different shapes and sizes, with various passageways leading to bathrooms and more bedrooms. Beams, standing timbers, original roof trusses, cob and lime plaster walls, large stone fireplaces, and sitting areas are features; bathrooms are large. The West bedroom has an antique four-poster bed. A recent addition is purpose built (in stone and timber) annexe cottages, some with disabled access, surrounded by an enclosed walled garden.

Rooms: 6 en suite. Double room from £50, single from £30.
Other Points: No smoking area. Garden. Children welcome. Car park.
Directions: From Bridgwater take the A39 towards Minehead. Approximately three miles out of Bridgwater turn left at Tincknell & Son into Blackmore Lane. Follow lane for one mile until you pass the Maltshovel pub. Blackmore Farm is 500 yards past the pub on the left. (Map 8, F5)

DULVERTON, SOMERSET

Prices: Set lunch from £12.
Hours: 10.00-17.00. Closed for one week in January.
Cuisine: Traditional English teas.
Other Points: Totally no smoking. Children welcome. Garden. Credit cards not accepted.
Directions: Junction 27/M5. Dulverton is on the A3223 that runs from north-west to south-east across Exmoor. (Map 4, C5)

Lewis' Tea Rooms
13 High Street, Dulverton, Somerset TA22 9HB
Telephone: +44(0)1398 323850

The village of Dulverton is a thriving tourist spot, especially from March to October, and this traditional English tearoom with its welcoming atmosphere and wonderful smells of home baking caters for everyone. With its cheerful façade made colourful by summer flower tubs and baskets, the interior, by contrast, is simple, roomy but traditional in looks, with cream walls, floral curtains and tablecloths, plus open fires in winter; in summer tables spill out into the enclosed rear garden. Owner Kathie Fuller does all the baking and there are some very yummy cakes on display - coffee and walnut, or strawberry cheesecake, for example, and the warm teabread is highly recommended. The wide choice of tea is correctly served: loose leaf with tea strainers and extra hot water. Also, there's a full English breakfast (popular with walkers and served until 3pm) soups, a selection of very filling rarebits, as well as homebaked ham and two fried eggs, cheese onion and tomato tart, mushrooms on toast, salads and traditional homemade puddings. All the bread and cakes are available for take away, and there is a bring-your-own wine policy.

The Crown Hotel

Park Street, Exford, Somerset TA24 7PP
Telephone: +44(0)1643 831554
info@crownhotelexmoor.co.uk
www.crownhotelexmoor.co.uk

The 17th-century coaching inn has been imaginatively styled; on one side you enter a pretty country hotel, on the other, a simple rural bar with hunting and shooting memorabilia, tables fashioned from wooden barrels, good bar food and well kept ales such as Exmoor Fox and Gold. The hotel offers country pursuit followers a touch of luxury with 17 very comfortable en suite bedrooms, all of which are tastefully furnished with quality pieces, and are very well equipped. And comfort and elegance extend throughout the cosy reception rooms. However, changes are under way since Hugo Jeune picked up the reins. There's much up-grading in hand: new colour schemes in the dining room, and on going bedroom refurbishment. Yet the character of the hotel is being retained studiously. Scott Dickson used to cook at Cameron House Hotel, Balloch, and comes with a high pedigree. His is a style that's modern, pan-European with a classical base, and very produce minded, with dishes such as garden pea boudin with braised leeks and roast loin of Exmoor lamb with rissole potatoes appearing on the nightly gourmet menu. Daily bar food is equally up to date.

Prices: Set five-course dinner £29. Main course restaurant from £15. Bar main courses from £7. House wine £11.50.
Hours: 11.00-14.30. 18.00-23.00. Sunday 12.00-23.00. Closed 25 December.
Food served: Restaurant from 19.00-21.30 Monday to Saturday. 12.00-14.00 Sundays. Bar food 12.00-14.30. 18.30-21.30. All day Saturdays and Sundays.
Rooms: 17 rooms, 16 en suite. Singles and doubles from £47.50.
Cuisine: Modern and Traditional French.
Other Points: No smoking area. Garden. Children welcome. Car park.
Directions: On B3224 midway between Simonsbath and A396 at Wheddon Cross south of Minehead. (Map 4, C5)

Exmoor White Horse Inn

Exford, Exmoor National Park,
Somerset TA24 7PY
Telephone: +44(0)1643 831229
linda@exmoorwhitehorse.demon.co.uk
www.devon-hotels.co.uk

Situated opposite the River Exe in the heart of this small village in the Exmoor National Park, the White Horse is a lovely creeper-clad 16th-century coaching inn. Popular among the walking fraternity and as a base for exploring Exmoor, the inn offers good value accommodation in bedrooms that reflect the character of the inn. All have a soft cottagey look that takes in soft pastel colours and floral fabrics. Downstairs in the comfortable, beamed and carpeted bar there are country-themed prints adorning the walls, open log fires and an extensive menu listing traditional pub meals; Sunday carvery lunches.

Prices: Set dinner £25 (3 courses). Main course from £9. Extensive bar snack menu from £6. House wine £8.45.
Hours: 07.30-23.30.
Food served: 12.00-14.30, 18.00-21.30.
Rooms: 26 en suite. Double room from £80, single from £40.
Cuisine: Traditional British.
Other Points: No smoking in the restaurant and food bar. Children welcome. Garden. Car park.
Directions: On B3224 midway between Simonsbath and Wheddon Cross (A396) south of Minehead. (Map 4, C5)

Prices: Set lunch £12.50. Main courses from £6.50. House wine £9.
Hours: 10.00-16.00 Monday to Saturday. Closed Sunday, Bank Holidays, Christmas and New Year.
Cuisine: Modern British.
Other Points: Totally no smoking. Dogs welcome, Children welcome. Car park.
Directions: Exit25/M5. From Taunton follow signs for Langport. At the Bell Inn in Curry Rivel, turn right and follow the signposts to Hambridge and Ilminster. After one and a half miles see Smokery sign on the left. (Map 4, C6)

Brown and Forrest Smokery Restaurant

Bowden Farms, Hambridge, Langport, Somerset TA10 0BP
Telephone: +44(0)1458 250875
brownforrest@btinternet.com
www.smokedeel.co.uk

Michael Brown started his smokery in a converted cider barn in the early 1980s and has combined fine smoked products with a fairly spacious café and retail shop with lots of smoked products on sale. As this is a small smokery, producing low volumes, more time and effort are spent on the smoking process. Salmon, for example, is hung in the traditional way and oak-smoked for 16 to 18 hours, eels are hot-smoked over beech and applewood to give a strong smokey flavour. And if you simply can't wait until you get home to try the wares, then the neat café, with its red-chequered tablecloths, provides the answer. Start with smoked eel on rye, then order a plate of smoked chicken, salad, new potatoes with homemade chutney, and finish with smoked cheddar or golden syrup bread and butter pudding, and you will come to the conclusion that Brown and Forrest is one of those great little finds. This is the kind of place where the friendly owner and staff, not to mention the food, will have you detouring back for more. It is worth noting that staff are happy to give interested visitors a brief tour of the smokery to explain the smoking process.

Royal Oak Inn

Luxborough, Dunster, Somerset TA23 0SH
Telephone: +44(0)1984 640319
royaloakof.luxborough@virgin.net

The new stewardship of James and Sian Waller and Sue Hinds reaffirms that Luxborough's Royal Oak is indeed in good hands. The two stone-clad public bars and adjacent patio attract a strong local following and events such as real folk nights (not of the Country'n'Western variety) have become a great draw. The connected dining-rooms are comfortably romantic and the food is well worth seeking out, note an evening meal that took in roast Crottin goats' cheese on toasted brioche, grilled turbot with clam and king prawn sauce and pear and frangipan tart accompanied by locally made ice cream. Exmoor ales, Cotleigh Tawny and Acorn from Palmers of Bridport, a versatile range of Somerset bottled ciders, and fairly priced wines by the glass all err on the side of generosity. Stay the night in cosy bedrooms tucked under the eaves, enlivened by country prints and with a friendly teddy bear propped up on the pillow. For those with a day's planned activities ahead, from exploring the moors on foot or touring the north Devon coast, a hearty breakfast is just the thing.

Prices: Main course restaurant from £11.75. House wine from £9.45.
Hours: 12.00-14.30. 18.00-23.00, 22.30 on Sunday.
Food served: 12.00-14.00. 19.00-21.00.
Rooms: 12 rooms, 11 en suite. Doubles from £65, singles from £55.
Cuisine: Modern British.
Other Points: No-smoking area. Dogs welcome. Garden. Children welcome. Car park.
Directions: Village signposted off B3224, three miles east of Wheddon Cross. Exit25/M5. (Map 4, C5)

The Talbot 15th Century Coaching Inn

High Street, Mells, Frome, Somerset BA11 3PN
Telephone: +44(0)1373 812254
roger@talbotinn.co.uk
www.talbotinn.com

Steeped in history, the Talbot stands at the heart of a unique feudal village, the desmaine of the Earl of Oxford and Asquith. Visitors take a step back in time as they enter the cobbled courtyard and pass through a massive oaken double doorway. Within, in the company of old prints, hop vines and attendant memorabilia, Roger Elliott and his experienced team provide an object lesson in what good inn-keeping is all about. Seasonal menus are safely traditional in content, everything from goats' cheese ciabatta and smoked salmon tagliatelli, perhaps, to generously-portioned calf's liver and bacon, and evening Brixham fish specials that might include fresh scallops grilled in their shells with coriander, and sea bass fillets with saffron and mussel sauce. Butcombe bitter is served direct from the cask, and quality house French and world-wide alternatives served by the glass. Stone steps lead to bedrooms whose facilities offer a taste of old-style country living with the added modern appointments of colour TVs, direct dial 'phones and brightly lit, practical bathrooms.

Prices: Main course from £10.95. Bar snack from £7.50. House wine £10.95. Sunday lunch £9.95.
Hours: 11.00-15.00. 18.00-23.00. Sunday 12.00-15.00. 19.00-22.30.
Food served: 12.00-14.00. 19.00-21.30.
Rooms: 8 en suite. Singles from £45.
Cuisine: Traditional British.
Other Points: No-smoking area. Dogs welcome. Garden and patio. Children welcome in the garden. Car park adjacent.
Directions: Village signposted off A362 Frome to Radstock road, half a mile north of Frome. (Map 4, C7)

Whites Hotel

Church Road, North Hill, Minehead, Somerset TA24 5SB
Telephone: +44(0)1643 702032
www.whites-hotel.co.uk

Tony and Linda Walford took over the former Beaconwood Hotel at the end of 2002 and spent almost six months on much refurbishment, giving an entire change of style, décor and direction. Now known as Whites Hotel, it's a pleasant house with a light airy feel that makes the most of big picture windows looking out over the town from its lofty position towards the northern slopes of Exmoor, and westerly over the full sweep of Blue Anchor Bay. Run with infectious good humour, there's a relaxed atmosphere within, and it makes a quiet place to unwind, whether in the informal Oyster Bar, the colourful, comfy library, or unstuffy dining room. Linda Walford is a clever cook, using prime ingredients in a nicely balanced, daily changing set menu that represents great value. Locally sourced produce includes organic leaves and fruit, meats from Hindon Exmoor Organic Farm, and Styles Farmhouse ice creams and sorbets. An understanding of simplicity lies at the heart of the cooking, thus pan-fried goats' cheese patties with Somerset apple and cider chutney, local organic lamb noisettes and cannellini beans in red wine served with new potatoes, and homemade apple crumble with clotted cream.

Prices: Set dinner £16. House wine £9.50.
Hours: Dinner served at 19.00.
Rooms: 10 en suite. Double room from £60, single from £42.
Cuisine: Traditional English.
Other Points: Totally no smoking. Children welcome. Garden. Car park.
Directions: Junction 24/M5. Close to St Michael's Church, off St Michael's Road. (Map 4, C5)

England - Somerset

England - Somerset

The Kings Arms Inn

Montacute, Somerset TA15 6UU
Telephone: +44(0)1935 822513
dearsley@supanet.com

A 17th-century Grade II listed hamstone inn stands opposite the church and Montacute House in a picturesque and unspoilt village. It was once an ale house, owned by the abbey, and later a coaching inn on the Plymouth-London route, where horses were changed before the gruelling climb up Ham Hill. Today's comfortable inn offers characterful accommodation in fifteen newly refurbished en suite bedrooms, all of which are spacious and well equipped; some sporting comfortable four-poster beds. Downstairs, the Windsor Room is a relaxing lounge, but the Pickwick Bar remains the centre of village life. Here, Greene King ales are served, alongside popular bar meals that range from homecooked ham sandwiches and beer-battered cod and chips to lamb hotpot and steak and kidney pie with shortcrust pastry. The evening carte is served in the intimate Abbey Room restaurant, offering smoked duck and mango salad, mussels in white wine, or Caesar salad to start. Mains could be grilled sea bass with crushed parsley new potato cake and prawn sauce, or oven roasted escalope of herb-crumbed lamb with buttered leeks and minted gravy, with rhubarb crumble or apple and cinnamon pie to finish.

Prices: Set lunch from £12.95, dinner from £19.95. Main course from £10.95. Bar meal from £6.95. House wine from £9.95.
Hours: 11.00-23.00. 12.00-22.30 on Sunday.
Food served: 12.00-14.30. 18.30-21.00 (from 19.00 on Sunday).
Rooms: 15 en suite. Single room £65, double from £80.
Cuisine: Modern British.
Other Points: No-smoking area. Children welcome. Garden. Car park.
Directions: Exit 25/M5. Take A3088 at Cartgate roundabout on A303, signed Montacute House. (Map 4, C6)

Wells Cathedral, Somerset

Phelips Arms

The Borough, Montacute, Somerset TA15 6XB
Telephone: +44(0)1935 822557
thephelipsarms@aol.com

Overlooking 'The Borough' or central square close to the entrance to Montacute House, this striking 17th-century hamstone building takes its name from the Phelips family who built the fine Elizabethan mansion that dominates the village. Owned by Palmers brewery and serving their IPA, Copper and 200 ales, it is a thriving village local, with a traditional pub interior featuring simple darkwood tables and chairs, cushioned benches, a huge stone fireplace with open log fires, and walls and shelves adorned with plates and jugs. In keeping with the homely atmosphere, bar food is simple and freshly cooked, ranging from pub favourites such as Somerset Brie ploughman's, filled baguettes and butchers sausages, egg and chips to cod fillet in homemade beer batter with chips, and fillet steak with pepper sauce. More interesting daily specials could include pork hock cooked in cider and apple gravy, queen scallops pan fried in garlic, and fresh brill topped with Lyme Bay scallops and grilled in lemon butter. In addition, there are four cosy, simply furnished en suite bedrooms, and a tranquil walled garden with flower borders for fine weather drinking. This unpretentious, well maintained local provides the perfect lunchtime refreshment spot prior to visiting Montacute House and surrounding gardens (NT).

Prices: Main course from £8. House wine from £9.
Hours: 11.30-14.30. 18.00-23.00.
Food served: 12.00-14.45. 18.00-21.00 (Sunday from 19.00).
Rooms: 4 en suite. Single from £35, double from £55.
Cuisine: Traditional British.
Other Points: No-smoking area. Garden. Car park.
Directions: Take A3088 at Cartgate roundabout on A303, signed Montacute House. Exit25/M5. (Map 4, C6)

Bowlish House

Wells Road, Shepton Mallet, Somerset BA4 5JD
Telephone: +44(0)1749 342022
enquiries@bowlishhouse.com
www.bowlishhouse.com

Jason Goy and Darren Carter took over this mid 17th-century Palladian fronted house in late 2000, continuing the tradition of running Bowlish House as a restaurant with rooms. As you can imagine with a house of this period, ceilings are high, there's wood panelling, a stained glass window halfway up the stairs, all offset by soft lighting from picture lights above paintings supplied by the local art gallery. The intimate restaurant leads through to a large conservatory, which, in turn, overlooks the well-maintained walled garden. Lighting is soft, tables laid with white linen, candles and fresh flowers - a vast antique mirror on one wall reflects the scene. Darren Carter delivers a simple, short menu that could open with chicken liver and wild mushroom parfait accompanied by red onion marmalade and aged balsamic vinegar, or tiger prawns in a rich sun-dried tomato and sour cream dressing. Main courses bring a classic steak and Guinness pie, or baked fillet of salmon with whole grain mustard and cream sauce, and there could be chocolate tart with vanilla ice cream to finish. Bedrooms are spacious, enhanced by large windows, good beds, comfortable chairs, quality furniture, and thoughtful extras such as good quality lotions and potions.

Prices: Set dinner £29.95. House wine £12.50.
Hours: 10.00-11.30 morning coffee. 15.00-17.00 afternoon tea.
Food served: 12.00-14.30. 18.30-21.30. Sunday 12.00-19.00.
Rooms: 3 en suite. Double room from £80, single occupancy £65.
Cuisine: Modern British.
Other Points: No-smoking area. Garden. Children welcome. Car park.
Directions: On the A371 Wells to Bath road. (Map 4, C7)

Burnt House Farm

Waterlip, West Cranmore, Shepton Mallet, Somerset BA4 4RN
Telephone: +44(0)1749 880280

Pam Hoddinott makes a marvelous hostess at this unusual farmhouse B&B, while her husband and son run the farm. Today, the building is crowned by a slate roof, it was the fire that destroyed the original thatch that gave the house its name. This is staying on the farm as it should be, with the added luxuries of a rear garden with a hot tub spa, loads of places to walk, and simply nothing is too much trouble. There's even a tiny fridge at the bottom of the stairs to keep such things as milk and your own wine. The house is full of charm, character, and clutter with memorabilia everywhere, plus low-beamed ceilings, pitch-pine floors, and an inglenook fireplace with a fire burning from autumn to spring. A full-size snooker table is in a separate games room. In the three intimate bedrooms lace canopied beds and lace accessories give a country cottage appeal; one room is ensuite, the other two have their own shower rooms. Great pride is taken in breakfast, which consists of freshly baked own bread (made with local organic flour), homemade jam and preserves, plus locally produced farmhouse butter, eggs and bacon.

Rooms: 3 rooms, 1 en suite, 2 with private showers. Prices from £25 per person.
Cuisine: Organic breakfasts.
Other Points: Totally no smoking. No pets. Garden. Children welcome. Car park.
Directions: From Shepton Mallet take the A361 east towards Frome. After Doulting village you enter Cranmore Parish. Turn left signposted Waterlip. Burnt House Farm is found half a mile on the left. (Map 4, C7)

Hours: Monday-Saturday 09.00-19.00 and Sunday morning.
Other points: National mail order service.
Directions: A30 Honiton/Exeter road, turn off at Fairmile, direction Talaton for 1.5m over crossroads at top of hill, shortly afterwards take road dropping to right, 0.5m to farm. Look for signs. (Map 4, C6)

Lashbrook Unique Country Pork

Drakes Arms Farmhouse, Bishopwood, Chard, Somerset TA20 3QW
Telephone: +44(0)1823 601005
john@lashbrookpork.co.uk
www.lashbrookpork.co.uk

John, Jim and the Carter family team farm barley, potatoes and pigs. From the pigs come the products the farm sells - pork, sausages and bacon from naturally reared free-range and native breeds, including a British Saddleback herd established 35 years ago, as well as Large Whites and Welsh. Working in collaboration with Chris Hill, the Carter family use a unique welfare friendly farming system which produces meat with quality and taste. The sustainable farming system allows the herd to rotate around the farm, rooting up weeds, waste corn, clearing up potatoes and creating fertility for the following crops. Barley straw is used for bedding, grain for feeding and the manure is composted and returned to the land. They produce some 15 types of sausages and burgers and these, together with their quality pork and bacon is delivered by mail order, direct from the farm. Lashbrook also participates in Crediton, Cullompton, and Ottery St Mary farmers' markets.

IN SEARCH OF AVALON

Tantalising glimpses of this glorious, undulating landscape rise from a lowland plain to just over 1,000 feet and effectively divide the spirit and character of north-west Somerset. Drive length: 59 miles

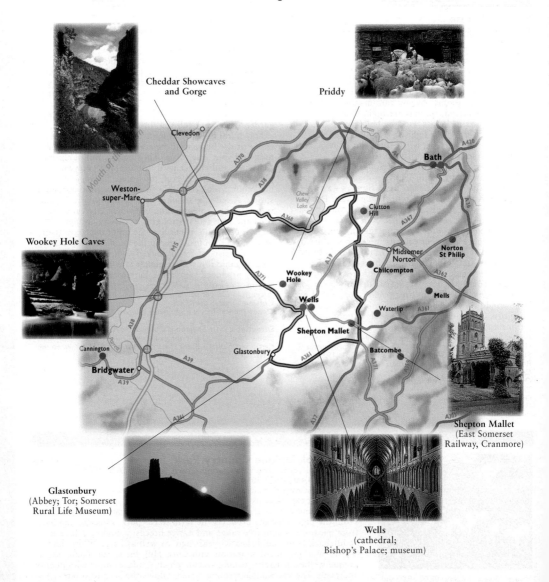

Cheddar Showcaves and Gorge

Priddy

Wookey Hole Caves

Glastonbury
(Abbey; Tor; Somerset Rural Life Museum)

Shepton Mallet
(East Somerset Railway, Cranmore)

Wells
(cathedral; Bishop's Palace; museum)

● Accommodation/Food

● Accommodation

● Food

🌙 Food Shop

To find the establishments marked here, look up the listing town marked on the map in bold in the town index on page 395

The Crown at Wells and Anton's Bistrot

Market Place, Wells, Somerset BA5 2RP
Telephone: +44(0)1749 673457
eat@crownatwells.co.uk
www.crownatwells.co.uk

The historic 15th-century inn with a connection to William Penn (founder of Philadelphia) is in sight of the Gothic cathedral and Bishop's Palace. The traditional, pubby Penn Bar is complemented by Anton's, a more contemporary wine-bar-cum-bistro. In the latter, dark-wood beams are offset by half pitch-pine walls hung with cartoons (originals by a well-known local cartoonist after whom the bistro is named), while stripped-pine tables, candles, newspapers, and subdued (evening) lighting offer an informal, relaxed, more up-to-date atmosphere. Anton's dishes of generous proportions continue the contemporary theme with the likes of chicken and wild mushroom pâté with caramelised onion jam, followed, perhaps, by rack of lamb with grain mustard crust and redcurrant gravy. A sharp lemon tart with vanilla ice cream or baked apple and raspberry crumble make a good finish. Blackboard specials run to fillet of cod with rösti potatoes, fennel and mushroom sauce. Good value 'Les Routiers' menu available at lunchtime and early evening Sunday to Thursday. A 30-plus wine list offers 12 by the glass, with most coming in under £20. Bedrooms are all en suite and are decorated in keeping with the old traditional inn. Some of the larger rooms at the front have four-poster beds.

Prices: Set price lunch from £9.50. House wine £9.95.
Hours: 12.00-15.00. 18.00-23.00. Monday to Sunday.
Food served: 12.00-14.30 18.00-21.30 (18.00-21.00 Sunday)
Rooms: 15 en suite. Double rooms from £60, single from £50. Family room from £90.00.
Cuisine: Mediterranean.
Other Points: No-smoking area. Children welcome. Car park.
Directions: Centre of Wells, in the Market Place. (Map 4, C6)

Fountain Inn and Boxer's Restaurant

1 St Thomas Street, Wells, Somerset BA5 2UU
Telephone: +44(0)1749 672317
eat@fountaininn.co.uk
www.fountaininn.co.uk

For 22 years, Adrian and Sarah Lawrence have worked hard at their 16th-century pub, initially built to house builders working on nearby Wells Cathedral. The bar offers the main focal point on entry, along with a welcoming fire, but what hits you is the unpretentious nature of the place. Dark-wood furniture, simple tablecloths and a floral carpet happily clashing with the terracotta walls offer an almost 'Chelsea Kitchen' cult-style, no-nonsense bistro atmosphere, within a pub setting. This place is all about food, and there's a profusion of blackboards displaying the daily specials such as a starter of warm crab tartlet lightly spiced with chilli, ginger and lime. The printed menu cranks out a lengthy repertoire of familiar and more contemporary dishes: speciality sausages with mash and red wine and onion gravy, lasagne bolognaise, and steaks. Main courses take in slow-roasted shoulder of lamb with red wine, garlic and rosemary, and duck confit with a medley of mixed beans. Portions are honest, robust, and prices reasonable. An 80-odd-bin wine list travels the globe with most bottles well under the £20 mark. Upstairs there's Boxer's Restaurant (scrubbed-pine tables and an air of country calm) serving the same menu.

Prices: Set lunch £9.75. Main course in restaurant from £7.25. Main course bar snack from £3.50. House wine £9.95.
Hours: 10.00-14.30. 18.00-23.00. 11.00-19.00 on Sunday. Closed 25-26 December.
Food served: 12.00-14.00. 18.00-22.00. Sunday 12.00-18.00.
Cuisine: Modern British.
Other Points: No-smoking area. Children welcome. Car park.
Directions: Junction 22/M5. In the city centre, 50 yards from the cathedral. (Map 4, C6)

Old Inn

Holton, Wincanton, Somerset BA9 8AR
Telephone: +44(0)1963 32002

A delightful spot to pause for a drink, the 17th-century Old Inn, in a peaceful setting not far from the A303, is a popular walking destination and a local favourite for good straightforward pub food. The character beamed bar, dominated by a large stone fireplace with log-burning stove, boasts ancient flagstones, upholstered wooden settles, large refectory tables and a clutter of bric-à-brac, including polished copper pots and pewter mugs, and a collection of key rings hanging from the beams by the bar counter. Sup a pint of local Butcombe ale, Otter Ale or Wadworth 6X and tuck into a traditional bar meal, perhaps a ploughman's lunch with locally produced farmhouse cheddar cheese, roast beef and horseradish sandwich, lasagne, homemade watercress soup, pork curry, or rump steak with all the trimmings. From the separate restaurant menu perhaps choose lamb cutlets with rosemary, homebaked ham with a mustard, cream and cider sauce, or peppered steak flamed in brandy and cream. Meat from locally reared animals is supplied by quality local butchers. Book for hearty Sunday roasts. There's alfresco seating on the flower-filled front terrace or in the raised rear garden.

Prices: Set menu £16.50. Main course from £8.25. Bar meal from £6.25. House wine £8.
Hours: 12.00-15.00. 18.00-23.00. 19.00-22.30 on Sunday.
Food served: 12.00-14.00. 19.00-22.00. Restaurant closed Sunday evening, bar meals available.
Cuisine: Traditional British.
Other Points: No-smoking in restaurant. Children welcome over 14 years old. Garden. Car park.
Directions: Just off the A303, in the centre of Holton village, two miles south-west of Wincanton. (Map 4, C7)

The Royal Oak

Withypool, Exmoor Natonal Park,
Somerset TA24 7QP
Telephone: +44(0)1643 831506

The 300-year-old whitewashed stone inn packs a lot of history: RD Blackmore stayed here in 1866 while writing *Lorna Doone*, and during the 1930s it was owned and run by Maxwell Knight the spy-master upon whom Ian Fleming based the character of 'M'. The place is full of character - low ceiling and thick black beams in the main bar offset by brass pots, black kettles, stags' antlers, fox heads, and hunting pictures. The Acorn restaurant is more formal, with white linen tablecloths and fully dressed tables. Good pub food extends to whisky homecured gravadlax with a grain mustard dressing, free-range chicken breast filled with red pepper mousse and served with a watercress sauce. Puddings could be strawberry meringue, or apple and raison crumble with crème anglaise. Exmoor Ale and Exmoor Gold are on handpump, and there's a large global selection of wines offering fair drinking at fair prices. Bedrooms are tastefully and individually decorated and come with biscuits, chocolate and tea trays; bathrooms have all been fitted with Victorian sinks and brass fittings. The pick of the rooms are two suites under the roof with their window seats, sofas, cushions and high arched beamed ceilings. Two pretty holiday cottages are also available.

Prices: Main course bar from £10. Main course restaurant from £12. House wine £9.75.
Food Served: 12.00-14.00. 18.30-21.30.
Rooms: 8 en suite. 2 cottages. Single from £60, double from £50.
Cuisine: Traditional and Modern British.
Other Points: Children welcome. Car park.
Directions: From Dulverton take the B3223 over the Moors and turn left in seven miles, signed Withypool. (Map 4, C5)

The Wookey Hole Inn

Wookey Road, Wookey Hole, Wells,
Somerset BA5 1BP
Telephone: +44(0)1749 676677
mail@wookeyholeinn.com
www.wookeyholeinn.com

From the outside, the early Victorian building looks like a typical rural pub. Within, the large interior with funky add-ons such as the orange retro couch and unusual wall lighting (designed by owner Mark Hey) indicate that this is more of a restaurant than a pub. Soft muted colours against white, lots of windows and skylights make for a light open-plan interior with blond wood tables and chairs well-spaced over wood or stone floors. A seagrass stairway leads to bedrooms decorated in muted colours, with interesting soft furnishings and lighting, contemporary art and big bathrooms. Reclamation yards have been scoured to give an interesting mix of old and new, juxtaposing, for example, a Victorian bathtub and square basin with a modern stainless-steel loo, and all rooms have video and CD players. Modern menus open with the likes of vegetable, fish or meat antipasto. Mains range from grilled sea bass with tapenade to roasted boneless maize-fed chicken with thyme, harissa and garlic, and puddings include a satisfying ginger pudding with ginger sauce. The wine list is short, with about half a dozen reds and whites under 20, but there are plans to expand and feature more top-end wines.

Prices: Main courses from £13. House wine £12.50.
Food Served: 12.00-14.30. 18.00-21.30.
Rooms: 5 en suite. Rooms from £70.
Cuisine: Modern British.
Other Points: Children welcome. Garden.
Directions: Follow the signs to Wookey Hole Caves off A371 between Cheddar and Wells. Exit22/M5 (Map 4, C6)

Essington Fruit Farm

Bognop Road, Essington, Wolverhampton, Staffordshire WV11 2BA
Telephone: +44(0)1902 735724
rmsimkin@farming.co.uk

Essington farm grows a wide range of pick-your-own and ready picked fruit and vegetables. Strawberries start the season in June and carry through to the end of July, and there are raspberries, tayberries, gooseberries, red and black currants. In the vegetable line they grow various cabbages, brussel sprouts on the stem, cauliflowers, broccoli and curly kale, with spinach, beetroot, carrots, onions, shallots, peas, broad, french and runner beans, leeks and sweetcorn, as well as ten varieties of potatoes. Pumpkin and squash are available in the autumn. There is, in addition, a tearoom and bakery.

Hours: Monday-Sunday: 09.00-21.00 (shorter out of season).
Other points: Parking. Children's play area. Garden plants. Tractor rides. Easy access for disabled.
Directions: From exit 1/M54, take A460 direction Wolverhampton and turn left at the second island. (Map 9, D2)

THE ROMANCE OF
LORNA DOONE COUNTRY

Part of Exmoor's beautiful National Park and the setting from RD Blackmore's classic novel
Lorna Doone. Along the way you'll discover a host of fascinating attractions with secret villages,
historic houses and delightfully unspoilt towns.
Drive length: 77 miles

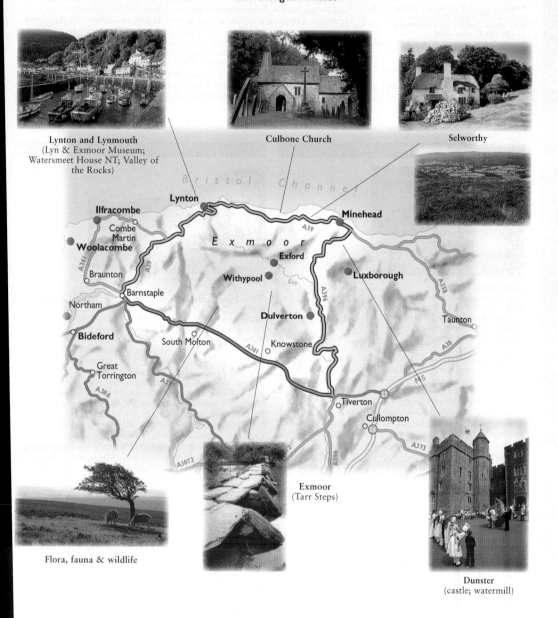

Lynton and Lynmouth
(Lyn & Exmoor Museum;
Watersmeet House NT; Valley of
the Rocks)

Culbone Church

Selworthy

Flora, fauna & wildlife

Exmoor
(Tarr Steps)

Dunster
(castle; watermill)

● Accommodation/Food

● Accommodation

● Food

🍃 Food Shop

To find the establishments marked
here, look up the listing town
marked on the map in bold in the
town index on page 395

Number 64

64 St Edward Street, Leek, Staffordshire ST13 5DL
Telephone: +44(0)1538 381900

Number 64 is a lovely house built by a local silk mill owner in 1747 to classic, clean lines, and set right in the centre of Leek. Tasteful and total refurbishment has created something more than your average townhouse hotel and restaurant. Incorporated into the building is an in-house bakery (selling to the public), a coffee lounge with an all-day menu, a vaulted, exposed-stone basement wine bar that's good for a simple snack and a glass of wine, a small, pretty restaurant and, currently, three bedrooms. In the kitchen Mark Walker follows a policy of total commitment to regional produce, delivering straightforward modern British cooking. His menu features starters of home-smoked pigeon, partnered by radicchio, chestnuts, tarragon and cream vinaigrette. Saddle of rabbit with pan-fried gnocchi pillows could follow, accompanied by peas, broad beans and thyme stock, or there could be pan-roasted salmon, hand-dived seared scallops, gingered baby carrots, potato tuilles and sorrel fish cream. Puddings include rhubarb crumble with cinnamon ice cream and rhubarb syrup, or a selection of local and regional cheeses. The wine list opens with two pages of global house wines; prices, even at the finer end are kind, with bottles rarely going over £20.

Prices: Cooked breakfast £5. Sunday lunch from £15 (2 course). Main course lunch from £6.25. Main course dinner from £14.50. House wine £9.95.
Hours: Snacks available 10.00-17.00. Lunch from 12.00. Dinner from 19.00. Closed Sunday evening and Monday.
Rooms: 3 en suite. From £65 per night.
Cuisine: Modern British.
Other Points: Restaurant no-smoking. Children welcome. Garden.
Directions: In the centre of Leek.
(Map 8, B6)

Old Boat

Kings Bromley Road, Alrewas, Staffordshire DE13 7DB
Telephone: +44(0)1283 791468
nawilson@hotmail.com
www.theoldboat.com

Under the guidance of Neil Wilson, this traditional looking pub is quickly establishing a solid local reputation as a restaurant. The bar and adjoining room display a timeless feel, aided by sturdy wooden tables and chairs, wood floors, a nautical theme (a river runs fairly close to the rear of the building), and a chalkboard displaying house wines, with Marston's Pedigree and Ushers, plus an occasional guest ale. The restaurant is different. Deep reds, contemporary paintings, beams, partly exposed brick walls, a fireplace stuffed with logs, all exude an intimate, cosy air. Here chef Richard Turner delivers an imaginative, well-balanced menu that specialises in seafood, say, langoustine ravioli with cappuccino of shellfish. In addition, a printed menu delivers the likes of potted duck with port jelly as a first course followed, perhaps, by loin of venison, poached pear and bitter chocolate sauce, with vanilla crème brûlée to finish. Meat is purchased from a local butcher who buys from farms within a ten mile radius and slaughters on his premises. Indeed, a great effort is made to buy most raw materials from the immediate area. The wine list is evenly global and impressive, with six house wines and some 20 bottles below £20.

Prices: Set dinner £13.95. Main course restaurant £7.95. Main course bar £3.95. House wine £9.95.
Hours: Open: 12.00-15.00. 18.30-23.00. Closed Sunday evening and first weekend after New Year.
Food served: 12.00-14.30. 18.30-21.30.
Rooms: Rooms on line from autumn 2003.
Cuisine: Modern British.
Other Points: No-smoking area. Garden. Children welcome. Car park.
Directions: Four miles north of Lichfield off the A38. (Map 9, C2)

The Holly Bush

Salt, Stafford, Staffordshire ST18 0BX
Telephone: +44(0)1889 508234
geoff@hollybushinn.co.uk
www.hollybushinn.co.uk

Thatched and dating from the 14th century, the attractive, flower-adorned pub is reputedly Staffordshire's oldest licensed premises and England's second oldest. Once a baiting house for asses, mules and ponies carrying salt to nearby Stafford and beyond, it maintains its historic charm throughout the cosy interior, with carved heavy beams, a planked ceiling, exposed brick walls, old oak furnishings, open fires and intimate alcoves charcterising the main bar. There's also a modern rear extension with comfortable settees. Landlord Geoff Holland is passionate about using fresh local produce and sources meat from W. M Perry, an Eccleshall butcher with his own abbatoir, and game from local shoots. Among the good value dishes on offer you will find homemade steak and kidney pudding, deep-fried cod with mushy peas, and local estate vension with red wine sauce. Alternatives include, braised ham hock with horseradish sauce, pork with apples and cider, slow-roasted lamb with redcurrant gravy and prime steaks, including a 20oz T-bone. Expect good lunchtime sandwiches and a chalkboard listing daily seafood specials, perhaps pan-fried monkfish with fennel, shallots, morels and crème fraîche, and herb-crusted salmon.

Prices: Main course from £6.95. House wine £7.25.
Hours: 12.00-14.30. 18.00-23.00. 12.00-23.00 on Saturday. 12.00-22.30 on Sunday.
Food served: 12.00-14.00. 18.00-21.30. 12.00-21.30 on Saturday. 12.00-21.30 on Sunday.
Cuisine: Modern and Traditonal British.
Other Points: No-smoking area. Garden. Car park.
Directions: Junction 14/M6. Four miles along A51 Stone to Lichfield road, or half a mile from the A518 Stafford to Uttoxeter road. (Map 9, C2)

The Swan Hotel

46-46a Greengate Street, Stafford,
Staffordshire ST16 2JA
Telephone: +44(0)1785 258142

The ancient Swan is steeped in history: Charles I slept here at the time of the Civil War, and Charles Dickens recorded a miserable night during the inn's dip in fortune in late Victorian times. All is well now, with refurbishment bringing the Swan back firmly as a focal point for this pleasant county town. Public areas extend to a contemporary café filled with lots of wicker chairs and comfy soft sofas, a stylish brasserie with marble topped tables, and a smart bar looking out onto a rear courtyard filled with wooden tables and chairs. In addition, all 27 bedrooms have a comfortable, contemporary look, are decorated in soft colours, some with a coffee and cream theme, and a mix of bath or shower rooms. Sizes vary and some rooms boast original features uncovered during renovations. Food in the brasserie is good with an effort made to buy local and regional produce. An expansive menu offers starters of confit duck salad with peppered oranges and walnut vinaigrette, mains of seared sea bass with pak choi, artichoke crème fraîche and lemon oil, and chocolate steamed pudding with chocolate sauce and caramel ice cream. The wine list is impressively set out and categorised by flavour; it offers a wide, evenly global selection at very reasonable prices.

Prices: Set lunch (2 courses) £9.95. Main course restaurant from £7. Main course (coffee shop) from £4. House wine £9.25.
Food served: 12.00-14.30. 17.30-22.00, Sunday until 21.00.
Rooms: 27 en suite. Double/twin from £85.
Cuisine: Modern British.
Other Points: No-smoking area. Garden. Children welcome.
Directions: Exit 13 and 14/M6. Situated on the High Street in Stafford town centre. (Map 9, C2)

The Swan Inn

Swan Lane, Barnby, Beccles, Suffolk NR34 7QF
Telephone: +44(0)1502 476646

Take Swan Lane off the A146 at Barnby to find this flower-adorned, pink-washed village local and, perhaps, the most extensive menu of fish and seafood to be found in a Suffolk pub. Unlike many, the quality and freshness here is first class thanks to pub owner and Lowestoft fish wholesaler, Don Cole, who supplies the pub with the best of the day's catch landed at the dock five miles away. Up to 80 different fish dishes are listed on the printed menu and an array of ever-changing blackboards in the bar. From local sprats traditionally smoked in Don's smokehouse, flour-fried slip sole, and fresh grilled sardines with garlic butter, the choice extends to longshore codling fillets, deep-fried in crispy batter, and turbot fillet in prawn and brandy sauce. The house speciality, however, is a 20oz Dover sole, simply grilled. In addition, expect to find oysters, dressed Cromer crabs, locally caught lobster, deep-fried fresh scampi and monkfish tails in hot garlic butter. All are accompanied with salad, new potatoes or chips and peas, and served throughout the traditionally furnished bar and restaurant. Both are crowded at lunch and dinner, so do book. A self-contained flat is available on a nightly basis.

Prices: Set lunch £13 and dinner £18. Main course restaurant from £7.95. Main course bar £3.95.
Hours: 11.00-15.30 (from 12.00 on Sunday). 18.00-23.30. Closed 25 December evening.
Food served: 12.00-14.00. 19.00-21.30.
Rooms: 3 en suite. Rooms from £40 per person.
Cuisine: Seafood.
Other Points: No-smoking area. Children welcome. Garden. Car park.
Directions: From the west or east come along the A146, turn into Barnby (left from the west) and follow signs to the inn. (Map 10, D8)

Queen's Head

The Street, Bramfield, Halesworth, Suffolk IP19 9HT
Telephone: +44(0)1986 784214
qhbfield@aol.com
www.queensheadbramfield.co.uk

Records show that a pub has stood on this site for over seven centuries. Now a prime mover locally in promoting 'real food' - listing the names and family history of the likes of Village Farm at Market Weston, Stonehouse Organic Farm at West Harling and the nearby Soil Association registered Elm House and Wakelyns farms - particular facilities offered, include real ale from Adnams, Suffolk's oldest brewer, eight wines by the glass plus several organic alternatives, a Birthday Club discount for listed regulars on the mailing list, and recycling facilities for everything from glass to used postage stamps, printer cartridges and toners. Not to be outdone, a typical daily changing menu lists Wakelyns Farm roast parsnip and parmesan soup with Metfield organic bread and Village Farm butter, Larchfield Cottage leek and bacon crumble, fresh-landed lemon sole with herb butter and Denham Estate venison steak with redcurrant, port and orange sauce. Alternative to lemon tart with Village Farm Jersey cream and homemade ice creams and sorbet are a British and Irish cheese selection direct from the Country Kitchen in Halesworth.

Prices: Set Sunday lunch £16.95. Main course from £5.95.
House wine from £7.95.
Hours: 11.45-14.30. 18.30-23.00. Sunday 12.00-15.00. 19.00-22.30. Closed 25 December evening, all day 26 December.
Food served: 12.00-14.00. 18.30-22.00. Sunday 19.00-21.00.
Cuisine: Modern British.
Other Points: No-smoking area. Dogs welcome. Garden. Children welcome. Car park.
Directions: On A144 between A12 and Halesworth, 10 miles west of Southwold. (Map 10, D7)

Earsham Park Farm

Harleston Road, Earsham, Bungay, Suffolk NR35 2AQ
Telephone: +44(0)1986 892180
routiers@earsham-parkfarm.co.uk
www.earsham-parkfarm.co.uk

The Victorian farmhouse stands surrounded by a lovely mature country garden and 600 acres of land, a good half mile up a private drive. Pass through the large front door into the long hallway and Bobbie Watchorn or her daughter will greet you and bring tea and scones. The guest sitting room is small and homely: lots of family photos sit on an antique cupboard and dresser, there are potted plants, a rug on ceramic tiles. The dining room has a real farmhouse kitchen feel to it. Set right in the middle is a beautiful antique table around which guests gather for an exceptional breakfast of sausages made locally to Bobbie's specification, local bacon, own eggs, and for dinner, which is by request. Two doubles and a twin room are all individual, comfortably furnished, and have thoughtful touches such as fresh milk with the hot drinks tray, biscuits and chocolate, and bottled water, and bathrobes. This is a no-smoking establishment.

Rooms: 3 en suite. Double room from £50, single from £36.
Other Points: Totally no-smoking. Children welcome. Garden. Car park.
Directions: Situated off the A143 Diss to Great Yarmouth road between Harleston and Bungay. (Map 10, D7)

Earsham Street Café

11-13 Earsham Street, Bungay,
Suffolk NR35 1AE
Telephone: +44(0)1986 893103

Celebrating their fourth year in 2004, Rebecca Mackenzie and Stephen David's stylish, unpretentious café-cum-restaurant has proved a hit in this pleasant, indeed quaint, market town. It's all set in a 17th century terraced house that has had an unfussy, rustic chic makeover that keeps in tune with the age of the building. But the philosophy of damn good food, fresh local ingredients and flexible dishes, is a style that's a bit of modern British meets Mediterranean. In the mornings and afternoons, life glides along with pots of tea and cakes, but at lunchtime and occasional evening openings, the place literally hums. Dishes on offer include roasted pigeon breast on beetroot salad, braised lamb shank with roasted garlic and chorizo, seared king scallops and bacon salad for lunch. Dinner brings pan-fried foie gras and black pudding with french beans and caramelised onions, then roast line-caught cod with spaghetti, steamed palourdes clams, artichokes, basil and crème fraîche, or magret of duck with porcini risotto, roast courgettes, fennel and truffle oil. A short wine list offers choice, value and good drinking, with nine offered by the glass. As we went to press, the deli was about to move to its own premises nearby - the restaurant will fill the resulting space.

Prices: Main course restaurant from £7.95. Main course snack from £3. House wine £11.50.
Hours: 09.30-17.00 Monday-Saturday. Open for dinner the last Friday and Saturday of every month 19.00-21.00. Closed Sunday, 25-26 December and 1-2 January.
Food served: 11.00-16.00.
Cuisine: Modern British/Mediteranean.
Other Points: No-smoking area. Dogs welcome. Garden. Children welcome.
Directions: (Map 10, D7)

St Peter's Hall

St Peter, South Elmham, Bungay, Suffolk NR35 1NQ
Telephone: +44(0)1986 782322
beers@stpetersbrewery.co.uk
www.stpetersbrewery.co.uk

Built in 1280 and extended in 1539 using 14th century architectural salvage from nearby Flixton Priory, the manor and surrounding farm buildings were refurbished in 1996 to provide the rather grand setting for a unique micro-brewery, and a highly individual bar and restaurant. Open at weekends only, the latter not only showcases the brewery's impeccable portfolio of bottled and draught beers, but offers a stylish menu created by chef Julian Williams. What's more, the ambience is unmatched anywhere else in the country. Cross the moat, enter a stone porch and drink and eat in high-ceilinged rooms filled with 17th and 18th century furnishings, notably some French choirstalls and a Bishop's chair, splendid Brussels tapestries, and fine stone fireplaces. Food, however, is right up to date, a typical lunch menu may list Jerusalem artichoke soup, or smoked haddock and watercress tart, served as a starter or main course, in addition to open sandwiches made with Metfield organic bread. From the evening carte, order game terrine with pear and Spiced Ale chutney, followed by braised oxtail with celeriac mash, and finish with pecan pie or a plate of British cheeses.

Prices: Main course dinner from £9.95. Lunch main course from £4.25. House wine £10.
Hours: 11.00-23.00 Friday-Saturday. 12.00-18.00 on Sunday. Closed Monday-Thursday (extended days during the summer months).
Food served: 12.00-14.30. 19.00-21.00.
Cuisine: Modern British/International.
Other Points: No-smoking area. Garden. Children welcome. Car park.
Directions: Brewery and Hall signed off the A144 Bungay to Halesworth Road, three miles south of Bungay. (Map 10, D7)

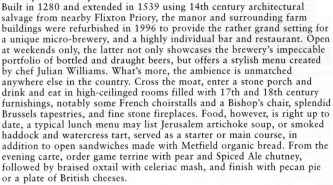

Prices: Set dinner, £19.95. Main course
restaurant from £12.75. Bar snack/light
lunch from £4.95. House wine £9.95.
Hours: 11.00-23.00. Closed Sunday
evenings from November to March.
Food served: 12.00-15.00 (from 12.30 on
Sunday). 18.30-22.00.
Rooms: 5 en suite. From £37.50
per person.
Other Points: No-smoking in the
restaurant and bedrooms. Garden and
terrace with heated canopies.
Well behaved children welcome.
Directions: On A1092 between Haverhill
and Long Melford. (Map 10. E6)

The George

★ ❚ ▯ ✕ ⬦

The Green, Cavendish, Sudbury, Suffolk CO10 8BA
Telephone: +44(0)1787 280248
reservations@georgecavendish.co.uk
www.georgecavendish.co.uk

The 600-year-old timber framed building stands at the corner of the
village green, remodelling creating a smart, stylish look. Jonathan and
Charlotte Nicholson took over this faded village boozer in July 2002, and
in a short space of time have managed a dramatic transformation.
Everything has been stripped back, so that wood, exposed brick and
standing timbers create a modern space offset by simple neutral colours.
That this is a dining pub is obvious, tables laid up for eating fill every
space, though there is a small bar area for those just wanting pint of
Woodford's Wherry or a glass of wine from a short, well annotated global
wine list. Food is keenly priced at lunch with a two or three course menu
delivering home cured gravadlax on brioche topped with poached egg,
roast pork steak with creamed cabbage, parsnip mash and sage jus, and
panna cotta with fresh winter berries. Otherwise, the carte could deliver
sautéed goats' cheese terrine with confit potato, black truffle and mache
salad, then Moroccan spiced lamb rump with roast sweet potato and
stuffed pimento. Upstairs, four stylish, keenly priced, en suite bedrooms
have been created.

The Fox and Goose Inn

❚ ▯ ✕

Church Road, Fressingfield, Eye, Suffolk IP21 5PB
Telephone: +44(0)1379 586247
foxandgoose@uk2.net
www.foxandgoose.net

Backing on to the churchyard and facing the village
pond, the magificent timber framed Fox and Goose
was built around 1500 as a Guildhall and later became
a pub. For more than a decade it was famous across
the region for fine food and wine, but recent times
have not been kind to the ancient fabric of the
building. In the summer of 2002 it was sold to Paul
Yaxley, a bold young chef who was undeterred by its
condition and former culinary fame. A comfortable
lounge with new carpets and deep sofas replaced the
drab bar, and vibrant colours, modern works of art
and an eclectic mix of dining tables have brightened up
the two heavily beamed dining areas. It is still very
much a restaurant, but with Adnams tapped from the
barrel and excellent value light and set lunch menus,
casual diners are made very welcome. Lunch on
smoked haddock, mussel and prawn stew, or try a
main dish of pork fillet with red cabbage, french beans
and red wine sauce. Dinner from the carte could
include ham hock and pork terrine with mustard seed
brioche, beef fillet with parsnip purée and shallot jus,
and plum tarte tatin with chilled rice pudding and star
anise anglaise.
Prices: Set lunch £12.95. Main course restaurant from £10.95.
Main course bar from £6.50. House wine £11.95.
Hours: 12.00-14.00. 19.00-21.00, until 21.30 Friday and Saturday.
Sunday 18.30-20.30. Food served during opening hours.
Closed Monday and 27-30 December.
Cuisine: Modern British with French influences.
Other Points: No-smoking area. Well behaved children. Car park.
Directions: Take the A143 Diss to Bungay road; turn off to take
the B1116 to Fressingfield, situated by the church. (Map 10, D7)

The Ship Inn

❚ ▯ ✕

Church Lane, Levington, Ipswich, Suffolk IP10 0LQ
Telephone: +44(0)1473 659573

Tranquil views over the Orwell estuary with its
bobbing boats and serene waterscape, and a nautical
ambience are among the attractions at this
immaculately whitewashed and impressively thatched
14th-century pub. Just six miles from Ipswich (signed
off the A45) it is a popular lunchtime venue, especially
in summer when the flower-festooned front and rear
terraces fill up early. The spick-and-span, low-ceilinged
bar is adorned with nautical bric-a-brac of all kinds,
including interesting photographs and a ship's wheel
on the walls. Both chef/patron Mark Johnson and his
wife Stella spent many years at the successful Angel
Inn at Stoke-by-Nayland (see entry) before heading
east to take on The Ship over a year ago. With hardly
a free table to found at lunch and dinner, it has proved
a great move, for Mark's twice daily changing
chalkboard menus offers imaginative meals prepared
from fresh local produce, notably locally reared meats,
seasonal salads and vegetables, venison from the
Suffolk Estate. A satisfying meal can be washed down
with an excellent pint of Adnams ale or one of eight
wines available by the glass.
Prices: Main course lunch from £6.95. Main course dinner from
£9.50. House wine from £9.25.
Hours: 11.30-14.30. 18.00-23.00. Sunday 12.00-15.00.
Closed Sunday evening.
Food served: 12.00-14.00. 18.30-21.30. Sunday 12.00-15.00.
Cuisine: Modern British.
Other Points: No-smoking area. Garden. Children welcome over
14 years old. Car park.
Directions: A14/A12 junction to Woodbridge. Follow signs to
Levington village via Bridge Road. (Map 10, E7)

The Crown and Castle ★♟🍷🅳✕⬦

Orford, Woodbridge, Suffolk IP12 2LJ
Telephone: +44(0)1394 450205
info@crownandcastle.co.uk
www.crownandcastle.co.uk

The former proprietors of Hintlesham Hall and the Fox and Goose at Fressingfield bought this run-down Victorian pub in 1999 and have recreated their vision of a modern, stylish inn and bistro. The location, adjacent to a Norman castle with stunning views across the Ore estuary, is perfect. In keeping with the setting, all eighteen bedrooms are light and refreshingly simple, yet with taste apparent in everything, from the choice of colours, fabrics, and large comfy beds. En suite bathrooms have quirky pebble-print tiles, luxury towels and toiletries. Downstairs, stripped wooden boards, polished tables and original artworks set the scene for some modern food that delves deep into Suffolk's rich larder. Casual lunches, also served on the terrace, may include Orford smoked trout with beetroot and horseradish relish, locally cured ham ploughman's, and a delicious crayfish and dill salad. At dinner, choose from the fixed-price menu, or, perhaps, Butley oysters with lemon chilli relish, and a robust dish of belly pork with Puy lentils and gingery greens from the short carte. Round off with Tuscan orange and almond cake with lime syrup and mascarpone. Well-chosen list of wines with tasting notes and bin end specials.

Prices: Main course restaurant meal from £13.50. House wine £12.
Hours: 11.00-17.30 (12.00 on Sunday). 18.30-23.00 (until 22.00 on Sunday). Closed 23-25 December and 5-9 January.
Food served: 12.00-14.00. 19.00-21.00 (later on Saturday).
Rooms: 18 en suite. Single room from £60, double from £75.
Cuisine: Global.
Other Points: No-smoking area. Children welcome. Patio. Car park. Pets welcome.
Directions: Take the A12 to Woodbridge and then follow the B1084 to Orford. (Map 10, E8)

Hollow Trees Farm Shop 🦢

Hollow Trees, Semer, Ipswich, Suffolk IP7 6HX
Telephone: +44(0)1449 741247
sally@hollowtrees.co.uk
www.hollowtrees.co.uk

Third generation farmers Sally and Robert Bendall run their farm shop as a local shop to the surrounding villages. It has grown from a roadside table to an extensive business offering home produced vegetables grown on 10 acres and ranging from peas, pumpkins, and beetroot to broccoli, sprouts and spinach. In addition, there's a wide selection of farm-grown orchard and soft fruits. The locally grown theme extends throughout the shop, as, with over 200 carefully chosen local and regional suppliers, they offer the best of Suffolk's food produce, among them honey, wines and beers, ice cream, apple juice, confectionery, jams and chutneys. Bread is delivered from a nearby bakery and there is a freezer centre selling pork, beef, lamb and chickens that have been bred on the farm. A farm trail allows you to wander around and see many of the animals and there is a plant centre and annual pumpkin festival.

Hours: Monday-Saturday: 08.30-17.45. Sunday: 09.00-15.00.
Other points: Parking. Children's play area. Garden centre. Easy access for disabled. Farm trail. Annual Pumpkin Festival.
Directions: From Bury St Edmunds find Lavenham. Left at Swan Hotel onto A1141 for 6 miles (signed on right). From Ipswich take A1071 to Hadleigh. Take A1141 right. After 2 miles left direction Lavenham (A1141). Farm is 1 mile on left. (Map 10, E7)

The Crown 🅸♟🅳✕⬦

High Street, Southwold, Suffolk IP18 6DP
Telephone: +44(0)1502 722275
crownhotel@adnams.co.uk

Adnams flagship, The Crown, is to be applauded for its success in bringing straightforward food, prime-condition beers, and excellent wines to the average spender. Its place, indeed, in local folklore is as valid today as it was to the 18th century founders of the original Nag's Head as it was formerly known. The maritime atmosphere of the town's past is echoed in a magnificent ship's binnacle, marine paintings and glazed screen in the Back Bar, whilst at the front, the Parlour is a buzzing mix of contemporary wine bar, brasserie and English village pub, and the centre of local life. Here, daily choices offer crab spring roll with Mersea oyster and seared scallop, as a precursor to pan-roasted hoki or John Dory fillets that mark out the emphasis on fresh fish. However, confit duck leg on herb crushed potatoes and fritata of roast peppers and sweet potatoes assuage alternative appetites, and a stack of Swiss chocolate mousse with white chocolate sails marries the nautical to the just plain naughty. Restaurant menus, set at two or three courses, add a further dimension to the kitchen's skills, while imaginatively selected wines and beautifully kept bedrooms simply underline the thread of quality that runs throughout.

Prices: Set lunch £20.50. Set dinner £29. Main course restaurant from £10. House wine £9.50.
Hours: 08.00-22.00.
Rooms: 14 en suite bar one. Double/twin from £110.
Cuisine: Modern British.
Other Points: No-smoking area. Garden. Children welcome. Car park.
Directions: Take A1095 off A12, 14 miles south of Lowestoft, for Southwold. (Map 10, D8)

England - Suffolk

The Angel Inn

🍷🅳✕🛋

Polstead Street, Stoke-by-Nayland,
Suffolk CO6 4SA
Telephone: +44(0)1206 263245

The Angel is a civilised 16th-century village inn offering good food and comfortable accommodation and retaining much of its original character (exposed brickwork, beams and two open fireplaces). Expect fresh flowers and candles on tables, a few antique pieces, a charming lounge area with deep sofas, and a gallery overlooking the high-ceilinged dining room, once the old brewhouse. An imaginative daily changing blackboard offers fresh fish and shellfish from East Coast ports, perhaps grilled sardines in oregano, freshly beer-battered haddock, and pan-fried squid with coriander, lemon and ginger. Game from Denham Estate are popular additions to the menu in winter, while other more typical choices include roast vension with red onion confit and juniper sauce, and steak and kidney pudding. Despite being constantly busy service remains courteous and efficient. Arrive early if you wish to eat in the bar as tables cannot be reserved. On warm summer evenings the sheltered rear patio provides extra, and much sought after, space to eat. The six individually furnished en suite bedrooms are due for refurbishment as we went to press.

Prices: Main course restaurant from £9.95. Main course bar from £7.15. House wine £8.90.
Hours: 12.00-14.30. 18.00-23.00. Sunday 12.00-22.30.
Closed 25-26 December and 1 January.
Food served: 12.00-14.00. 18.30-21.30.
Sunday 12.00-17.00. 17.30-21.30.
Rooms: 6 en suite. Double/twin from £69.50. Single from £54.50.
Cuisine: Modern British.
Other Points: No-smoking area. Garden. Children welcome over eight years old. Car park.
Directions: On B1068 between A12 north of Colchester and Sudbury. (Map 10, E7)

Southwold, Suffolk

The Bell Inn

🍺🍷🅳✕🛋

Ferry Road, Walberswick, Southwold, Suffolk IP18 6TN
Telephone: +44(0)1502 723109
bellinn@btinternet.com
www.blythweb.co.uk/bellinn

Just a stone's throw from the beach, this fine old inn has a history dating back 600 years. Low beams, open fires, flagged floors and high wooden settles have been a draw to artists and ghost writers - inspiring one of the most celebrated ghost stories of all time. Accommodation comprises six en suite bedrooms including the Sea View Suite, while its fame for good food is based on simply prepared local produce among which local fish and seafood take pride of place. Beers and the fine wines fittingly come from Adnams in Southwold, and the repertoire encompasses all manner of options from toasted brie and cranberry sandwiches, savoury vegetable crumble, and Walberswick fish pie in the bar, to romantic dinners in the candlelit restaurant on weekends. Weekly choices might include terrine of venison with juniper berries, sea bass fillets with fennel, mushrooms and chive beurre blanc or chicken breast with pancetta and Marsala sauce. Exotic fruit salad in spiced syrup or British, French and Italian regional cheeses with quince jelly, celery and walnuts bring up the rear.

Prices: Set lunch £16. Set dinner £17.50.
Main course restaurant from £7.25.
House wine from £7.95.
Hours: 11.00-15.00. 18.00-23.00.
Closed 25-26 December evening. Open all day every day from 21st July-31 August.
Food served: 12.00-14.00, Sunday until 14.30. 19.00-21.00
Rooms: 6 en suite with showers.
Double/twin from £70.
Cuisine: Modern British.
Other Points: No-smoking area. Dogs welcome. Garden. Children welcome. Car park. Boule court.
Directions: Take the A12 to Blythburgh, turn onto B1387 for Walberswick. Pub is at the end of the village green. (Map 10, D8)

The Stephan Langton Inn ★ 🍷 🚪 ✕
Friday Street, Abinger Common, Dorking,
Surrey RH5 6JR
Telephone: +44(0)1306 730775
www.Stephanlangton.co.uk

This is prime Surrey walking country and a popular pit stop is the Stephan Langton, a 1930s building named after the first archbishop of Canterbury, who was supposedly born in Friday Street. But don't expect crusty baguettes or steak and ale pie to accompany your pint of Adnams ale, for this is the domain of Jonathan Coomb who bought the pub in summer 2000 and comes with plenty of experience in London restaurants. He makes his own bread, pasta and ice cream on the premises, and sources first-class seasonal fruit and vegetables from George Allen and local farm shops. At lunchtime there could be hearty bowls of goulash soup, or a dish of pork confit with chorizo and chickpeas. Sensibly short and simply described supper menus are good value, drawing folk from far and wide for robust, full flavoured country cooking. Calf's liver, bacon and bubble-and-squeak, braised shank of lamb with mash and salsa verde, and monkfish tagine with merguez sausages and preserved lemons, are typical examples. Simple puddings could include chocolate brownie with crème fraîche. A blackboard lists some sound drinking with eight offered by the glass.

Prices: Main course from £11.50. House wine £10.25.
Hours: 11.00-15.00. 17.00-23.00. 11.00-23.00 on Saturday. 12.00-22.30 on Sunday.
Food served: 12.30-15.00. 19.00-22.00.
No food all day Monday & Sunday evening.
Cuisine: Modern British.
Other Points: No-smoking area. Children welcome. Patio. Car park.
Directions: From the A25 between Dorking and Guildford, take Hollow Lane (west of Wootton). After one and a half miles turn left for Friday Street. (Map 6, 5C)

The Villagers Inn 🚪 ✕
Blackheath Lane, Blackheath Village, Guildford,
Surrey GU4 8RB
Telephone: +44(0)1483 893152
kbranton@ringstead1.fsnet.co.uk

This country pub is situated in an area that has an air of timelessness about it - delightfully re-enforced by a large timber post used to tether horses taking centre stage in the pub's car park, the scattered hay and water trough indicating that it is still in demand. 'More used than the car park' according to Helen Scott, who, along with Kevin Brampton, has recently taken over this quintessentially English pub. The horse theme extends into the pub with blinkers, horse brasses and saddles jostling for wall and ceiling space alongside other rural memorabilia. Jason Lewis previously worked at Bibendum, and his food is good. Raw materials are locally sourced wherever possible, with fish (delivered daily) in summer and local game in winter finding their place in the kitchen's modern repertoire, perhaps crab and artichoke with herb oil, followed by roasted red snapper with curried Puy lentils and cucumber yogurt. The cooking style aims for bright flavours and timing is accurate in, say, sauté calf's liver and bacon with mustard mash, and roast quails, crêpe Parmentier and bordelaise sauce. A short list of wines includes five by the glass.

Prices: Main course restaurant from £9. Main course bar/snack from £7. House wine £10.95.
Hours: 12.00-15.00. 18.00-23.00. Friday to Sunday open all day.
Food served: 12.00-14.30. 18.00-22.00. Sunday 12.00-15.00.
Rooms: Available Spring 2004.
Cuisine: Modern British.
Other Points: No-smoking area. Dogs and horses welcome. Garden and Patio. Children welcome during the day. Car park.
Directions: M25 Junction 10. Take the A3 to Guildford then follow the A281 (Horsham Road) to Bramley and then the B2128 to Wonersh and turn left onto the A248. First right onto Blackheath Lane go through the village and straight across the crossroads. (Map 5, C4)

Bryce's 🍷 🚪 ✕
The Old School House, Ockley, Dorking, Surrey RH5 5TH
Telephone: +44(0)1306 627430
bryces.fish@virgin.net
www.bryces.co.uk

Owned by Bill Bryce since 1992, fish is the mainstay on the menus and ever-changing blackboards in both the informal, beamed and carpeted bar or in the more formal restaurant. Daily fish deliveries from London, and oysters, mussels and scallops from Loch Fyne Oysters and the Pure Oyster Company at nearby Faygate, with 'John the Crab', whose Selsey boat supplies first-class specimens, ensure quality and freshness. Enjoy a pint of Gales bitter in the bar with non-fishy dishes such as confit duck leg on mustard mash, or a farmer's platter of cheese and ham, or there could be Cornish plaice with lemon and parsley butter. The main fish event, however, is reserved for the set-price lunch and dinner menus, where imaginative specials may include seared tuna on lentil and mango salsa, monkfish wrapped in Parma ham with red onion jam, and thyme and red wine roasted salmon on herb couscous. The blackboard dessert list may list lemon panna cotta and banana, or wild berry and apple crumble. The wine list includes fourteen by the glass, although feel free to delve into 'Bryce's Special Cellar' for some classic vintages.

Prices: Set lunch £15.50 (two courses). Set dinner £25. Main course (bar/snack) from £7.50. House wine £11.50.
Hours: 12.00-15.00. 18.30-23.00. Closed Sunday evenings in November, January and February, 25 December and 1 January.
Food served: 12.00-14.30. 18.30-21.30.
Cuisine: Seafood.
Other Points: No-smoking in restaurant. Children welcome. Patio. Car park.
Directions: J9/M25. Eight miles south of Dorking on the A29 (Map 6, D5)

The Inn @ West End

42 Guildford Road, West End, Surrey GU24 9PW
Telephone: +44(0)1276 858652
greatfood@the-inn.co.uk
www.the-inn.co.uk

Gerry and Ann Price's refurbished pub-restaurant stands out. Originally called the Butcher's Arms (there was an abattoir opposite) then renamed the Wheatsheaf in the 1950s, the current name change has inspired locals to refer to it as the 'dot com'. However, the subtle inn sign depicting a scene from Othello extolling the virtues of drinking with an Englishman, is an indication that beyond the rather ordinary exterior lies a stylish, yet informal place, noted for a good wine list and great food. Light, modern and airy throughout, with wooden floors, creamy yellow walls, tasteful check fabrics, crisp linen clothed tables in the dining area, a warming wood-burner in the bar, and a relaxed, bustling atmosphere. Imaginative monthly menus, enhanced by daily specials, list an eclectic range of modern British dishes. There are good lunchtime light bites, and a sandwich menu to go with a pint of London Pride or Courage Best, or a glass of wine (seven by the glass) from an enthusiast's' list. Follow homemade breads and Welsh rarebit with grilled tomatoes and dressed leaves, with pan-fried calf's liver with mash, red onion marmalade and sage fritters. Round off with spiced apple crumble, or a plate of cheese.

Prices: Set lunch £18. Main course from £10. Main course bar from £6.
House wine £11.50.
Hours: 12.00-15.00. 17.00-23.00. 12.00-23.00 on Saturday. 12.00-16.00 and 17.00-22.30 on Sunday.
Food served: 12.00-14.30. 18.00-21.30. Sunday 12.00-21.30.
Cuisine: Modern British.
Other Points: No-smoking area. Children over 10 welcome in restaurant. Boules pitch. Dining patio. Car park.
Directions: On the A322 Guildford to M3 road, two miles south of J3/M3. (Map 5, C4)

Anchor Inn

Anchor Lane, Barcombe, Lewes,
East Sussex BN8 5BS
Telephone: +44(0)1273 400414
www.anchorinnandboating.co.uk

The white painted inn is on the banks of the River Ouse. The whole building has been completely revamped after extensive flood damage in October 2000, and now offers a 'mature' interior with lots of beams, wood and flagstone floors, bright, light decoration, warm lighting, open fires and a lovely atmosphere. The restaurant is similar in style, light and airy, but there is seating for diners in all areas of the bar. The menu offers classic pub staples such as chilli and lasagne. Daily specials are chalked up on a board and offer the likes of roast salmon with coriander and dill and homemade tomato soup for starters, followed by noisettes of lamb with rosemary jus, sirloin steak with Burgundy sauce, and chicken supreme. The wine list is predominantly French and offers ten wines by the glass. One of the biggest attractions, especially in summer, is the large riverside decking area with views directly to the river and the open countryside beyond. In addition, ancient boating rights stretching over two miles, mean that the inn has 27 rowing boats available for hire by the hour. And there are three cottage-style en suite bedrooms with a comfortable feel.

Prices: Set lunch and dinner £15. Bar main course from £6.50. House wine £10.95.
Hours: 11.00-23.00. 12.00-22.30 on Sunday.
Food served: 12.00-15.00. 18.00-21.00.
Rooms: 3, 1 en suite, 2 with private bathrooms. Prices start at £45 for single occupancy.
Cuisine: Modern British.
Other Points: No-smoking area. Garden. Licence for Civil Weddings. Children welcome. Car park. Fleet of 27 boats. Marquee events in the summer.
Directions: From Lewes take the A26 to Barcombe. (Map 6, D5)

Pilgrim's Restaurant

1 High Street, Battle, East Sussex TN33 OAE
Telephone: +44(0)1424 772314
www.foodrooms.co.uk

The Grade II listed building is a classic slice of old England, built in 1444, one of the earliest examples of a timber framed Wealden hall house. Bending through the low door, you enter into an impressive timbered entrance hall where drinks are served, with the low beamed dining room beyond. The overall combination of period features, classic furniture, open fires, beams, evening candles, modern art contrasting with ancient walls, and impressive chandeliers hanging from the ceiling, creates a wonderful atmosphere. The food is outstanding. Toby Peters is committed to using locally grown produce with the emphasis on fresh, natural and seasonal. Taste and flavour are paramount, evident in such dishes as double baked Golden Cross cheese soufflé with a sweet pepper coulis, or ceviche of local plaice, lime juice, coriander, chilli potato and red onion salad. For mains there may be best end of spring lamb, marinated artichoke, red onion potato cake and Marsala jus, with pudding of white chocolate and vanilla parfait with Marsala syrup. Under the same ownership and governed by the same sustainable philosophy, The Food Rooms, at 55 High Street, is a deli-cum-restaurant, opening for breakfast and lunch, and offering a good choice of dishes freshly prepared to eat at home.

Prices: Set lunch £17. Set dinner £19.50. Main course restaurant from £11.20. House wine £10.50.
Hours: 11.00-15.00. 19.00-00.30. Open all day for snacks. Closed Sunday evening and 25 December.
Cuisine: Modern British.
Other Points: No-smoking area. Garden. Children welcome. Private dining.
Directions: A21, follow the signs for Battle and Pilgrim's is located next to Battle Abbey. Public parking available behind the

The Greys

105 Southover Street, Brighton,
East Sussex BN2 9UA
Telephone: +44(0)1273 680734
chris@greyspub.com
www.greyspub.com

A brisk 12 minute walk from the station and seafront brings you to The Greys, an extraordinary pub that maintains a sound reputation for quality food and world-class live music. With its stripped pine and flagstone floors, low ceilings and soft lighting, there's an air of a mid-European café bar mixed in with the traditional accoutrements of a British pub. It makes for an intimate setting, with background music kept at a reasonable level, but it steps up a gear with live music events (folk/country/bluegrass) and one-man theatre shows on Sunday and Monday nights. Chris Beaumont and Gill Perkins, with the help of chef Ian 'Spats' Picken, have set about improving on an already successful recipe: menus change every two months and include dishes such as a miniature shepherd's pie, pork cutlet with gooseberry sauce and apple, and strawberry and claret jelly. Real ales include Harvey's from nearby Lewes, Ringwood Best and Timothy Taylor's Landord, there's a famous selection of Belgian beers - 15 at the last count - and a couple of organic wines on the short wine list.

Prices: Set lunch £15. Set dinner £17. Main course restaurant from £9. Main course bar/snack from £5.50. House wine £9.50.
Hours: 11.00-15.00. 17.30-23.00. Sunday 12.00-16.00, 19.00-22.30. Closed Monday lunchtime.
Food served: 12.00-14.30. 18.00-21.00 Tuesday - Thursday and Saturday. No food Monday all day, and Friday and Sunday evenings.
Cuisine: Authentic and original World Cuisine.
Other Points: Dogs welcome. Garden. Children welcome over 14 years old. Small car park.
Directions: M23/A23 to Brighton. Follow the signs to the City Centre. Southover Street is the first turning on the left from Richmond Terrace. (Map 6, D5)

Nineteen

19 Broad Street, Brighton, East Sussex BN2 1TJ
Telephone: +44(0)1273 675529
info@hotelnineteen.co.uk
www.hotelnineteen.co.uk

Mark Whiting's cool urban hideaway in Kemp Town delivers the kind of sequestered feeling that only comes at a so-called boutique hotel, the kind that makes you feel as if you're staying with old chums. This is a hip hotel too. Contemporary décor runs to a lot of white - duvets, walls, clean white bath or shower rooms - a great eye for modern art, and lovely touches such as a handful of sweeties by the bed, plasma screen TVs, stunning glass tables, CD and video players, and burners for aromatherapy oils. Everything has been thought through, from the lighting to the beds - three of which are built on glass bricks, which light up. Carefully bought breakfast ingredients show attention to detail and quality: free-range eggs accompany smoked salmon, and there are BLTs, salads, yogurts, juices and smoothies. Complimentary champagne ('not cava', insists Mark), is offered at weekends, and breakfast hours are very civilised. If the weather is fine, there's a bijou flower and plant filled patio off the breakfast room. The kitchen next door is available to guests to make their own tea or coffee. Massages, manicures, pedicures, and yoga sessions with a qualified instructor are part of a package that can be booked on arrival; the keynote of Nineteen is one of relaxation.

Rooms: 7 en suite. Rooms from £95 to £150 including breakfast. Champagne breakfast on Sundays.
Other Points: No smoking. Garden.
Directions: M23 onto A23 and head for Brighton town centre. Travel past the Pavilion on the right hand side. Keep left, turn left at the roundabout onto Marine Parade. Keep left again to turn left into Manchester Street, turn right into St James Street and the second right into Broad Street, Hotel Nineteen is the petrol green building on the left. (Map 6, D5)

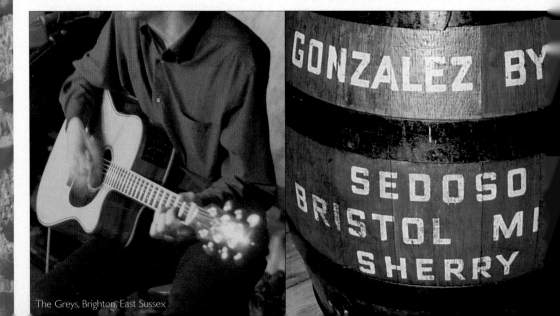

The Greys, Brighton, East Sussex

Why go to...Brighton

The 18th century fashion for sea bathing made Brighton, taking it from a small fishing village to the height of fashion when the Prince Regent (George IV), took up the place. His legacy is the extravagant oriental-gothic Royal Pavilion. The Victorians defined their era with the elegant West Pier - the mangled remains are part of the seascape. The 20th century gave us the tacky Palace Pier, with its fairground rides, Palace of Fun and Pleasure Dome. The Lanes (the core of the old fishing village) offer diverse bars, restaurants, antique, art, furniture, and clothes shops, and the town has a real buzz lent by a fairly bohemian crowd that takes in a thriving gay community and students from an art college and two universities.

Paskins Town House

18-19 Charlotte Street, Brighton, East Sussex BN2 1AG
Telephone: +44(0)1273 601203
welcome@paskins.co.uk
www.paskins.com

The fine four-storey Grade II listed building that makes up Paskins is at the heart of this East Cliff Regency area, one of eight conservation areas in Brighton recognised by the Department of the Environment as outstanding. Within, each bedroom is individually designed, ranging from the graceful elegance of a by-gone era, to a fresh, modern quirkiness. It's hard to decide between a plush deep-red room with vast antique four poster and impressive sofa, or Laura Ashley florals with brass bed and enormous, inviting mattress, and one of the light, bright modernistic rooms complete with unusual shaped mirrors, coloured headboard lights and Audrey Hepburn prints. Attention to detail is impeccable, down to vintage-style room phones or silver, sleek, space age ones where appropriate, and walls are flamboyantly decked out with old prints, modern art, theatre and cabaret posters. Breakfast in a fabulous art deco room is something to look forward to. Ingredients are from local Sussex farms with superb bacon, and sausages that can take in over fifty varieties in a year. For vegetarians, a breakfast of organic free-range eggs, mushrooms and tomatoes cooked and sprinkled with basil or oregano on toast is heavenly. The Vegetarian Society nominated Paskins Vegetarian Hotel of the Year 2001/02.

Rooms: 19 rooms, 16 en suite. Double/twin room from £35.
Cuisine: Farm fresh, local and mainly organic.
Directions: M23. At Brighton Pier proceed towards the Marina. Charlotte Street is approximately the 11th turning on the left. (Map 6, D5)

England - East Sussex

The Griffin Inn   ★ ♈ 🍴 ✕ ✎

Fletching, Uckfield, East Sussex TN22 3SS
Telephone: +44(0)1825 722890
www.thegriffininn.co.uk

The Pullan family's civilised 400-year-old inn is everything a village local should be, and more. It's a classic old-style country pub, full of oak-beams and panelling, blazing log fires and old furnishings. Excellent food is the major attraction, with a twice-daily changing chalkboard in the bar and a short, more imaginative carte on offer in the restaurant - all draw on local, mostly organic, suppliers. In the bar, expect confit of pork and mungbean terrine with plum chutney, and lamb shank cooked in red wine with parsley mash. There are homely puddings (rhubarb and ginger crumble) and first-rate English cheeses with fruit chutney. You must book in the restaurant. Here, rosemary and garlic crusted monkfish with saffron and dill cream, chargrilled beef fillet with haricot bean beignets, or local veal and game are typical offerings; on Thursday there's the 'fishtastic' menu. The impressive wine list runs to some 100 bottles with 15 offered by the glass. Ale drinkers will not be disappointed with the tip-top local brew from Harveys of Lewes. The eight individually furnished bedrooms may not be spacious, but all ooze character, with timbers, beams and sloping floors reflecting the age of the building; most have four-poster beds, and four are housed in the converted coach house.

Prices: Sunday set lunch £22.50. Main course bar meal from £8. Main course restaurant meal from £12. House wine £10.50.
Hours: 12.00-23.00. Closed 25 December.
Food served: 12.00-14.30. 19.00-21.30.
Rooms: 8 en suite. Double room from £85, single from £60, family room £120.
Cuisine: Modern British.
Other Points: Children welcome. Garden and Terrace. Car park.
Directions: One mile off the A272 between Maresfield and Newick, three miles north of Uckfield. (Map 6, D5)

Terre à Terre   ✕

71 East Street, Brighton, East Sussex BN1 1HQ
Telephone: +44(0)1273 729051
mail@terreaterre.co.uk

Philip Taylor and Amanda Powley's ground breaking vegetarian restaurant remains hard to pinpoint, even after a decade in business. This truly one-off place thinks about food in a way that other chefs do not. The cooking style is totally eclectic, with ideas drawn right across the Mediterranean to Central and Eastern Europe, the Far East and America, backed up by a kitchen confident enough to break culinary boundaries. Thus, a pête a brik is filled with minted cracked wheat, pressed sheep's cheese and preserved lemon, and served with saffron scented fennel, buttered string beans, and pickled apricots finished with tiger nut pesto. The house tapas plate is a great introduction to this unusual style - a starter for two to share or a satisfying lunch dish where a myriad of textures and culinary styles gives each mouthful an unpredictability that keeps interest buoyant. Right from the word go you notice the flavours, picking up on mint, cardamom, coriander, wasabi, tamarind. Other materials bolster strength: roast Jerusalem artichoke risotto served with truffled seasons mushrooms, a Madeira and balsamic reduction and sage and rootie chippers. The enthusiasts wine list is totally organic; it is worth checking the blackboard in the bar for current recommendations.

Prices: Main course restaurant from £11.95. House wine £12.75.
Hours: 12.00-22.30. Tuesday to Sunday, Monday 18.00-22.30. During the winter closed Mondays. Closed 24-26 December and 1 January.
Cuisine: Modern British and Vegetarian.
Other Points: No-smoking area. Garden. Children welcome.
Directions: Just off the seafront, close to Palace Pier. (Map 6, D5)

The Freemasons   🚪 ✕

38/39 Western Road, Hove, East Sussex BN3 1AF
Telephone: +44(0)1273 732043

The Freemasons has the most wonderful exterior: gold mosaic complete with Masonic Lodge symbol designs. The former 'Mason's drinking hole' is now well looked after by enthusiastic proprietors Tanya and D'Arcy Gander, who are quick to point out that gone are the days when you couldn't get a table until you had given your 'Lodge' number.
The interior has been transformed into a sleek, relaxed atmosphere where food comes first. Alcoves of leather seating, small leather stools and wooden flooring form a great backdrop for informal dining. The simple lines of the interior, although contemporary, are very sympathetic to the 1920's design of the building. From a menu designed around local supplies of fresh ingredients, look out for starters of Thai spiced mushroom soup, or salt and pepper deep-fried whitebait, with mains of parsley battered wing, chunky chips, peas and tartare sauce, or thyme marinated rump of lamb, Puy lentils and root vegetables served with boulangère potatoes. Tanya and her husband are dedicated to sourcing fresh ingredients locally - hence their keenness to support farmers markets.

Prices: Main course restaurant from £6. Main course bar from £3.50. House wine £10.50.
Hours: 12.00-23.00.
Food served: 12.00-21.00 and until 18.00 on Mondays.
Cuisine: Modern British.
Other Points: Outside seating during the summer. Children welcome until 19.00.
Directions: At seafront turn right at pier along A259 through Hove, then in a mile turn right at Lansdowne Street, then right into Western Road. (Map 6, D5)

The Rainbow Inn

Resting Oak Hil, Cooksbridge, Lewes,
East Sussex BN8 4SS
Telephone: +44(0)1273 400334

The combined talents of owner/entrepreneur Sebastian
Gorst and chef Luke Wilson have successfully
transformed this once run-down village local into a
stylishly refurbished pub-restaurant providing freshly
produced modern pub food. Built of brick and flint in
the 17th century, the Rainbow makes the most of its
attractive corner site, with rustic benches on a flower-
filled front patio and a sun-trap enclosed rear terrace
replete with teak furnishings, barbecue area, and
distant South Downs views. Inside, beyond the small
rustic bar, where you will find a cracking pint of local
Harveys ale, the civilised and warmly decorated dining
areas sport an eclectic mix of tables and chairs and a
relaxed and informal atmosphere. Menus change daily,
the chalkboard above the bar listing fresh Newhaven
fish and game in season. The printed menu offering,
say, seared scallops and yellow courgettes with sweet
chilli dressing, followed by chargrilled leg of local
lamb steak with ratatouille and garlic jus, or
homemade pork, chilli and garlic sausages with
cheddar mash and shallot jus. Good puddings range
from baked orange tart to homemade ice creams. The
short, carefully selected global list of wines
complements the menu. Two upstairs private dining
rooms are perfect for intimate dinner parties.

Prices: Set lunch (2 courses) £10.45. Main course restaurant from
£8.95. Main course bar/snack from £3.95. House wine £11.
Hours: 12.00-15.00. 17.30-23.00. Sunday 12.00-22.30.
Food served: 12.00-14.30. 19.00-22.00. Sunday 12.00-22.00.
No food Christmas Day.
Cuisine: Modern European.
Other Points: No-smoking area. Garden. Children welcome. Car
park. Private dining. Barbecue area.
Directions: M23/A23/A27 exit Eastbourne and Lewes. Situated on
the A275 between Lewes and Haywards Heath on the edge of
Cooksbridge village at Barcombe Fork. (Map 6, D5)

Jeake's House Hotel

Mermaid Street, Rye, East Sussex TN31 7ET
Telephone: +44(0)1797 222828
jeakeshouse@btinternet.com
www.jeakeshouse.com

The late 17th-century building - built originally by
merchant Samuel Jeake as a storehouse - exudes a real
sense of history. Jenny Hadfield has decorated each
room individually using fresh flowers and lots of deft
personal touches to create an elegant look that mixes
bold floral prints and striking colours with beams and
standing timbers, period pieces such as a grandfather
clock and a piano with highly polished antiques. An
open fire may greet you (as well as Jenny's cats) as you
come down to breakfast in the galleried hall of what
was once a meeting house used by the Quakers. Tuck
into local award-winning sausages, natural oak-smoked
kippers and haddock from Rye Harbour, devilled
kidneys, scrambled free-range egg with smoked
salmon, and bread and croissants from the High Street
baker, served with homemade preserves from the local
Women's Institute. An honesty bar operates in the
book-lined library; there are no evening meals served,
but reservations can be made for nearby restaurants.
Bedrooms are splendid with brass or mahogany beds,
drapes, cushions, and flowers and sparkling bathrooms
are equipped with luxurious towels. There's a private
car park, a real boon as parking in Rye is difficult.

Prices: Main course (bar/snack) from £4.50. House wine £10.50.
Rooms: 11 rooms, 10 en suite. Double room from £40 per person,
single from £37.
Other Points: No-smoking in the dining room. Children welcome
over 12 years. Car park.
Directions: Exit 10/M20 and follow signs for Brenzett, then
directions for Hastings and Rye. Parking in Rye is restricted, but
Jeake's House has its own private car park. (Map 6, D6)

Prices: Set lunch £10.95. Set dinner
£11.95. Main course restaurant from £5.95.
Main course bar from £3.50.
House wine £10.50.
Hours: 11.00-23.00. Sunday 12.00-22.30.
Food served: 12.00-14.30. 18.00-21.00.
Sundays from 19.00-21.30.
Rooms: 10 en suite. Double room from
£75, single from £45.
Cuisine: Modern British.
Other Points: No-smoking area. Dogs
welcome. Courtyard. Children welcome.
Directions: Off A27 into Chichester,
follow ring road to north of the city and
top end of North Street. (Map 5, D4)

The George & Dragon

North Street, Chichester, West Sussex PO19 1NQ
Telephone: +44(0)1243 785660
info@georgeanddragoninn.co.uk
www.georgeanddragoninn.co.uk

This lovely little pub in the centre of Chichester is a wonderful lunch time
stop-off, where scrubbed pine tables, soft green walls, pretty tiled
fireplaces and simple glass lanterns all make an inviting place for people
to enjoy a break. Around the central bar, you will find a refreshing cross-
section of visitors - shoppers, local businessmen, friends meeting for
lunch, and tourists - and Mike Burchett and his staff work hard to make
everyone feel welcome. Chef Shawn Tadd is keen to tell you that 'fresh is
best' as you enjoy a starter of toasted goats' cheese, pesto and lettuce
followed, perhaps, by lamb cutlets with rosemary and red wine gravy.
Where possible, Shawn uses produce from an organic garden, where he
also grows lettuces and herbs. He designs his menus around seasonal lines.
The slate-floored conservatory restaurant opens out onto a small patio,
which forms a wonderful barbecue area and sun trap. It's from here you
can see Mike Burchett's most recent handiwork - newly refurbished rooms
in the pub's old flint and brick stable block. Stylish accommodation is
painted in warm yellow with white bed linen and wonderful heavy pine
beds with wrought iron detail.

Purchases Wine Bar
31 North Street, Chichester, West Sussex PO19 1LY
Telephone: +44(0)1243 537352
thediningroom@forgehotel.com
www.forgehotel.com

Prices: Main course restaurant from £8.50. Main course bar/snack from £2.50. House wine £9.
Hours: 12.00-23.00. Closed Sunday.
Food served: 12.00-20.45.
Cuisine: Eclectic.
Other Points: Totally no smoking. Garden. Children welcome over 12 years old. Car park.
Directions: Park in public theatre car park and walk up into North Street. Purchases is on the left next to Laura Ashley. (Map 5, D4)

In Chichester, there is no shortage of beautiful buildings and sights, especially around Cathedral Close. But, until recently, there was a shortage of watering holes of the same calibre. When Neil Rusbridger set up a wine bar in rooms behind wine merchants Arthur Purchase & Son, he created an immediate hit. The small compact wine shop, founded in 1760, makes a marvellous entrance. Old photographs and portraits of the Purchase family are on the walls of the entrance hall and take you seamlessly past the shop and through to the wine bar at the back. Here deep red walls form a striking backdrop to more family portraits, a wonderful fireplace and an impressive grandfather clock. With a policy of sourcing as many ingredients locally from independent suppliers as possible, the simple pick-and-mix menu is an enticing read. Warm salad of grilled chicken breast is tossed with artichokes and mustard flavoured potatoes, or there's dressed Selsey crab. 'Tapas' come in the form of smoked breast of duck, silver anchovy fillets, hard boiled quails' eggs with mayonnaise and celery salt, and marinaded herring fillets, a perfect light summer lunch served in the courtyard garden. The choice of wines is excellent, prices are sensible enough to encourage exploration throughout.

England - West Sussex

The Royal Oak

Pook Lane, East Lavant, Chichester, West Sussex PO18 0AX
Telephone: +44(0)1243 527434
nickroyaloak@aol.com

Within a year of acquiring this tiny 200-year-old village inn Nick Sutherland extended the dining area and convered the rear barn and cottage into bedrooms, thanks to a thriving dining trade and demand for accommodation due to its proximity to Chichester, Goodwood and the new Rolls Royce factory. Flint-built and accessed via a pretty raised terrace, this pretty cottage comprises an open-plan bar and dining area with open log fires, leather sofas, fat cream candles on scrubbed tables, and ales tapped from the cask. The food is modern British in style, the main menu and daily blackboard additions featuring quality fish and meats from London markets and vegetables from local organic farms. Typically, a meal may begin with crispy crab cakes with sweet chilli, followed by Sussex pork and herb sausages, mash and balsamic onion jus, lamb steak with rosemary mash, or whole grilled lemon sole with chive butter. Lunchtime brings sandwiches and there are good homemade puddings. Very stylish bedrooms feature pastel décor, smart furnishings, flat-screen TVs, CD players and smart bathrooms with power showers.

Prices: Main course from £11. House wine £9.95.
Hours: 11.00-23.00. Sunday 12.00-15.00. Closed Sunday evenings and 25 December.
Food served: 12.00-14.30. 18.30-21.30. Sunday 12.00-14.30.
Rooms: 6 en suite. Double/twin from £70.
Cuisine: Modern and Traditional British.
Other Points: No-smoking area. Garden and Terrace. Car park.
Directions: Village signposted off A286 Midhurst road a mile north of Chichester.(Map 5, D4)

White Horse Inn

High Street, Chilgrove, Chichester, West Sussex PO18 9HX
Telephone: +44(0)1243 535219
info@whitehorsechilgrove.co.uk
www.whitehorsechilgrove.co.uk

Charles Burton dreamt of owning this magnificent inn when he worked here as a waiter in the 1970s; he realised that dream in 1998. Designed as a place to relax, the bar delivers something light and delicious from the menu - Italian-style open sandwiches, maybe, or scallops, Selsey crab, duck, rabbit and many other local specialities. It was former owner Barry Philips who made the White Horse famous for its wine cellars, and Charles has continued the tradition. A tiny corridor - one wall of which is a wine rack from floor to ceiling - leads through to the Chilgrove Restaurant. Here amongst the pink linen table cloths, and fresh flowers you can choose from two wine lists covering over 500 global wines, matched by marinated venison fillet with red onion marmalade and a rich fruit cappucino, and roast loin of lamb with rosemary and cepe mushroom sauce. Charles's own particular stamp has been the introduction of eight en suite bedrooms, all named after a premier wine and each is furnished in neutral colours with raw silk scatter cushions on the beds. Breakfast is another treat - delivered to your room in a country hamper filled with muffins, fruit, preserves, yogurt, fresh orange juice and coffee.

Prices: Main course from £9.50. House wine £10.
Hours: 11.00-15.00. 18.00-23.00. Closed Sunday evening, all day Monday. Check for seasonal variations.
Food served: 12.00-14.00. 19.00-22.00.
Rooms: 8 en suite. Single from £50.
Cuisine: Modern English.
Other Points: No-smoking area. Dogs welcome. Children welcome. Garden. Car park.
Directions: Take A286 Midhurst road north of Chichester and turn left on to B2141for South Harting and Chilgrove. (Map 5, D4)

Half Moon Inn

Glass House Lane, Kirdford, West Sussex RH14 0LT
Telephone: +44(0)1403 820223
halfmooninn.kirdford@virgin.net
www.the-halfmoon-inn.co.uk

Patrick and Francesca Burfields patience in their search for their dream pub truly paid off when they stumbled upon the Half Moon Inn tucked away in a sleepy village north of Petworth. Tile-hung and rose-adorned, with a rambling series of timbered and tiled dining areas, this attractive 16th-century pub more than fitted their requirements, despite its recent chequered past. Two years on, following complete and tasteful redecoration, and the introduction of imaginative modern menus, the Half Moon is thriving as a country dining pub. Although most tables are topped with linen cloths and quality glassware, you will find real ale on tap and an atmosphere that is relaxed and informal. In addition to grilled sardines with garlic butter, and Caesar salad, the lunch menu may feature smoked salmon risotto, and beer battered haddock with handcut chips, the repertoire built around produce carefully sourced from local suppliers. Updated classics on the evening menu may include roast duck with ginger and spring onion on saffron noodles. There's an interesting list of wines with four by the glass. Overnight accommodation is available in two homely and comfortable bedrooms (not en suite) on a dinner, bed and breakfast basis only.

Prices: Main course from £8.95. House wine £10.50.
Hours: 11.30-15.00 18.30-23.00. Closed Sunday evening and all Monday.
Food served: 12.00-14.00 and 19.00-21.00
Rooms: 2 rooms not en suite. Dinner, bed and breakfast from £130.
Cuisine: Modern British
Other Points: No smoking area. Garden. Children welcome. Car park.
Directions: Off the A272 between Billingshurst and Petworth. Follow signs at Wisborough Green to Kirdford. (Map 5, D4)

THE CROWN OF ENGLAND

Described as the 'Crown of England' poets and writers such as Rudyard Kipling and Hilaire Belloc have been captivated by its green hills and gentle beauty.
Drive length: 66 miles

Sheffield Park Gardens
(NT)

Michelham
Priory

Glynde Place

Bateman's
(Rudyard Kipling's
home - NT)

Firle Place

Charleston Farmhouse
(former home to members of
the Bloomsbury Set)

Alfriston
(Clergy House NT)

East Grinstead
Turners Hill
Royal Tunbridge Wells
Biddenden
Lamberhurst
Tenterden
Haywards Heath
Crowborough
Fletching
Heathfield
Rye
Glynde Place
Uckfield
South Downs
Battle
Cooksbridge
Barcombe
Lewes
Hailsham
Hastings
Bexhill
Brighton
Hove
Eastbourne
Newhaven
Beachy Head

● Accommodation/Food

● Accommodation

● Food

🍃 Food Shop

To find the establishments marked here, look up the listing town marked on the map in bold in the town index on page 395

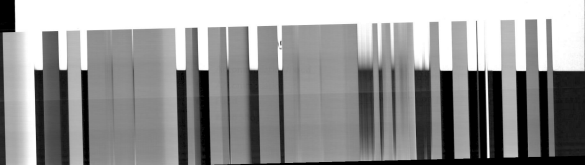

The Duke of Cumberland ⓓ ✕

Henley, Fernhurst, Midhurst, West Sussex GU27 3HQ
Telephone: +44(0)1428 652280
gaston.duval@btopenworld.com

Tricky to locate, this unspoilt 15th-century country pub, its brick and stone walls covered with roses and wisteria, is well worth the effort to find. The tiny rustic bars exude atmosphere in spades, helped by painted, panelled walls, low beamed ceilings, quarry-tiled floor, scrubbed pine tables and benches, and open log fires. Gas lamps, old indentures, and blue and white plates decorate the walls. Relying on fresh produce, including organic beef from local farms, bar food combines both the modern and the traditional, the latter including ploughman's lunches, homemade beefburgers, ham, egg and handcut chips, cod in 'hatter' batter, and a rump steak sandwich with horseradish. Alternatively, you may wish to order chicken liver parfait, pan-fried mackerel with cracked peppercorns and tomato compote, and rib-eye steak with anchovy butter. Specialities include grilled trout from the pub's own spring-fed pools and, given 24-hours notice, traditional roasts (rib of beef, leg of lamb, haunch of venison) are served as a joint to the table. In summer, order a pint of Youngs Bitter or Ballards Best, drawn straight from the cask, or a glass of local farmhouse cider.

Prices: Main course from £10.95. Main course (bar/snack) from £6.95. House wine £10.95.
Hours: 11.00-15.00. 17.00-23.00. 12.00-15.00. 19.00-22.30 on Sunday. 12.00-14.00 on 25 December.
Food served: 12.00-14.30. 19.00-21.30. No food Sunday evening.
Cuisine: Traditional and modern pub food.
Other Points: Children welcome. Garden. Car park.
Directions: The village is signposted off the A286 north of Midhurst. (Map 5, D4)

The Green Man ★ ◫ ♍ ⓓ ✕

Church Road, Partridge Green, Horsham,
West Sussex RH13 8JT
Telephone: +44(0)1403 710250

There is something very special about this red-brick roadside pub. For proprietor William Thornton, the pub is the fulfillment of a personal ambition - he used to drive past the run down pub when visiting his mother. When the building came up for sale, he bought it and the results are remarkable - especially for someone with no previous experience of running a pub. Refurbished with enthusiasm and taste, the place oozes stylish informality and reflects William's interests, through and through. His love of Spain can be found in everything, from the olive-patterned water jugs to the lashings of olive oil and bread on the table, and tapas on the menu (chorizo, anchovies, mussels in chilli oil, and squid in their own ink). The interior is highly individual, which makes it feel more like a home than a pub: prints, a wood-burning stove. There are cosy corners for small groups, and areas for larger parties to enjoy dinner. Food remains the central focus, with a typical meal opening with seared scallops and vegetable purée followed, perhaps, by pan-roasted duck breast with fig and port jus, red cabbage and dauphinoise potatoes, and an extraordinary glazed lemon tart with thyme essence and crème fraîche finishing things on a high note.

Prices: Set lunch £16. Set dinner £22. Main course restaurant meal from £7.95. Main course bar meal from £3.95. House wine £10.95.
Hours: 11.30-15.00. 18.30-23.00. Sunday 12.00-16.00. Closed Sunday evening.
Food served: 12.00-14.00 (Sunday until 14.30) 19.00-21.30
Cuisine: Modern British.
Other Points: No-smoking area. Dogs welcome. Garden. Children welcome over five years old. Car park.
Directions: On B2135 between A281 north of Henfield and A24 south of A272 junction. (Map 6, D5)

Prices: Set price lunch £16.25. Set price dinner £23.25. House wine £11.
Hours: 12.30-14.00. 19.00-21.30.
Rooms: 29 en suite. Double room from £151, single from £126.
Cuisine: Modern British.
Other Points: No-smoking area. Children welcome. Garden. Car park.
Directions: Exit 11/M23. Between Horsham and Crawley on the A624. (Map 6, D5)

Ghyll Manor ◫ ✕ ♫

High Street, Rusper, Horsham, West Sussex RH12 4PX
Telephone: +44(0)845 345 3426

The 17th-century manor house is set in nine acres of formal gardens and surrounded by 45 acres of parkland, yet the hotel's main entrance is just off Rusper's High Street with its pubs and several shops - a wonderful juxtaposition of style and atmosphere. The house retains a classic feel in public rooms that are divided into a series of comfortable, traditionally styled lounges, including a relaxed, bright, airy conservatory, and a charming small bar. Bedrooms in the main house are individual, and come with lovely period details and a few antiques; those in a converted stable mews set around a courtyard are spacious and modern with neat bathrooms. The old beamed restaurant is the setting for some modern British dishes. The menu is a mix of old favourites (terrine of chicken and vegetables, grilled Dover sole) and up-to-the-minute dishes, attractively prepared and plated. Meals might start with devilled veal sweetbreads, sautéed with garlic, fresh chillies and ginger and served with asparagus and sauce vierge. Main courses of grilled free-range chicken breast with a leek and truffle salad, or chump of South Down lamb, lead on to glazed coconut risotto or terrine of autumn fruits.

Old Tollgate Restaurant and Hotel

The Street, Bramber, Steyning, West Sussex BN44 3WE
Telephone: +44(0)1903 879494
info@oldtollgatehotel.com
www.oldtollgatehotel.com

Built on the site of a much older toll house, this extremely comfortably appointed roadside hotel is located a hundred yards or so off the A283 close to the village centre. It offers some very up-to-date and spacious accommodation arranged upstairs in the main building, as well as in a separate block just across the courtyard from the main entrance. Public areas comprise a very attractive lounge, as well as a split-level bar and carvery restaurant. The latter both have a very traditional air, with dark oak panelling a prominent feature. There's also a good emphasis on local produce in the carvery, with game from local shoots, locally smoked salmon and shellfish, and bread from a nearby baker. Bedrooms are all of very good size, but are even larger in the main building, where bed settees provide additional sleeping options, especially suitable for family use, with children under 14 accommodated free when sharing with their parents. All rooms have mini-bars and many feature bidets in the well-equipped bathrooms. Indeed, the relative degree of comfort provided in the bedrooms are akin to hotels rated higher than three stars. Those on business will appreciate the ample desk space provided.

Prices: Set lunch from £17.45. Set dinner £23.95. House wine £11.25.
Hours: 12.00-13.45. 19.00-21.30.
Rooms: 31 en suite. Rooms from £76.
Cuisine: Traditional English.
Other Points: No-smoking area. Children welcome. Garden. Car park. Licence for Civil Weddings.
Directions: On A283; in Bramber village, four miles from Shoreham-by-sea. (Map 6, D5)

Springwells Bed and Breakfast Hotel

9 High Street, Steyning, West Sussex BN44 3GG
Telephone: +44(0)1903 812446
contact@springwells.co.uk
www.springwells.co.uk

This imposing creeper-clad Georgian merchant's house stands at the very eastern end of the High Street. Reception is at the end of the narrow entrance hall; to reach it you pass a homely and comfortable lounge and the attractive breakfast room. To the rear of the ground floor is the bar that incorporates a further lounge-cum-conservatory area, which looks out over a neat walled garden. The whole place has a very traditional and well-maintained air; the owner obviously takes great pride in the place. Bedrooms, whether they be on the first or second floor, are well appointed and of good size, those on the first being somewhat larger, and with higher ceilings. Furnishings are of good quality and are in keeping with the building's character - two rooms have four-posters. Bedrooms at the back enjoy views over the garden, are quieter, and have a sunnier aspect too. On the top floor, a couple of rooms have to share a bathroom. As well as tea/coffee-making facilities and biscuits, a bowl of fresh fruit stands at the bottom of the stairs, and there's a fridge containing fresh milk and a few cans of beer at the end of the first-floor corridor.

Hours: Closed for two weeks over Christmas and New Year.
Rooms: 11 rooms, 9 en suite. Double room from £79, single from £35.
Other Points: Children welcome. Garden. Car park.
Directions: Off A283. (Map 6, D5)

Tulley's Farm

Turners Hill Road, Turners Hill, Crawley,
West Sussex RH10 4PE
Telephone: +44(0)1342 718472
shop@tulleysfarm.com
www.tulleysfarm.com

Winners of the 1999 Marks and Spencer Grower and Retailer of the Year Award, the Beare family have been farming here for over 60 years, and have seen many changes since they started with a small dairy herd. The extensive pick-your-own enterprise was developed in the early 1970s, and now offers a menu of crops and picking times that opens in April with rhubarb, goes onto all kinds of soft fruits from July to September, and closes in October with pumpkins. In 1992 the Farm Shop opened. In addition to a large selection of foods, including local and regional cheeses, the shop now offers a vast array of produce including spring and summer bedding plants and containers. Between July and September there is the famous Amazing Maize Maze to visit. The Farmhouse Kitchen opened in 1996, converted from a Victorian stable block. As you enter, you are confronted with a vast array of cakes and scones. The menu offers mainly sweet items, but filled jacket potatoes, sandwiches and a slice or two of quiche deliver some savoury options.

Prices: Main course from £5.25.
Hours: Tea and coffee served 10.00-17.00 in summer, 10.00-16.30 in winter. Lunch served 12.00-14.30.
Shop: 9.00-18.00. PYO daily from June to October.
Cuisine: Traditional English.
Other Points: No smoking area. Children welcome. Play area. Garden. Car park. Seasonal activities.
Directions: Exit 10/M23. Take the A264, then the B2028 to Turners Hill. (Map 6, D5)

Cherington Arms

Cherington, Shipston-on-Stour, Warwickshire CV36 5HS
Telephone: +44(0)1608 686233
www.hooknorton.tablesir.com/cheringtonarms

A small, quiet Cotswold village pub with a strong local feel, run by passionate and confident owners. The bar is deeply traditional in look with exposed brick walls, red stone tiled floor, an open fire, hop decorations and classic wooden pub furniture - a place to relax with a pint of Hook Norton. Chalkboards list special dishes of the day, backed up by a printed bar menu ranging from roast beef and horseradish sandwiches to baguettes filled with chargrilled steak and caramelised onions, and ploughman's of mature cheddar with salad, whole apples, pickles and a basket of bread. The restaurant is separate, a nice room with lots of character. In two tiers, one part has large oak pillars, carpeted floor, ceiling beams, and log burner, the other is wood floored with square wooden tables of varying sizes. A piano sits in the corner and hops decorate the walls. A well balanced menu, a mixture of traditional and modern British, delivers good country cooking along the lines of roasted pumpkin soup, followed by hay-baked rump of lamb with clapshot potatoes and rosemary jus. Sticky toffee pudding gets the thumbs up for dessert. The wine list is a small, evenly global and priced under £15.

Prices: Main course restaurant from £6.75. Main course bar/snack from £3.75. House wine £10.
Hours: 12.00-15.00. 18.30-23.00, 19.00-22.30 Sunday. Closed Monday lunch time.
Food served: 12.00-14.30. 19.00-21.30. No food Sunday evening.
Cuisine: Modern and Traditional British.
Other Points: No-smoking area. Totally no smoking in restaurant. Dogs welcome. Garden. Children welcome. Car park.
Directions: Exit 11/M40. Village signposted off A3400 between Chipping Norton and Shipston-on-Stour. (Map 9, E3)

Turmeric Gold

166 Medieval Spon Street, Coventry, Warwickshire CV1 1BB
Telephone: +44(0)2476 226603
info@turmericgold.co.uk
www.turmericgold.co.uk

"Turmeric Gold is situated in a truly gorgeous medieval street within the confines of the thoroughly modern and distressing Coventry Inner Ring Road", writes Jay Alam of his popular Indian restaurant. The building itself dates from the 15th century and transformation into a restaurant has lost none of its charm - exposed brick, beams and timber framework are enhanced by vibrant eastern colours and oriental antiques. The upstairs dining room has a particularly romantic feel with lots of hidden features and private dining areas. There are no new surprises on the menu, baltis and tandoori dishes show up forcefully alongside stalwarts such as chicken jalfrazi and various dhansak and bhuna dishes. What distinguishes the cooking, however, is that it is fresh tasting and light in oils. Fluffy naans, a selection of vegetarian dishes and a price range of set menus are also offered. An option is to be treated like a Maharaja for £55. This enables you to have as much food and drink as you like in a private lounging area which is covered in silk and can be draped over for privacy.

Prices: Set lunch £12.95. Set dinner between £28-£35. Main course from £10. House wine £8.75.
Hours: 12.00-14.00. 17.30-23.15. Friday and Saturday until 00.15, Closed Sunday lunch, 25-26 December.
Cuisine: Modern Indian.
Other Points: No-smoking area. Children welcome over three years old. Car park. Large private room.
Directions: Situated off the city ring road on junction 9, going towards Upper Well Street. Turn right at the second traffic lights onto Corporation Street. At the top of the street, turn right at the roundabout onto Medieval Spon Street. Turmeric Gold is found opposite Bonds night spot. (Map 9, D3)

The Fox & Hounds Inn

Great Wolford, Moreton-in-Marsh, Warwickshire CV36 5NQ
Telephone: +44(0)1608 674220
info@thefoxandhoundsinn.com
www.thefoxandhoundsinn.com

Like the relatively untouched village in which it stands, the 16th-century, stone-built Fox and Hounds remains delightfully unspoilt. The traditional interior exudes character through its polished flagstones, black-painted beams garlanded with hops and jugs, eclectic mix of old furnishings, and fine inglenook fireplace; in the small taproom you can play time-honoured pub games. Wendy Veale sources meat from a local butcher, game from nearby shoots and dairy produce from a local farm shop. Whereas the main bar and adjoining dining room offer traditional pub food along the lines of homemade soup, decent sandwiches, and ploughman's, more ambitious dishes are found on the daily changing blackboard. Starters of roasted Piedmont peppers topped with garlic, plum tomatoes, mozzarella and tapenade dressing, say, or monkfish wrapped in bacon with saffron mash and a garlic and tomato fondue. Strawberry pana cotta with fruits of the forest is highly recommended. The well-stocked bar dispenses five micro-brewery beers and an impressive range of 180 whiskies. Housed in a separate building are comfortable en suite bedrooms with stripped-pine furniture and modern facilities.

Prices: Main course from £9.25. House wine £12.95.
Hours: 12.00-14.30 Tuesday to Saturday. 12.00-15.00 Sunday. 18.00-23.00 Tuesday to Saturday. Closed all day Monday.
Food served: 12.00-14.00 Tuesday-Saturday (12.00-14.15 Sunday). 18.00-21.00 Tuesday-Friday (18.00-21.15 Saturday).
Rooms: 3 en suite. Double room from £60, single from £40.
Cuisine: Modern and traditional British.
Other Points: No-smoking area. Bedrooms non-smoking. Car park. Garden. Children welcome.
Directions: Exit 12/M40. Three miles east of Moreton-in-Marsh off the A44. (Map 4, A8)

The Howard Arms ★ 🍷 ◗ ✕ ⌁

Lower Green, Ilmington, Stratford-upon-Avon,
Warwickshire CV36 4LT
Telephone: +44(0)1608 682226
info@howardarms.com
www.howardarms.com

Ex-hoteliers, Robert and Gill Greenstock run this late
16th century Cotswold stone inn. It is a rambling
building, but the flagstoned bar and open-plan dining
area create a civilised look without sacrificing period
charm. Rare-breed pork and free-range chicken from
Chesterton Farm, Cirencester, locally grown vegetables,
proper bacon, local farm eggs, game in season, all
feature in a repertoire that acknowledges country roots
and understands modern urban tastes. A typical menu
could offer fillet of John Dory, braised endive and
lemon butter sauce, contrasted by a classic beef, ale
and mustard pie. Desserts are made on the premises
except ice cream (which is from Rocombe), so expect
steamed chocolate sponge, chocolate sauce and clotted
Jersey cream to finish. The Genesis ale on handpump is
made in the neighbouring village, and there is always a
guest ale, say Black Sheep. The small wine list offers a
dozen or so house wines from around the world, all
available by the glass. Three individually decorated,
stylish en suite bedrooms are furnished in a
comfortable, antique country house chic that sets a
high standard for pub accommodation.

Prices: Sunday set lunch £18.50. Main course from £9.50.
House wine £11.50.
Hours: 11.00-14.30. 18.00-23.00. 12.00-15.30. 18.00-22.30 on
Sunday. Closed 25 Dec, 1 Jan and evening of 26 & 31 Dec.
Food served: 12.00-14.00. 19.00-21.00 (until 21.30 Friday and
Saturday). 12.00-14.30. 18.30-20.30 on Sunday.
Rooms: 3 en suite. Double room from £84.
Cuisine: Eclectic mix of traditional and world.
Other Points: Mainly no smoking (no-smoking in bedrooms). Car
park. Garden. Children welcome over 8 years old.
Directions: J15/M40. Two miles north west of Shipston-on-Stour
off A3400, eight miles south of Stratford. (Map 8, D7)

Simpson's Restaurant ★ 🍷 ✕

101-103 Warwick Road, Kenilworth,
Warwickshire CV8 1HL
Telephone: +44(0)1926 864567
info@simpsonsrestaurant.co.uk
www.simpsonsrestaurant.co.uk

Simpson's stands out. The neat creamy-yellow building
smartened by railings and neat topiary is set apart
from the chain stores, estate agents and charity shops
that make up Kenilworth's main thoroughfare. Within,
the contemporary look of mustard and green, with
shades of brown, beige and cream, modern paintings,
prints, cartoons, and mirrors covering the walls, is
matched by a gregarious and sophisticated atmosphere.
The classy, assured cooking of Andreas Antona and his
team, headed by Luke Tipping, matches the setting.
Cooking of this quality comes with a price tag, but
fixed-price menus are a bargain, especially those
offered at lunch. Note this summer lunch that began
with ham hock and foie gras terrine and celeriac
remoulade, was followed by pavé of Loch Duart
salmon with a zesty pink grapefuit and orange sauce,
accompanied by white asparagus and endive
marmalade, and finished with exotic fruit soup with
mango sorbet and basil. The set dinner provides the
opportunity to try house specialities such as torte of
Salcombe crab with Loch Fyne smoked salmon,
creamed avocado and gazpacho coulis. The wine list is
sensibly arranged in ascending order of price and
offers a broad, thoughtful spread with plenty of good
drinking to suit all pockets.

Prices: Set lunch £15 (2 courses) and £20, dinner £30. Main course
from £17.95. House wine £15.
Hours: 12.30-14.00 19.00-22.00. Closed Sunday, Monday and the
last two weeks of August.
Cuisine: Classical French with Modern influence.
Other Points: No-smoking area. Car park.
Directions: On the main high street in the centre of Kenilworth.
(Map 8, D7)

Prices: Main course from £8.
House wine £7.95.
Hours: 17.00-23.30.
Cuisine: Indian.
Other Points: Children welcome.
Car park.
Directions: Two miles south east of
Solihull. Exit5/M42. (Map 9, D2)

Cafe Saffron ✕

1679 High Street , Knowle, Solihull, Warwickshire B98 0RL
Telephone: +44(0)1564 772190

The location, just one mile from junction five of the M42, makes this
evening-only Indian restaurant an ideal pit stop. It is easy to find on the
High Street, with its modern-looking, open glass fascia, and stand out
orange logo over the door. It is obvious that this is an Indian restaurant
with a difference, moving away from the traditional curry house theme
through a more contemporary, minimalist look, with modern prints, and
warm orange-plastered walls lending a bistro feel. And the kitchen pays
more attention to detail, preparation, and look, with fresh meat and
poultry purchased from local butchers, and many herbs and spices
imported directly from Calcutta, and freshly ground on site. What is
familiar, however, is the long list of curry house favourites, delivering
dishes from India, Pakistan and Bangladesh. Classic starters such as
chicken shashlick, or prawn pathia puri, for example, with tandoori grills,
and curries such as bhuna, korma, dopiaza, passanda, jalfrezi and rogan
josh, making up the list of main courses. It provides a comforting,
something-for-everyone security of choice, but look to the list of
specialities for a more varied selection.

Harvard House, Stratford-upon-Avon, Warwickshire

The Boot Inn 🍷🍴

Old Warwick Road, Lapworth, Warwickshire, B94 6JU
Telephone: +44(0)1564 782464
www.thebootatlapworth.co.uk

Modern brasserie style dishes highlight the specials board and stylish menu at this smartly refurbished, red-brick pub beside the Grand Union Canal, just minutes from the M42 (J4) and within easy reach of Birmingham, Warwick and the NEC. Bustling bars sport an interesting mix of rustic tables and bench seating, rug-strewn quarry-tiled floors, impressive flower arrangements and a lively atmosphere, while the contemporary upstairs restaurant has a civilised dining ambience. Expect adventurous pub food with a distinct Mediterranean flavour, the choice ranging from crevettes, aïoli and rocket and onion tart with balsamic vinegar and Parmesan on the list of 'first plates' to roast lamb rump with baby onions and chorizo, and chargrilled chicken with chilli jam, basil and mango. Classic British dishes are given a modern twist, perhaps calf's liver with roast garlic, caramelised onion mash and smoked bacon. On the 'Puds and Stickies' menu you may find baked chocolate fondant with mint ice cream, accompanied by glass of Campbells Rutherglen Muscat from the excellent global list of wines. Impressive sandwich and filled baguette menu. Summer alfresco dining can be enjoyed on the attractive side terrace. Friendly service from an international, polo-shirted team of staff.

Prices: Main course restaurant from £9. House wine £11.50.
Hours: 11.00-23.00. Sunday until 22.30.
Food served: 12.00-14.30. 19.00-22.00. Sunday 12.00-15.00. 19.00-21.00.
Cuisine: Modern European.
Other Points: Dogs welcome. Garden. Children welcome. Car park.
Directions: Exit4/M42. Take A3400 from Hockley Heath south west for two and a half miles; Lapworth signposted left. (Map 9, D3)

The Crabmill 🍷🍴

Preston Bagot, Claverdon, Warwickshire B94 6JU
Telephone: + 44(0)1926 843342
www.thecrabmill.co.uk

A stylish Italian influence permeates the modern menus and the interior at this 15th century, brick-and-timber, former cider mill, peacefully located beside a leafy lane deep in Shakespeare country. Comfortably upmarket and appealing to a well-heeled clientele, expect to find a contemporary and often bustling bar area, replete with steely bar, wood floors and mirrored mustard walls, and a cosy, spilt-level lounge with leather sofas and deep armchairs. The main attraction, however, is the rustic Italian food served in the three individually themed and candlelit dining rooms, each divided by heavy beams and standing timbers. The Red Room (also known as the 'rude room') sports slightly risqué caricature pictures. Starters or light meals come in the guise of seared squid with chorizo, tomato and rocket, and smoked haddock tart with caramelised onions and mustard. For a main course, consider lamb rump with truffle dauphinoise and wilted red chard, fillet steak with confit garlic, onion and olive oil mash, or a daily fish special of whole lemon sole with lemon butter and crushed black pepper. Add in imaginative bar meals, upmarket sandwiches, decent wines, and a super summer garden and you have it all.

Prices: Main course restaurant from £10. Main course bar/snack from £4.95. House wine £12.50.
Hours: 11.00-23.00. Sunday 12.00-18.00.
Food served: 12.00-14.30. 18.30-21.30. Sunday 12.30-15.30.
Cuisine: Modern European.
Other Points: No-smoking area. Dogs welcome. Garden. Children welcome. Car park.
Directions: Exit16/M40 and Exit4/M42. (Map 9, D3)

The King's Head

21 Bearley Road, Aston Cantlow, Stratford-upon-Avon,
Warwickshire B95 6HY
Telephone: +44(0)1789 488242

Sensitive and stylish refurbishment in 2000 of this impressive, black and
white timbered Tudor building, set in an ancient village deep in the heart
of Shakespeare country, transformed it into one of Warwickshire's finest
destination dining pubs. Historic charm and modern styling blend
perfectly in the tastefully rustic interior, with lime-washed low beams,
huge polished flagstones, painted brickwalls, old scrubbed pine tables,
scatters cushions on antique settles, and crackling log fires setting the
relaxing scene in which to savour some innovative pub food. Sit where
you want, order a pint of Abbot Ale or a glass of decent wine (eight
available), and tuck into rustic breads, roast garlic and extra virgin olive
oil, or chicken liver parfait with spicy plum chutney. Follow with chilli
and lemon chicken served with olives, sun-dried tomatoes and rosemary,
or braised gammon hock on carrot and swede mash with parsley liquor, or
tuck into the King's Head famous duck supper. Alternatively, look to the
chalkboard for 'fishy specials', perhaps monkfish with salad niçoise and
herb oil, and the day's choice of sandwiches.

Prices: Main course restaurant from
£9.95. Bar snack from £4.60.
House wine £10.95.
Hours: 11.00-15.00. 17.30-23.00. Saturdays
from 11.00-23.00 and Sunday 12.00-22.30.
Food served: 12.00-14.30. 19.00-22.00.
Sunday 12.30-15.00. 19.00-21.00.
No food Christmas Day.
Cuisine: Modern British.
Other Points: No-smoking area. Dogs
welcome. Garden. Car park.
Directions: Five miles from Stratford-
upon-Avon; one mile off the main A34
Stratford to Birmingham road. (Map 5, A3)

The One Elm

1 Guild St, Stratford-upon-Avon,
Warwickshire CB37 6QZ
Telephone: +44(0)1789 404919
theoneelm@peachpubs.com
www.peachpubs.com

Hot on the heels of the success of their first pub
venture, the Rose and Crown in Warwick (see entry),
Lee Cash and Victoria Moon officially opened this,
their second acquisition, in July 2003. In a prime
location in the town centre, a stroll from the river and
theatre, it mirrors the chic, contemporary look and
style of menus to be found in Warwick. Opening at
9am for coffee and breakfast sandwiches, there is an
informal, almost continental feel about the place,
especially in the stylish front lounge area with its wood
floor, bright painted walls, leather sofas and low tables
displaying the day's newspapers. Beyond the central,
open-to-view kitchen is the more formal dining area.
From a deli chalkboard above the bar offering tapas-
style starters or nibbles of charcuterie, cheese, fish,
antipasti, and rustic breads, both lunch and dinner
menus list interesting modern pub food. Enjoy starter
or main course size Caesar salad or begin with pan-
fried sardines with ratatouille or wild mushroom
tagliatelle. Follow with spiced shoulder of lamb with
roast squash and mint yogurt, and round off with dark
and white chocolate terrine. Well chosen global list of
wines with eight by the glass.

Prices: Main course restaurant from £7.50. Main course bar/snack
from £1.35. House wine £10.50.
Hours: 09.00-23.00. Sunday 09.00-22.30.
Cuisine: Modern European.
Other Points: Dogs welcome. Garden. Children welcome.
Car park.
Directions: Exit15/M40. Town centre (Map 5, A3)

Aladdin's Indian Brasserie

4 Main Road, Tiddington, Stratford-upon-Avon,
Warwickshire CV37 7AZ
Telephone: +44(0)1789 294491

Located in a small shopping parade in a well-heeled
village, Aladdin's could expect to do good business.
The spacious, richly decorated jade and claret interior
is as far removed from your average curry house as is
possible, and designed more as a destination eating
place; prices reflect this. There's also extremely
courteous service, as well as a menu of old favourites
and interesting specials.

Prices: Set price dinner £30. House wine £8.75.
Hours: 17.30-24.00. Closed 25 December.
Cuisine: Indian.
Other Points: Children welcome.
Directions: Situated in Tiddington's Main Street (Map 9, E3)

Prices: Set lunch £10 (2 course Monday-Friday). Main course from £5.95. Snack from £3.95. House wine £12.
Hours: 11.00-23.00. 12.00-22.30 Sunday. Closed 25 December and 1 January.
Food served: 12.00-15.00. 17.30-22.00. food serving hours are flexible.
Cuisine: Modern British.
Other Points: No-smoking area. Dogs and children welcome. Large garden. Childrens play area. Car park.
Directions: Junction 15/M40. Just off the A4177 country lane running between Warwick and Solihull, four miles from Warwick town centre. (Map 9, D3)

The Durham Ox

Shrewley Common, Shrewley, Warwick, Warwickshire CV35 7AY
Telephone: +44(0)1926 842283
info@durham-ox.com

Ross Saunders and Andrew Whiffen are the duo responsible for the contemporary makeover of this pub, in particular, bringing to the kitchen a pedigree that takes in Barbados's Sandy Lane and Lone Star restaurants. This is the type of place where a tractor can be found parked next to a Ferrari. Indeed, the cream coloured brick facia overlooks loads of space for cars plus a massive beer garden next to a 'horse park' that provides waitress drinks service to the well-shod and mounted. The food, both in its sourcing and preparation, is taken seriously, with as much fresh produce as possible procured locally and presented in two styles: 'classical' and 'contemporary'. From the former comes grilled calf's liver with crisp bacon and sweetcorn and spring onion pancake; the latter might run to seared scallops with duck confit, rocket and balsamic dressing. Team with Abbott Ale or Speckled Hen, or one of up to two dozen chosen wines by the glass. This is one of the best pubs to have come out of the highly competitive area of Warwickshire and was voted Food Pub of the West Midlands in May 2003.

The Rose and Crown

30 Market Place, Warwick, Warwickshire CV34 4SH
Telephone: +44(0)1926 411117
roseandcrown@peachpubs.com
www.peachpubs.com

Lee Cash is a chef with a passion, and together with his partner Victoria Moon is rapidly establishing this 18th-century inn as a destination for food and accommodation. Main draws are inspired touches such as leather sofas bordering a long, low-slung coffee table displaying a selection of the day's newspapers, and a policy of opening early to attract people throughout the day. There's a dedicated dining area, but all tables are kept free of cutlery to encourage a mix of drinkers and diners. A deli plate chalkboard offers small tapas-style portions of cheeses, hams, salami, marinated anchovies and peppers and rustic breads. There is also a soup of the day and risotto of the week. Two printed menus offer a wide selection of options to suit the occasion and time of day, opening at 8am with breakfast sarnies, then offering deep-fried calamari, salmon niçoise, sausage of the week and mash, seafood chowder, and Aberdeen Angus rib-eye steak and chips with peppercorn sauce. An extensive wine list offers an evenly global supply of wines with six by the glass. Five minimalist-style bedrooms are tastefully decorated in different colour schemes and are comfortably equipped and appointed.
Prices: Main course restaurant from £7.50. Main course bar/snack from £6.50. House wine from £10.50.
Hours: 08.00-23.00, until 22.30 on Sunday. Closed 25 December.
Food served: 08.00-22.00.
Rooms: 5 en suite. Doubles/twins from £65.
Cuisine: Modern British.
Other Points: Dogs welcome. Garden and terrace. Children welcome. Parking opposite. Private dining available.
Directions: In the centre of Warwick, Market Square. (Map 9, D3)

Horns of Boningale

Holyhead Road, Wolverhampton WV7 3DA
Telephone: +44(0)1902 372347
horns@boningale.freeserve.co.uk

In a pretty rural location, but readily accessible on one of the main roads from Wolverhampton to Telford, the Horns is a large bustling place with an old fashioned feel. The beamed interior with traditional pictures and prints attracts a mix of folk, drawn by the array of real ales and wines, and by the reworked pub classics. These run to dishes such as the Horns' famous homemade steak and kidney pudding and stir-fries, which are listed on the lengthy good value menu offered in the various bar areas and more formal restaurant. There is an outdoor eating space set in the attractive gardens, and inside roaring fires; whether warming yourself up in the winter or basking in the sun, the atmosphere is spot on. The whole place has a traditional yet upbeat feel of which the owners are justly proud.
Prices: Main course bar meal from £8. House wine £8.50.
Hours: Open for lunch and dinner daily.
Cuisine: Modern British.
Other Points: Children welcome.
Directions: On the A464 towards Telford, at Boningale, just off the A41. (Map 9, D2)

San Carlo

4 Temple Street, Birmingham B2 5BN
Telephone: +44(0)121 633 0251

Situated in a narrow back street off the city centre stands the Birmingham original of a small Italian chain with branches in Leicester and Bristol. From the outside you find a very modern Mediterranean façade of marble and glass, reflected within by a spacious dining area that is light and bright, with mirrors decorating the walls, white ceramic-tiles on the floor, and potted plants and small trees adding colour. This is a busy, buzzy restaurant, with an energetic atmosphere; none the less professional staff cope remarkably well under pressure. The focus is on simple, clean flavours and prices, the cooking a cut above the norm for a city-centre eaterie majoring in pizzas and pasta. In addition, there are risottos, soups, and salads, as well as main courses of trattoria classics such as pollo sorpresa, scallopa milanese, and saltimboca alla romana. Blackboard specials extend an already wide choice, offering some very good fresh fish dishes; look out for excellent lobster Thermidor, crevettes in garlic butter, and spaghetti shellfish. There's a selection of well-priced Italian wines, with good choice by the glass and France and the new world bringing up the rear.

Prices: Main course from £11. House wine £11.20.
Hours: 12.00-23.00.
Cuisine: Italian.
Other Points: No-smoking area. Children welcome.
Directions: In the centre of the city. (Map 9, D2)

The Orange Tree

Warwick Road, Chadwick End,
Birmingham B93 0BN
Telephone: +44(0)1564 785364
www.theorangetree.co.uk

The Orange Tree is the jewel in the crown of this select group of country dining pubs operated by Paul Hales and Paul Salisbury. Set back from the A4141, this stylishly refurbished old inn exudes contemporary charm. From the smart cream painted and timbered exterior to the modern, perhaps minimalistic décor of the beautifully reworked interior, the Orange Tree impresses; indeed, has set the trend that numerous pubs are trying to follow across the West Midlands. The rustic country setting and the simple, restrained interior is matched by an interesting and unusual, Italian-inspired menu. Authentic wood fired pizzas and robust meat dishes, either cooked on an in-view rotisserie spit, perhaps spit chicken with balsamic and accompanied by confit garlic and mash, partnered by lamb rack with saffron potatoes, chorizo and broad beans from the stove, draw the crowds. Further favourites include homemade pasta dishes such as linguine with shrimps, chilli and lemon grass, delicious warm salads, and fishy specials like whole plaice with white beans, garlic and Parmesan. An Italian deli-style counter displays a superb range of breads, cheeses and olive oils. The interesting wine list offers good value and a global choice.

Prices: Main course restaurant from £7.95. House wine £11.95.
Hours: 11.00-23.00.
Food served: 12.00-14.30. 18.00-22.00. Sunday 12.00-16.30.
Cuisine: Modern European.
Other Points: Dogs welcome. Garden. Children welcome. Car park.
Directions: Exit5/M42. On the A4141, four miles south east towards Warwick. (Map 9, D3)

Prices: Set lunch £15. Main course from £9.50. House wine £10.95.
Hours: 10.00-23.00 Monday-Wednesday. 10.00-24.00 Thursday-Saturday. 10.00-22.30 on Sunday. Closed 25 December evening.
Food served: 12.00-14.30. 18.30-22.00 Monday to Saturday. 12.00-15.00 on Sunday.
Rooms: 12 en suite. Double from £72.50, single £62.50.
Cuisine: Modern European.
Other Points: No smoking area. Children welcome. Terraced area. Car park
Directions: Two miles from exit 5/M42 on A4141. After Knowle village turn right for Dorridge. (Map 9, D2)

The Forest

Station Approach, Dorridge, Solihull, Birmingham,
West Midlands B93 8JA
Telephone: +44(0)1564 772120
info@forest-hotel.com
www.forest-hotel.com

Style and simplicity, and definitely no showing off - that's how Tracy and Gary Perkins run their extraordinary town-centre operation. Directly opposite the station, the red-brick of the Victorian former station hotel gives way to an easy-on-the-eye modern look where cool, urbane styling runs from the open-faced bar right through to the bang-on-the-nail brasserie. James Pye has taken over in the kitchen, continuing the trend for food that is noted for elegant simplicity. From an ingredient led, no-nonsense menu, come starters of risotto of pea, mint and mascarpone cheese, or perfectly timed pan-roasted scallops with watercress purée and red wine reduction. Typically good main courses run to breast of Gressingham duck, thyme rösti, spring greens and blueberry jus, backed up by side orders of cauliflower purée with gruyère cheese and great pommes frites. Puddings such as warm fresh cherries and Kirsch ice cream are executed with skill. The set menu served on Monday and Tuesday evenings includes a glass of house wine and is definitely a bargain. The well-balanced wine list (arranged by style) is fairly priced. Twelve bedrooms include a number that are restrained and minimalist with an unmistakable sense of style.

The Cock Inn ⎹ ▯ ✕

Bulls Lane, Wishaw, Sutton Coldfield, Birmingham
Telephone: +44(0)121 313 3960

Paul Hales and Paul Salisbury's 'Orange Tree-style' makeover of run-down village boozers continues apace with the recent addition of the Cock Inn to their small and rather upmarket group of country dining pubs. Backing on to open fields in the sleepy village of Wishaw, this cracking country pub is a clone of the locally famous Orange Tree at Chadwick End (see entry). The amazing success of the OT concept, which appeals to Birmingham's young and well heeled pub-goers, has seen the stylish interior décor and food operation marketed as a brand, with further openings planned for the Home Counties. Beyond the tasteful cream and beige look for a spacious and very contemporary interior. Expect plush leather sofas, matching deep armchairs, modern wood tables and a fresh, minimalist feel. Sutton Coldfield residents need only drive to Wishaw to experience the Italian-inspired food that put the Orange Tree on the local culinary map. From 'little dishes' like Parmesan and chive soufflé, delicious warm salads and fresh pasta meals, the modern, simply described menu lists home-fired pizzas, perhaps 'salsiccia piccante' with chorizo, mozzarella and jalapeño peppers, robust main courses like rib-eye steak with blue cheese and onion butter, and spit-roast meats.

Prices: Main course restaurant from £7.95. House wine £11.95.
Hours: 12.00-23.00.
Food served: 12.00-14.30. 18.00-22.00.
Cuisine: Modern British with Italian influences.
Other Points: Garden. Children welcome. Car park.
Directions: Exit9/M42. Village signposted left off A446, two miles north of M42. (Map 9, D2)

The Kings Arms ▯ ▯ ✕

Monkton Farleigh, Bradford-on-Avon,
Wiltshire BA15 2QH
Telephone: +44(0)1225 858705
enquiries@kingsarms-bath.co.uk
www.kingsarms-bath.co.uk

Set in the heart of the conservation village of Monkton Farleigh, just a short drive from both Bradford-on-Avon and Bath, this striking stone-built inn dates back to the 11th century when it functioned as a retreat for a nearby monastery. With its impressive stone-arched doorway and stone mullion windows it is clear that the Kings Arms packs a lot of history and, of course, ghosts; the place is said to be haunted by a monk, a miner and a wailing woman. Heavy beams, dark red-painted walls and a stone-flagged floor give period character to the Chancel Bar, but the restaurant, with wall-hung tapestries, church pews, candelabras, and sturdy wooden tables adorned with pewter plates, has a rather ecclesiastical look. Note that the massive inglenook fireplace in the restaurant is, reputedly, the largest in Wiltshire. Homecooked food takes in the traditional in the bar: ham, two fried eggs and chips, or beer-battered haddock with chips and mushy peas. In the evening, the kitchen puts the emphasis on modern British dishes, notably coriander crusted loin of pork with pink peppercorn sauce, and homemade chicken Kiev on creamed spinach. Blackboards feature fresh fish and game dishes.

Prices: Set Sunday lunch £13.50. Main course (restaurant) from £9.60. Main course bar from £6.25. House wine £9.50.
Hours: 12.00-15.00. 17.30-23.00. 12.00-23.00 on Saturday. 12.00-22.30 on Sunday.
Food served: 12.00-14.45. 18.30-21.30 12.00-21.30 on Saturday.
Cuisine: Modern British
Other Points: No-smoking area. Children welcome. Garden. Car park.
Directions: A4 east from Bath, then right on A363 for Bradford-on-Avon. Go under the railway bridge and turn left in two and a half miles for Monkton Farleigh. (Map 8, F6)

Prices: Set lunch/dinner £15.20 (2 courses). Main course from £12.95. Main course bar £4.95. House wine £11.95.
Hours: 11.00-15.00. 18.00-23.30. 11.00-16.00. 18.00-24.00 on Saturday. 12.00-17.00. 18.00-22.30 on Sunday.
Food served: 12.00-14.00. 18.00-21.30.
Cuisine: Modern British, Traditional French.
Other Points: No-smoking area. Children welcome. No dogs. Garden. Car park.
Directions: J16/M4. A3102 towards Wootton Bassett, then follow B4042 Malmesbury road for five miles. (Map 4, B7)

Three Crowns ⎹ ▯ ✕

The Street, Brinkworth, Swindon, Wiltshire SN15 5AF
Telephone: +44(0)1666 510366
www.threecrowns.co.uk

The 200-year-old Three Crowns is a bustling dining pub that attracts supporters from miles around. The traditional pubby bar, furnished with a variety of old and new pine, features two remarkable tables created from huge 18th-century bellows and is the spot for lunchtime snacks, namely enormous ploughman's lunches and filled double-decker rolls. A comprehensive list of main courses is displayed on a huge blackboard that dominates one wall of the pine-furnished conservatory dining extension. Few people leave dissatisfied: portions are more than generous, and food quality is well above average. The ambitious (and elaborately described) dishes make good use of local produce. Rack of English lamb, for example, is served with white wine and cream, flavoured with mint and garnished with pear and rosemary jelly. Good fish options include supreme of halibut poached in white wine with sweet coconut milk, chillies and fresh lime juice, and traditional pie lovers will be torn between classics such as steak and kidney, or veal and mushroom. All main courses are accompanied by a large dish of six vegetables. Round off with a delicious homemade pudding or a plate of cheese from an impressive cheeseboard selection. An ever-improving list of wines now offers around 12 by the glass.

Revolutions Cafe Bar and Restaurant

66 New Road, Chippenham, Wiltshire SN15 1ES
Telephone: +44(0)1249 447500
sanddwebb@aol.com

A firm favourite with the residents and the office workers of Chippenham, this town-centre brasserie-style restaurant oozes contemporary good looks. Sandie and Doug Webb take their policy of buying produce from local suppliers seriously, so much so that menus give credit to their beef and organic egg producers. Prices are kind too, with light lunch dishes such as a 'delicious' chicken salad with cashew nuts, pumpkin seeds, lemon and basil dressing, or steak sandwich with the emphasis on Dijon mustard mayo, lettuce and tomato, priced at just under a fiver, with even cheaper options to be had amongst sandwiches and filled jacket potatoes. Good value, too, can be found in the daily changing, set evening menu where modern ideas deliver simply conceived dishes with the emphasis on freshness. Pork tenderloin with an apricot stuffing and cider gravy, makes appealing main course, with savoury goats' cheese and tomato tart a bright start. Although licensed, a bring-your-own wine policy has proved very popular and is encouraged, but if you forget the house Australian is £7.95, and there's a decent selection of lager, beer and spirits. A highlight of 2003 was winning the Taste of the West's Silver Award for Wiltshire.

Prices: Lunch time menu from £2.95. Set dinner £14.95. House wine £7.95.
Hours: Open and food served from 09.00. Closed Monday evening and all day Sunday.
Cuisine: Modern British.
Other Points: No-smoking area. Children welcome.
Directions: Exit 17/M4. Take the dual carriageway towards Chippenham and follow the signs to the town centre. Turn left through the railway arches and just before the first crossing Revolutions is on the right hand side. (Map 5, C2)

The Angel

Angel Lane, Hindon, Salisbury, Wiltshire SP3 6DJ
Telephone: +44(0)1747 820696
eat@theangel-inn.co.uk
www.theangelhindon.fslife.co.uk

Penny Simpson's handsome former coaching inn dates from the 18th century. A warm welcome awaits in the cosy, pine furnished bar, where a log fire burns in the huge brick fireplace and deep red walls are adorned with Victorian prints. Beyond lies the stylish long dining room, furnished with sturdy tables and huge photographs; an added feature is the glass-fronted open-plan kitchen. Matthew Laughton cooks robust, modern food using fresh produce, including fresh Brixham fish, quality meats from Aubrey Allen, Neal's Yard cheeses, and local organic vegetables. Contemporary, brasserie-style dishes (for a light meal in the bar) include chargrilled open ciabatta sandwiches or hot crab galette with french bean and watercress salad and sorrel butter sauce. For something more substantial, try whole plaice with caper sauce, calf's liver with leek mash, crispy bacon and mustard sauce, or Goan-style prawn and cashew nut curry with spicy rice. Steamed orange and cardamom pudding with ginger custard or hot banana and custard tart with chocolate ice cream make a fine finish. Refurbishment is on going in the seven well furnished and appointed en suite bedrooms.
Prices: Set lunch £18.50. Main course from £10. Main course (bar/snack) from £4.50. House wine £10.
Food served: 12.00-14.00. 19.00-21.00. Closed Sunday evening, 26 December and 2 January.
Rooms: 7 en suite. Double room from £55, single from £47.40. Family from £95.
Cuisine: Modern British.
Other Points: No-smoking area. Garden/courtyard. Children welcome in the bar. Car park.
Directions: One mile off the A303 on the B3089 towards Salisbury, 10 miles west of Salisbury. (Map 5, D2)

The Red Lion

1 High Street, Lacock, Wiltshire SN15 2LQ
Telephone: +44(0)1249 730456

An imposing Grade II listed red-brick Georgian building standing opposite the entrance to Lacock Abbey and the Fox Talbot Museum in the centre of a timeless National Trust village. Agricultural implements and sturdy old furniture adorn the rambling beamed bar with its fine stone fireplace and mixture of flagstones and bare boards strewn with Turkey rugs. Accommodation, for those wishing to linger in this charming historic village, is in four delightful upstairs bedrooms; three enjoy views down an ancient narrow street lined with timbered buildings. Each sport comfortable mahogany or brass beds, antique furniture and attractively tiled en suite facilities; two with shower only. Unencumbered by phones (or radio/alarms!) they make for a restful overnight stay. A gravelled rear garden has abundant shrubs and flowers and picnic tables. Lacock is amongst England's most beautiful villages and you may recognise the medieval streets as the backdrop to several televison costume dramas, notably Jane Austen's *Pride and Prejudice* and *Emma*. Make time to visit Lacock Abbey..
Prices: Main course restaurant from £6.95. Main course bar meal £4.25. House wine £8.25.
Hours: 11.30-14.30. 18.00-23.00. 12.00-14.30 and 19.00-22.30 on Sunday. Closed 25 December and 1 January evenings.
Food served: 11.30-14.30. 18.00-21.00. 12.00-14.30 and 19.00-21.00 on Sunday.
Rooms: 6 en suite. Double/twin room £75, single £55.
Cuisine: Modern British.
Other Points: No-smoking area. Dogs and children welcome. Garden. Car park.
Directions: Lacock is signed off A350 midway between Chippenham and Melksham. Exit 17/M4. (Map 5, C2)

The Hatchet

🍷 🍴 ✗ 🛏

Lower Chute, Andover, Wiltshire SP11 9DX
Telephone: +44(0)1264 730229

This idyllic, thatched country pub is situated down a web of narrow lanes in a sleepy hamlet. Built in the 16th century as three cottages, it is full of old-world charm with heavily beamed ceilings, flagstone floors, intimate alcoves with oak tables and wheelback chairs, and an enormous inglenook that takes up a whole wall. The cosy rural feel to the pub is maintained in the intimate, low-ceilinged restaurant. Extensive menus list a broad range of traditional bar and restaurant meals. Round off a good walk with a pint of Otter and a plate of homemade liver and bacon, steak and stout pie, lime and chilli chicken or smoked haddock pasta, or tuck into a hearty filled baguette or a cheddar ploughman's. In the evening, relax in the restaurant and follow warm goats' cheese salad or smoked salmon salad with baked sea bass with lemon and herbs, pork medallions with mustard sauce, rack of lamb or seasonal local game dishes. Housed in a modern cottage to the rear of the pub are four light and airy new bedrooms, all furnished and decorated to a high standard and featuring modern en suite bathrooms.

Prices: Main course restaurant meal from £7.25. Main course bar meal from £6.25. House wine £9.75.
Hours: 11.30-15.00. 18.00-23.00.
Food served: 12.00-14.00. 18.30-21.45.
Rooms: 6 en suite. All rooms from £50.
Cuisine: Modern European.
Other Points: No-smoking in the restaurant. Garden. Children welcome. Car park.
Directions: The Chutes are signposted north off A342 at Weyhill west of Andover, two miles from A303 (Map 5, C3)

The Barleycorn Inn

🍴 ✗

Collingbourne Kingston, Marlborough, Wiltshire SN8 3SD
Telephone: +44(0)1264 850368

With four real ales on handpump and menus listing good traditional pub food, this 17th-century coaching inn is a welcome pit stop for travellers using the A338 south of Marlborough. Since their arrival three years ago, David and Heather Wheeler have neatly refurbished the place in modern style, creating a convivial bar area with pastel yellow walls, wooden floors and comfortable furnishings, and a modern dining room in deep blue, stripped wooden floors, linen tablecloths, and contemporary art covering the walls. Food is homecooked and good value, the lunchtime choice including filled baguettes and jacket potatoes alongside steak and mushroom pie and locally-made sausages with mash and onion gravy. Evening dishes range from Spanish-style mussels cooked in tomato, basil, garlic and cherry tomato and red onion tart to orange and thyme-marinated salmon, pork medallions with brandy and cream, and rib-eye steak with pepper sauce. Good summer garden with popular barbecue evenings.

Prices: Set lunch £15 and dinner £20. Main courses from £7.25. Main course (bar/snack) from £4. House wine £6.50.
Hours: 12.00-15.00. 19.00-23.00. Until 22.30 on Sunday. Closed 25 and 26 December evening and 1 January.
Food served: 12.00-14.15. 19.00-21.15.
Cuisine: Modern and Traditional English.
Other Points: No-smoking area. Garden. Children welcome over 14 years old. Car park.
Directions: Exit 14/M4. On the A338, midway between Swindon and Salisbury, 10 miles south of Marlborough. (Map 5, C3)

The Pear Tree

🍷 🍴 ✗ 🛏

Top Lane, Whitley, Melksham, Wiltshire SN12 8QX
Telephone: +44(0)1225 709131

There is a studied air of rusticity to The Pear Tree. Country pub it remains with its cosy bar and cushioned window seats conducive to the enjoyment of a pint of Wadworths; but brand new bedrooms come on stream in August 2003. Its major focus, however, remains the food which echoes the rustic approach and confidently makes use of local produce and prime ingredients. Backed up by sound knowledge and cooking techniques the prodigious output from the kitchen runs daily from prawn and haddock fishcakes with rouille and rocket salad and chargrilled Mediterranean vegetable tart with pesto dressing, to Capricorn goats' cheese baked in filo pastry with beetroot relish, and seared tuna loin in sesame and ginger crust with mango salsa. Results, often surprising yet never boring, have established this as a deservedly popular venue: the ales are well-kept and always interesting, while the selection of wines by the glass deserves of special mention. And what a pleasure to note service that is professional and knowledgeable without losing sight of the friendliness and welcome that marks out for success this new breed of country dining pub.

Prices: Set lunch from £14. Main course from £12.50.
Hours: 11.00-15.00. 18.00-12.00.
Food served: 12.00-14.00, until 14.30 on Sunday. 18.30-21.30.
Rooms: Rooms will be available from August 2003.
Cuisine: Rustic European.
Other Points: No-smoking area in restaurant. Garden. Children welcome. Car park.
Directions: Whitley is signposted off A365 on B3353, a mile west of Melksham. Exit 17/M4. (Map 5, C2)

The Vine Tree 🍷🍴

Foxley Road, Norton, Malmesbury, Wiltshire SN16 0JP
Telephone: +44(0)1666 837654
info@thevinetree.co.uk
www.thevinetree.co.uk

Weary M4 drivers in search of rest and refreshment should note that this sleepy country pub is just four miles north of junction 17. The secluded 18th-century mill is set in unspoilt Wiltshire countryside, has a tranquil sun-trap summer terrace, a two-acre garden for kids to let off steam and, more importantly, a growing reputation for innovative modern pub food. Equally, it is popular with local drinkers in search of a decent pint or one of 20 wines by the glass. Partners Tiggi Wood and Charles Walker have smartened up the part stone-flagged interior, furnishing it in attractive pine and maintaining the open fires and evening candlelight. Eclectic menus draw on global influences, although fish from Cornwall is a speciality, as is local game in season, and where possible, they use organic produce. Starters and light meals may include soup with home-baked bread, and local sausages with bubble and squeak and mustard sauce. For something more substantial try pot-roasted partridge with white bean casserole, or fishy specials like chargrilled tuna with olive and red papper tapenade. For pudding try the white and dark chocolate torte. Impressive Sunday lunch menu and popular summer barbecues.

Prices: Main course from £10.50. Snacks from £6.95. Sunday lunch £15.95 (£12.75 for 2 courses). House wine £10.50.
Hours: 12.00-15.00. 18.00-23.00. (Supper license until 24.00). Open all day on Sunday. Closed 25 December.
Food served: 12.00-14.30 (until 15.00 at weekends). 19.00-21.30 (until 22.00 Friday and Saturday). Seasonal opening hours.
Cuisine: Traditional and Modern British.
Other Points: No-smoking area. Dogs welcome. Children welcome. Play area. 2 acre garden and terrace. Large car park.
Directions: Exit 12/M4. Take A429 towards Cirencester, turn left in one and a half miles, signed Grittleton. In Norton turn right to Foxley, bear right over ford to pub. (Map 12, E7)

The Seven Stars Inn 🍷🍴

Bottlesford, Woodborough, Pewsey,
Wiltshire SN9 6LU
Telephone: +44(0)1672 851325
sevenstars@dialin.net

Interesting pub food with a distinct Gallic flavour can be savoured at this rambling, thatched and creeper-clad pub lost down narrow country lanes in the heart of the Vale of Pewsey. Inside, you will find a delightful beamed and panelled bar with quarry tile flooring, a comfortable mix of antique settles and country furniture, and winter log fires. Enjoy locally-made organic cider, West Country real ales or decent French wines with one of the hearty dishes prepared by the enthusiastic, inspired French chef/patron Philippe Cheminade. Choices range from Brittany fish soup, moules marinière, fillet of pork normande, beef bourguignon, and confit of duck, to more traditional dishes like smoked salmon salad Niçoise, venison and mushroom pie, whole Dover sole, Quantock duck with pink peppercorns, cream and brandy, and Sandridge farmhouse sausages with garlic mash and onion gravy. Expect local game in winter and fresh seafood on the menu in summer. Homemade puddings and an excellent French cheese board for those with room. Those calling in for a pint and a snack will not be disappointed with the soups, filled baguettes and croque monsieur that are always available.

Prices: Set Sunday lunch £16. Main course from £10.95. House wine £10.25.
Hours: 12.00-15.00. 18.00-23.00. Sunday 12.00-15.00. Closed Sunday evening and all day Monday.
Food served: 12.00-14.00. 19.00-21.30.
Cuisine: Traditional French.
Other Points: No-smoking area. Garden. Well behaved children welcome. Car park.
Directions: From Pewsey travel to Woodborough and turn left to Bottlesford. (Map 4, B8)

The Bell 🍴🍷🍴

The Square, Ramsbury, Marlborough, Wiltshire SN8 2PE
Telephone: +44(0)1672 520230
www.thebellatramsbury.co.uk

This fine old coaching has been the focal point in the village since the 17th century. Its exterior is unassuming, but inside, the large bar and adjoining dining room have been refurbished in a light and contemporary style. Expect rag-washed walls, deep sofas fronting a wood-burning fire and a wealth of sporting memorabilia in the bar, while the restaurant sports smart clothed tables, open log fires and subtle spotlighting. Jeremy Wilkins took over the pub just as we went to press. However, this is how we found the pub at our last visit. Food is taken seriously and utilises local butcher meats, game from the Ramsbury estate and daily deliveries of fish from Poole. Modern interpretations of classic pub dishes feature on the main menu, perhaps grilled sardines with ginger, lemon and fresh coriander, or pan-fried calf's liver and bacon with a soya sherry and ginger dressing. Simpler bar food staples include filled ciabatta (roasted vegetables with honey), smoked haddock kedgeree, and local sausages with onion gravy. A trio of real ales changes regularly, and might well feature local West Berkshire Good Old Boy. Good list of wines with a fine wine section; 6 available by the glass. New owners as we went to press; please check opening and food times as details may change.

Prices: Set lunch £15. Set dinner £19.75. Main course restaurant from £6.95. Main course bar from £6.50. House wine £11.50.
Hours: 11.30-15.00. 18.00-23.00. Sunday 12.00-16.00. 18.00-22.30. Closed Monday lunchtimes.
Food served: 12.00-14.00. 19.00-21.30. Tuesday to Sunday.
Other Points: No-smoking area. Dogs welcome. Garden. Chidlren welcome. Car park.
Directions: Exit 14/M4. Take the A338 to Hungerford and then the B4192; Ramsbury is signposted left. (Map 5, C3)

Carpenters Arms

♥ 🍺 ✕

Easton Town, Sherston, Malmesbury,
Wiltshire SN16 0LS
Telephone: +44(0)1666 840665

Since taking over this 300-year-old former farmhouse in July 2001, Keith Britton and Karen Myers have revitalised the fortunes of this once downmarket boozer; it's now a great community pub with thriving cribbage and boules teams. Sit in one of the rambling interconnecting rooms, all nicely modernised with wooden floors, a good mix of sturdy benches, chairs and tables, some of the latter sporting blue-checked tablecloths and napkins, with tasteful bric-à-brac on high shelves. Lunch ranges from crusty filled baguettes, Wiltshire ham ploughmans, or beer battered cod and chips, to homemade pies, burgers and chilli. With meats supplied by Skidmores, Sherston's award-winning butcher, asparagus and free range chicken from local farms, the evening menu lists such dishes as chicken with smoked bacon and mozzarella cheese and barbecue sauce, rib-eye steak with port, Stilton and cream sauce, and seasonal game from Badminton Estate. Look to the blackboard for seasonal dishes and daily fresh fish options. There are good homemade puddings, local ice creams, fine cheeses from Wiltshire Tracklements, a short global list of wines, and four real ales on handpump.

Prices: Main course from £6.95. Bar meal from £4.50. House wine £9.95.
Hours: 12.00-14.30 (from 10.00 on Saturday). 17.30-23.00. 12.00-15.00 and 19.00-22.30 on Sunday.
Food served: 12.00-14.00 (until 14.30 on Sunday). 19.00-21.00. No food Sunday evening.
Cuisine: Modern British.
Other Points: No-smoking area. Children welcome. Garden. Car park.
Directions: Junction 16/17/ M4. Take the B4040 from Malmesbury heading towards Chipping Sodbury. (Map 8, E2)

The Sun Inn

♥ 🍺 ✕

The Street, Lydiard Millicent, Swindon,
Wiltshire SN5 3LU
Telephone: +44(0)1793 770425
thesuninn@yahoo.co.uk
www.cotswoldinns.co.uk

This late 18th century pub is situated in a pretty conservation village on the outskirts of Swindon close to Lydiard House and Park. With its large garden and heated terrace, it's a popular summer destination, while the recently refurbished interior with its tiled and wooden floors, open fires and exposed timbers, retains much of the building's original charm and character. Food is freshly prepared from local produce, with meat supplied by Harts specialist butchers in Cricklade, smoked fish from Severn and Wye Smokery (see entry), and first-class vegetables from Mise en Place in Cirencester. Well presented lunch dishes may include warm ciabattas (smoked salmon and scrambled egg or three Italian cheeses with tomatos and basil), pasta with tomato and chorizo, Wiltshire ham, egg and chips, and liver and bacon with mash and onion gravy. Evening additions may feature sautéed mussels with chilli, oriental Thai-style squid, rack of lamb with leek and herb mash with rosemary gravy, West Indian seafood with basmati rice, mustard baked chicken with honey sauce, and lemon baked tuna with pesto dressed salad. Short global list of wines (eight offered by the glass), and four handpumped real ales.

Prices: Early dinner set menu £11.95 (Sunday-Wednesday). Bar meal/snack from £4.25. Main course from £7.50. House wine £9.50.
Hours: 11.30-15.00. 17.30-23.00 (from 18.00 on Saturday). 12.00-22.30 on Sunday. Closed 25 December evening.
Food served: 11.30-14.30 (until 15.00 on Sunday). 18.30-21.30 (until 21.00 on Sunday).
Cuisine: Modern and Traditional British and European.
Other Points: No-smoking area. Children welcome. Garden. Car park.
Directions: Junction 16/M4. Situated in the village of Lydiard Millicent, about three miles to the west of Swindon. (Map 5, C2)

Howard's House Hotel

🍺 ✕ ✎

Teffont Evias, Salisbury, Wiltshire SP3 5RJ
Telephone: +44(0)1722 716392 or 716821
enq@howardshousehotel.com
www.howardshousehotel.com

Prices: Set lunch £22.50 and dinner £23.95. Main course from £14. House wine £13.25.
Hours: 12.00-14.00. 19.00-21.30. Closed Friday lunch. Reservations only.
Rooms: 9 en suite. Double room from £145, single from £95. Four poster £165.
Cuisine: Modern British.
Other Points: No-smoking in restaurant. Children welcome. Garden. Car park.
Directions: Due west from Salisbury towards Wilton and Chilmark, off B3089 towards Hindon and A303. (Map 5, D2)

Howard's House Hotel, built in 1623 as a dower house, is surrounded by large well-tended lawns, the perfume from the cottage garden flowers drifting into the house through open windows in summer and the theme is picked up by filling all rooms with fresh flowers. In the sitting room you can relax on the large overstuffed sofas where, in winter, the large stone fireplace blazes with logs. Upstairs, nine en suite bedrooms are luxuriously decorated (some have four-poster beds) all have bathrobes, are spacious and comfortable with particularly good views of either the garden or the surrounding countryside. Boyd McIntosh heads up the kitchen, delivering his brand of sophisticated, ambitious cooking. Quality and freshness of raw materials are a match for any, and what makes his food interesting as well as good to eat are the well-tuned accompaniments. The set menu is a real bargain, delivering confit of Gressingham duck leg with red onion marmalade and poppy seed vinaigrette, then seared breast of cornfed chicken with wild mushroom and coriander risotto and port wine jus and, to finish, banana baked Alaska with mango coulis. Prices reflect the pedigree of the wine list, but the list of house wines offers fair drinking and good value.

The Compasses Inn 🍷🛏✕🗘

Lower Chicksgrove, Tisbury, Wiltshire SP3 6NB
Telephone: +44(0)1722 714318
thecompasses@aol.com

A timeless air pervades this attractive, 16th-century thatched inn. An old cobbled path leads to the latch door and the charmingly unspoilt bar has a low-beamed ceiling, partly flagstoned floor and an assortment of traditional furniture arranged in secluded alcoves. Various farm tools and tackle from bygone days adorn the bare walls and a roaring wood-burning fire warms the bar in winter. Alan Stoneham has retained the services of chef Toby Hughes, who continues to produce an imaginative daily changing menu of sound modern British dishes, utilising organic vegetables and first-class meat from local farms. From lunchtime-only filled foccacia, or ham, egg and chips and salads, the blackboard menu may feature starters of smoked duck and red onion tartlet and mushroom and rosemary soup. Main course choices range from steak and kidney pie with suet crust, beef fillet with Madeira and mushrooms, and roast shoulder of lamb with red wine, molasses and soy, to tuna with mango salsa, and whole plaice with lemon and pesto dressing. Popular puddings may include brioche bread-and-butter pudding. The four upstairs bedrooms have been comfortably refurbished; all have smart new en suite facilities, with the best room tucked beneath the heavy thatch.

Prices: Set lunch £15. Set dinner £19. Main course from £7.95. House wine £9.95.
Hours: 12.00-15.00 (15.30 on Sunday). 18.00-23.00. Closed Sunday evening and all day Monday, 26 December and Tuesday after each Bank Holiday Monday.
Food served: 12.00-14.30. 19.00-21.30.
Rooms: 4 en suite. Double/twin from £65.
Cuisine: Modern British.
Other Points: No-smoking area. Garden. Children welcome. Car park.
Directions: Chicksgrove and the Compasses signposted off the A30 between Wilton and Shaftesbury. (Map 5, D2)

The Angel Coaching Inn 🛏✕🗘

High Street, Heytesbury, Warminster, Wiltshire BA12 0ED
Telephone: +44(0)1985 840330
angelheytesbury@aol.com
www.angelheytesbury.co.uk

Sympathetic refurbishment by Jeremy and Anna Giddings of this former 17th-century coaching inn has created a fine all-round inn that combines stylishly comfortable accommodation and imaginative modern pub food. Either reserve a table in the main bar, (old beams, terracotta walls, scrubbed tables, fine prints and a splendid open fire), or sink into a deep sofa with a drink in the lounge before eating in the lighter, more modern, formal restaurant. The menu, however, remains the same, a changing chalkboard of modern British dishes that make the most of prime local produce. Start, perhaps, with queen scallops and Jerusalem artichoke salad with a hazelnut dressing. Go on to fillet of Wiltshire pork stuffed with pistachios and apricots and served with vanilla dauphinoise, and finish with apple and cinnamon crème brûlée with apple crisps or a plate of local cheeses including Cropwell Bishop Stilton and Cornish Yarg. Complete the experience and stay overnight in one of the tastefully decorated, well-appointed bedrooms; all have good en suite facilities and one has a handmade four-poster bed.

Prices: Main course restaurant from £7.95. Main course bar meal from £4.95. House wine £11.95.
Hours: 11.30-23.00. 12.00-22.30 on Sunday. Closed 25 December.
Food served: 12.00-14.30. 19.00-21.30. 12.00-14.00. 19.00-21.00 on Sunday.
Rooms: 8 en suite. Double room from £65, single from £50, family room from £90.
Cuisine: Modern British.
Other Points: No-smoking area. Children welcome. Car park.
Directions: Village signed off A36 four miles east of Warminster. (Map 4, C7)

The Crown and Trumpet Inn 🛏✕🗘

Church Street, Broadway, Worcestershire WR12 7AE
Telephone: +44(0)1386 853202
info@cotswoldholidays.co.uk
www.cotswoldholidays.co.uk

Tucked away behind the green close to the parish church in one of England's most picturesque villages, the Crown and Trumpet looks the quintessential Cotswold inn, built of local golden stone in the 17th century and postcard pretty with roses around the door. The equally charming yet unpretentious interior, with its beamed and timbered bar sporting antique high-backed settles, exposed stone walls and blazing winter log fires, attracts folk from far and wide for the chatty atmosphere, a good choice of well kept ales (try the locally brewed Stanway Bitter), and traditional homemade pub food. Good value dishes include chicken liver and wild mushroom pâté, cheese and asparagus flan, steak and kidney pie, steaks, local butcher's faggots, and nursery puddings such as treacle tart and bread and butter pudding with locally made ice cream. Hearty roasts are a major draw on Sundays. Worth knowing in this tourist honeypot for its five cottagey bedrooms. Although simply furnished, all are clean and cosy, with patchwork quilts, brass beds, and en suite bathrooms.

Prices: Main course bar meal from £5.50. House wine £9.95.
Hours: 11.00-15.00. 17.00-23.00. Weekends 11.00-23.00 (until 22.30 on Sunday).
Food served: 12.00-14.15. 18.00-21.15. Weekends 12.00-15.00. 17.30-21.30.
Rooms: 5 en suite. Double room from £48, single from £45.
Cuisine: Traditional British.
Other Points: Children welcome. Garden. Car park.
Directions: Village just off A44 between Moreton-in-Marsh and Evesham. Exit9/M5. (Map 9, E2)

Malvern hills, Worcestershire

The Crown and Sandys Arms

Main Road, Ombersley, Droitwich,
Worcestershire WR9 0EW
Telephone: +44(0)1905 620252
enquries@crownandsandys.co.uk
www.crownandsandys.co.uk

Wine merchant and delicatessen-owner Richard Everton has transformed this Dutch-gabled, 17th century former coaching inn. Stylish and buzzing, it offers a striking mix of traditional and modern, with the bar featuring stone-flagged floors, low beams and huge fireplaces, and the classy bistro full of zebra-print chairs and marble-topped tables; the Louis XV Restaurant is more formal. The attraction, other than tip-top local ales, a superlative wine list and the informal atmosphere, is the interesting, competitively priced modern British food. Local lines of supply, including first-class produce from the deli, dictate a repertoire of dishes that range from tried and tested favourites at lunchtime (braised steak and kidney with red wine and mushrooms, hot beef baguette) to the imaginative Thai-style fish and crab cakes with chilli jam, or pan-fried pheasant breasts with mustard and whisky sauce on the choice of evening specials. On going improvements has seen the refurbishment and opening (August 2003) of five spacious bedrooms. Expect huge pine beds, tasteful fabrics, digital TV with modem points, and en suite facilities - two with roll-top baths and separate power showers.

Prices: Set dinner £15.95. Main course restaurant from £8.95. Main course bar/snack from £5.95. House wine £10.50.
Hours: 11.30-15.00. 17.00-23.00. Weekends open all day.
Food served: 12.00-14.30. 18.00-22.00. Sunday all day 12.00-21.00.
Rooms: 5 en suite. Double/twin between £75-£95.
Cuisine: Modern European.
Other Points: No-smoking area. Garden. Children welcome until 20.30. Car park.
Directions: Exit6/M5. Take the A449 signposted to Kidderminster and follow the signs to Ombersley. (Map 8, D6)

Rose & Crown

Church Lane, Severn Stoke, Tewkesbury,
Worcestershire WR8 9JQ
Telephone: +44(0)1905 371249

The classic black and white timber-framed country pub has 16th-century origins and is set over looking the village green right by the River Severn. The popular locals' bar delivers a strongly traditional 'pubby' look and the rear dining area sports beams, leaded windows and rural knick-knacks. All in all, this cracking pub exudes a timeless atmosphere. It's part of the Pineapple Pub Company, a small but growing group noted for a fresh, young outlook. Indeed, much personality has been stamped on the Rose and Crown through a laudable hands-on attitude, good service and fresh food that's simply cooked and backed up by local real ales such as Highgate Fox's Hob, and interesting wines. As much local produce as is practical (ranging from locally baked breads to Severn and Wye Valley vegetables and salad stuff), is supplemented by local game in winter, and single herd lamb and steaks from Ledbury. This results in up-to-date pub food. The lunch menu brings a cold platter of mature cheddar, baked ham, chutney and crusty bread, or Thai fish cakes on a mixed salad with lemon aïoli. The carte delivers the likes of pan-seared Gressingham duck breast with a blueberry and juniper sauce.

Prices: Main course restaurant from £8.95. Main course bar from £5.50. House wine £9.95.
Hours: 12.00-15.00. 18.00-23.00. Sunday 12.00-22.30. Open all day during the summer.
Food served: 12.00-14.30. 18.00-21.30. Sunday until 15.00 and 21.00. Food served all day at weekends during the Summer.
Cuisine: Modern English and Mediterranean.
Other Points: No-smoking area in restaurant. Dogs welcome in the garden. Garden. Children welcome. Car park.
Directions: Exit1/M50. On the A38 between Tewkesbury and Worcester. (Map 8, D6)

The Fountain Inn

Oldwood, St Michaels, Tenbury Wells,
Worcestershire WR15 8TB
Telephone: +44(0)1584 810701
enquiries@fountain-hotel.co.uk
www.fountain-hotel.co.uk

After 20 years in corporate pub management, Russell Allen decided it was time to buy his own pub and do things his way. Three years on and he has certainly made his name at the Fountain, a traditional black and white 17th-century inn. He has totally refurbished the interior and sympathetically extended the pub, installing an impressive (and very live) shark tank in the low-beamed bar. Press coverage following a shark attack on the head chef's arm boosted trade considerably, and now diners come from miles around, tucking into the likes of baked tuna marinated in garlic, olive oil and spice, while watching the leopard sharks, blue-spotted stingray and Hawaiian tangs patrolling the tank. Seafood is, of course, big business here, with fish bought direct from Birmingham market on a daily basis, but other produce is sourced more locally, notably Herefordshire beef and game from Bowket's of Tenbury, home-grown organic herbs and vegetables, and handmade local cheeses from Hereford. With food served all day, the menu caters for all tastes, and that ranges from Worcestershire ploughman's, and beef and ale pie, to salted sea bass, and blackened red snapper. Excellent real ales include their award-winning Fountain Ale.

Prices: Main course from £6.95. Sunday lunch £12.95. House wine £9.95.
Hours: 11.00-23.00. Monday to Saturday. 12.00-22.30 Sunday.
Food served: 09.00-21.00 daily.
Rooms: 11 en suite. Double/twin room from £39.50.
Cuisine: Traditional British.
Other Points: No-smoking in the restaurant. Children welcome. Garden. Car park. Shark aquarium.
Directions: Junction 5/M5. One mile from Tenbury Wells on the A4112 Leominster road. (Map 8, D5)

Peacock Inn

Worcester Road, Tenbury Wells, Worcestershire WR15 8LL
Telephone: +44(0)1584 810506
james.vidler@btconnect.com
www.thepeacockinn.com

The rambling, ivy-clad 14th-century inn is set smack on the borders of three counties - Worcestershire, Shropshire and Herefordshire. With views across the River Teme and unspoilt orchards, the Peacock boasts a charming interior that comprises several beamed and comfortably furnished rooms, notably the oak-panelled lounge with its huge inglenook and relaxing dining atmosphere. A separate locals bar serves ten wines by the glass and local Hobsons Best Bitter on tap. To the rear, a high-vaulted dining room offers a bistro-style menu that includes fresh pasta dishes and good homemade pizzas. In the lounge bar the modern menu highlights local produce, notably excellent fish fresh from Birmingham market, such as fillet of sea bass with scallops and beurre blanc sauce, or freshly battered cod and chips. Further soundly cooked dishes may include crab cakes with spicy mango chutney, a salad of scallops and bacon with sherry dressing, with mains of strips of fresh salmon marinated in a teriyaki sauce and served on a bed of noodles, or fillet steak with Roquefort and brandy sauce. To finish try, perhaps, the lemon tart with raspberry coulis.
The Peacock also offers overnight accommodation in three en suite bedrooms, including two with four-poster beds.

Prices: Set lunch £15 and dinner £18. Main course from £10. Main course bar/snack from £8. House wine £9.
Hours: 11.00-15.00. 18.00-23.00.
Food served: 12.00-14.15.18.15-21.15.
Rooms: 3 en suite. Double/twin room from £70.
Cuisine: Traditional British/French.
Other Points: No-smoking area. Children welcome. Garden. Car park.
Directions: Exit6/M5. Two miles east of Tenbury Wells on the A456 Worcester Road. (Map 8, C5)

Old Rectifying House

North Parade, Worcester, Worcestershire WR1 3NN
Telephone: +44(0)1905 619622

A rather trendy new addition to Worcester's pub/dining scene from the Pineapple Pub Company, a small but growing group noted for its fresh, young outlook. The old former pub, with parts dating from the 17th century, is close to the city centre, set on the banks of the River Severn. It has been fortified against possible flooding and opened out to reveal an interior of brickwork, beams, and flag floors, enhanced by modern lighting and bright decor with plenty of well-spaced pine tables. It is the place for informal lunches and dining in a buzzy wine bar atmosphere. Plentiful seasonal produce, available through Worcester markets, provides Evesham asparagus, Hereford strawberries, and poultry from Golden Valley. Look, too, for fresh salmon, whole trout and sea bass, and monkfish tail. A typical alternative might be chargrilled chicken supreme filled with Parma ham and brie with a saffron and chive cream and butter sauce. Lighter lunches range from filled ciabattas to a single course fish or meat special with salad and bread. Top-of-the-range dishes include bouillabaisse and a peerless fruits de mer for two. Service is attentive and generally slick, with staff displaying a decent knowledge of the global wine list.

Prices: Main course restaurant from £9.95. Main course bar from £4.95. House wine £9.95.
Hours: 12.00-23.00. Sunday from 12.00-22.30. Closed 25 December and 15.00-18.00 during the Winter.
Food served: 12.00-14.30. 18.00-21.45. Sunday from 12.00-21.00.
Cuisine: Modern British/Mediterranean.
Other Points: No-smoking area. Children welcome.
Directions: Exit6/M5. Follow the signs for the city centre and the A449. The pub is on the riverbank by the River Severn and Worcester bridge. (Map 9, E2)

Georgian Tea Rooms

56 High Street, Old Town, Bridlington,
East Yorkshire YO16 4QA
Telephone: +44(0)1262 608600

After Bath, the Old Town of Bridlington tucked away a mile inland from the better-known bustling seaside resort has the most complete Georgian High Street in Britain, a source of pride and tourism for the town. Indeed, fans of *The Royal*, a spin off of *Heartbeat*, may recognise the street as part of the series was filmed here. Diane Davison's Georgian Rooms, an old-fashioned tearoom in that very High Street, is set on the ground floor of a grade II listed building, forming part of a three-floored antique emporium. There's plenty of space in rooms painted in striking yellows and greens and filled with highly polished wooden tables; there's a separate room for smokers, plus a fantastic big garden dominated by a central fountain. Breakfast starts the day, a full English perhaps, or a breakfast bap filled with sausage or bacon, with snacks running to filled jacket potatoes, salads, toasted sandwiches, as well as those teashop stalwarts of toasted teacakes and mushrooms on toast. Everything is of a very high quality, including homemade cakes and pastries.

Prices: Main course from £3.45. House wine £8.99.
Hours: 10.00-17.00. 10.00-15.00 on Sunday. Closed for two weeks over Christmas and New Year.
Cuisine: Traditional English.
Other Points: No-smoking area. Children welcome. Patio and garden.
Directions: In Bridlington's Old Town. (Map 12, E8)

The Charles Bathurst Inn

Arkengarthdale, Richmond,
North Yorkshire DL11 6EN
Telephone: +44(0)1748 884567
info@cbinn.co.uk
www.cbinn.co.uk

Dr John Bathurst, physician to Oliver Cromwell, was the original owner of Arkengarthdale, (above Swaledale on the edge of the Pennine Way) around 1650 - the inn was named after his son. Reopened in 1996, it retains many period features that blend well with open fires and a warm atmosphere, creating a small hotel of commendable quality. Local wood, stone and antique pine are used to good effect in both bar and restaurant where residents can eat, drink and relax in company of a regular cast of colourful characters. True to such tradition, proprietors Charles and Stacy Cody rely almost exclusively on local staff and suppliers, reflected in their Black Sheep beers from Masham, locally shot grouse, Swaledale lamb and fish delivered regularly from Hartlepool. Look to the mirror menu, written up daily at the end of the bar, to find the best of the day's shopping: mussel chowder; duck terrine with cumberland sauce; 'five fish' cakes with hollandaise sauce; shank of lamb on lentil potato cake; and baked cod steak with sun-dried tomatoes and cream.

Prices: Main course restaurantl from £8. Bar snack from £3.85. House wine £8.95.
Hours: 11.00-23.00. Sunday 12.00-22.30. Closed lunch Monday to Thursday from December until February half term, then open 15.00-23.00.
Food served: 12.00-14.00. 18.30-21.00.
Rooms: 18 en suite. Double/twin room from £70.
Cuisine: Modern pub food.
Other Points: No-smoking area. Dogs welcome. Children welcome. Car park.
Directions: Leave A1 at Scotch Corner and take A6108 to Richmond. Follow B6270 to Reeth and turn left along unclass for Langthwaite. (Map 11, D5)

Helm

Askrigg, Leyburn, North Yorkshire DL8 3JF
Telephone: +44(0)1969 650443
holiday@helmyorkshire.com
www.helmyorkshire.com

Barbara and John Drew have lived in their late 17th-century farmhouse for 16 years, and a warm welcome, comfortable stay and fantastic food are their main priorities. Public rooms include a stone-flagged, beamed dining room with wood-burning stove and a residents' lounge with an open fire. The rotating summerhouse is designed as a painting and drawing base and Barbara, as an illustrator, is on hand to give informal advice. There are three small bedrooms, one with Victorian furniture, burgundy colours and a shower room, another a small twin-bedded room, and a double bedded room with floral everything, plus a roll-top bath. The extensive breakfast menu ranges from a traditional Yorkshire breakfast to Raj kedgeree and Whitby kippers; the sausage selection is truly remarkable. There is no choice at dinner but likes and dislikes of guests will be catered for. A typical meal may be blue Wensleydale and broccoli in a Helm fresh herb pastry tartlet, followed by fillet of sea bass, spinach and spring onion mash with a tomato crème and accompanied by seasonal vegetables, with rhubarb meringue roulade to finish The 46 bin wine list is extensive for such a tiny place but prices are keen and the choice well considered.

Prices: B&B. Dinner available if ordered 24 hours in advance. Set dinner £20. House wine £12.85.
Hours: Closed mid November until after the New Year.
Rooms: 3 en suite. Double room from £33.50, single from £51.
Cuisine: Modern British.
Other Points: Totally no smoking. Children welcome over 10 years old. Garden. Car park.
Directions: M6/A1M. From the A684 at Bainbridge turn towards Askrigg. At the T junction turn right and take the first left turn to Helm. (Map 12, D5)

The Austwick Traddock

Yorkshire Dales National Park, Via Lancaster,
North Yorkshire LA2 8BY
Telephone: +44(0)15242 51224
info@austwicktraddock.co.uk
www.austwicktraddock.co.uk

A romantic, elegant Georgian country house set in the unspoilt village of Austwick surrounded by the Yorkshire Dales National Park. The Traddock was built in the 18th century for the Ingilby family who contributed much to the development of this area of North Yorkshire and Cumbria. New owners, Bruce and Jane Reynolds, have kept many of the original features, keeping the interior stylish, inviting and comfortably furnished with traditional antiques, comfy sofas and open log fires. Eleven individual and classically decorated bedrooms include modern en suite bathrooms and many thoughtful touches such as flowers, fruit, shortbread, and sherry. Careful, unpretentious cooking is built around notably fresh, often seasonal, ingredients - local and organic where possible - and runs to cream of wild mushroom soup, for example, or pheasant served with a Calvados cream sauce. Quality ingredients are matched by attractive presentation: melted organic goats' cheese and avocado salad served on toasted focaccia with beetroot crisps and chilli jam, roast rack of Mansergh Hall lamb with roast shallots and fondant potatoes. Puddings maintain the momentum with a light raspberry shortcake sable with whipped cream and raspberry coulis.

Prices: Set dinner £23.
House wine from £11.
Food served: 18.30-21.00 Wed - Thurs.
Sun 13.00-19.00. Closed for lunch (except Sun), and Sun, Mon and Tue evenings.
Rooms: 11 en suite. Double/Twin £45.
Single £42.
Cuisine: Modern and Traditional British.
Other Points: No-smoking area. Garden. Children welcome. Car park.
Directions: Exit34/M6. From the M6 or M1, take the A65. Austwick is located midway between Skipton and Kirkby Lonsdale, two and a half miles north-west of Settle. (Map 11, E5)

Three Hares

Main Street, Bilbrough, North Yorkshire YO23 3PH
Telephone: +44(0)1937 832128
enquiries@thethreehares.co.uk
www.thethreehares.co.uk

Expect a fresh and stylish new look to the interior of this 18th-century coaching inn, now a well-respected dining pub-restaurant. The restaurant, with its beamed roof, stone floor, white table cloths, blue glasses, modern artwork and evening candles, incorporates the old village forge and is a striking setting in which to sample some serious pub food. Equally appealing is the beamed bar, replete with flagged floor, cushioned pew benches, fresh flowers, and hand-pulled Yorkshire ales. Local and seasonal produce help to give the food its particular identity and menus display imagination and attention to detail. In the bar, follow game terrine with spiced chutney and homemade brioche, with duck leg confit, blue cheese risotto and wilted greens.
Additional restaurant choices may include seared squid and chorizo sausage with herb linguine and spring onion and ginger dressing, sea bass on basil pesto mash with grilled pancetta and roasted root vegetables, and duck with roast figs and braised mustard Puy lentils. To finish, try the white chocolate and raspberry cheesecake or a plate of excellent Yorkshire cheeses served with homemade chutney. An extensive wine list has wines of the month and eight by the glass.

Prices: Main course from £12.50. Bar meal from £7.95.
House wine £10.
Hours: 12.00-15.00. 19.00-23.00.
Closed all Monday and Sunday evening.
Food served: 12.00-14.00. 19.00-21.00 (until 15.00 on Sunday).
Cuisine: Modern British/traditional English.
Other Points: No-smoking area. Dogs welcome. Children welcome. Garden. Car park.
Directions: Located off the A64, just outside York (towards Leeds). Turn into Bilbrough from either direction off the A64. (Map 12, E6)

The White Lion Inn

Cray, Buckden, Skipton, North Yorkshire BD23 5JB
Telephone: +44(0)1756 760262
admin@whitelioncray.com
www.whitelioncray.com

Built in the 1700s and originally a drovers' inn, the White Lion stands in superb countryside beneath Buckden Pike, 1,100ft above sea level - the highest pub in Wharfedale. Hand-pulled ales such as Moorhouses Pendle Witches Brew or Timothy Taylor's Landlord and hearty homecooking draw ramblers off the many surrounding trails for rest and refreshment. On wild winter days bag a seat by the open range in the welcoming beamed and stone-flagged bar and enjoy the traditional atmosphere of this unspoilt Dales inn. Alternatively, try your luck at the time-honoured game of Ring-the-Bull. Good honest bar food is cooked to order and features thick-cut sandwiches alongside homemade soups, black pudding with apple sauce, steak and mushroom pie, venison casserole with red wine, root vegetables and a red wine and pimento gravy, local butcher steaks with all the trimmings, and whole Kilnsey trout with lemon and dill butter. Simple en suite bedrooms are clean and comfortable, equipped with solid pine furnishings, beverage trays and good local information. Wake up to spectacular views, eat a hearty Yorkshire breakfast and enjoy invigorating moorland rambles straight from the front door.

Prices: Main course bar meal from £7.95. Lunch main meal from £2.95. House wine £11 (litre).
Hours: 11.00-23.00. Sunday 12.00-22.30.
Closed 25 December to general public, open for residents.
Food served: 12.00-14.00. 17.45-20.45.
Rooms: 8 en suite. Double/twin from £60.
Cuisine: Traditional and Modern British.
Other Points: No-smoking area. Children welcome. Garden. Car park.
Directions: From Skipton take the B6160 towards Aysgarth; the inn is about 20 miles north-west of Skipton. (Map 12, D5)

Devonshire Fell

Burnsall, Skipton, North Yorkshire ND23 6BT
Telephone: +44(0)1756 729000
reservations@thedevonshirearms.co.uk
www.devonshirehotels.co.uk

The scenery is spectacular, the former gentlemen's club for local mill owners nestling in the hillside and looking out over the River Wharfe. The Duke of Devonshire's hotel was given a trendy makeover, in 1999, with the urban chic lines, cool colours and sleek modern design in the bright reception/ bar area setting the tone. In summer, it is a very popular weekend wedding venue. Our room was quite small, but stylish, with views to the fells and to the roof, which was covered in Astroturf with fake sheep (nice touch). Rooms are similar in style, ours painted in muted salmon and mustard tones with matching checked fabrics, a roll top bed and Mark Rothko print. Bathrooms are gorgeous, we had striking red mosaic tiles, tongue and grove painted in eggshell, and a sunflower-head shower. It is not surprising to find the local environment playing its part in the formation of the menus, with the estate supplying game, fish, vegetable, herbs, fruit, and eggs from rare-breed hens, with contributions from local suppliers. There was a pleasing simplicity to a meal that opened with bresaola and rocket salad, went on to black bream, balsamic dressing and olive tapenade, and finished with an intense chocolate tart.

Prices: Main course from £11.50. House wine £11.95.
Hours: 11.00-23.00.
Food served: 11.30-14.30 (12.00-15.00 Sunday) 18.30-22.00 (18.30-21.30 Sunday)
Rooms: 12 en suite. Double room from £110, single from £70.
Cuisine: Modern British.
Other Points: No-smoking area. Children welcome over 1 year. Garden. Car park. Licence for Civil Weddings. Private Room.
Directions: On the B6160 6 miles north of A59, 11 miles east of Skipton. (Map 12, E5)

Brownlow Arms

Caldwell, Richmond, North Yorkshire DL11 7QH
Telephone: +44(0)1325 718471

Peering from behind four large conker trees Tim Johnstone's Brownlow Arms at first glance looks like a conventional village pub. In the summer colourful flowers hang from window boxes and pots, and a couple of tables await customers who want to sit outside. Inside there are two bars and three rooms where comfortable seats, low beams, roaring winter fires and hunting scenes on the walls create a lovely intimate air. What makes it less conventional, however, is the really outstanding traditional food. Bar meals can be as reassuring as steak and kidney pie in flaky pastry, or as modish as tagliatelle with dill, scallops and smoked salmon in cream and wine sauce. Good lines of supply provide outstanding local beef for the steaks listed on the restaurant menu, whilst game from neighbouring estates produces breast of pheasant wrapped in bacon and stuffed with herb and vegetable duxelle and served with a port, cranberry and redcurrant sauce. Local Yorkshire beer such as John Smith's or Theakstons are excellent accompaniment to all this, and there's an exceptional wine list with some good things from South Africa and the USA, as well as old world favourites.

Prices: Main course bar meal from £6.50. Main course restaurant meal from £9.50. House wine £9.00.
Hours: 12.00-15.00. 18.00-23.00. Sunday 12.00-22.30.
Food served: 12.00-14.30. 18.30-21.30 Sunday 12.00-20.00. During the winter Thursday and Friday lunch only.
Cuisine: Modern British.
Other Points: Children welcome.
Directions: From the A66 east of Scotch Corner take the B6274 north to Winston. (Map 12, D6)

Abbey Inn

Byland Abbey, Coxwold, York YO61 4BD
Telephone: +44(0)1347 868204
jane@bylandabbeyinn.com
www.bylandabbeyinn.co.uk

The atmospheric ruins of the 12th-century Byland Abbey stand opposite this creeper-clad inn, and they both enjoy a tranquil in-the-middle-of-nowhere rural position off the main Thirsk to Helmsley road. Flagstone floors, polished boards, exposed stone walls, oak beams and a big, open roaring fire are all complemented by heavy Jacobean dining chairs, stripped-oak tables, candlesticks, stuffed birds and objets dart. In addition, the book-lined library can be used for private dining; it is all very civilised. The menu is classic modern British, with local ingredients shaping the repertoire. Baby leek and cheese bread and butter pudding may open proceedings on the dinner menu. Among main courses, look for pan-fried escalope of venison haunch with redcurrant glaze and sweet onion compote. The global wine list offers helpful tasting notes. The three bedrooms are stunning: two have great Abbey views, the third looks on to hills and farmland, each is spacious with fabulous beds, and a mix of beams, soft colours and well-chosen period furniture giving a chic, country look. TVs with video, bathrobes, aromatherapy oils and fresh fruit, and smart en suite bathrooms are part of the package.

Prices: Main course from £7.95. House wine £11.50.
Hours: 12.00-15.00. 18.30-23.00. Closed Monday lunch and Sunday evening.
Food served: 12.00-14.00. 18.30-21.00 Tuesday to Saturday.
Rooms: 3 en suite. Double room from £80-£120.
Cuisine: Modern British.
Other Points: No smoking area. Garden. Children welcome. Car park.
Directions: From A1 take the A168 towards Thirsk, then A170 and A19 towards York. In two miles turn left to Coxwold, then left for Byland Abbey. (Map 12, D6)

ALL CREATURES GREAT AND SMALL

Leave the M6 at junction 37 and follow the A64 through the heart of the Yorkshire Dales, the third largest of Britain's eleven national parks and a land of snug cottages, drystone walls and tumbling waterfalls.
Drive length: 62 miles

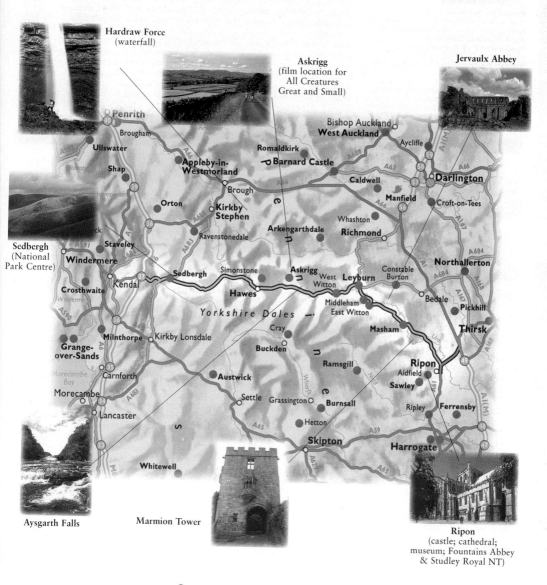

Hardraw Force
(waterfall)

Askrigg
(film location for
All Creatures
Great and Small)

Jervaulx Abbey

Sedbergh
(National
Park Centre)

Yorkshire Dales

Aysgarth Falls

Marmion Tower

Ripon
(castle; cathedral;
museum; Fountains Abbey
& Studley Royal NT)

● Accommodation/Food

● Accommodation

● Food

🦪 Food Shop

To find the establishments marked
here, look up the listing town
marked on the map in bold in the
town index on page 395

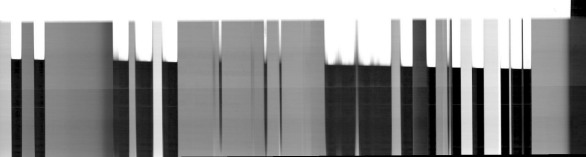

The Durham Ox

Westway, Crayke, Easingwold, North Yorkshire YO61 4TE
Telephone: +44(0)1347 821506
durhamox@btopenworld.com
www.thedurhamox.com

Michael Ibbotson's unassuming 300-year-old inn stands on the hill of 'Grand Old Duke of York' fame and affords magnificent views across the Vale of York to York Minster from the rear cottage bedrooms and garden. Beyond the locals' bar, there's a traditional lounge bar (interesting carved panelling and a pair of worn leather chairs fronting the huge inglenook), and a separate, more formal dining room. Choose a bottle of wine from the array of bottles and bin-ends on the dresser, or order a pint of Theakstons XB, to accompany daily specials of local game hotpot with winter vegetables, mussels with chorizo, thyme and white wine, or pan-seared bass on a tomato tart with rocket and pesto. Regular dishes include homemade soups, the Durham Ox platter of cheeses, hams and pickles with homebaked bread, rib-eye steak with pepper sauce, and local sausages and mash. Good sandwiches, homemade puddings (chocolate and orange torte with crème anglaise), and an excellent cheeseboard, served with fruit cake, chutneys and port. Comfortable, well equipped accommodation is split between the inn and adjacent cottages; all have brass beds, settees, CD players and smart, compact bathrooms. One luxury self-contained cottage suite is ideal for a family or friends sharing.

Prices: Set dinner 18.00-19.00. Main course from £11.95. House wine £10.65.
Hours: 12.00-15.00. 18.00-23.00, Saturday 23.30. Closed 25 December.
Food served: 12.00-14.30 (Sun until 15.00). 18.00-21.30 (Sat 22.00, Sun 20.30).
Rooms: 8 en suite. Double/twin from £80. Single from £60.
Cuisine: Modern British.
Other Points: No-smoking area. Garden. Children welcome. Car park.
Directions: From York take the A19 north to Easingwold, go through the Market Place and head west signed Crayke. (Map 12, E6)

The Black Bull Inn

Main Street, Escrick, North Yorkshire YO19 6JP
Telephone: +44(0)1904 728245
www.theblackbullinn.net

Head south along the A19 from York to find Escrick and the Black Bull, a very traditional village inn that brings a friendly welcome from the Hall family and comfortable overnight accommodation. All ten bedrooms, one with four poster, are freshly decorated with pastel colours and matching furniture, and are well equipped with TV, alarm clocks, tea-making facilities and toiletries. The en suites with power showers are very well fitted, and as with the rest of the accommodation are meticulously clean. Bedrooms are good value and make a peaceful country alternative to the city centre hotels, yet you are only a ten minute drive from York. Downstairs, log fires warm a traditional bar that's filled with polished tables and pew bench seating, and there's an adjoining restaurant. Printed lunch and dinner menus list classic homecooked pub dishes, ranging from filled Yorkshire puddings and sizzling skillets with peppered steak, or sweet and sour chicken, to hearty grills and steak and ale pie with shortcrust pastry topping. Daily specials extend the choice to include pork medallions in a cream and whisky sauce or chicken cooked with coconut and cream. Salads, hot sandwiches and vegetarian dishes are also available.

Prices: Main course from £8. Sunday lunch £7.95. House wine £8.50.
Hours: 12.00-14.30. 17.00-23.00. Sundays from 12.00-22.30.
Food served: 12.00-14.30. 18.00-21.30; until 22.00 on Saturday. 12.00-20.30 Sunday.
Rooms: 10 en suite. Single room from £42, double from £65, four poster £70.
Cuisine: Traditional pub food.
Other Points: No-smoking area. Children welcome. Car park.
Directions: Five miles south of York on the A19. (Map 12, E7)

The Plough Inn

Main Street, Fadmoor, Kirkbymoorside,
North Yorkshire, YO62 7HY
Telephone: +44(0)1751 431515

This spick-and-span pub stands by the triangular green in this picturesque hamlet on the very edge of the North Yorkshire Moors with distant views to the Wolds and the Vale of Pickering. It is a great local, serving a splendid pint of Black Sheep Bitter in its snug little bar replete with black-tiled floor, simple wall benches and wood-burning old range. However, it is becoming increasingly popular for some imaginative pub food. Neil Nicholson sources meat from local farms and butchers, fresh vegetables from Kirkbymoorside, and fish is delivered direct from Hartlepool. Dinner may begin with smoked Scottish venison served with a rocket, spinach and endive salad with a bramble jelly dressing, or a fricassée of king scallops and wild mushrooms with a creamy champagne, chive and garlic sauce. For main course, try the slow-roasted shank of lamb with red wine and rosemary sauce, braised beef brisket joint with port and shallot sauce, or roast pheasant with bacon braised barley and whisky cream sauce. Firm favourites include freshly battered haddock with homemade tartare sauce or fillet steak au poivre. Good-value two-course lunch and Early Bird menus are also available.

Prices: Set lunch £11.25 (two courses). Set Early Bird dinner £14.50. Main course from £9.50. House wine from £10.95.
Hours: 12.00-14.30. 18.30-23.30. 19.00-23.00 on Sunday. Closed 25-26 December and 1 January.
Food served: 12.00-13.45. 18.30-20.45 (from 19.00 on Sunday).
Cuisine: Traditional and Modern pub food.
Other Points: No-smoking area. No dogs. Children welcome. Garden. Car park.
Directions: Head north from Kirkbymoorside (off A170) for one and a half miles turn left and fork left to Fadmoor. (Map 12, D7)

General Tarleton Inn

Ferrensby, Knaresborough,
North Yorkshire HG5 0QB
Telephone: +44(0)1423 340284
gti@generaltarleton.co.uk
www.generaltarlton.co.uk

This 18th-century former coaching inn is run by John
Topham and partner Denis Watkins, owner of the
famed Angel Inn at Hetton (see entry). There's a varied
choice of modern British dishes on the brasserie-style
menu, Tuscan terrine, for example, or rustic fish soup,
perhaps an open sandwich of cream cheese, smoked
salmon, bacon and mango chutney. Mains bring confit
of duck and Toulouse sausage, Lancashire hotpot and
gateau of provençale vegetables with herb salsa, and
puddings may include warm chocolate mousse, apple
tart with caramel ice cream, or, as an alternative, a
plate of Yorkshire cheeses. Food is served throughout a
rambling, low-beamed bar which boasts open fires, a
comfortable mix of country furnishings and some cosy
nooks and crannies, and in summer you can eat in the
light and airy covered courtyard. The adjacent dining-
room, formerly a granary, offers a separate set menu.
The well-chosen list of wines includes a dozen by the
glass. Housed in a more recent extension are 15
uniformly decorated bedrooms. All are well appointed
with pine furnishings, quality fabrics and en suite
bathrooms (bath and shower).

Prices: Set lunch £17.50. Set dinner £25. Main course from
£10.50. House wine £11.75.
Hours: 12.00-15.00. 18.00-23.00, until 22.30 on Sunday.
Closed 25 December.
Food served: 12.00-14.00. 18.00-21.30. Restaurant closed Sunday.
Rooms: 14 en suite. Double/twin £84.90. Single £74.95.
Cuisine: Modern British.
Other Points: No-smoking area. Dogs welcome (not in the bar).
Garden. Children welcome. Car park.
Directions: From the A1 at Boroughbridge take the A6055
towards Knaresborough. (Map 12, E6)

The Downcliffe House Hotel

The Beach, Filey, North Yorkshire YO14 9LA
Telephone: +44(0)1723 513310
info@downcliffehouse.co.uk
www.downcliffehouse.co.uk

Filey is a charming, unspoiled coastal town, and the
Downcliffe Hotel, right on the beach, is a great place
for a peaceful break. Nick and Caroline Hunt have put
a lot of effort into creating a comfortable homely,
family feel without sacrificing style. Public areas are
smart and there's a real fire in the bar and in the
restaurant. Bedrooms are of a good size, all are en
suite, some with four-poster beds, and are decorated in
the Victorian style that runs through the whole house.
Most rooms have views overlooking Filey's six miles of
golden sands, taking in Flamborough Head to the tip
of Filey Brigg. With its separate entrance, the
restaurant has its own identity, more of a restaurant at
the seaside than a hotel dining room. The menu reflects
the proximity to the sea with some sparkling fresh fish,
but also acknowledges the farms that surround Filey.
Thus, the strongly modern British menu may offer crab
fishcakes with garlic mayonnaise to start. Next, there
could be Yorkshire coast haddock grilled with butter
and lemon, or Downcliffe lamb chops with crushed
potatoes, pan juices and mint. A speciality is the grand
platter of fruits de mer.

Prices: Set dinner £20. Main course from £10. House wine £10.
Hours: 12.00-14.00. 18.00-19.00. No food Sunday and Monday
evening. Closed December-February.
Rooms: 11 en suite. Double room from £88, single from £44,
family room from £132.
Cuisine: Seafood/British.
Other Points: No-smoking area. Sea front terrace. Children
welcome. Car park.
Directions: Leave the A165 taking the A1039 and follow to the
centre of Filey. Drive through the centre and down Cargate Hill and
turn right along the sea front. (Map 12, D8)

Prices: Main course from £11. Main
course bar meal from £5.
House wine from £9.80.
Hours: 17.00-21.30. Saturday 12.00-21.30.
Sunday 12.00-21.00.
Closed 25 December, 26 December
evening and 1 January evening.
Cuisine: Modern British.
Other Points: No-smoking area.
Children welcome. Garden. Car park.
Directions: Junction 48/A1. Great
Ouseburn is off the B6265, midway
between Boroughbridge and Green
Hammerton. (Map 12, E6)

The Crown

Great Ouseburn, York, North Yorkshire YO26 9RF
Telephone: +44(0)1423 330430

The Crown stands in a picturesque village, conveniently close to the A1,
and is the epitome of a classic Yorkshire pub, chock full of character and
interesting memorabilia, notably that of the Tiller Girls dancing troupe
who began their careers at this bustling and cheerfully friendly free house.
Despite its traditional appearance, food is well above average for a pub,
with various menus offering imaginative modern British dishes. From the
extensive dining room carte you may begin with seared king scallops with
crispy prosciutto and tomato and basil dressing, before moving on to a
memorable 'Moby Dick' fresh haddock in crisp beer batter, or rack of
lamb with redcurrant and rosemary sauce. In the bar, opt for chargrilled
British steaks, served with handcut chips, the Crowns legendary steak, ale
and mushroom pie, homemade fishcakes with dressed leaves, or chicken
and bacon Caesar salad. Leave room for the apple and blackberry crumble
or savour a fine selection of Yorkshire farmhouse cheeses, perhaps
handmade Swaledale goat or Richmond smoked. The well-annotated,
wide-ranging wine list has been thoughtfully put together, offering good
tasting notes and ten wines by the glass.

The Star Inn ★ ♥ ⁊ ▯ ✕ ◭

High Steet, Harome, Helmsley,
North Yorkshire YO62 5JE
Telephone: +44(0)1439 770397
www.thestaratharome.co.uk

Andrew and Jacqui Pern have transformed an empty and neglected village local into one of the finest pub-restaurants in Britain. Indeed, Andrew's culinary talents haven't stopped at delivering outstanding pub food - an organic food shop-cum-deli is a recent development. The single thatched building is delightful within, with low-beamed ceilings, wonky walls, hand-carved oak furniture (by Mousey Thompson), and a splendid log fire. There is a separate, beautifully decorated dining-room where booking is essential. The cooking makes full use of homegrown herbs and seasonal produce comes from a select network of local suppliers. Short, weekly-changing menus, enhanced by daily specials, blend imaginative modern ideas with bold and vibrant flavours, evident in a meal that could open with fresh dressed Whitby crab, celeriac coleslaw, tomato and lobster oil dressing with avocado purée. Next, lavender roast leg of Helmsley lamb with its own brochette, roasted peppers, red onions and Madeira jus, and a trio of burnt creams with a hot blackcurrant toddy. Accommodation, in eleven tastefully furnished bedrooms, is first-class, three are in a thatched 15th-century cottage nearby. Wake up to a delicious breakfast hamper; cooked breakfasts are extra, served in the 'Piggery'.

Prices: Set lunch £20 and dinner £30. House wine £11.95.
Hours: 12.00-23.00. Closed Monday.
Food served: 11.30-14.00. 18.30-21.30. 12.00-18.00 on Sunday.
Rooms: 11 en suite. Double/twin room from £90.
Cuisine: Modern British/Regional.
Other Points: No-smoking area. Children welcome. No dogs. Garden. Car park.
Directions: The Star is two and a half miles south-east off the A170 between Helmsley and Kirkbymoorside. (Map 12, D7)

Ascot House ▯ ✕ ◭

53 Kings Road, Harrogate,
North Yorkshire HG1 5HJ
Telephone: +44(0)1423 531005
admin@ascothouse.com
www.ascothouse.com

It may be one of the smaller hotels among Harrogate's many, but Ascot House has much to recommend it. Its town-centre location means that it is just a short stroll to the conference and exhibition centre, shops and attractions, yet pleasant gardens give a peaceful air. The small, informal reception area neatly sums up the hotel's pleasantly relaxed style, backed up by a lounge filled with plump sofas and armchairs and overlooking the garden, and a pleasant lounge bar looking on to a pretty patio balcony. There are 19 very well-kept bedrooms, each individually styled in soft colours, and with every extra. Further reasons to stay can be put down to some sound cooking which caters for a wide range of tastes and offers value for money. The set-dinner menu runs to grilled lamb chops accompanied by a warm red onion marmalade, and chicken breast wrapped in smoked bacon and served with Madeira sauce. A typical meal from the carte could include chargrilled vegetable terrine with a balsamic dressing, and roasted pork fillet with apple and onion chutney, and Marsala wine sauce. The wine list lingers longest in France. Private car parking is a bonus.

Prices: Set price dinner £16.50. House wine £9.95.
Hours: 19.00-20.30. Closed 1 January and 25 January - 9 February.
Rooms: 19 en suite. Double room from £80, single from £55.
Cuisine: Traditional and Modern English.
Other Points: No smoking area. Children welcome. Small garden. Car park. Licence for Civil Weddings.
Directions: Follow signs for town centre/conference and exhibition centre of Harrogate. This will bring you to Kings Road, drive past the exhibition centre and the hotel is on the left, immediately after the open park area as you drive up the hill. (Map 12, E6)

Prices: Set lunch from £15. Set dinner from £24. Main course restaurant from £18.50. Main course bar/snack £10.75. House wine £10.75.
Hours: 12.00-14.00. 18.30-23.00.
Food served: 12.00-14.00. 18.30-21.30.
Rooms: 25 en suite. Doubles from £120.
Cuisine: Modern British.
Other Points: No-smoking area. Dogs welcome. Garden. Children welcome. Licenced for civil weddings at Ripley Castle.
Directions: Three miles north of Harrogate on the A61. (Map 12, E6)

Boars Head Hotel ★ ▯ ⁊ ♥ ▯ ✕ ◭

Ripley, Harrogate, North Yorkshire HG3 3AY
Telephone: +44(0)1423 771888
reservations@boarsheadripley.co.uk
www.boarsheadripley.co.uk

An historic coaching inn, formerly The Star, that stands at the head of the stone-walled approaches to Thomas Ingilby's Ripley Castle. In 1900, all the old village pubs were closed on Sundays by the zealous Sir William Ingilby, an action that eventually left the place dry for 71 years. Yet, such was the rejoicing at the re-opening of The Boars Head in 1990, that the vicar arrived to bless the beer pumps. Today's thoroughly stylish hotel boasts every modern comfort in sumptuous bedrooms filled with antiques, plush soft furnishings and homely touches such as toy boats in baths. The best of modern British cooking is evidenced by breast of duck with Seville orange marmalade, or seared scallops with sweet pea pesto and pickled mushrooms. Bistro alternatives include stir-fried marinated beef in black bean sauce, award winning venison sausages on cranberry mash, and red bream fillet on spiced ratatouille and sun-blushed tomato risotto with shaved Parmesan. Round off perhaps with blackcurrant panna cotta with mango coulis or a noteworthy assortment of British farmhouse cheeses. Wines by the glass come from vineyards as diverse as the Murray/Darling rivers of Australia and Chile's Central Valley, home of Sir Thomas's own Reserve Chardonnay.

Courtyard Restaurant

1 Montpellier Mews, Harrogate, North Yorkshire HG1 2TQ
Telephone: +44(0)1423 530708
www.courtyardrestaurant.net

The tiny restaurant, situated in a former stable mews overlooking the Montpelier Quarter cobbled streets lined with bow-fronted shops, old-fashioned gas street lamps, antique shops is famous as the restaurant that launched the career of chef Simon Gueller. Its an attractive, welcoming place, decorated in creams, with white tablecloths covering small, close-set tables, and one wall covered by a large glass mirror on which special dishes of the day are scrawled. Food is modern in concept, ranging from a fashionable pan-seared queen scallops, celeriac and fennel purée, coriander and basil cream, to a classic fillet of beef, pommes Anna, buttered spinach, tomatoes, shallots and red wine jus. A set menu offered at lunch and in the early evening could bring a well-made ham hock terrine with first-class homemade ketchup and frisé and herb salad. Then slow-cooked roast belly pork with a rich, unctuous sauce, to follow, served with crunchy oriental vegetables and hoi sin sauce. Iced white peach parfait, pear and orange syrup makes a worthwhile finish. This is good value cooking, using fresh ingredients and based on sound cooking skills. Service is very efficient and the wine list is wide-ranging and not greedy on prices.

Prices: Set lunch and dinner £14.95. Main course from £9.95. House wine £11.50.
Hours: 12.00-14.30. 18.30-21.30. Closed on Sunday.
Cuisine: Modern English.
Other Points: Totally no smoking. Garden and courtyard.
Directions: In Harrogate town centre, located in the Montpellier Quarter, near Valley Gardens. (Map 12, E6)

Simonstone Hall

Simonstone, Hawes, North Yorkshire DL8 3LY
Telephone: +44(0)1969 667255
info@simonstonehall.co.uk
www.simonstonehall.com

Plum in the middle of Upper Wensleydale, near the market town of Hawes, is an imposing early 18th-century house surrounded by gardens that blend into moorland, and bills itself as offering 'rest and relaxation at its very best'. It is an elegant retreat with original panelling, ornate fireplaces and large windows overlooking glorious scenery. Portraits, hunting scenes, and large mirrors cover walls, rugs are strewn over floors, and lovely period furniture takes in swan-backed chairs in the sitting room, some highly polished barley-twist side tables, and graceful beds in suitably plush bedrooms with good-sized bathrooms and lots of thoughtful extras. The bar has a quirky, pubby interior and offers an intersting menu, perhaps black pudding with red onion marmalade topped with grilled goats' cheese, with braised lamb shank, mashed potatoes and gravy as a main course, and sticky toffee pudding to finish. In stark contrast, the restaurant is an elegant, romantic room, with cream panelling covered with paintings and mirrors, and crisp. Here, country-house cooking takes in seared king scallops, watercress salad, crisp Parma ham and an orange and thyme dressing, to start, followed by pan-fried duck breast with stir-fried pak choi and bean sprouts and a gingered pink grapefruit sauce.

Prices: Set price three course dinner £35. House wine £10.50.
Hours: 12.00-14.00 and 18.30-21.00.
Rooms: 20 en suite. Double/twin from £120, single from £60.
Cuisine: Traditional and Modern British.
Other Points: No smoking area. Children welcome. Garden. Car park. Licence for civil weddings.
Directions: Hawes is on the A684 west from the A1 at Bedale. East from the M6 at junction 37. (Map 12, D5)

Pheasant Hotel

Harome, Helmsley, North Yorkshire YO62 5JG
Telephone: +44(0)1439 771241
binks-harome.freeserve.co.uk

The setting is quintessentially English: beside a duck pond in a pretty Yorkshire village. The two former cottages and the village blacksmith's shop that make up this country hotel have blended into a style that ranges from cottagey (the beamy, flagged floored bar) to country house (the pleasant conservatory section of the restaurant and chintzy lounge). Bedrooms are quite spacious, neatly decorated in cottage-style, and very well equipped; most look out over the duck pond. This is a comfortable place to stay, the lounge has an open fire, and the views onto the pond with its ducks and geese are pleasant and relaxing. In one of the Pheasant's courtyard buildings is a small heated swimming pool, which is as unusual for the location as it is extremely popular with guests. Food in the restaurant is very traditional, the daily changing menu offcring the likes of cream of asparagus soup, roast breast of Gressingham duckling with apple sauce and onion stuffing, or poached fillet of fresh Scarborough sole with parsley sauce, and blackberry and apple pie to finish.

Prices: Set dinner £22.50. House wine £7.50.
Hours: 12.00-14.00. 19.30-20.30. Closed December, January and February.
Rooms: 12 en suite. Double room from £140, single from £70. Includes breakfast and dinner.
Cuisine: Traditional English.
Other Points: No smoking area. Children welcome over 8 years. Garden. Car park. Indoor heated swimming pool.
Directions: Take the A170 from Helmsley towards Scarborough. After 0.25 miles turn right for Harome. (Map 12, D7)

Wombwell Arms

Wass, Helmsley, North Yorkshire YO61 4BE
Telephone: +44(0)1347 868280
thewombwellarms@aol.com
www.thewombwellarms.co.uk

Originally built as a grainstore for nearby Byland Abbey, a 17th-century Cistercian abbey, this old whitewashed stone pub lies tucked away in a small hamlet at the foot of the Hambleton Hills. Susan and Andy Cole have created a relaxed atmosphere within. Four connecting rooms sport a mix of flagstone and red-tiled flooring, some exposed stone walls, original beams, attractive watercolours and stripped pine furnishings. In addition, you will find good real ales on draught - Timothy Taylor Landlord and Black Sheep Bitter - and an interesting list of wines with tasting notes and eight by the glass. Imaginative bistro-style food is listed on a huge blackboard in the main bar. Freshly prepared from local ingredients wherever possible, expect hearty lunchtime soups (parsnip and celery), hot goats' cheese salad with red onion marmalade, and ciabatta sandwiches. For something more substantial try the game casserole, Masham sausages with mash and grain mustard, rabbit cooked with cider and apples, fresh mixed seafood platter, or the popular lasagne cooked with three cheeses and red wine. Upstairs, the three cottagey bedrooms have been comfortably refurbished with red carpets, pine furnishing and all feature smart new en suite facilities with quality tiling and fittings.

Prices: Set lunch £20. Set dinner £25. Main course from £7.95. House wine £10.80.
Hours: 12.00-15.00. 18.30-23.00. Closed Sunday evenings and all day Mondays from January until end of March.
Food served: 12.00-14.00. 19.00-21.00 (until 21.30 Saturday and Sunday).
Rooms: 3 en suite. Doubles from £62.
Cuisine: Modern British.
Other Points: No-smoking area. Dogs welcome in bar only. Garden. Children welcome. Car park.
Directions: From the A19 York to Thirsk road go east through Coxwold. Pass Byland Abbey to reach Wass. (Map 12, D7)

Wrangham House Hotel

10 Stonegate, Hunmanby, near Filey,
North Yorkshire YO14 0NS
Telephone: +44(0)1723 891333
info@wranghamhouse.co.uk
www.wranghamhouse.co.uk

A vicarage from 1754 until 1954, this unpretentious family-run country hotel stands in the shadow of All Saints Church. Its most famous incumbent was Francis Wrangham, a correspondent of William Wordsworth and the man responsible for renovating and extending the house, adding the current dining room and the rooms above primarily to accommodate its library. Beautifully proportioned day rooms have been tastefully furnished with lots of comfortable armchairs and boast log fires and views on to the two acres of wooded garden. Meals are served in the spacious, strikingly decorated dining room that offers a short menu of updated country-house cooking. The set-price dinner menu takes in Caesar salad or smoked trout with avocado and shrimp mousse, and goes on to roasted rack of lamb with redcurrant coulis, and breast of Barbary duck in a red wine, button onion and mushroom sauce. The wine list has something for most tastes, and prices are very reasonable, rarely going over £15. Four of the smart, traditionally styled bedrooms are located in an adjacent converted coach house, where one on the ground floor is equipped for guests with disabilities.

Prices: Set dinner £19.50 and £16 (2 courses). Main course bar/snack from £4.95. House wine £10.75.
Hours: 19.00-21.30. No food on Sunday.
Rooms: 12 en suite. Double room from £70, single from £42.
Cuisine: Contemporary British.
Other Points: No-smoking area. Children welcome over 12 years old. Garden. Car park. Licence for Civil Weddings.
Directions: Nine miles south of Scarborough via the A165, then the A1039. (Map 12, D8)

The Stone Trough Inn

Kirkham Abbey, Whitwell-on-the-Hill, York,
North Yorkshire YO60 7JS
Telephone: +44(0)1653 618713
info@stonetroughinn.co.uk
www.stonetroughinn.co.uk

Lovely views of Kirkham Abbey and the Derwent valley are to be had from this well-kept pub, and Castle Howard (of Brideshead Revisited fame) is ten minutes away. The bar area is split in two sections with big farmhouse tables, plenty of open fires, flagstone floors and fresh flowers. Exposed stone walls, nooks and crannies and lots of little knick-knacks add to the relaxed, homely atmosphere. Here, the bar menu offers homemade fishcakes with a flat parsley butter sauce, chargrilled sirloin steak on thyme sauté potatoes with a peppercorn and blue cheese butter, or lunchtime sandwiches, and classic puddings. The restaurant goes in for a more smart-casual look with big, cloth-covered tables and softer lighting. Chef/proprietor Adam Richardson and his head chef Charlie Lakin use as much local produce as possible, giving a strong regional identity to the food. Starters, for example, might feature pan-fried pigeon breast and black pudding on bubble and squeak cake with a Madeira jus, with mains offering roast whole boned partridge with lemon thyme and jumbo raisin stuffing and sloe gin and peppercorn sauce. There's a good rounded, global wine list with some 60 wines.

Prices: Main course restaurant from £10.95. Main course bar from £6.95. House wine £9.95.
Hours: 12.00-14.30. 18.00-23.00.
Closed 25 December and Monday except Bank Holidays.
Food served: 12.00-14.00. 18.30-20.30 Tuesday-Saturday. 12.00-14.15 on Sunday.
Cuisine: Modern British.
Other Points: No-smoking area. No Dogs. Garden. Children welcome. Car park.
Directions: One and a half miles off A64 between York and Malton, near Castle Howard, overlooking Kirkham Abbey. (Map 12, E7)

Lastingham Grange

★ 🍴 ✕ 🛏

Lastingham, Kirkbymoorside, York,
North Yorkshire YO62 6TH
Telephone: +44(0)1751 417345
reservations@lastinghamgrange.com
www.lastinghamgrange.com

The village of Lastingham, tucked away in a small valley on the edge of the North Yorkshire Moors, is very pretty and the 17th century former farmhouse epitomises it all: peaceful, rural, elegant and exuding an air of timelessness and solid values of genuine hospitality. Everything is tidy with well-maintained flower baskets and planters, the formal and wild gardens beyond are delightful. The entrance is welcoming and the Wood family, whose home the Grange has been for nearly 60 years, put visitors immediately at ease. Public areas and bedrooms are spacious and furnished in soft colours with antiques, ornaments, and paintings. Bedrooms and en suite bathrooms are in pristine condition and offer much comfort, although the floral print wallpapers in some bedrooms may strike one as old-fashioned, but it is that timeless air that distinguishes the character of the hotel and makes it so appealing. The dining room has a romantic feel. Four course dinners are built around local produce and may include Waldorf and grapefruit salad, and ragout of kidneys in red wine.

Prices: Set lunch £17.75 (4 courses), dinner £35.50 (5 courses).
Main course from £12.50. House wine £7.75.
Hours: 12.00-13.45. 19.00-20.30 (20.00 on Sunday).
Closed December to the beginning of March.
Rooms: 12 en suite. Double room from £210, single from £115 (dinner, bed & breakfast).
Cuisine: Traditional English.
Other Points: No-smoking area. Children welcome. Garden. Car park.
Directions: From Pickering take the A170 towards Kirkbymoorside for five miles. Turn off right towards Appleton-le-Moors and Lastingham; follow the road and turn right by the church after 75 yards turn left up the no through road for 400 yards. (Map 12, D7)

The Blue Lion

🍴 ✕ 🛏

East Witton, Leyburn, North Yorkshire DL8 4SN
Telephone: +44(0)1969 624273
bluelion@breathemail.net
www.thebluelion.co.uk

Since his arrival in 1990, Paul Klein has successfully created one of the finest inns in North Yorkshire, offering twelve comfortable and individually furnished en suite bedrooms and quality modern pub food that draws the crowds from miles around. Choose between a short carte in the intimate, antique-furnished dining room or the ambitious bar menu of classy modern dishes chalked on boards above the striking stone fireplace. (As you can't book a table in the bar, it's best to arrive early.) First-class ingredients appear in starters like crispy fried squid with chilli and coriander salsa. Equally appealing main courses might range from pan-fried cod with seafood risotto, to roast chump of lamb with Mediterranean vegetables and pesto mash. Puddings may feature dark chocolate tart with orange sorbet. For a light snack (not Sunday lunchtime) there are decent sandwiches. A good pubby atmosphere takes in locals at the bar quaffing Black Sheep and Theakston ales, and a relaxed dining ambience in the two candle-lit bar rooms. Tasteful prints and paintings, rustic high-backed antique settles, old Windsor chairs, rug-strewn flagstones and a blazing log fire set the evocative scene. Wines are an impressive global list of over 100 wines with some 20 by the glass.

Prices: Main course from £15. Main course bar meal from £11.50.
House wine £10.50.
Hours: 12.00-23.00.
Food served: 12.00-14.00. 19.00-21.00. No food 25 December.
Rooms: 12 en suite. Singles from £53.50, doubles from £69.
Family rooms from £89 plus £10 per child.
Cuisine: Traditional British.
Other Points: Children welcome. Garden. Car park.
Directions: On the A1608 between Leyburn and Ripon.
(Map 12, D5)

The Sandpiper Inn

🍷 🍴 ✕ 🛏

Market Place, Leyburn, Wensleydale, North Yorkshire DL8 5AT
Telephone: +44(0)1969 622206
hsandpiper99@aol.com

Just a stone's throw from Leyburn's pretty market square stands this 17th-century stone cottage, a pub for just 30 years, its flagging fortunes revived in 1999 by the arrival of Jonathan Harrison, who left the stress of grand hotel cooking in favour of this homely market town pub-with-rooms. A wood-burning stove, cushioned wall benches and low dark beams create an unspoilt and traditional atmosphere in the bar, while the simple, yet stylish dining area hints at Jonathan's modern approach to pub dining. Listed on a twice daily changing blackboard, light lunchtime options may include onion and cider soup, fishcakes with chive and parsley sauce, and Yorkshire ham with local farm eggs and fried potatoes. However, dinner reveals the true expertise in the kitchen, with a repertoire of well-balanced modern British dishes featuring the best local produce available, notably locally shot game, Wensleydale heifer beef and home-grown herbs. Typical main courses range from grilled bream on creamed leeks and garlic, to braised rabbit with wild mushrooms and thyme. For pudding try the lemon tart with lime sorbet. Those in need of a comfortable bed should look no further than the two smart upstairs bedrooms. Both are tastefully furnished and equipped with quality en suite facilities.

Prices: Main courses from £10.50.
House wine £10.
Hours: 12.00-14.30 and 18.30-21.00 from Tuesday to Thursday (until 21.30 Friday and Saturday). 12.00-14.00 and 19.00-21.00 on Sunday. Closed Monday.
Rooms: 2 en suite. Double room from £65, single from £55.
Cuisine: Modern British.
Other Points: No-smoking in the restaurant. Car park. Garden.
Directions: Just off Market Square in Leyburn. (Map 12, D5)

England - North Yorkshire

Wensleydale Heifer Inn

Main Street, West Witton, Leyburn, North Yorkshire DL8 4LS
Telephone: +44(0)1969 622322
info@wensleydaleheifer.co.uk
www.wensleydaleheifer.co.uk

This well-heeled inn dates from 1631 and is mentioned in James Herriot's books about the area - the perfect base for exploring All Creatures Great and Small country. Deep sofas and armchairs around a huge log fire set the cosy scene in the comfortable front lounge, while beams and settles characterise the small and intimate bar areas beyond. Visitors can choose to eat in the informal bistro with its terracotta walls and modern pine furnishings, or in the spacious, more formal restaurant, which has a period feel with beams, dark wood pews and heavy window drapes. Meals range from simple lunchtime snacks of Yorkshire ham ploughman's and a Wensleydale cheese sandwich with homemade granary bread, to traditional pub meals in the bistro, for example seafood pasta, liver and onions and haddock and chips. More inventive dishes listed on the restaurant carte may open with Stilton and quince pâté or hot black pudding with bacon and tomato salad, with pan-fried tuna with tomato and sweet pepper salsa or lamb casserole to follow. Traditional puddings include bread and butter pudding and fruit crumble. Smart, newly refurbished bedrooms - four with four-posters - feature antique furnishings and well appointed en suite facilities.

Prices: Main course from £8.95. Main course bar from £4.95. House wine £9.50.
Hours: 11.00-23.00.
Food served: 12.00-14.00. 18.30-21.00.
Rooms: 9 en suite. Double room from £36 per person, single from £60.
Cuisine: Traditional British.
Other Points: No-smoking in the bedrooms. Children welcome over 12 years old. Garden. Car park.
Directions: Follow the A684 from Leyburn towards Hawes for about three and a half miles. (Map 12, D5)

The White Swan

Market Place, Middleham, Leyburn, North Yorkshire DL8 4PE
Telephone: +44(0)1969 622093
whiteswan@easynet.co.uk
www.whiteswanhotel.co.uk

Refurbishment and first-class interior design have brought real style to Helen and Paul Klein's Tudor coaching inn which stands in the cobbled market square in the shadow of the Middleham's ruined castle. The original oak beams, polished flagstones and winter log fires have been carefully preserved in the front bar, a popular retreat for the local racing fraternity, where tip-top Black Sheep ales and well chosen wines by the glass accompany enjoyable modern British pub food. Using quality Yorkshire produce, notably handmade Masham sausages, Bedale meats, game from nearby shoots, and local Wensleydale cheeses, the daily blackboard menu may list beef in Black Sheep pie, lamb cutlets with horseradish mash and red wine sauce, and an excellent bowl of bouillabaisse, served with rouille and croutons. Mains range from black pudding and bacon risotto, and crisy duck leg confit with braised red cabbage, to beer battered cod and chips, and chargrilled rib-eye steak with garlic butter. The refurbished en suite bedrooms feature quality fabrics and furnishings. In the same ownership as the Blue Lion at East Witton (see entry).

Prices: Set lunch £12.95. Set dinner £14.95. Main course restaurant from £10.95. Main course bar from £5.95. House wine £9.50.
Hours: 11.30-23.00. Sunday 12.00-22.30.
Closed 25 December lunch.
Food served: 12.00-14.15. 18.30-21.15.
Rooms: 12 en suite. Double/twin from £59.
Cuisine: Modern British.
Other Points: No-smoking area. Dogs welcome. Garden. Children welcome.
Directions: From A1 north/south exit Masham and follow the A6267 to Masham and remain on the A6267. (Map 12, D5)

The Wyvill Arms

Constable Burton, Leyburn, North Yorkshire DL8 5LH
Telephone: +44(0)1677 450581
www.wyvillarms.co.uk

Popular with visitors to Constable Burton Gardens just along the road, this creeper-clad former farmhouse enjoys lovely views across the Ure Valley to the distant Dales from its attractive landscaped gardens. On cooler days, the relaxing beamed and part-carpeted and stone-flagged interior, with its comfortable upholstered alcoves, carved stone fireplaces and plaster ceilings, and collections of local photographs and hunting paintings, fills quickly with diners eager to sample the range of homemade food listed on printed and blackboard menus. Using local produce, notably herbs and vegetables from the pub garden, a typical evening menu may list braised lamb shank with garlic and rosemary, calf's liver with smoked bacon and port gravy, and chicken breast with leek, bacon and Stilton sauce, alongside daily fish specials. Lighter lunchtime meals include decent sandwiches (try the hot beef baguette), pasta and risotto dishes of the day, steak and onion pie with handcut chips, and local Wensleydale cheese ploughman's. Good ales from Black Sheep and Theakston and a good-value list of wines with 10 by the glass. Homely overnight accommodation is available in three well-equipped en suite bedrooms, all with soothing country views.

Prices: Main courses from £9. House wine £9.95
Hours: 11.00-15.00 and 18.30-23.15 daily.
Food served: 12.00-14.15. 18.30-21.00. Sunday 19.00-21.00.
Rooms: 4 en suite. Double room £56, single £34.
Cuisine: Modern British and French.
Other Points: No smoking area. Car park. Garden. Children welcome.
Directions: The Wyvill Arms lies between Leyurn and Bedale on the A684. (Map 12, D5)

Wrightson & Company

Manfield Grange, Manfield, Darlington,
North Yorkshire DL2 2RE
Telephone: +44(0)1325 374134
ed.wrightson.wines@onyxnet.co.uk
www.thatwineclub.com

Simon Wrightson runs one of the nicest, best informed
wine businesses anywhere in the North of England.
Wrightson & Co offers the best kind of old-fashioned
personal service for private clients, as well as guiding
and supplying some of the top restaurants in the
region, providing expert advice, an impressive selection
of domaine-grown European wines and an outstanding,
innovative selection of New World wines. Bi-annual
wine tastings take place at Manfield Grange, and the
business publishes an attractive annual wine list with
sensible and helpful guidance on the selection, laying
down and drinking of wine.

Hours: 09.00-17.30. Closed Saturday and Sunday and
Bank Holidays.
Directions: A1(M)/ Junction 56. Manfield Grange is in the village of
Manfield, three miles from junction 56 on the A1(M), taking the
B6275 signed Piercebridge. (Map 12, D6)

The Appletree Country Inn

Marton, Pickering, North Yorkshire YO62 6RD
Telephone: +44(0)1751 431457
appletreeinn@supanet.com
www.appletreeinn.co.uk

Take a loss-making village boozer and transform it into
a stylish, money-making modern dining pub within a
year, and one that holds its own against several stellar
performers in the neighbourhood. Impossible? Not for
chef TJ Drew and partner Melanie Thornton. They
have done just that to this refurbished old stone pub
tucked away in a sleepy hamlet below the North
Yorkshire Moors. Innovative monthly menus make the
most of quality local produce. Arrive for dinner and
follow excellent homemade breads with Yorkshire
game terrine with chutney and toasted brioche. Move
on to venison suet pudding with red onion marmalade
and juniper gin jus. For pudding, opt for the unusual,
warm blackberry soup with homemade vanilla ice
cream. First rate lunches range from spiced crab cakes
with oyster sauce and tomato salsa and Marton goose
and crispy bacon salad, to roast suckling pig on
mustard mash with apple sauce and sage jus. All are
served throughout the informal and very comfortable
bar/restaurant, with its deep red walls, heavy beams
and open fires, and neatly adorned with polished tables
and hundreds of candles. In addition, expect quality
wines (twelve by the glass), Yorkshire ales, and a shop
counter laden with homemade goodies.

Prices: Main course dinner from £10.50.
House wine £9.95.
Hours: 12.00-14.30 (until 15.00 on Sunday). 18.30-23.00.
Closed Tuesday, 25 December and three weeks in January.
Food served: 12.00-14.00. 18.30-21.30. 12.00-15.00
and 19.00-21.30 on Sunday.
Cuisine: Modern British.
Other Points: No-smoking area. Children welcome. Garden.
Car park.
Directions: From Kirkbymoorside on the A170 towards
Scarborough, village signposted right. (Map 12, D7)

The Black Sheep Brewery

Wellgarth, Masham, North Yorkshire HG4 4EN
Telephone: +44(0)1765 689227
sue.dempsy@blacksheep.co.uk
www.blacksheep.co.uk

Set up in 1992 by Paul Theakston, a member of Masham's famous
brewing family, in the former Wellgarth Maltings, Black Sheep has
enjoyed continued growth. This includes brewing and bottling five award-
winning real ales and developing an excellent visitor centre where you will
discover how Black Sheep brew 12 million pints a year. The brewery now
supplies well over 600 free houses within an 80-mile radius of Masham.
Follow a fascinating tour of the brewhouse with a perfect pint and a meal
in the spacious, split-level bar-cum-bistro, with its wooden floors, bright
check-clothed tables, brewery equipment and informal atmosphere. At
lunchtime, tuck into wholemeal sandwiches of ham and Black Sheep
chutney, say, and steak and Riggwelter pie, one of the blackboard specials,
perhaps rack of local lamb with rosemary, Black Sheep Bitter and
redcurrant sauce. The more imaginative evening menu (Wednesday -
Saturday) may offer honey-glazed duck confit with port sauce and fillet
steak with caramelised shallots and bordelaise sauce, with homemade
puddings or local Wensleydale cheese to finish. Afterwards, visit the Black
Sheep shop and buy some bottled ale to take home.

Prices: Lunch main course £5.95. Evening
main course from £8.95.
House wine £9.95.
Hours: 10.30-14.30 and evening until
23.00. Closes at 17.00 on Monday, Tuesday
and Sunday. Closed 25-26 December and
10 days in January.
Cuisine: Traditional and Modern British.
Other Points: No-smoking area. Children
welcome. Car park.
Directions: Masham lies midway between
Ripon and Leyburn on the A6108.
(Map 12, D6)

Lovesome Hill Farm

Lovesome Hill, Northallerton, North Yorkshire DL6 2PB
Telephone: +44(0)1609 772311
pearson1hf@care4free.net

The Yorkshire Dales of James Heriott's *All Creatures Great and Small*, and *Heartbeat's* North Yorkshire Moors, sandwich Mary and John Pearson's working farm. Sheep, cows, pigs and hens, 156 acres of farmland, and a location 200 yards from Wainright's Coast to Coast walk, are added attractions. This is a welcoming place. Expect to be fed well, from the moment Mary ushers you into the lounge with a tray of tea and homemade biscuits on arrival. Breakfast supplies eggs from the farm, local honey, sausages and bacon, homemade marmalade and lemon curd. Dinner is built around local supplies too, and can run to homemade soups, chicken in tarragon or pork with apricots, served with locally grown vegetables, and raspberry Pavlova to finish. There is one bedroom in the main house; the rest are in a barn conversion. However, this is attached to the main house, so there is no need to go outside. A neat cottage style with floral prints, some canopied beds, and neat touches distinguish the rooms, which are all en suite. Gate Cottage sleeps two and offers the flexibility of bed and breakfast or self catering.

Prices: Set dinner £16.
Rooms: 6 en suite. Double room from £48, single from £26, family room £78.
Cuisine: Traditional English.
Other Points: No-smoking area. Children welcome. Garden. Car park.
Directions: Four miles north of Northallerton on the A167 towards Darlington, on the right hand side. (Map 12, D6)

The Golden Lion

6 West End, Osmotherley, Thirsk,
North Yorkshire BL6 3AA
Telephone: +44(0)1609 883526

Peter McCoy, formerly of that famed McCoys (Tontine Inn) at Staddlebridge, joined forces with two partners in 1996 to buy this old stone inn. Set on the green overlooking the market cross, it has proved a successful venture, appealing to walkers hiking the Lyke Wake Walk, as well as those in search of imaginative, good value cooking. Expect a lively and bustling atmosphere in the cosy, wood-panelled bar, with its whitewashed stone walls, cushioned pew bench seating, log fire, and inviting evening candlelight. Booking is advisable; essential at weekends when the upstairs dining room provides extra covers. Christie Connelly presides over the bar, dispensing pints of Hambleton Bitter and Taylor Landlord and distributing menus with efficent aplomb. Simple, clean and full-flavoured dishes range from fresh sardines in olive oil, creamy lemon risotto with caramelised onions, and a tureen of chunky fish soup for a snack or starter, to steak and kidney pie with suet crust, simply grilled sea bass with potatoes and peas, or homemade chicken Kiev with green salad and handcut chips. Puddings include sticky toffee pudding and lemon and passion fruit pavlova; decent coffee to finish.

Prices: Main course from £6.50-£13.95. House wine from £12.
Hours: 12.00-15.30 (until 16.30 Saturday and Sunday) 18.00-23.00. Closed Christmas Day.
Food served: 12.00-16.00. 18.00-22.00.
Cuisine: Modern Pub Food.
Other Points: No-smoking area. Children welcome.
Directions: Off the A19 north of Thirsk. (Map 12, D6)

The Fox and Hounds

Main Street, Sinnington, Pickering, North Yorkshire YO62 6SQ
Telephone: +44(0)1751 431577
foxhoundsinn@easynet.co.uk
www.thefoxandhoundsinn.co.uk

Beyond its attractive stone frontage of this 18th-century coaching inn lies a comfortably modernised interior, including a neat rear extension housing bedrooms and a well-appointed dining room. Of the two front bars, the carpeted lounge, with its beams, panelling and open fire, has a warm and welcoming atmosphere and there's a separate locals' bar. Thornton-le-Dale butcher Charlie Hill supplies the locally-farmed beef, the superb black pudding, and handmade sausages, while game is sourced from local shoots, and herbs come from the pub's own garden. A short list of daily specials (roast Goosnargh duck with tarragon and orange sauce, local venison with plum chutney, port and red wine jus) supplements the extensive carte. Begin with marinated pigeon breast with shallot confit, fig tarte tatin and rosemary pesto, move on to monkfish wrapped in pancetta with sweet capsicum coulis and balsamic reduction, and finish with raspberry and passion fruit panna cotta with lime syrup, or a selection of Yorkshire farmhouse cheeses. Newly refurbished bedrooms are equipped with either antique or modern pine furnishings, have compact tiled bathrooms, and all the usual modern-day comforts.

Prices: Sunday lunch £14.25. Main course from £9.75. House wine £11.50.
Hours: 12.00-14.30. 18.00-23.00. Check for seasonal variations. Closed Christmas Day.
Food served: 12.00-14.00. 18.30-21.00.
Rooms: 10 en suite. £25 per person including breakfast.
Cuisine: Modern British.
Other Points: No-smoking area. Dogs welcome. Garden. Children welcome.
Directions: Three miles west of Pickering off the A170 towards Thirsk. (Map 12, D7)

The White Swan

Market Place, Pickering, North Yorkshire YO18 7AA
Telephone: +44(0)1751 472288
welcome@white-swan.co.uk
www.white-swan.co.uk

Originally built as a four-room cottage in 1532, and quickly extended as a coaching inn, the White Swan has been run with genuine enthusiasm by the Buchanan family for almost 20 years. Old-fashioned courtesy is the style in the intimate, wood-panelled snug bar, where locals congregate for pints of Black Sheep ale. The recent refurbishment of the lounge, with its deep, comfy sofas and blazing log fire, and the twelve individually decorated bedrooms is impressive. Visitors can expect brass and carved wood beds, tasteful coordinating fabrics and smart bathrooms with thick towels and luxury toiletries. This level of quality and attention to detail extends to the kitchen. Using fresh Whitby fish, local meat and game, cooking is simple, contemporary, but unpretentious - Yorkshire dishes given a modern twist. Bar lunches move beyond sandwiches and ploughman's to more imaginative ideas - served throughout the inn. A typical dinner may begin with spiced mussel soup with saffron crispbreads and basil, then roast belly pork with apple sauce and glazed baby root vegetables, with glazed lemon tart with lime ice cream and brandy snap, or Yorkshire farmhouse cheeses to finish. The impressive wine list offers eight by the glass and a specialist section of over fifty exceptional St Emilion wines.

Prices: Main course from £9.95. House wine £12.50.
Hours: 10.00-15.00. 18.00-23.00 Tuesday-Thursday. 10.00-23.00 Monday, Friday and Saturday. 11.00-16.00. 19.00-22.30 Sunday.
Food served: 12.00-14.00. 19.00-21.00.
Rooms: 12 en suite. Double room from £110, single from £70, family room from £125.
Cuisine: Modern British.
Other Points: No-smoking area. Children welcome. Garden. Car park.
Directions: Inn located in the centre of town, off the A169 between Scarborough and Thirsk. (Map 12, D7)

Nags Head Inn

Pickhill, Thirsk, North Yorkshire YO7 4JG
Telephone: +44(0)1845 567391
enquiries@nagsheadpickhill.freeserve.co.uk
www.nagsheadpickhill.freeserve.co.uk

Raymond and Edward Boynton have been welcoming visitors to their extended, former 17th-century coaching inn for 30 years. Synonymous with Yorkshire hospitality at its best, and popular with the racing fraternity, visitors can retreat to the beamed and comfortably furnished lounge, or the tie-adorned main bar, at any time of day for refreshment. Two blackboard menus show Raymond's varied repertoire which utilises the best available produce - local game and asparagus in season, Doreen's black puddings, and quality butcher meats. For a bar snack, try the salmon, prawn and cod fishcake, or a choice of sandwiches (available all day). Interesting and often adventurous main meals extend the choice to whole grey mullet with black bean sauce, pheasant with root vegetables and game gravy, and duck with lime and gin sauce, plus traditional puddings such as burnt Oxford cream. You will also find immaculately-kept real ales, monthly wine selections (also offered by the glass), vintage armagnacs and an array of 40-odd malt whiskies, all the domain of Edward who oversees the choice and quality with pride and passion. Seventeen bedrooms are split between the main building, the next-door house and a cottage, which can also be let in its entirety.

Hours: 11.00-23.00. Closed Christmas Day.
Food served: 12.00-14.00. 18.00-21.30.
Rooms: 17 en suite. Double/twin from £70, single from £45.
Cuisine: Modern British.
Other Points: No smoking in restaurant. Garden. Car park.
Directions: In the centre of Pickhill just off the A1 between Boroughbridge and Catterick. (Map 12, D6)

Yorke Arms

Ramsgill, Harrogate, North Yorkshire HG3 5RL
Telephone: +44(0)1423 755243
enquiries@yorke-arms.co.uk
www.yorke-arms.co.uk

The imposing, creeper-clad manorial façade hints at an interesting history. The transition from an ecclesiastical farm building to a shooting lodge for the premier family of the area adds interest to an elegant interior of polished stone flag floors, open fires, panelling and oak beams. Now a smart yet relaxed restaurant with rooms, Frances and Bill Atkins acknowledge the local community for whom the Yorke Arms was once the village pub by running an intimate bar that serves up character in spades and Black Sheep on hand pump. Yet the cooking in the restaurant draws visitors from afar with accomplished dishes that deploy a wide range of skills. While the workmanship is detailed, the wow comes from direct hits on the plate: striking combinations such as Yorkshire potted beef, ham hock and foie gras terrine served with asparagus velouté and beetroot relish, or roast turbot contrasted by an intense lemon relish and celery, turnip and sweetcorn chowder. An enterprising wine list combines interest and value throughout. Bedrooms are well appointed; superior rooms have their own sitting area, and one spacious ground floor room comes with a magnificently carved four poster bed.

Prices: Set Sunday lunch £25. Main course from £15. Main course bar meal from £8.50. House wine £14.95.
Hours: 10.00-15.00. 18.00-23.00 (22.30 on Sunday).
Food served: 12.00-14.00. 19.00-21.00.
Rooms: 14 en suite. Double room from £90 per person per night for dinner, bed and breakfast.
Cuisine: Modern British.
Other Points: No-smoking area. Children welcome over ten years old. Garden. Car park.
Directions: From Ripon take the B6265 to Pateley Bridge. Turn right over the River Nidd, signed to Ramsgill. (Map 12, F6)

KITCHEN
WISDOM

Elizabeth Carter visits Frances Atkins, whose culinary workshop is guaranteed to change the way you think about food and cooking

Question: *what do you do when you give a dinner party?*
Answer: *first get out the recipe books.*

"Wrong", says Frances Atkins, chef/patron of the Yorke Arms at Ramsgill in North Yorkshire. "You go to the supermarket and you choose the finest, freshest, best looking ingredients, then come home and decide how you are going to prepare them."

The stylish, creeper-clad restaurant-with-rooms (see page 235), is set in a stunning part of North Yorkshire. It is a perfect setting for a two-day culinary workshop that has been designed to make us question the way we cook, and to make us think about food, taste and flavour in a different way. It's a revelation. You could almost say that when Frances Atkins makes an omelette, she doesn't break eggs — she breaks your very notion of what an omelette may be.

Her message is simple: we need to concentrate far more on the quality and flavour of our ingredients, rather than messing about with it when we cook — in other words, it is far braver, and more sensible, to cook

236

Frances Atkins Culinary Workshop, The Yorke Arms Restaurant with Rooms, Ramsgill in Nidderdale, Pateley Bridge, North Yorkshire.

simple, superb food. And you'll find the most practical advice that you'll ever receive on organising your time so you can actually enjoy your own dinner parties.

A break between running restaurants was the catalyst – Frances did some entertaining at home and found it "awfully hard work". It inspired her to teach basic skills in order to take the mystery out of cooking. She has found it "much more creative and stimulating than showing people how to make terrines". The key is working with fresh, seasonal ingredients, especially in summer which, she feels, always seems to be brief. "It makes so much sense to make the most of seasonal ingredients when you are entertaining friends."

The workshop opens with a questionnaire, sent on booking, which is designed "to reveal the importance of food in your life" and to find out just what you are aiming to achieve. It is the answers to the questionnaires that shape the course. Frances doesn't set out to be comprehensive; she suggests shortcuts, perhaps by showing how to make instant stock, reducing and finishing it, or how to reduce and freeze in ice cube trays for later use, and advises on what to keep in the fridge for ease, speed and good presentation. She firmly believes in set weekly tasks – Sunday afternoon tasks, she calls them. "Work out how long it takes you to go to Marks and Spencer to buy prepared salads and sauces," she explains. "Then, imagine using that time, say a few hours on a Sunday, for basic preparation instead, so you have your own ready made on a weekly basis in your fridge".

Basically, you learn how to do this, alongside the principles of a professional kitchen, with sauces made up, stocks ready, all ingredients prepared. You are shown how to buy and present, how to organise your fridge at home, how to plan, design and deliver well presented fresh food. Groups are small – no more than four people – and work alongside the brigade in the restaurant kitchen. Here they make pasta and risotto, bone out meat, make a soufflé ("getting the timing right"), basic sauces, simple stocks, oils, vinaigrettes, and learn how to treat fruits for dessert. The theory is that you will learn to be organised when in your own kitchen with guests. For the group, part of the thrill is working alongside skilled chefs in a Michelin starred kitchen.

Above all, the idea is to have an enjoyable time. The class is planned around dishes of the day in the restaurant, so that each pupil contributes, making the dishes with the chefs. Lunch, ultimately, includes what they have been making ("we get some strange shapes"), so that flavour is understood. A more relaxed dinner in the evening (with non-cooking partner, perhaps) reinforces this philosophy.

Most people who are vaguely competent in the domestic kitchen believe that they can invent new dishes. The idea of throwing a little bit of this or that into a well-designed recipe makes them quiver with anticipation, But, without the aid of cookbooks, what would you do with a list of ingredients such as aubergine, peas, stick beans, rabbit and fresh cod. Most of us would come up with pretty pedestrian dishes that said more about our cooking skills, or lack of them, than how we thought about taste, flavour and texture. Give the same list to Frances and instant ideas include cod served with a little soufflé with the beans dressed with a pre-made sauce, say horseradish vinaigrette, the aubergine pan-fried with the zest of a lemon and served with mozzarella, tomato, pomegranate seeds and puddles of herb oil. It is this ability to think laterally, and the simple skills to carry it off, that she teaches so well.

This unpretentious cookery course does exactly what it sets out to do – there are no gimmicks and no trickery. What you see is what you get, and what you get it is an inspiring reminder that wonderful food is often waiting in unexpected places, and that it can open up a whole new world of flavour. You will leave inspired.

The Hack & Spade Inn

Whashton, Richmond, North Yorkshire DL11 7JL
Telephone: +44(0)1748 823721
hackandspade@ukonline.co.uk

The 17th-century pub looks like an old-fashioned country local but as you walk in you get a pleasant surprise. Jeremy Jagger and Joanna Millar have really taken a lot of care in the planning and design of the place. Original beams, a stone-flagged floor, open fire and, in the restaurant, prettily laid, highly-polished tables, set the scene. In one corner stands an old Aga, with a 1950s radio, and there's an old black telephone on the bar. The menu is chalked up on boards, but there are additional printed menus, and dishes are dictated by the seasons and by whatever local farmers can supply. Thus, to start, there could be a choice of grilled black pudding on a mustard and goats' cheese mash topped with a tomato and chilli jam. Then pan-fried pork fillets on a chive mash with a creamy mushroom and brandy sauce, with bread and butter pudding or local cheeses with homemade chutney to finish. Bar snacks take in open sandwiches, potatoes filled with the likes of gammon ham and chutney, and salads. A good selection of well-priced bin ends complements a short, well-annotated and globally-ranging wine list that struggles to get above £16.

Prices: Lunch from £5, 3 course dinner £18. Main course from £7.25. Bar snack from £4.50. House wine £9.50.
Hours: 12.00-14.00. 19.00-21.00.
Closed Monday all day, Sunday evening, 25-26 December and the first week of January.
Cuisine: Traditional/Modern British.
Other Points: No-smoking area. Children welcome. Car park.
Directions: Whashton is signed south off A66 five miles west of Scotch Corner and A1. (Map 6, C5)

Why go to...Scarborough

The oldest seaside resort in the country first attracted visitors in the early 17th century, drawn by the newly discovered mineral springs. The Victorians called it the Queen of the Watering Places. Anne Brontë died here in 1849 - her tomb can be seen at the Church of St Mary. After World War II workers from the industrial heartland discovered North Bay's clean sands, quiet parks and gardens, adding a layer of kitsch amusement arcades, kids' entertainment and the miniature North Bay Railway which runs up to the Sea Life Centre. More genteel is the South Bay, where faded Regency and Victorian hotels look onto an esplanade from which a hydraulic lift idles down to the beach. All the traditional ingredients of an

Mallard Grange ★ ⌂

Aldfield, Fountains Abbey, Ripon,
North Yorkshire HG4 3BE
Telephone: +44(0)1765 620242
maggie@mallardgrange.co.uk
www.mallardgrange.co.uk

Five centuries of history are packed into Mallard
Grange, and current incumbants, the Johnson family,
have farmed here since 1933. Maggie Johnson is the
kind of person who is more than willing to go that
extra mile for all her guests, for this is the kind of
farm B&B that gives you a real feeling of getting away
from it all. Come back from a day of sightseeing or
walking to a big log fire roaring away in a roomy
sitting room that's filled with comfortable sofas and
thoughtful touches. In addition, well-equipped,
comfortable bedrooms look out on to sprawling lawns.
Two are in the main house and two in a converted
barn and they all have big beds, antique furniture,
sofas, and good bathrooms with large double showers.
In the beamed breakfast room, everyone sits around a
highly polished table set with fresh flowers, and tuck
into sausages made by the farm next door, own eggs,
award winning black pudding from Thirsk, local bacon
and smoked haddock, Whitby kippers, and homemade
jams and marmalade. Such is the commitment to local
produce, all suppliers are listed on the breakfast menu.

Hours: Closed Christmas and New Year.
Rooms: 4 en suite. £30-£35 per person per night.
Other Points: Totally no smoking. Garden. Car park.
Directions: Take the B6265 from Ripon towards Pateley Bridge.
Go past the entrance to Fountains Abbey. Mallard Grange is on the
right hand side, two and a half miles from Ripon. (Map 12, E6)

The Sawley Arms and Cottages ▮ ✕ ⌂

Sawley, Fountains Abbey, Ripon,
North Yorkshire HG64 3EQ
Telephone: +44(0)1765 620642

Immaculately kept and enduringly popular, this fine
old-fashioned dining pub lies tucked away in a quiet
village five miles south west of Ripon. June Hawes has
been here for over 34 years and has built up an
excellent reputation for good food, friendly hospitality
and more recently for quality overnight
accommodation in a newly built stone cottage.
Regulars have their preferred tables in the four
interconnecting, comfortably furnished little rooms,
each with winged armchairs, cushioned settles and
attractive plates and prints; there's also a cosy snug bar
with coal fire. Daily specials supplement June's varied
menu that is built around prime local materials,
including smoked Nidderdale trout. Expect a good
range of fresh cut sandwiches, delicious soups and
snacks or starters like salmon, celeriac and herb
pancake, and crab salad. In the evening one end of the
pub takes on a more restaurant feel, and choice
extends to steak pie with buttercrust pastry, corn-fed
chicken with creamy mushroom sauce, and halibut
with prawns and white wine. Available, on a self-
catering basis, the two very comfortable cottage suites
feature spacious lounges, fully equipped kitchens and
spotless en suite bathrooms with power showers and
bathrobes, and plenty of cosseting extras.

Prices: Main course bar meal from £7. Main course restaurant
meal from £10. House wine £9.95.
Hours: 11.30-15.00. 18.30-21.00.
Closed Sunday and Monday evening and 25 December.
Rooms: 2 cottage apartments sleeping two persons each. Prices
from £250. There are seasonal price variations, please call ahead.
Cuisine: Traditional and Modern British.
Other Points: No-smoking area. Garden. Car park.
Directions: Take the B62665 from Ripon and turn at Risplith into
Sawley village. (Map 12, E6)

Golden Grid Fish Restaurant ★ ✕

4 Sandside, Scarborough, North Yorkshire YO11 1PE
Telephone: +44(0)1723 360922
www.goldengrid.co.uk

This lovely example of a northern seaside resort restaurant is a
Scarborough landmark; a great place for very fresh fish. The restaurant
has been in John Senior's family for 110 years, reputedly Scarborough's
oldest seafood restaurant. The support comes from tourists and locals
alike, drawn as much by the unrivalled views of Flamborough Head from
the upper floors (reservations are recommended for window tables), as by
the bustling, busy atmosphere. The fish couldn't be fresher, with Atlantic
cod, haddock and plaice served with mushy peas and chips, and lemon or
Dover sole and halibut offered either grilled, herbed or meunière. Shellfish
comes in the guise of a simple crab, split in two and served with brown
bread and lemon, or try a fantastic fruits de mer platter with lobster, crab,
oysters and a selection of other shellfish. That old-fashioned northern
tradition of high tea lives on in the Golden Grid's speciality farmhouse
ham and egg tea, and it's home to the Greenlay 1873 secret recipe
sausage, which features in the all-day big breakfast. Game from Wykeham
Estates shoots makes a seasonal appearance, and even the butcher gets a
mention on the menu, so proud are they of the quality of their meat.

Prices: Main course from £5.
House wine £9.
Hours: 11.00-19.30 winter. 10.00-22.30
summer. Winter hours are flexible
due to weather.
Cuisine: Seafood.
Other Points: No-smoking area.
Children welcome.
Directions: Located on the harbourside
adjacent to the fish pier. (Map 12, D7)

The Kingfisher

Oxmoor Lane, Biggin, Sherburn-in-Elmet,
North Yorkshire LS25 6HJ
Telephone: +44(0)1977 682344
www.kingfisher-seafood-brasserie.co.uk

The Kingfisher (formerly The Blacksmith's Arms) has served the rural hamlet of Biggin for many years. Jem Sales, a former catering college lecturer who knew the pub well, took it over in 2002 and has created a very pleasant, informal restaurant, but still caters for anyone wanting to pop in for a drink. Fresh pale cream walls under red pantiles and a lovely country garden with a pond and fruit trees make the place look inviting. The entrance has retained its country pub air: the small bar offers Black Sheep Bitter and Old Speckled Hen and an additional traditional stone-flagged bar displays the blackboard menu. The three connected areas of the dining room combine to give a feeling not only of space but also of intimacy with half timbered and cream walls, low beams and candles creating a relaxed, rural atmosphere. As the name suggests, menus features fish and seafood from the East Coast Fleet, though local meat and game from Bramham Estate are available, with cheeses from the Yorkshire Dales. Much thought has gone into the wine list with house wines sourced directly from France.

Prices: Main course restaurant from £11.50.
Main course bar/snack from £8.50. House wine £9.75.
Hours: 12.00-14.00. 18.30-21.45. Sunday 12.00-19.00.
Closed Monday.
Cuisine: Eclectic.
Other Points: No-smoking area. Garden. Children welcome. Car park.
Directions: Exit33/M62. Travel on the A1 heading north. Take the Sherburn-in-Elmet exit on the B1222 for nine miles heading towards Cawood. Turn left for Biggin.
(Map 12, E6)

The Angel

Hetton, Skipton, North Yorkshire BD23 6LT
Telephone: +44(0)1756 730263
info@angelhetton.co.uk
www.angelhetton.co.uk

Old settles, a kitchen range, open fires, polished wood, rich colours, prints and paintings, this 400-year-old drovers inn glows with care. Move on into the restaurant and the high back chairs and crisp linen deliver a style that is more refined, without losing sight of the fact that this is a pub. This year, Denis and Juliet Watkins are celebrating twenty years at the Angel, and their enthusiasm remains undimmed. The food, especially, lifts the place well above the local norm with a well-constructed restaurant carte and a bar-brasserie menu. Blackboard specials in the bar mix award winning sausages and onion gravy with queen scallops baked in garlic butter and gruyère. There are always little moneybags (filo purses filled with seafood and served with lobster sauce), followed by gutsy dishes such as slowly cooked confit shoulder of lamb. The kitchen gets the chance to show off in the restaurant with a soft herb-crusted halibut layered with grain mustard, mushroom duxelle, tomato fondue and served with a lobster chive sauce. The in-depth wine list is as impressive as it is value for money. Five luxury suites in a converted barn opened in July 2003.

Prices: Set Sunday lunch £22 and set Saturday dinner £32.50.
Main course from £10.50. House wine £11.95.
Hours: 12.00-14.00. 18.00-22.30 Monday-Thursday. 12.00-14.30 Saturday and Sunday. 18.00-23.00 on Friday, 23.30 on Saturday and 22.00 on Sunday.
Food served: 12.00-14.00. 18.00-21.00 (until 21.30 on Saturday and 20.30 on Sunday).
Rooms: 5 studio suites. Double/twin room from £120.
Cuisine: Modern British
Other Points: No-smoking area. Car park.
Directions: Hetton is signposted off B6265 Grassington road, four miles north of Skipton. (Map 12, E5)

Prices: B&B. Dinner by prior arrangement.
Set dinner £29.50 (4 course).
Rooms: 3 rooms, 2 en suite. Double room from £48 per person, single from £58.
Other Points: Totally no smoking. Children welcome over 12 years old. Garden. Car park.
Directions: Travel south on the A19 from Thirsk for two miles; there are two three foot high white posts on the right hand side marking the drive entrance.
(Map 12, D6)

Spital Hill

York Road, Thirsk, North Yorkshire YO7 3AE
Telephone: +44(0)1845 522273
spitalhill@amserve.net
www.wolsey-lodges.co.uk

To find Spital Hill keep a sharp look out for two white posts on the A19 Thirsk to York road, one mile south of the intersection with the A168/A170, then follow a private road through some lovely countryside. The original Georgian farmhouse was extensively remodelled in Victorian times. Within, Ann and Robin Clough have created an impression of subtle elegance by a clever blend of period furniture, curios, watercolours, open fires and over-stuffed sofas. The dining room has panelling, leather dining chairs and a communal table around which everyone gathers for breakfast and dinner. Evening menus are based on local supplies and could include homegrown asparagus, pork fillet in a port wine sauce with dates and walnuts, local cheeses, and tarte florette lemon mousse. Attention to detail extends to homebaked breads. Bedrooms are as well presented as the food. All are individual but space, period furniture and extras such as robes, mineral water, fresh fruit and homemade shortbread make up for the lack of TV. Close to the main house is an elegantly decorated self catering cottage with two double bedrooms. Surrounding gardens and parkland cushion the house and cottage, giving a real sense of peace and tranquillity.

Allerston Manor House

Allerston, Thornton le Dale, North Yorkshire YO18 7PF
Telephone: +44(0)1723 850112
routier@allerston-manor.com
www.allerston-manor.com

The rural village of Allerston consists of a pub, a church, farmhouse and some dozen houses, and ancient Allerston Manor. The classical Queen Anne façade hides the remains of a 14th century Knights Templar hall on the site of an old castle. In the drawing room there's a magnificent marble fireplace, guarded by two marble lions, but it is the beamed dining room that occupies the original hall; it also contains an immense stone fireplace. Here meals are served at a large mahogany table. Menus are tailored to ones likes and dislikes, with good country cooking taking in baked mushrooms with Stilton on a crisp leaf salad, tender beef and black pepper casserole, or a vegetarian dish of baked butternut squash with black pilau rice. Ice creams are homemade, or there could be lemon curd bake for pudding. For breakfast, eggs come from the manors own hens, there's homemade jam, with fishcakes and kedgeree in amongst the usual choices. The house has a spacious feel and this comes over in very well equipped, traditionally styled bedrooms that sport big spacious wardrobes and lots of extras such as electric blankets and bowls of sweets.

Rooms: 3 en suite. Double and twin rooms £70-£90, single occupancy £50-£70.
Other Points: Totally non smoking. Children welcome over 12 years. Garden. Parking.
Directions: From the A64 (east of Malton) take the B1258. On leaving Yedingham turn left and then immediately right (signed to Allerston). In Allerston take the driveway on the right just after Church Lane.
(Map 12, D7)

The Star Country Inn & Restaurant

Weaverthorpe, Malton,
North Yorkshire YO17 8E
Telephone: +44(0)1944 738273
info@starinn.net
www.starinn.net

For this small rural community nestling in a peaceful Wolds valley, the Star is the heartbeat of Weaverthorpe, and the friendly atmosphere owes as much to contented and garrulous locals as to the warmth of the welcome. Located next to the parish church and dating from 1786, the Star is a rustic place, with old farming implements hanging from beams, and ales such as Taylor Landlord, Slaters Supreme, and Tetley drawn from old brass handpumps. Good country cooking too, with jugged Yorkshire hare, and rabbit pie with pan haggety making seasonal appearances, or there could be seared salmon with lime and coriander, or Brompton sausages served with sautéed onions and ale enriched sauce on the daily changing specials board. All red meats, notably prime steaks, are sourced from a local farm butcher. The five cottagey bedrooms upstairs have a simple, unpretentious, yet comfortable appeal, there are different levels, little nooks and crannies, and bags of character.

Prices: Set lunch £12.95 and dinner £18. Main course restaurant meal from £9.75. Main course bar from £7.25. House wine £10.25.
Hours: 12.00-15.00 (until 16.00 on Saturday and Sunday). 19.00-23.00. Closed Monday lunch and all day Tuesday.
Food served: 12.00-14.00 (until 15.00 on Sunday). 19.00-21.30 (until 21.00 on Wednesday and Thursday).
Rooms: 3 en suite. Double room from £50, single from £26.
Cuisine: Modern British.
Other Points: No-smoking area. No dogs. Children welcome over six years old. Garden. Car park.
Directions: From the A64 travel east to Scarborough. Bypass York and Malton. Continue 11 miles to Sherburn. Turn right at the lights and travel four miles to Weaverthorpe. (Map 12, E7)

Prices: Smokery and shop.
Hours: 09.00-16.00 Monday to Saturday. 10.00-12.00. 13.30-14.30 Sundays. Closed Christmas, 1 January.
Directions: Walk down the 199 steps from Whitby Abbey and turn right up a cobbled street. The shop is 200m on the right. (Map 12, D7)

Fortune's Kippers

22 Henrietta Street, Whitby,
North Yorkshire YO22 4DW
Telephone: +44(0)1947 601659

In the old part of Whitby, up a cobbled street underneath the Abbey ruins, is a small, slightly ramshackle shop that just pokes out of a row of houses. It is here, at the back of the shop, that some of the best kippers in the north of England are smoked: meatier in taste than anything that can be bought in a supermarket, and where you can taste the smoking and not some artificial approximation. The smoking has been done in exactly the same way since 1872, using sawdust and wood shavings, and has been run by five generations of the same family. Barry Brown is currently at the helm - a man passionate about keeping old values alive. In the small shop they display old photos of the smokery, as well as photos of the numerous foodie celebs, such as Clarissa Dickson Wright, Gary Rhodes, and Rick Stein, who have visited in the past. It is necessary to visit the shop to purchase the kippers as mail order is not available.

Magpie Café

14 Pier Road, Whitby, North Yorkshire YO21 3PU
Telephone: +44(0)1947 602058
ian@magpiecafe.co.uk
www.magpiecafe.co.uk

The queues are legendary. 'Often the queue of people waiting to enter the restaurant have to make way for deliveries of halibut, salmon, or boxes of live lobsters fresh off the boats landing at the quayside opposite' writes Ian Robson of his Whitby institution. There has been a Magpie Café in Whitby since the 1900s, but the now famous black and white 18th century building has only been its home since 1937. The extensive repertoire takes in Whitby kippers (smoked by Nobles of Henrietta Street) or a perfect Magpie trio (Whitby sole and salmon poached in a light white wine and butter sauce with griddled king scallops). Their renowned fish and chips, either haddock or cod, are served in small, regular or large sizes. The quality speaks for itself and extends to carefully sourced meat used in traditional dishes of local pork, sausage, egg and chips, or own-boiled ham with homemade coleslaw, and steak pie. Portions are in the grand Yorkshire tradition, as are puddings such as jam roly-poly and trifle, but our favourite is Yorkshire gingerbread served with Wensleydale cheese. The short wine list is global and keenly priced, and there's a good selection of bottled beers.

Prices: Main course from £5.95. House wine £8.95.
Hours: 11.30-21.00. Closed 25-26 December, 1 January and from mid January-early February.
Cuisine: Seafood.
Other Points: Totally no smoking. Children welcome.
Directions: Directly opposite the fishmarket on Whitby's historic harbourside. (Map 12, D7)

Northbeach Cafe

The Sea Wall, Whitby,
North Yorkshire YO21 3EN
Telephone: +44(0)1947 602066
manager@northbeachcafe.co.uk
www.northbeachcafe.co.uk

This is a courageous development: a former art-deco style pavilion, built in1933 on the sea wall and totally neglected for decades. It was scheduled for demolition when Darren Archibald spotted its potential. Restored to its original style, a contemporary café has been created serving light meals and refreshments throughout the day and offering good bistro style dishes in the evening; in addition, the flat roof now has a barbecue for fine weather, operating mostly at weekends. And it has proved very popular. The informal style of the place, combined with excellent service led by Rebecca Archibald (with sister-in-law Alison Halidu managing the business) draws the crowds (and there's the added attraction of being able to watch the sunrise and sunset). The menu emphasis, especially in the evening, is on local seafood, which could not be fresher, and meats and other raw materials are sourced locally; Fortune's Kippers (see entry) are suppliers, for example. There is a good choice of mostly modern wines and bottled beers and prices for both food and drink are very reasonable. One has to walk down the cliff path to reach the promenade, but transport can be arranged if needed.

Prices: Set lunch £11.95. Set dinner £19.85. Main course restaurant from £9.95. Main course bar/snack from £4.95. House wine £9.50.
Hours: 10.00-17.00. Open 1 November-16 March Friday, Saturday and Sunday only. Café open 10.00-17.00 weekends and Restaurant open Friday and Saturday 19.00-23.00.
Food served: 10.00-16.30. 19.00-21.00. All day 17 March-31 October. May close Monday/Tuesday evenings when quiet.
Cuisine: Modern British.
Other Points: Totally no smoking. Garden. Children welcome.
Directions: Exit45/A1M. Take A64 to York, then Malton, then A169 Whitby. Situated at base of west cliff on the sea wall. (Map 12, D7)

Prices: Set lunch £10. Main course from £8.95. House wine £10.95.
Hours: Food served from 08.30am all day.
Rooms: 11 en suite. Single room from £30, double from £56, family from £80.
Cuisine: Global.
Other Points: No-smoking area. Children welcome. Car park.
Directions: In the centre of Whitby. Head over the Old Swing Bridge heading east. Take the second left, a cobbled street, the White Horse is 20 metres along on the right hand side.
(Map 12, D7)

White Horse and Griffin Hotel

Church Street, Whitby, North Yorkshire YO22 4BH
Telephone: +44(0)1947 604857
reception@thewhitehorse.activehotels.com
www.whitehorseandgriffin.co.uk

You may have to look hard to ensure you are at the right place - Whitby's first coaching inn has a small narrow entrance with the name discreetly written in the curved plasterwork high above. Within, the place retains the feel of an earlier time, with old floorboards, low-beamed ceilings, narrow corridors, stone-flagging, chunky farmhouse tables and a large Yorkshire range filled with blazing logs. Upstairs is the breakfast room, which is used as a smart restaurant in the evenings, the wooden tables laid up with crisp white table linen, fresh flowers and candles. Fish is a strength on the menu, and ranges from Whitby cod in beer batter, to their special seafood medley (a delicious mix of hot and cold seafood). There's also traditional dishes such as North Yorkshire beef casserole. Bedrooms just ooze character and are beautifully designed with old sea chests, original fireplaces, and the odd beamed ceiling; one room still has a jail door incorporated into it. In addition, there are big comfortable beds, CDs, stereos, soft chairs. For 50 years the building was neglected, used by trawlermen as a fisherman's store. The hard work that Stewart Perkins has put into the place is nothing short of incredible.

England - North Yorkshire

The Spice Box

152 High Street, Boston-Spa, West Yorkshire LS23 6BW
Telephone: +44(0)1937 842558
www.thespicebox.com

Hugh Mansford owns the acclaimed Three Hares at Bilborough (see entry) and, in expanding his empire, has bought this intimate, atmospheric restaurant that was established by Karl and Amanda Mainey. In a former life the building was a chemist's shop and the two dining rooms still contain the wooden medicine drawers lining the walls. Sound country cooking is to be seen in a bistro menu that offers terrine of local rabbit and brandied Agen prunes, with herb salad, crisp chorizo and walnut dressing, and mains of fillet of red bream, creamy dill mash, wild mushroom and basil sauce. There's a bargain set lunch and dinner menu, perhaps tarte tatin of slow roasted tomatoes and shallots, shaved Parmesan and sherry vinaigrette, and foil-baked chicken parcel with peppers, red onions, lemon, garlic, rosemary, thyme and a generous splash of white wine. Choice is extended by the carte (green pea and scallop soup, steamed lemon sole fillets with cucumber, dill and glazed with brown shrimps and hollandaise), and Jaffa Cake pudding or chilled banana soufflé with Ovaltine ice cream make an interesting finish.

Prices: Set lunch and dinner £17.95. Main course from £9.50. House wine £10.95.
Hours: 12.00-14.00. 19.00-21.30.
Closed all day Sunday and Monday and 26 December-first week of New Year.
Cuisine: Classical British and European.
Other Points: Totally no-smoking. Children welcome.
Directions: South of Wetherby, just off the A1. Follow the sign for Boston-Spa. (Map 12, E6)

Weavers Bar - Restaurant

13/17 West Lane, Haworth,
West Yorkshire BD22 8DU
Telephone: +44(0)1535 643822
weavers@amserve.net
www.weaversmallhotel.co.uk

Set in the heart of this Pennine village made famous by the Brontë sisters, sits this cluttered restaurant carved out of three weavers' cottages. It offers period charm, bric-a-brac and goodwill in spades. Colin and Jane Rushworth have a down-to-earth approach to running a restaurant. A simple approach defines the cooking style with a high proportion of local ingredients used in blackboard specials of breaded and fried breast of local farm chicken, wild garlic and butter, apricot couscous and North African sauce making a point with prime raw materials and good technique. Without being over ambitious, the kitchen reveals a knowledge of modern ideas on a printed restaurant menu that delivers sesame, ginger and rhubarb dressing served with a shredded Lune Valley duck, and Morecambe Bay brown shrimps and sorrel butter with west coast lemon sole. Ginger parkin pudding with treacle toffee sauce and homegrown rhubarb ice cream, is an irrisible pudding. The global wine list is keenly priced. Three bedrooms are reached via a narrow staircase. They are well-designed, decent-sized rooms with quality fabrics, writing desks, novels on the bedside tables, comfortable chairs, and old-fashioned lights.

Prices: Set lunch and dinner £16. Main course from £11.95. House wine £11.50.
Hours: 12.00-14.00. 18.30-21.00. Closed all day Monday, Tuesday and Saturday lunch, Sunday evening and 26 December-5 January.
Rooms: 3 en suite. Double room from £85, single from £55.
Cuisine: Modern and Traditional British.
Other Points: No-smoking area. Children welcome.
Directions: Exit 24 or 26/M62 then A629. Take B6142 to centre of village, find the Parsonage Museum Car Park, Weavers backs on to it. (Map 12, E5)

Prices: Set lunch £9.95 and £12.95. Main course from £13.95. House wine £10.95.
Hours: 12.00-14.00. 19.00-21.00 (until 10.00 on Saturday).
Closed Sunday and Monday.
Rooms: 5 en suite. Double room from £70, single from £60.
Cuisine: Modern British.
Other Points: No-smoking area. Children welcome. Garden. Car park.
Directions: From A62 to Oldham take B611 to Milnsbridge and Golcar. At the Kwik Save, Milnsbridge, turn left at traffic lights into Scar Lane. One mile up the hill on the right. (Map 12, F6)

The Weavers Shed Restaurant with Rooms

Knowl Road, Golcar, Huddersfield, West Yorkshire HD7 4AN
Telephone: +44(0)1484 654284
info@weaversshed.co.uk
www.weaversshed.co.uk

It looks like a large stone house from the outside, but thick stone walls and flagstone floors within give some clue to its cloth mill ancestry. This is a civilised place, in a part of Yorkshire where folk understand value for money, this is exactly what the kitchen delivers: good value for very fair cooking from a menu built around local and home-grown supplies. There is much praise for the evident concern of both Tracy and Stephen Jackson that everything should be just right. Menus from stellar restaurants at home and abroad line one wall in the bar, the atmosphere is unhurried, and service is invariably friendly and attentive. Ideas are not lacking - a risotto of spring vegetables is given the right balance by whole herb leaves served on the side. Sound ingredients are matched by enjoyable, flavourful sauces: for example, chargrilled fillet of local beef, served with mashed potatoes, red cabbage, green beans, and oxtail sauce. The set lunch is a bargain. Five en suite bedrooms are stylishly decorated with the emphasis on simple colours and lots of extras such as sherry, half bottles of wine, and shortbread.

Dimitris Mediterranean Restaurant and Tapas Bar

Simpsons Fold, Dock St, Leeds, West Yorkshire LS10 1JF
Telephone: +44(0)113 246 0339
leeds@dimitris.co.uk
www.dimitris.co.uk

The Manchester original (see entry) may have a more bohemian and laid-back atmosphere, but the younger Leeds branch is more upbeat. The former bakery in a cobbled street has been transformed with a look that mixes simplicity with a touch of rural chic. Terracotta walls, sporting black ancient Greek imagery, contrast with bare brick, wood floors, and a fantastic old wooden ceiling - it is all lifted by lots of natural lighting flooding through big windows. The menu is the same as Manchester, with only daily specials and the occasional lunch menus differing. This means popular dips, keftedes (lambmeat balls with tomato sauce) and grilled Cypriot cheese among the Greek dishes, goats' cheese and sun-dried tomatoes with olives and couscous, mushrooms in garlic butter, and steak au poivre among the more general Mediterranean offerings. Mezes such as the Kalamata platas and the mega mezzes are brilliant set-menu deals for two or more people, and the good fresh food at affordable prices policy ensures a popular following. Dimitris is a lively place with excellent, professional service. The wine list takes a popular global view and includes a few well-priced Greek wines; prices are mainly under £15.

Prices: Set lunch from £9.95. Set dinner from £13.95. House wine £10.95.
Hours: 11.00-23.15. Closed 25-26 December and 1 January.
Cuisine: Mediterranean and Greek.
Other Points: Children welcome. Car park, evenings only.
Directions: Two minutes walk from Leeds City station. Over Leeds bridge and past the Malmaison Hotel. Take the first left at the Adelphi pub into Dock Street. (Map 12, E6)

Mill Race Organic Restaurant

2 Commercial Road, Kirkstall, Leeds, West Yorkshire LS5 3AQ
Telephone: +44(0)113 275 7555
enquiries@themillrace-organic.com
www.themillrace-organic.com

This relaxed, laid-back organic restaurant is made up of early 19th century cottages close to Kirkstall Abbey grounds. All ingredients, including beer and wines, are certified by the Soil Association, UK Farmers and Growers, or similar international certifying bodies. Upstairs is a casual, relaxed sitting room, filled with deep sofas and is the only place where you can smoke. Downstairs, the dining room has big windows with frosted glass at the bottom to shield everyone from the sight of the traffic outside. The upbeat, contemporary menu opens with seared savoury cheesecake with four cheeses and honey beetroot salad. Main courses range from breast of chicken stuffed with almond and saffron on bubble and sqeak polenta with raisin and black olive sauce, to Thai noodles with peanut sauce and deep-fried tofu, served with a spicy carrot and lemon salad. Blackboard evening specials bring the likes of Yorkshire reared pork chop with apple and sage mash with a creamy cider sauce. After this chocoholics should head straight for the triple chocolate cheesecake with dark chocolate sauce and chocolate ice cream. The well-annotated organic wine list ranges far and wide and is reasonably priced.

Prices: Main course from £10. House wine £10.95.
Hours: 17.30-22.00 Tuesday-Saturday. 12.00-15.00 on Sunday. Closed Monday.
Cuisine: Modern British.
Other Points: No-smoking area. Children welcome.
Directions: Two miles from the centre of Leeds on the A65 Skipton road; close to Kirkstall abbey and opposite Kirkstall Leisure/sports centre. (Map 12, E6)

The Millbank

Millbank, Sowerby Bridge, Halifax, West Yorkshire HX6 3DY
Telephone: +44(0)1422 825588
millbankph@ukonline.co.uk
www.themillbank.com

Christine and Paul Halsey's stylishly modernised old stone pub stands on a steep hill above Sowerby Bridge with great views over rolling Yorkshire countryside. The contemporary reworking of a traditional pub interior cleverly combines log-burning fires, flagstone floors and old wooden church pews with chunky modern furniture, stripped wooden floors, bold colours, abstract art, and a smartly decked terrace that makes the most of the pastoral view. Matching this relaxing and cosmopolitan style is an imaginative modern European menu that draws the crowds. The emphasis is on the use of fresh local produce simply prepared. Sausage of confit chicken and sweetbread with flageolet beans and pancetta may feature among starters on the evening carte. For main course try a dish of Holy Island lobster ravioli with asparagus, vermouth and tarragon, or Hartshead Moor pheasant with creamed lentils and pistachios, and finish with banana and walnut pudding with caramel sauce and banana cream. Excellent snacks in the bar may include braised oxtail with mash. The wine list is usefully divided by style, and there are 10 by the glass, as well as a good range of bottled Belgian beers.

Prices: Set lunch and dinner £13.90. Main course from £9.50. Bar meal from £7.95. House wine £9.95.
Hours: 12.00-15.00 Wednesday-Saturday. 17.30-23.00 Tuesday-Saturday. 12.00-22.30 on Sunday. Closed all day Monday, Tuesday lunch and the first two weeks of October.
Food served: 12.00-14.00. 17.30-21.30 Tuesday-Thursday. 18.00-22.00 Saturday. 12.30-15.30 Sunday. No food Sunday evening.
Cuisine: Modern European.
Other Points: No-smoking area. Children welcome. Garden.
Directions: J22/M62. Take the A58 towards Sowerby Bridge, then

The Old Bridge Inn

Priest Lane, Ripponden, Halifax, West Yorkshire HX6 4DF
Telephone: +44(0)1422 822595

Cottage-style flower boxes create a vivid splash of colour against the whitewashed stone walls of this historic 14th-century inn, set beside a cobbled packhorse bridge over the River Ryburn. Easy to miss as there is no inn sign, but once inside you may find a welcoming log fire burning in each of the three comfortable bar areas, which retain their medieval charm of crooked walls, original beams and nice old furniture. In fact, the modern world intrudes little into the current interior, which remains delightfully unspoilt and free from noisy machines, music, or a pool table. Instead, Yorkshire's oldest hostelry offers traditional hospitality and good homecooked food, including an excellent-value weekday buffet lunch, or homemade soups and freshly-cut sandwiches. The main blackboard menu (available weekday evenings and weekend lunchtimes only) may list lamb, aubergine and lentil curry, fishermans pie, and traditional meat and potato pie with pickled red cabbage, and homemade puddings like tangy lemon tart. A good showing of real ales includes tip-top northern brews from Timothy Taylor and Black Sheep. In addition, there is a good selection of foreign bottled beers and a global list of wines with a dozen offered by the glass.

Prices: Buffet lunch £9.50. Main course from £6. House wine £9.25.
Hours: 12.00-15.00. 17.30-23.00. 12.00-23.00 Saturday and Sunday.
Food served: 12.00-14.00. 18.00-21.30. No food on Saturday and Sunday evening.
Cuisine: Traditional home-cooked English.
Other Points: No-smoking area. Children welcome until 20.00. Garden. Car park.
Directions: J22/M62. From here follow signs for Ripponden/Halifax. Take the first right after the traffic lights in Ripponden, then first left. (Map 12, F5)

Shibden Mill Inn

Shibden Mill Fold, Shibden, Halifax,
West Yorkshire HX3 7UL
Telephone: +44(0)1422 365840
shibdenmillinn@zoom.co.uk
www.shibdenmillinn.com

While retaining an appealing rustic tone, this white painted, rambling old inn has succeeded admirably at the difficult task of being simultaneously a simple pubby brasserie, a restaurant with serious aspirations, and a rather fine place to stay the night. This is a class act with Adrian Jones heading the kitchen, bringing skill and finesse to the cooking. Simplicity appears to be the key to the operation, and good ingredients (much of it local) and clear, well defined flavours are to be seen in a starter of crayfish tails with a refreshing salad of radish and french bean salad, in roast skate with bubble and squeak, and an astonishing grilled honeycomb apple with cider granita. A self-proclaimed champion of British produce, Adrian makes the best of fine materials. His take on British classics includes his version of cod fish fingers, pickled onions and salad cream, and English tapas, served in the bar. Own-baked bread deserves a special mention. Wines are well chosen, with a Connoisseur Collection adding weight. There are twelve bedrooms, all comfortably decorated with warmth and style and well appointed with dressing gowns and TV videos (there's a well-stocked video library in reception).

Prices: Main course from £10. Main course bar meal from £8. House wine £9.95.
Hours: 12.00-15.00. 17.30-23.00. Saturday 12.00-23.00. Sunday 12.00-22.30.
Food served: 12.00-14.00. 18.00-21.30 Monday to Saturday. 12.00-19.30 Sunday.
Rooms: 12 en suite. Singles from £60, doubles from £72.
Cuisine: Modern British.
Other Points: Children welcome. Garden. Car park.
Directions: Exit26/M62 on A 58; turn right into Kell Lane at Stump Cross Inn (near A6036 junction), then pub signposted. (Map 12, E5)

Rose and Crown

Cop Hill, Slaithwaite, Huddersfield,
West Yorkshire HD7 5XA
Telephone: +44(0)1484 844410

This large, white-painted former farmhouse, lies hidden in the heart of Last of the Summer Wine country, a sibling of the nearby Rams Head at Denshaw (see entry, Saddleworth). It is a popular watering hole for local farmers and walkers who fill the traditional bar in search of a decent pint of Black Sheep Bitter. Food is equally important, the extensive blackboards listing homecooked pub food that utilises fresh seasonal produce with seafood and winter game considered specialities. Dishes range from starters of dressed crab with lemon mayonniase, potted duck with poached pear and mulled wine, and seared scallops on sun-dried tomato risotto, to mains of battered haddock with handcut chips, wild boar steak with roasted root vegetables and pan juices, and a hearty beef stew. Puddings include rum and raisin rice pudding and a traditional sticky toffee pudding with caramel sauce. Good lunchtime sandwiches - smoked chicken and bacon club. The newly converted barn houses a private dining or function room.

Prices: Main course from £8.95. House wine £7.95.
Hours: 12.00-14.30. 18.00-22.00 Monday to Saturday. Sunday and Bank Holidays 12.00-20.30. Drinks only on 25 December.
Cuisine: Modern British with seafood and game specialities.
Other Points: No-smoking area. Children welcome. Garden. Car park. Separate Dining room available for parties.
Directions: From Huddersfield at exit 23 (M62) follow A640 towards Rochdale. Turn left and follow road for half a mile. Take the right fork down Laund road and continue for three miles. (Map 12, F5)

SCOTLAND

Loch Kinord Hotel

Ballater Road, Dinnet, Ballater,
Aberdeenshire AB34 5JY
Telephone: +44(0)13398 85229
stay@kinord.com
www.kinord.com

This former Victorian coaching inn occupies a
prominent location on the A93, in the heart of Royal
Deeside. The owners appear to have a good grasp of
what a Scottish hotel ought to offer, which includes
comfortable, stylish surroundings and good food.
Roast breast of woodland pigeon with glazed
vegetables, crisp pancetta and brown butter dressing,
or own made ravioli of mushroom with an Arran
mustard and whisky cream typify starters in the
restaurant. Mains run to honey roasted duck with
clapshot potato, roasted leeks and cardamom scented
jus, or thyme-roasted chump of lamb leg with fondant
potato and chargrilled Mediterranean vegetables, with
rich chocolate tart with chocolate sorbet and apricot
compote for pudding. The well-annotated wine list has
wide appeal and very reasonable prices; six wines are
offered by the glass. Bedrooms are all en suite, are very
well maintained and stylishly decorated, with under
12s free in their parent's room. There is live music in
the bar on Friday evenings and lots of local colour.

Prices: Main course from £9. House wine £9.
Hours: 12.00-14.00. 18.00-21.00.
Rooms: 15 not all en suite. Rooms from £30 per person.
Cuisine: Modern Scottish.
Other Points: No-smoking area. Children welcome. Garden.
Car park. Licence for Civil Weddings.
Directions: On the main A93, Aberdeen to Braemar Road, in the
village of Dinnet, midway between Aboyne and Ballater.
(Map 16, F7)

The Station Restaurant

Station Square, Ballater, Aberdeenshire AB35 5RB
Telephone: +44(0)13397 55050

The little town of Ballater is well known for its close
association with the Royal Family (eight miles away in
Balmoral Castle). No more so than the small cream
and red wooden railway station that welcomed royals
and their guests from the 1860s until its closure in
1966. However, the now disused station has fallen into
good hands. Nigel Franks, hotelier and train
enthusiast, has bought the station's refreshment rooms
and transformed them into a fun, informal restaurant.
Many of the original features including wood panelling
and a smoked glass ceiling still exist and are tastefully
offset with wicker chairs, marble tables and green
palms. And if only all railway food could be as good.
Opening for breakfast with porridge and cream, french
toast or a full Scottish monty, and moving on through
cakes and cappuccino, to light dishes of sweetcorn
fritters with bacon, roasted tomatoes and rocket, or a
more substantial crispy beer-battered haddock with
french fries and a green salad, the Station has a
something-for-everyone appeal. Blackboard daily
specials extend the choice, raw materials are sourced
locally, and there is a homely appeal to the cooking –
we would return just for the straight-out-of-the-oven
scones, the best we had ever tasted.

Prices: Main course from £6. House wine £12.
Hours: 09.00-17.00. 18.00-21.00. Seasonal variations.
Cuisine: Scottish.
Other Points: Totally no smoking. Children welcome. Car park.
Directions: In central Ballater, the old royal station. (Map 16, F7)

Prices: Set lunch £16.50. Set dinner
£29.50. House wine £14.50.
Hours: 12.00-14.00. 19.00-21.00. Closed
25 December evening-30 December.
Rooms: 21 en suite. Double room from
£90, single from £60.
Cuisine: Modern Scottish/French.
Other Points: No-smoking area. Children
welcome. Garden. Car park. Licence for
Civil Weddings. Tennis court. Croquet.
Directions: From Banchory take A93 then
A980 towards Torphins for approximately
two miles. Raemoir House is across the
crossroads. (Map 16, F7)

Raemoir House Hotel

Raemoir, Banchory, Aberdeenshire AB31 4ED
Telephone: +44 (0)1330 824884
relax@raemoir.com
www.raemoir.com

The classical mansion, set at the end of a winding drive, is surrounded by
3,500 acres of parkland and forest of Royal Deeside. Within, it's a visual
feast: a low-lit corridor of lamps, candles, draped curtains and vases of
scented flowers, the bar (a glorious room giving on to the garden), the
morning room where high ceilings and impressive marble fireplace strive
to make this a grand room, but family photographs, books, and a muted
colour scheme leave a calming and relaxed impression. One of the more
unusual rooms is the oval ballroom, now the restaurant. It is a tranquil
place where the cooking is distinguished by clean flavours and precise
technique. This might mean an early summer meal of seared loin of tuna
with a herb salad and gazpacho dressing, fillet of sea bass with herb
couscous, peas, broad beans and a spinach cream, and rhubarb tart with
its own sorbet and light syrup to finish. The bedrooms are just as lavish,
perhaps the flagship is the Old English Suite with an Elizabethan four-
poster bed. There is more luxurious accommodation in a small annexe
that lies behind the main house. This is the original Raemoir House, now
known as the Ha' Hoose and dates from the 16th-century.

Banff Springs Hotel

Golden Knowes Road, Banff,
Aberdeenshire AB45 2JE
Telephone: +44(0)1261 812881
team@banffspringshotel.co.uk
www.banffspringshotel.co.uk

The location is stunning. Open views reach right across the Moray Firth, there are nearby cliff top path walks, secluded coves, pristine beaches and sandy caves - this is the place to view the Northern Lights, superb sunsets and the Moray Firth dolphins. The privately owned Banff Springs is a relatively small, modern hotel - just 31 ensuite bedrooms - large enough to create a buzz, small enough to offer good, friendly service. The air-conditioned restaurant and brasserie, for example, offer superb views with local suppliers providing all poultry, fish, and meat, with fresh local beef and seafood a speciality on the internationally inspired menu.

Prices: Set dinner £25. House wine £11.50.
Hours: 12.00-14.00. 18.00-21.00 (brasserie 17.00-21.00).
Rooms: 31 en suite. Double room from £63, superior single from £45, single from £36.
Cuisine: Modern Scottish.
Other Points: Children welcome. Garden.
Directions: On the western outskirts of Banff on the A98 Fraserburgh-Elgin road. (Map 16, E7)

Loch Melfort Hotel

Arduaine, Oban, Argyll & Bute PA34 4XG
Telephone: +44(0)1852 200233
reception@lochmelfort.co.uk
www.lochmelfort.co.uk

On a clear day the view across the Sound of Jura is quite magnificent, and the hotel's claim to have the 'finest location on the west coast' is hard to dispute. The main frame of the Edwardian house has been much extended, but Nigel and Kyle Schofield manage to conjure up an image of life that has gone unchanged for decades. A keen eye for décor has updated colours and fabrics, with, for example, the popular bistro (the Skerry) taking on a bright, breezy Mediterranean look. Bedrooms in the main house are spacious and some have spectacular loch views; cheerful rooms in the Cedar Wing are simpler. Food in the restaurant is very good, specialising in locally caught fish and seafood, much of it collected straight from the boat in front of the hotel. Meat and game are also locally sourced. Dinner could bring local shellfish bisque or twice-baked Dunshyre Blue soufflé, followed by grilled fillet of sea bass with sautéed asparagus and sugarsnaps, tomato and chive butter sauce, or roast gigot of Barbeck lamb on a ring of clapshot with redcurrant jus. A well-annotated wine list spans a good range of styles and prices.

Prices: Set price dinner £25-34. House wine £12.50.
Hours: 12.00-14.30. 19.00-21.00. Restaurant open evenings only. Closed 4-22 Jan.
Rooms: 26 en suite. Double/twin from £90, single from £55.
Cuisine: Modern Scottish.
Other Points: No-smoking area. Dogs welcome. Children welcome. Garden. Car park.
Directions: 19 miles south of Oban on the A816. (Map 13, C3)

Greenbank Guest House

Arrochar, Argyll & Bute G83 7AL
Telephone: +44(0)1301 702305
shirleyandsam@cluer101.freeserve.co.uk

This 19th century house is now a small, attractive guesthouse and ideal for those on a limited budget. Right in the centre of Arrochar, the place is bustling in summer, peaceful in winter. Views from the dining room and some of the bedrooms are wonderful, taking in the famous Cobbler Mountain as well as Loch Long. Everything is well maintained, with a cosy feel to the lounge and bar area; the four en suite bedrooms are warm and homely. Food is available all day, with a series of menus ranging from snacks and light lunches to a full carte. Scotch broth, mussels from the Isle of Mull, and fried Loch Fyne herring in oatmeal and haggis and neeps are typical choices.

Prices: Set lunch and dinner £10.95. Main course from £7. House wine £9.95.
Hours: 11.00-20.00 November-March. 11.00-22.00 rest of year. Closed 25 December and 1 January.
Rooms: 4 en suite. Double room from £37, single from £22 including breakfast.
Cuisine: Traditional Scottish/seafood.
Other Points: No-smoking area. Children welcome. Garden. Car park. Licence for Civil Weddings.
Directions: On the A83, opposite Cobbler Mountain. (Map 14, C5)

Turning bags at the oyster farm, Loch Fyne

CAIRNDOW, ARGYLL & BUTE

Loch Fyne Oyster Bar and Seafood Restaurant

Cairndow, Clachan, Argyll & Bute PA26 8BL
Telephone: +44(0)1499 600236
info@loch-fyne.com
www.loch-fyne.com

Home of the late John Noble's renowned oyster fishery, the original Loch Fyne has one of the most beautiful settings of any restaurant in the British Isles - on the edge of the largest sea loch in Scotland. From the windows of the simple, wood-themed brasserie-style restaurant one can see where oysters and mussels are grown, and the smoke house is located just behind the restaurant. The taste of oysters fresh out of the salt water is memorable, but smokery products are outstanding too, especially own-smoked salmon, as well as some particularly good smoked cod's roe, or smoked haddock poached in milk and served with an egg. The basic philosophy of serving very fresh fish from the loch with little embellishment works well and the grilled or poached fish of the day is consistently and immaculately timed. Chargrilled halibut, for example, arrives with lemon and parsley butter. Isle of Mull cheddar is an alternative to homemade puddings. In addition, the old-style Highland bar makes the perfect lunch pit stop for some simple fish dishes, on one of the most lovely drives in Scotland. Some 27 wines are listed, with eight by the glass.

Prices: Main course from £10. House wine £9.95.
Hours: 09.00-20.30 Easter to October. 09.00-17.00 October to Easter, phone for weekend and evening bookings. Closed 25-26 December and 1-2 January.
Cuisine: Seafood.
Other Points: No-smoking area. Children welcome. Car parks.
Directions: A82 from Glasgow/M8 to A83 Campbeltown road. Situated at the head of Loch Fyne. (Map 13, B4)

CARDROSS, ARGYLL & BUTE

Ardardan Estate Farm Shop & Nursery

Cardross, Argyll & Bute G82 5HD
Telephone: +44 (0)1389 849188
www.ardardanestate.co.uk

When a compulsory order for road widening was put on the Montgomery's Brown Egg Farm Shop on the other side of the Clyde, they put the cash boost from the council and their 20 years of experience into a farm estate some 30 minutes away. Now, after four years of hard work, their super farm shop, along with its small plant nursery, walled garden, woodland walks and working farm is drawing folk from Glasgow and further afield, as it is en route for the Highlands via Loch Lomond. The farm has sheep, free-range chickens and bantams, and a few Highland cows, and they grow their own summer fruit. In the farm shop they stock a huge variety of Scottish produce: clover and heather honey, free-range eggs, fruit and vegetables in season (not all locally grown), locally made cakes and biscuits, homemade jams and chutneys, smoked and cured meats and fish, and a wide range of organic ice creams including Orkney ice cream. There's also the option of picking your own strawberries and raspberries in season. The coffee shop next to the plant nursery serves light lunches from a menu built around traditional Scottish food such as homemade soups, and bakery goods are available.

Hours: 10.00-16.00.
Closed Christmas Day, Boxing Day and 1-3 January.
Cuisine: Light lunches.
Other Points: No-smoking area. Dogs welcome. Children welcome. Garden. Car park.
Directions: M8 motorway, go over the Erskine Bridge. Two miles from Cardross on the A814 towards Helensburgh. (Map 14, C5)

Prices: Meals from £4.90.
Hours: 10.00-17.00. Closed 25 December.
Cuisine: Modern Scottish.
Other Points: Totally no smoking.
Children welcome. Garden.
Directions: From the A82 follow the signs
for Luss. The café is next to the church in
the centre of the village. (Map 14, C5)

Coach House Coffee Shop

Loch Lomond Trading Co Ltd, Luss, Loch Lomond,
Loch Lomond Trossachs National Park, Argyll & Bute G83 8NN
Telephone: +44(0)1436 860341
enquiries@lochlomondtrading.com
www.lochlomondtrading.com

The atmosphere is homely, warm and welcoming at this super old-style
coach house. With its preponderance of exposed beams, rustic huge stone
fireplace, and solid wooden tables and chairs, you are hard pressed to tell
that this is a new building. Although quite large, the coffee shop has a
cosy feel, and is set in the centre of one of the most visited villages on the
banks of Loch Lomond. Open all day, it caters for everyone. The kilted
Gary Grove and his wife Rowena offer an ever-revolving repertoire.
Scones, cakes such as caramel apple granny or Skeachan fruit cake, light
lunches of homebaked quiche with coleslaw, salad and fresh bread, or
stokies (traditional soft bread rolls) filled with egg mayonnaise from their
own free range Black Rock hens, form the bedrock of the menu. Haggis,
neeps and tatties, and bacon and courgette pasta make filling lunch
dishes; indeed, portions are generous. There's a separate menu offering a
wide range of espressos, cappuccinos and lattes, speciality teas and
smoothies. Unlicensed.

Lodge on Loch Lomond

★ ▯ ✕ ✑

By Alexandria, Luss, Argyll & Bute G83 8PA
Telephone: +44(0)1436 860201
res@loch-lomond.co.uk
www.loch-lomond.co.uk

On the edge of Luss, the long, linear building (built
some 12 years ago), hugs the shore of Loch Lomond,
every window making the most of the setting. The
hotel is entirely pine clad, including all 30 bedrooms,
the atmosphere is Scottish without the tweeness that
often accompanies the tartan, the welcome warm, and
the views across Loch Lomond are spectacular.
Bedrooms range from standard and executive rooms
with sitting areas to the President Carter Suite, which
has its own separate sitting room. In addition, all
bedrooms have their own sauna, as well as smart
modern bathrooms; magnificent views are standard.
A lack of pretension, coupled with meticulous
attention to detail, characterises the running of both
hotel and restaurant. In the latter, among winning
interpretations of established ideas, haggis and black
pudding parfait has appeared with apple and pear
chutney, and three fish kedgeree with a soft poached
egg on the set price dinner menu. Mains deliver the
likes of pan-seared Shetland salmon with a white
tomato risotto, tapenade and basil dressing, or a range
of steaks from quality aged grass-fed Aberdeenshire
beef with classic accompaniments. The wine list is a
well annotated global tour with plenty of good
drinking.

Prices: Set lunch £10.95. Set dinner £21.95. Main course restaurant
from £12. Main course bar/snack from £6. House wine £11.95.
Hours: 12.00-17.00 (until 16.00 on Sunday). 18.00-21.45.
Rooms: 45 en suite. Double/twin from £85. Single from £50,
family room from £110.
Cuisine: Modern British.
Other Points: No-smoking area. Dogs welcome. Children
welcome. Garden. Car park. Licence for Civil Weddings.
Directions: On the A82 on the western shores of Loch Lomond.
(Map 14, C5)

Fishermen's Pier Fish and Chip Van

✕

Raraig House, Tobermory, Argyll & Bute PA75 6PU
Telephone: +44(0)1688 302390
jeanette@scotshop.biz
www.silverswift.co.uk/chipvan

For traditional fish-and-chip junkies, things don't get
any better than Jeanette Gallagher and Jane MacLean's
take-away fish and chips from this seafront fish-and-
chip van on Tobermory's Fisherman's Pier. Here for 13
years now, they occupy an amazing setting in a unique
position overlooking Tobermory Bay, famous for the
sinking of a galleon from the Spanish Armada in 1588.
Fish comes straight off the boats and into the van
where it is cooked to order. At times, the queues are
long (even in bad weather), but always good
humoured.

Prices: Average price of meal £3.80.
Hours: 12.30-21.00. Closed Sunday and January, February, March.
Cuisine: Seafood.
Directions: On the Fisherman's Pier in Tobermory. (Map 13, B3)

Cosses Country House ★ 🛏✕🍴
Ballantrae, South Ayrshire KA26 OLR
Telephone: +44 (0)1465 831363
staying@cossescountryhouse.com
www.cossescountryhouse.com

The beautiful country house, tastefully converted from a former small shooting lodge, is set amid woodland in a little quiet valley. It's full of antique furniture, chintzy covers and curtains, lovely paintings, flowers and is a find in an area not known for its culinary highlights. It is not unusual for Glaswegians to make the one-hour drive and stay the night at this very up-market B&B, just to have dinner. Susan Crosthwaite's famous breakfasts are also a draw. The small stable block has also been converted into two bedrooms (mini-suites, really, with their own sitting rooms and bathrooms). The one bedroom in the house has a lovely outlook over the garden, but this room is slightly smaller. Susan takes great care in ensuring that raw materials are local or home-grown. A typical dinner might include natural smoked cod risotto with fresh asparagus, fillet and loin of Ayrshire lamb roasted with garlic and ginger and served with a Madeira and redcurrant sauce, and strawberry and elderflower shortcakes with Melba sauce. There's a good selection of wines from France and the new world. For devotees of Susan's cooking see her book, *A Country Cook's Garden in South West Scotland*.
Prices: Set dinner £25 (4 courses). House wine £8.20.
Hours: Drinks at 19.30, dinner served at 20.00 or when guests require. Occasionally closed 25 December-2 January, phone to check.
Rooms: 3 en suite. Double room from £38-£45. £10 single supplement. Family room from £100.
Cuisine: Scottish.
Other Points: No-smoking area. Garden. Children welcome over 12 years old. Car park. Games room with snooker and table tennis.
Directions: Take the A77 from Glasgow or Stranraer. South of Ballantrae take the inland road, at the caravan sign. Cosses is two miles along on the right hand side. (Map 13, E4)

Auchen Castle Hotel and Restaurant 🛏✕🍴
Beattock, Moffat, Dumfries & Galloway DG10 9SH
Telephone: +44 (0)1683 300407
reservations@auchen-castle-hotel.co.uk
www.auchen-castle-hotel.co.uk

Built in Scottish baronial style in1849 for General Johnstone, and later the home of Sir William Younger, this is a house with real character, outside and in. First, the view over 30 acres of lush gardens, mature woodlands and its own trout loch, to green hills beyond is glorious and restful. Next, the house with ornate period features and classically proportioned, spacious rooms, is run along old-fashioned lines, with attention paid to good service. Bedrooms are split between the lodge and the main house, but all are very well equipped and appointed with every amenity. Public rooms are elegant. The restaurant delivers a traditional menu that could open with chicken liver pâté with oatcakes, go on to grilled haddock with prawn sauce, and finish with fruit pie and cream or a selection of Scottish cheeses. The wine list offers affordable drinking with a number of bottles under £20.
Prices: Table d'hote £25. Main course from £14.95. House wine £14.95.
Hours: 19.00-21.00. 12.00-14.00. Sunday lunch. Closed Monday-Saturday lunch.
Rooms: 25 en suite. Singles from £48-£75, doubles from £55-£95.
Cuisine: Traditional British.
Other Points: No-smoking area. Children welcome. Garden. Car park. Licensed for civil weddings.
Directions: Exit15/M75. Two miles from Moffat. (Map 14, E6)

Prices: Set Sunday lunch £13.25. Set dinner, 5 courses £27.50. Main course restaurant from £12.75. Main course bar/snack from £6.25. House wine £12.50.
Hours: 12.00-14.00. 19.00-20.30. Closed from the first Saturday in December to the second last Saturday in February.
Rooms: 20 en suite. Double from £114.
Cuisine: Modern British.
Other Points: No-smoking area. Dogs/children welcome. Garden. Car park.
Directions: Auchencairn is on the A711 between Dalbeattie and Kirkcudbright. On reaching Auchencairn turn along the Shore Road for two miles. (Map 14, F6)

Balcary Bay Hotel 🛏✕🍴
Shore Road, Auchencairn, Castle Douglas, Dumfries & Galloway DG7 1QZ
Telephone: +44(0)1556 640217
reservations@balcary-bay-hotel.co.uk
www.balcary-bay-hotel.co.uk

For nearly two decades Graeme Lamb has slowly enhanced his hotel, creating space and comfort. The entrance hall-cum-reception leads to a large, comfortably appointed oak-panelled lounge with open fire and fine bay views. Off this is a residents' lounge, furnished in full country house rig, with a separate cocktail bar and terrace overlooking the sea – popular for pre-dinner drinks and good value light meals at lunchtime. Three new superior bedrooms are on the ground floor – original bedrooms are on the first and second floors – all are roomy, furnished and equipped to a particularly high standard, but those overlooking the bay are the pick. There are fantastic views from the pastel-coloured dining room whose windows look over the sea as well as the gardens. Here, the emphasis is firmly on flavour and quality. Local produce features strongly on menus that include starters of ravioli of fresh lobster and pickled dill served with braised Puy lentils, and mains of rosette of local beef fillet and sautéed mushrooms. Similarly, the wines are well chosen and represent the classic and new wine producing areas of the world.

Prices: Set dinner £16.50 served at 19.00. House wine £9.95.
Hours: Closed 24 December - 2 January.
Rooms: 7 en suite. Double/twin from £35. Single from £45. Prices are per person.
Other Points: No-smoking area. Dogs welcome. Garden. Children welcome. Car park.
Directions: M74. Leave the motorway on the A75 to Dumfries. Follow the signs to Castle Douglas, after nine miles go through the village of Crocketford, turn right on the A712. Craigadam is two miles along on the right hand side. (Map 14, F6)

Craigadam

Castle Douglas, Dumfries & Galloway DG7 3HU
Telephone: +44(0)1556 650233
enquiry@craigadam.com
www.craigadam.com

The substantial, 300-year-old whitewashed farmhouse is set a couple of hundred yards back from the A712 that heads west to New Galloway and Newton Stewart. There are views southwards over rolling hills and distant views northwestwards to the higher Galloway hills. Cecilia Pickup runs Craigadam as a charming guesthouse, but with the space, style and service of a country house, while Richard, her husband, runs the farm that operates organically. This conveys the dedication they bring to their businesses: guests benefit from the attention to detail in bedrooms and public rooms and from the quality of produce used. An excellent set dinner is served that may include locally smoked salmon, home-reared lamb, or estate game, with own-grown vegetables, homebaked bread and regional cheeses. All seven bedrooms and ensuite bathrooms are generously proportioned and furnished - many have french doors opening onto a gravelled courtyard – and are decorated in different styles, oriental or Rennie Macintosh, for example. Public rooms are also spacious, with the bay windowed lounge being particularly comfortable. The dining room is grand with a massive communal oak table, off this is a room with a full-size snooker table and honesty bar

Trigony House Hotel

Closeburn, Thornhill, Dumfries,
Dumfries & Galloway DG3 5EZ
Telephone: +44(0)1848 331211

This attractive, tastefully decorated and spacious creeper-clad old house is noted for restful surroundings and an unfussy approach. The lounge, for example, has a wood-burning stove, comfortable sofas and looks out onto the garden, and the lounge bar, where meals may be taken as an alternative to the non-smoking dining room, is warmed by an open fire. Menus make a virtue of simplicity, as owner-cum-chef Adam Moore is proud of his top quality materials provided by a network of suppliers, including the neighbouring farm, which is certified organic. Added to this, the kitchen garden is coming back to life as the gardens are restored to their former glory. Thoughtful and well-balanced starters might include a straightforward salad of goats' cheese and garden beetroot with a sun-dried tomato dressing. The choice at main course might be between braised shoulder and pan-fried fillet of organic black-faced lamb with flageolet bean, aubergine and basil, or organic Galloway beef braised with wild mushrooms, red wine and served with buttered noodles. There are eight en suite bedrooms of different sizes and style, but all are attractively decorated and furnished. Most have king-sized beds, enjoy views over the gardens and rolling countryside; housekeeping standards are high.

Prices: Main course restaurant from £10.50. Main course bar/snack from £7.90. House wine £10.50.
Hours: 17.30-20.30.
Rooms: 8 en suite. Double/twin from £80. Single from £40.
Cuisine: Modern European.
Other Points: No-smoking area. Dogs welcome. Garden. Children welcome. Car park.
Directions: M74/M6. Take the M6 north until Gretna Green then turn left onto the A75 towards Dumfries and Stranraer. Turn onto the A76 to Kilmarnock for 12 miles heading north. (Map 14, E6)

Garden House Hotel

Sarkfoot Road, Gretna, Dumfries & Galloway
DG16 5EP
Telephone: +44(0)1461 337621
enquiries@gardenhouse.co.uk
www.gretna-weddings.net

Just across the Scottish Border, the Garden House takes its cue from that famous blacksmith's shop a couple of miles away. This is the place for modern Gretna weddings, complete with a Japanese water garden and with several stylish honeymoon suites to choose from. However, spacious, well-equipped bedrooms that offer real value for money, and a state-of-the-art swimming pool with sauna and steam room, act as a lure for weary travellers too; families, in particular, will find the hotel a useful stopping point on a journey north or south. The lounge and dining room are bright and open-plan. In the latter, a traditionally robust country house menu delivers something for everyone, be it salads such as Waldorf and Caesar, meats from the chargrill, say fillet steak with crushed black peppercorn sauce, or rack of lamb with redcurrant sauce, and fish in the guise of lemon sole with basil and herb butter, or Solway salmon steak with a lemon and herb crust. Some 80 or so wines make a good effort to keep prices within reason.

Prices: Main course from £11. House wine £8.25.
Hours: 12.00-14.00. 19.00-21.00.
Rooms: 38 en suite. Bed and Breakfast from £42.50 per person.
Cuisine: Modern British.
Other Points: Children welcome. Garden. Car park. Licence for Civil Weddings.
Directions: On the A74, just across the Scottish border. (Map 14, F7)

Steam Packet Hotel

Harbour Row, Newton Stewart, Isle of Whithorn,
Dumfries & Galloway DG8 8LL
Telephone: +44(0)1988 500334
steampacketinn@btconnect.com
www.steampacketinn.com

John Scoular and his family have been here for 22
years, constantly modernising and improving this
harbourside inn that takes its name from the paddle
steamer that plied between the Galloway coast and
Liverpool during Victorian times. Large picture
windows take in yachts and inshore fishing boats, as
well as the comings and goings of folk in what is
considered one of the prettiest natural harbours in this
part of Scotland. The split bar, one side with wood-
burning stove, serves Theakston XB on handpump, and
has a relaxed, laid-back atmosphere. Seven
comfortable, well-equipped bedrooms, two of them deluxe rooms overlooking the harbour, are all en suite,
and very good value for money. Fish, landed on the
doorstep, dictates the menu, served in the beamed,
comfortable dining room and conservatory.
Chalkboards are scrawled with the daily catch, dishes
such as pan-fried brill with a beetroot compote, or sole
with lime and sea salt, complemented by local seasonal
game, such as venison steak with black pudding and
port wine jus. Bar snacks take in haddock and chips,
smoked fish pie and filled rolls, all freshly made to
order. The well-annotated wine list tours most of the
wine-growing regions of the world.

Prices: Set lunch £10 and dinner £15. Main course from £7.
House wine £10.50.
Hours: 11.00-23.00 (until 24.00 on Friday and Saturday). 12.00-
23.00 Sunday. Bar closed 25 Dec and 14.30-18.00 from Oct to Mar.
Food served: 12.00-14.00 18.30-21.00.
Rooms: 7 en suite. Double room from £50, single from £25.
Cuisine: British, seafood as a speciality.
Other Points: No-smoking area. Children welcome. Garden.
Directions: South of Newton Stewart on A714 and A746 to
Whithorn, then take B7004 to Isle of Whithorn. (Map 14, F5)

40a Heriot Row

40a Heriot Row, Edinburgh EH3 6ES
Telephone: +44 (0)131 226 2068
diane@heriotrow.com
www.heriotrow.com

The garden flat of a Georgian townhouse five minutes
from the centre of Princes Street may make an unlikely
bed and breakfast. There's a tiny patio filled with
exotic and unusal plants and across the road is the 3-4
acre private Queen Street Garden, to which guests have
access. The spacious, beautifully decorated B&B is on
two light and airy levels. There's a long, light hallway
and large drawing room with wall-to-wall bookcases
and antiques, the place to relax in the evening over a
complimentary glass of whisky. One bedroom, a twin,
is on this floor, a lovely cosy room with an en suite
shower room; the second en suite bedroom is on the
lower ground floor. Both rooms have tea trays, mineral
water and a little decanter of whisky. The dining room
is also on the lower level, making use of the old cellar
and decorated with painted stone walls, bookcases
covering one wall, light cream paintwork, an antique
dining table and sideboard. Here, Diane Rae serves
breakfast, using as much homemade produce as
possible, and the local butcher and fishmonger supply
sausages, bacon, and kippers. This is a real gem, and,
if you like cats, you will love this place.

Rooms: 2 en suite. Double room from £50 per person,
single from £60.
Cuisine: Local Scottish.
Other Points: No-smoking area. Garden. Children welcome.
Directions: From Princes Street take a left at Fredrick Street and
then the third left after the gardens. Heriot Row is at the end of
the block on the left. (Map 14, C7)

Prices: Set lunch £10.95 and dinner
£21.95. Main course from £10.25.
House wine £9.95.
Hours: 12.00-14.30. 17.30-22.00 (22.30 on
Friday and Saturday, 21.30 on Sunday).
Closed 25-26 December, 1-2 January and
second Sunday of January.
Cuisine: Modern Scottish
Other Points: Smoking allowed after
14.00 and 22.00. Bring your own wine
policy, £1 corkage. Children welcome.
Directions: Turn off Princes Street up
Frederick street. Howe Street is a
continuation of Frederick Street.

A Room in the Town

18 Howe Street, New Town, Edinburgh EH3 6TG
Telephone: +44 (0)131 225 8204
john.tindal@btconnect.com
www.aroomin.co.uk/thetown

A Room in the Town captures the feeling of history evoked by this
cobbled street and it is a popular spot, drawing in customers with a
bright, colourful daytime look, and by lowering the lights and bringing
out the candles in the evening. With a few exceptions all produce is
obtained from small, independent local suppliers and producers, such as
MacSweens for haggis and Tombuie smoked cheese from the Perthshire
Hills. The menu offers bistro fare with a contemporary twist: roast
chicken, chorizo and couscous salad with an avocado and corn salsa, or
pink peppercorn and mustard crusted tuna garnished with a chunky
Niçoise vinaigrette. A Highland element is evident in the cooking too,
with the likes of smoked haddie and black pudding dauphinoise topped
with peppered goats' cheese, or haggis, neeps and tatties, accompanied by
heather honey roasted shallots, and cassis soaked brambles with lemon
meringue ice cream. Scottish cheeses are teamed with hot gooseberry
chutney and oatcakes. Value for money is a major factor, combined with
generous portions and use of fresh produce. A mixed selection of mostly
new world wines includes two by the glass.

A Room in the West End and Teuchters Bar

🚪 🚰 ✕

26 William Street, Edinburgh EH3 7NH
Telephone: +44 (0)131 226 1036
john.tindal@btconnect.com
www.aroomin.co.uk/thewestend

Go in the evening to this bar-cum-restaurant and you will be knocked backwards by the sheer vitality of this venture. The traditional bar sports a large oval drinks counter, chunky tables, and wooden floors; the basement restaurant has candles on the wood tables, soft spots, a massive wall mural of Scottish characters enjoying themselves, and a breezy informal atmosphere. Value for money is a major part of the success of this operation, but the inspired BYO policy adds to the popularity. However, a side order of one of over 50 malt whiskies is a popular option, and a good percentage of beer is from the famous Caledonian Brewery, including the award winning IPA Deuchars. But there is a wine list too, and it offers a couple by the glass and a mixed selection of mostly new world wines. Since this is a sister restaurant to A Room in Town (see previous entry), the style of food is very similar: bistro fare with a contemporary twist. This translates as haggis stuffed salmon coated in couscous and served with fresh local asparagus, and pan-fried escalope of veal in an Arran mustard crust with Parmesan mash and rosemary jus.

Prices: Set lunch £10.95 and set dinner £21.95 for parties of 12 or more. Main course from £10.25. House wine £9.95.
Hours: 12.00-14.30. 17.30-22.00 (22.30 on Friday and Saturday, 21.30 on Sunday). Closed 25-26 December, 1-2 January and second Sunday of January.
Cuisine: Modern Scottish.
Other Points: Children welcome.
Directions: West end of Princes Street along Shandwick Place. Along Shandwick Place turn down Stafford Street and then left into William Street. (Map 14, C7)

The Blue Parrot Cantina

✕

49 St Stephen Street, Edinburgh EH3 5AH
Telephone: +44(0)131 225 2941
blue.parrotcantina@virgin.net

This tiny little basement restaurant is situated in the bustling Stockbridge area of the city. Décor is bright and simple: alternate walls painted dark blue or dark red; a wooden floor; wooden chunky tables and chairs; Mexican-style iron wall candle sconces. With only nine tables, the dining room can either be very intimate, quiet and cosy - usually midweek - or absolutely buzzing at weekends. The menu does not change that often as Fiona Macrae finds the unusual dishes they create draw people again and again, but you won't find your usual chilli-con-carne or tacos here. This is modern Mexican cooking, taking in starters of home-made bean and vegetable soup, or seafood ceviche marinated with lime and orange juice with cold avocado, chilli and coriander. Mains include strips of sirloin marinated with orange, lime juice, oregano and smoked chipotle chillies and pan-fried with capsicum and onion. Fruit chimi (kahlua liqueur with apple, banana or pineapple wrapped in flour tortillas, deep fried and served with cream), or pecan pie make good puddings. There's a good range of cocktails, tequilas, and predominately new world wines, with only the house French being offered by the glass.

Prices: Main course from £7.70.
House wine £9.25.
Hours: 17.00-23.00. Monday-Thursday and Sunday. 12.00-23.00. Friday and Saturday. Closed 25 December and 1 January.
Cuisine: Modern Mexican.
Other Points: Children welcome.
Directions: In the centre of Edinburgh. (Map 14, C7)

Britannia Spice

✕

150 Commercial Street, Britannia Way, Leith, Edinburgh EH6 6LB
Telephone: +44(0)131 5552255
info@britanniaspice.co.uk
www.britanniaspice.co.uk

Down in the newly converted Leith Docks, close to the Royal Yacht Britannia and the new Ocean Terminal, this former whisky bond has been converted into a modern, open, yet intimate Indian restaurant. In the nautically themed dining room, blonde wood tables, dark blue chairs, and sunken ceiling spots, create a sense of light and space in the contemporary setting. The restaurant has many supporters. Indeed, the menu, which explores Northern Indian, Bangladeshi, Nepalese and Thai cuisines, constantly changes, with new dishes added every few weeks to provide this regular clientele with new choices. From Nepal there could be spicy trout roasted with fried mushrooms, tomatoes, green chilli, mustard seeds and fresh herbs, with its counterpart from Bangladesh of freshwater fish marinated in spices and herbs. Thailand supplies a popular green curry of chicken or, from North India, chicken kebab with hot spices and a ginger-based sauce with fresh coriander. There's also tikka masala, billed as the Queen's favourite dish, in chicken, lamb and prawn versions, as well as biryanis, and a decent selection of vegetarian dishes. The wine list offers a balance of wines from the traditional European vineyards and the new

Prices: Main course from £6.95.
Hours: 12.00-14.15 Monday to Saturday. 17.00-23.45 daily.
Cuisine: Indian and Thai.
Other Points: No-smoking area. Children welcome. Car park.
Directions: In Leith, follow road signs for the Ocean Terminal or the Royal Yacht Britannia. (Map 14, C7)

Cafe Provencal

34 Alva Street, Edinburgh EH2 4PY
Telephone: +44(0)131 220 6105

This super little café-cum-bistro-cum-shop encompasses all things French. Huge ceiling to floor windows open up to allow tables to spill out onto the pavement and the décor reflects the south of France: walls are a bright yellow, the floor wood, the chairs slate-grey metal with fancy artwork and padded in terracotta or dark blue. Along one wall is bar-style seating (useful for singletons). The day starts at 8am with coffee and a croissant or patisserie, and runs with an all-day menu rapide (until 6.30pm) with soup, pasta, assiette of cheese and crudités, various warm and cold salads, filled baguettes, croissants and rolls, and so on. Alternatively, lunch and dinner bring an excellent value set menu which offers the likes of salad composée, saucisse de Toulouse with garlic and chive mash potato, onion marmalade and vegetables, chocolate and caramel ice cream gateau and coffee. The menu maison delivers bouillabaisse, chicken fillet sautéed in a rich tomato and basil sauce with a mixed pepper couscous, or pan-fried Scottish sirloin steak with a mushroom and tarragon sauce, salad leaves and French fries, and crème brûlée and coffee for £19.75. The short, keen list of wines is anchored firmly in France.

Prices: Set lunch and dinner £19.75. House wine £10.40.
Hours: 08.00-20.00 Monday to Wednesday. 08.00-23.00. Thursday to Saturday. 12.00-18.00 Sunday. Closed 25-26 December and 1-2 January.
Cuisine: French.
Other Points: Children welcome.
Directions: Five minues walk from the west end of Princes Street. (Map 14, C7)

Cafe Royal Circle Bar and Oyster Bar Restaurant

19 West Register Street, Edinburgh EH2 2AA
Telephone: +44(0)131 556 1884
caferoyale@snr.co.uk

This great Edinburgh institution was founded as a bar and restaurant in 1817 and has occupied its present location since 1862. It's a glorious example of the Victorian and Baroque, especially the elaborate plasterwork, gilding, mahogany panelling, hand painted windows depicting sporting life in the 19th century, and the famed Doulton Murals of the technological heroes of the time. Divided into two, the bar, with its dark-brown leather banquet-style seating serves a short, informal menu that delivers very good sandwiches, seafood chowder, and braised shank of lamb with rosemary and honey sauce. In the richly decorated restaurant, the emphasis is on fresh fish, shellfish and game. First courses typically include a salad in some form – perhaps grilled langoustine with a salad of marinated spring onion, young fennel and tomato vinaigrette. Variations on traditional themes might include plump, sweet, pan-seared scallops partnered with crab risotto and a light ginger and vermouth sabyon. Likewise a pairing of collops of wild Highland venison with a bitter chocolate and red wine jus is a typical example of the regularly changing carte. France is the anchor for the wine list with Italy, Spain and new world wines adding variety.

Prices: Main course restaurant from £15.50. Main course bar/snack from £4.95. House wine £9.
Hours: 11.00-23.00. Thursday 11.00-24.00. Friday and Saturday until 01.00. Closed 25 December.
Food served: 12.00-14.00. 19.00-22.00. Bar food available 11.00-22.00 and Sunday 12.30-22.00.
Cuisine: Seafood and Game.
Other Points: Children welcome in the restaurant only.
Directions: Just off the south-east corner of St Andrew's Square, close to Princes Street. (Map 14, C7)

Daniel's Bistro

88 Commercial Street, Leith, Edinburgh EH6 6LX
Telephone: +44 (0)131 553 5933

This open-all-day, seven-days-a-week bistro is a boon to this part of town. Daniel's overlooks the reconstructed Leith Docks, occupies a converted warehouse and is strikingly bright and modern with beech tables, chrome chairs, spotlights, and a semi-open-plan kitchen. Indeed, the main part of the restaurant is almost conservatory-style, with one whole wall made up of floor-to-ceiling windows; even the roof is glass with canvas awnings to protect against the glare of the sun. A variety of all-day eating options runs from late breakfast of croissants, Danish pastries and coffee, through a value-for-money lunch to a carte that offers French bistro classics such as moules farcies, and entrecôte steak au poivre. This is simple, direct cooking, overseen by Daniel Vencker, who hails from Alsace. He pays homage to his home by offering specialities such as tarte flambé, charcuterie alsacienne, and jarret de porc l'ancienne. Desserts are mainly French stalwarts: tarte tatin, gateau opera, but cranachan flies the Scottish flag. The wine list is predominantly French, but other wine-producing regions of the world get a look in. There are five by the glass, as well as a good selection of beers.

Prices: Set lunch £7.65. Main course from £7.50. House wine £10.95.
Hours: 12.00-14.30. 17.00-22.00 (22.30 on Saturday). Closed 25-26 December and 1 January.
Cuisine: Traditional French.
Other Points: No-smoking area.
Directions: City district of Leith near the Docks and Ocean Terminal. Halfway along Commercial Street towards Royal Yacht Britannia on the right hand side. (Map 14, C7)

EDINBURGH

Duck's at le Marche Noir

2/4 Eyre Place, Edinburgh EH3 5EP
Telephone: +44(0)131 558 1608
bookings@ducks.co.uk
www.ducks.co.uk

Ducks are everywhere at Malcolm Duck's eponymous restaurant: from the small ornaments on the tables (which sometimes go missing) to the Emma Bridgewater side plates. The room is a pleasant one to sit in: the fairly intimate space has large picture windows allowing lots of natural daylight (candlelit at night), and wooden panelling painted racing car green contrasting with textured mustard-gold walls hung with small French country scenes. Duck's is something of an Edinburgh institution, building up loyal support for the refined modern bistro-style cooking that ranges wide. Starters may take in a delicate chargrilled vegetable and goats' cheese mousse terrine with balsamic and port reduction, and a contemporary take on moules marinière (served in a lemon grass, coconut and coriander broth). Among main courses, pan-fried sea bass on pickled carrot and toasted coconut salad, red pepper and orange salsa shows an inventiveness that is matched by pork, sage and mozzarella saltimbocca with fig and apple compote and red wine jus. The carte changes monthly, and bargain set lunches change every five weeks or so. Though its strength lies in France, the wine list also contains some well-chosen new world bottles and a notable selection of halves.

Prices: Main course £11.50-£22. House wine £10.
Hours: 12.00-14.30. 19.00-22.00 (21.30 on Sunday evenings). Closed Monday, Saturday and Sunday lunch and 25-26 December.
Cuisine: Modern European.
Other Points: Children welcome.
Directions: 15 minutes walk from the city centre. (Map 14, C7)

EDINBURGH

Grain Store Restaurant

30 Victoria Street, Old Town, Edinburgh EH1 2JW
Telephone: +44 (0)131 225 7635
contact@grainstore-restaurant.co.uk
www.grainstore-restaurant.co.uk

The Grain Store blends well into a pretty, curved row of converted stores. Within, it has the shape of a cellar (although it is definitely not at basement level), with very old stone walls and an arched stone ceiling. There's an informal, rustic feel to the décor, but at the same time an understated elegance is lent by polished wooden floorboards, a mix of halogen lights and table candles and high-backed chairs with velvet seats. Carlo Caxon has owned the restaurant for 11 years and, in keeping with the style of the restaurant, his is quite a laid-back approach. The menu changes every six to eight weeks and has a very conscious awareness of organic and local seasonal produce. Lunch has a tapas theme: people can try a number of smaller dishes such as starters of carpaccio of beef with Parmesan and balsamic, and mains of confit of chicken, braised apples and tarragon, and confit of duck, bean sprouts, spring onion, sherry and soy. Dishes work because they are carefully considered, as in haunch of hare with a confit of the leg, cabbage and juniper, taken from the carte. The well-annotated wine list is predominately French, with an occasional new world.

Prices: Set lunch from £10. Set dinner £20.50. House wine £11.90.
Hours: Monday to Thursday 12.00-14.00. 18.00-22.00. Friday, Saturday and Sunday 12.00-15.00. 18.00-23.00 (22.00 Sunday). Closed 26 December, 1 January, and one week early January.
Cuisine: Modern Scottish.
Other Points: Children welcome.
Directions: Half way along Victoria Street, adjacent to Ian Mellis Cheese shop, on the first floor. (Map 14, C7)

EDINBURGH

Maison Bleue

36-38 Victoria Street, Edinburgh EH1 2JW
Telephone: +44(0)131 226 1900
www.maison-bleue.co.uk

A funky French bistro that has hit the ground running as far as the citizens of Edinburgh are concerned, with its blending of contemporary style, relaxed, bustling atmosphere, and imaginative take on food. Indeed, it is said that some pages of *Harry Potter and the Philospher's Stone* were written here. The bargain set menu, available at lunch and in the early evening, is rooted firmly in France, with a style that's typified by Provençal-style seafood croquettes with rocket salad, and slow-cooked lamb casserole with butter beans, spinach and white wine. But it's the tapas-style grazing menu of dishes to mix and match that has caught on. From a repertoire that roams the world, you can sample: vegetable tempura; Vietnamese nems (crispy rice pancakes with fresh crab, shrimp, garlic, mint and Chinese greens); goats' cheese boulettes with jalapeño fritters and guacamole; homemade duck confit; marinated seared tuna steak (in olive oil, garlic, chilli, ginger, coriander and served with spicy rice); and prime 10oz steaks with a choice of sauces. The wine list offers a good selection of predominately French wine, but a few new world choices help to match the extensive range of dishes on offer.

Prices: Set 2 course lunch £9.50. Main course from £8. House wine £9.90.
Hours: 12.00-15.00. 17.00-23.00. Longer opening hours during the Edinburgh festival. Closed 24-26 December.
Cuisine: Modern French.
Other Points: No-smoking area. Children welcome.
Directions: Just off Grassmarket between the Royal Mile and Grassmarket. (Map 14, C7)

Merchants ☐ ✕

17 Merchant Street, Edinburgh EH1 2QD
Telephone: +44 (0)131 225 4009
www.merchantsrestaurant.co.uk

The old kilt warehouse, situated in a tiny little dead end street close to the Royal Mile, can be difficult to find, but once found, never forgotten. Stone walls have been painted a bright red which, as the ceiling is quite low, beamed and black, and the windows few, makes for clever lighting both day and night (aided by large mirrors which help the light to diffuse nicely). Varnished rustic floorboards have just the right feel, yet white linen, cream napkins, white crockery and fine glassware lend a look that teeters on the formal/informal; it's a striking contrast of styles. The set lunch and dinner menus change every couple of weeks or so, and good use is made of local and seasonal produce. Thus crown of quail is filled with an apricot stuffing and served with sesame seed and honey dressing. Mains run to medallions of Angus fillet topped with wild mushrooms and offset by a rich red wine and port sauce, saddle of lamb stuffed with black pudding with onion jus, or pan-fried fillet of halibut and ratatouille. The short wine list opens with a pair of house French at £10.50, and prices remain under £20 throughout most of its varied international selection.

Prices: Set lunch £12.50. Set dinner £23.50. House wine £10.50.
Hours: 12.00-14.00. 18.00-22.00. Closed Saturday lunch and all day Sunday, 26 December and 2-3 January.
Cuisine: Modern Scottish.
Other Points: No-smoking area.
Directions: In Edinburgh old town; just off the Grassmarket.
(Map 14, C7)

Peter's Cellars ☐ ✕

11a-13a William Street, Edinburgh
Telephone: +44(0)131 226 3161

This small basement restaurant in a smart West End shopping street has been in existence for 20 years, albeit with several changes of hands. Suzanne Brown, the current proprietor, is the goddaughter of the original owner and worked as manager for the previous one; she therefore knows what does and does not work. It is certainly a place that has built up a good following. The bar is a popular local hangout, used as just that, despite only accommodating ten people. The restaurant proper, however, is unusual in that nearly all the tables are in their own little mahogany-style booths with wrought iron rails around the top and little checked curtains – very popular with couples. The short, weekly changing set menu is built around what basic materials are available from local suppliers. The kitchen is not ambitious, content to offer favourite combinations such as chargrilled sirloin steak with sauce au poivre, and breaded pork and brie schnitzel with a lemon and thyme reduction. Starters offer terrines, soups, and beer battered cauliflower and broccoli florets with chilli jam, with individual summer puddings, or iced vanilla parfait with a blackcurrant coulis among the desserts.

Prices: Set lunch £9.95. Set dinner £21. House wine from £8.50.
Hours: 12.00-01.00. Sunday from 12.30-23.00.
Food served: 12.00-14.30. 17.00-22.00. Sunday 12.30-14.30. 17.00-21.30. Closed 26 December and 1 January.
Cuisine: Scottish.
Other Points: No-smoking area. Children welcome.
Directions: In the West End of Edinburgh. (Map 14, C7)

Prices: Main course restaurant from £9.80. One course and coffee £5, between 12.00-15.00 and 17.00-19.00.
Hours: Summer hours, 12.00-22.30, until 23.00 on Friday and Saturday. Winter hours, 12.00-15.00. 17.30-22.30, until 23.00 Friday-Sunday. Closed Monday during the winter, over Christmas and 31 December evening.
Cuisine: Traditional French.
Other Points: Children welcome.
Directions: In the centre of Grassmarket. (Map 14, C7)

Le Petit Paris ✕

38-40 Grassmarket, Edinburgh EH1 4DU
Telephone: +44(0)131 226 2442
petitparisrestaurant@hotmail.com
petitparis-restaurant.co.uk

A super little restaurant set against a backdrop of the towering rocky cliff face of Edinburgh Castle. The outside is painted blue and white with blackboards helping to draw attention to incredibly good value lunch or pre theatre menus. Within, the theme continues – all things French with old photographs, old French signs – plus scrubbed wood floors, five tables upstairs and eight in the cosy basement room. The specials menu offering a £5 one-course lunch (or pre theatre) with coffee, changes daily, the repertoire including 7oz rib-eye steak, baked chicken legs with Basquaise sauce, or pork fillet with a mustard grain sauce. Equally, the main menu never strays beyond the boundaries of French classicism. This is the place to rediscover forgotten favourites such as a straightforward version of fish soup with rouille and croutons, boudin noir with a special Limousin mustard, snails in garlic and Pernod sauce, coq au vin (properly done and marinated in wine for 48 hours), and baked saddle of rabbit with a Dijon mustard sauce. Desserts are equally traditional, perhaps crème brûlée, or chocolate fondue, and there is a French cheese selection. The all French wine list is to the point and keenly priced.

Regents House Hotel
3/5 Forth St, Edinburgh EH1 3JX
Telephone: +44(0)131 556 1616
info@regenthousehotel.co.uk
www.regenthousehotel.co.uk

This small, homely hotel-cum-guest house is made up of two Georgian houses that have been knocked into one; the strong period feel of the properties has been retained. For example, those windows that are long and large have sumptuous curtains, whereas those that are small have a more cottagey feel about them. In some bedrooms patchwork bedspreads add appeal to the homeliness of the establishment. Although some rooms are small (but reserved for single occupancy), nearly all have ensuite shower facilities, and in addition there are family rooms catering, in one instance, for up to five. Given the location (only ten minutes walk from Princes Street and the centre of Edinburgh) this is good value for money in a city where prices can be extremely high. In addition, the main dining room where breakfast is served, opens as a teashop during the day, offering traditional Scottish teas and high teas, backed up by home-made soups, sandwiches and a selection of cakes, pastries and scones.

Hours: Closed five days over Christmas.
Rooms: 17 rooms, all en suite bar two. Singles from £35, doubles from £65, family rooms from £70.
Cuisine: Traditional Scottish.
Other Points: Totally non-smoking. Chldren welcome. Garden.
Directions: In the centre of Edinburgh. (Map 14, C7)

Suruchi Too
121 Constitution Street, Leith, Edinburgh EH6 7AE
Telephone: +44(0)131 554 3268
suruchires@aol.com
www.suruchirestaurant.co.uk

There is a lot to like about this Indian restaurant at the foot of Leith Walk. It occupies a former whisky warehouse and pungent smells from the kitchen complement the energetic decoration of Indian fabrics, mirrors, dramatically enlarged photographs of Indian scenes, and the huge leather camel adorned with Rajasthan decorations. Herman Rodrigues hails from Jaipur in Rajasthan, his chefs have trained in India, and he is intensely proud of the fact that he uses as many Scottish ingredients as possible in his food, especially venison, salmon, and even haggis. Indeed, an Indian interpretation of Scottish produce is a unique feature of the kitchen. Currently, the food is presented buffet style, at a fixed price, and this is proving very popular. Each day there is a selection of four starters, such as pakora, samosas, fritters and kebabs, four main courses, normally two chicken and two lamb, with four vegetarian side dishes of, say, chana masala, masala bhindi, aubergine masala, or shabnam. There is always plain and pilau rice, poppadums, naan bread, as well as a host of traditional thali and four desserts. As an alternative, there is another branch of Suruchi at 14a Nicholson Street, opposite the festival theatre, offering a very comprehensive carte.

Prices: Set lunch £6.95. Set dinner £14.95. Main course from £8. House wine £9.95.
Hours: 12.00-14.00. 17.30-23.30. Closed Christmas Day.
Cuisine: Traditional Indian.
Other Points: No-smoking area. Children welcome.
Directions: At the bottom of Leith walk straight over the lights into Constitution Street and Suruchi Too is 200 yards along on the right hand side. (Map 14, C7)

Teviotdale House
53 Grange Loan, Edinburgh EH9 2ER
Telephone: +44 (0)131 667 4376
teviotdale.house@btinternet.com
www.teviotdalehouse.com

Elizabeth and Willy Thebaud (she is Scottish, he is French) have run this charming, very stylish B&B for three years, and the large terraced house on a residential road ten minutes from the city centre makes a restful base for visitors exploring the Scottish capital. All the bedrooms are individually decorated and show great attention to detail, however, all follow a smart, well thought through chintzy theme, with matching headboards or pelmets; five rooms have small compact en suite shower rooms. The two remaining rooms have adjacent bathrooms and come with bathrobes. All have hot drinks trays, TVs, and hairdryers, and large, fluffy towels. The dining room looks out through a picture window onto the back garden, it's light and pleasant, filled with light pine furniture, golfing pictures and memorabilia (golfing lessons, and green fee bookings can be arranged at 20 different courses). Breakfast is excellent, with a choice of teas or herbal infusions, porridge, compote of dried fruits, prunes in nectar, free-range eggs, Ayrshire cured bacon and locally made sausages, oatcakes, and homemade scones.

Rooms: 7 rooms, 2 not en suite but private facilities. Single from £32 per person. Double from £28 per person, family from £25 per person.
Other Points: Totally no smoking. Dogs welcome by prior arrangement. Children welcome.
Directions: A720. Leave the city bypass at Straition junction and head towards the city centre for 2.1 miles. Fork left, Mayfield Road, for one mile. Go through the traffic lights at Mayfield church and then take the first left. (Map 14, C7)

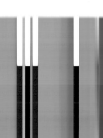

Inveresk House

3 Inveresk Village, Musselburgh, Edinburgh EH21 7UA
Telephone: +44(0)131 665 5855
chute.inveresk@btinternet.com

This is a large house dating from the 15th century with lots of history attached: Oliver Cromwell stayed here before the Battle of Dunbar in 1653, there are Roman remains in the gardens, and ghosts (of course). The interior has a wonderful lived-in feel, full of antiques, heavy drapes and large colourful oil paintings (done by owner, Alice Chute). The dining room is enormous, rugs cover bare boards, there are dark sideboards, a long dining table and painted bamboo-style chairs. Here Alice serves wholesome, hearty breakfasts. The drawing room immediately upstairs is equally large, and this is where a grand piano is housed, as well as large comfy sofas, antique tables, more pictures, and a fire on chilly days. Bedrooms range from a roomy family room, with antique furniture and a Victorian-style bathroom with a huge, deep bath with overhead shower, to a double room with more modern en suite facilities, plus a separate smaller double room, which also may be used by a family. A final bedroom has a double bed and two single beds, and has its own modern shower room. All rooms have TV, hot drinks trays, large cream fluffy towels and toiletries.

Hours: Closed 23-27 December.
Rooms: 3 en suite. Singles from £45, doubles from £70.
Other Points: Totally no smoking. Garden. Children welcome. Car park.
Directions: Before entering the village of Musselburgh at the top of the hill, turn sharp right towards St Michaels Church. Take the second entrance on the right; go past two cottages and follow the road round to the right, signposted Inveresk House. (Map 14, C7)

Seasons Coffee Shop

7 Kirk Street, Kincardine-on-Forth,
Fife FK10 4PT
Telephone: +44(0)1259 730720

There's a decidedly homely, cottagy feel to Leslie Mitch's tiny bistro-cum-coffee shop. The old fireplace is covered with cards and gifts, many of them local crafts, there's a small corner shelf display, with further displays of gifts laid out on the small window sills and hanging on the walls. It is all attractively done with the added bonus of the coffee shop being totally non smoking. The little shop front with its food counter and seating for 25 does good business dispensing not just good home cooked food to eat at anytime during the day, but also takeaways. The menu is short and straightforward, delivering soup, perhaps an excellent carrot and ginger, followed by a generous prawn sandwich made with chunky brown bread, or there are hot paninis with mixed salad, say roast beef and mustard, or bacon rolls, and filled baguettes. Cakes and homemade scones extend the range with three wines offered by the glass.

Hours: 08.00-16.00.
Closed Sundays, 25-26 December and 1-4 January.
Cuisine: Coffee shop, sandwiches and homemade cakes.
Other Points: Totally no smoking.
Directions: In the centre of Kincardine. (Map 14, C6)

Unicorn Inn

★ ▶ ✕

15 Excise Street, Kincardine-on-Forth, Fife FK10 4LN
Telephone: +44(0)1259 739129
info@theunicorn.co.uk
www.theunicorn.co.uk

Right next to Kincardine Bridge, in the oldest part of town, this lovely village inn dating back to 1639 has undergone extensive refurbishment, creating a modern dining pub that has retained its classic feel. At ground level is a lounge that features leather sofas in soft browns and slate blues around an open fire, and the more casual of two dining areas, The Grill Room. Coffee and sandwiches or afternoon tea with warm home-made scones can be taken all day, but its greatest asset lies in the beef cuts from the Duke of Buccleuch estates that score highly for quality and flavour. Additional selections take in pork-and-ale sausages, and classic puddings. Open on selected evenings only, you'll find the Red Room restaurant upstairs, romantically fitted out with deep red, gold-tasselled curtains and tables clothed in white linen. Nightly menus depend on the market's best available fresh seafood, meat and game. Start, perhaps, with Loch Linnhe langoustines and wild mushroom and guinea fowl terrine, then sea bass baked in olive oil and crushed garlic, or local venison medallions with sweetened haggis and red wine sauce. Local strawberries set in pink champagne or Scottish and Irish cheeses round things off.

Prices: Main course in the Red Room from £10.95. Main course in the Grill from £6.95. House wine £10.50.
Hours: 12.00-14.00. 18.00-21.00 Tuesday-Sunday. Red Room Seafood restaurant open weekend evenings. Closed on Monday.
Cuisine: Scottish and Irish.
Other Points: No-smoking area. No dogs. Garden. Children welcome. Car park.
Directions: From the south, cross Kincardine Bridge, then take the first then the second left. (Map 14, C6)

Inn at Lathones ★ ✕ ⬧

By Largoward, St Andrews, Fife KY9 IJE
Telephone: +44(0)1334 840494
lathones@theinn.co.uk
www.theinn.co.uk

Nick and Jocelyn White have built up this 400-year-old coaching inn, offering a mix of ancient and modern charm. The tiny reception has an old-fashioned shop fronted bow-window room which houses the extensive award-winning wine cellar, the large lounge has stone walls, a mix of leather and upholstered chairs, coffee tables, table lamps and bow windows, one facing the roadside, the other the courtyard. Executive bedrooms are situated in the adjoining coach house. Standard bedrooms, on the other side of the courtyard, are smaller and have en suite shower rooms. The dining room blends elegance with informality. With low beamed ceilings, this old part of the house oozes a relaxed atmosphere. Here, a typical dinner could open with pan-fried, hand-dived scallops with a beetroot dressing (also available as a main course), go on to jugged leg of duck accompanied by a sauce flavoured with truffle extract, and finish with iced lemon soufflé. At lunchtime, the Market Menu offers good-value. The wine list is always being updated with plenty of scope regarding price to suit all pockets; five are available by the glass.

Prices: Set lunch £12 and dinner from £25. Main course from £14.
House wine £11.50.
Hours: 12.00-14.30. 18.00-21.30.
Closed two weeks in January.
Cuisine: Modern European.
Other Points: No-smoking area. Children welcome. Garden. Car park. Licence for Civil Weddings.
Directions: On the A915 midway between St Andrews and Leven, 5 miles south of St Andrews. (Map 14, B7)

Art Lovers' Café ▯ ✕

House for an Art Lover, Bellahouston Park,
10 Dumbreck Road, Glasgow G41 5BW
Telephone: +44(0)141 353 4779
info@houseforanartlover.co.uk
www.houseforanartlover.co.uk

In 1901 Glasgow's most famous son, Charles Rennie Mackintosh, entered a competition to design a grand house in a thoroughly modern style – a 'House for an Art Lover'. However, the house was not constructed in his lifetime, the building started in 1989 and was completed six years later. Set in the heart of Bellahouston Park, it is a venue for corporate and private dining with the Art Lovers' Café situated on the ground floor. Three large arched windows create a light, bright space, enhanced by white linen table cloths, light wood floors and monthly exhibitions of contemporary Scottish paintings. Noted for being child friendly, this is a relaxed place, open throughout the day for just a coffee and pastry, or light snacks of toasted bagel with Loch Fyne salmon. Elegant three course lunches have as much to do with good value as ability and acumen. Choice may include terrine of ham hock, braised cabbage and root vegetables, cornichons and their juices with, say, roasted fillet of sea bass, broth of fennel, mussels and tomato to follow, and an open tartlet of Bramley apples, fresh egg custard and cinnamon ice cream to finish. The very limited wine selection is keenly priced.

Prices: Set lunch from £13.45. Main course restaurant from £8.50. Snacks from £4.50. House wine £13.50.
Hours: 10.00-17.00. Closed 25-26 December and 1-2 January.
Food served: 12.00-15.00.
Cuisine: Modern Scottish.
Other Points: No-smoking area. Dogs welcome on terrace only. Children welcome. Garden. Car park. Licenced for Civil Weddings. Changing art exhibitions.
Directions: Exit 23/M8. At top of slip road turn left, then next

---

City Merchant ▯ ✕

97-99 Candleriggs, Glasgow G1 1NP
Telephone: +44(0)141 5531577
citymerchant@btinternet.com
www.citymerchant.co.uk

Part of the charm of this family-owned restaurant is that it continues to be a safe bet for a good meal in a pleasant, welcoming environment. Tony Matteo is an ambitious owner and has chalked up nearly 16 years of bonhomie, offering a modern Scottish menu with a strong line in seafood. However, various menus take in game in season, meat and vegetarian foods, complemented by daily-changing blackboard specials. Starters on the carte, for example, may include Loch Etive mussels in wine, garlic, onion and parsley, or Dingwall haggis with neeps and tatties, followed by baked cod fillet with herb pesto crust and basil oil, or rack of lamb with ceps and rosemary jus, with warm bread and butter pudding layered with marmalade and sultanas and served with sauce anglaise to finish. A daily changing menu that's fixed price at each course (and offered from noon until 6.30pm) is a simple affair, perhaps offering chicken liver and game pâté, roast chicken in bacon with haggis parfait and bell pepper cream, and clootie dumpling with whisky and oatmeal ice cream. Cheeses are regional and the well annotated, short wine list makes a point of finding good drinking for less than £20.

Prices: Set lunch £13.50. Main course from £7.50.
House wine £12.50.
Hours: 12.00-22.30. Closed Sunday, 25-26 December and 1-2 January.
Cuisine: Seafood/modern Scottish.
Other Points: No-smoking area. Children welcome over 5 years old.
Directions: Take exit 15, east or west bound on M8 and follow signs for Glasgow Cross. Turn right into Ingram Street, then second left into Candleriggs. The restaurant is 500 yards east of George

Kama Sutra

331 Sauchiehall Street, Glasgow G2 3HW
Telephone: +44(0)141 332 0055
cats@harlequin-leisure.co.uk
www.harlequin-leisure.com

Glasgow, named 'Curry Capital of the UK' in 2002, has taken the Harlequin Group restaurants to heart. This sibling of Mister Singh's India (see entry below) is another style-led restaurant from the group. Lots of modern ironwork, wooden floors, cream walls upstairs, terracotta downstairs, kilim-style banquet covered seating, and terracotta and dark blue high backed chairs, add up to a look that is more modern European than Indian. Swathes of hessian fabric create 'curtains' to break the room and there are mosaic domed indented ceilings and wrought iron baskets hanging from the walls. The lunchtime buffet, also available on Monday evenings, is a huge hit, and although the extensive main menu roams the Indian sub-continent, it contains few surprises, although chicken tikka roma is an Italian-style twist on an old favourite. However, a few examples from the north-east frontier, offering an Indo-Chinese flavour in dishes such as a vegetarian Tibetan ting-sa, or Himalayan hotpot add interest. House wines are offered by the litre and in different glass sizes.

Prices: Buffet lunch £5.95, buffet dinner £10.95. Pre-theatre £7.95. Main course from £6.50. House wine £10.50.
Hours: 12.00-12.00 (12.30 on Friday and Saturday).
Cuisine: Modern Indian.
Other Points: Children welcome.
Directions: From the east exit at junction 18 on the M8. (Map 14, C5)

Langs Hotel

2 Port Dundas Place, Glasgow G2 3LD
Telephone: +44(0)141 333 1500
reservations@langshotels.co.uk
www.langshotels.co.uk

Light, colour and contemporary design (large windows, slate floors, soft leather furniture) combine to make this new-generation Glasgow hotel both chic and comfortable. Colour co-ordinated floors capture the cool big city style well, offering standard bedrooms, suites and split-level apartments. Standard rooms are compact, but PlayStations, CDs, ironing boards, TV are neatly hidden in the furniture, and every room has a modem connection, as well as chrome and glass bathrooms with jet showers. A plethora of eateries, includes the B-Bar for all-day food, and Oshi, a bold space serving Oriental-style food . Good-value express lunches and pre- and post-theatre menus are worth noting. The centrepiece is Las Brisas: a soft-coloured dining room of oatmeal, pale grey and blues, combined with striking lighting, has an understated elegance. Ambitious menus bring contemporary influences to bear on a fundamentally classical style of cooking. This can produce some elaborate constructions - braised oxtail, foie gras and duck terrine, caramelized nectarines and quince jelly, for example - although there are simpler yet equally appealing ideas, including roast partridge breast, sarladaise potato, braised cabbage and charcuterie sauce.

Prices: Set lunch £11 and pre-theatre set dinner £11.95 and £13.50. Main course from £12.75. House wine £11.95.
Hours: 12.00-14.00. 17.00-22.00.
Rooms: 100 en suite. Double room from £55 per person, suite from £70 per person, single room from £90.
Cuisine: Euro-fusion and Mediterranean.
Other Points: No-smoking area. Children welcome. Licence for civil weddings. Oshi Spa with treatments to energise and relax.
Directions: J16/M8. At the top pf West Nile Street, opposite Glasgow Royal Concert Hall next to Buchanan Bus Station. (Map 14, C5)

Mister Singh's India

149 Elderslie Street, Glasgow G3 7JR
Telephone: +44 (0)141 221 1452

This unusual Indian restaurant on the edge of town, heading towards the West End, has built up considerable support over the past few years. It is by no means a standard looking curry house, the waiters in black and white kilts see to that. Wrought-iron railings divide a two-tier room that's all light wood floors with a stark white and dark blue colour scheme. The extensive menu (with blackboard specials ringing the changes) opens with a familiar selection of tandooris, pakoras (including one made with haggis) poori or dosas and generously portioned main courses offer the familiar kormas, biryanis, and masalas. Thalis are a popular lunch choice and there is an easy option set menu. In addition, a few European dishes are on offer for those who cannot or will not eat curry! Service is splendid and the extensive wine list has prices to suit all pockets. Part of the Harlequin Restaurant Group whose restaurants all have their own unique theme and a good standard of Indian cooking (see Kama Sutra above).

Prices: Set lunch £6.95. Set dinner £14.95. Pre-theatre menu £8.25. Main course from £6.95. House wine £9.65.
Hours: 12.00-24.00. (from 14.30 on Sunday). Closed 1 January.
Cuisine: Indian.
Other Points: No-smoking area. Children welcome.
Directions: M8. Exit at Charing Cross. (Map 14, C5)

Mulberry's ★ ◻ ✕

42 Munro Place, Anniesland, Glasgow G13 2UW
Telephone: +44(0)141 9592722

In 1999, Denis Shankland realised a dream to open his own restaurant (after spending 20 years with Textile World), and the result is a great find in a rather extraordinary place: a 50-seater restaurant in a converted business unit on a small industrial estate. However, as soon as you walk in the door, the welcoming atmosphere, soft lighting and the theatre of an open-to-view kitchen soon cast their spell. The cooking offers a generous slate of appealing dishes from country style to cosmopolitan, prepared with flair and passion. The menu changes daily (based on what produce is available at market) and everything, from rolls to ice cream, is made from scratch. Pan-fried pork loin served on a Stornoway black pudding with apple sauce could open a meal that goes on to roast saddle of new season Scottish lamb filled with garlic and rosemary stuffing, and finish with rhubarb and ginger crumble with sauce anglaise. The lounge bar menu runs firm favourites such as a proper prawn cocktail with finest quality prawns and marie rose brandy sauce. Note that it can be hard to find a table at the latter end of the week; it is necessary to book at least two weeks in advance.

Prices: Set lunch £11.95, set dinner £18.95 Tuesday to Friday. House wine £12.50.
Hours: 12.00-15.00. 19.00-22.00 (late on Friday and Saturday). Closed for dinner on Sunday and all Monday.
Cuisine: Scottish.
Other Points: No-smoking area. Children welcome. Car park.
Directions: Off the Great Western Road at Anniesland; after approximately 300 yards turn left into Esso Garage and then left again through to the lane. (Map 14, C5)

George Square, Glasgow

Prices: Set lunch £9.50. Set dinner £12.50. Main course restaurant from £13.50. House wine £12.50.
Hours: 12.00-14.30. 18.00-23.00. Closed 1-2 January, 25-26 December and Easter Monday.
Cuisine: Italian.
Directions: Exit18/M8. Follow signs for West End along Great Western Road, travel over Kelvinbridge and La Parmigiana is on the left. (Map 14, C5)

La Parmigiana ◻ ✕

447 Great Western Road, Glasgow G12 8HH
Telephone: +44(0)141 334 0686
s.giovanazzi@btclick.com
www.laparmigiana.co.uk

Walk into this small restaurant near Glasgow's West End, and you could imagine yourself to be in an Italian courtyard. Terracotta tiles, faux arched windows, roof tiles and a cheerful yellow colour scheme make up this very personal restaurant with the congenial atmosphere helped along by charming, well-trained staff. Given the size of the kitchen, the menu is sensibly pared down and is changed quarterly, but there is a policy of using seasonal produce. In the past, when trying to extend and change more frequently, Sandro Giovanazzi found that his regulars knew what they liked and resisted too much change, demanding the great regular dishes back. Thus lobster ravioli with cream and basil, beef carpaccio with Parmesan shavings and rocket salad, or chargrilled Minch scallops with lemon and olive oil are regular starters. Other good things to be had include fillet of beef with crushed peppercorns and tarragon cream, or risotto with porcini mushrooms, Parmesan and cream. Fish is also a reliable bet, perhaps zuppa of mixed fish and shellfish with bruschetta. Finish with crème brûlée with calvados and caramelised apples. Set price menus at lunch and dinner are very good value.

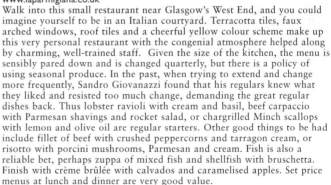

The Pot Still

154 Hope Street, Glasgow G20 0TB
Telephone: +44(0)141 333 0980
ken@thepotstill.co.uk
www.thepotstill.co.uk

With such atmosphere and character, it is easy to believe that the polished wooden floor, dark red leather seating, wood panelling and dusky pink-painted walls hung with sepia pictures hasn't changed much since the Pot Still opened in 1835. It's certainly a Glasgow legend, a traditional city-centre pub that was run from 1870 to 1981 by several generations of the McCall family. The bar extends along one whole wall and houses over 300 malt whiskies (a great draw for visitors as some are hard to find elsewhere). In addition, there's a good selection of real ales, with at least two to four quality cask ales changing twice a week, but you can always expect McEwan's 80/- and Caledonian Deuchars IPA. Every couple of months whisky tastings are held and the £50 ticket price sounds good value, given the fact that £6,000 worth of whisky can be drunk in one night. The food is very simple, typical pub staples of baked potatoes, baguettes, homemade soup, steaks, burgers, steak and ale pies, and liver and onions, but is served all day, so is worth noting just for that.

Prices: Main course bar/snack from £3.95.
Hours: 11.00-23.00. Until 12.00 Friday and Saturday. Closed 25 December and 1 January.
Food served: All day until just before closing.
Cuisine: Traditional British.
Directions: Hope Street is one way running north to south between Argyll Street and Cowcaddens. The pub is at the junction of West Regent Street. (Map 14, C5)

Sandyford Hotel

904 Sauchiehall Street, Glasgow G3 7TF
Telephone: +44 (0)141 334 0000
www.sandyfordhotel.glasgow.com

Derek and Colin McMillan's unpretentious West End city hotel is, as their brochure states, "interestingly different", offering stylish, value-for-money accommodation to all who appreciate being within walking distance of a host of Glasgow's major attractions. Throughout the hotel there's a warm, opulent feeling. The lobby area has lavish cream drapes and deep sofas and chairs in dark blue, matching the thick carpet. Bedroom corridors, as well as the original sweeping staircase, are painted a dark red with contrasting white paintwork, but the bedrooms themselves are simply decorated with crisp, white duvets and sheets and walls papered a discreet cream. All rooms have a simple dressing table-cum-desk arrangement, TV, tea trays, telephone and hair dryer, and bathrooms are predominately showers only. One way the McMillans keep down costs is by providing bed and breakfast only. Served in the basement dining room, it is partly self-service, with compotes, cereals, and fruit juices, but the full Scottish breakfast, including porridge, is cooked to order (and it is included in the room price).

Rooms: 55 en suite. Singles from £32, doubles from £52, family rooms from £70.
Other Points: No-smoking area. Children welcome.
Directions: Exit 18/M8 signposted Charing Cross. At the traffic lights go straight across, next lights turn right into Berkeley Street. Follow the road round and take first left into Sauchiehall Street. Hotel is 200 yards down on the first bend. (Map 14, C5)

Altnaharra Hotel

By Lairg, Altnaharra, Highland IV27 4UE
Telephone: +44(0)1549 411222
altnaharra@btinternet.com
www.altnaharra.com

The Mugford family arrived at this remote 19th century inn, on a single-track road 30 miles from Bonar Bridge, in the summer of 2002. They have continued the tradition of running this hotel with an enthusiasm and style that suits the traditional fishing and shooting guests, as well as making all visitors and locals equally welcome. This is important, as the hotel is the centre of a small rural community that is just about as remote as you can get in the British Isles. The surrounding area is memorable for its great vistas, spectacular mountains and numerous lochs, and Altnaharra is regarded as one of the best salmon and trout fishing hotels in the Highlands, offering a truly comprehensive range of fishing. The several public areas, lounge bar, lounge and library are welcoming with open fires, comfy seating, flowers, plants, and fishing memorabilia. The hotel is open throughout the day and will happily provide light refreshments or meals, and the daily changing limited choice dinner menu features locally sourced meat and game. Bedrooms are en suite and are quite spacious and very comfortably furnished, but you have to go to the library to watch TV.

Prices: Set dinner £30 (4 courses). House wine £14.50.
Hours: 07.30-21.30 (flexible).
Rooms: 15 en suite. Rooms from £40 per person.
Cuisine: Modern Scottish.
Other Points: No-smoking area. Dogs welcome. Children welcome. Garden. Car park.
Directions: From Inverness, take the A9 for Wick. At Bonar Bridge, follow the A836 towards Tongue; hotel is between Lairg and Tongue. (Map 16, C5)

SHIMMERING LOCHS
AND GLORIOUS GLENS

Scotland's west coast is the gateway to a breathtaking world
of beautiful lochs and glens in this magnificent Highland region of Scotland.
Drive length: 47 miles

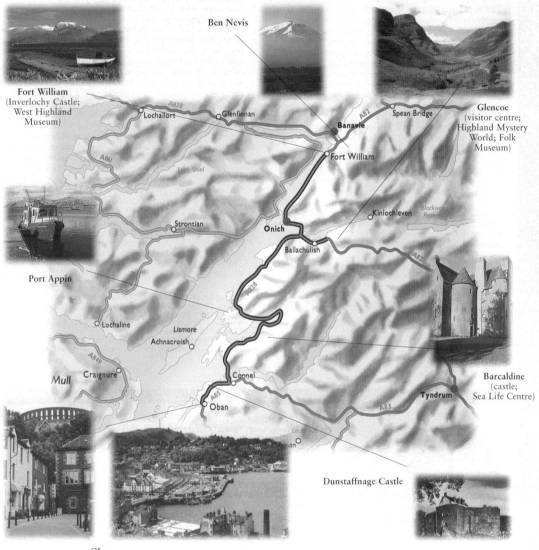

Ben Nevis

Fort William
(Inverlochy Castle;
West Highland
Museum)

Lochailort   Glenfinnan

A830

Banavie

A82

Spean Bridge

Glencoe
(visitor centre;
Highland Mystery
World; Folk
Museum)

A861

Loch Shiel

Fort William

Kinlochleven

Blackwater
Reservoir

Strontian

Onich

Ballachulish

A82

Port Appin

A828

Lochaline

Lismore
Achnacroish

A849

Mull   Craignure

Connel

Tyndrum

A85

Oban

A85

Barcaldine
(castle;
Sea Life Centre)

Dunstaffnage Castle

Oban
(McCaig's Tower;
Rare Breeds Farm)

● Accommodation/Food

● Accommodation

● Food

🥄 Food Shop

To find the establishments marked
here, look up the listing town
marked on the map in bold in the
town index on page 395

Applecross Inn

★ ◨ ✗ ◢

Shore Street, Applecross, Strathcarron,
Highland IV54 8LR
Telephone: +44(0)1520 744262
www.applecross.net

The cosy interior complete with wood burners and
comfortable dining areas is more popular than you
would imagine after traversing one of the highest and
most exhilarating routes in Britain. The latterday
reputation of Applecross has been founded on the
admirable Judith Fish and, more recently, the culinary
talents of Robbie Macrae who prepares and cooks the
excellent local produce available, predominantly
seafood, with great style. The value-for-money food in
the bar, usually available all day, comes with a punchy
self confidence, delivering an exemplary beef burger
with great chips, as well as a proper seafood cocktail
made with local prawns or squat lobster. The very
fresh seafood takes in pan-fried king scallops from
Loch Toscaig, with garlic butter, crispy bacon and rice.
The set dinner menu in the dining room (booking
recommended) could run to local wild salmon with
hollandaise sauce, alongside the likes of Applecross
estate venison casseroled in red wine. Bedrooms may
be small, but they are charming with splendid sea
views and are extremely good value for money when
you consider the excellent Highland breakfast in the
morning. Note that those rooms not en suite have
adjacent bathrooms.

Prices: Set dinner £20. Main course restaurant from £10.95.
Main course bar/snack from £6.05. House wine £7.30.
Hours: 11.00-23.00. Closed Christmas Day and New Years Day.
Food served: 12.00-21.00.
Rooms: 7 rooms, 3 en suite. Singles from £30, doubles from £60.
Cuisine: Traditional Scottish and Seafood.
Other Points: No-smoking area. Children welcome. Dogs
welcome. Garden. Car park.
Directions: From Lochcarron follow the Wester Ross coastal trail
over the famous Bealach na Ba, (Pass of the Cattle). (Map 15, E3)

Glen Loy Lodge Hotel

✗ ◢

Banavie, Fort William, Highland PH33 7PD
Telephone: +44(0)1397 712700
glenloy.lodge@virgin.net
www.smoothhound.co.uk/hotels/glenloyl.html

In the five years that Pat and Gordon Haynes have
been here, the house has been redecorated in tasteful
and individual style, rooms have been filled with
original artwork, ornaments and personal touches,
much of them sympathetic to the period, and furnished
throughout with arts and crafts pieces from 1880 to
1935. The sun room is a lovely room to sit and watch
the ever-changing light over Ben Nevis. The sitting
room is cosy with a large log fire and a television (for
those who can't switch off from the outside world).
Very comfortably styled bedrooms are all en suite, the
majority are a good size, well equipped with hot drinks
trays (real ground coffee), mineral water and good
toiletries. The set, daily changing dinner menu is given
out at breakfast, so alternatives can be readily
provided. The repertoire is built around local supplies:
asparagus and smoked salmon soufflé, fillet of
Aberdeen Angus steak with sherried mustard sauce,
then Scottish farmhouse cheeses (Sweet Milk and
Brierly from Wester Lawrenceton Farm, mature
Cairnsmore and Dunsyre Blue) with rhubarb créme
brûlée to finish. The list of soundly chosen wines, with
France in the ascendancy, picks off many a fine
producer.

Prices: Set price dinner £26 (4 course). House wine £10.55.
Hours: Dinner at 19.30.
Open by arrangement in Winter.
Rooms: 7 en suite. Double room from £80, single from £40.
Cuisine: Modern Scottish.
Other Points: Totally no smoking. Garden. Car park.
Directions: Four miles north of Banavie on the B8004.
(Map 13, A4)

Old Ferryman's House

◨ ✗ ◢

Nethy Bridge Road, Boat of Garten, Highland PH24 3BY
Telephone: +44(0)1479 831370

Elizabeth Matthews runs her extraordinary B&B, one of the smallest
establishments in Les Routiers membership, with tremendous style. The
traditional stone-built former ferryman's cottage is just across the River
Spey from Boat of Garten. In addition to three small but perfect pine-
furnished bedrooms, a diminutive bathroom, a tiny sitting room warmed
by a wood-burning stove, and filled with flowers, books and magazines,
there's a breakfast room for just six people, and a lovely enclosed garden
bursting with tubs, planters and borders of cottage garden flowers. No TV
is a bonus for those wanting a complete break from the norm, as are
flexible breakfast times for a traditional Scottish grill-up with homemade
bread and preserves, or oak-smoked kippers, Scotch pancakes, or
kedgeree. Afternoon tea is also included in the B&B price, so look
forward to homemade bran teabreads, shortbread and flapjacks.
Residents will eat very well at dinner, starting perhaps with smoked
venison and homemade mayonnaise, or cullen skink, followed by wild
venison Stroganoff, or organic Gloucester Old Spot pork, with herbs,
vegetable and salad leaves from the garden in season. Lovely puddings,
such as rhubarb and banana crumble, or baked apples with heather honey.

Prices: Set price dinner £17.
Hours: From 19.00. Check for closures
in winter.
Rooms: 4. Double room from £42,
single from £21.
Cuisine: Modern Scottish.
Other Points: No smoking. Children
welcome. Garden. Car park. Credit cards
not accepted.
Directions: Follow main road through
Boat of Garten and across the River Spey;
house immediately on right. (Map 16, F6)

Comar Lodge

Glen Affric, Cannich, Highland IV4 7NB
Telephone: +44(0)1456 415251
ianmure@aol.com
www.comarlodge.co.uk

The location in Cannich Glen by the River Glass could hardly be bettered, with salmon and trout fishing available and loch fishing at Glen Affric. The pretty white house was built in 1740 by Roderick Chisholm and is the ancient seat of the Chisholm Clan; it is rumoured that Bonnie Prince Charlie hid here after his defeat at Culloden. Original features include the lounge fireplace bearing the date 1740. The house is neat and well kept, modest rather than luxurious, in that relaxed home-from-home style that is a feature of good fishing hotels. Two comfortable, en suite, family sized bedrooms are on the top floor, offering fine views of the river and the hills beyond, with a third bedroom with wash basin and private toilet on the middle floor. Breakfast only is provided, a magnificent Highland feast that will set you up for the day. With just three bedrooms offering remarkable value for money and the easy hospitality that Ian and Jane Mure practice effortlessly, booking is essential. Although popular with fishing folk, walkers and climbers are drawn here, lured by the close proximity of 13 Munros.

Prices: Dinner by prior arrangement. £15 set menu including cheese and coffee.
Rooms: 3 en suite. Double room from £22, single from £20.
Cuisine: Bed and Breakfast.
Other Points: Totally no smoking. Children welcome. Garden. Car park. Credit cards not accepted.
Directions: Take the A82 from Inverness to Drumnadrochit, then the A831 to Cannich. The house is on the left, 400 yards after leaving Cannich. (Map 15, F4)

Mallin House Hotel

Church Street, Dornoch, Highland IV25 3LP
Telephone: +44(0)1862 810335
mallin.house.hotel@zetnet.co.uk
www.users.zetnet.co.uk/mallin-house

There is nothing especially historic about the modest, unprepossessing family-run hotel in the heart of Dornoch, but it fits well within its surroundings. The style starts off with service, which is very friendly and efficient, and continues through the interior, where carefully chosen furniture and fabrics blend with tradition. Local prints cover walls in public areas, the bar is a suitably convivial place, well stocked with single malts, and offers very good bar food such as fresh salmon salad, or battered haddock and chips. Ten comfy bedrooms are decorated with simplicity, with comfort uppermost; all have modern bathrooms and stunning views across the Dornoch Firth. Food in the restaurant specialises in fresh local seafood (and very good steaks), with starters including a creamy traditional cullen skink. Main courses take in west coast lobster, or meat options of local wild mountain venison marinated in red wine and herbs and panfried, or roasted loin of spring lamb served with haggis mound and a Drambuie and grain mustard cream sauce. The wine list offers a sound selection of French and new world wines; most try to please by staying below £20.

Prices: Bar meal from £6.95. House wine £9.95.
Hours: 18.30-21.00. 12.00-14.00 on Sunday.
Rooms: 10 en suite. Double room from £25 per person, single from £29.
Cuisine: Scottish/seafood.
Other Points: Children welcome. Garden. Car park.
Directions: 40 miles north of Inverness off the A9 in the town centre. (Map 16, D5)

Benleva Hotel

Drumnadrochit, Inverness, Highland IV63 6UH
Telephone: +44(0)1456 450080
enquiry@benleva.co.uk
www.benleva.co.uk

Stephen and Allan Crossland, with James Beaton, bought the Benleva in November 2001 and immediately implemented a programme of improvements and refurbishment. Indeed, the old place is scrubbing up nicely, the injection of new blood and ideas just what was needed. Two homely, rustic bars serve cask-conditioned ales, including Isle of Skye Brewery ales, there's a super range of malt whiskies - note the rare cask-strength one - and bar food is served all day until 9pm, with the emphasis firmly on local produce. In the evening the dinner menu kicks in, offering cullen skink, Kilmore haggis with Glen Ord whisky sauce, or Stornaway black pudding with apple sauce and berry salad, followed by fresh Isle of Skye scallops with bacon, tomato and spring onion, Black Isle lamb cutlets with thyme, lemon and garlic butter, or Lochaber venison steak served with a berry sauce. Clootie dumpling or sticky toffee pudding bring up the rear. The six unpretentious bedrooms are all en suite and have hot drinks trays and TVs.

Prices: Main course from £9. House wine £8.95.
Hours: 12.00-12.00. Until 01.00 Thursday and Friday and 23.00 on Sunday.
Food served: Bar snacks only during the day; restaurant open from 18.30-21.00.
Rooms: 6 en suite. Singles from £25, doubles from £20 per person per night. Family room from £50.
Cuisine: Modern Scottish.
Other Points: No-smoking area. Children welcome. Dogs welcome. Garden. Car park.
Directions: Just off the A82 on the Fort William to Inverness road. Well signposted. (Map 16, F5)

DRUMNADROCHIT, HIGHLAND

FORT AUGUSTUS, HIGHLAND

Loch Ness Lodge Hotel

Drumnadrochit, Inverness,
Highland IV63 6TU
Telephone: +44(0)1456 450342
info@lochness-hotel.com
www.lochness-hotel.com

The solid yet romantic-looking stone Highland lodge was built in 1740, and set high enough to get wonderful views overlooking the River Enrick and its valley. There is also the proximity to Urquhart Castle and Loch Ness (the hotel is part of the Original Loch Ness Monster Exhibition Centre complex). Directly opposite the hotel is a 9th century Viking battle site. The welcome is genuinely enthusiastic and down to earth, backed up by open peat fires, wood panelling, and traditional furnishings. An industrious kitchen bakes its own bread and pastries, and sources local and regional Scottish produce for a traditional repertoire that includes local Moray pork, vegetables from an organic garden in the village, game from local estates, and an excellent selection of local and regional cheeses. Expect Lochaber chicken breast stuffed with tarragon and olive emince, or tian of Moray Firth smoked salmon served with potato and horseradish salad to start. Then, perhaps, casserole of West Highland venison, pan-fried pavé of West Coast salmon with mashed potatoes and parsley butter sauce, or a selection of Aberdeen Angus steaks with a choice of sauces. The short, annotated wine list is global in outlook, listed by style, and reasonably priced.

Prices: Set dinner £22.50. Main course from £8.95. House wine £8.95.
Hours: 12.00-14.30. 18.30-21.30. Closed November-Easter.
Rooms: 50 en suite.
Cuisine: Traditional Scottish.
Other Points: No-smoking area. Children welcome. Garden. Car park. Licence for Civil Weddings. Coffee shop and visitors centre.
Directions: Off A82 in Drumnadrochit 14 miles south west of Inverness. (Map 16, F5)

The Loch Inn

Canalside, Fort Augustus, Highland PH32 4AU
Telephone: +44 (0)1320 366302
www.lochinnlochness.com

On the banks of the Caledonian Canal at the heart of the village, this former bank building and Post Office dating from around 1820, was converted into a pub in 1985. It's a stylish, well-run alehouse with flagstone floor, stone walls, open fires at either end, Dutch elm tables and chairs and a popular bar where guest ales might include Nessie's Monster Mash from Tomintoul. Best Scottish traditions underpin the bar menus with fish from Malaig, beef products approved by the Scottish Beef Guild, and Glenuig cheeses all a feature. Wild venison pâté comes with bannocks and redcurrant jelly; grilled Orkney salmon with mango and paw-paw salsa; while steak burgers and aged char-grill cuts are pure Aberdeen Angus. Mid-week summer evenings feature Scottish folk music, out on the loch-side in fine weather, overlooked by the best tables in the upper Gilliegorm Restaurant. Taste of Scotland menus here might feature smoked oysters in champagne jelly, rack of hill lamb with juniper and heather honey jus and Loch Ness Mud Pie, rounded off with Highland Gaelic liqueur coffee and traditional tablet.

Prices: Set lunch £7.95. Set dinner £12.50. Main course restaurant from £9. Bar snack from £5.95. House wine £8.95.
Hours: 12.00-15.00. 18.00-22.00.
Closed 25 December, 1 January. Restaurant closed end of October to March.
Cuisine: Traditional Scottish.
Other Points: No-smoking area. Totally no smoking in restaurant. Garden. Children welcome. Car park.
Directions: Take the A82 from Inverness or Fort William; situated right in the heart of the village on the banks of the Caledonian canal. (Map 15, F4)

Why go to...Loch Ness

Loch Ness is undeniably scenic with heather-clad mountains sweeping down to the wooded shoreline. Yet if it weren't for the legendary monster you would probably drive past without a second glance, especially as the A82 (running southwest along the western side of the loch to Fort William), gives little opportunity to pull over. 'Nessie' has been around a long time, first mentioned in St Adamnan's 7th century biography of St Columba and culminating in the famous incident in 1961 when 30 hotel guests saw a pair of humps break the water's surface and cruise for half a mile before submerging. Drumnadrochit is the centre of 'Nessie' hype – with the pick of the offerings being The Official Loch Ness Monster Exhibition, and where cruises on the *Nessie Hunter* can be booked.

Palio Pasta and Pizza
26 Queensgate, Inverness, Highland IV1 1DJ
Telephone: +44(0)1463 711950
info@palioinverness.com
www.palioinverness.com
Carol and Michael Cracknell describe their informal Italian-style restaurant as "a taste of the Mediterranean in the middle of Inverness", and their simple formula of good value and lively, fresh flavours has won them fans aplenty. The former bank premises make a chic setting for such an informal town-centre eatery, not that there is anything slapdash about it: service does everything properly and efficiently, and the menu caters successfully to a wide range of tastes. The two-course business lunch is a terrific bargain, offering soup or garlic bread, then smaller portions of main-course pasta dishes, perhaps, or half of any pizza, or omelette, with salad, and coffee to finish, all for £5.95. The theatre of an open-to-view kitchen adds to the atmosphere, and the carte runs to grilled goats' cheese and tomato on crisp Italian bread, chargrilled tuna steak with a tomato, olive, Parmesan salad, and smoked salmon tortellini. Pizzas include a very popular quattro formaggi and il toscano: sun-dried tomatoes, artichoke, peppers, olives, roasted courgettes, mozzarella and tomato. The wine list is short, Italian and eminently fairly priced. House wine, for example, is £10.50.
Prices: Set lunch £5.95 (2 courses) and dinner £9.95 (2 courses including a large glass of wine). Main course from £4.80. House wine £10.30.
Hours: From 1st October to 30th April, 12.00-14.15. 17.30-22.00. From 1st May to 31st September, 12.00-22.00 Monday-Thursday. 12.00-23.00 Friday and Saturday. 17.30-22.00 Sunday .
Cuisine: Italian/Mediteranean style.
Other Points: No-smoking area. Children welcome.
Directions: In the city-centre next to the main post office. (Map 16, E5)

Prices: Set lunch £12.50 and dinner £22.50. Main course restaurant from £8.95. House wine £11.
Hours: 11.00-24.00 (weekends until 01.30) Closed 6 January to end of January.
Food served: 12.00-14.00. 18.00-21.00.
Rooms: 9 en suite. Double/twin from £36 per person, single and family room from £46 per person.
Cuisine: Modern Scottish.
Other Points: All rooms non-smoking. Children and dogs welcome. Car park.
Directions: Take the A86 through Kingussie towards Newtonmore; hotel is on

The Scot House Hotel
Newtonmore Road, Kingussie, Cairngorms, Highland PH21 1HE
Telephone: +44(0)1540 661351
enquiries@scothouse.com
www.scothouse.com
Kristin Grantham purchased this typically Scottish Highland stone built hotel, a former manse, early in the summer of 2003 and brings with her a wealth of international hotel experience. Although it is the first hotel she has owned, she has all the right attributes to making Scot House both welcoming and successful. Off the spacious reception lobby is a well-appointed lounge bar – a popular locals' bar – and, being in Speyside, a malt whisky list is not unsurprisingly promoted. From here proceed to an attractive dining room that can comfortably accommodate some 20 guests. Here, a set dinner offers the likes of Scottish smoked salmon salad, and roast duck with cranberry and red wine sauce, with smoked breast of duck with onion marmalade, and monkfish tails pan-fried with fresh cream, garlic butter and Pernod choices from the carte. Light, airy and well-equipped bedrooms on the first and second floors are well proportioned with good quality furnishings, fabrics, and good views. Some of the en suites are small but they are well planned and very well maintained. Throughout the hotel service is both friendly and professional, with attention to detail evident throughout.

Park House ✗ ✿

Station Road, Lairg, Highland IV27 4AU
Telephone: +44(0)1549 402208
dwalker@park-house30.freeserve.co.uk
www.fishinscotland.net/parkhouse

The home-from-home welcome from Mr and Mrs
Walker, the atmosphere and service, all please visitors
to this elegant Victorian-style guest house on the
outskirts of Lairg. The location is a bonus: the quietly
situated house overlooks Loch Shin and the view from
the dining room window is perfect. This is an unusual
house in that it offers very affordable accommodation,
which is combined with some serious field sport
activities. Whether fishing for brown trout, salmon or
sea trout, shooting woodcock or grouse, or stalking for
red, roe and Sika deer, all can be arranged with prior
notice. The three bedrooms are spacious with good en
suite facilities and are very comfortably appointed with
TVs and tea trays. Magnificent breakfasts are hearty,
and evening meals (by prior arrangement) are built
around local and regional produce such as fresh sea
fish, local salmon and trout, Scottish beef, game in
season, and regional cheeses. The championship golf
course at Dornoch and those of Golspie, Brora and
Tain, are all within easy driving distance.

Hours: Residents only.
Rooms: 3 en suite. Double room from £46, single from £28.
Cuisine: Traditional Scottish.
Other Points: No-smoking area. Children welcome. Garden.
Car park.
Directions: On the A836 in Lairg. (Map 16, D5)

Foyers Bay House ▯ ❦ ✗ ✿

Lower Foyers, Loch Ness, Inverness,
Highland IV2 6YB
Telephone: +44(0)1456 486624
carol@foyersbay.co.uk
www.foyersbay.co.uk

Although built in the late 19th century by the British
Aluminium Company for the manager of the local
smelter, this solid house is now a traditionally styled
guesthouse run with great enthusiasm by Otto and
Carol Pancirolli. The setting makes the most of the
Loch Ness views, and the grounds are set amid forests,
nature trails and adjoin the famous Falls of Foyer.
Five bright and spacious bedrooms in the main house
mix smart fabrics with good-quality furniture and
gleaming en suite bathrooms. Within the grounds are
six semi-detached lodges with large balconies and
garden furniture, three bedrooms (one double, one
twin, one bunk), fully fitted kitchen, and lounge.
The Café Conservatory overlooks the loch and offers
light meals, snacks, cakes and coffee, with more
substantial menus available in the evening. Scottish
rollmop herrings or homemade straciatella could
precede homemade ragout of Highland venison or
sirloin steak mâitre d'hôtel, with toffee crunch pie and
cream to finish.

Prices: Set dinner from £10.95. Main course from £5.95.
Wine from £7.50.
Hours: 12.30-16.00 (snacks only). 19.00-20.00. Closed for lunch
on Tuesday and Friday. Closed 6-26 January.
Rooms: 5 en suite. Double room from £48, single from £30.
Cuisine: Scottish/Continental.
Other Points: Children welcome over 5 years old. Garden.
Car park.
Directions: From Inverness take the B862 to Dores, then fork
right along B852 to Foyers. (Map 16, F5)

Allt-nan-Ros ▯ ✗ ✿

Onich, Fort William, Highland PH33 6RY
Telephone: +44(0)1855 821210
lr@allt-nan-ros.co.uk
www.allt-nan-ros.co.uk

The lovely family hotel is set on the seashore and the fabulous panoramic
views across Lochs Levin and Linnhe to the mountains beyond from all
rooms (except one bedroom) are just one of the glories of a stay here.
Within, it is neat and well ordered, with personal service from excellent
long-serving staff headed by James and Fiona Macleod. The bar and
lounge are homely, with a roaring fire lit in the white marble fireplace in
the bar on colder days. Bedrooms are spacious, with five rooms on the
ground floor offering disabled access; two in particular are fully converted
with properly equipped bathrooms. Other rooms vary in style, but all
have pretty fabrics and are decorated and maintained to a very high
standard, with superior rooms offering CD players, as well as the
standard electric blanket. There are two, light, cottagey bedrooms in the
converted stables. The dinner menu is short, simple and steers clear of
overelaboration, with prime raw materials meticulously sourced. Locally
smoked salmon, the Macleods own smoked venison, good local seafood
including Mallaig cod with wilted spinach and their own grain mustard
sauce, game from Letterfinlay Game, own-grown herbs - the list is endless.

Prices: Set price lunch £15 and dinner
£30. House wine £12.95.
Hours: 12.30-13.30 and 19.00-20.30.
Rooms: 20 en suite. Double room from
£150, single from £75. Prices include
dinner, bed and breakfast.
Cuisine: French and Scottish.
Other Points: No smoking area.
Children welcome. Garden. Car park.
Directions: Ten miles south of Fort
William on the A82. (Map 13, A4)

Prices: Main course from £12. Bar snack from £6.75. House wine £7.95.
Hours: 11.00-23.00.
Closed New Years Day
Food served: 12.00-14.30)(from 12.30 on Sundays). 18.00-21.30.
Rooms: 11 en suite rooms in hotel and 4 cottages. £40 per person bed and breakfast.
Cuisine: Modern Scottish.
Other Points: No-smoking area. Garden. Children welcome. Licenced for civil weddings.
Directions: Seven miles north round the coast from Kyle of Lochalsh. (Map 15, F3)

The Plockton Hotel ★ ◧ ✕ ◿

Harbour Street, Plockton, Highland IV52 8TN
Telephone: +44(0)1599 544274
info@plocktonhotel.co.uk
www.plocktonhotel.co.uk

The Pearson family's uniquely converted inn is fully committed to caring for its guests; from fresh flowers in the lobby and hot water bottles in the beds to limited edition Hamish MacDonald prints on the walls and cosseting sofas to flop into. Day-rooms include a stone-walled leather furnished reception lounge, a non-smoking snug, two bars with open fires and log-burning stove, a friendly fusion of cask ales, fine wines and finer malts, and the new restaurant. Food reflects the hillsides, sea and mountains of the area. Locally caught shellfish landed at the pier daily, west coast fish from Gairloch and Kinlochbervie, hill-fed lamb and Highland beef from the butcher's in Dingwall and locally-made west Highland cheeses feature on comprehensive, daily changing menus. House specialities embrace traditional fish and chips, alongside cream of smoked fish soup, pints of prawns and the celebrated Plockton Smokies of smoked mackerel baked with cream, tomato and cheese topping. There is casserole of Highland venison with juniper berries, Highland beef steak platters and daily vegetarian options, all at blinkingly generous prices. Real food and wine, real value and real Highland hospitality conspire together to make this a place that's hard to leave.

The Shieldaig Bar ◧ ✕ ◿

Shieldaig by Strathcarron, Wester Ross, Highland IV54 8XN
Telephone: +44(0)1520 755251
tignaneileanhotel@shieldaig.fsnet.co.uk

Connected (literally) to Tigh an Eilean Hotel, this is the locals' bar of Shieldaig village, standing on the banks of Loch Torridon with stunning views of islands and hills to the open sea beyond. Built in 1800 to encourage local fishing in the area, it has stayed true to its founders' foresight for over 200 years: seafood and shellfish are as fresh as it comes with the Tigh an Eilean's newest custodians sourcing hand-dived scallops and clams, fish from Kinlochbervie and creel-caught crab and lobsters straight from the jetty. They also make their own bread and chips, obtain their salads and soft fruits locally and provide homemade soup and sandwiches right through the day. In addition, there are daily specials such as fresh crab bisque, haggis with whisky cream, poached Scottish salmon with Drambuie and dill sauce and, perhaps, heather cream cheesecake for pudding. From courtyard tables visitors can observe the herons, seals and otters out in the bay or roam the rock pools in search of crabs and limpets. There are regular sessions of live traditional music and, when night settles in, comfortable overnight accommodation next door.

Prices: Bar main course from £6.25.
Hours: April to October, 11.00-23.00. Sunday 12.30-22.00. November to March, 11.00-15.00. 17.00-23.00 (Sunday 12.30-22.00).
Food served: 12.00-14.30, Sunday from 12.30. 18.00-20.30
Cuisine: Scottish Seafood.
Other Points: No-smoking area. Garden. Children welcome. Car park.
Directions: Centre of village off the A896 Lochcarron to Kinlochewe road. (Map 15, E3)

Brae Guest House ✕ ◿

Shore Street, Ullapool, Highland IV26 2UJ
Telephone: +44(0)1854 612421

Mr and Mrs Ross run the longest established guesthouse in Ullapool - in residence for some 45 years - it is also one of the nicest in Scotland. The seafront Victorian property was originally two houses and two shops and everything is of a very high standard, from the genuinely warm welcome on arrival, to the nine homely, comfortable bedrooms and the excellent traditional breakfast in the morning. The setting, on the front overlooking Loch Broom, is splendid and Brae House is within easy walking distance of the village centre and the Stornoway ferry. Although the Rosses no longer offer evening meals, there are several restaurants in Ulllapool that they would be happy to recommend. The guesthouse is open from May to September only.

Prices: Main course from £5.50.
Hours: 17.30-21.30. Closed October to May.
Rooms: 11, 9 en suite. Double room from £26 per person, single from £24.
Cuisine: Traditional Scottish.
Other Points: No-smoking area. Children welcome. Car park.
Directions: In the centre of Ullapool. (Map 15, D4)

Port Royal Hotel Russian Tavern

37 Marine Road, Kames Bay, Port Bannatynne, Isle of Bute PA20 0LW
Telephone: +44(0)1700 505073
stay@butehotel.com
www.butehotel.com

Three miles north of Rothesay, in the pretty village of Port Bannatyne, Norwegian-born Dag Crawford and his wife Olga, a Russian palaeobotanist, are establishing themselves as a new breed of innkeepers, describing themselves as running a 'pre-revolution Russian tavern'. The Georgian building is in a stunning location, overlooking Kames Bay with views to the Cowal Hills. It's an amiable place, the friendliness is genuine, and service relaxed. Dag cooks a brasserie-style menu of dishes that have a strong Russian accent - the beef Stroganoff is considered outstanding, but gets strong competition from blini with marinated herring, smoked trout and caviar, and spicy Russian sausage served with apple, latkas, red cabbage and sauerkraut. Local produce plays a big part, notably Highland beef and fish and langoustines from the bay. A typical dinner of langoustine soup, halibut steak in cream and white wine sauce with new potatoes, mushrooms and artichokes, with fresh fruit, cream and ice cream filled Russian Pavlova, is remarkable value. To drink, try a 'pint' of Vaucluse wine (£5), one of the excellent real ales from Scottish micro-breweries, or even a glass of Imperial Russian stout. Upstairs, there are five unpretentious, good-value bedrooms, two are en suite.

Prices: Set lunch and dinner £17. Main course £9. Main course (bar/snack) from £5.50. House wine £5.
Hours: 11.00-01.00 (until 02.00 on Saturday). Closed 1-21 November.
Rooms: 5 rooms, 2 en suite. Rooms from £22 per person, £26 for an en suite.
Cuisine: Traditional Russian.
Other Points: No-smoking area. Children welcome. Beachfront. Car park. Golf course at the rear.
Directions: Three miles north along the coast road from the Rothesay (ferry) on the Isle of Bute. (Map 13, C4)

Hotel Eilean Iarmain

Eilean Iarmain, Isle Ornsay, Sleat, Isle of Skye
IV43 8QR
Telephone: +44(0)1471 833332
hotel@eilean-iarmain.co.uk
www.eileaniarmain.co.uk

Built in 1888 as an inn, the magnificent setting beside a fishing harbour draws visitors. Simplicity and style go hand in hand here - there's an element of the cosy traditional, juxtaposed with a great deal of rural chic. The 16 bedrooms are all smartly individual, one has a canopy bed from nearby Armadale Castle, and there are four suites in the converted stables. In the often bustling timber-clad bar you can sample over 30 local malt whiskies, including their own blend Te Bheag, hear Gaelic spoken, and tuck into some first-rate bar food, perhaps lunchtime sandwiches and homemade soups, or hearty casseroles, prime steaks and fresh local fish. The dining room has a civilised air with candles and fresh flowers. Local seafood includes oysters from the hotel's own beds, shellfish from their private stone pier, and game, especially venison, from the estate. A typical five-course dinner could include hand dived scallops, seared and served with a salad of organic leaves and herbs, cream of celery and pear soup, steamed fillet of plaice with red fish mousse, tartare potato mash and a dill flavoured butter sauce, Scottish cheeses, and brandy snap basket of Chantilly cream, berries and fruit.

Prices: Set lunch £16.50. Set dinner £31. House wine £15.85.
Hours: 08.00-23.00.
Food served: In the bar 12.00-14.30. 18.30-21.00. In the restaurant 19.30-21.00.
Rooms: 4 suites in restored stables at £200, 12 en suite. Double/twin room from £60 per person, single occupancy £90.
Cuisine: Modern Scottish.
Other Points: No-smoking area. Children welcome. Garden. Car park.
Directions: 40 miles from Portree and seven miles from Broadford on the A851. (Map 15, F3)

The Stein Inn

MacLeod's Terrace, Stein, Waternish, Isle of Skye
IV55 8GA
Telephone: +44(0)1470 592362
angus.teresa@steininn.co.uk
www.steininn.co.uk

Skye's oldest inn stands on the shores of a quiet sea loch with stunning views over the water to the Hebrides. Combine this peaceful location with the charm of a traditional flagstoned bar, hearty food prepared from fresh local produce, comfortably refurbished bedrooms, and glorious never-ending sunsets, then you have the perfect place to stay if touring the island. Expect a warm welcome from Angus and Teresa MacGhie and a well stocked bar that dispenses quality ales brewed on the island with a menu of over 80 malt whiskies. Enjoy a dram of Talisker on wild winter nights beside the open peat fire, or sup a pint of Isle of Skye Cuillin Red by the shore on balmy summer evenings. Angus makes good use of local seafood and Highland lamb, beef and venison in preparing his daily changing menus. Choices range from traditional staples like homemade pea and ham soup and decent sandwiches (try the fresh local crab) to Dunvegan langoustine salad, fresh Talisker oysters, West coast mussels steamed in cider and sage, whole sea bass with vermouth and tarragon sauce, and venison pie. Leave room for sticky toffee pudding or a plate of wonderful Scottish cheeses.

Prices: Main course from £5.25. House wine £7.65.
Hours: 11.00-24.00. Sundays 12.30-23.00. Closed 25 December and 1 January.
Food served: 12.00-16.00. 18.00-21.00.
Rooms: 5 en suite. Double room from £25.
Cuisine: Traditional British.
Other Points: No-smoking area. Children welcome. Dogs welcome. Garden. Car park.
Directions: Seven miles north from Dunvegan (B886); 22 miles from Portree; 55 miles from Skye Bridge. (Map 15, F2)

Brough House

Milton Brodie, Forres, Moray IV36 2UA
Telephone: +44(0)1343 850617
annlawson@librario.fsnet.co.uk

Rosemary Lawson's charming, secluded country house is set in delightful gardens and countryside well off the beaten track for most tourists - it is worth seeking out. The minute you set foot in the classic entrance hall with its black and white tiled floor, the welcome is warm. First and foremost, this is a family house, tastefully furnished with beautiful period pieces, knick-knacks, and pictures. There's a very comfortable sitting room, a dining room with a highly polished dining table where a magnificent breakfast is served family style (with dinner by arrangement) and three, spacious en suite bedrooms filled with delicately painted Japanese furniture and lots of thoughtful touches. Indeed, everything here is lovely, with a perfect garden and some very pleasant walks in the immediate vicinity.

Prices: B&B. Dinner by prior arrangement. Set dinner £20.
Rooms: 3. Double room from £35 per person, single from £45.
Other Points: No-smoking area. Garden. Car park. Credit cards not accepted.
Directions: Turn north off A96 two miles 4 miles east of Forres, signed East Grange. In 1 mile go right over hump-backed railway bridge; Brough House at junction in half a mile. (Map 16, E6)

Minmore House

Glenlivet, Moray AB37 9DB
Telephone: +44(0)1807 590378
minmorehouse@ukonline.co.uk
www.minmorehousehotel.com

Lynne and Victor Janssen have created a peaceful and idyllic spot. From the warm welcome at the front door, the elegant hallway leads through to a lovely, wood panelled sitting room with books, and a selection of over 100 whiskies from the small bar. In the dining room, mahogany tables are beautifully arranged with fresh garden flowers, crisp white linen and low candlelight. The set four-course dinner menus change every day and make the best of prime raw materials and vegetables from the hotel's organic vegetable garden; even the water is from a natural spring - also used by the Glenlivet Distillery next door. Roasted pepper soup could be followed by seared king scallops baked in prawn sauce, with mains of fillet of Aberdeen Angus served with parisienne potatoes, balsamic green beans and honey and whisky glazed baby carrots, finishing with hot apple and tarragon soufflé with Calvados cream. Upstairs, the bedrooms are luxurious and beautifully decorated with each room named after a whisky. A capacity for making you feel at home is apparent in each room, with a collection of chocolates and a small bottle of whisky on each dressing table.

Prices: Light lunch from £7. Set dinner £35 (4 courses). House wine £15.95.
Hours: 12.00-14.30. Dinner served from 20.00. Closed February and one week in October.
Rooms: 10 en suite. £65 per person bed and breakfast. £97.50 per person for afternoon tea, dinner, bed and breakfast. Suites £120 per person.
Cuisine: French.
Other Points: No-smoking area. Children welcome over 10 years old. Garden. Car park. Three miles of fly fishing.
Directions: Follow A9 to Aviemore, then A95 and B9008 towards The Glenlivet Distillery; Minmore House is just before the distillery. (Map 16, F6)

Prices: Main course lunch from £7.50. Main course dinner from £14.95. House wine £10.95.
Hours: 12.00-14.00. 18.30-21.00. Closed Sunday and Monday, first two weeks of January and last two weeks of August.
Cuisine: Modern Scottish.
Other Points: Totally non-smoking. Children welcome over 10 years old. Car park.
Directions: Next to the river in the centre of Perth. (Map 14, B6)

63 Tay Street Restaurant

63 Tay Street, Perth PH2 6NN
Telephone: +44(0)1738 441451
www.63taystreet.co.uk

This immediately likeable contemporary restaurant mixes spring colours and fresh flowers with blond wood, white linen-clad tables with blue upholstered chairs, and offers a superb view across the Tay to the Kinnoull Hills through large windows. Jeremy Wares brings an impressive CV to this, his first solo venture, with time spent in some splendid London and Scottish establishments contributing to the essentially classic style that underpins his cooking. However, the finely tuned repertoire fizzes with lively up-to-date ideas, partnering seared Skye scallops with tomato risotto and onion grass, say, or corn-fed breast of chicken with confit of root vegetables, cocottes, and lemon and garlic sauce. Primary materials are well sourced and properly treated, be it haunch of Perthshire venison with choucroute, potato gnocchi and red wine jus, or pan-fried fillet of halibut with shallots, white beans and wild mushroom ragout. To finish, there may be poached rhubarb shortbread with crème chantilly. Carte prices are fixed for each course, with the same principle applied to a very good value set lunch that could bring spaghetti of Skye prawns with chilli and coriander, Tay Street fish cake with spinach, tomato confit and beurre blanc, and raspberry crème brûlée.

ANYONE FOR A
WEE DRAM?

*Anna Burges-Lumsden travels the
Scottish whisky trail and learns
about nosing, the optimum tasting
temperature, and never to add ice.*

Dry, green, mellow, round and sharp are but a few terms that may not instantly spring to mind whilst sipping a whisky and coke in your local. However, should you wish to acquire the skills to enable such identification of flavours, whilst learning the art of 'nosing' your favourite tipple, then head for the hills and valleys of the famous Malt Whisky Trail in bonnie Scotland for an adventure steeped in history and enveloped in outstanding beauty.

The earliest record of distilling in Scotland dates from 1494 when 'the water of life' or, as it was first known, *uisge beatha*, was lauded for its medicinal qualities, being prescribed for the prolongation of life, the preservation of health, and for the relief of palsy, colic and even smallpox. However, primitive equipment and lack of sound scientific knowledge rendered much of the spirit produced in the early days so potent as to be occasionally life threatening! But knowledge was quickly acquired and distilling methods dramatically improved to ensure that whisky has now become inextricably woven into the fabric of Scotland's history, culture and customs.

With regards to etiquette, there remain endless disputes as to the correct method for tasting the fiery water. Traditionalists maintain that there are only two things one should add to a measure of scotch, the first is water and the second is more scotch. Some believe the addition of pure spring water serves to open the bouquet whilst enhancing the distinctive aroma and prolonging the drinking experience. A few whiskies, especially the older ones, and those bottled at 40%, give their best without adding water as it is believed that your own saliva will act as a sufficient dilutant. Whisky at proof strength, however, anaesthetises the nose and sears the tongue, rendering you incapable of effectively evaluating the sample, and therefore must always be taken with water. The question of ice provokes further debate. Serving whisky in this state is said to close down the flavour-bearing chemicals and so is inadvisable if you want to appreciate the aroma of the whisky to the fullest.

Now to the concept of 'nosing' – a pastime which many argue constitutes no less than 40% of the entire pleasure of whisky. Whisky tasting is performed principally via the nose – a far more acute organ than the tongue – although the two interrelate as the sample is swallowed. It is said that whisky is best appreciated at the equivalent room temperature of an old-fashioned Scottish parlour (15° C) and must be tasted from a 'snifter' which allows you to swirl the spirit and gather the aromas round the rim.

Due to an abundance of the purest fresh water and a fortunate coincidence of perfect climate and geology, half of Scotland's distilleries have evolved among the northern foothills of the Grampian Mountains to form the famous Malt Whisky Trail. Arriving in Aberdeen, your first port of call should be the home of Chivas Royal and the oldest working distillery of the Highlands – Strathisla Distillery in Keith and open April to October. Just 58 miles from Aberdeen, you will discover the art of the blender by tutored whisky nosing, and the relaxed pace of a self-guided tour, before sitting back and sipping a beautifully crafted dram in luxurious comfort..

Venture 29 miles north west along the A96 and you will discover the smallest working distillery in Moray which is open all year round. Benromach Distillery was founded in 1898, but for many years suffered countless closures and ownership changes. But 1993 saw the arrival of Gordon & MacPhail who renovated the distillery and transformed it to its former glory. Five years later the distillery was officially opened and visitors were first welcomed in 1999. Enjoy the guided tours, tasting and the exhibition or relax in the "wee nook" and travel the historical journey of the creation of Benromach Distillery and Malt Whisky Centre.

For a perfectly preserved time capsule of the distiller's craft, visit the last distillery to be built in the nineteenth century – Dallas Dhu Historic Distillery. Despite being no longer in production, it has been preserved for posterity as a traditional and historic industrial museum under the aegis of the Scotland's Historic Buildings and Monument Directorate. Nestled between the Findhorn and the Lossie rivers, it is believed that the name derives from the Gaelic for 'black water valley' although it is not certain whether this refers to the colour of the water or derives from an earlier brand name for a

Delight in the surrounding splendour as you plunge into the undulating hills of Speyside on route to the only malt whisky distillery pioneered by a woman. Cardhu Distillery in Knockando (also known as Cardow or Cardoor), derives from the Gaelic for 'black rock' and was established in 1824 by a local farmer, John Cumming. Prior to this time, illicit distilling was clearly apparent, but it is said that John Cumming relied on the aromas of his wife's home baking to conceal the presence of a still from the excise men! The unique, unhurried and unchanging method of distillation, coupled with magnificent fresh mountain spring water, yields a malt of the subtlest flavour and silkiest texture. Cardhu malt matures for 12 years in specially selected oak casks, during which time it mellows to develop the smooth, sensuous flavour that defines the award winning Johnnie Walker blends. The distillery is open all year.

Between mid-March and the end of October, visit the wild and lonely setting of The Glenlivet Distillery near Tomintoul, established in 1824 by George Smith, one of the first to take out a government license to legally distil on Speyside. Savour a complimentary dram of the finest Glenlivet, 12 year old malt, whilst enjoying a guided tour of the distillery and the vast bonded warehouse where the famous spirit matures to a whisky of infinite subtlety and grace.

Near Dufftown, you will discover the home of one of the world's most favourite tipples and one of the very few Scottish whisky companies still remaining in the hands of its founder, the Glenfiddich Distillery. Established by William Grant in 1887, Glenfiddich represents the time-honoured method of making malt whisky and is the only Highland single malt to be distilled, matured and bottled at its own distillery. Using a single source of water ensures Glenfiddich's unique purity of taste. It is open all year except between Christmas and Near Year.

Savour the sights, sounds and smells of the bustling workshops at the multi award winning Speyside Cooperage in Craigellachie. It has been owned and run for three generations by the Taylor family and forms an essential part of the Malt Whisky Trail as you can watch the highly skilled coopers and apprentices practising their ancient crafts of restoration. Each year nearly 100,000 oak casks are repaired here although many beyond repair are used to create the delicious smoky flavour of Scottish smoked salmon.

And finally, from mid-March to mid-October, in a sheltered glen, in the heart of malt whisky country, you will find the only distillery named after its owners - Glen Grant Distillery in Rothes. Marvel at the magnificent shining copper stills which produce the light, floral malt whisky which is "different by tradition" and take a stroll through the spectacular Victorian Woodland Garden, originally created by Major Grant, where you can enjoy a wee dram from Major Grant's secret whisky safe.

Something in the region of 20 million gallons of whisky – that's 160 million bottles – evaporate into the atmosphere each year, which may explain why visitors find the air of Scotland so delightfully invigorating! A little suggestion – come, test this theory for yourself.

Let's Eat ★ ✕

77-79 Kinnoull Street, Perth PH1 5EZ
Telephone: +44(0)1738 643377
enquiries@letseatperth.co.uk
www.letseatperth.co.uk

Since opening Let's Eat in 1995, Tony Heath and Shona Drysdale have won many supporters, drawn by their sheer delight in the cooking of produce from Scotland's natural larder. Venison, for example, comes from the Rannoch Moors and nearby Eassie Farm supplies beautiful asparagus and sea kale. These prime raw ingredients are translated in a confident way, bringing on such dishes as terrine of pigeon, chicken and black pudding with spiced apple and cumberland sauce, and grilled fillets of sole with chive mash and a sorrel sauce. Classic techniques, seen in prime fillet of Angus beef with truffled wild mushroom, potato cake, button onions, creamed spinach and a Madeira and red wine sauce, are deployed to good effect. But there are homely touches too, as in grilled black pudding and bacon with sautéed lamb's liver, mashed potato, onion gravy and poached egg. Textures are well managed - herb crusted loin of local lamb, served with gratin potatoes and rosemary jus, nicely contrasted with confit of lamb shoulder. Puddings are equally impressive, note a perfect honey, whisky and oatmeal parfait with delicious local strawberries and a tuile biscuit. The wine list is quite extensive and very well priced, with a number offered by the half bottle.

Prices: Main course lunchtime from £9.50. Main course dinner £13.95. House wine £11.
Hours: 12.00-14.00. 18.30-21.45. Closed Sunday, Monday, two weeks in January and last two weeks in July.
Cuisine: Modern British.
Other Points: No-smoking area. Children welcome.
Directions: In the centre of Perth on the junction of Atholl Street and Kinnoull Street. (Map 14, B6)

Over Kinfauns ★ ◇

Over Kinfauns, Kinfauns, Perth PH2 7LD
Telephone: +44(0)1738 860538
b&b@overkinfauns.co.uk
www.overkinfauns.co.uk

The 19th-century stone-built traditional Scottish farmhouse is set in two acres of gardens through which the Coronation Walk runs. This was the route taken by the ancient kings of Scotland, travelling from Falkland Palace to Scone Place to be crowned. Within, lavish attention to detail teams elegant colours such as creams, buttermilks, yellows and pinks with tasteful antique furnishings, and fresh flowers are everywhere. All three en suite bedrooms are stylish and have amazing views over the Perthshire glens. The breakfast-cum-dining room is bright and modern in style, with Continental wrought-iron chairs with cushions and a custom-made dining table. This is the setting for Anne Maclehose's modern British cooking of fine-quality raw materials (much of it sourced locally, with seasonal fruit and vegetables from the garden), all treated in an imaginative yet straightforward, uncomplicated manner. A typical meal could open with warm red onion tart on a bed of herb salad with Parmesan shavings and warm bread, then roast leg of Scottish lamb with a redcurrant gravy, served with Aga potatoes and seasonal vegetables, with fresh fruit pavlova and a selection of regional cheeses to finish.

Prices: Set dinner £25.
Hours: Dinner served 19.30-20.00.
Rooms: 3 en suite. Double room from £70, single from £45.
Cuisine: Modern British.
Other Points: Totally no smoking. Children welcome over 12 years old. Garden. Car park.
Directions: From Perth take A90 towards Dundee. In two and a half miles turn left to Kinfauns, then left again in 300 yards. (Map 14, B6)

Prices: Set lunch £12. (2 courses). Set dinner £32.50 (8 courses). Bistro main course from £12. House wine £9.50.
Hours: 11.00-14.30. 18.00-21.30. Closed Tuesday and month of January.
Rooms: 5 en suite. Double from £60.
Cuisine: Modern British.
Other Points: Totally no smoking. Children welcome. Car park.
Directions: Take B8079 off A9, 5 miles north of Pitlochry. In Blair Atholl take Golf Course Road by Tilt Hotel; restaurant in 50 yards. (Map 14, A6)

The Loft Restaurant ✕ ◇

Golf Course Road, Blair Atholl, By Pitlochry, Perth & Kinross PH18 5TE
Telephone: +44(0)1796 481377
theloftrestaurant@amserve.com
www.theloftrestaurant.co.uk

At first sight the Loft is an unusual complex, made up of a restaurant, bistro, and swimming pool. But once up the external staircase, the old beams, stone walls and oak flooring of the restaurant create a cosy atmosphere. It is also the place to try the cooking of Britain's youngest head chef. When chef Paul Collins departed, 16-year old Daniel (son of owner Stuart Richardson), took over the kitchen; even Paul described him as a 'frighteningly good chef'. He seems undaunted by his new position and, with great enthusiasm, delights in telling that he gets venison from 'up here', pointing to the hills behind, and wild garlic from 'over the road'. He also gathers wild mushrooms, found in dishes such as ravioli of wild mushrooms, and roast quail served with Madeira sauce. This could be followed by saddle of local roe deer Wellington, and parfait of vanilla, poached fruits, five spice sabayon, with caramel soufflé with its own ice cream to follow; ice creams are a trademark of the restaurant. There's also the option of sampling Daniel's cooking in the less formal Bistro of the Loft. Here, amongst the rough plastered walls, wooden tables and bar, perhaps a main course of risotto of smoked haddock, leeks and parsley.

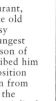

Bridge of Cally Hotel

Bridge of Cally, Blairgowrie, Perth & Kinross PH10 7JJ
Telephone: +44(0)1250 886231
jeff@bridgeofcallyhotel.com

This old drover's inn set in a lovely wooded spot with grounds extending over many, many acres along the banks of the River Ardle, is now a popular sporting hotel. Bedroom numbers have increased from nine to eighteen, the dining room has been remodelled, a conservatory added, and new furniture installed throughout. The use of fresh colours creates a modern feel, especially in the dining room where the colour combination of buttermilk and marigold blends with chairs covered in an oak leaf pattern of pale pink or green. The conservatory makes the most of the riverside location, there's a comfortable sitting room, and the bar is warm and inviting - a fun, friendly place used by locals, and a perfect place for a pint of Speckled Hen or one of a magnificent selection of single malts. Food is served in the bar or the dining room, with menus built around the likes of local venison sausages, wild venison, local lamb, and locally smoked trout, and offering, say, garlic mushrooms in a cream sauce to start, with confit of duck to follow. Good value bedrooms are nice, bright, and comfortable, with light wood furniture, modern bathrooms, and all the usual extras, except room phones.

Prices: Set lunch £15 and dinner £20. House wine £9.95.
Hours: 11.00-23.00 (until 23.45 on Friday and Saturday).
Food served: 12.00-21.00.
Rooms: 18 en suite. Double room from £60, single from £40.
Cuisine: Traditional Scottish.
Other Points: No-smoking area. Children welcome. Garden. Car park.
Directions: Six miles north of Blairgowrie on the A93 heading for Braemar.
(Map 14, B6)

The Conservatory

Ballachallan, Cambusmore, by Callander, Perth & Kinross FK17 8LJ
Telephone: +44(0)1877 339190
enquiries@ballachallan.co.uk
www.ballachallan.co.uk

Well established as a bed and breakfast, noted for good hearty breakfasts (including home-range duck and hen eggs), and jolly good dinners by request, the next obvious move was to create a restaurant. The Conservatory restaurant was built on the side of the house, including a patio that accommodates diners in specially created marquee-style tents with heating; if the weather is good, the sides roll up. The original dining room is incorporated into the restaurant and makes a cosy alternative to the light filled conservatory, especially on winter evenings when the log burning stove is lit. The menu is predominantly fishy (crab bisque, pan-fried scallops, grilled tuna steak in lemon juice, whole oven baked lemon sole, fish and shellfish stew with crusty bread), but for meat eaters, there are locally bred steaks, or a spicy Barcelona chicken. The kitchen likes to keep things simple, so flavours stand out and saucing is restrained. And such is the fame of the Ballachallan breakfast that it is now served to the public – there is good passing trade. For overnight accommodation, three cottage bedrooms have twin beds, lovely views, and private bath or shower rooms.

Prices: Main course restaurant meal from £7.95. Main course bar meal from £5.95. House wine £8.75.
Hours: 12.00-14.00. 18.00-21.00. Closed 24 December-28 February.
Rooms: 3 en suite. Room from £50.
Cuisine: Scottish with traditional French influence
Other Points: No-smoking area. Garden. Children welcome over one years old. Car park.
Directions: One and a half miles east of Callander or five miles west of Doune on the A84. (Map 14, B5)

The Lade Inn

Kilmahog, Callander, Perth & Kinross FK17 8HD
Telephone: +44(0)1877 330152
steve@theladeinntrossachs.freeserve.co.uk
www.theladeinn.com

In the past, this warm, traditional pub was noted for basic pub food. Slowly, things are changing under the new management with good use made of the excellent produce that is available locally such as Highland beef, and seafood from suppliers around Scotland. There are always going to be pub favourites, but now they are freshly prepared and well presented. At present, there is a bar menu as well as a dining menu, but plans are afoot to change the dining room into a comfy seating area, with large sofas and chairs, where people can delve into huge bowls of shellfish chowder and crusty bread, or enjoy a selection of tapas. The decor will probably have a Mediterranean feel, but the rest of the pub will retain its traditional look. There is a good selection on the specials' board, dishes such as salad of Mannbury smoked venison, or goose breast with onion marmalade. Pork fillet with apples and sage, topped with Highland black pudding, or lamb steaks with sun-dried tomato and pesto are typical main courses. A good selection of real ales, such as Lomond Gold, Ben Nevis, Meridian and Greenmantle, change every month or so.

Prices: Main course restaurant from £11.50. Main course bar from £6.50. House wine £9.95.
Hours: 12.00-14.30. 17.30-23.00. Saturday and Sunday 12.00-23.00. Closed 1 January.
Food served: 12.00-14.30. 17.30-21.00. Saturday and Sunday 12.00-21.00.
Cuisine: Modern British.
Other Points: No-smoking area. Dogs welcome. Garden. Children welcome. Car park.
Directions: Exit10/M9. Follow the signs to Crianlarich and Callander on the A84. Kilmahog is 1 mile west of Callander. (Map 14, B5)

The Royal Hotel

Melville Square, Comrie, Perth & Kinross PH6 2DN
Telephone: +44(0)1764 679200
reception@royalhotel.co.uk
www.royalhotel.co.uk

This 18th-century coaching inn has a country house atmosphere, with period antiques, paintings and stylish soft furnishings complemented by the Milsom family and their staff's cheerful, helpful hospitality. The beautifully appointed bedrooms, including three four-poster suites, feature furnishings by local craftsmen, rich fabrics and luxurious toiletries. Dining options are divided between the intimate Royal Restaurant, a conservatory-style brasserie and the cosy Lounge Bar that, along with a wood-and-stone public bar, is a focus of the local community and offers a warm welcome to all comers. Here, home-made venison-and-leek burgers, fish cakes with hot tomato sauce or haggis hash brown and whisky sauce may be washed down with a glass of ale or one of a wide range of Highland malts. Dinner can be a fixed-price three-course affair or taken from a seasonal carte that makes full use of the markets' seasonal produce from fresh fish, meats, and game to Tobermory cheddar, spiky tasting salad greens and luscious summer berries from the local fruit farm.

Prices: Set dinner £26.50. Main course restaurant from £9.75. Main course bar from £5.95. House wine £8.95.
Hours: 11.00-23.00 (until 23.45 Friday and Saturday). Sunday 12.00-23.00.
Food served: 12.00-14.00. 18.30-21.00.
Rooms: 11 en suite. Double/twin £55 per person. Single £70. Four poster suite from £75 per person.
Cuisine: Modern and Traditional English.
Other Points: No-smoking area. Dogs welcome. Children welcome. Car park.
Directions: From the A9 at Greenloaning take the A822 heading for Crieff; then the B827 to Comrie. (Map 14, B6)

The Pend

5 Brae Street, Dunkeld, Perth & Kinross PH8 OBA
Telephone: +44(0)1350 727586
molly@thepend.sol.co.uk
www.thepend.com

The Georgian townhouse is of some charm, situated just off the main street of this attractive Perthshire village, right on the banks of the River Tay. On three floors, all rooms are decorated to a high standard with great attention to detail, including antique furniture featuring in the lounge-cum-dining room as well as in the very comfortably appointed bedrooms. In lieu of a bar, a fully equipped drinks cabinet works on an honesty basis, and attention to detail is such that drinks trays in bedrooms are equipped with fresh milk and a choice of teas. The foundation of the cooking is assiduous attention to detail. Locally, even homegrown vegetables, soft fruits, local cheese, Tay salmon, Perthshire game and smoked salmon from the Dunkeld smokery just across the road appear on the set, four course dinner menu. There could be roast haunch of Perthshire venison in game sauce, pudding of coffee and rum gateau, and cheese served with homemade oatcakes. There is an appealing lack of pretentiousness about the place: the small scale allows for genuine friendliness and it is easy to feel at home. In the past, the whole house has been taken over for small weddings or fishing and shooting parties.

Prices: Set dinner (4 course) from £20.
Rooms: 3. £30 per person bed and breakfast. £50 per person dinner bed and breakfast.
Cuisine: Traditional with French and Italian influences.
Other Points: No-smoking area. Dogs welcome. Children welcome. Car park.
Directions: 12 miles north of Perth on A9. Cross river into Dunkeld and take second right into Brae Street. (Map 14, B6)

Loch Tummel Inn

Strathtummel, By Pitlochry, Perth & Kinross PH16 5RP
Telephone: +44(0)1882 634272

Michael Marsden explains that his hostelry (a former coaching inn built by the Dukes of Atholl), where mobile phones are out of range and TVs ordered on request, is a place for stopping, taking in the view, and rediscovering your forgotten childhood senses of taste, touch and smell. Even on a wet summer evening the green and burgundy colour scheme with cream walls decorated with deer antlers and maps makes the bar (a former stable room) feel cosy. Here, against a backdrop of magnificent views of the loch, a dinner menu built around local lines of supply is served. This is good country cooking with a typical meal producing smoked venison with avocado and walnut oil, followed by Scottish lamb shank braised with tomatoes and peppers, and a 'fantastic' rhubarb and fudge crumble. From the guests' sitting room furnished with comfy sofas and warmed by a log fire, a small staircase leads to six bedrooms furnished in exquisite good taste (even the door plaques are beautifully painted). Breakfast is served above the bar in the old hayloft, which also doubles as a restaurant, and includes salmon smoked by the Marsdens in their own smokery.

Prices: Main course from £10. House wine £4.80 (half litre).
Food Served: 12.15-13.30. 18.15-20.30.
Closed from end October - the week before Easter.
Rooms: 6 rooms, 2 with private bathrooms. Single from £50, double from £75. Family room £100.
Cuisine: Traditional Scottish.
Other Points: No-smoking area. Children welcome. Garden. Car park.
Directions: From Pitlochry take the Blair Atholl road (A9) At Garry Bridge turn left onto the B8019 for eight miles. (Map 14, A6)

Port Na Craig Restaurant ✗

Port Na Craig, Pitlochry, Perth & Kinross PH16 5ND
Telephone: +44(0)1796 472777
www.portnacraig.com

Nestling by the river, and beneath the Festival Theatre,
the Port-na-Craig is a rose-covered stone building that
has been an inn since 1650. The elegant yet simple
restaurant is accessed through a pretty cobbled
courtyard. The building may be old, but there is
nothing old and rustic about the restaurant or its
owners, the Thewes family. Son Bertie is out front
'pouring', and his brother Jamie behind the scenes
cooking; they make a dynamic team. The pale yellow
walls of the restaurant create a lovely airy atmosphere.
The dark green blinds, benched wall seating covered in
subtle local tweed, and fresh flowers from the garden
make a stylish impression that doesn't detract from the
fantastic views of the River Tay from the restaurant's
cottagey windows. Although elegant there is nothing
pretentious about the place. Jamie trained at
Ballymaloe and it shows in a repertoire built around
seasonal local produce that takes in medallions of
venison loin with cinnamon and redcurrant sauce. Fish
comes in the guise of very fresh langoustines dressed in
mint butter with mayonnaise, new potatoes and salad.
Honeycomb ice cream with fruit coulis makes a good
finish.

Prices: Main course from £9. House wine £10.50.
Hours: 12.30-14.00. 18.00-21.00. 13.00-14.30 on Sunday. Closed
Sunday evening, all day Monday and 24 December-late February.
Cuisine: Modern British.
Other Points: Totally no smoking. Children welcome over
eight years old. Garden. Car park.
Directions: Follow signs to Port-Na-Craig and Pitlochry Festival
Theatre; restaurant just below theatre on riverbank. (Map 14, A6)

The Pend, Dunkeld, Perth & Kinross

Prices: Main course from £5. Main course
snack from £2.95.
House wine £2.70 for a small bottle.
Hours: 08.30-17.30.
Closed 25-26 December and 1 January.
Cuisine: Traditional Scottish.
Other Points: No-smoking area. Children
welcome. Patio. Car park.
Directions: On the A82, in the centre of
the village. (Map 14, B5)

Green Welly Stop Restaurant ☕ ✗

Tyndrum, Crianlarich, Perth & Kinross FK20 8RY
Telephone: +44(0)1838 400271
thegreenwellystop@tyndrum12.freeserve.co.uk
www.thegreenwellystop.co.uk

A brilliantly located outdoor equipment shop and all-day café that makes
a perfect pit stop on the way to Oban or Fort William (located just before
the road divides). It's a lively, third generation family business; the café
specialises in good, homely Scottish dishes with everything made on the
premises. Local supplies dictate the menu, which offers fresh soups made
daily, perhaps Scotch broth, cream of kail (traditional winter vegetable
soup), or cullen skink. The baking is excellent, with scones ranging from
plain, through fruit, treacle, and cheese, to cherry, with date and walnut
slice, banana loaf, Border tart and Orkney Broonie making choice
difficult. Main courses include haggis 'n' neeps, as well as crofters stew
(diced lamb with vegetables in a rich sauce) and Hebridean leek pie - all
are full of flavour. Desserts include boozy bread and butter pudding or
Atholl brose trifle. There's an amazing selection of whiskies, locally
smoked salmon, haggis and Scottish preserves on sale in the shop, as well
as own-made snacks to go. With racks of waterproof gear, this is the place
to stock up if the variable Scottish weather has caught you out - Barbour
and green wellies are to the fore.

WILD BORDER COUNTRY

The Borders between Carlisle and Edinburgh contains some of the wildest and most spectacular scenery to be found anywhere in Britain.
Drive length: 101 miles

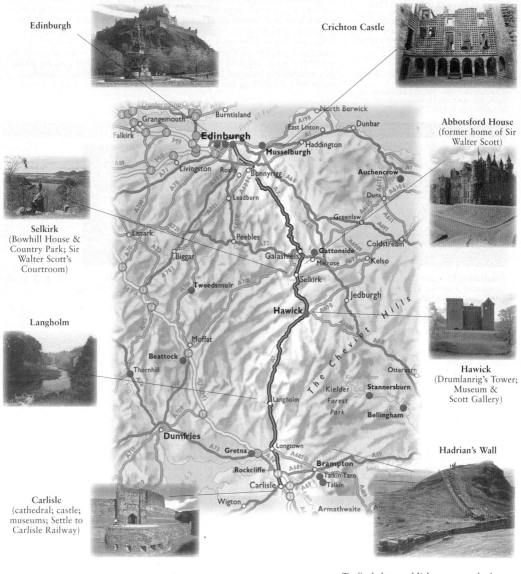

Edinburgh

Crichton Castle

Abbotsford House
(former home of Sir
Walter Scott)

Selkirk
(Bowhill House &
Country Park; Sir
Walter Scott's
Courtroom)

Langholm

Hawick
(Drumlanrig's Tower;
Museum &
Scott Gallery)

Hadrian's Wall

Carlisle
(cathedral; castle;
museums; Settle to
Carlisle Railway)

● Accommodation/Food

● Accommodation

● Food

🌶 Food Shop

To find the establishments marked
here, look up the listing town
marked on the map in bold in the
town index on page 395

Craw Inn

★ 🅓 ✗ ✧

Auchencrow, Berwick-upon-Tweed, Scottish Borders TD14 5LS
Telephone: +44(0)18907 61253
info@thecrawinn.co.uk
www.thecrawinn.co.uk

Derived from the Gaelic name *auch na craw* meaning 'valley field,' the hamlet is surrounded by unspoilt countryside with the Lammermuir Hills rising to the west. Dating from the 18th century, this cosy country pub offers comfortable, sensibly priced bedrooms, all with private modern facilities, good food and wines, and warm hospitality. The bar is well stocked with real ales, a wide range of malt whiskies and some decent wines. In the attractive dining room, robust dishes are built around the best local produce. With fish sourced from Eyemouth, shellfish from St Abbs, lamb from the Lammermuir Hills and game from local dealers, the cooking has a fresh, regional appeal. Expect dishes like pheasant stuffed with haggis and Drambuie sauce, game casseroled in a rich mulled wine marinade, an impressive seafood platter (24 hours notice), and prime Aberdeen Angus fillet steak with a brandy and peppercorn sauce. For pudding try the mulled plum sponge pudding with rum sauce or excellent Scottish cheeses supplied by Ian Mellis in Edinburgh. Soups, pâtés, steak pie, and freshly battered cod are available in the bar. There's a lovely patio with a babbling brook, for summer imbibing and al fresco meals.

Prices: Restaurant main course from £12.50. House wine £9.90.
Hours: 12.00-14.30. 18.00-23.00. 12.00-24.00 on Saturday. 12.30-23.00 on Sunday.
Food served: 12.00-14.00. 18.00-21.00. 12.30-14.30. 19.00-21.00 on Sunday.
Rooms: 3 rooms, 2 en suite, 1 with private bathroom. Double/twin room £35 per person, single £37.50. Two day break offers.
Cuisine: Scottish.
Other Points: No-smoking area. Children welcome. Garden. Car park.
Directions: Follow inn sign off the A1 at the B6437 junction, 15 miles north of Berwick upon Tweed. (Map 14, C8)

Fauhope House

✗ ✧

Gattonside, Melrose, Scottish Borders TD6 9LU
Telephone: +44(0)1896 823184
fauhope@bordernet.co.uk

Ian and Sheila Robson's stunning home offers three en suite bedrooms within the main house, all beautifully and individually decorated, as well as a double and twin-bedded room in an adjacent cottage (which can also be let for self-catering). The house is over 100 years old, and the gardens surrounding it are a sight to behold: terraces, African wrought-iron birds, croquet lawn, tennis court and stunning views over the River Tweed to Melrose, with the Eldon Hills in the distance, are so alluring that many visitors stay two or three nights. Within, rooms are furnished with lovely antiques and stunning art, while the smell of garden flowers from magnificent floral arrangements linger throughout. The dining room is a beautifully appointed room, with polished tables, silverware and crystal. Here, breakfast is served, with homemade preserves and local produce forming the backbone of the menu. Dinner can be arranged with notice, again using home-grown and local produce where possible.

Prices: Meals by prior arrangement.
Hours: Residents only.
Rooms: 3 en suite. Double room from £54, single from £32.
Cuisine: Bed and Breakfast.
Other Points: No smoking area. Children welcome. Garden. Car park.
Directions: On entering Gattonside from A68, turn right immediately past 30mph sign, right again, and up long drive. (Map 14, D7)

Mansfield House Hotel

🅟 🅓 ✗ ✧

Weensland Road, Hawick, Scottish Borders TD9 8LB
Telephone: +44(0)1450 360400
ian@mansfield-house.com
www.mansfield-house.com

This handsome Victorian mansion on a hillside overlooking Hawick combines old world charm with 21st-century credentials: a kitchen strong on up-to-date ideas, and comfortable bedrooms, all wrapped in a large, mature garden. The house has been in the MacKinnon family since 1985 and they successfully combine the character of a large house with the commercial needs of a small hotel. The sitting room is classical with ornate cornicing, open fire and comfy sofas and chairs, and there is a traditional-looking bar for informal bar meals. The majority of the bedrooms are of a good size, are well decorated, and have comfortable chairs and a table in front of the TV. In the kitchen, Sheila MacKinnon relies on local seasonal produce. These materials are fashioned into regularly changing dinner menus that could take in new seasons asparagus with crispy Cumbrian ham, capers and black olive balsamic dressing, or plainly grilled new season's lamb chops teamed with crushed new potatoes and mint. Rhubarb tart or coffee date pudding make satisfying, if filling, desserts. Bar meals are simpler, but equally appealing, the wine list a good mix of France and the new world at keen prices.

Prices: Set lunch £19.50. Set dinner £25. House wine £9.50.
Hours: 12.00-14.00. 19.00-21.00 (until 20.00 on Sunday). Lounge bar 17.30-21.00.
Rooms: 12 en suite. Double room from £60, single from £42, family room from £75.
Cuisine: Traditional Scottish.
Other Points: No-smoking area. Garden. Children welcome. Car park. Licence for Civil Weddings.
Directions: Take A7 to Hawick, then A698 to Denholm/Jedburgh; hotel one mile on right. (Map 14, D7)

Crook Inn

Tweedsmuir, Scottish Borders ML12 6QN
Telephone: +44(0)1899 880272
thecrookinn@btinternet.com
www.crookinn.co.uk

The poet Robbie Burns wrote *Willie Wastle* while
staying at this famous old drovers' inn and locally
born John Buchan set many of his novels in the area -
the glorious Tweed Valley countryside. Scotland's
oldest licensed coaching inn, dating from 1604, it is a
strange but winning amalgam of old stone-flagged
farmers' bar with open fire and bags of character, and
1930s pure art deco in ocean liner-style lounges.
Today's visitors are guaranteed a warm welcome from
Gordon and Susan Bell. As well as providing
comfortable accommodation in five en suite bedrooms
with lovely valley views, the inn offers local Broughton
ales on tap, a good selection of single malts, and
delicious homecooked food with supplies of beef and
lamb provided by a local farmer. Dishes range from
chicken liver pâté with plum chutney, steak pie, Crook
Pillows (cheese, mushroom and leek parcels), Arbroath
haddock and chips, haggis with whisky cream sauce,
and Borders shepherds pie in the bar, to herb-crusted
salmon with herb butter sauce, and sirloin steak with
Drambuie cream sauce.

Prices: Set dinner £15. Main course bar meal from £7.
House wine £10.
Hours: 11.00-24.00. Sunday 12.00-24.00
Closed 25 December and third week in January.
Food served: 12.00-14.30. 17.30-21.00.
Rooms: 5 en suite. Double room from £57, single from £38.50.
Cuisine: Traditional Scottish.
Other Points: No-smoking area. Children welcome. Dogs
welcome. Garden. Car park.
Directions: On the A701 Moffat to Edinburgh road, 16 miles
north of Moffat. (Map 14, D6)

Puddleducks

Hillfoots Road, Blairlogie, Stirling FK9 5PX
Telephone: +44(0)1259 761467
thesecretgarden1@tinyworld.co.uk
www.puddleduckstearoom.co.uk

Think quaint, think whitewashed cottage with roses
round the door, and you have Puddleducks, a super
little tearoom (actually two rooms with a veranda
overlooking the Ochil Hills for those days when you
can sit outside). Each room is painted tongue and
groove, soft summery yellows and pinks, has varnished
wood floors and little round tables with checked cloths
on them, and there's a fine array of cakes in one of the
sideboard glass-fronted cabinets. The veranda looks on
to a stunning two acre garden with a stream spanned
by a Japanese-style bridge, little pagodas, weeping
willows, and an amazing array of plants and bushes.
For the keen gardener there's a small garden shop.
Isabel Mitchell has strong links with America, and
many of her cakes have American themes or are based
on traditional American recipes. Everything is freshly
made each day, and blackboard specials include
homemade soup and two or three hot dishes that
change each day, perhaps warm chicken and mango
salad with a warm coconut dressing in a croissant.
There's also quiche and salads, and sandwiches, with a
multitude of fillings, offered on a selection of different
breads.

Hours: 10.30-16.30 Monday to Saturday. 12.00-16.30 Sundays
Call to confirm hours for Christmas and New Year.
Cuisine: Tearoom.
Other Points: No-smoking area. Garden.
Supervised children welcome. Car park.
Directions: On A91 in Blairlogie, 4 miles north of Stirling.
(Map 14, C6)

Prices: Sunday lunch £11.95. Set dinner
£19.95 (4 courses). House wine £8.50.
Hours: 11.00-23.00. Closed 26 December.
Cuisine: Seafood.
Other Points: No-smoking. Children
welcome. Garden. Car park. Licence for
Civil Weddings.
Directions: On the island of Benbecula,
on the Airport over road, 5 minutes from
the ferry. (Map 15, E1)

Stepping Stone Restaurant

Benbecula, Balivanich, Western Isles H57 5DA
Telephone: +44(0)1870 603377

In the group of islands that make up the Western Isles, Benbecula is
regarded as a stepping stone between North and South Uist, hence this
restaurant's name. Due to its central location in the island chain, the small
town makes an ideal base and Benbecula airport has regular flights to and
from Stornoway, Barra and Glasgow. The Stepping Stone is just opposite
the airport entrance. This bright, cheerfully decorated building with
wooden interior, houses the Food Base, which is an informal cafe serving
all day snacks, sandwiches, takeaways and homebaking, and more
substantial meals such as fish and chips, overlooked on the slightly raised
levels by the no-smoking restaurant, Sinteag. Here, three or five-course
meals are served, with the repertoire built around locally caught fish
presented in a simple style, be it fillet of sole with a shrimp sauce, or
scallops with bacon and cheese.

WALES

The Fruit Garden

Groesfaen Road, Peterston-Super-Ely, Cardiff
South Glamorgan CF5 6NE
Telephone: +44(0)1446 760358

Linda and Charles George run about five acres of pick-your-own with the ready-picked fruit sold in their farm shop. The season opens with asparagus, grown in half an acre and sold ready-picked and graded into sprue, cooking and mixed - a crop that takes the Georges through to mid-June. Their land, described as 'top grade loam on a south facing well drained site and well suited to soft fruit' grows several varieties of strawberries, potted cane raspberries, gooseberries, tayberries, blueberries, red and white currants, and black berries as well as jostaberries - a blackcurrant goosberry cross that makes good jam. Ice cream started as an extra, purely for the visitors and limited to strawberries and cream, but proved so successful it has grown into a business with its own dedicated ice cream parlour supplying delis and restaurants.

Hours: PYO: June-July: daily 09.30-19.00.
Directions: At Peterston-Super-Ely off exit 34/M4, or A48 at 'Five Mile Lane', 'Sycamore Cross'. (Map 7, D2)

Glanrannell Park Country House

Crugybar, Llanwrda, Carmarthenshire SA19 8SA
Telephone: +44(0)1558 685230
enquiry@glanrannellpark.co.uk
www.glanrannellpark.co.uk

The glorious setting in 23 acres of wooded parkland with gardens, a trout lake, and abundant wildlife including a red kite eyrie, is undoubtedly Glanrannell's chief asset. In the three years that they have been here, Richard and Lucy Golding have worked hard to remove all traces of the rather run-down 1970s-style hotel that was the building's previous incarnation, removing, for example, the old bar and replacing it with a sideboard that provides drinks on an honesty system. There's plenty of day room space with two comfy lounges and bedrooms have been updated with soft furnishings and colours. En suite bathrooms are being remodelled as funds allow. Richard deals in precise cooking, wise to his limitations as a self-taught cook. Although dinner is optional, most guests take the uncomplicated, no choice, three-course menu with its canny appreciation of well-sourced local ingredients, as word has got around that the food is good. Indeed, the simplicity is a positive bonus: note a late spring meal of coarse tomato soup, terrific Carmarthenshire pork loin with mustard cheese crumble dressed with fresh asparagus, followed by baked apple with homemade cinnamon ice cream; it couldn't be faulted.

Prices: Set dinner £21.50 and £17.50 (2 courses). House wine £9.
Hours: Dinner served at 19.30. No food on Sunday.
Rooms: 7 en suite. Double room from £40 per person, single from £55.
Cuisine: Modern British.
Other Points: No-smoking area. Children welcome over eight years old. Garden (23 acres of grounds). Car park. Lake.
Directions: Off the A40 midway between Llandeilo and Llandovery. Take the A482 signposted to Lampeter and follow the signs to the house. (Map 7, D3)

Harbourmaster Hotel

Pen Cei, Aberaeron, Ceredigion SA46 0BA
Telephone: +44(0)1545 570755
info@harbour-master.com
www.harbour-master.com

Built in 1811, the Grade II listed building once controlled a thriving harbour traffic. Carefully retained inside is the original linen-fold panelling hung with sepia prints of former glory days that are in stark contrast to its total transformation into a sparkling 21st-century small hotel and brasserie. At the helm now are Welsh-speaking Glyn and Menna Heulyn who have charted a new course unthinkable a few short years ago. The seven ultra-modern, ship-shape quarters lead off central, spiral stairs, each with their own colour schemes in sea and sky colours: recessed lighting, power showers and space-age radio alarms are somehow entirely appropriate to the setting. Downstairs in the bar and brasserie real ale and carefully chosen wines stimulate spontaneous bonhommie in front of the open fire and the erudite Anglo-Cwmreig menus are an object lesson in what fine use can be made of local produce. Leaving aside organic free range eggs, Shirgar butter with the home-baked breads, Talybont preserves, Carmarthen ham and all manner of sea foods direct from the jetty, a chosen dinner of Pant Mawr cheese with lemon relish, black beef fillet with dauphinoise potato, wild mushrooms and spinach, rounding off with passion fruit torte on a raspberry coulis could simply not be faulted.

Prices: Main course restaurant from £10.95. House wine £10.50.
Hours: 12.00-15.00. 18.00-23.00. Closed 24 December-18 January.
Food served: 12.00-14.00. 18.30-21.00. Restaurant closed Sunday evening and Monday lunch.
Rooms: 7 en suite. Double/twin from £85. Single from £45.
Cuisine: Modern Welsh.
Other Points: No-smoking area. Totally no smoking in bedrooms. Car park at rear.
Directions: From Aberystwyth take the A487 towards Cardigan. (Map 7, D3)

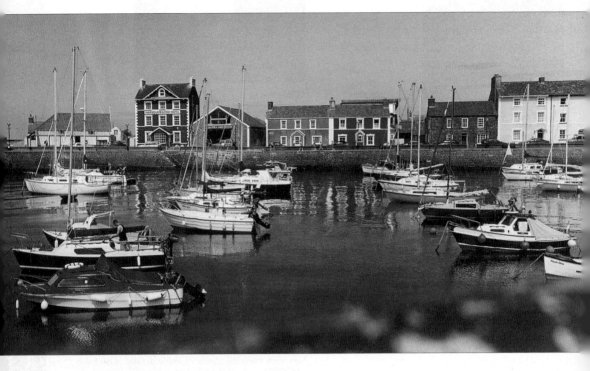

*Map in hand, Martin Greaves travels
to West Wales and discovers a land of
legend, language, and the perfect hotel*

A SENSE OF PLACE

West Wales: the name conjures up the coastal glories of Pembrokeshire and Cardigan, the estuaries of the Teifi, Mawddach and Dyfi. For those who know no other way, there is always the motorway to the western tip of Swansea and dual carriageway to Carmarthen and Haverfordwest beyond. Coast-hugging roads then run from Fishguard, via Cardigan, Aberystwyth, Aberdyfi and Porthmadog to the Lleyn Peninsula, Caernarfon and Anglesey. But, believe you me, there are highways and byways that criss-cross this wonderful land, from which you will return to motorway-bound Middle England in endless chorus of "no-one ever told me all this was here".

Certainly, if you are in possession of a good road map and a willingness to learn your way around, those who are brave enough will travel to the very heart of Red Kite country at Rhayader and follow the Elan Valley road past its escalation of Victorian reservoirs, or over the memorable single-track mountain road that emerges onto a high escarpment at Devil's Bridge overlooking Aberystwyth. Then, halfway up this scenic coastline stands the handsome John Nash designed Georgian town of Aberaeron. Across from its sheltered inner harbour, beloved of Dylan Thomas in the 1940s and the retirement home of late-lamented Welsh tenor Sir Geraint Evans, stands the Grade II listed former harbourmaster's house that guards the western approaches that look out over Cardigan Bay.

Not that many years ago, in this writer's memory, the pungent odours of chips and vinegar at The Harbourmaster pub virtually overwhelmed the saltier shoreline aromas of seaweed and crushed crab-shell,

and the counter of Will Willis's Fish on the Quay, (next door to which you still can buy the best honey ice cream in the Principality). But you notice The Harbourmaster for different reasons now. Rescued from near-dereliction with a new roof and months of renovation, it stands resplendent at the far end of Quay Parade sporting a new-found deep-purple hue and offering its own subtle blend of traditional inn-keeping and, true to its original roots, definitive Welsh hospitality.

Under the watchful eye of its energetic young owners, Glyn and Menna Heulyn, the transformation took place over eight months in the winter of 2001/2, inspired by a sympathetic local architect, interior designer and team of local builders and craftsmen who toiled non-stop in all weathers to create a minor modern masterpiece. The blend of traditional and trendy within is little short of phenomenal. A tiny bar preserves the wood panelling and black-and-white photographs of days of yore; here guests can lounge in front of the cast-iron range or perch on solid-hewn wood blocks as they nurse a pint of real ale, fine wine, sparkling spring water or Welsh organic elderflower cordial.

Opposite, the dining area is implacably modern with its wood-block floor, walls of aquamarine, bright fishy motifs and an almost garish oil of the quayside by local artist Davis Davidson. Menus are presented in both Welsh and English, echoing the multi-lingual banter in the bar as well as a certain egalitarianism that increasingly plays so great a part in dining out these days.

The food itself celebrates the glorious country that spreads inland from this coast and abounds with everything good from its agrarian economy: milled organic flour; farm butter; Nantclyd organic free range eggs; bacon from Dragon Farm, Bethania; Goetre Farm sausages; Rachael's organic yogurts; home-made preserves from Tal-y-bont. Fish and shellfish come from the Bay and Black beef from Welsh Hook butchers at Fishguard. Indeed, the daily fish selection listed on large chalkboards just about says it all: Carlingford oysters, Aberaeron herring with chilli and lime but

and Cardigan Bay lobster with hollandaise, dressed Pembrokeshire potatoes and mixed Tan-yr-allt leaves from the nearby organic farm of that name.

If such a concept is seen as bold, then the design of the bedrooms is just another eye-opener. Of the epithets recently applied – minimalist, modern chic, boutique - none quite fits the bill. The very nature of the building and its location instinctively creates the theme: the colours of the sea and sky unify, while porthole-style windows enhance its nautical look. Yet the rooms themselves shine with unfussy modernity. There are steely up-to-date bedside CD players, wonderfully comfortable beds and fully tiled, brightly-lit bathrooms and showers that are the bees' knees.

At the heart of the operation are the Heulyns: born and brought up locally, yet cool, well travelled and in touch with modern trends. They are in the process of fulfilling a long-held ambition to return to their roots. From their joint former careers in financial services, marketing, media and public relations they have brought to the business an overview and a passion that many of their peers embedded in the hospitality industry could well learn from. And with this has come a certain celebrity that, in a single year, has extended far beyond Wales. They have brought to The Harbourmaster a new generation of customer, eagerly and thoroughly enjoying what is to be found there.

We found Aberaeron in the early summer of 2003 to be full of self-confidence and permeated with a sense of fun. During its 7th annual Seafood Fair, with vehicular access diverted away from Cadwgan Place and Pen Cei, there were upwards of 5,000 in a single day enjoying the shellfish and cookery stalls, the beach art, crab fishing, mackerel barbecues, shanty singers and (yes) whelk-racing. A few penn'orth of yachts bobbed in the harbour at high water and a few bob more of classic Welsh beer was consumed. At its heart, The Harbourmaster proudly (and rightly) took its place; and Aberaeron is that much better for it. West Wales at its best? You'd better believe it!

Hazeldene Guest House

South Road, Aberaeron, Ceredigion SA46 0DP
Telephone: +44(0)1545 570652
hazeldeneaberaeron@tesco.net
www.hazeldeneguesthouse.co.uk

Jackie and John Lewis have completely refurbished their Edwardian sea captain's home, yet have retained period features such as ornate fire surrounds and pilasters, offsetting it all with antique furniture. Immediately noticeable is the warm, personal welcome, an instant reassurance of the style with which this charming B&B is run. The lounge is full of comfy sofas and armchairs, with plenty of reading matter, local information (and wide screen TV). Every care is taken in the three en suite bedrooms, with attention to detail evident in lush soft furnishings, toiletries, towels, colour TV and hot drinks tray (but no phones) and gleaming bathrooms. Breakfast is taken in the dining room and really does run the range of goodies with the menu listed in English and Welsh; dinner is available by arrangement only. Would that there were more B&Bs of this undoubted quality - and at prices that are highly competitive for the area.

Prices: B&B. Dinner £15, occasionally and by prior arrangement.
Hours: Closed October-March.
Rooms: 3 en suite. Double room from £52, single from £30.
Other Points: Totally no smoking. Garden. Car park.
Directions: Quarter of a mile from the A487. Turn off the High Street of Aberaeron by the 'Square Field'. (Map 7, D3)

Hive on the Quay

★ 🍵 ✗

Cadwgan Place, Aberaeron, Ceredigion SA46 0BU
Telephone: +44(0)1545 570445

On many a mad March morning one might be blown clear off the sea wall adjacent to Aberaeron's sheltered inner harbour. Yet, come Easter and the approaching summer, fishing boats float in quietly to deliver the coast's finest fruits de mer to the Holgate family's harbour-side fish shop and the freshest crabs and lobsters imaginable to their peerless seasonal quayside café. As described, the Hive is a busy, swarming place, yet it's the production of incomparable honey ice cream the best, arguably, in the Principality, that threatens to steal the show. There is, however, as much to admire in the friendly and informal all-day teashop which serves hearty lunches of daily special dishes, as well as a splendid buffet of unusual soups and chowders, salads, free-range chicken, savoury and sweet plate pies. Don't miss the braised knuckle of Welsh lamb, or the huge black cherry meringue sundae. Smaller portions of the specials are available to anyone of any age (delighting older customers). Evening meals are served in August from 6pm-9pm with similar menus to those detailed above. Sarah Holgate and her team make their own bread and cakes and use almost entirely organic produce, eggs and cheeses.

Prices: Main course from £4.50. Snack from £2.
House wine £10.25.
Hours: Restaurant open 12.00-15.00 from Spring Bank holiday to mid-September. 18.00-21.00 only in August. Café menu available 10.30-17.00 and 10.30-21.00 in August. Closed in Winter.
Cuisine: British (especially Welsh) and regional European.
Other Points: No smoking in the restaurant. Courtyard. Children welcome.
Directions: At the end of the M4. Continue to Carmarthen via Llandysul to the A487 coast road to Aberaeron. Take the first left after the river bridge to the harbour and the Hive. Street parking available. (Map 7, D3)

Ambassador Hotel

Promenade, Llandudno, Conwy LL30 2NR
Telephone: +44(0)1492 876886
reception@ambasshotel.demon.co.uk

The Williams family offer three generations of experience in running this marvellously traditional Victorian seafront hotel. Jim and Freda Williams started the business in 1946, and the running of the hotel has now passed to Nigel Williams, who maintains a firm hands-on policy that ensures visitors return year after year. Spacious lounges are traditional in looks, there are two plant-filled sun verandas, and the bar is a convivial spot at night. The restaurant offers set-price dinners that aim to please both cautious and adventurous guests, so you'll find fruit juices and a standby boiled ham or beef salad, as well as roast salmon with a mustard and Welsh cheese crust, mushroom sauce and horseradish mashed potato. There's also a very good-value set lunch menu. Bedrooms vary in size, the best being very spacious indeed, but all are light, decorated in soft colours and well thought out; all enjoy sea views.

Prices: Set lunch £6.95 and dinner £15.25. House wine £9.80.
Hours: 11.45-13.45. 18.30-19.30.
Rooms: 57 en suite. Rooms from £31 per person.
Cuisine: British.
Other Points: No-smoking area. Children welcome. Garden. Car park.
Directions: Leave A55 and take the A470 to Llandudno. Follow to Promenade, turn left towards the pier. (Map 7, B3)

Why go to...Llandudno

The Victorian Edward Mostyn's speculative venture to create a seaside resort for the upper middle classes was a huge success. He laid down the street pattern and leaseholders had to submit proposed buildings for approval – which accounts for the extraordinary variety of Victorian architecture, and its remarkable homogeneity as a town. Substantial hotels, erected from the 1850s, attracted an elite clientele; it was here Lewis Carroll met Alice Liddell, the daughter of friends and inspiration for *Alice in Wonderland.* Don't be put off by the traditional nature of the town – and its promenading devotees. Llandudno is an outstanding example of a Victorian seaside resort, remarkable for having retained its nineteenth century character.

Dunoon Hotel

Gloddaeth Street, Llandudno, Conwy LL30 2DW
Telephone: +44(0)1492 860787
reservations@dunoonhotel.co.uk
www.dunoonhotel.co.uk

Over fifty years of family tradition have gone into creating a charming, old-fashioned seaside hotel, a tradition to be continued by new owners Rhys and Charlotte Williams, long-standing, second-generation friends of the previous owners. Young and enthusiastic, they have sensibly embraced a philosophy of 'if it ain't broke, don't fix it', retaining long serving staff and (almost) an appreciation of what Llandudno did best in its Victorian hey-day. The splendid gable-ended mansion, set a block-or-two back from the sea front, is one of many fine examples of Victorian architecture that define this wonderfully traditional resort town. Bedrooms are solidly comfortable and well equipped, oak-panelled public rooms include the Welsh Dresser Bar - sporting a magnificent cooking range. There's a pleasant reading lounge and a more intimate panelled lounge with open fire and cosy corners, in addition to a pool table and solarium. Chandeliers, panelling and magnificently draped windows define the formal restaurant where Mark Martin produces set price five-course dinners, say, mussels in concasse of leek, peppers, tomato and cream, pea and ham soup, pan-fried breast of chicken with chorizo, steamed syrup sponge and English and Welsh cheeses.

Prices: Set Sunday lunch £11.75 (5 courses + coffee) and set dinner £15.50 (5 courses + coffee). House wine £10.50.
Hours: 13.00-14.00. 18.30-20.00. Closed end of December-mid March.
Rooms: 50 en suite. Double room from £64, single from £47.
Cuisine: Traditional British.
Other Points: No-smoking area. Children welcome. Garden/patio. Car park.
Directions: Turn left off Llandudno Promenade near Pier. Continue straight on at the roundabout; hotel is 200 yards on the right. (Map 7, B3)

Queen's Head

Glanwydden, Llandudno Junction, Conwy LL31 9JP
Telephone: +44(0)1492 546570
enquiries@queensheadglanwydden.co.uk
www.queensheadglanwydden.co.uk

Housed in an 18th-century former wheelwright's cottage and workshops, the Queen's Head retains its place at the centre of village life, with a well-frequented locals' bar where real ale is king and a comfortable, sectioned lounge where food is ordered and hastily delivered from the clearly visible, well-organised kitchen. Long one of the area's instigators of the daily blackboard menu, this offers in their seasons the freshest Conwy crab and lobster, skate and sea bass from the Bay, spring new potatoes and summer soft fruits from farther up the Valley. Many appetisers may double as a substantial snack; as in crispy confit duck leg with red onion marmalade, and pea and smoked pancetta risotto with Parmesan shavings. Alternatively there are giant open sandwiches such as Coronation chicken and mushroom vol-au-vents with hollandaise and gruyère topping. From the grill come pork and stilton sausages, Welsh lamb cutlets with plum and soured cherries, and rich local beef and wild mushrooms in a short-crust pastry pie. Home-made cheesecake and fruity Pavlova from the chilled dresser, or gooey hot pecan pie effortlessly transform an informal evening out into a feast of indulgence.

Prices: Main course from £7.95. Bar/snack from £4.95. House wine £10.95.
Hours: 11.00-15.00. 18.00-23.00 (22.30 on Sunday).Closed 25 December.
Food served: 12.00-14.15. 18.00-21.30. Sunday until 21.00.
Rooms: Storehouse cottage sleeps two. £100-£125 for B&B. Self-catering rates available.
Cuisine: Pub food.
Other Points: No-smoking area. Children welcome over seven years old. Car park.
Directions: Follow Penrhyn Bay signs off the A470 Conwy (A55) and Llandudno. (Map 7, B3)

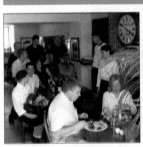

The Kinmel Arms

St George, Abergele, Conwy LL22 9BP
Telephone: +44(0)1745 832207
lynn@watzat.co.uk
www.thekinmelarms.co.uk

Rejuvenated after a period of closure in the 1990s, this fine village dining pub, marches on under the touch of Lynn Cunnah-Watson. Amid country furniture and polished wood floors, everything operates on clean, uncluttered lines around a slate topped bar with its range of quality real ales, wines of the month and exceptional value bin ends. Meals may be taken anywhere - in the cosy lounge, a quieter segregated dining area or the sunny conservatory. From a seasonally adjusted menu, orders are taken with an enthusiasm and confidence matched by the prodigious kitchen output of Weston Holmes. A major medal winner in the 'Cater-Wales' food fair at Llandudno in spring 2003, his signature dish of Welsh beef fillet with stuffed courgette, caramelised leeks, sautéed root vegetables and roast garlic and shallot jus is exemplary. Alongside a range of sandwiches and snacks, traditional Caesar salad prepared 'the Kinmel way' or ' boat sinking battered cod' with tartare sauce make for a more than adequate lunch, with perhaps slow roast lamb shank on honey and mustard mash a mainstay of a full-blown evening feast. Look out for smoked duck breast salad, bacon-wrapped chicken on savoury red pepper sauce on the boards.

Prices: Set lunch on Sunday £11.95. Main course restaurant from £9. Main course bar from £4. House wine £9.95.
Hours: 12.00-15.00. 19.00-23.00. Sunday 12.00-17.30. 19.00-22.30. Closed Monday.
Food served: 12.00-14.00. 19.00-21.30.
Cuisine: Traditional British.
Other Points: No-smoking area. Children welcome before 21.00. Patio. Car park.
Directions: Exit16/M56. A5517 and A550 to A55; St George is 2 miles south east of Abergele. (Map 7, A4)

Barratts Restaurant at Ty'n Rhyl

167 Vale Road, Rhyl, Denbighshire LL18 2PH
Telephone: +44 (0)1745 344138
ebarratt5@aol.com

It is not hard to believe that the building housing Mr and Mrs Barratt's long-running restaurant-with-rooms dates from 1672: panelling and a fireplace constructed from the bedstead of Catherine of Aragon, Henry VIII's first wife, testify to the fact. The ivy-covered house is set in an acre of walled gardens and has a cosy lived-in feel, with tapestries and rich colours complementing highly polished dark wood and a rich mix of collectables and bric-à-brac. Upstairs, the three en suite bedrooms are all spacious, and individually decorated, some with lovely French beds dating from 1872 and Louis XV-style furniture. Downstairs, the bar is filled with over-stuffed sofas, and the restaurant has high ornate ceilings and 10 prettily laid tables. The cooking style, however, is far from antique. Instead it shows a preference for a broadly contemporary way of doing things. The three-course set menu offers the likes of wonton of freshly cooked crab meat with crab sauce. Main courses take in lemon sole filled with spinach and spring onion with ginger sauce, and specialities include Denbigh lamb, Welsh Black beef, and Conwy Bay mussels. The wine list has a wide global choice with bottles all under £20.

Prices: Set dinner £15. Sunday lunch £10. Main course restaurant from £9.50. House wine £9.95.
Hours: 12.00-14.00 Sunday. 19.00-21.30 Monday to Saturday. Residents only on Mondays. Closed one week in February.
Rooms: 3 en suite. Double/twin from £70, singles from £35.
Cuisine: Modern British.
Other Points: No-smoking area. Children welcome. Garden. Car park.
Directions: From A55 take the Rhyl slip road onto the A525 into Rhyl. Pass Sainsbury's and follow the road for quarter of a mile. Barratts is on the right hand side. (Map 7, A4)

Drapers Café-Bar

Tweedmill Factory Outlets, Llannerch Park, St Asaph,
Denbighshire LL17 0UY
Telephone: +44(0)1745 731005
enquiries@tweedmill.co.uk
www.tweedmill.co.uk

Tweedmill Factory Outlets, graded a star attraction by
the Welsh Tourist Board, was, as the name suggests,
once a mill weaving tweed. The conversion includes the
100-seater Drapers Café Bar, a bright, clean, cheerful
space filled with plants, pine furniture and boasting a
large, south-facing patio with beautiful views across an
area designated as being of outstanding natural beauty.
Food (offered at very reasonable prices) is taken
seriously here, and everything on the premises is made
from fresh produce delivered daily. Daily specials could
take in leek and potato soup, or chicken liver pâté,
grilled chicken breast filled with Welsh cheese,
wrapped in smoked bacon and served with a leek
sauce, followed by meringue nest with fresh
strawberries and cream. Snacks and light meals run to
scrambled eggs with smoked salmon, cheese, chive and
bacon bagel, chestnut and mixed bean savoury loaf,
and filled jacket potatoes.

Prices: Main course from £4.95. House wine £6.50.
Hours: 09.30-17.00 (Thursday 19.00, Sunday 16.00).
Closed 25 December.
Cuisine: Modern British.
Other Points: No-smoking area. Children welcome. Patios.
Car park.
Directions: Two miles south of St. Asaph on the A525 to Denbigh.
Follow the tourist signs from A55. (Map 7, A4)

Mike Williams

12-14 High Street, Caergwrle, Wrexham,
Flintshire LL12 9ET
Telephone: +44(0)1978 761078

There's always a lot of friendly banter going on
between the butchers and their customers at this classic
butcher's shop, which has been in the same family for
28 years (with son now training to take over). They
even close for an hour at lunchtime. What
distinguishes this shop is that every piece of properly
hung meat is certified, so its origin is guaranteed. Mike
Williams adheres to the Black Labelling scheme, which
proves the origin of the meat and verifies that this is
what is being sold. Butchers like Mike Williams are a
dying breed, but the quality of their meat is unrivalled
- support them. Specialities include Welsh Black and
Rose beef, own-cure bacon and homemade burgers and
sausages. Business comes from as far afield as Chester
and occasionally from the south. Alongside the meat
business, they also serve as a greengrocers.

Hours: 09.00-17.50. Closed on Sundays.
Closed between 13.00-14.00.
Cuisine: Speciality butchers.
Directions: Five miles along the A542 on the Wrexham
to Mold Road. (Map 8, B5)

Penhelig Arms Hotel

Aberdyfi, Gwynedd LL35 0NA
Telephone: +44(0)1654 767215
info@penheligarms.com
www.penheligarms.com

Prices: Set lunch, 2 course from £10.95.
Set dinner £24. Main course restaurant
from £8.95. Bar snack from £4.95.
House wine £10.
Hours: 11.30-15.30. 17.30-23.00, Sunday
from 18.00-22.30. Closed 25-26 December.
Food served: 12.00-14.30. 18.30-21.30.
Rooms: 14 en suite. Double/twin from
£114 including dinner.
Cuisine: Welsh and Seafood.
Other Points: No smoking in restaurant
or bedrooms. Dogs allowed.
Children welcome. Garden. Car park.
Directions: A493 to Aberdyfi from the
A487 in Machynlleth. (Map 7, C3)

Formerly known as 'Y Dafarn Fach' (The Little Inn) and dating back to
the 18th century, constant updating and improvements over the last 15
years have restored its rightful place amongst the finest of Welsh inns.
Typically, in the Fisherman's Bar, where locals and visitors alike
congregate to enjoy traditional ales and imaginative, locally procured bar
food, wine-loving Robert Hughes has introduced a 'verre de vin' system
that enables up to a dozen wines by the glass to be served fresh from the
bottle in prime condition. This is a true 'local' also, in that fresh fish,
meats, fruit, vegetables and bakery goods all arrive at the door from local
suppliers, featuring within minutes, it seems, on the daily changing menus
that provide such excellent value for money. Diners are charged simply by
the amount they eat from a host of choices: grilled brochette of mixed
fish, Welsh black sirloin steak with peppercorn sauce, and panna cotta
with fresh fruit, being typical temptations to indulgence. The Penhelig
Arms just gets better and better: returning guests, genuinely greeted as old
friends in ever-increasing numbers, request their favourite rooms and the
staff who seem to stay for years enter into the spirit of its relaxed family-
run ambience.

The Bistro

Church Street, Barmouth, Gwynedd LL42 1EW
Telephone: +44(0)1341 281009
bistro.barmouth@btinternet.com
For many, this tiny-fronted, 18-seater restaurant on the main street has reassuring virtues - a cosy, romantically lit interior and generally much chatter between tables. Val Brown does all the cooking (apart from the bread and the bought in speciality ice creams), while husband Gordan supervises out front, dispensing bonhomie and good wines from a sensibly short, quality wine list. Raw materials are good: Conwy and North Sea fish delivered from Llandudno, the local butcher providing the likes of spring lamb and aged beef, with organic herbs and salad stuffs from local growers. There is a comforting familiarity about field mushrooms stuffed with garlic and parsley butter, or Hereford chicken breast topped with bacon and cheese and served with a creamy cider, chunky apple and rosemary sauce, but it is also worth exploring the fish specials: sea bass fillets with citrus butter and lemon and coriander sauce, for example. Vegetarians are catered for, with, say, mushroom tortellini with a creamy cheese sauce, sun-dried tomatoes and pesto. Colourful planters and window boxes extends a certain 'Frenchness', and the Bistro attracts a loyal clientele - that means that booking, especially at weekends, is a must.
Prices: Main course restaurant from £10.50. Vegetarian main course from £8.50. Starter from £3.95. House wine £8.95. Special dietary requirements with advance notice.
Hours: 19.00-20.30, until 21.00 on Saturday.
Closed Sunday to Thursday October-December.
Closed January-March. Closed lunch and all day Wednesday.
Cuisine: Traditional British with Mediterranean influences.
Other Points: Totally no smoking. Children welcome.
Directions: In the town centre. Some street parking which is free at night. (Map 7, C3)

The Black Bear Restaurant and Inn

Betws Newydd, Usk, Monmouthshire NP15 1JN
Telephone: +44(0)1873 880701
Hidden down country lanes, and dedicated for over a decade to 'Food by Molyneux', The Black Bear has the outward appearance of a Dickensian inn that time forgot. Indeed, it is 'the food and the man' that draws a steadfast band of regular diners here to enjoy his touches of eccentricity, produce drawn exclusively from the day's shopping and unexpected food combinations and flavours that are the mark of a man who lives for his passion; somewhat quirky, always inventive and often genuinely surprising. Everything Stephen Molyneux finds locally he uses to good effect, and when it runs out he'll substitute a handy alternative; the best illustration of this being his inclusive 'whatever comes out of the kitchen' tasting menu that might include a Provençale tartlet, whole Dover sole with lime jelly glaze and Greek yogurt and honey ice cream with dark butterscotch sauce. Plans for the year ahead include two en suite bedrooms, designed to be utilitarian rather than luxurious. You will be one of the family and made to feel totally at home - dogs, muddy boots and all - for there is simply no standing on ceremony here.
Prices: Sunday lunch £12.95. Set dinner £23. Main course restaurant from £12. Bar snack from £5. House wine £10.
Hours: 12.00-14.00. 18.00-23.30. 12.00-22.00 on Sunday. Closed Monday lunch.
Food served: 12.00-14.00. 18.00-22.00.
Rooms: 2 en suite. Double/twin from £50, single from £25.
Other Points: No-smoking area. Dogs welcome. Garden. Children welcome. Car park.
Directions: Exit24/M4. A449 to Usk, then B4595 towards Abergavenny; village signposted in two miles. (Map 8, E5)

Prices: Set menu £15. House wine £9.
Hours: 11.00-23.00. 12.00-22.30 on Sunday.
Food served: 12.00-14.30. 18.30-21.30.
Rooms: 23 en suite. Double room from £55, single from £44. Family room from £65.
Cuisine: Modern British.
Other Points: No-smoking area. Children welcome. Patio. Car park opposite.
Directions: Chepstow town centre; turn left in front of St. Mary's Church and left at the end of the public car park. Hotel car park on the right. (Map 8, E5)

The Beaufort Hotel

Beaufort Square, Chepstow, Monmouthshire NP16 5EP
Telephone: +44(0)1291 622497
info@thebeauforthotel.co.uk
www.beauforthotelchepstow.com
A family-owned and run former coaching inn (with a traffic-free approach opposite the town-centre War Memorial) that possesses a true sense of community. Popular with local rugby fanatics (Cardiff is 40 minutes by train) and turf enthusiasts on race days, the bar decor includes former silks of racing legend Lester Piggott who won his first professional race at Chepstow. In addition to traditional bar food, fresh fish and daily specials, both fixed-price menus and the carte exhibit a welcome emphasis on fresh seasonal produce. A typical meal from the latter may feature chicken liver and brandy pâté with onion marmalade, followed by pan-seared duck with port and redcurrant sauce, or roast rack of lamb with apple pie or raspberry syllabub to finish, all washed down with real ales and varietal wines, several by the glass. Best bedrooms are in the newly completed extension, housed over a purpose-built function suite with self-contained bar and kitchen. Free parking is to the rear with over-flow space at night opposite St Mary's Church.

THE WONDERFUL WELSH BORDERS

The remote border country of England and Wales offers
a varied range of landscapes with mountains, river valleys and forest.
Drive length: 82 miles

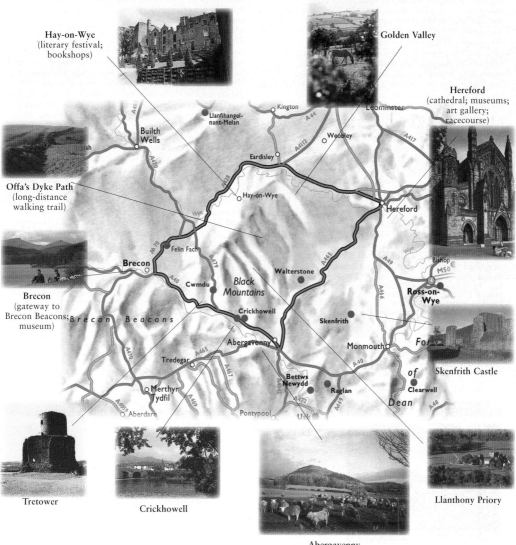

Hay-on-Wye
(literary festival;
bookshops)

Golden Valley

Hereford
(cathedral; museums;
art gallery;
racecourse)

Offa's Dyke Path
(long-distance
walking trail)

Brecon
(gateway to
Brecon Beacons;
museum)

Tretower

Crickhowell

Llanthony Priory

Skenfrith Castle

Abergavenny
(castle; museum)

● Accommodation/Food

● Accommodation

● Food

🥄 Food Shop

To find the establishments marked
here, look up the listing town
marked on the map in bold in the
town index on page 395

The Beaufort Arms Coaching Inn and Restaurant

High Street, Raglan, Monmouthshire NP15 2DY
Telephone: +44(0)1291 690412
thebeauforthotel@hotmail.com

The Lewis family have brought a fresh new look to the this proper 16th century coaching inn. While outstanding period features include a huge fireplace taken from Raglan Castle across the road, and an impressive heavily carved oak bar in the lounge, renovation has introduced a modern feel, best summed up in the restaurant where contemporary colours complement heavy beams. However, open fires and a warm welcoming atmosphere are a traditional reflection of a vibrant, acclaimed inn that is very much at the heart of things in this community minded village. Chef Ellis Masters is committed to using first-class ingredients sourced from local suppliers. Bar menus comprise simple things such as freshly baked rustic sandwiches of Welsh ham and green salad alongside inventive modern dishes listed on the daily specials board; overall quality and presentation is well above average for an inn. In the restaurant imaginative cooking produces highlights such as lemon-infused smoked salmon, torn leaf salad and dill crème fraiche, and seared, marinated lamb with fine green beans, warm basil and mint oil on a red wine deglaze. 15 en suite bedrooms are strikingly modern.

Prices: Main course restaurant from £10.95. Main course bar/snack from £5.75. House wine £8.95. Set Sunday lunch.
Hours: 11.00-23.00. Sunday 12.00-22.30.
Food served: Lunch daily in lounge bar. Dinner 18.00-21.00 (20.30 on Sunday) in the restaurant and lounge.
Rooms: 15 en suite. Double/twin room from £55, single from £45 and family from £75.
Cuisine: Modern British.
Other Points: No-smoking restaurant. Terrace garden. Children welcome. Car park. Private dining area.
Directions: One minute from the junction of the A40 from Abergavenny and the A449 to Monmouth. (Map 8, E5)

The Bell at Skenfrith

Skenfrith, Abergavenny, Monmouthshire NP7 8UH
Telephone: +44(0)1600 750235
enquiries@skenfrith.co.uk
www.skenfrith.co.uk

This handsome black and white painted 17th century coaching inn stands by a bridge spanning the River Monnow. Careful restoration over the last few years by Janet and William Hutchings has made a feature of Welsh slate floors, the charming open-plan bar and dining area with fireside easy chairs and coffee tables, and eight luxuriously appointed, en suite bedrooms with their magnificent river or mountain views. Most people come to eat either in the bar or the separate restaurant. A commitment to local produce is a strong point, with fish from Abergavenny, Welsh black beef and lamb, and regional Welsh cheeses. Bar lunches bring rare roast beef or Gloucester Old Spot pork open sandwiches, braised lamb shank with creamed potatoes and onion cream sauce, and rhubarb crumble and local clotted cream. In the dining room, the set dinner menu is noted for interesting combinations of, say, tiger prawns and seared scallops, chorizo, pickled mango and rocket with blueberry maple viniagrette, and roast fillet of turbot served with fennel and artichoke risotto cake, oyster, mussels, roasted vine tomato and gribbiche.

Prices: Sunday lunch £17.50. Main course from £10.20. Main course bar/snack from £5.50. House wine from £10.
Hours: 11.00-23.00. Closed for two weeks end of January, early February and Mondays from November-March.
Food served: 12.00-14.30. 19.00-21.30.
Rooms: 8 en suite. Double/twin from £90. Single from £75, family room from £140.
Cuisine: Modern British.
Other Points: No-smoking in restaurant and bedrooms. Dogs welcome. Garden. Children welcome. Car park.
Directions: From A40 at Monmouth take A49 towards Hereford. In 3 miles turn left onto B4521 towards Abergavenny; Skenfrith signed on left. (Map 8, E5)

Greyhound Inn Hotel

Llantrissant, Usk, Monmouthshire NP15 1LE
Telephone: +44(0)1291 672505
enquiry@greyhound-inn.com
www.greyhound-inn.com

The Greyhound was originally a traditional 17th-century Welsh longhouse and later a staging post for coaches travelling between Wales and England. Conversion of the former stables has produced ten spacious en suite bedrooms, all decorated in a cottage style that suits both the building's nature and rural location. Ground floor rooms open on to private patios in a garden setting and all rooms are well equipped with modern comforts. In the main house, noted for open fires and a comfortable atmosphere, visitors will find a printed bar menu detailing traditional pub favourites alongside interesting homecooked specials listed on a daily changing chalkboard. Using fresh produce from well-sourced suppliers, including venison from the Welsh Venison Centre, game and fish from Vin Sullivan in Abergavenny, and smoked products from Minola Smokery at nearby Triley Mill, typical choices may feature Usk salmon, venison and ale pie, lamb shank with red wine and rosemary, and fish pie.

Summer alfresco imbibing is a real treat among the colourful flower borders and hanging baskets of the Greyhound's award-winning garden - Wales in Bloom Gold Award 1998-2002. A stone barn houses a country pine and antique shop.

Prices: Set lunch and dinner £16. Main course restaurant from £10. Main course bar meal from £6.50. House wine £10.80.
Hours: 12.00-14.15. 18.00-22.30. Closed for dinner on Sunday and 25-26 December.
Rooms: 10 en suite. Double room from £66, single from £49.
Cuisine: Traditional Welsh.
Other Points: No-smoking area. Children welcome. Garden. Car park.
Directions: Exit 24/M4. Usk town square, second left, follow signs to Llantrissant for 2.5 miles. (Map 8, E5)

Three Salmons Hotel 🅳✕⌷

Bridge Street, Usk, Monmouthshire NP15 1RQ
Telephone: +44(0)1291 672133
3salmons.hotel@talk21.com
www.3-salmons-usk.co.uk

Tracy Lewis and Clive Hughes are very keen, hands-on owners at this well above-average town-centre inn, and with their team spend time, effort and resources on constant improvements. There's also a good sense of community amongst the locals - the sort of place where you pop in for a pint of Hancock's HB or Abbot Ale and catch up on the gossip. The kitchen works hard in its effort to up the stakes to quality pub dining, but is well aware of local tastes and thus continues to offer plenty of steak and chips and liver and bacon for local palates. Otherwise there could be Thai spiced crab cakes with a mild chilli oil, shank of braised lamb with couscous, or asparagus and Yfenni cheese tartlet with coriander cream on a menu that is available in both the paneled, mirrored bar and the more formal restaurant. Comfortable accommodation makes this a great weekend break destination. Bedrooms are freshly decorated and nicely up to date, and there's plenty of information provided for touring the Wye Valley castles, Cardiff shopping, golf and outdoor activities.

Prices: Lunch from £5.95. Main course restaurant from £9.95. Main course bar/snack from £4.95. House wine £10.95.
Hours: 11.00-23.00. Sunday 12.00-22.30.
Food served: 12.00-15.00. 17.00-19.00.
Rooms: 24 en suite. Double room from £95. Single from £75. Family from £110.
Cuisine: Modern European.
Other Points: No-smoking area. Garden. Children welcome. Car park. Licensed for civil weddings.
Directions: Exit 24/M4. A449 to Usk; hotel on main street by junction with B4598 to Abergavenny. (Map 8, E5)

Inn at the Elm Tree 🅳✕⌷

St Brides Wentlooge, Newport NP10 8SQ
Telephone: +44(0)1633 680225
inn@the-elm-tree.co.uk
www.the-elm-tree.co.uk

This stylish inn is in the midst of the Wentlooge Flats, an area of special scientific interest offering protection to rare and varied fauna, flora and wild life. Modern extensions have transformed this old traditional farm and 19th-century barn. Confident styling mixes the old and the new through the tiled flooring, muted colours and log fire of the small lounge and bistro. Here, an all day menu delivers sandwiches such as home boiled ham and salad, or Penclawdd cockles, eggs and bacon; afternoon tea brings crumpets and scones. Amid the slightly art deco look of wrought iron and glass in the dining room, an imaginative carte offers pan seared king scallops with pea pancake, minted pea purée and tomato and lemon dressing, followed by marinated rack of Welsh salt marsh lamb and honey roasted parsnip puree, petite ratatouille, caper and rosemary butter. Bedrooms are top drawer – high tech enough with ISDN and modems – and ranging in design from a country look of solid pine to elegant iron and brass beds, waterbeds and four posters.

Prices: Main course restaurant meal from £12. Main course bar/snack from £7.50. House wine £10.50.
Hours: 11.00-23.00. Sunday 12.00-22.30.
Closed for a few days around Christmas and New Year.
Food served: 12.00-14.30. 18.00-21.30 (until 22.00 on Friday and Saturday). 12.00-15.00. 18.00-19.30 on Sunday.
Rooms: 10 en suite. Double room from £80, single from £80. Family room from £120.
Cuisine: Modern British/Welsh/European.
Other Points: No-smoking area. Dogs welcome. Garden. Children welcome over 12 years old. Car park.
Directions: Exit 28/M4. Take A48 towards Cardiff; pass first roundabout to Asda and take next right, then at T junction turn right for two miles. (Map 8, F5)

The Wolfe Inn 🍷🅳✕⌷

Wolfscastle, Haverfordwest, Pembrokeshire SA62 5LS
Telephone: +44(0)1437 741662
eat@the-wolfe.co.uk
www.thewolfe.info

Gianni di Lorenzo is a leading light in the Pembrokeshire Food Growers' Association, his sourcing of local produce and suppliers is a feature of daily-updated menus that won a Wales 2002 True Taste Award. Typical brasserie lunch and supper dishes include home-cured salmon with mead and soured cream, 'cawl cymraeg' with Llangloffan cheese and yes, tagliatelli Putanesca with charcuterie and juicy black olives. From the carte at night, diners might go for goats' cheese and Carmarthen ham brioche, followed by steamed brill with cockle and laverbread cream, and a host of sticky, liqueur-soaked desserts. Cheeses on display are pure Welsh; best value wines are true Italian from a list that includes a 50-bin personal collection. Draught ales and a simple snack in the front-facing bar are 'simply no problem' with low calorie, vegetarian and children's choices all readily available. Throughout the inter-linked dining areas away from the road a sensible 'as-you-like-it' policy offers an intimate Victorian parlour, the joviality of the hunting room or simple relaxation in a leafy conservatory. Cosy accommodation that includes a self-contained unit in the adjacent Hay Loft finally obviates any decision on who's to drive!

Prices: Set Sunday lunch £12.95. Main course restaurant from £12.50. Main course bar from £6.95. House wine £10.50.
Hours: 12.00-15.00. 18.00-23.00, until 22.30 Sunday. Open all day July and August.
Food served: 12.00-14.30. 18.30-21.30, until 21.00 on Sunday.
Rooms: 3 en suite. £30 per person, £35 per person at weekends.
Cuisine: Modern British.
Other Points: No-smoking area. Garden. Children welcome. Car park.
Directions: Exit29/M4. Beside A40 mid-way between

Wolfscastle Country Hotel ★✗⬦

Wolfscastle, Haverfordwest, Pembrokeshire SA62 5LZ
Telephone: +44(0)1437 741225
enquiries@wolfscastle.com
www.wolfscastle.com

Well hidden from the main A40 coast road by a host of forestation, yet less than half-an-hour's drive from the Fishguard ferry, stands this Welsh stone country house - family run for some 25 years now. Its greatest virtue has always been an ability to stay abreast of the times, as evidenced by recent bedroom extensions (in what were once squash courts) that are among the most spacious and comfortable in the county. In addition to state-of-the-art television, video players, and soft furnishings that have a lived-in feel, proprietor Andrew Stirling's pet 'toys' include finger-touch bedside lighting. Equally aware of current trends, daily-changed menus follow an 'eat what you like, where you like' policy that sees traditional lambs' liver and onions rubbing shoulders with Pembrokeshire Gressingham duck with a bigarade sauce, offered in both the clubby bar and a restaurant that echoes whispers of yesteryear. The day's sweet list might include profiteroles with ice cream and hot chocolate sauce and iced orange and espresso mousse with Tia Maria syrup. Highly recommended as a base for touring the fabulous Pembrokeshire coastline or a restful stop over on the way to or from the Emerald Isle.

Prices: Main course from £8.50. House wine £10.
Hours: 12.00-14.00. 19.00-21.00. Advisable to pre-book. Closed 24-26 December.
Rooms: 20 en suite. Double room from £79-£105, single from £49-£69.
Cuisine: Welsh.
Other Points: No-smoking in bedrooms and dining room. Children welcome. Garden. Car park. Licence for civil weddings.
Directions: Signed off A40 midway between Haverfordwest and Fishguard. (Map 7, E2)

Lion Hotel & Restaurant ⬛✗⬦

Berriew, Welshpool, Powys SY21 8PQ
Telephone: +44(0)1686 640452

The 17th-century half timbered 'magpie' inn at the centre of a quiet village five miles south west of Welshpool, is a real local, run for the last year by easy going, hands-on young owners Tim Woodward and Susan Barton. They have made a good fist of refurbishment in the two cosy bars, the lounge bar, informal bistro dining area, and the more formal timbered dining room (now hung with striking black and white photographs), and are now turning their attention to the seven en suite bedrooms under the rafters. Sensibly, while upgrading bedrooms, they have reduced the ludicrous bed and breakfast prices they inherited, and now offer very good value for money. Local produce features with good results on daily menus that are offered throughout the pub, whether staples such as pan-fried garlic mushrooms, chicken curry, and steaks, or chef's specials of whole grilled lemon sole, and slow-roast Welsh lamb shoulder with garlic, rosemary, red wine and mint gravy. Wines are a fairly-priced listing from around the world, with three by the glass. Bass and Worthington are always available, backed up by imaginative guest ales.
Prices: Set lunch from £10.95. Main course restaurant from £6.95. Main course bar/snack from £3.25. House wine £10.
Hours: 12.00-15.30. 18.00-23.00 (until 22.30 on Sunday).
Food served: 12.00-14.00. 19.00-21.00. No food Sunday evening.
Rooms: 7 en suite. Single room from £55, double from £70.
Cuisine: Traditional English with French influence.
Other Points: No-smoking area. Garden patio. Children welcome.
Directions: Village signposted off A483 Newtown to Welshpool road. (Map 7, C4)

The Felin Fach Griffin Inn ★⬛✗⬦

Felin Fach, Brecon, Powys LD3 0UB
Telephone: +44(0)1874 620111
enquiries@eatdrinksleep.ltd.uk
www.eatdrinksleep.ltd.uk

Charles Inkin has rapidly established a new beacon in the Brecons. Unmissable beside the main Builth Wells road, their revitalised inn has an ochre hue. Inside, the building has been opened out to form inter-linked dining areas around a single, central bar. Look for flagstone floors, open fire-places, stripped pine beams and doors, and particularly the Aga cooker retained in an inglenook of what was formerly the farmhouse kitchen. With assorted dining and refectory tables, a glorious assortment of antique chairs and walls spotted with black and white photographs and pastoral memorabilia, anticipation of exciting dining is raised. The best of local supplies appear on daily updated chalkboard menus, which their authors reluctantly refer to as 'eclectic'. Choices include pan-fried scallops with asparagus and black pepper butter, and minute steak of Welsh Black beef with chips and béarnaise sauce from the lunch menu. Dinner brings loin of wild venison, red cabbage and dauphinoise potatoes. Extensions and modifications have led to the addition of bedrooms that exhibit a similar flair for interior design with bright, eye-catching colours and a contemporary feel. Do not, however, think 'pub' in terms of dropping in for a quick pint and a sandwich.
Prices: Main course from £10. House wine £10.75.
Hours: 12.00-15.00. 19.00-23.00. Closed Monday lunch.
Food served: 12.30-14.30. 19.00-22.00 (until 21.00 on Sunday).
Rooms: 7 en suite. Double room from £92.50, single from £57.50. Four poster room £115.
Cuisine: Modern British.
Other Points: No-smoking area. Children welcome. Garden. Car park.
Directions: Four miles north of Brecon on the A470. (Map 7, E4)

The Talkhouse 🍷🍷🅿️✕◇

Pontdolgoch, Caersws, Powys SY17 5JE
Telephone: +44(0)1686 688919
info@talkhouse.co.uk
www.talkhouse.co.uk

The stylish remodelling of this formerly run-down coaching inn has created a smart restaurant with rooms, although the bar retains its old coaching inn feel – and is the only room in which smoking is allowed. The Green Room is a peaceful, beamed sitting room for residents and guests, and the three bedrooms are Laura-Ashley-styled with brass bedsteads and good, modern bathrooms. The restaurant has conservatory-style french windows leading to a summer dining patio, where produce-led food is served in the atmosphere of candlelight, fresh flowers, and just a hint of background music. A light lunch might bring a baguette filled with local Welsh sirloin and homemade onion marmalade, or creamy seafood risotto with basil pesto and fresh seasonal vegetables. The kitchen aims for a recognisably contemporary cooking style and is powered by a sense of adventure. Thus, slow cooked shoulder of lamb is partnered with roast root vegetables, shallots, potato purée and confit of garlic, and glazed Barbary duck with caramelised apple, date and balsamic sauce. Warm chocolate mousse with wild lime and toasted coconut ice cream, is an interesting dessert. There are six "wines of the month" offered by the glass.

Prices: Set lunch £21.50 and dinner £26. Main course restaurant from £10.50. Main course bar/snack from £6.50. House wine from £14.

Hours: 12.00-14.00. 19.00-21.00. Closed Sunday and Monday, and the whole of January.

Rooms: 3 en suite. Double/twin from £80. Single from £70.

Cuisine: Modern British.

Other Points: No-smoking area. Garden. Dogs welcome in the garden.

Directions: On the A470 six miles west of Newtown, on the left past the railway bridge. (Map 7, C4)

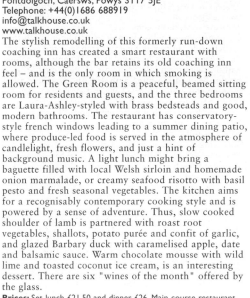

Brecon

Prices: Main course from £15. Bar meal from £7. House wine £8.95.

Hours: 11.00-15.00. 18.00-23.00.

Food Served: :12.00-14.00. 19.00-21.30.

Rooms: 35 en suite. Double room from £72, single from £55. Family room from £102.

Cuisine: Modern/eclectic.

Other Points: No-smoking area. Dogs welcome. Children welcome over seven years old. Garden. Car park.

Directions: Centre of Crickhowell on A40 between Abergavenny and Brecon. (Map 8, E5)

Bear Hotel ★🍷✕◇

High Street, Crickhowell, Powys NP8 1BW
Telephone: +44(0)1873 810408
bearhotel@aol.com
www.bearhotel.co.uk

The Bear somehow ignores the passage of time whilst forever staying abreast of the best trends and traditions of good innkeeping. Continual improvements have seen expansion deep into its 15th-century fabric, unearthing along the way ever more beams and fireplaces, stone-faced walls, nooks and crannies. Through the original arched entrance, former stables have been converted into a colourful courtyard of thoroughly up-to-date bedrooms and across the sheltered rear garden self-contained honeymoon suites nestle under the trees. Very much a hub of local community, the fiercely traditional bars always have a buzz about them - a perfect location for light lunches featuring spicy Thai prawn cakes with sweet chilli dip, Welsh rarebit on toasted olive bread and daily specials such as braised lamb and leeks in rosemary and red wine. Top-class cask ales and well chosen wines by the glass are ideal to complement the hearty fare. More extensive menus in the separate, more formal dining-rooms display solid reliance on local suppliers for Brecon lamb and venison, market-fresh fish and plentiful supplies of Welsh cheeses. Here we have enjoyed baked cod wrapped in smoked salmon, calves' liver and bacon with onion gravy and some sumptuous desserts epitomised by the trade-

Glangrwyney Court

Glangrwyney, Crickhowell, Powys NP8 1ES
Telephone: +44(0)1873 811288
glangrwyney@aol.com
www.glancourt.com

The lovely Georgian House is approached by a tree-lined drive and surrounded by gorgeous gardens. Christina Jackson is the perfect host, proud of her home in which visitors are treated as personal guests. Supremely comfortable lounges, with a preponderance of chintz, are complemented by five opulently decorated en suite bedrooms that are quite romantic; all have lovely views over the grounds. Only breakfast is served, but sourcing is impeccable, using the Black Mountain Smokery, local honey, vegetables and fruit; for dinner there are plenty of pub and restaurant options in Crickhowell and there is a pub nearby. However, Glangrwyney Court does have a residential drinks licence. Although Mrs Jackson declares that she runs her B&B as a hobby (she has no brochures to send out), it has, nevertheless, proved a runaway success over the nine years she has been doing this, and offers very good value for money.

Prices: Set dinner £20.25. Main course from £12.50. House wine £10.
Rooms: 5 rooms, 4 en suite, 1 with private bathroom. Double room from £60, single from £45. Family rooms £85.
Other Points: No-smoking area. Children welcome. Garden. Car park. Boules and croquet.
Directions: Two miles east of Crickhowell off A40. (Map 8, E5)

The Farmers Arms

Cwmdu, Crickhowell, Powys NP8 1RE
Telephone: +44(0)1874 730464
cwmdu@aol.com
www.thefarmersarms.com

This unassuming white-painted roadside inn with the French-style shuttered windows stands at the edge of the Brecon Beacons National Park. Deceptively roomy within, there is an immediate air of welcome in the bright, beamed bar hung with dried hops, where a log-burning stove and polished Welsh flagstones confirm the impression of a happy place in caring hands. Fronting house with a witty semblance of order is Sue Lawrence while the master of his kitchen, Andrew, cooks in full view as the foil of a well-worked balancing act. Home-made cawl with a cheese croute or duck liver and brandied apricot pâté for starters amply suffice for a lunchtime snack, alongside smoked haddock and onion fishcakes, Glamorgan cheese sausages on piquant tomato sauce and maybe roast pork loin with stuffing, crackling and a sweet apple tartlet. Up a gear at night in the informal candlelit dining-room, customer favourites include sea bass fillets with courgette spaghetti on a tarragon beurre blanc, and confit duck leg and dry-fried breast laid over soy noodles with a teasing citrus and rum sauce. Sunday lunch is a leisurely, multi-option affair (booking advised) and strictly limited accommodation is available by arrangement.

Prices: Main course restaurant £9.95. House wine £9.95.
Hours: 12.00-15.00. 18.30-23.00, Sunday 19.00-22.30. Closed Mondays except Bank Holidays.
Food served: 12.00-14.00 (Sunday until 15.00). 19.00-21.30.
Cuisine: Traditional Pub Food.
Other Points: No-smoking area. Dogs welcome in bar only. Children welcome. Car park.
Directions: From Crickhowell travel west on A40 for one and a half miles, then turn right along A479 for 3 miles to Cwmdu. (Map 7, E4)

The Red Lion Inn

Llanfihangel-nant-Melan, New Radnor, Powys LD8 2TN
Telephone: +44(0)1544 350220
enquiries@theredlioninn.net
www.theredlioninn.net

It is certainly not difficult to drop in to the Red Lion as its basic floor space is a significant level below the main road and one is more likely to see the wheels than the driver of a passing tractor or charabanc. Within, its recent makeover is remarkable, and stylish; a somewhat minimalist new dining-room in stainless steel and glass and new in-house bedrooms that are little short of sumptuous in fitments and decor. On newly styled dining menus credit is given prominently to suppliers of single herd meats, Welsh cheeses, organic vegetables and free-range eggs all sourced locally; with fresh bread bought virtually next door - the only item not prepared and cooked on the premises. Seafood, however is chef Dillon's forte offering, for instance, organic salmon on mussels and saffron sauce, and roast monkfish with Pernod and prawns. Alternatives might include a trio of Welsh cheese dumplings with orange dressing and Brecon beef fillet with green peppercorn sauce. Walkers and hikers, however, are equally welcome to drop in for a pint, with muddy boots left at the door and inexpensive, if rather more spartan, accommodation available in the adjacent annexe.

Prices: Main course from £10. House wine £8.50.
Hours: 12.00-14.30. 18.00-23.00. 22.30 on Sunday.
Rooms: 7 en suite. Double room from £45, single from £30. Family rooms from £55. Prices vary between main house and annexe rooms.
Cuisine: Modern British/Mediterranean.
Other Points: No-smoking area. Children welcome. Garden. Car park.
Directions: On A44 Leominster to Aberystwyth road. Nine miles west of Kington and 15 miles east of Rhayader. (Map 8, D5)

Welcome To Town Country Bistro & Bar ★ ⬗ ⬥ ◫ ✕

Llanrhidian, Gower, Swansea SA3 1EH
Telephone: +44(0)1792 390015
www.thewelcometotown.co.uk

The 300-year-old whitewashed country inn-cum-bistro is situated on the Gower Peninsula overlooking the Penclawdd Cockle beds. Noted for friendly service and a relaxed atmosphere, fresh produce is essential to the kitchen's aspirations, and in this part of Wales, nature's larder is a particularly handy resource: locally grown asparagus, cockles from Penclawdd, seasonal lobsters, laver bread, salt-marsh lamb, Welsh Black beef, cheeses from Swansea market. As an example of what all this bounty adds up to on the plate, look no further than pan-fried local sewin with braised samphire and laver bread sauce. Seafood can turn up in a starter of mackerel escabeche, or again in a main course of pan-fried wild sea bass with creamed potatoes and garden peas. A roast saddle of Welsh lamb may be simply served by some Niçoise vegetables, and a fillet of Welsh Black beef with buttered spinach and fondant potato. Everything stays on an even keel, right through to desserts, such as fresh fruit vacharin with passion fruit sorbet, or a smooth, delicate vanilla panna cotta with local strawberries. Bread, baked on the premises, is delicious, and the same attention to detail extends to homemade ice creams and sorbets. The well-chosen house wine is especially good value.

Prices: Set lunch £14.95. Main course restaurant from £11. Main course bar/snack from £6.50. House wine £11.
Hours: 12.00-14.00. 19.00-21.30. Closed Sunday and Mondays except Bank Holidays.
Cuisine: Modern British.
Other Points: No-smoking area. Garden and Patio. Children welcome. Car park.
Directions: Exit47/M4. A484 to Gowerton and B4295 via Penclawdd to Llanrhidian, approximately ten miles. (Map 7, E3)

ABERTHAW, VALE OF GLAMORGAN

The Blue Anchor ⬗ ◫ ✕

East Aberthaw, Vale of Glamorgan CF62 3DD
Telephone: +44(0)1446 750329
www.blueanchoraberthaw.com

Stories of pirates and contraband abound at the stone-built, thatched Blue Anchor that has an unbroken history back to 1380 and where evidence remains of ancient tunnelling down to the nearby shore-line. Its interior is a warren of inter-linked rooms with tiny doorways, narrow passages and stairs that lead nowhere, stone fireplaces under vast oak lintels and a central bar that attracts swarms of real ale buffs. Family-owned and run for over 40 years, the property includes a three-acre kitchen garden and owns the private shoot that provides winter game. Simple lamb-and-leek casserole, spicy beef curry and pheasant breast in apple and cider cream sauce, are supplemented at lunch by sandwiches and jacket potatoes in time-honoured tradition with peripheral apple and raspberry tart, assorted regional cheeses and things for kids and vegetarians. Head, however, for dinner up another stairway to a roomy dining-room under the eaves where chefs' specials à la carte include poached Wye salmon with fresh asparagus, rack of Welsh lamb with grain mustard crusting, and chicken supreme in coconut and tarragon sauce. There is a further range of fixed-price menus, including Sunday lunch, and a balanced list of mainly European wines at prices that won't jeopardise the mortgage.

Prices: Sunday lunch £11.75. Set dinner £13.95. Main course restaurant from £9.50. Bar snack from £3.25. House wine £9.95.
Hours: 11.00-23.00. Sunday from 12.00-22.30.
Food served: 12.00-14.30. 19.00-21.30 Monday to Saturday. Restaurant closed Sunday evening.
Cuisine: Pub food.
Other Points: Dogs welcome. Garden. Children welcome. Car park.
Directions: Exit33/M4. A4232 and A4226 follow the signs to Cardiff Airport and then the B4265 to Llantwit Major. (Map 7, F4)

WREXHAM

The Boat Inn ⬥ ◫ ✕

Erbistock, Wrexham LL13 0DL
Telephone: +44(0)1978 780666
www.theboatinn.co.uk

A lane runs past the Victorian church and leads to the Boat Inn, converted from two 16th-century ferryman's cottages and set in a superb, peaceful position on the banks of the River Dee. The interior is equally enchanting. Sit by the kitchen range in the low-beamed bar and sample a pint of Tetleys or Old Hooky, or follow the stone-flagged corridor through to the airy conservatory, with its views of the river and passing swans, and on to the high-ceilinged modern restaurant extension with its marble-topped tables and wicker chairs. The kitchen puts great store by good-quality local produce: open sandwiches, fishcakes, salads and Dee salmon are a big draw for lunch. From the more adventurous evening carte, choice extends to sautéed scallops and asparagus with cracked peppercorn dressing or red pepper and chicken terrine with beetroot and lime relish among the starters. Mains take in rack of Welsh lamb with red wine jus, baked monkfish wrapped in Parma ham with an oregano and sun-dried tomato sauce, or fillet steak with Madeira and mushroom sauce. Puddings may include homemade pecan pie served with local Erbistock ice cream, and white chocolate cheesecake.

Prices: Main course from £9.95. Bar food from £7.95. House wine £11.95.
Hours: 12.00-23.00. Closed Sunday evenings and 1 January.
Food served: 12.00-14.30. 18.30-21.00 (until 21.30 on Friday and Saturday).
Cuisine: Traditional British.
Other Points: Children welcome. Garden. Car park. Dogs Welcome. No Credit Cards accepted. Licence for Civil Weddings.
Directions: From Ruabon take the A539 and follow signs for Whitchurch. After two and a half miles turn down a single track road. (Map 8, B5)

Wales • Swansea/Vale of Glamorgan/Wrexham

IRELAND

IRELAND REVISITED

Ireland has never had it so good, writes Hugo Arnold. Everyone will tell you the number and quality of restaurants and cafes has grown enormously and with it standards have increased along with the much-trumpeted Celtic Tiger. Much of this is true, yet with any kind of significant growth, along with the good things comes a certain amount of not so good.

Ireland sees itself as being a prime tourist destination but, as many other countries have found, world events have led to a significant downturn in numbers. This has led to a refocusing on the domestic market and an increasingly healthy questioning of what, as a nation, we are trying to be. Top of the list for residents and visitors alike is pricing. We are seen as being expensive and as with any image it gets increasingly hard to shrug that off regardless of whether it is true or not. At the moment it is too often true. The focus of Les Routiers in Ireland has been to concentrate on value, seeking out establishments that have really focused on doing what they do well regardless of whether they are pitched at the high, middle or lower end. The surprising thing is how many there are. Looking round the country those who diligently get on with being the best are seeing customers, many of whom return. This idea of a mature market, where repeat business forms the core focus is, many argue, where Ireland should be focusing its main efforts. Whether you are a bed and breakfast in the wilds of Connemara, or a restaurant in a large urban area, success in the long run is driven not by the one-off visitor, but by those who keep returning.

Dublin is seeing significant change too. Over the last year there have been several high-profile closures, The Commons and Pacific being the most notable. But there have been some impressive openings concentrating on the middle market. The likes of Dunne and Crescenzi and The Unicorn have both been around for some time, but their whole approach – casual dining, an equal importance given to a relaxed easy atmosphere – is so much in keeping with what is happening world wide.

Customers are looking for value for money and this search is coupled with an enthusiasm for eating out regularly. Gone – at least on an everyday basis – is the need to have something to celebrate. It may be soup and salad, but this still means that as a customer you want the soup and salad to be good. This understanding on the part of the establishment is what has become so crucial in the last few years. Money, travel, and the simple reality of greater experience, mean the contract between customer and survivor now has greater hope of success as well as greater risk of failure. This Guide is about those places that not only realise this, but actively work with enthusiasm not just to meet this challenge, but to exceed it.
Les Routiers might once have been about the little out of the way brasserie known only to those French travellers on the inside track. These days, it is more about making sure you are permanently travelling on

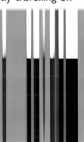

The Beams Restaurant

59 Dublin Street, Carlow, Co Carlow
Telephone: +353(0)59 913 1824
the.beams@ireland.com

Betty O'Gorman's small, intimate town centre restaurant packs a lot of history. Built in 1716 as a coaching inn, it went on to become a high-class grocer, spirit broker and tea blender, owned by the Duggan family from 1916-1972. Huge wooden beams testify to the age of the building. An industrious kitchen, headed by Romain Chall who has been with Betty from the start, bakes its own bread, scones, biscuits and pastry, grows a large percentage of fruit and vegetables, buys farm eggs, local meat, handmade farmhouse cheeses, and fish comes straight from Dunmore East. It all adds up to good country cooking given a slight modern twist. A plate of crispy bacon and white pudding is served with warm potato salad, for example, and smoked salmon and fresh salmon terrine is accompanied by sun-dried tomato mayonnaise. From the same set menu comes cornfed chicken breast with Serrano ham and cheese on champ and served with a herb sauce. The carte offers hot crab cakes with lemon and horseradish cream, and pork medallions with wild mushroom and cream sauce. The wine list is especially strong in Burgundy and Bordeaux.

Prices: Set dinner €38.50 (4 courses). Main course restaurant from €16. House wine from €18.
Hours: 19.00 until close. Closed every lunchtime and all day Sunday and Monday. Closed two weeks from 25 December, one week at the beginning of July and all Bank Holidays.
Cuisine: Modern Irish.
Other Points: No-smoking area. Children welcome (no children's menu).
Directions: In the centre of Carlow town beside the crossroads of Tullow Street and Dublin Street. (Map 20, B6)

Barrowville Town House

Kilkenny Road, Carlow Town, Co Carlow
Telephone: +353(0)59 914 3324
barrowvilletownhouse@eircom.net
www.barrowvillehouse.com

Randal and Marie Dempsey have run their listed Regency townhouse and home as a guesthouse for the last 13 years. Set in its own private grounds, just 300 metres from Carlow town centre, location and setting are perfect. The drawing room is a finely proportioned room with a welcoming open fire and grand piano, and bedrooms are comfortable and individually decorated with a mixture of antiques and fixed furniture, with hot drinks tray, telephone and television in all rooms. Breakfast, served in the conservatory, is a feast. Local produce features, as does some excellent homebaking. Start with the buffet, perhaps mixed nuts, cereal, yogurts, a selection of fresh seasonal and dried fruits, as well as smoked salmon and a wonderful cheese board, then a traditional Irish breakfast, pancakes or kippers. Home baking takes in scones and brown bread, and Marie's own jams and marmalade.

Prices: Guesthouse.
Rooms: 7 en suite. Double/twin from €37.50-€40 per person, single room from €45-€50. Prices include breakfast.
Other Points: Garden. Car park.
Directions: From travelling south on the N9, 300 metres from the town centre at the traffic lights on the right. Travelling north, 50 metres before the first set of traffic lights on the left. (Map 20, B6)

Lord Bagenal Inn

Leighlinbridge, Co Carlow
Telephone: +353(0)59 972 1668
info@lordbagenal.com
www.lordbagenal.com

The Kehoe family's renowned old inn is located just off the main M9 Waterford-Carlow road on the banks of the river Barrow and has its own private marina. This relaxing family run hotel offers a homeliness and hospitality that is characteristic of James Kehoe. The kitchen keeps up with modern trends without ignoring the popularity of old favourites like the oysters and mussels, crabs and scallops, the homemade pâtés, steaks and fine fresh fish. A hugely popular carvery lunch is served in the bar, and bar food is available all day. In the restaurant the set four-course dinner could bring carrot and coriander cream soup, Dunmore East crabmeat with mango, red onion and avocado salsa, roasted shank of lamb, coriander mash and mint pesto, finishing, perhaps, with tangy lemon tart with citrus coulis. The wine list should certainly generate some contented murmurs. James is justifiably proud of his collection. Old world traditional styles are balanced by new word charmers, all helpfully annotated with many offered at attractive prices. Twelve smart bedrooms offer good value for money, the best have canopied beds, but all rooms are spacious, well designed and maintained, with 24-hour room service.

Prices: Set dinner from €35 (5 courses). Main course restaurant meal from €22. Main course bar meal from €11. House wine from €18.
Hours: 12.00-14.30. 18.00-22.00. 12.00-21.00 on Sunday. Open for Breakfast 07.30-11.00. Closed on 25 December.
Rooms: 12 en suite. Rooms from €55 per person sharing. Single supplement applies.
Cuisine: Modern Irish.
Other Points: No-smoking area. Children welcome. Garden. Car park. Private Marina.
Directions: Situated in Leighlinbridge just off the main N9 Dublin/Waterford road. (Map 20, C6)

Polo'D Restaurant

Main Street, Ballyconnell, Co Cavan
Telephone: +353(0)49 952 6228
polodrestaurant@hotmail.com

An old blackened oven forms the lintel over one of the doors to this cosy, intimate country restaurant. The ground floor is finished in two sections in typical old-world Irish-style, with exposed rafters, stone and subdued red rendered walls and hanging lantern-style lamps. Upstairs, a pine ceiling and timber floors lend a more modern look. While the décor maintains a traditional ambience, Paul O'Dowd produces a modern repertoire of imaginative dishes. Considerable emphasis is placed on locally produced meats and fresh vegetables delivered on a simply described, ingredient led menu. Combinations are as simple as steamed smoked salmon with herb butter sauce, or mixed salad with bacon, smoked duck and avocado, and grilled turbot and sea trout with scallops and chive sauce. Rack of lamb comes with red wine and port, and breast of chicken with white wine and mushroom sauce. Homely desserts include pear poached in cinnamon with caramel sauce and chocolate pudding in chocolate sauce with ice cream. The wine list covers old and new world wines and prices are reasonable.

Prices: Set dinner €35. Main course from €22.50. House wine €18.
Hours: 19.00-21.30. Closed Sunday, Monday and 25-26 December.
Cuisine: Modern Irish.
Other Points: No-smoking area. Children welcome over 10 years old.
Directions: N3. Ballyconnell is situated on the N87 which is linked to the N3 Cavan to Enniskillen road. Top right hand side of the main street in Ballyconnell. (Map 18, E5)

The Oak Room Restaurant

Cavan Crystal Building, Dublin Road,
Cavan, Co Cavan
Telephone: +353(0)49 4360099/436 2748

The restaurant is an integral part of a large red-bricked Georgian-style building on the site of the old Cavan Crystal factory. The décor is a striking combination of old style exposed timbers set against warm orange colours - the modern colour scheme reflecting Norbert Neylon's culinary skills. He represented Ireland in the best apprentice chef category in Versailles in 1996, and is keenly interested in the seasonality of food and in using local ingredients; in season he serves pheasant, woodcock, snipe, mallard and duck from Cootehill. Thought is given to the composition of each dish, as in a starter of seared salmon, for example, served with sesame and herb-scented noodles, horseradish and dill sauce, or a main course of pan-fried sea bass with a tomato and fennel tartlet, seafood tortellini and lobster bisque. A lot of work goes on in the kitchen, but prime materials are at the heart of it and the cooking is technically sound. Puddings are as well conceived as the rest, with cherry panna cotta served with white chocolate ice cream and lime syrup among them. The well-annotated wine list is a thoughtful selection of reasonably priced old and new world wines.

Prices: Sunday lunch €19.50. Set dinner (5 courses) €35.50.
Hours: 12.30-14.30 Sundays only. 18.30-22.00, Sunday until 21.00. Closed for lunch every day except Sunday, 24-26 December.
Cuisine: Modern Irish.
Other Points: No-smoking area. Children welcome.
Directions: On the Link road between Cavan town and the Dublin/Enniskillen road roundabout half a mile south of Cavan town. (Map 18, E5)

Hyland's Burren Hotel

Ballyvaughan, Co Clare
Telephone: +353(0)65 707 7037
hylands@eircom.net
www.hylandsburrenhotel.com

The building dates from the 18th century and is located in this picturesque village on the shores of Galway Bay amidst the wild splendour and breathtaking scenery of the Burren. The bygone charm of the hotel, teamed with modern day facilities and old-fashioned turf fires, give an immediate sense of warmth and hospitality. The reception area and restaurant have wooden floors and furniture, further lending to the rustic, homely atmosphere. The comfortable bedrooms are all en suite and offer multi-channel TV, tea trays and all the expected amenities. All day bar food offers the likes of chicken and bacon salad, and roast salmon with Cajun spices. Dinner, served in the restaurant, delivers a good selection of traditional and modern Irish food that takes in a wide range of seafood, but meat, poultry and vegetarian options are also available. Start, perhaps, with Atlantic seafood chowder, go on to oven baked sea bass with black olive and chive butter, or rack of lamb with herb and garlic crust and port sauce, and finish with a platter of Irish cheeses. The well-annotated wine list offers varied drinking at fair prices.

Prices: Set lunch €17 and dinner €32.50. Bar main course from €9.50. Restaurant main course from €14.95. House wine €16.
Hours: 11.00-23.30 Monday-Wednesday. Until 00.30 Thursday-Saturday and 23.00 on Sunday. Closed 23-25 December.
Food served: 12.30-21.00.
Rooms: 29 en suite. Single from €70, double from €90.
Cuisine: Traditional and Modern Irish.
Other Points: No-smoking in restaurant. Children welcome. Patio. Car park.
Directions: Located in the centre of the village of Ballyvaughan on the N67. (Map 19, B3)

Monks Bar and Restaurant

The Old Pier, Ballyvaughan, Co Clare
Telephone: +353(0)65 7077059
monkspub1@eircom.net
www.monkspub.com

Follow the road through Ballyvaughan village to The Old Pier. This is about all you need to know before you stumble across this jewel of a quayside pub at the heart of the Burren - a land of terraced mountains, sunken valleys, hidden caves, exotic flowers and, scattered everywhere, the relics of its stormy past. There are several smallish, low-ceilinged, white walled interconnecting rooms with wooden country-kitchen furniture and blazing open fires, creating a cosy atmosphere in which to enjoy some superb local seafood. There will be few, if any, surprises on the menu: seafood chowder, oysters by the half or full dozen, and crab claws in garlic butter set the scene. Follow with smoked salmon platters, plain or with prawns or crab, baked garlic mussels, or chef's catch of the day; and open sandwiches on homemade whole wheat brown bread consisting of yet more salmon, prawns and crabmeat. A short selection of wines includes the popular quartet of quarter bottles from France and Chile that slide down so easily with seafood. To follow there will be a dessert of the day, often featuring locally-picked fresh fruits in summer. Wednesday and Saturday nights see traditional live music (June to October).

Prices: Set lunch €15. Set dinner €18. Main course restaurant from €9.50. Main course bar from €7. House wine €17.50.
Hours: 11.00-23.30. (24.30 Thursday-Saturday). Closed Good Friday and 25 December.
Food served: 12.00-20.30.
Cuisine: Seafood.
Other Points: No-smoking area. Garden. Children welcome.
Directions: Through the village to the Old Pier. (Map 19, B3)

Rusheen Lodge

Ballyvaughan, Co Clare
Telephone: +353(0)65 7077092
rusheen@iol.ie
www.rusheenlodge.com

The McGann family has owned this charming guesthouse for 15 years. Now run by Karen McGann, it is set in a valley surrounded by the Burren Mountains - famous for extraordinary rock formations and the unique diversity of its flora - and the house itself is pristine, bright with flowers in the perfect garden outside and meticulously maintained within. Nine generously proportioned bedrooms are comfortably appointed and individually designed, with desk and dressing tables, easy chairs, and lots of prints and fresh flowers. The easy hospitality of the house extends to generous breakfasts that take in a magnificent full Irish as well as treats such as Burren smoked salmon and scrambled eggs, and local smoked ham. Ballyvaughan village has many restaurants for evening meals and the local pubs are renowned for their traditional music.

Prices: Guesthouse.
Hours: Closed 14 November to 13 February.
Rooms: 9 en suite. Double/twin from €35. Single from €52. Family room from €80.
Other Points: No-smoking area. Garden. Children welcome. Garden.
Directions: N67. Three quarters of a kilometre from Ballyvaughan village on the N67 Lisdoonuarna road. (Map 19, B3)

Hal Pino's

7 High Street, Ennis, Co Clare
Telephone: +353(0) 6568 40011
halpinosrestaurant@eircom.net
www.halpinos.com

Derek Halpin's Hal Pino's has only one obstacle to overcome - its first floor location. The restaurant is wonderfully central, just beside the statue of Parnell in the heart of the town, and shares a frontage (window) with O'Halloran's pub. At the top of the stairs you walk into a space that is roomy, stylish and welcoming. Walls are used as an art gallery, in the corner is a leather sofa that begs to be lounged in; here you can stop for a drink and unwind before moving to tables which are simply but perfectly set. Service is first class and there is no sense of hurry. The food philosophy is good, ingredients simply prepared and sympathetically showcased to allow flavours to shine through. There are several menus ranging from a carte, a set menu, a seafood menu that changes with availability, and a bargain-price Early Bird selection. From the carte, expect chargrilled wild salmon with wilted spinach and prawn vinaigrette, herb-crusted rack of Irish lamb accompanied by sweet parsnip and ginger puree, wholegrain mustard and honey sauce, with lemon meringue tartlets to finish. The wine list is well chosen and reasonably priced and there are occasional late-night jazz sessions.

Prices: Set dinner €30. Main course from €14. House wine €17.
Hours: 17.00-22.00. 17.00-22.30 on Friday and Saturday. Lunch by arrangment. Closed 25 December.
Cuisine: Rustic and Modern Irish.
Other Points: No-smoking area. Children welcome. Car park. Live music. Art Gallery.
Directions: In the centre of Ennis just off the main square at the top of Parnell Street. (Map 19, B3)

Henry's Delicatessen 🍷✕

Abbey Street Car park, Ennis, Co Clare
Telephone: +353(0)65 682 2848

Henry Benagh, West Clare resident, but American born, originally opened a deli in another part of Ennis, but three years ago moved to these larger premises on the banks of the River Fergus. Of modern design, with large glass fronted windows and simple, wood furniture within, the place has a clean, fresh and open look, but it's really more of a sandwich and coffee bar than a deli. Fresh sandwiches are made to order, from a complex muffaletta (ham, salami, provolone cheese, green olives, pickle and olive oil), to a straightforward bacon, lettuce and tomato. There are six choices of homemade ice cream (made with full fat cream), and the quality of Henry's coffee is outstanding - he makes a mean cappuccino. Tuesday to Saturday evenings, Henry opens as a pizzeria. All the pizzas are made in house, include the usual favourites and, of course, some new combinations - asparagus and goats' cheese with oregano, perhaps. Salads such as Greek or Caesar are freshly made. The wine list is simple with just two prices, one for a bottle and one for a glass. There are three white and three red wines on offer: two from Chile and four from Italy.

Prices: Main course from €10 and €4.50 during the day. House wine €17.
Hours: 10.30-18.30. 19.00-23.00. Closed Monday evening and all day Sunday.
Cuisine: Sandwiches and pizzas.
Other Points: No-smoking area. Children welcome. Public car park.
Directions: In the centre of Ennis town on the banks of the River Fergus in the bottom end of Abbey Street car park. (Map 19, B3)

Cherry Tree Restaurant 🍷✕

Lakeside, Ballina, Killaloe, Co Clare
Telephone: +353(0)61 375688

The restaurant occupies an enviable setting on the banks of the River Shannon with plate glass windows making the most of the views. The bar area boasts leather armchairs, and a striking sloping ceiling supported by cross beams - all contained in a chic, light space offset by contemporary paintings. Harry McKeogh's highly accomplished cooking is both classical and innovative with ingredient-led menus based on sound, seasonal and often organic supplies, say, ravioli of duck confit with cider sauce, seared black pudding and apple compote or poch-grillé lobster with shellfish cappucino asparagus, fèves and purée of petit pois. Such fine materials are treated with confidence, assurance and understanding. Chargrilled, organic Irish asparagus is simply accompanied by roast pepper vinaigrette and Parmesan. For a main course, loin of spring lamb is teamed with pommes fondant, baby vegetables and jus, or fillet of black bass with crab crust, lobster chorizo cream and frogs' legs. Finish with lemon tart made with unwaxed organic lemons, cassis sorbet, candied lemon and clotted cream. The separate vegetarian menu is an exemplar of how such a thing should be done. The instructive wine list roams byways and highways to bring flavourful, food friendly wines to table.

Prices: Main course from €27. House wine €17.65.
Hours: 18.00-22.00. Closed Monday and Sunday, 24-25 December, St Stephens day, last week of January and first week of February.
Cuisine: Modern Irish.
Other Points: No-smoking area. Children welcome over 7 years old. Garden. Car park.
Directions: Travelling on the N7 Dublin-Limerick road, turn right at Birdhill for Killaloe. The restaurant is next to the Lakeside Hotel in Ballina village. (Map 19, B4)

Waterman's Lodge Hotel 🛏🍷✕♻

Ballina, Killaloe, Co Clare
Telephone: +353 (0)61 376333
info@watermanslodge.ie
www.watermanslodge.ie

This elegantly sprawling, single storey house with its long, sun-embracing façade, makes good use of its location on the Ballina side of the River Shannon overlooking the historic town of Killaloe. Within, there's the feel of a country house with polished wood floors, rugs, and a lovely sitting room situated in what used to be an inner courtyard (now glazed over) with a mix of sofas and armchairs in striking fabrics, large lamps, small side tables and soft cream coloured panelling. The bar has a terrific atmosphere, successfully blends tartan with polished dark wood, and attracts some local custom. Spacious bedrooms, some with magnificent brass bedsteads, are stylishly decorated, have good closet space, sofas, dressing tables and other thoughtful touches. Modern bathrooms come with bathrobes. A meal in the dining room might include timbale of crab and avocado topped with salmon mousse with tomato and coriander dressing, followed by Barbary duck breast served on a leek and pink grapefruit marmalade with a Cassis jus, with poached pear, white wine and almond cream to finish. France dominates the wine list, which includes a handful of half bottles and house wines from France and Chile.

Prices: Set lunch €21. Set dinner €42. Main course from €26. House wine €19.
Hours: 12.30-19.00. 19.00-21.30. Closed 23-25 December.
Rooms: 10 en suite. Singles from €90, double room from €150-€180, family room from €190.
Cuisine: Irish.
Other Points: No-smoking area. Children welcome. Garden. Car park.
Directions: 12 miles from Nenagh on the N7 and 17 miles from Limerick. (Map 19, B4)

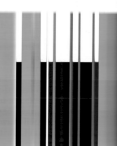

Barrtra Seafood Restaurant ♉♈✕
Lahinch, Co Clare
Telephone: +353(0)65 7081280
barrtra@hotmail.com

Located just outside Lahinch on the Miltown Malbay
road, down a little lane you come upon a small,
cottage-style house, overlooking Liscannor Bay. The
relaxed and intimate restaurant makes the most of
beautiful views over the water through a large window
and a small conservatory area. To the left is a snug
little room, which serves as a bar. Paul and Theresa
O'Brien are passionate about the food they serve; she
cooks, he's out front. Everything is made in- house,
including their breads. The kitchen's enterprising way
with seafood extends to smoked salmon with capers
and Liscannor Bay chowder. But menus are not
exclusively fishy. Meat main courses take in sirloin
steak with onion and pepper sauce, and a vegetarian
option of gnocchi with regatto cheese, tomatoes and
spinach. Peak condition Irish cheeses are a fine
alternative to softy fudgie brownie with homemade ice
cream and hot chocolate sauce. There's a carte, a good
value set dinner menu and a three course set early
dinner menu is served from 5pm to 6.30pm. Fifty or so
well chosen wines, which major in France, include a
good selection of half bottles and offer prices and
styles to suit all tastes and pockets.
Prices: Main course from €19. Set dinner €35. House wine €14.
Hours: 17.00-22.00. Closed Monday evenings, January and
February.
Cuisine: Modern Irish.
Other Points: No-smoking area. Children welcome. Garden.
Car park.
Directions: From Lahinch follow the signposts to Miltown Malbay
road, the N67. About one and a half miles along this road take a
right hand turn down a small road to Barrtra Restaurant.
(Map 19, B3)

Linnanes Lobster Bar ♉ ♌ ✕
New Quay, Burrin, Co Clare
Telephone: +353(0)65 7078120

This unassuming old cottage bar and diner is situated
just 500 metres off the main Galway road. It has
sliding doors at the back, which open virtually on to
the rocks and bring the magnificent seascape across
Galway Bay right inside. In winter, it is inward
looking, as visitors cluster around the peat fire
clutching pints of Guinness. It has rightly attracted
attention for the quality of its seafood. From the pier
opposite, Ocean West Fishery supplies the pick of each
day's landed catch, while speciality salmon and oyster
products come down from the Kinvara smokery, and
meat dishes are available alongside the long list of fish
and seafood specialities. Fresh lobster, sold by the
pound, can be ordered in advance, though the seafood
platter is arguably the pick, offering Pacific oysters,
clams, crab, smoked salmon and prawns, for two or
more. Then there is seafood chowder, open sandwiches,
and freshly cooked dishes such as steamed mussels, and
crispy crab cakes. Brown bread is freshly baked on the
premises. Suitable house wines come by both half and
quarter bottles, while Chablis and Chianti Classico
come in a price range that won't break the bank.
Prices: Main course from €11.00. House wine €14.25.
Hours: 12.30-21.00.
Closed Good Friday and 25 December.
Food served: 12.30-21.00.
Cuisine: Traditional Irish.
Other Points: No-smoking area. Garden. Children welcome.
Car park.
Directions: Off the main Kinvara Ballyvaughan road on journey
from Galway to Lisdoonvarna. (Map 19, A3)

Spanish Point Restaurant ♉♌✕✎
Ballycotton, Co Cork
Telephone: +353(0)21 4646177
spanishp@indigo.ie

John and Mary Tattan have been running their informal seafood
restaurant with five good value, comfortable en suite bedrooms since
1992, and have built up a sound local reputation. The house was built in
the late 19th century on the seaward side of the road giving clear views
across the bay, the property of the Presentation nuns, hence the local
nickname - the convent. The main part of the restaurant is in a wooden
conservatory, with wooden floors and outside is a timber-decked patio.
There is a cosy bar and off this another conservatory area where pre-
dinner drinks are served. Fish comes straight from their own trawler, and
Mary is proud of the fact that they bake all their own bread and use as
much local produce as possible. This is good, simple cooking that takes in
goujons of lemon sole with a basil and lime mayonnaise. Main courses
range from grilled wild salmon with straw potatoes and chive butter, to
pan-fried John Dory, chorizo mash with a pineapple and chilli salsa. Meat
eaters might opt for roast fillet of lamb with beetroot and feta cheese tart,
cider, onion and apple sauce.

Prices: Set lunch €22. Set dinner €39. Main
course restaurant from €22. Main course
bar/snack from €10. House wine €18.
Hours: 12.30-15.00 Sunday only. 18.30-
21.30. Sunday from 19.00.
Rooms: 5 en suite. Double/twin from €40
per person sharing. Prices
include breakfast.
Cuisine: Modern Irish.
Other Points: No-smoking area. Dogs
welcome. Garden. Children welcome.
Private beach.
Directions: From the N25 turn off either
at Midleton or Castlemartyr. (Map 20, E5)

Ashlee Lodge

Tower, Blarney, Co Cork
Telephone: +353(0)21 438 5346
info@ashleelodge.com
www.ashleelodge.com

John and Anne O' Leary's beautiful house is located just outside Blarney. With ten individually furnished rooms and suites (plus one fully accessible disabled room with private entrance), an indoor sauna, and Canadian hot tub, it is an ideal place to relax in elegant surroundings. All the rooms are named after famous Irish golf courses and come fully equipped with king size beds, wide screen TVs, radios and CD units, as well as modem access; bathrooms are luxurious and suites are equipped with whirlpool baths. Attention to detail extends to the fact that the O'Learys have taken the time to add all the little bits and pieces that you may have missed when packing. Also, there's a lovely, relaxing drawing room and breakfast is served in the bright and cheerful breakfast room - a real feast with a hearty breakfast buffet selection, and dishes cooked to order. The O'Learys take great pride in their guesthouse and try to accommodate every need, indeed going that one step further by offering transport, be it golfing or dining out for the evening. Also offered are holistic treatments such as aromatherapy, Reiki, reflexology and massage, but by appointment only.

Prices: Main course bar from €8. House wine €13.50.
Rooms: 10 en suite. Double/Twin room from €100, single from €70. Family room from €130.
Other Points: No-smoking area. Dogs welcome. Garden. Children welcome. Car park.
Directions: R617. Located in Tower vilage, 2 kilometres outside Blarney on the main Killarney to Blarney road. (Map 19, D4)

Blairs Inn ★ ♥ ▯ ✕

Cloghroe, Blarney, Co Cork
Telephone: +353(0)21 4381470
blair@eircom.net
www.homepage.eircom.net-blair

An outstanding example of a real, traditional Irish family pub just five minutes from the famous Blarney Woollen Mills in a secluded riverside setting. John Blair's friendly hospitality and great character permeates the building and his wife Anne, with chef Raphael Delage, cook great Irish food using the best raw materials - they are passionate promoters of small food producers. Food is served throughout the day. In the bar this covers lunchtime soups, sandwiches, and cold plates, to the more substantial casserole of lamb in Murphy's Stout sauce served in the evening. The restaurants, known as the Snug and the Pantry, are just as the names suggest - cosy, warm, a homely atmosphere brought about by a rustic look of wooden seating and low ceilings. Light is low with candles dotted around and there are lots of fresh flowers. Interesting combinations are the distinctive style of the menus here. Quality Kenmare seafood and Co Cork farm produce provide the foundations for the Blair's much talked about food. Fish is a strength, be it whole bass with beurre blanc sauce, or baked salmon with saffron mash and red pepper coulis. However, there could also be old style saddle of wild boar with red wine jus.

Prices: Main course from €20.95 (dinner) and €11.95 (lunch). Main course bar from €11.95. House wine €18.75.
Hours: 12.30-15.30. 18.30-21.30. Closed 25 December and Good Friday.
Cuisine: Modern Irish.
Other Points: Children welcome until 19.30. Garden. Car park.
Directions: Five minutes from Blarney on the R579. (Map 19, D4)

An Sugan Seafood Restaurant ♥ ▯ ✕

Wolfe Tone Street, Clonakilty, Co Cork
Telephone: +353(0)23 33498
sineadocrowley@hotmail.com

This colourful pub sums up everything that makes Clonakilty such a delightful place to visit; there's a genuinely friendly welcome and a well deserved reputation for excellent bar food. There's a wealth of options on the menu, whose main dishes through the day run to thirty or more; but, it is the evening menu that really says it all. There is salmon and shrimp parfait, baked cod with herb crust, and salmon escalope in filo pastry amongst the options. Informal lunch dishes offer fresh whiting with salad and fries, and salmon-and-potato cakes. Meaty alternatives almost inevitably include traditional bacon and cabbage, chicken breast in Madeira sauce and roast sirloin of beef. At the top of the range come an Atlantic seafood filo pastry basket and, subject to availability, lobster an Sugan, flamed in brandy and tomato sauce with mushrooms and shallots. Prime sirloin comes with herb butter, green peppercorns, or Cognac sauce. Appetisers would suffice equally as a snack: terrine of Clonakilty puddings with tomato chutney, or deep-fried Gubeen cheese with cranberry relish. This scarcely suggests that simply dropping by for a pint of 'the black stuff' would come free of any temptation to indulge in a great deal more.

Prices: Set dinner from €20. Main course restaurant and bar evening meal from €13 . Main course bar from €6. House wine €15.
Hours: Open and food is served: 12.30-21.30. Closed 25-26 December and Good Friday.
Cuisine: Irish and Seafood.
Other Points: No-smoking area. Garden. Children welcome.
Directions: On the left hand side as you enter Clonakilty from Cork. (Map 19, E3)

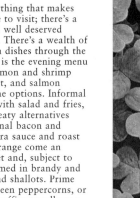

Ireland - Co Cork

WatersEdge Hotel ★ ♟ ✗ ♫
(next to Cobh Heritage Centre), Cobh, Co Cork
Telephone: +353 (0)21 481 5566
info@watersedgehotel.ie
www.watersedgehotel.ie

Margaret and Michael Whelan have built a modern, elegant hotel reflecting the Victorian splendour of historic Cobh. The bright yellow painted hotel is located in Yacht Club Quay beside the Cobh Heritage Centre, right on the water's edge, looking out to Spike Island and Haulbowline Island, the Irish naval base. All the bedrooms are individually styled - cheerful, with bright colourful furnishings and white wooden furniture - and provide a high standard of comfort; several have views over the water. Wood floors and tables, elegantly covered chairs, ceiling to floor windows and fresh flowers, create a striking impression in Jacob's Ladder, the hotel restaurant. Large windows provide a beautiful view of the water. Modern Irish cooking delivers Thai spiced crab and prawn cakes with a mango-lime salsa and caper mayonnaise, oven roasted rack of lamb, root vegetable purée, beetroot and mint jus, followed by Jacob's raspberry tiramisu, served with crème anglaise. During the summer it is possible to sit out on the balcony and overlook the water. This small 19 bedroom hotel is a find, offering elegance and comfort and run by friendly, efficient owners and their staff.

Prices: Main course restaurant meal from €15. Main course bar/snack from €7.50. House wine €17.95.
Hours: 12.30-15.00 (until 14.30 in the Winter). 18.30-21.30. Closed 22-27 December, after breakfast on the 1 January to re-open on 4 January.
Rooms: 19 en suite. Double room from €50 per person, single from €80, family room from €135.
Cuisine: Modern Irish and Seafood.
Other Points: Totally no smoking. Children welcome. Car park.
Directions: Next to Cobh Heritage Centre. (Map 19, E4)

Café Paradiso ♟ ♟ ✗
16 Lancaster Quay, Western Road, Cork, Co Cork
Telephone: +353(0)21 4277939
info@cafeparadiso.ie
www.cafeparadiso.ie

A unique experience, which must be observed, tasted and touched, is a view many take of Denis Cotter's restaurant, a Cork landmark delivering vivid modern dishes, with the emphasis on sound raw materials. The cooking is skilled and dedicated, the quality of materials and the work required to garner them impressive. The fact that meat plays no part is somehow not an issue - you simply just don't notice. The food avoids the stodge and heavyweight flavours of much vegetarian cooking and uses ingredients intelligently to provide seasoning and balance and a real lightness of touch. Examples might be a starter of ravioli of Knockalara sheeps' cheese, currants and pine nuts in a plum tomato, basil and olive oil broth, or a main course lemon, mint and scallion risotto with broad beans, roasted beetroots and mature Oisin goats' cheese. Oriental spicing and vivid contrasts of flavours and textures are combined in vegetable sushi with pickled ginger, wasabi and a dipping sauce and tempura of cauliflower and aubergine, as well as sweet chilli-glazed pan-fried tofu with pak choi in a coconut-lemongrass broth and sesame-dressed fresh noodles. The wine list shows the same dedication, the range of modern producers is impressive, with a good choice of organic and half bottles.

Prices: Set lunch €27. Set dinner €36. Main course lunch from €13. Main course dinner from €18.50. House wine from €20.
Hours: 12.30-15.00. 18.30-22.30.
Closed Sundays and Mondays and over Christmas for 10 days.
Cuisine: Modern Vegetarian.
Other Points: No-smoking area. Children welcome.
Directions: Opposite Jury's Hotel and a five minute walk from University College Cork. (Map 19, D4)

The Douglas Hide ♟ ▮ ✗
63 Douglas Street, Cork, Co Cork
Telephone: +353(0)21 4315695
douglashide@eircom.net

Aoife and Tadhg O' Donovan bought this small pub in 1999, carried out extensive renovation and named it the Douglas Hide (a pun on Douglas Hyde, the first President of Ireland). Small, intimate, and contemporary looking, it is now more restaurant in style than pub; this is really a restaurant where you can have a pint. An unfussy style of cooking allows everyone to enjoy the best local produce, including organic and free-range produce when available, with Cork's English Market supplying fish - there's also wild Irish game in season, and west Cork cheeses, including Gubeen and Mileens. A warm salad of chicken livers and O'Flynn's sausage, or chilli prawns with a pineapple and coriander salad, are typical starters. Free range farmyard duck could follow, teamed with red onion confit and a black olive cream sauce, or almond crusted free-range breast of chicken, accompanied by mushroom risotto with a citrus vinaigrette. Chalkboards display the fish and vegetarian dish of the day. Finish perhaps with espresso pudding with tiramisu ice cream, or chocolate and strawberry tart with crème anglaise. The short wine list darts around the globe and is very good value.

Prices: Main course restaurant from €15. House wine €17.
Hours: 12.00-14.00. 18.00-23.30. Thursday to Saturday until 00.30. Closed 25-26 December, Good Friday.
Food served: 12.00-14.30. 18.00-21.00. Friday and Saturday until 22.00. No food Saturday lunchtime.
Cuisine: Modern Irish.
Other Points: No-smoking area. Children welcome before 20.00.
Directions: Opposite the South Preservation Convent on Douglas Street, five minutes walk from South Mall over Parliament Bridge. (Map 19, D4)

Farmgate Cafe ★ 🍷 🍵 ◗ ✕
Old English Market, Princes Street,
Cork, Co Cork
Telephone: +353(0)21 4278134

The English Market is the epicentre of food in Cork and was recently voted by *The Observer* as one of the top ten food markets in the world. Founded over 200 years ago, it has traditionally been the place to buy meat, fowl, fish, vegetables and fruit, and is one of the last remaining areas where classics such as tripe and drisheen can be purchased, both dishes served in the Farmgate Café upstairs. This straightforward eatery, the brainchild of sisters Maróg O'Brien and Kay Harte, certainly makes the most of its location. (Kay runs this Cork venture, Maróg the original Farmgate Restaurant in Midleton, see entry.) The menu is dictated by the availability of local and fresh food in the market below. Indeed, the market is their larder: fish, for example, comes to table straight from the famous fish stalls, oysters directly so. And they do it justice: classic Irish cooking taking in lamb's liver and bacon, Irish lamb stew, smoked bacon and cabbage, corned mutton and caper sauce, as well as plates of locally smoked salmon, and local cheeses with Farmgate chutney. It's open for breakfast and lunch, with cakes and breads from their patisserie served all day.

Prices: Main course restaurant from €10. House wine €18.
Hours: 08.30-17.30.
Closed 25-26 December, 1 January, Good Friday.
Cuisine: Modern European and Traditional Irish.
Other Points: No-smoking area. Children welcome.
Directions: Off Patrick Street in Cork City. (Map 19, D4)

The Franciscan Well Brew Pub ▐
North Mall, Cork City, Co Cork
Telephone: +353(0)21 4210130

Built on the site of an Franciscan monastery and well dating from 1219, legend has it that the water here has miraculous and curative properties. No wonder a brand new brewery opened here in 1998. Old traditions in forming classic beer styles such as ale, stout and wheat beer have been combined with modern technology to produce varietals that are naturally brewed and free of chemical additives and preservatives. The brew pub houses three serving vessels, openly visible behind the bar, that dispense directly to the serving taps. There is Blarney Blonde in the style of German Grolsch lager, caramel-flavoured Rebel Red fortified with challenger and fuggles hops, and Shandon Stout with a creamy, roasted malt character, in the classic Cork style. Seasonal specialities include Bellringer Winter Warmer and Purgatory Pale - which may be self-explanatory. Book up for brewery tours, private parties in the function room, and look out for the regular beer fests, which generally include an all-day barbecue in the beer garden.

Hours: 15.00-23.30 Monday-Wednesday. 15.00-24.00 on Thursday. 15.00-24.30 on Friday and Saturday. 16.00-23.00 on Sunday.
Directions: Head straight down north Main Street, cross over the North Gate Bridge and then turn left. (Map 19, D4)

Lotamore House 🛏
Tivoli, Cork, Co Cork
Telephone: +353(0)21 4822344
www.lotamorehouse.com

Located in Tivoli, on the main road into Cork city, just minutes from the city centre, this elegant Georgian house is owned and run by Mairead Harty as a guesthouse. After undergoing major refurbishment, Lotamore is now beautifully appointed. First impressions of an elegant house are immediately backed up when you walk in the front door and see a lovely antique desk (used as a reception) behind which is an impressive staircase leading up to the bedrooms and a striking stained glass window. Really fabulous bedrooms have antique furniture and beautiful bed linen, and the house is tastefully and lavishly decorated with a peaceful and relaxed atmosphere. Breakfast includes full Irish and a buffet selection, including homemade museli, toasted granola, freshly made brown bread, freshly squeezed orange juice and a choice of fresh and poached fruits.

Prices: Guesthouse.
Hours: Closed 20 December - 7 January.
Rooms: 20 en suite. Double/twin from €120. Single from €75. Family room from €150.
Other Points: No-smoking area. Garden. Children welcome. Car park.
Directions: N8 and N25. Lotamore is on the left hand side of the dual carriageway. (Map 19, D4)

THE TIMES

As the legendary Cork restaurant Café Paradiso celebrates its tenth birthday, owner Denis Cotter reflects on what a difference a decade makes.

Its hard to believe that Café Paradiso reached its tenth birthday in 2003. When we first opened, we thought that perhaps we would amuse customers and ourselves for a few years, then either crash financially or get bored and move to a better climate. Some people thought it was a daft enterprise anyway: a vegetarian restaurant that wanted out of the wholefood industry and wanted to be taken seriously in the restaurant main stream. And in Cork?

In fact, Cork was the perfect place. The city (and county) has a very open-minded food culture, and has always supported individuals who went about things in their own idiosyncratic way. Around the time Café Paradiso opened, Seamus O'Connell opened his highly single-minded Ivory, which was closely followed by Toby Simmonds' eccentric notion of importing olives, and little else but olives, to sell to a Cork public which had, until then, shown little demand for the things!

However, if that were all there was to it, an attempt to make a mark, we would indeed have become bored and moved on. The energy and interest needed to carry on, to improve and move forward came from the relationships we formed with vegetable growers and distributors, and with cheese makers. Once we had started (tentatively) to buy the produce of Hollyhill Farm, there was a gradual but enormous shift of power in the menus of Paradiso. They produced distinctive rocket, watercress, black kale, many varieties of beans and peas, baby beetroots, pumpkins and Swiss chard unseen since our time in New Zealand, courgette flowers, yams, gooseberries and more – the produce was erratic, unique and, most of all, seasonal.
This, in turn, caused a shift in power in our menus, away from clever recipe-based dishes, getting the ingredients where we could, to a style of cooking based on the produce available at the time. This is not only the most demanding, but also the most rewarding way to cook. Each season brings its joys and its challenges, indeed every day of each season does. When it rains heavily, there are no strawberries, courgettes are a summer treat, as celeriac is in winter, and the glut of sugar snaps must be adapted to as much as the sudden ending of their season.

THEY ARE A' CHANGING

The pleasure of cooking with, and feasting on, the bounty of the best produce available in its perfect time, is on another plane from trying to make decent grub from expensive but weary stuff that budgets dictate you have to be mean with, despite its poor quality. Cooks can no longer work with such rubbish and, thankfully, consumers have had enough of it.

In Café Paradiso, it seems that the first years were only a learning period, a time of finding our place - not in the narrow restaurant scene as we had naively wanted, but in the wider food culture. I believe this reflects the biggest and most important development in food in recent years. There is a renewed perception of the produce and those who produce it as the most important element of the food chain. Restaurants and retailers are, at best, a medium between the producer and the consumer. This is illustrated best in the growth of farmers' markets, where people go, not in search of bargains or because they like to shop at dawn in the rain, but for fresh, local food from producers they can connect with. The industrialisation of food sold us the notion of cheapness, constant supply and uniform quality, albeit bland and dull, as the principle qualities in food. There is a very strong sense in the air that people have tired of it, and we are moving on, or perhaps back, to a time when local broad beans and Swiss chard are prized more highly than flabby, out-of-season Peruvian asparagus.

This new energy in the food culture is coming from an unusual coincidence of the interests of producers, consumers and cooks; and it is an increasingly conscious effort to repair the connections that have been torn by years of making do with the depressing products of the industrialisation of food. This isn't just wishful thinking. It is visible as a new enthusiasm and confidence in vegetable growers and other food producers, those who were often previously perceived as eccentric outsiders: a sense that they are no longer working alone or in struggle against the public drift. Instead, there is the hugely energising feeling that if they can produce it, if we can cook it, the consumers are crying out for local, seasonal food; food that makes all of us feel part of the culture rather than victims of it.

This is a wonderful environment and a wonderful time to be working with food. I would be one of the last to say that Cork, or indeed Ireland as a whole, is anywhere near to being a food nirvana, but there is a

Pi Restaurant

Courthouse Chambers, Washington Street,
Cork, Co Cork
Telephone: +353(0)21 4222860
info@pirestaurant.com
www.pirestaurant.com

Situated in the courthouse chambers, opposite the
refurbished circuit courthouse in the heart of the
Washington Village area of Cork, Pi's has a welcoming
feel, its aspirations egged on by a band of loyal
supporters. The quality of materials is top notch, with
fish and organic foods delivered from Cork's famed
English Market, cheese and meat locally sourced, and
game making its seasonal appearance. This is an all
day café-cum-restaurant, with breakfast taking in all
the usual big fry-up suspects, as well as kippers,
poached egg wrapped in Parma ham on french toast,
and breakfast rolls to take away. The lunch and
afternoon menu includes such promising ideas as green
papaya salad with crispy fish cakes, and tuna, salmon
and prawn sandwich (made with brown soda bread)
with garlic mayonnaise, salad and cherry tomatoes, as
well as burgers, a lengthy pizza list, Thai curries and
steaks. There's a good value Early Bird set menu before
the dinner carte kicks in with duck confit, salad and
aromatic dressing, and rack of lamb, polenta, roast
peppers and port jus. There's a something-for-everyone
appeal to Pi, prices are reasonable, and the well-
annotated wine list roams the world in search of good
value drinking.

Prices: Set lunch €20. Set dinner €50. House wine €19.50.
Hours: 08.30-22.30. Sunday 12.00-22.00.
Closed Good Friday, 25 December and 1 January.
Cuisine: Modern European.
Other Points: No-smoking area. Children welcome.
Directions: Go up Washington Street and turn right across the
Courthouse. (Map 19, D4)

Nakon Thai Restaurant

Tramway House, Douglas Village, Cork, Co Cork
Telephone: +353(0)21 436 9900
www.nakonthai.com

Named after the southern Thai province of Nakon-si
Thammarat (City of Kings), David and Sineerat
McGreal's Nakon Thai is located in the village of
Douglas. It is a small and intimate restaurant offering
good, unpretentious Thai cooking using authentic
ingredients. Indeed, the kitchen delivers competent
renditions of Thai favourites: chicken satay, fish cakes
with a sweet plum sauce, and classic pad Thai noodles.
Tom yam gung (spicy soup with black tiger prawns)
comes with a full set of spices, gai phad king is a
savoury combination of stir-fried chicken breast with
fresh ginger, black Thai mushrooms, onion and spring
onion, or there could be squid marinated in garlic and
black pepper and stir-fried with a blend of Thai herbs.
All beef used is locally sourced, and appears in such
dishes as nua phad krapow - stir-fried with garlic,
chillies and sweet basil leaves, and panang nua, sliced
in a curry sauce with coconut milk and herbs. There is
a lengthy, reasonably priced wine list as well as Singha
beer, and Premium Thai beer. Service is friendly and
efficient.

Prices: Set dinner €22.95. Main course restaurant from €13.25.
House wine €14.95.
Hours: Food served: 17.30-23.00. 17.00-22.00 on Sunday.
Closed 24-26 December and Good Friday.
Cuisine: Thai.
Other Points: No-smoking area. Children welcome. Car park.
Directions: Opposite the Rugby Club in Douglas village.
(Map 19, E4)

The Heron's Cove

The Harbour, Goleen, Co Cork
Telephone: +353(0)28 35225
suehill@eircom.net
www.heronscove.com

Prices: Main course from €19.50. Wine
from €12.
Hours: Food served daily from 19.00.
Reservations only October-April.
Closed 25 December and 1 January.
Rooms: 5 en suite. Double room from
€35 per person, single from €35.
Cuisine: Irish.
Other Points: Garden. Car park.
Directions: Turn off the N71 and follow
the R592 to Goleen. Turn left down to the
harbour. (Map 19, E2)

Sue Hill's waterside restaurant-with-rooms overlooks a private cove in one
of the most beautiful locations. This is a magical place where seals,
choughs, kittiwakes and gannets are common sights, and dolphins, whales
and basking sharks are frequent visitors. The cooking utilises organic
vegetables, fish landed at Goleen harbour, Irish cheeses, Clonakilty black
and white puddings, Bantry Bay mussels and smoked fish; an impressive
list of local producers. That and Sue's determination to keep prices
reasonable are laudable features. The carte can start with warm west Cork
duckling salad, or the popular locally smoked salmon platter, followed by
Roaring Water Bay scallops or chargrilled fillet steak, with Cashel Blue
rarebit. Desserts are also a real treat with homemade ice creams, and
Heron's Cove cream lime pie. You choose your own wines from the rack
and it is opened at your table; whites are replaced with a bottle from the
cooler. Five en suite rooms are cosy and very well maintained. The
restaurant is open only in the evenings, and only by prior booking from
November to May.

The Old Bank House

11 Pearse Street, Kinsale, Co Cork
Telephone: +353(0)21 4774075
oldbank@indigo.ie
www.oldbankhousekinsale.com

This grand old Georgian house was once the first bank in Kinsale - the bank manager and his family lived on the upper floors. Now run as a guesthouse, period details such as high ceilings, large windows and fireplaces are striking features, and are complemented by antique furniture and original art. Fifteen years of running a guesthouse to very high standards has honed Michael and Marie Reise's hospitality skills, and it is the extra little personal touches, especially in the comfortable, beautifully appointed bedrooms, that make all the difference. Each room is a blend of Georgian good looks and modern comfort and most of the 17 bedrooms have views of the harbour town - "the oldest town in Ireland." Michael is a Master Chef, dedicated to using only organic and local produce as much as possible. His breakfasts are excellent, ranging from farm eggs, local bacon, black pudding, tomato and mushrooms, to various omelettes, smoked haddock and french toast with maple syrup, as well as homemade brown bread and marmalade.

Rooms: 17 en suite. Double/twin room from €170. Family room from €245.
Other Points: No-smoking area.
Directions: On the right hand side at the start of Kinsale town, next to the Post Office. (Map 19, E4)

Farmgate Restaurant and Country Store

Coolbawn, Midleton, Co Cork
Telephone: +353(0)21 463 2771

Maróg O'Brien has run her lovely little restaurant and farmshop for 20 years and it draws visitors from far and wide, as much for the appealing local produce in the shop (organic fruits and vegetables, cheeses, and wonderful home baking) as for the delicious food in the restaurant. This can range from simple lunchtime sandwiches of local smoked salmon, salads, a plate of Irish cheese, or grilled minute steak with garlic butter and salad, and deep-fried squid with chilli provençale, to more elaborate evening meals served on Thursday, Friday and Saturday nights. The ingredient led menus belie the skill behind the dishes, they are not overworked but starters of moules marinière or warm spicy chicken salad, stand out for their fresh, vibrant flavour. Main courses include grilled strip loin of beef with a perfect béarnaise sauce, and pan-seared monkfish with chargrilled red pepper sauce. Finish with vanilla bavarois with a little cream and florentines, or white chocolate meringue gateau. The wine list is well spread with a particularly strong showing in France and the Antipodes. This is a comfortable, relaxed place with some striking sculptures. A sister restaurant to the Farmgate Café, Cork (see entry).

Prices: Main course restaurant from €18. Main course bar/snack from €10. House wine €18.
Hours: 12.00-16.00. 18.30-21.30.
Closed all day Sunday, Monday-Wednesday evenings, Bank Holidays, 25-26 December and 1 January.
Cuisine: Traditional Irish and Modern European.
Other Points: No-smoking area. Garden. Children welcome.
Directions: Follow the signs for the Irish Distillery off the Waterford to Cork road. (Map 19, D4)

Glenview House

Midleton, Co Cork
Telephone: +353(0)21 4631680
glenviewhouse@esatclear.ie/info@glenviewmidleton.com
www.glenviewmidleton.com

When you turn into the winding, tree-lined drive, past glimpses of lawn tumbling down into woodland, it is all Ken and Beth Sherrard's work; even the restored classic Georgian farmhouse is down to their immense vision. In the 1960s, Ken heard that 16 houses in Dublin's Fitzwilliam Square were going to be pulled down and he shipped the lot to Glenview. The magnificent front door, the mantlepiece over the log-burning stove in the marble-tiled hallway, the delicate staircase, all came from those houses. It's a family home too, with photos, dogs, a drawing room filled with comfy sofas, armchairs, and magazines. Rugs cover bare boards, there's period furniture, fresh flowers and a very warm, lived-in feel. In the dining room there's a huge mahogany table for communal breakfasts with eggs from Beth's 80 hens. Dinner, by request, has no real menu but good homecooking runs to tomato and red pepper soup, beef casserole in red wine, and lemon and strawberry syllabub. One of the three magnificent, spacious bedrooms has an amazing *fin de siècle* bath/shower contraption with sunflower head and sideways pin shower. Thoughtful touches include jars of instant coffee, Lemsip, Aspirin, sewing kit. The coach house has two self-catering cottages.

Prices: Set dinner €40. House wine €20.
Hours: Dinner served at 20.00. Book 24 hours in advance.
Rooms: 7 en suite. Double room from €65-€70 per person, single from €83.
Cuisine: Country House Cooking.
Other Points: No-Smoking area. Children welcome. Garden. Tennis. Ample secure parking.
Directions: Take the L35 (R626) from Midleton to Fermoy. After two and a half miles turn right at the T junction for Fermoy. A quarter of a mile down the road turn left marked for Glenview House. The house is three miles down. (Map 19, D4)

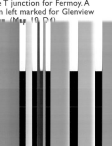

COLOURFUL CORK
AND THE RING OF KERRY

Ireland's wild and windswept coastline takes in Bantry Bay, the Ring of Kerry and the Dingle Peninsula,
a glorious corner of the country renowned for its beautiful scenery and magnificent views.
Drive length: 362 miles

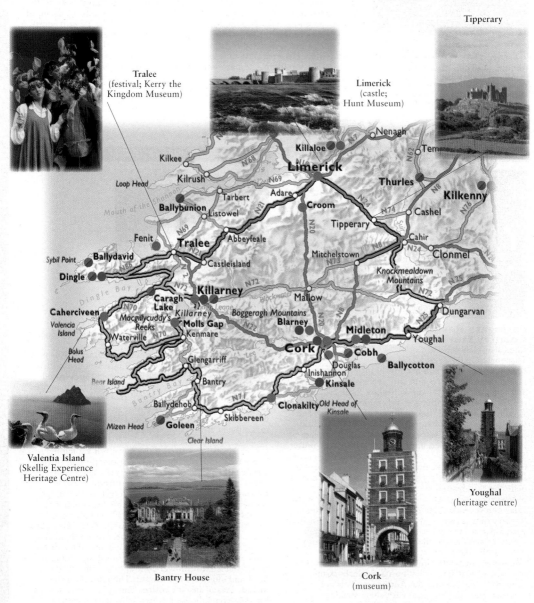

Tipperary

Tralee
(festival; Kerry the
Kingdom Museum)

Limerick
(castle;
Hunt Museum)

Nenagh

Killaloe

Kilkee

Limerick

Tem

Loop Head

Kilrush

N69

Thurles

Kilkenny

Tarbert

Adare

Kilrush

N68

Ballybunion

Listowel

Croom

Cashel

N76

Fenit

Abbeyfeale

Tipperary

Cahir

N74

Clonmel

Sybil Point

Ballydavid

Tralee

Castleisland

Mitchelstown

N24

Dingle

Killarney

Knockmealdown
Mountains

N25

Caragh
Lake

Killarney

Mallow

N72

Caherciveen

Macgillycuddy's
Reeks

Molls Gap

Boggeragh Mountains

Dungarvan

Valencia
Island

Blarney

Bolus
Head

Waterville

Kenmare

Midleton

Youghal

Bear Island

Glengarriff

Cork

Cobh

Ballycotton

Bantry

Douglas
Inishannon

Kinsale

Ballydehob

Clonakilty

Old Head of
Kinsale

Mizen Head

Goleen

Skibbereen

Clear Island

Valentia Island
(Skellig Experience
Heritage Centre)

Youghal
(heritage centre)

Bantry House

Cork
(museum)

● Accommodation/Food

● Accommodation

● Food

🥄 Food Shop

To find the establishments marked
here, look up the listing town
marked on the map in bold in the
town index on page 395

Mill Park Hotel 🛏 🍷 ✕ ⬧

The Mullins, Killybegs Road,
Donegal, Co Donegal
Telephone: +353(0)73 22880
millparkhotel@eircom.com
www.millparkhotel.com

Situated in its own private grounds on the outskirts of the picturesque town of Donegal, this eye catching hotel is set in well-maintained gardens and has its own private car park and leisure centre. A mill wheel stands beside the entrance with a stream and little waterfall passing underneath. Within, open fires greet you in the Granary area, an open-plan combination of reception, restaurant and bar, where beamed ceilings and floors that are a mix of wood and Chinese slate, give a feeling of years of character. The spacious bedrooms are in contrast to the olde worlde look of the public areas. Rich warm colour schemes blend with modern, stylish furniture; there are comfortable beds and more than ample storage areas. All rooms are equipped with hot drinks trays, hairdryer, multi-channel TV and trouser press. Two eating areas supply plenty of choice, with one small, intimate no-smoking dining room, while the main open-faced, bustling Granary Restaurant has the feel of an old mill.

Prices: Set lunch €17.25. Main course bar from €8.80. Main course restaurant from €16.50. House wine €14.
Hours: 13.00-15.00. Sunday lunch open until 17.00. 18.00-21.30. Closed 24-26 December.
Rooms: 43 en suite. Double room from €110, single from €115.
Cuisine: Irish.
Other Points: No-smoking area. Children welcome. Garden. Car park.
Directions: From Donegal town centre take the Killybegs route until you arrive at the roundabout. Take the second exit which is the Letterbarrow exit off the roundabout. (Map 17, C4)

Why go to...Co Donegal

Situated in the northwest of Ireland, surrounded on three sides by the Atlantic Ocean, Donegal is a beautiful county with dramatic cliff scenery (geologically a continuation of the Highlands of Scotland) and a very irregular coastline broken by Lough Swilly, Sheep Haven, Boylagh Bay, Gweebarra Bay, and Donegal Bay. Rich in early remains, the most interesting is, perhaps, the Grianan of Aileach, a large circular stone fort, built about 1700 BC as the stronghold of the kings of Ulster, the O'Neills. In Donegal town, the O' Donnells castle (where the famous Irish chieftan Red Hugh O' Donnell lived) is another must see, the famous St Patrick's Purgatory pilgrimage takes place on Station Island in the middle of Lough Derg, and Garton is the birthplace of St Columba (521-597).

Castle Murray House Hotel

🛏 🍷 ✕ 📖

St John's Point, Dunkineely, Co Donegal
Telephone: +353(0)74 9737022
castlemurray@eircom.net
www.castlemurray.com

The location is unbeatable: on the coast road of St John's Point, one mile from the main road between Killybegs and Donegal Town and overlooking the magnificent McSwynes Bay. The view is breathtaking, taking in the surrounding Donegal Mountains and a ruined castle; a long conservatory fronts the house and makes the most of the panorama, as does the restaurant on the seaward side, and all ten spacious, individual bedrooms have magnificent views. Marguerite Howley bought the hotel in the spring of 2002, winning friends with her generosity, hospitality, and cooking that emphasizes robust flavours - it all adds to the homely feel. Produce embraces locally caught fish that's delivered to the back door still alive. Sound skills translate this into favourites such as a starter of prawns and monkfish in garlic butter - something of a speciality - with a main course of, say, steamed black sole with lobster brandy cream. Or there could be roast rack of lamb accompanied by port cream and morels, and grilled corn-fed chicken stuffed with peppers and mushrooms. Strawberry and champagne jelly with strawberry sorbet makes an equally appealing dessert.

Prices: Set lunch €23. Set dinner €46. House wine €19.
Hours: 19.00-21.30. Sunday 13.30-15.30. 18.30-20.30.
Closed middle of January for one month. Closed Monday and Tuesday during low season.
Rooms: 10 en suite. Double/twin from €96. Single from €70.
Family room from €130.
Cuisine: French and Irish.
Other Points: No-smoking area. Dogs welcome. Garden.
Car park.
Directions: N56. 15 minutes from Donegal town in Killybegs direction. One mile off the main road for St John's Point.
(Map 17, C4)

McGrory's of Culdaff

🛏 🍷 📕 ✕ 📖

Culdaff, Inishowen, Co Donegal
Telephone: +353(0)74 9379104
info@mcgrorys.ie
www.mcgrorys.ie

An inn in the true sense of the word, with accommodation, restaurant and bar making up this long established family business. It is probably most famous for its music, which includes traditional Irish sessions, but bedrooms are modern in comforts, reflect the style of the original building in design and décor, and take in a family suite. The close proximity to the Atlantic is reflected in both bar and restaurant menus. Local seafood chowder is a bar favourite, served with wheaten bread, or there could be wild mussels and Donegal oysters, with O'Doherty's Black bacon served with Filligans tomato relish and prime Irish steaks making meaty alternatives. The contemporary menu in the restaurant conjures up some intriguing dishes, teaming monkfish with fennel and Black bacon, and serving white crab meat with plum tomatoes and lime mayonnaise. Locally sourced Inishowen lamb comes as noisettes with herb crust and redcurrant sauce, or there could be a classic fillet steak Café de Paris. Some four dozen wines offer a decent cross section of styles and good value.

Prices: Set dinner €28. Main course restaurant from €14. Main course bar/snack from €7.50. House wine €15.
Hours: Food served: 12.30-20.00 bar food.
18.30-21.30 Tuesday to Sunday Restaurant.
Closed: Restaurant closed Mondays and Tuesdays during the winter.
Closed 23-26 December.
Rooms: 10 en suite. Double/twin from €90. Single from €55.
Family room from €90.
Cuisine: Modern Irish.
Other Points: No-smoking area. Children welcome. Car park.
Traditional Irish music sessions in this famous music venue.
Directions: On the R238 between Moville and Malin Head.
(Map 18, B6)

Castle Grove Country House Hotel

🍷 ✕ 📖

Castlegrove, Letterkenny, Co Donegal
Telephone: +353(0)74 51118
reservations@castlegrove.com
www.castlegrove.com

The Sweeney family's handsome Georgian house was built in the late 17th century and the mile long drive through a parkland of mature trees ensures complete seclusion. Views are assured as it occupies a very sheltered position looking out over Lough Swilly. First impressions of a grand old home are justified. Spacious public rooms are pleasantly furnished, with impressive period details and striking colours adding to the effect. All 14 en suite bedrooms have retained individual character and are very well furnished and appointed with soft colours and floral fabrics, easy chairs, and period-style furniture. Local produce is a feature of the menu served in the formal restaurant with roast chicken and quail terrine, apple and walnut salsa and balsamic dressing, opening a typical meal. Main courses are likely to include chargrilled fillet of Donegal prime beef with salsa verde, crunchy celeriac and roast pine kernel and red wine jus, or seared fillets of sea bass layered with smoked haddock, green asparagus tips and chive white wine sauce. Finish with an unusual warm sticky chocolate pudding with fudge sauce and melon ice cream. The French dominated but appealingly varied wine list is kindly priced and there is a reasonable selection of halves.

Prices: Set lunch €22. Set dinner €30, or 5 course €45. House wine €16.
Hours: Lunch served from 12.30. Dinner served from 18.30. Closed 20-30 December.
Rooms: 14 en suite. Double/twin from €110. Single from €45.
Cuisine: Modern European.
Other Points: No-smoking area. Garden. Children over 12 years welcome. Car park.
Directions: From Letterkenny follow the signs to Ramelton, after approximately two and a half miles follow the signs to Castle Grove. (Map 18, C5)

Rathmullan House

Rathmullan, Co Donegal
Telephone: +353(0)74 9158188
info@rathmullanhouse.com
www.rathmullanhouse.com

The original house was built in the 1760s as a bathing place for Bishop Knox of Derry. Later, in the early 19th century, it became the country residence of the Batt family who were linen brokers and founders of the Belfast bank - now the National Irish Bank. Bob and Robin Wheeler bought the house in 1962 and converted it to a country house hotel. Now semi-retired, Rathmullan is run by their sons, William and Mark, and daughter-in-law Mary. It's a gracious place, set above the shores of Lough Swilly with a beautiful garden that stretches down to a deserted sandy beach. Within, fine art, antiques, comfy chairs and sofas vie with open log fires to create a relaxing atmosphere: a luxurious house full of quality but without formality. There are three tastefully furnished sitting rooms and a pavilion-like dining room with an unusual tented ceiling. Here, good country house cooking produces asparagus soup with black truffle oil and chives, boned, stuffed leg of rabbit with Clonakilty black pudding, sage, bacon and thyme mash with Madeira jus, and lemon and mango syllabub parfait served with pineapple cooked in caramel. Bedrooms vary, ranging from superior and standard to economy and single rooms. There's also an indoor heated swimming pool.

Prices: Set dinner €45. Main course restaurant from €22.50. House wine €18.
Hours: Food served: 19.30-20.45. Saturday 19.00-21.00. During 2004 closed from January until Easter for refurbishment
Rooms: 24 en suite. Double/twin from €66. Single and family rooms from €77.
Cuisine: Traditional and Modern Irish.
Other Points: No-smoking area. Garden. Children welcome. Car park. Indoor swimming pool. Outside tennis courts.
Directions: R247. From Letterkenny go to Ramelton. Turn right at the bridge to Rathmullan. Go through village and gates are on the right hand side. (Map 18, B5)

Ariel House

50-54 Landsdowne Road, Ballsbridge, Dublin 4, Co Dublin
Telephone: +353(0)1 668 5512
reservations@ariel-house.net
www.ariel-house.net

Ariel House is an historic listed Victorian house built in 1850 which has been carefully restored over the years, evoking the mid 19th century with its high ceilings, ornate plasterwork, Waterford glass chandeliers and weighty antique furniture. You mark the distinctive hospitality immediately on arrival, starting with tea or coffee and homemade scones served in the imposing drawing room. All 37 comfortable rooms are en suite, filled with a collection of fine Victorian and period-style furniture such as the huge wardrobe and four-poster bed in one of the junior suites. These are beautifully ornate, sturdy pieces that complement the comfortable rooms well. Bathrooms, too, are fairly spacious, decked out in white and black, with bath and shower, Spa Therapy lotions and potions and a complimentary pack of those things often forgotten: toothbrush, toothpaste, shaving foam. Although there's a hot drinks tray in some rooms, there's a complimentary tea and coffee room service. Breakfast is served in the bright breakfast room (half of it is a conservatory) to a background of classical music. Also available is 'Source of Life at Ariel House': Simon O'Connor is a trained complementary therapist who offers reflexology and Swedish massage amongst other treatments.
Rooms: 37 en suite. Double room from €40, single from €79.
Other Points: Totally no smoking. Garden.
Directions: From Dublin city centre and Stephens Green go straight down Baggott Street onto Pembroke road. Pass over the junction on to Lansdowne Road. (Map 20, A7)

Avoca Café

11-13 Suffolk Street, Dublin, Co Dublin
Telephone: +353(0)1 672 6019
info@avoca.ie
www.avoca.ie

Avoca Handweavers' newest store is located just off Grafton Street and includes a basement food hall where all the home baked products and freshly made dishes available in the restaurant can be purchased for takeaway. Of course, there are other specialist gourmet foods and cookery books available, including their own Avoca Café Cookbook, and the store sells everything from clothing to household furnishings. The second floor Avoca Café has table service and is hugely popular. Dishes could include Thai broth, confit of duck salad, homemade beef stew with mashed potato, and mushroom, a large choice of house salads, and a selection of Avoca breads with various dips, hummus, pesto, and sun-dried tomato; a healthy option breakfast is also available. There is a selection of red and white wine in quarter, half and full bottles, plus organic apple, tomato, cranberry and grapefruit juices, freshly squeezed orange juice and a range of fruit smoothies to choose from. Team with the legendary homemade Avoca desserts, especially their famous scones and biscuits. This is a perfect place to drop in for morning coffee, lunch, or afternoon tea.
Prices: Main course restaurant from €9.50. House wine €18.
Hours: 10.00-17.30. Sunday 11.00-17.30.
Shop open 10.00-18.00 Monday to Wednesday and Saturday, 10.00-20.00 Thursday and 11.00-18.00 Sunday.
Closed 25-26 December.
Cuisine: Traditional and Modern Irish with International influences.
Other Points: No-smoking area. Children welcome. Craft shop.
Directions: Turn left into Suffolk Street from the bottom of Grafton Street. (Map 20, A7)

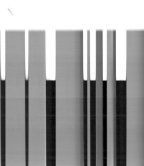

Beaufield Mews Restaurant, Gardens and Antiques

Woodlands Avenue, Stillorgan, Dublin, Co Dublin
Telephone: +353(0)1 2880375
beaumews@iol.ie
www.beaufieldmews.com

Dublin's oldest restaurant has been carved out of an 18th-century coach house and stables. It's an idiosyncratic, family run establishment, open for dinner only (except lunch on Sunday), with a very traditionally styled bar that's full of beams, dark wood furniture, and looks out into a very pretty garden - an ideal spot for summer drinks before dinner. Upstairs is a treasure trove of an antique shop and it is worth finding time to take a look - daily opening is in tune with the restaurant times. The set five-course menu could offer smoked mackerel with potato and horseradish, or chicken and bacon terrine with creamy peppercorn and lemon dressing to start. Roast glazed loin of pork marinated with rich rosemary and cider jus, or traditional spiced beef on a bed of spinach mash with cinnamon and port wine jus could follow, with baguette and butter pudding laced with Baileys to finish. The carte, however, stretches further, into a duo of smoked salmon and gravadlax, onion and dill blini with Dalkey mustard dressing, and boned half duck on a bed of fruit, herb and nut stuffing, served with Beaufield orange sauce.

Prices: Set dinner €30.95 (+12.5% service, 5 courses). Main course from €16. House wine €16.
Hours: 18.30-24.00. Sunday 12.30-17.00. Closed Monday, Bank Holidays and Good Friday.
Food served: 18.30-22.00. 12.30-14.45 on Sunday.
Cuisine: Modern European.
Other Points: No-smoking area. Garden. Car park.
Directions: Along the N11 Stillorgan dual carriageway, direction south, just four miles from the city centre. (Map 20, A7)

Bella Cuba Restaurant
11 Ballsbridge Terrace, Dublin 4, Co Dublin
Telephone: +353(0)1 660 5539
info@bella-cuba.com
www.bella-cuba.com

Juan Carlos Jimenez and his family opened Ireland's first and only Cuban restaurant in 1999. It's a small, cosy, intimate room, located at the top of two flights of narrow stairs, seats just 24, and delivers authentic Cuban food. Look out for a selection of Cuban rice, especially moros y cristianos (black beans and rice with pieces of roast pork), and classic dishes such as ropa vieja, shredded beef combined with aromatic vegetables and served with a spiced tomato sauce and red wine. Starters include Havana meat pies in aubergine and tomato salsa, traditional black bean soup, and sofrito steamed mussels - sofrito being a Cuban staple, a mixture of garlic, onions, bell peppers, dry white wine and parsley. Some excellent seafood dishes include spicy garlic shrimp with piquillo peppers, butter and rum and a great seafood enchilada of shrimp, crabmeat, mussels, swordfish and snapper with sofrito. Caribbean jerk of lamb, or chicken with chorizo stuffing, are other interesting main courses. The small bar in one corner produces some great daiquiris and mojitos as well as Cuban cigars, and a global selection of good value wines from a 50-bin wine list.

Prices: Set dinner €20 (2 courses). Main course restaurant from €17. House wine €18.
Hours: 17.30-22.30. Thursday to Saturday until 23.00
Cuisine: Cuban.
Other Points: Children welcome over four years old until 19.00.
Directions: In the heart of Ballsbridge between the RDS and Herbert Park Hotel. (Map 20, A7)

Bewley's Café
11-12 Westmoreland Street, Dublin 2, Co Dublin
Telephone: +353(0)1 6355431
manager@weststbewleys.ie
www.bewleys.com

All Bewley's Cafés are instantly recognisable through their trademark mosaic front and distinctive maroon awnings; their sticky buns were immortalised by the poet Brendan Kennelly. This fast-paced branch, close to Trinity College, seats 300. The balcony area is home to a stained glass creation by Pauline Bewich, the window looking out on the main room of the café. This Bewley's has also become an exhibition centre for many Irish artists, with all works for sale; a quick walk around will give views of paintings in unusual settings. It's also a popular spot for the traditional Irish breakfast (served all day) for which Bewley's are famous. There is, in addition, good value soups, carvery items such as silverside of beef with chive sauce, or honey roast ham with parsley sauce. Specials of cottage pie or meatballs in pepper sauce extend choice, and there are traditional puddings such as rice pudding with hot jam sauce.

Prices: Main course from €9. Small bottle House wine €4.25.
Hours: 7.00-19.00. Closed 25-26 December.
Cuisine: Traditional Irish.
Other Points: No-smoking area. Children welcome.
Directions: Just off the south side of O'Connell Bridge, right on the Liffey. (Map 20, A7)

Ireland - Co Dublin

CITY CHARMS AND MOUNTAIN GRANDEUR

Pass from a city of renowned Georgian architecture and associations with literary giants such as Joyce, Wilde, Swift and Shaw to a land of bleak glens, remote mountain scenery, and friendly, embracing hills.
Drive length: 302 miles

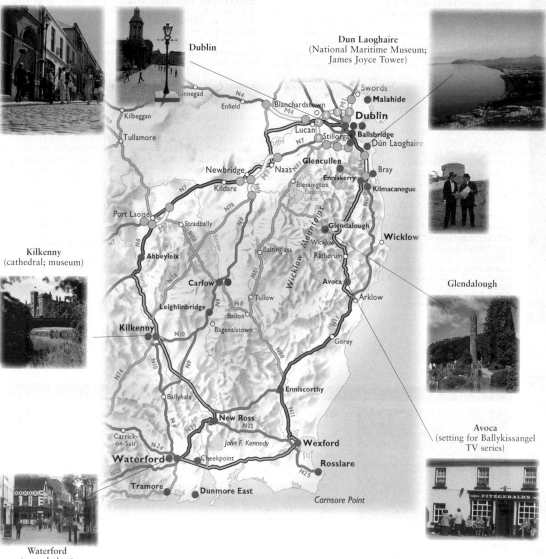

Dun Laoghaire
(National Maritime Museum; James Joyce Tower)

Dublin

Kilkenny
(cathedral; museum)

Glendalough

Avoca
(setting for Ballykissangel TV series)

Waterford
(crystal glass)

- ● Accommodation/Food
- ● Accommodation
- ● Food
- 🥄 Food Shop

To find the establishments marked here, look up the listing town marked on the map in bold in the town index on page 395

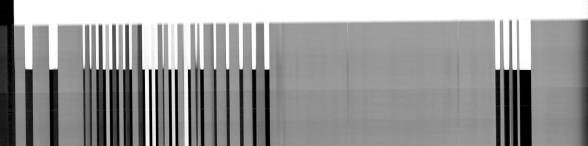

Bewley's Oriental Café

78 Grafton Street, Dublin 2, Co Dublin
Telephone: +353(0)1 6355470
manager@graftonst.bewleys.ie
www.bewleys.com

It's a great location on Dublin's most fashionable street, and this bustling, multi-tiered 385-seater flagship is the only Bewley's in the city to stay open late. The main room, with its magnificent stained glass windows by the early 20th century Irish artist, Harry Clarke, is lovely, with wooden stairs linking various levels; our favourite is the area with tables looking out over Grafton Street. Throughout, Bewley's maintain a tradition of supporting Irish craft: light fittings, bronze counter tops, mirrors, hand-painted tiles, for example. This is the place for traditional Irish cooking, and although famed for all day breakfasts, just the spot for a light lunchtime snack, or cake and coffee. A new addition is the introduction of Harry Clarke menus, with smoked haddock fish cakes bound with potato spiked with chilli, and served with a tomato and sweet chilli sauce, perhaps, or chicken, leek and bacon pie. In the evening the Harry Clarke Room offers an evening buffet with perhaps roast Shannon salmon and spinach or Irish organic beef and potatoes. Bewley's wide selection of teas, coffees, and chocolates are also for sale here.

Prices: Main course from €9.60.
Hours: 07.30-23.00. Closed on 25 December.
Cuisine: Traditional Irish.
Other Points: No-smoking area. Children welcome.
Directions: Half way between Trinity College and St Stephen's Green. (Map 20, A7)

Botticelli Restaurant

1-3 Temple Bar, Dublin 2, Co Dublin
Telephone: +353(0)1 672 7289
botticelli@eircom.net

Located in the heart of Temple Bar, this bright and airy restaurant with its tiled floors, minimalist décor and big windows overlooking the canal, is noted for straightforward, unpretentious Italian cooking that has a genuine feel to it. Owner Piero Cosso firmly believes in using the best ingredients in order to produce the best food. All breads, pizza, gnocchi, ravioli and desserts are made on the premises, the ice cream is made in Botticelli's ice-cream parlour-cum-coffee shop, which is next door, and only Italian wines and Italian cheeses are used. Set lunches offer remarkable value, ranging from just a slice of pizza to minestrone soup and minute steak with chips, salad and bread. From the carte, carpaccio di filletto, or gnocchi sorrentina with tomato, mozzarella, basil and Parmesan, and diced veal in extra virgin olive oil, white wine and aromatic herbs, followed by homemade lemon ice cream makes a perfect meal. The range of pizzas is good, and they are treated with respect, based on top quality materials and extra virgin olive oil. Service is charming and utterly professional.

Prices: Set lunch €8. Main course restaurant from €9. House wine €15.75.
Hours: 13.00-24.00. Closed Good Friday, 25 December.
Cuisine: Italian.
Other Points: No-smoking area. Children welcome.
Directions: Just off the square in Temple Bar. (Map 20, A7)

Brewery Bar

Guinness Storehouse, James Street, St James Gate,
Dublin 8, Co Dublin
Telephone: +353 (0)1 4084800
customer.service@diageo.com
www.guinness-storehouse.com

A visit to the home of Guinness has been described as the high point of any trip to Dublin: at the Storehouse you will discover all there is to know about the world-famous beer. Housed in an old grain storehouse opposite the original, still-operating St James's Brewery, it is a dramatic story that begins over 250 years ago and ends 21st-century-style in Gravity, the sky bar, with its unparalleled view over the City - and an excellent complimentary pint of 'the black stuff'. For those wishing to linger longer, there is the bright and spacious Brewery Bar with its bold contemporary design and a short but varied menu of things to go with Ireland's finest ale. Anything, in fact, from oysters with chilli shallots and Guinness bread, and wild mushroom risotto with goats' cheese and spicy tomato sauce, to Limerick glazed bacon with buttered kale and champ potatoes, and baked salmon fillet with saffron cream sauce. To follow, there is even Guinness white and dark chocolate mousse, or a simple caffè latte with chef's homemade biscuits. St James's Brewery brews an astonishing 4-5 million hectolitres of Guinness a year. Almost 50% of all beer consumed in Ireland - four million pints a day- is produced here.

Prices: Starter from €4.
Main course from €9.80.
Hours: 10.00-17.00.
Food served: 12.00-16.00.
Cuisine: Irish and Modern European.
Other Points: No-smoking area.
Children welcome. Car park.
Directions: At the rear of the Jame's Gate distillery just off James Street.
(Map 20, A7)

La Cave

28 South Anne Street, Dublin 2, Co Dublin
Telephone: +353(0)1679 4409
lacave@iol.ie
lacavewinebar.com

One of the oldest wine bars in Dublin has mercifully never been updated, so there's charm in spades. Enter from the street and head down to the wine bar and restaurant. The black bar houses some 300 or more well-chosen wines with global leanings, but with a French bias; some 30 wines are sold by the glass, 30 by the half bottle. Mirrors, books, old wine bottles, pictures and postcards are scattered around the deep red walls and on the odd shelf, and a low cream and mustard ceiling and soft lighting caps the tiny 25-seater restaurant. It's certainly atmospheric and visitors have been warmly welcomed for the past 14 years by husband and wife team, Margaret and Akim Beskri. This is a place where you can have anything from a glass of wine to a light snack or full meal. Classic French food is served all day and finishes with a late night menu served after 11pm. Menus offer value and quality, with lunch bringing baked goats' cheese salad with a walnut oil dressing, and Toulouse sausage with red onion confit. A typical dinner could open with warm salad of lamb's kidneys with a rocket salad, then roast sea bass with chorizo and basil sauce.

Prices: Set lunch €15 and dinner €29.50. Main course from €16. House wine €16.
Hours: 12.30-23.00. Monday to Saturday. 18.00-23.00 Sunday. Closed 25-26 December, Good Friday and Bank Holiday lunchtimes.
Cuisine: Classic French.
Other Points: No-smoking area. Children welcome.
Directions: Just off Grafton Street. (Map 20, A7)

Cornucopia

19 Wicklow Street, Dublin 2, Co Dublin
Telephone: +353(0)1 677 7583
cornucopia@eircom.net

This vegetarian restaurant, a short walk from Grafton Street, was opened by Deirdre McCafferty some seventeen years ago and has built up a loyal band of supporters over the years. There's an easy informality to the place, with self-service food dispensed from a counter behind which boards list breakfast, main dish and salad choices. Tables are wooden, and there are counter tops with stools around the large window so that you watch the world go by in busy Wicklow Street; during the summer tables and chairs spill outside. Breakfast could be anything from an omelette with caramelised red onion, fresh herbs, and oven roasted tomato, or vegetarian sausage, to french toast, homemade baked beans and stuffed field mushroom. Lunch is an extremely busy time with soups, salads, and main courses such as African chickpeas, spinach and sweet potato casserole served with chilli and coriander couscous, or Puy lentil, leek and pumpkin pie topped with olive oil and herb mash, drawing the crowds. Dinner is a more relaxed affair. Organic wines are available by the glass and bottle, non organic by the quarter. Service is friendly and helpful.

Prices: Main course from €9.95. House wine by the glass €4.50.
Hours: 08.30-20.00, until 21.00 on Thursdays and 19.00 on Sundays.
Closed 25-27 December, 1 January and Easter Sunday.
Cuisine: Vegetarian.
Other Points: No-smoking area. Children welcome.
Directions: Just off Grafton Street. (Map 20, A7)

Dunne and Crescenzi

14 South Frederick Street, Dublin 2, Co Dublin
Telephone: +353(0)1 675 9892

Dunne and Crescenzi, is an Italian restaurant-cum-wine bar, located close to Grafton Street, and owned and run by husband and wife team Eileen Dunne and Stefano Crescenzi. It's very atmospheric inside, all wood with bare tables and plain wood floor with the walls covered in boxed shelving filled with bottles of Italian wine (100 to choose from), pasta, olive oil, all of which can be purchased to take away. There's a relaxed, informal air to the place - you can drop in for just a glass of wine, coffee and dessert, as well as a more formal lunch or dinner; the day's specials are written up on a blackboard. In May 2003, next door but one, the Crescenzi's opened another restaurant and deli. It's smaller and much more intimate, but otherwise run in the same style. Here you can purchase anything that is on the menu, Italian cooked meats, cheese, pasta, coffee, olives, preserves, olive oils. Eileen makes regular visits to Italy to source the products and in addition, supports small producers who are committed to producing good quality products and "who are passionate about what they do." There is a wonderful atmosphere in both vibrant, bustling places.

Prices: Set lunch €15. Set dinner €25. Main course restaurant from €6.50. Main course bar/snack from €6.50. House wine €10.
Hours: 12.00-22.30.
Closed Sundays and from 25 December for two weeks.
Cuisine: Italian.
Other Points: No-smoking area. Children welcome.
Directions: Close to Grafton Street and parallel to Dawson Street. (Map 20, A7)

Egan's House

7 Iona Park, Glasnevin, Dublin 9
Telephone: +353(0)1 830 3611
info@eganshouse.com
www.eganshouse.com

Patrick and Monica Finn both gave up medical careers to run this elegant early 20th century house as a charming guesthouse. Built by the architect Alexander Strain as his own home, it is situated in a quiet residential area close to the Botanic Gardens, Phoenix Park and Dublin Zoo, convenient for the city centre and just a 15 minute drive from Dublin Airport. Modernisation was completed in 2002, en suite bedrooms have been designed to a very high standard with red walls and carpets, thick quality bed quilts, and chunky pine furniture. TVs come with videos, and there are power showers in the spotless bathrooms. The drawing room has a large winter fire, comfy sofas and a piano, while the large breakfast room has lovely original cornice work on the high ceiling with a crystal chandelier. All breakfasts are cooked to order. There are plenty of pubs and restaurants in the vicinity that serve dinner. Internet access is a great plus, as is free parking.

Hours: Closed 21-27 December.
Rooms: 32 en suite. Double room from €98, single from €29. Family room from €120.
Other Points: No-smoking area. Children welcome. Garden. Car park. Lounge with TV/video and stereo. Internet access
Directions: From the airport take the Drumcondra road (M1). Before the railway bridge turn right (St. Alphonsos Road) then take the fourth turn right to Egans. (Map 20, A7)

Locks Restaurant

1 Windsor Terrace, Portobello,
Dublin 8, Co Dublin
Telephone: +353(0)1 454 3391

Locks has been owned and run by Claire Douglas for over 23 years, and has a reputation for serving consistently good food at fair prices. On two levels, the whole place is comfortably furnished with cushioned red and green benches and chairs, white linen-clad tables, Turkish cushions, and a low coffee table beside an open fire. Paintings cover the white wood panelled walls and there are plants, rugs and mirrors, all in all creating a comfortable contemporary feel. Narrow uneven stairs lead upstairs to some funky loos and on again to a further part of the restaurant. The contemporary cooking has absorbed plenty of influences from around the world, organic vegetables are served in summer and fish and game are specialities. Good set menus cover lunch and dinner with the likes of goats' cheese salad, followed by sea bass and lemon sole with pesto beurre blanc and warm bean salad. From the carte comes roast duck, Chinese leaves, shiitake broth, pineapple and chilli. Service is wonderfully 'old school' from staff with more than 40 years of waiting experience. Wines are predominantly French with a fine Bordeaux selection, but there's plenty of good drinking for under €30.

Prices: Set lunch €28.95. Set dinner €48.95. Main course from €34.95. House wine €23.15.
Hours: 12.30-14.00. 19.00-22.30. Closed Saturday lunch, Sunday, all public holidays and 25 December-6 January.
Cuisine: Contemporary.
Other Points: No-smoking area. Children welcome.
Directions: Half way between the Portobello and Harolds Cross bridges on the banks of the Grand Canal, 15 minutes on foot from the city centre. (Map 20, A7)

O'Connells in Ballsbridge

Bewley's Hotel, Merrion Road, Ballsbridge,
Dublin 4, Co Dublin
Telephone: +353(0)1 647 3304
info@oconnellsballsbridge.com
www.oconnellsballsbridge.com

Run independently from Bewley's Hotel, O'Connell's is owned and run by Tom O'Connell. Moving with the times, he has developed the large restaurant along bistro lines. His aim is to provide the best quality modern Irish food at reasonable prices. There's a refreshing flexibility to the food, with good set menus and Early Bird options, plus an obvious commitment to excellence both on the menu and on the plate (an Australian wood-burning oven cooks beef and salmon, for example, which are carved in front of you). This simple, ingredient led food has natural flavours uppermost. Witness an Early Bird menu that opened with wood-oven grilled garlic and parsley bread, and Adrian Sweeney's oak smoked salmon with horseradish cream and cucumber pickle. Then grill roasted Ballybrado Farm organic loin pork chop served with a fresh herb stuffing, apple compote and a light, sweet Dijon mustard sauce. Puddings come in the form of an Irish coffee meringue and a 'just right' lemon crème brûlée. An impressive but unintimidating wine list favours France in the main (note the Petits Chateaux page), but there are some decidedly useful contributions from other wine growing regions in the old and new world.

Prices: Set lunch €18.45. Early set dinner €25. Main course from €14.95. House wine €18.95.
Hours: 12.30-14.30. 18.00-22.30. Sunday 12.30-15.00. 18.00-21.30. Closed from evening of 24-27 December lunch.
Cuisine: Traditional and Modern Irish.
Other Points: No-smoking area (totally no smoking in the restaurant). Children welcome. Garden and courtyard. Car park.
Directions: On the junction of Simmonscourt and Merrion road in Ballsbridge. Opposite the Four Seasons Hotel. (Map 20, A7)

O'Neills ⬚ ♇ ▯ ✕

2 Suffolk Street, Dublin 2, Co Dublin
Telephone: +353(0)1 679 3656
mike@oneillsbar.com
oneillsbar.com

Centuries of Dublin republican history surround the
world-renowned O'Neill's, just around the corner from
Guinness's St James Gate brewery, and trade has
flourished uninterrupted for over 300 years. Formerly
in the hands of the Coleman family, the premises finally
converted to their present name in August 1927 and
have operated under Michael J. O'Neill's direction for
the last 46 years. Beers aplenty from the Dublin
Brewing Company - Darcy's Stout, Revolution Red and
Maeve's Crystal beer - all tell their own story; while
today's worldly-wise diner will find a dozen eclectic
wines by the glass with which to slake a city thirst.
Food served throughout the day runs the gamut of
roasts from the carvery (right up to 10pm on Sundays),
through a traditional range of grills, pies and Irish stew
to massive sandwiches and burgers. More structured
daily lunches take in oak smoked salmon, and potato
and herb soup, followed by Cajun spiced chicken
stuffed with mushrooms and cream cheese, or plaice
fillets steamed with salmon and tarragon mousse. Then,
for those oblivious of dietary constraints, chocolate
orange cheesecake, chunky apple pie and formidable
Irish cheeses - smoked Gubeen, Cashel Blue, Milleens
and Laviston.

Prices: Set lunch from €16.50. Main course from €9.25.
House wine €14.95.
Hours: 10.30-23.30, until 00.30 Thursday to Saturday.
Closed 25-26 December and Good Friday.
Food served: 11.30-20.00. Friday 11.30-16.30. Sunday 12.30-22.00.
Cuisine: Modern European and Traditional Irish.
Other Points: No-smoking area. Children welcome. Sandwich bar.
Directions: Conveniently situated in the heart of Dublin opposite
Dublin Tourism centre on Suffolk Street. (Map 20, A7)

The Long Room, The Old Library, Trinity College Dublin

Hours: Closed 18 December-7 January.
Rooms: 7 en suite. Rooms from €50.80
per person sharing. Seasonal price
variations. Prices include full Irish breakfast
and tax.
Other Points: No-smoking area.
Garden. Children welcome.
Directions: N11. Follow the signs for
South City to Baggot Street which
becomes Pembroke Road, Turn right onto
Raglan Road and Raglan Lodge is on your
left. (Map 20, A7)

Raglan Lodge

10 Raglan Road, Ballsbridge, Dublin 4, Co Dublin
Telephone: +353(0)1 660 6697

Dublin's residential areas were built during the 1860s and Ballsbridge
emerged as a well-planned suburb of wide, tree-lined streets with smart
red-brick houses fronted by impressive gardens. More recent times have
seen this fashionable suburb come to house diplomatic missions and
commercial institutions. But, fortunately, the atmosphere of a sedate
residential area has been retained on one of Ballsbridge's most attractive
streets, and Raglan Lodge offers visitors a quiet respite from the hustle
and bustle of the city. The poet, Patrick Kavanagh, who wrote the famous
ballad *On Raglan Road* lived down the road at number 19 from 1940-
1943. In later years Raglan Lodge was divided into flats and allowed to
deteriorate. But in 1987 the house was rescued and converted into an
elegant guesthouse. Helen Moran, here since 1991, provides a high level
of comfort and service - rooms are well proportioned with high ceilings,
and the seven en suite bedrooms are extremely comfortable and breakfast
is renowned.

Shanahan's on the Green ★ � ✗
119 St Stephen's Green, Dublin 2, Co Dublin
Telephone: +353(0)1 407 0939
www.shanahans.ie

Shanahan's at 119 St Stephens Green shares, along with its neighbour at number 120, the distinction of being one of the two surviving purpose-built townhouses in Dublin. Now, this graciously restored Georgian house is one of Dublin's most luxurious restaurants. Based on American steakhouse and seafood restaurants, it has beautifully proportioned rooms featuring original 18th century plasterwork, rich lighting and period antiques. It is spread over three floors and includes a ground floor lounge - The Oval Office - decorated with memorabilia from 18 American presidents. There's a strong American inflection to the menu too, with sautéed garlic shrimp, and Newport chicken broth, but a very contemporary degree of precision is brought to the cooking. Steaks are a speciality, the meat is certified Irish Angus beef and includes a New York strip sirloin, a bone-out rib eye, and a classic tournedos Rossini. Seafood brings sizzling black west coast mussels, or broiled Galway oysters Rockefeller (with spinach, smoked bacon, Pernod and hollandaise), or a main course of red mullet and Bere Island scallops with fennel purée, seared foie gras and orange consommé. The wines are listed by style, a good mix of old and new world, and are carefully chosen with quality and price much in evidence.

Prices: Main course from €36. Wine from €29.
Hours: 18.00-22.00, until 23.00 Thursday to Saturday. Open 12.30-14.15 Friday lunch.
Closed everyday for lunch except Friday. Closed Christmas, Bank Holidays and Good Friday.
Cuisine: American style steakhouse.
Other Points: No-smoking area.
Directions: On the west side of St Stephen's Green. Between Eircom House and the College of Surgeons. (Map 20, A7)

Unicorn Restaurant ♉ ☕ ✗
12b Merrion Court, Merrion Row, Dublin 2, Co Dublin
Telephone: +353(0)1 676 2182
unicorn12b@eircom.net

Informal, fashionable Italian restaurant that is a Dublin institution, in existence for almost 60 years and famed for its lunchtime buffet-style antipasto bar. The location is a lovely, secluded spot just off St Stephen's Green, and doors open onto a terrace used for fine weather dining. In addition, there's a popular piano bar and you can also drop in for morning coffee or afternoon tea. This may be classic Italian cooking, but it is done with style, conviction and a sound grasp of technique. This is the place to order vitello tonnato from the lunchtime antipasto bar (either as a starter or main course), or pasta such as linguine carbonara, then breast of chicken parmigiana, or ossobuco milanese with polenta. Dinner brings chargrilled polenta with gorgonzola, seafood chowder, and fritto misto, or scaloppa di vitello Holstein. The wine list is almost entirely Italian, an enterprising selection with just a handful of choices from France and the new world. Service is slick, polite and unstuffy.

Prices: Main course restaurant lunch from €12.50. Main course restaurant dinner from €10.20. House wine €25.
Hours: 12.30-16.00. 18.00-23.00, until 23.30 Friday and Saturday. Closed Sunday, Good Friday, all Bank Holidays and 25 December-2 January.
Cuisine: Italian.
Other Points: No-smoking area. Private dining. Piano bar. Live music every Wednesday and Thursday in the restaurant.
Directions: East of St Stephen's Green. (Map 20, A7)

101 Talbot Restaurant ▯ ♉ ✗
101 Talbot Street, Dublin 1, Co Dublin
Telephone: +353(0)1 8745011

Margaret Duffy and Pascal Bradley's Northside restaurant (a rarity in itself) is close to the Abbey, Peacock, Gate and Liberty Hall Theatres and is popular with a theatrical/artistic crowd. Art on the walls changes regularly and the overall décor matches the busy, informal style of the place. There's a Mediterranean slant to the modern Irish cooking with a variety of menus, including a carte, offering a broad range of dishes from roast mushroom, aubergine and tomato bake served with rocket and mozzarella cheese, basil oil and tapenade potatoes, to chargrilled salmon with roast red pepper, lemon and coriander dressing. Good value set menu choices might include tomato and goats' cheese tarte tatin, and roast fillet of pork with cashew and Parmesan crust with red wine sauce. Pasta dishes feature strongly, perhaps tagliatelle served with olives, roast tomatoes and walnuts in olive oil dressing, or chicken, roast mushroom and pea cream sauce, and in addition, an early bird menu offers starter, main course and coffee for €20. The wine list is a short, global selection offering good value drinking, and there's a decent selection of half bottles. Children are welcome before 8pm.

Prices: Set dinner €27.50 (3 courses + coffee) and €20 (2 courses + coffee before 20.00). House wine €16.75.
Hours: 17.00-23.00.
Closed Sunday, Monday, Bank Holidays and for one week at Christmas.
Cuisine: Mediterranean and Modern Irish.
Other Points: No-smoking area. Children welcome before 8pm.
Directions: Nearest main road is O'Connell Street. Three minutes walk from the Spire in the direction of Connolly Station. Upstairs on the right over 'Hairy Legs' clothing store. (Map 20, A7)

Caviston's Food Emporium

59 Glasthule Road, Sandycove, Dun Laoghaire, Dublin, Co Dublin
Telephone: +353(0)1 280 9245
info@cavistons.com
www.cavistons.com

Located in Glasthule, between Dun Laoghaire and Dalkey, south of
Dublin, Caviston's is a deli that sells everything from vegetables and
cooked meats to farmhouse cheeses. But it is for its fish and shellfish that
the place is renowned. Off the food shop is a small, upscale restaurant, its
walls hung with modern art, that serves the freshest fish. It is open for
lunch, from Tuesday to Saturday, with three sittings: at noon, 1.30pm and
3pm; booking is advisable. The menu changes every couple of days, but
could include deep-fried lemon sole in tempura batter, or tian of crab and
avocado to start. Mains may feature such dishes as cod fillet in tomato
sauce, or roast monkfish fillets with basil pesto, accompanied by salad
leaves and baby potatoes. The wine list concentrates mainly on white
wines chosen with an eye to value and food friendliness. There's a good
selection of wines by the glass, and some half bottles.

Prices: Set lunch between €30-€50.
Hours: 3 sittings - 12.00-13.30. 13.30-
15.00. 15.00-finish, Tuesday to Friday.
Saturday sittings - 12.00-13.45. 13.45-15.00.
15.00-finish. Closed Sunday, Monday and
two weeks from the 20th December.
Cuisine: Seafood.
Other Points: Totally no smoking.
Children welcome.
Directions: Located in Glasthule
between Dunlaoire and Dalkey south of
Dublin city. (Map 20, A7)

Johnnie Fox's

Glencullen, Dublin Mountains, Co Dublin
Telephone: +353(0)1 295 5647
info@johnniefoxs.com
www.johnniefoxs.com
www.jfp.ie

Although quite touristy, Johnnie Fox's is the
quintessential 'Irish pub' and drunk or sober, you'll
always have a good time here. Décor wise, it's what
many 'Irish' pubs would style themselves on, only this
pub has all the original bric-a-brac collected over the
past 200 years or so. It's also a bit of a maze, which is
very apparent as you wander through rooms that
tumble into one another, walking over saw-dust
covered black flagstones, past open fires in original
hearths fuelled by traditional peat and coal. On top of
the unique charm is the pub's splendid array of dishes
on a carte which runs all day and specialises in
seafood. Head chef Paul Davies delivers dishes such as
mahi mahi, or scallops in beurre blanc and fresh dill
sauce, or an impressive sea trout (almost overlapping
the plate). Meat is also on the menu, perhaps prime
mountain beef steaks, and there's a huge range of
vegetarian options. Own homemade Irish whiskey
cake, apple pie, treacle bread, and white soda bread,
are delicious and there's an interesting and varied
global wine list. One very popular attraction is the live
'hooley': a four-course meal with live music and
traditional Irish dancing from 7.30pm to midnight.

Prices: Main course from €14.50. House wine €18.
Hours: 10.30-23.30. 12.00-23.00 on Sunday. Closed Good Friday
and the 25 December.
Food served: 12.30-21.30.
Cuisine: Traditional and Seafood.
Other Points: Children welcome. Car park.
Directions: From Dublin take N11 south. At the Loughlinstown
Hospital roundabout go right around and go back on your journey.
Turn left at the Silver Tassie Pub and you will come to a T Junction,
turn right at this junction. Take first left and follow mountain road

Cruzzo Bar & Restaurant 🍴🍷✕

Malahide Village, Malahide, Dublin, Co Dublin
Telephone: +353(0)1 845 0599
info@cruzzo.ie
www.cruzzo.ie

The waterside bar and restaurant is built on a platform set high above the water on columns. On entering, there's a ground floor piano bar and a large staircase leads up to the spacious restaurant, which enjoys picturesque views of Malahide Marina. It's relaxed, informal and full of people enjoying themselves. The kitchen delivers contemporary Irish cooking using local fish, meat, and vegetables and comes up with some interesting combinations, such as five spiced chicken liver pâté and date chutney, alongside more traditional grilled sirloin steak, roast onions and peppercorn sauce. Options on the light lunch menu include seafood chowder, goats' cheese fritter with cranberry sauce, open grilled chicken wrap served with mayo, rocket tomato salad, and braised beef in Guinness and mushrooms with baby roast parsnips. Good puddings include vanilla bean cheese cake and berry compote, and warm pear and almond tart with sauce anglaise. There are interesting early evening set menus and the lengthy wine list is a well-annotated global selection with a decent range of halves and a good value wine of the month.

Prices: Set lunch from €23. Set dinner from €37.50. Main course restaurant from €17. House wine €21.50.
Hours: 12.30-14.30. 18.00-22.00, Sunday 18.00-21.30.
Closed all day Monday, Saturday lunch, Good Friday, 25-26 December.
Cuisine: Modern European.
Other Points: Children welcome. Car park. Private dining.
Directions: From M50 follow the signs to Malahide Road. Turn left and follow the signs to the Village, go left at the lights and straight through to Marina Village.
(Map 20, A8)

Red Bank House and Restaurant 🍴🍷✕🛏

5-7 Church Street, Skerries, Co Dublin
Telephone: +353(0)1 8491005
redbank@eircom.net
www.redbank.ie

The tree-lined seaside town just north of Dublin Airport is in golfing country, with as many as 30 courses within a driver and sandwedge of each other. Larger-than-life TV chef Terry McCoy settled here 20 years ago, his richly decorated restaurant occupying an old banking hall. Real thought goes into the menus, which are a celebration of flavours and styles, and dominated by seafood. A seasonal menu might deliver razor fish, or scallops Lambay Island. Rich classics such as lobster Thermidor or baked crab Loughshinny are hugely satisfying, and this is the place to order Dublin Bay prawns. Other favourites include Drogheda smoked loin of pork and or fillet steak Ardgillan Park. An excellent Irish cheese board is an alternative to the legendary dessert trolley. An extensive and well-researched wine list helpfully presents characterful and well-priced options with a diversity of styles. Terry and his wife, Margaret, have refurbished and extended their guest accommodation. It now has 18 well-equipped bedrooms. It is a short distance from Dublin airport and is located near the DART, (light rail train) which takes you into Dublin city centre.

Prices: Set lunch €26 and dinner €30. Main course from €17. House wine €20.
Hours: 18.30-22.00. Sunday lunch 12.30-16.30. Restaurant closed 24-27 December.
Rooms: 18 en suite. Double room from €90, single from €65. Family room from €135.
Cuisine: Modern Irish.
Other Points: Garden.
Directions: From Dublin Airport/Dublin take the N1 north through Lissen Hall Interchange. Follow the N1 to Blakes Cross,

Paddy Burkes 🍴🍷🚪✕

Clarinbridge, Galway, Co Galway
Telephone: +353(0)91 796226
info@paddyburkesgalway.com
www.paddyburkesgalway.com

Eight miles south of Galway on the Limerick road stands this legend, named after the man who was celebrated for introducing the virtues of oysters to the area, and who hosted the first Clarenbridge Oyster Festival in 1954. His guest list over the years reads like a Who's Who of the great and good with Irish connections, from Bing Crosby and Burl Ives to Princesses Margaret and Grace of Monaco. The menu remains unchanged to this day: natural oysters, baked and florentine oysters; Clarenbridge mussels grilled with garlic and breadcrumbs; Galway Bay chowder; and Irish salmon. The original 'festival' comprised 34 guests and an accordion raced there by taxi from Kinvara: these days 10,000 visitors from all over Ireland and abroad consume over 50,000 oysters at the annual bash. Any other day of the year, diners will encounter brochette of king scallops with béarnaise sauce, and saffron-flavoured medallions of monkfish. The main menu now also extends to include fillet steak with pepper sauce, honey-roast duckling in orange and grenadine, and rack of Irish lamb with rosemary stuffing and jus rôti. Open sandwiches of smoked salmon and sirloin steak fill out choices through the day, when Guinness and plentiful wine can be quaffed.

Prices: Set lunch €17.50. Set dinner €30. Main course from €20. Main course bar from €15. House wine €16.
Hours: Open and serving food: 12.30-14.30. 18.00-22.00. Bar food 14.30-22.00 and Sunday 15.30-22.00.
Closed Good Friday and 25 December.
Cuisine: Modern Irish and Seafood.
Other Points: No-smoking area. Garden. Children welcome. Car park.
Directions: N18. Situated on the main N18 in the village of Clarenbridge. Eight miles south of Galway on the Limerick Road.
(Map 19, A4)

GLORIOUS GALWAY
AND THE HILLS OF CONNEMARA

Taking in some of Ireland's finest scenery ranging from coastal vistas
to Ireland's rural heartland with a string of remote settlements on the way.
Drive length: 469 miles

Croagh Patrick

Sligo

Connemara National Park

Galway
(cathedral)

Ennis
(abbey; museum)

Boyle
(Abbey;
Lough Key Forest Park)

Birr Castle Demesne

Bunratty Castle

● Accommodation/Food

● Accommodation

● Food

● Food Shop

To find the establishments marked
here, look up the listing town
marked on the map in bold in the
town index on page 395

Abbeyglen Castle

Sky Road, Clifden, Connemara, Co Galway
Telephone: +353(0)95 21201
info@abbeyglen.ie
www.abbeyglen.ie

A drive along the famed Sky Road, slowly ascending from Clifden and swiftly descending to the sea, brings Abbeyglen Castle Hotel into view. Set in beautiful gardens, majestically overlooking Clifden Bay with a mountainous backdrop lent by the Twelve Bens, the grand crenellated façade gives way to a surprisingly homely, comfortable interior with cosy sofas randomly placed and many open fires. Built in 1832, the castle fell derelict during the famine and was rescued by the Hughes family in 1969; indeed, the character and charm of Paul and Brian Hughes fills the air. Bedrooms are individually and charmingly decorated with great views, and there are seven spacious suites. In the restaurant local ingredients add flavour to Kevin Conroy's cooking, be it locally caught fresh wild salmon, scallops, mussels, crab and turbot or Connemara lamb. Menus pleasingly blend classic and fashionable, say a lobster Thermidor from the carte, or oven-roasted guinea fowl with red onion marmalade and port wine and raisin sauce from the set dinner menu. The wine list is divided by style delivering a good-value round-the-world selection.

Prices: Set dinner from €44. Main course restaurant from €23. House wine €20.25.
Hours: Food served: 19.15-21.00.
Closed 5th January and 1st February.
Rooms: 38 en suite. Double/twin from €99, single from €129. Prices are per person and include dinner and breakfast.
Cuisine: International and French
Other Points: No-smoking area. Garden. Children welcome over 12 years old. Car park.
Directions: N59 west, 50 miles from Galway. (Map 17, F1)

Byrne's Mal Dua House

Galway Road, Clifden, Connemara, Co Galway
Telephone: +353(0)95 21171
UK freephone: 0800 904 7532 USA Toll free: 1866 8919420
info@maldua.com
www.maldua.com

Peter and Aideen Byrne's Mal Dua House is ideally located on the main road going into Clifden. Their charm and hospitality extends to please even the most discerning of guests. The house is set in expansive, well-manicured lawns and garden. The bay windows of the immaculate dining room look out over the garden towards a stone bridge with a stream flowing through. Here breakfast is served: freshly squeezed juices, fresh fruit, regional Irish cheeses, kippers, pancakes, smoked salmon, and cold meats, as well as a traditional Irish breakfast. Porridge with Irish Whisky and Honey is a real treat. Dinner in the evening specialises on locally sourced seafood, such as Connemara scallops or smoked salmon, with rack of Connemara lamb, studded with herbs and accompanied by Irish champ and Irish mist sauce something of a speciality. Thirteen spacious bedrooms are individually decorated with soft colours and co-ordinating fabrics, and come with different combinations of single and double beds. There are lots of thoughtful extras such as luxurious thick towels in gleaming bathrooms and lots of lotions and potions, and not just a trouser press, but a tie press too.

Prices: Set dinner €35. Main course from €19.95. House wine €16.50.
Hours: Food served: 18.30-21.00.
Rooms: 13 en suite. Double room from €100, single from €80, family room from €140.
Cuisine: Modern Irish.
Other Points: Totally non smoking. Children welcome. Garden. Car park.
Directions: One kilometre from Clifden. From Galway follow the N59 to Clifden. Hotel is located on right as you approach the town. (Map 17, F1)

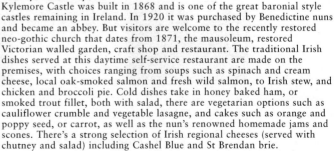

Kylemore Abbey & Garden

Kylemore, Connemara, Co Galway
Telephone: +353(0)95 41146
info@kylemoreabbey.ie
www.kylemoreabbey.com

Kylemore Castle was built in 1868 and is one of the great baronial style castles remaining in Ireland. In 1920 it was purchased by Benedictine nuns and became an abbey. But visitors are welcome to the recently restored neo-gothic church that dates from 1871, the mausoleum, restored Victorian walled garden, craft shop and restaurant. The traditional Irish dishes served at this daytime self-service restaurant are made on the premises, with choices ranging from soups such as spinach and cream cheese, local oak-smoked salmon and fresh wild salmon, to Irish stew, and chicken and broccoli pie. Cold dishes take in honey baked ham, or smoked trout fillet, both with salad, there are vegetarian options such as cauliflower crumble and vegetable lasagne, and cakes such as orange and poppy seed, or carrot, as well as the nun's renowned homemade jams and scones. There's a strong selection of Irish regional cheeses (served with chutney and salad) including Cashel Blue and St Brendan brie.

Prices: Main course from €6.30.
Hours: 09.30-17.30.
Closed Good Friday and Christmas week.
Cuisine: Traditional Irish and European.
Other Points: Totally no smoking. Garden. Children welcome. Car park. Free shuttle bus service to the garden. Garden Tea House. Craft Shop.
Directions: N59. The Abbey is two and a half miles from Letterfrack on the N59 from Galway. (Map 17, F2)

Killeen House ★ ⬥

Bushypark, Galway, Co Galway
Telephone: +353(0)91 524179
killeenhouse@ireland.com
www.killeenhousegalway.com

Killeen House was built in 1840, is set in 25 acres of private grounds and gardens on the shores of Lough Corrib, and is very conveniently located on the outskirts of Galway City on the main Clifden Road. Catherine Doyle recently extended her home with much thought, style, and sympathy, but it is the little touches that give that extra special feel. The drawing room and dining room, for example, which overlook the garden, are beautifully appointed with antiques and have a wonderful mix of luxury and comfort, and throughout the whole house exquisite local handmade rugs are strewn. The six spacious bedrooms are fabulously furnished, each themed in a different period: Victorian, Edwardian, Regency, and Art Nouveau, and all ooze quality and relaxation.
In addition, caring hospitality is uppermost. Breakfast includes fresh juice, grapefruit, natural yogurt and pinhead oatmeal porridge, and a choice of cooked breakfast, as well as own-made soda bread, scones and preserves, plus gold and silver cutlery to complement the beautiful china.

Prices: Guesthouse.
Rooms: 6 en suite. Double/twin from €140. Single from €100. Family room from €180.
Other Points: Garden. Children welcome over 12 years old. Car park.
Directions: On the N59, the main Clifden Road. Killeen House is four miles from Galway city centre and half way between Galway city and Moyeullen village. (Map 19, A3)

McDonagh's Seafood House 🍷 ✕

22 Quay Street, Galway, Co Galway
Telephone: +353(0)91 565001
mcdonaghs@tinet.ie
www.mcdonaghs.net

It is quite fair to state that a visit to Galway is not complete without eating at McDonagh's, it is part of Galway's tradition, "the best source of fresh fish and seafood in Galway," exclaims the New York Times. Established in 1902, it is an unusual place, which developed and progressed over the years as part of PJ and Mary McDonagh's efforts to satisfy their customer's requirements and change in taste. It started as a fish shop and also sold fish and chips. The restaurant and its wider selection of seafood came later. Now divided in two, with a fish and chip shop on one side where you are guaranteed the best chips (potatoes are cut on the premises) and your fish is cooked to order. The table-service restaurant (homely and extremely helpful) on the other side offers an extensive range of fish simply cooked. From the menu comes black sole, turbot, John Dory, silver hake or brill, served grilled and accompanied by dill sauce, or poached in white wine and cream sauce. There are cold plates of smoked salmon, barbecued monkfish tails, scallops and prawns, as well as shellfish platters, stuffed wild mussels, and daily specials. Don't be surprised if you have to queue.
Prices: Main course restaurant from €8 - €36. Main course bar/snack from €5.50. House wine €12.50.
Hours: Restaurant 12.00-15.00. 17.00-22.00. Closed Sunday during November - May. Closed 25-26 December and 1 January. Fish and Chips available 12.00-24.00. Sunday 17.00-23.00.
Cuisine: Traditional Irish Seafood.
Other Points: No-smoking area.
Directions: At the bottom of Quay Street. (Map 19, A3)

Íragh Tí Connor 🛏 🍷 ◻ ✕ ⬥

Main Street, Ballybunion, Co Kerry
Telephone: +353(0)68 27112
iraghticonnor@eircom.net
www.golfballybunion.com

John and Joan O'Connor's country house is an impressive, ivy-clad 19th century building set in its own walled gardens, a couple of minutes walk to the beach, and close to Ballybunion's world-famous golf links. John has completely restored the home where he grew up and has combined the old world with up to date conveniences. The house was originally a bar which John has stylishly maintained. Soft colours, open fires, and period furniture distinguish public rooms, while extremely spacious bedrooms are elegantly furnished. In the elegant restaurant, with grand piano, seafood is a speciality, lobster fresh from 100 metres offshore via the restaurant's sea tank, all baking and preserves are done in house, and local artisan cheeses are carefully sourced. A typical meal could open with Irish smoked salmon served with seasonal leaves and a caper dressing or baked goats' cheese topped with cranberry chutney and go on to parcel of grilled monkfish wrapped with parma ham, garnished with asparagus tips on a herb champ potato with wholegrain mustard sauce, or fillet of beef cooked to your liking and topped with a creamy garlic sauce, to be followed by a selection of house desserts.
Prices: Set lunch €18. Main course restaurant meal from €16. Main course bar meal from €9. House wine €18.
Hours: 17.30-21.30. 13.00-21.30 on Sunday. Closed 20-31 December.
Rooms: 17 including 3 mini suites. Double room from €190, single occupancy from €150.
Cuisine: Modern Irish.
Other Points: No-smoking area. Children welcome. Garden. Car park.
Directions: On the N69 north coastal route from Limerick to Tralee, at the top of Main Street. (Map 19, C2)

QC's Seafood Bar & Restaurant

Number 3, Main Street, Cahirciveen, Co Kerry
Telephone: +353(0)66 9472244
info@qcbar.com
www.qcbar.com

It is hard to believe that this stone-fronted building in Cahirciveen's main street once sold only potatoes and Guinness. Kate and Andrew Cooke opened the doors to their renovated bar and restaurant in 2000, making the most of the 18th century stone fireplace and featuring timber washed up on local beaches in the bar area and in the make up of the bar counter. Fish is the thing here, all supplied from the family business. Fresh crab meat and claws, cooked with fresh garlic, chilli, Spanish onion and tomato, or pan-seared baby squid with caramelised onions and salsa verde could appear amongst starters. Monkfish and prawns, a main course, served with sliced garlic and chilli sauce, is a house speciality, or there could be grilled Dover sole, served on the bone with lemon butter. Wild Kerry salmon (smoked in the family owned factory), fish cakes with sweet chilli vinaigrette, or straightforward fish and chips appear on the bar menu. Meat is from the local butcher, roast lamb shanks say, served with red wine reduction and straw potatoes, or roast half duck with peach compote and salsa verde. Expect own baked bread, regional cheeses, and reasonably priced global wines.

Prices: Set lunch €18. Set dinner €35. Main course restaurant from €16.50. Main course bar/snack from €11.50. House wine €16.50.
Hours: 12.00-14.30. 18.00-21.30. Closed Sunday lunch and 7 January to 12 February.
Cuisine: Modern European with Spanish influences.
Other Points: No-smoking area. Garden. Children welcome. Car park.
Directions: N71. In the centre of town, the stone fronted building on the right hand side as if coming into town from Waterville. (Map 19, D1)

Doyles Seafood Restaurant and Townhouse

John Street, Dingle, Co Kerry
Telephone: +353(0)66 9151174
cdoyles@iol.ie
www.doylesofdingle.com

Doyles Seafood Bar was established in 1974 and is one of the country's premier seafood restaurants, putting Dingle firmly on the map as a foodie destination. It is now owned and run by Sean and Charlotte Cluskey. Local seafood remains the main attraction, and the Cluskeys have wisely changed very little, retaining the flagstone floors and old pine furniture, and continuing to build the menus around the catch landed by the Dingle boats. In the kitchen, the cooking is straightforward, emphasising the freshness of the ingredients used. Start with platter of cured and smoked seafood, or warm potato and herb pancake. Then move on to Carmelised king scallops or Doyles trilogy of prime cuts (grilled medallion of beef fillet, pork and lamb with béarnaise, apple, and port wine sauces). Adacent to the restaurant is a lovely old townhouse with high quality accommodation including a Victorian drawing room and eight stylish, traditionally furnished bedrooms with luxury marble bathrooms.

Prices: Set dinner €30. Main course from €19.95. House wine €19.95.
Hours: 18.00-22.00. Closed on Sunday and mid December to mid February.
Rooms: 12 en suite. Double room from €128, single from €119.
Cuisine: Seafood.
Other Points: No-smoking area.
Directions: On approaching Dingle town take the third left off the roundabout into 'the Mall'. At the junction turn left into John Street. Doyles is the red and white building on the left. (Map 19, D1)

Heatons House

The Wood, Dingle, Co Kerry
Telephone: +353(0)66 9152288
heatons@iol.ie
www.heatonsdingle.com

On the harbour road overlooking Dingle Bay and convenient for the marina, stands this stylish, family run guesthouse noted for great views and fabulous accommodation. This is all down to the hard work of Cameron and Nuala Heaton who are natural and experienced hosts and work hard to create the air of a gracious family home. Indeed, Heaton House makes a great base for touring this magnificent part of Ireland, a place The National Geographic calls 'the most beautiful place on Earth.' All sixteen bedrooms are light, spacious and very well maintained and equipped, lavish attention to detail extends to brass beds in some rooms, and armchairs and coffee tables throughout; rooms range from standard and deluxe, to junior suites. In the morning look forward to an incredible breakfast prepared by the Heatons's daughter Jackie: cold meats, Irish cheese, porridge topped with Drambuie, brown sugar and cream, fresh fish, local smoked salmon, Dingle kippers, homemade sausages, and local black and white pudding all appear on the amazing menu, alongside homemade breads, scones and preserves.

Hours: Closed 24-26 December and 2 weeks in January.
Rooms: 16 en suite. Double room from €39 per person, single from €49.
Other Points: Totally no smoking. Children welcome over 8 years. Garden. Car park.
Directions: Take the harbour road out of Dingle and Heaton House is 500 yards past the marina at the front of Dingle town. (Map 19, D1)

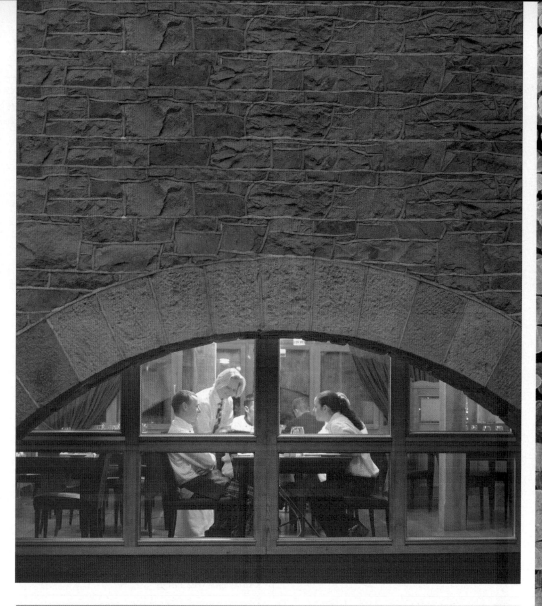

DINGLE PENINSULA, CO KERRY

Gorman's Clifftop House and Restaurant

🍷 🍴 🛏

Glaise Bheag, Dingle Peninsula, Ballydavid, Co Kerry
Telephone: +353(0)66 9155162
gormans@eircom.net
www.gormans-clifftophouse.com

Vincent and Sile Gorman's beautiful house is located on the Slea Head scenic drive, in one of the most westerly points in Europe, overlooking the vast Atlantic ocean. This is a most stunning location and every season brings it own special qualities. Vincent Gorman's family settled this land in the 18th century and his wife, Sile proudly proclaims that she came here on holiday over 20 years ago and, if anything, loves it more than ever. Now a fluent Irish speaker, it would not be unusual to hear Sile speak the odd "cupla focal" as this is also a Gaeltacht area , where Irish is the first language of the local people. Every room at Gorman's pays homage to the landscape offering breathtaking views of mountains or ocean. The spacious bedrooms are furnished in pine offset by hand-thrown pottery lamps and tapestry wall hangings. Superior rooms boast king-size beds and Jacuzzi baths. Comfort oozes everywhere. Downstairs, guests can gather around the fire to read or chat, dine handsomely on Vincent's home baked bread, organic produce (some home grown), Irish Hereford beef, Atlantic fish landed daily, wild salmon (fresh and locally smoked), and excellent local cheeses.

Prices: Set dinner €37.50.
House wine €18.50.
Hours: 18.30-21.00.
Rooms: 9 en suite. Double room from €100, single from €75. Family room from €125.
Cuisine: Modern Irish and seafood.
Other Points: No-smoking area. Children welcome. Garden. Car park. Bicycle hire.
Directions: From Dingle harbour go left to the roundabout west of town, straight across. Travel for eight miles towards An Fheothanach. Keep left but do not turn left. The sea is on the right, Gorman's is on the left. (Map 19, D1)

The Tankard Bar & Restaurant 🍴🍷◗✕

Kilfenora, Fenit, Tralee, Co Kerry
Telephone: +353(0)66 7136164 or 7136349
tankard@eircom.net
traleebaygoodfoodcircle.com

Mary and Jerry O'Sullivan's pub and restaurant dates back quite a few hundred years (the O'Sullivan's are relatives of the original owners) and claims to be the oldest bar in the area. Seafood is on the doorstep, with fresh crab and apple salad, steamed mussels, seafood platter, and the day's local catch featuring on the bar snack menu, alongside lots of familiar choices such as homemade burgers, steaks and sandwiches. In the restaurant, fish and seafood cookery again takes a prominent role, delivered in a modern Irish style from a classic base. Dishes such as seafood mornay, or a straightforward grilled half lobster with lemon butter, could open a meal that goes on to Clonakilty scallops pan-fried with an extra virgin olive oil pesto, Clonakilty black pudding and wild rice timbale, or Dover sole filled with pan-fried cabbage, prawns and bacon and served with beurre blanc. Meat choices bring a good steak selection, or rosemary crusted rack of lamb with a honey and rosemary sauce; there's also a pasta and vegetarian menu. A preference for France shows up on the wine list, but there is plenty of choice from other wine growing countries.

Prices: Set lunch €20. Set dinner €30. Main course restaurant from €13.50. Main course bar/snack from €4.75.
Hours: 12.00-22.00. Closed Good Friday.
Cuisine: Modern Irish
Other Points: No-smoking area. Garden. Children welcome. Car park. Games room.
Directions: 7 kilometres on the bayside of Tralee, a bright yellow building. (Map 19, C2)

Cahernane House Hotel 🍷🍴✕◇

Muckross Road, Killarney, Co Kerry
Telephone: +353(0)64 31895
cahernane@eircom.net
www.cahernane.com

Now owned and run by the Browne family, the relaxed manor house hotel replete with antiques was the seat of the Herbert Family, Earls of Pembroke, and is well matched by an aristocratic wine list and very sound cooking. The term country house is for once absolutely accurate, the last quarter mile to the house is through a tunnel of greenery which frames the long, private avenue. In addition, own grounds and parkland, which stand on the edge of Killarney's National Park (an area of outstanding natural beauty with lakes, mountains and woodland walks close by) guarantees a sense of place and atmosphere. However, the house is just minutes from Killarney town centre. The 38 bedrooms offer a range of styles and choice with spacious suites and junior suites with antique furniture, jacuzzis and, in some, private balconies. Those in the newer wing are simpler in style but equally spacious and well appointed. In the Herbert Room Restaurant Patrick Kerry delivers appealing menus that make the most of local, seasonal produce in a contemporary style. Service is smooth and hitch-free.

Prices: Set lunch €30. Set dinner €45. Main course restaurant from €25. Main course bar from €10. House wine €23.50.
Hours: 19.00-21.30. Sunday lunch 12.30-14.30.
Closed Monday to Saturday lunchtimes, 22 December - 10 January.
Rooms: 38 en suite. Double/twin from €200, Single from €120. Family room from €250.
Cuisine: Modern Irish.
Other Points: No-smoking area. Garden. Children welcome. Car park.
Directions: N71. On the Muckross Road, ten minutes walk from Killarney town. (Map 19, D2)

Rooms: 4 en suite. Double/twin from €190. Single supplement €50. Price includes breakfast.
Other Points: Totally no smoking. Garden. Children welcome over six years old. Car park.
Directions: From Killarney town on the N71 take the first left after crossing the metal bridge there is a small sign on the right hand side, Mill Road. Coolclogher House is quarter of a mile along the road on the right hand side. (Map 19, D2)

Coolclogher House ◇

Mill Road, Killarney, Co Kerry
Telephone: +353(0)64 35996
info@coolclogherhouse.com
www.coolclogherhouse.com

It took Maurice and Mary Harnett six years to restore their house. It's located on the edge of Killarney town and set in a 68 acre walled estate that boasts superb gardens and mature parkland; the house is reputed to have been built by Pugin. Mary's vibrant character and joie de vie fills the air, reflected in the lavish care and attention she has given to polished wooden floors, the placing of luxurious rugs, antique furniture, the tending of open fires, and the fresh flowers that are everywhere. It induces a cosseting feeling that envelopes visitors immediately on arrival. One of the loveliest parts of the house is the original conservatory, built around a 170-year-old specimen camellia. There are just four bedrooms, but all are spacious, beautifully appointed rooms with big beds, fine linen and magnificent bathrooms, It goes without saying that views from each bedroom are superb. This is a lovely place, with a private, exclusive feel. Indeed, it is possible to take the house for exclusive use. It is within easy walking distance of Killarney National Park, and there is a working farm with horses, cattle, sheep and hens on the estate.

The Laurels 🍷🍽️✕

Main Street, Killarney, Co Kerry
Telephone: +353(0) 643 1149
olearyc@idl.ie
www.the-laurels.com

Con and Kate O'Leary's, self-styled restaurant and 'singing pub' has stood at the heart of Killarney for just under a century and has been in the same family ownership for fully half of that time. Amongst other sports beloved of its singing, drinking clientele is that of dog-racing; from here the family-owned Kilbrean Boy travelled to Wimbledon back in 1930 to triumph at the first-ever Laurels greyhound meeting - and of such things are legends made. Alongside hospitality here that borders on the legendary, expect to find the best traditional fare around, prepared with not a little flair entirely from local ingredients. Bantry Bay mussels come in a tureen of white wine, garlic and fresh cream with home-made soda bread, Irish stew with crusty home-baked rolls. These happily rub shoulders with dishes of decidedly more up-to-date persuasion, such as bruschetta topped with roasted vegetables and mozzarella, and beef fajitas with salsa, guacamole and sour cream dips. Party goers are promised the best pizza in town, side orders of home-made 'champ'; German pils by the litre; and fairly-priced wines from around the globe. And transcending all, what is guaranteed is the craic. Regular cabaret entertainment - telephone for details for forthcoming shows.

Prices: Main course restaurant from €9. Bar meal from €7.95. House wine €14.50.
Hours: 10.30-23.30, Thursday - Saturday until 00.30. Sunday 12.30-23.00. Restaurant closed November to April. Call ahead for seasonal changes.
Food served: 12.00-15.00. 18.00-21.30 Monday to Saturday.
Cuisine: Traditional Irish and International.
Other Points: Children welcome.
Directions: Centre of Killarney. (Map 19, D2)

The Old Presbytery Restaurant ⭐🍷🍴✕

Cathedral Place, Killarney, Co Kerry
Telephone: +353(0)64 30555
oldpresbytery@eircom.net
www.oldpresbytery.com

Gerry Browne and Mary Rose Hickey converted this old presbytery into a stylish, contemporary restaurant. It stands opposite the early 19th century St Mary's Cathedral and since opening in 2001, has built up a loyal following for its commitment to local produce. The cooking strikes a contemporary cord, its repertoire taking in starters such as millefeuille of goats' cheese, grilled aubergine, crispy wonton pastry, mango and red onion salsa, or roast sea bass and mixed pepper terrine, balsamic reduction, chive and mustard cress salad. Main courses range from fish such as wild salmon served with pickled vegetables, crispy rösti and red wine sauce, to rolled stuffed breast of chicken with bacon crust, sauté cabbage, tomato pesto and sage and port jus, and braised Kerry lamb shank, rosemary mash, honey glazed vegetables, tarragon and wholegrain mustard sauce. A selection of Irish farmhouse cheeses is a savoury alternative to caramelised lemon tart and lime sorbet, or melting chocolate cake with white chocolate sauce and vanilla ice cream. The wine list favours Bordeaux, Burgundy and the Rhone, but there are some good selections from Italy, Spain and the new world.

Prices: Set dinner between 18.30-19.00 €23 (2 courses). Main course restaurant from €18.50. House wine €21.
Hours: 18.30-22.00.
Closed Tuesday, 7 January - 1 February and Monday-Wednesday from 1 November to 17 March.
Cuisine: Modern European.
Other Points: No-smoking area. Garden. Children welcome. Car park. Prviate dining area.
Directions: Opposite St Mary's Cathedral and adjacent to the National Park. (Map 19, D2)

Caragh Lodge ⭐🍷✕🍽️

Caragh Lake, Killorglin, Co Kerry
Telephone: +353(0)66 9769115
caraghl@iol.ie
www.caraghlodge.com

Graham and Mary Gaunt's Victorian fishing lodge, stands in a lovely garden on the shore of Caragh Lake and is less than a mile from the Ring of Kerry. Generous hospitality and attention to detail make this a special place. Day rooms are furnished with period and antique furniture and decorated with quiet good taste, with pictures, porcelain, fresh flowers, polished wood, and log fires. Bedrooms in the main house or the garden cottage reveal great attention to detail; garden rooms have spectacular views, overlooking grounds filled with magnolias, rhododendrons, azaleas, camellias and many rare and sub-tropical shrubs. There's a tennis court in the grounds, boating and brown trout fishing on the lake, and no less than five championship golf courses are a short drive away. Overlooking the lake, the dining room features the finest Irish cuisine, freshly caught wild salmon (locally smoked or fresh), Kerry lamb and garden grown vegetables. The evening menu can also feature a locally made cheese from Wilma's Farmhouse Cheeses, organic green salad with grilled goat's cheese and raspberry vinaigrette, and homebaked breads

Prices: Main course from €22. House wine €22.
Hours: 19.00-20.30. Closed mid Octobber to the end of April.
Rooms: 15 en suite. Double room from €180, single from €130. Suite from €325.
Cuisine: Modern Irish.
Other Points: No-smoking area. Children welcome over 12 years old. Garden. Car park. Sauna.
Directions: Caragh Lodge is located just off the N70. Travelling from Killorglin towards Glen Beigh and take the road signposted for Caragh Lodge. Turn left at the lake, the lodge is on your right. (Map 19, D2)

Avoca Café

Molls Gap, On the Ring of Kerry, Co Kerry
Telephone: +353(0)64 34720
www.avoca.ie

Avoca Handweavers on the Ring of Kerry enjoys a spectacular location in Molls Gap and is the perfect place to indulge in a little shopping and superb cooking and baking. The Gap itself is named after Moll Kissane, who reputedly ran a shebeen (a hostelry of dubious reputation). The store is set high on a rocky ridge, overlooking mountains, rivers, green fields and the famous lakes of Killarney. As in all the Pratt family's Avoca Cafes the range of wholesome foods is varied and delicious, with the restaurant self-service and all dishes made on the premises. Popular dishes include fish pie, shepherds pie, chicken and mushroom pie, quiches, lentil and nut loaf, chicken and pork terrine, fresh and smoked salmon, and a selection of freshly made salads. There is a huge selection of desserts - banoffi pie, pear tart, strawberry meringue roulade, chocolate roulade, jam and fresh cream scones, Bakewell slices, coffee cake, fruit cakes, muffins, chocolate and orange cake, rhubarb and mixed berry crumble, mixed berry tart, and apple pie (and that's to name but a few). Wine includes a selection of quarter bottles.

Prices: Main course restaurant from €9.50.
Hours: 09.30-17.00. Closed 8 November - 10 March.
Cuisine: Traditional and Modern Irish with International influences.
Other Points: No-smoking area. Children welcome. Craft shop.
Directions: Located on the Ring of Kerry. (Map 19, D2)

Café Sol

William Street, Kilkenny, Co Kilkenny
Telephone: +353(0)56 64987
cafesolkk@eircom.net

Purchased over a year ago by Hugh Bergin, he is cleverly carrying on all that is good about Café Sol. All day food, the resolutely homecooked dishes based on fresh raw materials and, if possible, organic, has made the café's reputation. Breakfast is served until noon, and includes a full Irish with free range eggs and Clonakilty black pudding, as well as buttermilk pancakes with crispy bacon and maple syrup, and cinnamon flavoured french toast with homemade jam and cream. Lunch brings sandwiches such as mature cheddar with homemade tomato chutney, and cooked dishes of salmon and prawn dauphinoise, or local Lavistown sausages with Bramley apple sauce and champ. Blackboards list the day's specials, there are fresh salads, puddings such as very chocolatey brownies with chocolate sauce and cream, and an extensive takeaway menu that ranges from breads, soups, sauces, and pâtés, to quiches, savoury dishes and puddings. Dinner is a slightly more formal affair, perhaps cold salad of quail escabeche, then seared saddle of venison with ginger confit, thyme, honey and soy sauce with wild mushroom couscous. There are set lunch and dinner menus and the wine list is short, global and reasonably priced.

Prices: Set lunch €12. Set dinner €20. Main course restaurant from €14. House wine €13.80.
Hours: 10.00-17.00. 18.30-21.45, until 22.00 Friday and Saturday. Closed Sunday and Monday evening.
Cuisine: Modern Irish with Mediterranean influences.
Other Points: No-smoking area. Children welcome.
Directions: William Street is opposite the City Hall on the High Street. (Map 20, C6)

Lacken House

Dublin Road, Kilkenny, Co Kilkenny
Telephone: +353(0)56 776 1085
res@lackenhouse.ie
www.lackenhouse.ie

The Victorian dower house is located on the edge of Kilkenny. It was built in 1847, home to Lord Viscount Montmorency. In early 1924 it became a private nursing home. Since its establishment as a guesthouse and restaurant in 1983, Lacken House has established a sound reputation for good food and wine a reputation new owners, Jackie and Trevor Toner, are maintaining. The kitchen takes an eclectic approach to all things gastronomic, offering on the set menu a salad of smoked venison, red pepper marmalade and cumin tuile, or tempura trout with chilli salad, soy sauce and tomato coulis. First rate local produce is handled well, be it roast rack of Kilkenny lamb with a herb crust and tomato farci, or monkfish tail served with creamy curried mussels from the short carte. Bread, biscuits, ice creams and sorbets are made in house, and Irish farmhouse cheeses make an alternative to warm chocolate fondant with mint ice cream. In addition to an affordable slate of some 50 wines, there's Kilkenny brewed Smithwicks beer, plus beer from nearby Carlow Brewing Company. The twelve bedrooms vary in size and outlook, but all are pleasantly decorated in a comfortable, thoughtful style.

Prices: Set dinner €39. Main course restaurant from €20. House wine €19.50.
Hours: 18.30-22.00 Tuesday to Sunday. Closed Sundays during the winter. Closed Mondays and 24-26 December.
Rooms: 12 en suite. Double/twin from €120. Single from €75, family room from €165.
Cuisine: Irish and European.
Other Points: No-smoking areas. Garden. Children welcome. Car park.
Directions: In Kilkenny City on the main Carlow to Dublin road (N7). (Map 20, C6)

Quinn's Tea Rooms
Main Street, Abbeyleix, Co Laois
Telephone: +353(0) 502 31020
mariequinn@eircom.net

Marie Quinn carries on the tradition of homestyle
baking that her mother Eileen, known to all as "the
duchess" started some 20 years ago. Today, this busy
little tearoom offers cakes, scones, tarts such as
rhubarb (made with homegrown rhubarb), quiches,
sandwiches and much more. Everything is made on
site, from the lunchtime soup of the day, lasagne,
and fish and chips, to the brown bread and rolls that
are used for sandwiches of ham, cheese or chicken.
A highlight is breakfast, served from 7.30am, which
ranges from a full working breakfast of bacon, egg,
sausage, tomato, hash brown, beans, black pudding,
mushrooms, and toasted homemade bread, to a roll
of bacon, egg and sausage. Bread and butter pudding
is a treat.
Hours: 07.30-18.00 Monday to Friday. 08.00-18.00 Sunday and
09.00-18.00 Sunday. Closed between Christmas and New Year.
Cuisine: Traditional Irish.
Other Points: No-smoking area. Dogs welcome on leads in the
garden. Garden. Children welcome.
Directions: On the main Dublin to Cork road in Abbeyleix town.
(Map 20, B6)

Croom Mills
Croom, Co Limerick
Telephone: +353(0)61 397130
croommills@eircom.net
www.croommills.ie

Croom Mills is the brainchild of Mary Hayes and her
husband Plunkett. On the one hand, it is a fascinating
visitor attraction enhanced by its lovely waterside
location and its giant 16-foot cast iron millwheel. As
well as the many interesting exhibits (some
interactive), there's an audio-visual presentation that
tells the story of grain milling. Admission to the visitor
centre is free. On the other hand, the complex houses
the Waterfront Bistro, a self-service restaurant serving
morning coffees, pastries baked on the premises, and a
carvery-style lunch. The Mill Race Restaurant, which
overlooks the mill wheel and is open for dinner, makes
the most of beams and wooden pillars with an easy
contemporary look to match the modern Irish cooking.
Typical main courses are smoked salmon and mussel
risotto with a hint of spring onion, or rack of lamb
with red pepper mash and grape jus. There's a good,
early evening set menu, own-made ice creams, regional
Irish cheeses, and a globally inspired wine list.
There is also the Corn Loft Gift and Craft Gallery with
a superb range of craft and giftware, and the
Miller Inn Pub.
Prices: Set lunch €16.50. Set dinner €20.95. Main course
restaurant from €16. Main course bar/snack from €7.95. House
wine €16.
Hours: 09.00-21.30 Wednesday to Saturday. 09.00-18.00 Monday,
Tuesday and Sunday.
Millers Inn open 17.00 until close Monday to Thursday and 12.00
until close Friday - Sunday. Closed Good Friday, 25-26 December.
Cuisine: Modern European.
Other Points: No-smoking area. Garden. Car park.
Directions: N20. 400 metres off the N20 on the R516 in the

Hush @ Aubars
49/50 Thomas Street, Limerick, Co Limerick
Telephone: +353(0)61 317799
padraic@aubars.com
www.aubars.com

When Padraic Frawley returned to Ireland some five years ago, he set out
to transform an old city centre pub into a lively bar, restaurant and
nightclub. The popular Aubars is the result. Hush is a smaller, more
intimate, trendy wine bar and bistro within Aubars, but with its own
separate entrance. Contemporary in style, there is cream leather seating,
modern art on the walls, and an excellent range of global wines displayed
behind a bar counter, with house wines from Chile, Australia and
Argentina. Open at 8.30 in the morning for coffee and croissants, the day
proceeds to lunch with a soup and sandwich menu that runs alongside a
carte whose modern credentials of, say, steamed mussels with coconut
milk, ginger, chilli, lemongrass and fresh coriander, are tempered by more
classical offerings such as grilled brill with an asparagus and pea risotto
and sauce vierge. If chocolate fondant with raspberries and mascarpone
doesn't appeal, there's farmhouse biscuit with ice cream and butterscotch
sauce. An exceptionally good value Early Bird menu is offered nightly
from 5.30pm-7pm seven days a week, as well as a set dinner menu.

Prices: Set dinner €40. Set early bird
dinner €22. Main course restaurant from
€14. Main course bar/snack from €11.
House wine €19.
Hours: 12.00-16.30. 17.30-21.30.
Closed Good Friday and 25 December.
Cuisine: Modern European.
Other Points: No-smoking area.
Children welcome.
Directions: Located centrally on Thomas
Street just off O'Connell Street.

Fitzpatricks Bar & Restaurant

Jenkinstown, Rockmarshall, Dundalk, Co Louth
Telephone: +353(0) 42 937 6193
fitzpatricks@ireland.com
www.fitzpatricksrestaurant.com

All manner of awards have been heaped on this fine country hostelry. It's set against the picturesque background of the Cooley Mountains, stands at the heart of the renowned Tain walking trail in County Louth, is a haven for golfers and fishermen, and handy for glorious beaches nearby. Tastefully displayed within is a remarkable collection of artefacts and memorabilia, and the warmth and hospitality of owners and staff is exceptional. For those just wanting a quiet drink there's the atmospheric Shann-Ronan Bar and adjacent beer garden, while in both lounge and restaurant food choices offer the best freshly-caught Carlingford seafood, locally grown vegetables and soft fruits and breads, desserts and petit fours baked on the premises. The menu runs literally to pages, from a comprehensive carte and full vegetarian options, through to the legendary Sunday lunch extravaganza. Traditional fish and chips rubs contrasts with chargrilled marinated salmon and prawns provençale, or steak and Guinness pie with beef Stroganoff, or rib-eye with peppercorn and herb crust. Still this leaves space for open sandwiches, full afternoon tea with scones, and fresh raspberry and lemon brûlée.

Prices: Set lunch €22.50. Main course restaurant from €23. Main course bar €14. House wine €17.50.
Hours: 12.30-22.00. Sunday 12.30-15.00. Closed Mondays and three days over Christmas period.
Food served: 12.30-22.00.
Cuisine: European and Irish.
Other Points: No-smoking area. Garden. Children welcome over three years old. Car park. Private dining room for up to 30 people.
Directions: Belfast to Dublin road N1. From Dublin take the Carlingford road from Dundalk. Fitzpatricks is five miles along the Carlingford Road on the left hand side. (Map 18, E7)

Crockets on the Quay

Quay Village, Ballina, Co Mayo
Telephone: +353 (0)96 75930/75940
info@crocketsonthequay.ie
www.crocketsonthequay.ie

On the outskirts of Ballina Quay Village, stands a stylish waterfront pub and restaurant. Owned and ably run by the Murphy family, this is a real find. As you enter you encounter a traditional Irish bar with open fire that often has Irish music sessions. To the rear is a comfortable lounge area off which is the restaurant. White-painted stone walls and modern furnishings distinguish the restaurant, which has its own separate entrance. Gina Murphy and her husband Pádraig run an industrious kitchen. They bake their own bread and focus on local produce, especially locally caught fish, producing a contemporary repertoire with plenty of wide-ranging ideas. Starters might be crispy open ravioli with home smoked salmon on an onion soubise and a snap pea broth. Main courses vary from wild Moy salmon with cucumber relish and confit of lime, to Quay Pit Country beef medallions with stir-fried tiger prawns and vegetables in a filo basket, with blue cheese and pepper cream. Puddings might feature Bailey's and Malteser soufflé. Sound, reasonably priced wines start with Italian and Chilean house wines.

Prices: Set lunch €20 and dinner €35. Main course from €17. Bar meal from €9.50. House wine €16.
Hours: 12.30-00.30 Monday-Wednesday. Until 24.00 on Sunday, 01.30 on Thursday and 02.00 on Friday and Saturday.
Food served: 12.30-20.30 for bar food. 18.00 until late in the restaurant. 12.00-14.30 on Sunday. Closed 25 December and Good Friday. No food served 26 December.
Cuisine: Modern Irish.
Other Points: No-smoking area. Children welcome until 19.30. Car park.
Directions: Leaving Ballina on the Sligo road turn left at the traffic lights. Follow the river to the quay, Crockets is on the right. (Map 17, D3)

Downhill House Hotel

Ballina, Co Mayo
Telephone: +353(0)96 21033
info@downhillhotel.ie
www.downhillhotel.ie

This family owned and managed hotel is set in tranquil landscaped gardens near the banks of the River Moy, one of Ireland's richest salmon and trout fishing rivers. Bedrooms are comfortable with all the modern amenities and there's a smart four-poster suite. With the Eagles Health and Leisure Club, the Downhill has excellent facilities for families, with a 50 foot oval swimming pool (from which you can enjoy spectacular views of the Brosna River and Falls from the poolside loungers), a childrens' pool, Jacuzzi, steam room, sauna, and gymnasium, in addition to three floodlit all-weather tennis courts, table tennis, squash and snooker. The kitchen treats dishes in a straightforward manner, with raw materials drawn from local suppliers such as the local smokery for trout, mackerel and salmon, game from nearby shoots, and locally made cheeses. The set dinner could see chicken and mushroom vol-au vent, consomme with port, medallions of fillet of pork diane with a fresh fruit Pavlova to finish. Modest pricing is a feature of the French-led wine list.

Prices: Set lunch €13 and dinner €29. House wine €11.
Hours: 13.00-14.15. 19.00-21.15. Closed 22-26 December.
Rooms: 60 en suite. Double room from €75.50 per person, single from €98.
Cuisine: Traditional Irish.
Other Points: No-smoking area. Children welcome. Garden. Car park.
Directions: From Dublin to Ballina, go as far as Ballisadare on the N4 then the A59 to Ballina. (Map 17, D3)

Knock House Hotel

Ballyhaunis Road, Knock, Co Mayo
Telephone: +353(0)94 9388088
info@knockhousehotel.ie
www.knockhousehotel.ie

This impressive purpose built hotel is located in the grounds of the International Shrine at Knock, a site of pilgrimage for many years. Open since 1999, Knock House was designed architecturally to blend with the surrounding countryside and sit fittingly alongside the shrine and church. The open plan, rectangular stone-faced building (built from local limestone) with two curved, low-rise bedrooms sections leading from both sides, is contemporary in style, sparsely decorated and furnished, with a clutter free feel. Comfortable up-to-date bedrooms are very well equipped with peaceful country views; there is excellent wheelchair access. The central part of the building has a glass wall to the rear providing lovely views of the surrounding countryside and a door leads outside to a seating area looking over the fields. In the Four Seasons Restaurant, influences from Europe and beyond are evident in starters of Mayo coast fresh mussels steamed the Mexican way with fresh chilli, lemon, coriander and onion, and savoury mushroom vol au vents. Dinner proceeds with a soup or sorbet, before main courses ranging from grilled fillet of sea trout with lemon butter, to roast stuffed leg of Mayo lamb. As a finale, there might be homebaked apple and cranberry crumble. Wines are a good mix of European and new world bottles.

Prices: Set lunch €20. Set dinner €35. House wine €19.
Hours: 12.30-15.00. 18.00-22.00.
Rooms: 68 en suite. Double/twin from €100. Single from €70.
Cuisine: Traditional Irish.
Other Points: No-smoking area. Garden. Children welcome. Car park.
Directions: In the grounds of the International Shrine. (Map 17, E3)

Ardmore Country House Hotel & Restaurant

The Quay, Westport, Co Mayo
Telephone: +353(0)98 25994
ardmorehotel@eircom.net
www.ardmorecountryhouse.com

Located near Westport Quay, overlooking Clew Bay, Pat and Noreen Hoban's small family run hotel has great style and a tremendous sense of luxury. All 13 bedrooms have been refurbished to a wonderfully high standard, each is individual with striking colour schemes, and quality furnishings. Most bathrooms have a separate walk-in power shower and bath, and there are plenty of thoughtful extras. Public rooms take in a restaurant that is bright, airy, and a comfortable Oyster Bar for pre and post prandial drinks. Pat does the cooking, presenting classic menus with the emphasis firmly on seafood. Oysters and lobsters are locally sourced, smoked salmon comes from Connemara, and during the game season, there's woodcock, snipe and pheasant, all of which are from local shoots. At its best, the food treads a successful familiar path, offering black and white pudding partnered by apple compote and whole grain mustard sauce, and pan-fried hake with red pepper vinaigrette. An extensive wine list offers both new world wines and classic French favourites.

Prices: Set dinner €40 (5 courses). Main course restaurant from €19. House wine €19.50.
Hours: Food served: 19.00-21.00
Closed mid January until March and Sundays during the low season.
Rooms: 13 en suite. Double/twin from €75. per person. Single from €125.
Cuisine: Classic menus with emphasis on seafood.
Other Points: Smoking only in the bar area. Garden. Children welcome over 12 years old. Car park.
Directions: One and a half kilometres from Westport town centre in the direction of the Quay. (Map 17, E2)

Hudson's Bistro

30 Railway Street, Navan, Co Meath
Telephone: +353(0)46 29231

An informal, down-to-earth feel characterises Richard and Tricia Hudson's bustling town-centre restaurant on two floors, which delivers a cheerful, informal bistro style of food in a warm and friendly atmosphere. The food covers all bases in an enthusiastic, eclectic manner that can produce starters of hummus and deep-fried crispy potato skins with aïoli dip, as well as marinated chargrilled chicken with lime and coriander dressing. What sets it all apart is that flavours are well defined, Richard's light and imaginative style drawing applause for its mix of exotic and down-to-earth ideas. Dishes such as Ho Chi Min chicken that's marinated in citrus juices, chargrilled, and then served with a sauce of lemongrass, citrus juices and chillis with rice and stir-fry vegetables. An Early Bird menu is offered between 6-7pm, perhaps the ever popular spicy chicken wings, followed by beefsteak strips, chargrilled, tossed with salsa verde and caramelised onions, rolled in flour tortillas and served with salad. Puddings are good too, especially the fudge cream: full cream yogurt and cream, flavoured with Amaretto and topped with praline hazelnuts. Wines are grouped by style, the selection wide ranging, and mark-ups are restrained.

Prices: Set dinner (early bird menu) from €20-€30. Main course from €18. House wine €16.75.
Hours: 18.00-22.00 Tuesday-Thursday. 18.00-23.00 on Friday and Saturday.
Closed Monday and major religious festivals.
Cuisine: Modern Irish.
Other Points: No-smoking area. Children welcome.
Directions: N5. Turn left into the town centre and right at the roundabout. The restaurant is on the left. (Map 18, F6)

Waterford Crystal

Waterford City

ROSCOMMON, CO ROSCOMMON

Gleeson's Townhouse & Restaurant

🚩🍷☕✕🗒

Market Square, Roscommon
Telephone: +353(0)90 6626954
info@gleesonstownhouse.com
www.gleesonstownhouse.com

The location is ideal - in the centre of Roscommon, next door to the tourist office and county museum and overlooking the town's historic square. If you are seeking comfort, value for money and good home cooking and baking, this is the place, for Eamonn and Mary Gleeson have lovingly restored their listed 19th century townhouse (formerly known as The Manse) to a very high standard. The combination of 19 well equipped and appointed bedrooms, an all-day café, separate restaurant (the Manse) mixed in with the Gleesons' charming hospitality creates a relaxed buzz. Food in the café ranges from a full-blown cooked breakfast, Caesar salad and pasta carbonara to various steaks and baked potatoes. In the restaurant, dishes are built around local supplies, say starters of seafood chowder, or Toulouse sausage with mustard mash, tomato and herb jus. Mains take in roast rack of local lamb with herb and mustard crust and red wine jus, or grilled salmon, lemon and parsley sauce with tomato salsa. There's a good regional cheese selection along the lines of Cashel Blue, Gubbeen, Boilie soft goats' cheese and Carrigaline. Value for money extends to the wine list with its fair choice and broad selection.

Prices: Set lunch €13.95. Set dinner €25. Main course restaurant from €15.95. Main course bar/snack from €7.50. House wine €15.
Hours: 12.30-14.30. 18.30-21.00. Friday and Satruday until 22.00. Cafe open 08.00-18.00 seven days. Closed 25-26 December.
Rooms: 19 en suite. Double/twin from €55-€70 per person. Single from €52.50. Family room from €55.
Cuisine: Modern Irish.
Other Points: No-smoking area. Dogs welcome. Garden. Children welcome. Car park.
Directions: From Dublin, take N6 to Athlone, then the N61 to Roscommon. From Sligo, N4 to Boyle, then the N61. (Map 17, F4)

THURLES, CO TIPPERARY

Horse & Jockey Inn

🚩🍷🍸✕🗒

Thurles, Co Tipperary
Telephone: +353(0) 504 44192
horseandjockeyinn@eircom.net
horseandjockeyinn.com

Located in the heartland of Tipperary, close to Holycross Abbey and the Rock of Cashel, the inn that gives its name to the village itself has been trading continuously for over 250 years. Such generations of experience, combined with rich limestone land and a clean environment, are the perfect ingredients for Ireland's horse industry (racing stables nearby) and, as its name suggests, this is a popular meeting place where visitors can expect to rub shoulders with key players in the sport. Public areas encompass spacious lounges and a bar leading to a stylish yet informal dining-room of polished tables, Queen Anne chairs, and evening candles, while the bedrooms and suites are individually furnished and equipped with state-of-the-art facilities. Prime ingredients permeate menus, from Cashel breads used in such classic hot sandwiches as The Bookmaker (grilled steak) and chicken ciabatta with tomato salsa, to house special dishes that include seasonally available pan-fried scallops in wine and tomato sauce and traditional bacon-wrapped chicken stuffed with black pudding mousse.

Prices: Set lunch €13. Set dinner €25. Main course restaurant from €13. Bar meal from €7. House wine €13.
Hours: Food served: 12.00-15.00. 17.00-22.00. Sunday 12.30-14.30. 16.00-21.00.
Rooms: 30 en suite. Double/twin from €140, singles from €70 and family rooms €150.
Cuisine: Irish and European.
Other Points: No-smoking area. Garden. Children welcome. Car park.
Directions: N8. Midway between Cork and Dublin on the N8. Five miles north of Cashel. (Map 20, C5)

Inch House Country House and Restaurant

Thurles, Co Tipperary
Telephone: +353(0)504 51348/51261
inchhse@iol.ie
www.tipp.ie/inch-house.htm

John and Nora Egan's beautiful manor house was built in 1720 and is set on a working farm, testified by the barley and wheat growing by the side of the lane as you drive up. Restoration over the years has been extensive and on entering, you are struck by the beauty of the oak staircase, the stained glass window, and the lovely homely feel. Five comfortable bedrooms are all individually decorated with fine antique furniture and a real sense of peace and tranquillity. In the dining room off the entrance hall, the modern country house-style of cooking is another attraction. A typical day's menu might open with spicy black and white pudding, served with caramelised onions and a sherry vinegar sauce, or roast quail with herb stuffing and plum sauce, followed by fish, perhaps medallions of monkfish with a white wine and chive cream sauce, or meat, say, roast rack of lamb with a garlic and herb sauce. A French orientated wine list, with nods to other wine growing regions of the world, offers fair value, opening with house wines from €16. Glorious breakfasts can include crêpes with maple syrup, grilled kippers, and Irish farmhouse cheeses.

Prices: Set dinner €40 (5 courses). House wine €16-18.
Hours: Food served: 19.00-21.30.
Closed Sunday, Monday and Christmas week.
Rooms: 5 en suite. Double/twin from €105. Single from €60.
Cuisine: Modern European.
Other Points: No-smoking area. Garden. Children welcome over ten years old.
Directions: N8. From Thurles take the Nenagh Road, travel for four miles to crossroads; go straight over for 300 yards and the Inch House is on your left. (Map 20, C5)

The McAlpin's Suir Inn

Cheekpoint, Waterford, Co Waterford
Telephone: +353(0)51 382220/182
frances@mcalpins.com
www.mcalpins.com

Dunstan and Mary McAlpin, with their family, run a professional operation where standards are high and there is a wealth of warmth and friendliness. This has been a pub for almost 300 years, and owned by the McAlpin family since 1971. However, even today it is basically the same building the Bolton family built in the 17th century. This little lime-washed pub can be found at the end of a winding drive down to the coast at Cheekpoint. Full of character, it has low ceilings, rustic tables and chairs, and old prints and plates decorating the walls. No reservations are taken, so if seats are not available you just wait. And it is worth it. Seafood is a speciality and evening meals are served from 5.30pm. There are crab claws or mussels in garlic butter, smoked salmon with salmon mousse or seafood vol-au-vent to start. Then oven-baked king scallops in cheese and white wine, a real treat we thought, there's a good seafood platter, crab bake, seafood pie, as well as meaty dishes of pan-fried beef fillet with black pepper and mushroom sauce, or chicken breasts in fresh ground spices, served with rice and chutneys.

Prices: Main course from €12. House wine €15.
Hours: 17.45-21.45.
Closed Sunday and Christmas to mid-January.
Cuisine: Seafood and meat dishes.
Other Points: No-smoking area. Children welcome over six years old.
Directions: From Waterford city follow the signposts to Dunmore East passing the hospital. Continue for two miles until you reach the Passage East turn off; follow signs for Cheekpoint. Continue straight down to the harbour and McAlpin's is on the left hand side facing the river (Map 20, D6)

Prices: Set lunch €18.50 and dinner €35. Main course from €19.95. House wine €15.
Hours: 12.30-14.15 (until 16.00 Wednesday-Saturday). 18.30-22.00. Restaurant closed 3 January-3 February. Tuesday & Wednesday November to March.
Cuisine: Modern/French.
Other Points: No-smoking area. Children welcome over ten years old. Car park.
Directions: From Waterford follow directions to Dunmore East. As you enter the village the inn is on the left after the garage. (Map 20, D6)

The Strand Inn

Dunmore East, Co Waterford
Telephone: +353(0)51 383174
strandin@iol.ie
www.thestrandinn.com

Edwina and Mike Foyle have owned this 16th century inn for over 35 years. The setting is glorious: right on the beach looking over a small expanse of golden sands, rocks and sea with views onto Hook Lighthouse, the oldest in Europe. The bar is a real local - coal fire, smoky, laid-back atmosphere - other bars have a younger feel, a pool table fills one, the other is dominated by a large TV, a venue for live blues, jazz or funk, but there are quieter lounge areas, kitted out with bamboo furniture and soft pastel colours. Bar food is good, everything is made on the premises including some delicious black treacle bread to complement homemade soups, scampi, chowders and burgers. The restaurant is strong on the very fresh seafood landed at the harbour opposite, but it does beef and game very well, too. Edwina Foyle puts a modern spin on things: spicy Toulouse sausage, Puy lentils and pebble mustard dressing, perhaps, or mains of baked monkfish tails with a farce of garlic salami and onion with a vermouth and white wine sauce. A keenly-priced, global wine list offers six by the glass. Such is its popularity, in the summer it is advisable to

Majestic Hotel

Tramore, Co Waterford
Telephone: +353(0)51 381761
info@majestic-hotels.ie
www.majestic-hotels.ie

Annette and Danny Devine own and run this striking all-white and glass hotel fronting Tramore Beach. With three miles of Golden Beach, Tramore is one of Waterford's most well known seaside resorts. This is an ideal family location and guests have the use of Splashworld's health and leisure club, which is situated across the road from the hotel. In addition, seven golf courses are within a 15 minutes drive. Live entertainment is extremely popular during the summer months. Public rooms include a conservatory and dining room which offers a wide range of dishes, specializing in local fish and steaks. Bedrooms are comfortable, with all modern facilities and overlook the sea. Or you can just relax on the patio overlooking the boating lakes, where locals and visitors meet.

Prices: Set lunch €16.50. Set dinner €23.
Hours: 12.30-15.00. 18.30-21.00.
Rooms: 60 en suite. Double room from €90, single from €70.
Cuisine: Irish/continental.
Other Points: No-smoking area. Children welcome. Patio and conservatory.
Directions: R675 from Waterford, ten minutes drive. (Map 20, D6)

Arlington Lodge Country House Hotel

John's Hill, Waterford, Co Waterford
Telephone: +353(0)51 878584
info@arlingtonlodge.com
www.arlingtonlodge.com

Maurice Keller has created a striking hotel in Waterford, where attention to detail is the key to success. The gracious 17th century house was formerly the Bishop's palace, and after extensive renovation, opened in early 2001. As you enter through a red brick wall entrance with imposing gates, you see a beautiful old house with a stained glass door and tall windows; to the right a conservatory restaurant has been added. Throughout the hotel antiques and paintings, chosen by Maurice, complement the style and character of the house. The atmosphere is one of easy informality. The snug-like bar with its rich, warm colours, stained glass window, curios and memorabilia, is both relaxing and intimate. In the Robert Paul Restaurant the menu is modern Irish. Dishes such as leek and brie tartlet, beetroot salsa and wild rocket, and supreme of chicken with stir-fried greens champ and Madeira are typical examples. A real effort has been made to source wines from less fashionable producers, though popular classics feature as well. Each of the luxurious bedrooms is individually decorated, furnished to create true comfort and offering state-of-the-art facilities.

Prices: Set lunch €22.50 and dinner from €38. Main course from €19. Snack from €5.65. House wine €20.
Hours: 12.30-14.30. 18.30-21.00. Closed 24-27 December.
Rooms: 20 en suite. Double room from €140, single from €80.
Cuisine: Modern Irish with International influences.
Other Points: No-smoking area. Children welcome. Garden. Car park.
Directions: Located in Waterford city. Go over the bridge in Waterford and turn left down the quay. At the third set of traffic lights turn left. Continue to the next set of lights and go straight over. Go up John's Hill for approximately half a mile and Arlington Lodge is on the right. (Map 20, D6)

Prices: Main course from €6.95. House wine from €17.50.
Food served: 10.00-18.00.
Closed 25 December and Good Friday.
Cuisine: Eclectic.
Other Points: Garden. Children welcome. Nightclub.
Directions: Opposite the Tower Hotel beside Reginalds Tower. (Map 20, D6)

Axis Mundi

The Mall, Waterford, Co Waterford
Telephone: +353(0)51 875041

Reginald's Tower is ancient and has a section of the original 9th century town wall fully preserved in the interior. As a restaurant it has had a chequered history, but new owner Michael Tierney, proprietor of the Centenery Stores in Wexford (see entry), has grandly renamed the place and re-established it as one of the city's busiest spots. Expect a modern, sophisticated environment, which acknowledges its ancient heritage, yet features a contemporary design with wooden floors, metal surfaces, earthy colours, subtle lighting and modern Scandinavian artwork An all-day food operation serves the spacious dining area with prime raw materials sourced by a keen kitchen brigade. Best value is to be found among the daily lunch specials, say, cream of minestone soup with homemade brown bread, pork escalope on Parmesan mash, or garlic and chive chicken with seared aubergine and pesto sauce. Apple pie and cream could be offered as dessert of the day. For starters and snacks there might be tossed Caesar salad, or crab meat beignets with lemon dressing, while main dishes run to lemon sole with ginger and asparagus, and sirloin or fillet steaks with optional garlic or peppercorn sauces.

Gatchell's Restaurant at Waterford Crystal   ♛ ☕ ✕

Waterford Crystal, Kilbarry, Waterford, Co Waterford
Telephone: +353(0)51 332575
visitorreception@waterford.ie
www.waterfordvisitorcentre.com

Gatchell's Restaurant is situated in the Waterford Crystal Visitor Centre and is a lively, contemporary day time self-service restaurant run by Paula Prendeville. It offers a wonderful opportunity for lunch or morning coffee after a tour of the world-famous crystal factory.

Paula cooks, using raw materials based, where possible, on local produce and the menu is divided into soups, hot food, salads and desserts. Among its offerings might be excellent roast pepper and tomato or cream of vegetable soup, chicken fillet with wholegrain mustard and Parmesan cheese sauce, or smoked and fresh salmon fish cakes. Salads range from a vegetarian roulade to Caesar salad, with desserts taking in a fresh berry torte or banana and walnut cake, as well as an indulgent chocolate fudge gateau. There's a limited choice of wine. Tables are well spaced, the room well appointed, and service is friendly and efficient.

Prices: Main course restaurant from €9. House wine €15.50.
Hours: 09.00-17.00.
Food served: 12.00-14.30
Cuisine: Selection of soups, salads, hot food and sandwiches.
Other Points: No-smoking. Children welcome. Car park. Tourist information office. Bureau de Change. Gallery and Shop.
Directions: Situated in the Waterford Crystal Visitors Centre. (Map 20, D6)

Manifesto Restaurant   ◨ ♛ ✕

Custume Place, Athlone, Co Westmeath
Telephone: +353(0)902 73241
info@manifestorestaurant.com
www.manifestorestaurant.com

Alan Rooney has created a smart, stylish restaurant in the heart of Athlone. The centrally located first-floor restaurant features dark grained wood, marble and mirrors. Fresh fish from Galway market appears either battered in a light tempura with bubble and squeak and drizzled with a soy and ginger infusion, or as a trio from the sea: battered and grilled annd served on garlic butter mash with fresh herbs. Meat appears in the guise of Rudds black pudding with red onion marmalade and seeded mustard aïoli, steaks, slow braised lamb shank, and oven roasted chicken breast wrapped in Parma ham with mushroom risotto and basil oil. Light dishes of, say, Caesar salad, smoked salmon bagel, and Cajun chicken and lemon risotto are available at Saturday lunch. Australian and French house wines open a global selection that offers fair drinking at fair prices.

Prices: Set lunch £16.95 Friday-Sunday.
Hours: 12.30. 16.00-22.30. Closed for lunch Monday-Thursday, 25 December, 1 January and Good Friday.
Cuisine: Traditional Irish.
Other Points: No-smoking area. Children welcome.
Directions: From Dublin take the N4 to Kinnegad westwards and then the N6 to Athlone. (Map 18, F5)

Ireland - Co Westmeath

Wineport Lodge

Glasson, Athlone, Co Westmeath
Telephone: +353(0)906 439010
lodge@wineport.ie
www.wineport.ie

Husband and wife team, Ray Byrne and Jane English's Wineport Lodge is really a waterside restaurant-with-rooms. There is cedar decking running along the length of the lough-facing front, where guests have the option of arriving by boat. The interior ranges from a traditional, cosy sofa-stuffed bar with open fire, to a spacious, nautical-themed dining room. The food is no less comforting than the surroundings. Signature dishes and house specialities could include whole lobster and a selection of fresh fish with three sauces on the side or seared fillet of Irish Angus beef, sundried pepper and auburn herb salsa. Local produce like baked Glasson mushrooms with goats' cheese and chorizo and Rudds organic black pudding salad with minted new potatoes and softly poached egg also feature. The menu gives some clue to the speciality of this restaurant, and the well-annotated wine list, listed by region, combines modern classics as well as bottlings from new generations, mixed with a few classic French offerings. The ten-bedroom wing is considered a model of its kind and rooms are named after some of the world's great wines. Each of the bedrooms enjoy superb views over the Lough, are tastefully and stylishly decorated, air-conditioned, and have a private balcony.

Prices: Set lunch €30 and dinner €55. Main course from €25. House wine €15.
Hours: 13.00-15.00. 18.00-22.00. 15.00-21.00 on Sunday. Closed Saturday and Sunday lunch and 24-26 December.
Rooms: 10 en suite. Double room from €220, single from €175.
Cuisine: Modern Irish.
Other Points: No-smoking area. Garden. Children welcome. Car park.
Directions: Take Longford/Cavan exit (N55) off the main Dublin-Galway road (N6). After three miles, fork left at the Dog and Duck pub. Lodge one mile on left. (Map 18, F5)

Gallery 29 Cafe

16 Oliver Plunkett Street,
Mullingar, Co Westmeath
Telephone: +353(0)44 49449
corbetstown@eircom.net

The building dates from the 19th century, and restoration has retained the original façade with the interior refurbished and extended to incorporate a 50 seater cafe whilst featuring much of the early architectural elements. It is decorated in muted tomes, complemented by old wooden furniture. Sisters Ann and Emily Gray's philosophy is "to source the highest quality fresh raw materials to create good honest food cooked with passion and attention to detail." Free range eggs, meats, poultry, and organic fruit and vegetables are sourced from local producers and the seasonal, but not overly elaborate menu changes weekly. Breakfast opens proceedings with the likes of baked potato cake with tomato and crispy bacon, or pancakes with lemon and sugar. Lunch brings daily specials and fillet of Irish chicken stuffed with roast peppers on a tangy Thai green curry sauce and served with baked potato, herb butter and house salad, as well as freshly baked focaccia bread filled with tandoori chicken, or Mediterranean vegetables. Scones, breads, cakes and tarts are house specialities. For dinner there could be seared medallions of monkfish in a creamy Pernod and dill sauce, or Barbary duck breast in sesame crumb with a zesty Thai dressing.

Prices: Set lunch €18. Set dinner €22. Main course restaurant from €9. Main course snack from €7. House wine €15.
Hours: 12.00-16.00. 19.00-21.00. Closed Sunday and Monday, 25 December - 7 January. Breakfast served: 09.00-12.00.
Cuisine: Modern Irish with European/Asian twist.
Other Points: No-smoking area. Children welcome. Air-conditioning.
Directions: Take any of the three exits from the Mullingar by pass to the town centre. Gallery 29 Cafe is about 50 yards from the Market Square on the main street. (Map 18, F5)

An Tintain Restaurant

Main Street, Multyfarnham, Co Westmeath
Telephone: +353 (0)44 71411
antintain@ireland.com

Jack and Caroline Sleator have settled into this single storey, granite-stone building just off the road linking Dublin with the west. Aided by chef Mervyn O'Connor, they have created a real gem of a restaurant with rooms. An Tintain is Gaelic for homestead or fireside, and an open fire burning in a granite stone fireplace greets everyone on arrival. There's a traditional feel to the place, in keeping with the beamed ceilings, but the kitchen has a more modern approach. The midlands is meat country and superb fillet of Irish beef comes with basil mash and confit tomato, while medallions of pork are stuffed with mixed herbs and served with pan-fried apple sauce. However, fish is delivered daily, and seafood chowder or seafood pot au feu could open a meal. The wine list is a good value collection from around the world, offering fair drinking at fair prices. Eight en suite bedrooms are to the rear of the restaurant, all furnished in pine with every amenity. The ancient village of Multyfarnham is the site of a 13th century Franciscan friary - only the church remains, but is well worth a visit.

Prices: Set lunch €22. Set dinner €32. Main course from €16. House wine €17.
Hours: 18.00-21.30, Wednesday-Saturday. 12.30-15.30 Sunday. Closed Monday and Tuesday.
Rooms: 8 en suite. Single from €45, double from €70, family room €85.
Cuisine: Global.
Other Points: No-smoking area. Children welcome. Garden. Car park.
Directions: Nearest town is Mullingar, take the N4 to Sligo. (Map 18, F5)

Monfin House

St John's, Enniscorthy, Co Wexford
Telephone: +353 (0)54 38582
info@monfinhouse.com
www.monfinhouse.com

Monfin House, a classically proportioned late Georgian house surrounded by gardens, is situated on the outskirts of town. Chris and Avril Stewart have put a lot of hard work into refurbishment, capturing the spirit and character of the house, yet offering a very comfortable, relaxed environment. This is the place for those looking for peace and tranquillity. Two of the four bedrooms have four-poster beds, and bathrooms come with either antique baths or modern whirlpools. Bathrobes are supplied and attention to detail runs to good quality crisp cotton sheets. Breakfast, and dinner on request, is served at a magnificent highly polished table in the traditional, Georgian-style dining room which features a sparkling cut-glass chandelier and an open fire. Particular attention is paid to using local and organic produce where possible and a typical, no choice dinner could open with fresh crab claws in a cream and Parmesan sauce. Main course of, say, roast breast of cornfed chicken with a mustard sauce could be accompanied by broccoli, green beans and honeyed turnips, with raspberry meringue roulade and a selection of cheeses to finish. There's good drinking to be had on the reasonably priced wine list.

Prices: B&B. Dinner by prior arrangement. Set dinner €35. House wine €18.
Hours: Closed Christmas.
Rooms: 4 en suite. Double room from €130, single from €65.
Cuisine: Irish.
Other Points: No-smoking in bedrooms. Children welcome over eight years old. Garden. Car park.
Directions: Outside Enniscorthy town. Follow the main road to New Ross, take the first left after the grain mill. Monfin House is approximately half a mile up the road on the right hand side. (Map 20, C7)

Kennedy's Bar and Martha's Vineyard Restaurant

5 South Quay, New Ross, Co Wexford
Telephone: +353 51 425188
kennedysbar@eircom.net
kennedyspub.com

Kennedy's Bar, opened in 2002 by Richard Rice and Barry Kent, is named after the most celebrated Irish American of them all. President John F Kennedy stood on this quay during his visit in 1963 and legend has it that the grandfather of the Kennedy clan partook of his last pint of Guinness in this very pub before setting sail from New Ross Quay for the New World. A speciality restaurant, Martha's Vineyard, serving seafood fresh from Duncannon Pier now shares the site, while Kennedy's menu ploughs a more traditional furrow. You will, of course, still find seafood chowder with toasted pine nuts, in company of such pub favourites as bacon and cabbage, traditional sausages with colcannon and red onion gravy, and beef and Guinness pie. But a touch of modernity has now arrived in the shape of Cajun chicken wraps and suchlike. Upstairs in Martha's Vineyard, choose from black mussels with tomatoes, bacon and cream or crab claws in garlic and lime butter to start, and follow with roast rack of lamb with honey and herb crust and a red wine jus, or warm seafood platter.

Prices: Main course restaurant meal from €21. Main course bar meal from €6.50. House wine €18.
Hours: 12.00-21.45.
Closed Good Friday and 25 December.
Cuisine: Contemporary Irish.
Other Points: No-smoking area. No dogs. Children welcome. Car park.
Directions: N25. Follow all signs to Dunbrody Famine Ship, the bar is directly across the road. (Map 20, C6)

Kelly's Resort Hotel

Rosslare, Co Wexford
Telephone: +353(0)53 32114
kellyhot@iol.ie
www.kellys.ie

The first hotel in Ireland to offer all-inclusive holidays is a place with packages sold mainly on a weekly basis. But, in recent years, shorter stays have become available. Established as a hotel in 1895, Kelly's is situated on five miles of sandy beaches in an area famed for enjoying the best of Ireland's variable weather. Should that fail, however, the Aqua Club, with its sauna, outdoor Canadian hot tub, and two swimming pools, is one of the country's most exclusive leisure developments. Paintings by Ireland's leading artists adorn the walls of public rooms, the main bar has a big, open log fire, the Ivy Room has dancing to live music, and there is a resident's lounge, reading room, and card room. Jim Aherne heads the kitchen, delivering a menu that's built around prime raw materials, including locally grown vegetables, fish from Kilmore Quay, Wexford Beef, and the hotel's own lamb. A typical meal could begin with Clarenbridge mussels in Chablis sauce, go on to pan-fried medallions of Kilmore monkfish with fennel, and finish with summer berry and almond cream flan. The bistro provides more casual meals. The wine list is an impressive collection from France, but other wine producing regions are covered.

Prices: Set lunch €25. Set dinner €39. Main course bar/snack from €5. Main course restaurant meal from €17 dinner/€13 lunch. House wine €20.
Hours: 13.00-14.00. 19.30-21.00. Closed 7 December to 20 February.
Rooms: 99 en suite. Double room from €66, single from €76.
Cuisine: Irish, French and Italian.
Other Points: Totally no smoking. Children welcome. Garden. Car park.
Directions: Follow the N25 from Rosslare Europort turning off at the sign for Rosslare Strand. The hotel is located in the

The Centenary Stores

Charlotte Street, Wexford, Co Wexford
Telephone: +353(0)53 24424

Popularly known as 'The Stores' by the locals, this cavernous pub and dining venue dates from 1898 when it opened on the centenary of the 1798 Irish Rebellion. It stands solidly on the waterfront and remains monumentally unaltered, though within there is nothing dated about its modern layout and up-to-date food. While local fish and meats, bakery, and dairy products are the mainstay of the menus, their interpretation leans towards wraps of sesame chicken, tuna and sweetcorn on warm focaccia, and bowls of Caesar salad. Daily special dishes include the inevitable fish chowder, honey and mustard baked bacon with apple and onion fritters, and four-cheese fritters with bacon-and-onion chutney, followed perhaps by bread and butter pudding. Much is made of the coffee selection with tasting notes. This is a hugely popular meeting place, the service is supremely efficient and the staff extremely helpful; note that lunchtimes are always very busy. Traditional Irish music sessions are every Sunday from 12.30-2.30pm; also on Wednesday nights between May and September from 9.30pm.

Prices: Main course from €8.45. House wine €16.50.
Hours: From 10.00. Closed Sunday, Good Friday and 25 December.
Food served: 10.00-18.00.
Cuisine: Modern European and Irish.
Other Points: Garden. Children welcome.
Directions: N25. (Map 20, D7)

Heavens Above the Sky and the Ground

112/113 South Main Street, Wexford, Co Wexford
Telephone: +353(0)53 21273

On entering this charming pub the decor of wooden floors, tables, benches and the wealth of traditional pub memorabilia makes you feel as if you have stepped back in time. But this is a popular and stylish speciality bar whose evening attraction is the regular ceilidhs featuring traditional Irish music. More liquid claims to fame include a beer menu of bottles from around the world, such as Indian Cobra, Mexican Corona, and Budvar and Staropramen from the Czech Republic. Irish ale aficionados will take delight in sampling their own bottled O'Hara's, Curim and Moling. The restaurant, Heaven's Above, opens in the evenings and is not short on speciality suppliers of its own: Jimmy Meyler for fish; Richie Doyle the butcher, Fanci Fungi of Wexford, and so on. Such prime ingredients are put to good use in the nightly menus. These might include smoked haddock and crabmeat fishcake, venison with aubergines and a light sage jus, or Atlantic cod with saffron beurre blanc. As an added bonus, diners can choose their wine from a range of over 300 different types in the Sky and the Ground wine shop and bring it into the restaurant with no additional charge for corkage.

Prices: Set lunch €15. Set dinner €29. Main course restaurant from €13.95. House wine €15.
Hours: Open and food served: 12.30-15.00. 17.00-22.00. Sunday 16.00-21.00. Only open for lunch during July and August and during the Wexford Opera Festival. Closed Good Friday, 25-26 December.
Cuisine: Modern Irish.
Other Points: No-smoking area. Garden. Children welcome. Private function room, wine shop and off license.
Directions: In the centre of Wexford. (Map 20, D7)

Westgate Design

28a North Main Street, Wexford, Co Wexford
Telephone: +353(0)53 23787
keith@westgatedesign.ie

The Jordan family's craft shop and daytime restaurant is located on Wexford's main shopping thoroughfare and sells a wide range of designer craftware, including pottery, furniture, jewellery, and leather goods. On the ground floor is a two-tiered self-service restaurant, sporting a balcony effect and very bright and airy décor, where freshly cooked foods and up to 20 fresh salads are displayed on huge counters. Blackboard menus list the day's specials, perhaps monkfish skewers, or bacon and cabbage, and an Irish breakfast is served all day. There's also a selection of sandwiches, baps and panninis, and lots of homemade cakes and puddings, including bannoffi pie, pear tart and carrot cake. There's a relaxed atmosphere, but lunchtime is particularly busy.

Prices: Main course restaurant from €8. House wine €15.
Hours: 09.00-18.00. Closed Sunday
Cuisine: Traditional Irish.
Other Points: No-smoking area. Dogs welcome. Children welcome.
Directions: On the main street in Wexford. (Map 20, D7)

Avoca Café at The Old Mill, Avoca Village

The Old Mill, Avoca, Co Wicklow
Telephone: +353(0)402 35105
info@avoca.ie
www.avoca.ie

This is where Avoca Handweavers originated. Owned and run by the Pratt family, it is well known for its beautifully woven clothing and accessories. Much of the fabric seen in this, and all the other Avoca stores, is woven here at the restored mill. The mill itself dates from 1723 and is the oldest working mill in Ireland. Visitors are welcome to see the whole weaving process first hand by touring the mill and admission is free. There is also a self-service café which, like all the Avoca cafés, provides a wide selection of straightforward food and homemade desserts. Hot dishes change daily but could include vegetarian frittata, spinach and pine nut quiche, and chorizo and mozzarella pizza. The cold menu runs to oak-smoked trout, sweet chilli salmon, and chicken breast with sesame seeds or barbecued, all served with a selection of salads. There's also a Weaver's Lunch which is particular to this café only, consisting of three Irish cheeses, homemade soup and homemade brown bread. There is also a short selection of wine in quarter, half and full bottles together with a selection of juices and flavoured waters. And all the famous desserts are homemade.

Prices: Main course restaurant from €9. House wine €18.
Hours: 09.30-17.00.
Closed 25-26 December.
Cuisine: Traditional and Modern Irish with International influences.
Other Points: No-smoking area. Dogs welcome. Garden. Children welcome. Car park. Historic working mill.
Directions: N11. Turn off the N11 at Rathnew and follow the signs to Avoca. (Map 20, B7)

Barracuda Steak and Seafood Restaurant

Strand Road, Bray Seafront, Bray, Co Wicklow
Telephone: +353(0)1 276 5686
barracuda@eircom.net
www.barracuda.ie

Situated on the seafront, above the National Aquarium this steak and seafood restaurant delivers a menu that's a familiar run through some classic favourites. However, on the ground floor, is a lovely contemporary lounge area with comfortable seating; the restaurant is above. Smoked salmon cornets are filled with crab meat and jumbo prawns and served with a chive and lemon cream, crab cakes are spiced, deep-fried and served with salsa. Main courses bring a Dover sole meunière, served on the bone with dauphinoise potatoes, or there's tempura of cod with steak fries and tartare sauce. Meat options include five ways with steaks, including surf and turf, or there could be honey-glazed Barbary duck with honey and orange sauce and creamy mash, and Cajun chicken with a spicy cream sauce. A popular brunch is served at weekends with Caesar salad, eggs Benedict and a joint of the day. The wine list runs to some three dozen keenly priced bins, all available by the glass.

Prices: Set lunch between €19-€21. Set dinner €21. Main course restaurant from €19.25. Main course bar/snack from €6. House wine €19.
Hours: 12.00-15.00. 17.00-23.00.
Closed Good Friday, 25-26 December.
Cuisine: Steak and Seafood.
Other Points: No-smoking ara. Children welcome. Car park. Sun terrace.
Directions: (Map 20, B8)

Powerscourt Terrace Café

Powerscourt House and Gardens, Enniskerry, Co Wicklow
Telephone: +353(0)1 204 6066
www.avoca.ie

Powerscourt House and Gardens is situated 12 miles south of Dublin and is one of the world's great gardens, stretching over 47 acres. The Powerscourt Terrace Café, owned by the Pratt family of Avoca Handweavers, is located in the 18th century Palladian house overlooking the magnificent gardens and fountains. The bright, airy café is self-service and extends to a large outdoor eating area that's immensely popular in summer. The menu changes daily and might include hot dishes such as Mediterranean lamb, beef and orange casserole, salmon and asparagus encroute, sweet potato and ham tart, nut and lentil loaf, and chicken curry filo. The selection of cold dishes takes in home baked ham, smoked trout fillet, pork, chicken and apricot terrine and a large selection of salads. An extensive range of homecooked desserts adds up to a difficult choice, but could include lemon tart, strawberry Normandy, strawberry meringue roulade, plus lots of cream cakes and homemade biscuits and scones. There is also a selection of red and white wine in quarter, half or full bottles. The house and gardens are open all year with guided tours and audio-visual presentations available.

Prices: Main course restaurant from €9.50. House wine €18.
Hours: 10.00-17.00, Sunday until 17.30. Closed 25-26 December.
Cuisine: Traditional and Modern Irish.
Other Points: No-smoking area. Children welcome. Outdoor terrace. Car park. Private dining.
Directions: N11. (Map 20, B8)

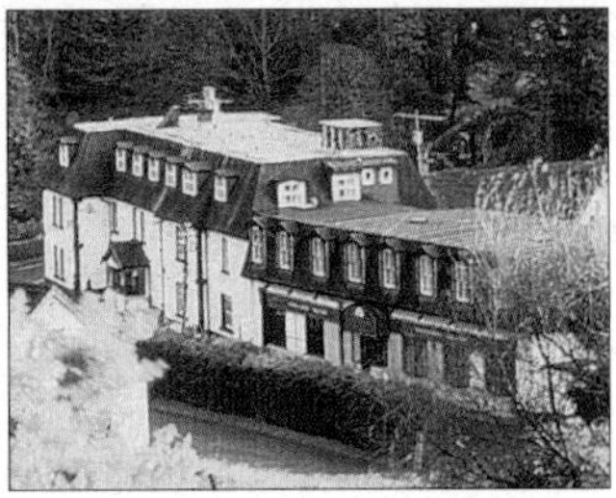

The Glendalough Hotel

Glendalough, Co Wicklow
Telephone: +353(0)404 45135
info@glendaloughhotel.ie
www.glendaloughhotel.com

Situated in the heart of the wooded valley of Glendalough (the Valley of the Two Lakes), this splendid 19th century building has been enlarged and the interior sympathetically restored; it is now a hotel run by the Casey family. Smart en suite bedrooms are spacious, very well maintained, have satellite TV and splendid peaceful views over the surrounding hills. There's a classic Irish pub, the Glandalough Tavern, and the Glendasan River Restaurant makes good use of fresh local produce. Expect starters of grilled St Tola goats' cheese on wheaten bread with tomato and basil pesto, or a rabbit and cognac terrine teamed with citrus fruit salad and Cumberland sauce. Main courses extend to oven roasted Barbary duck breast with baked red cabbage and a raisin and caramel glaze. This is a popular choice for conferences and weddings and Glendalough itself is a popular tourist destination, drawn by the beauty of the area and the remains of an early 6th century monastry. Also, the hotel is close to Avoca, where the BBC series *Ballykissangel* was filmed.

Prices: Set lunch €20 and dinner €35. Main course from €9.95. House wine €16.
Hours: 12.00-15.00. 19.00-21.30. Closed December and January.
Food served: 12.00-15.00. 17.30-20.30.
Rooms: 44 en suite. Rooms from €65 per person.
Cuisine: Ethnic, Irish and Continental.
Other Points: No-smoking area. Children welcome. Garden. Car park. Meeting room.
Directions: From the N11 at Kilmaconague turn right for Roundwood, travel straight for Annamoe, Caragh and into Glendalough. (Map 20, B7)

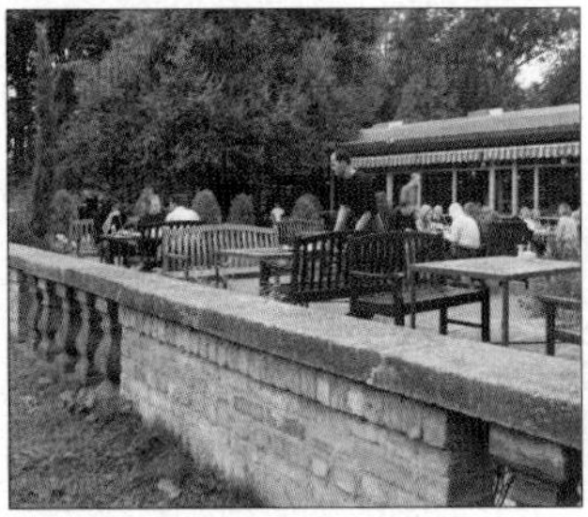

Avoca Terrace Café

Kilmacanogue, Bray, Co Wicklow
Telephone: +353(0)1 286 7466
www.avoca.ie

This store in Kilmacanogue is the flagship of Avoca Handweavers, set in the grounds of the old Jameson (of whiskey fame) Estate, in a lovely setting, with scenic gardens and walkways. The store is located at the gateway to county Wicklow and is a famous stopping off point for visitors to the area. This is an interesting place to visit with much to see and with shopping opportunities in the store, especially for Avoca's beautifully woven fabrics, clothing and accessories, and there is a welcome chance to recuperate in the self-service terrace café with seating in the terrace garden outside. The food here runs to tomato and basil soup, smoked salmon and trout terrine, Avoca fish pie, quiches, pizza, smoked chicken, asparagus and brie melt, sweet chilli salmon and spiced couscous, and homecooked ham. There's a large selection of house salads and the display of desserts is astonishing, ranging from apple pie, and lemon cheesecake, to fresh fruit flans, orange and chocolate cake, and scones.

Prices: Main course restaurant from €9.50. House wine €15.
Hours: 09.30-17.30. Saturday and Sunday 10.00-17.30. Closed 25-26 December.
Cuisine: Traditional and Modern Irish with International influences.
Other Points: No-smoking area. Garden and outdoor terrace. Children welcome. Car park. Craft shop.
Directions: N11. On the N11 signposted before Kilmacanogue village. (Map 20, B8)

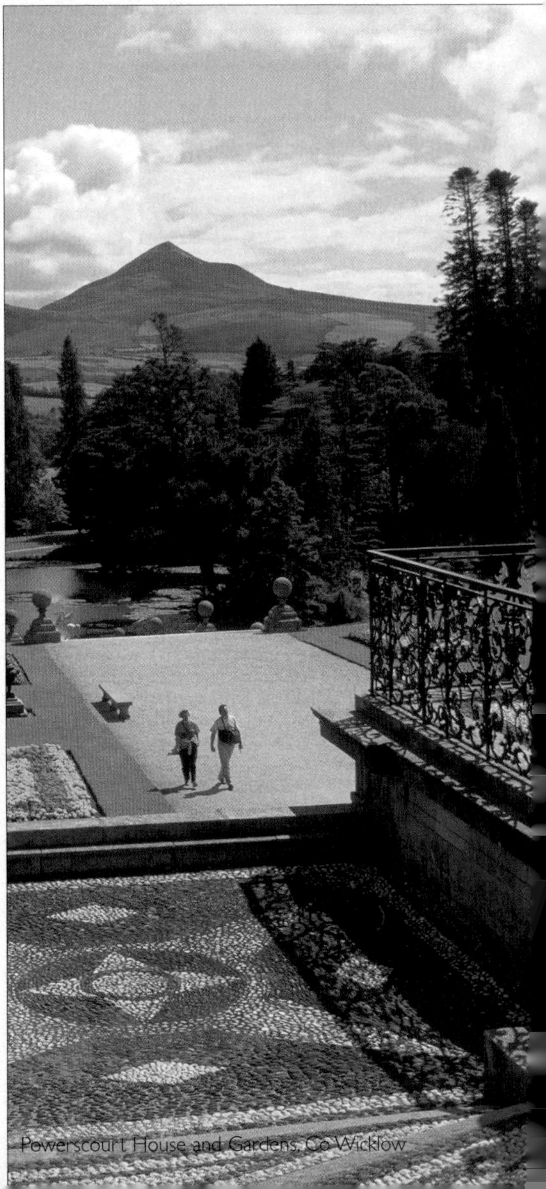

Powerscourt House and Gardens, Co Wicklow

Feasts

39 Dublin Road, Belfast, Co Antrim BT2 7HD
Telephone: +44(0)2890 332787
craignash@compuserve.com

The bright blue exterior canopy, sunny yellow interior walls, and tiled floor are a smart backdrop to this small, bustling, centrally located café and deli, offering modern Italian and British cuisine. A large blackboard lists all day snacks and more substantial lunches - their speciality is pasta and sauces, made on the premises daily and available to mix and match, eat in or take away. Choose your shape, say rigatoni or fusilli, and then add a sauce such as old favourites carbonara or bolognese, or the more imaginative chargrilled artichoke with lemon and cream. Delicious homemade scones and gorgeous crunchy biscotti baked to their own special recipe, along with fresh pastries made daily, are hard to resist, and old-fashioned ginger beer is served as well as a good range of real coffees and smoothies. Running along one wall of the café is the smart deli section with top quality dry goods and a good range of Irish cheeses such as Gubeen and Ardrahan as well as classics of Vignotte and Brie de Meaux. At Christmas, Feasts do a range of excellent bespoke hampers.

Prices: Set lunch £10-15. Main course from £6. Not licensed.
Hours: 09.00-18.00.
Closed Sunday, 25-26 December and for 3 days around 12 July.
Food served: All day. Pasta from 12.00.
Cuisine: Modern Italian and British.
Other Points: No-smoking area. Chldren welcome.
Directions: On the right hand side of Dublin Road going out of Belfast. Opposite Burger King and the UCG Cinema. (Map 18, C8)

Madison's Hotel

59-63 Botanic Avenue, Belfast,
Co Antrim BT7 1JL
Telephone: +44(0)28 90509800
info@madisonshotel.com
www.madisonshotel.com

This hotel, bar, restaurant and nightclub is located on a tree-lined avenue in the heart of Belfast's 'boulevard society'. The exterior has a Parisian art deco feel and within, the lobby, dominated by an oversized designer leather sofa, has a striking deep red colour scheme. There are 35 rooms, accessible by lift, and painted in sunny tones with contrasting blue print fabrics; bathrooms are large. Breakfast offers a vast choice: kippers; smoked salmon and scrambled eggs; bacon and melted cheese croissants; and a big breakfast with soda bread accompanied by a generous cafetière of coffee and complimentary newspapers. The restaurant is modern, bustling and decked out in an eclectic mix of suede and velvet, wrought iron, dark wood, vibrant paint, mosaics and mirrors. Some wonderful huge canvasses by artist, Jessica Levy, hang on the upper walls. Here, the menu is modern and wide ranging with dishes such as chicken Caesar salad with maple bacon, hoi sin duck with Asian greens, and baked darne of salmon with parsley and black pepper crust and hollandaise sitting alongside more traditional steaks. New world wines are modestly priced at under £15. Staff are eager to help and the level of service throughout is faultless.

Prices: Main course from £10.95.
Hours: 12.00-22.00. Closed July 12th.
Rooms: 35 en suite. Double room from £65, single from £50.
Cuisine: Global.
Other Points: No smoking area. Children welcome.
Directions: M2, in to Belfast centre. On Botanic Avenue, just before you get to Queens University. (Map 18, C8)

McHughs Bar and Restaurant

29-31 Queen's Square, Belfast, Co Antrim BT1 3FG
Telephone: +44(0)28 90509999
info@mchughsbar.com
www.mchughsbar.com

Located in a dock area adjacent to the River Lagan, close to the Custom House, under the shadow of the Albert Clock and built between 1710 and 1720, McHughes claims to be the oldest building in Belfast. Now, with its striking red façade and featuring live music at weekends in the below sea level basement bar, it successfully mixes old and new. Some walls expose original brick, others are washed in rust and mustard tones, floors are stone, and tables heavy wood. Large sculptural light fittings adorn the ceilings, colourful works of art from the Terry Bra Collection adorn the walls, and ornate carved wood decorates the staircase. Bar meals (soup and sandwiches) are served throughout the day and an evening menu is served in the 100-seater mezzanine restaurant. Popular wok-fried dishes (chicken and tiger prawn tails with garlic ginger paste and noodles) are backed up by pan-fried duck with parsnip rösti and caramelised beetroot, and braised lamb shank with champ and garlic and mint pesto. Starters run to shellfish risotto, fishcakes with lime and coriander crème fraîche, steamed rope mussels with ginger cream sauce, or goats' cheese and red pepper crostini with balsamic syrup.

Prices: Main course from £6. House wine £9.45.
Hours: 12.00-24.00. 12.00-01.00 on Saturday. Closed 25 December.
Food served: 12.00-15.00. 17.00-22.30 Monday-Friday. Sunday 12.00-21.00. Sunday carvery 12.00-17.00.
Cuisine: Traditional Irish with Oriental influences.
Other Points: Children welcome. 2 function rooms available for hire.
Directions: Beside the Albert Clock and Custom House. (Map 18, C8)

Dunadry Hotel & Country Club

2 Islandreagh Drive, Dunadry,
Co Antrim BT41 2HA
Telephone: +44(0)28 94434343
reservations@mooneyhotelgroup.com
www.mooneyhotelgroup.com

Just a 20-minute drive from central Belfast and very close to the international airport, the intriguing all white building looks modern even though it is converted from the remains of the village that grew up around an 18th century linen mill. The conversion has been sympathetic with original features still intact and all public rooms are very stylish. It makes an impressive hotel complex with fully equipped leisure facilities that run to a state-of-the-art fitness suite, solarium, and indoor swimming pool, all set in 12 acres of woodland. Leading off the reception lobby is a large open-plan bar with a grand wooden-galleried staircase and there is a beamed conservatory set around an inner landscaped garden. Many of the 83 bedrooms overlook the garden: impressively large, especially superior rooms, which have a contemporary feel: pale wood, leather headboards, lilac and grey tones. There are two places to eat, the Linen Mill restaurant and Mill Race bistro. The former offers a sophisticated formal environment, the latter a sleek, modern look for more casual occasions. Here, a typical bistro meal could produce deep fried brie with mango coulis, followed by ginger and lime duck, with profiteroles and hot chocolate sauce to finish.

Prices: Set lunch £15.95. Set dinner £24. House wine £12.50.
Hours: 12.00-14.00. 19.30-22.30. 12.30-14.30 on Sunday. Closed Sunday and Monday evening.
Rooms: 83 en suite. Single from £70, double £90, family room £90.
Cuisine: Traditional and modern Irish.
Other Points: No-smoking area. Children welcome. Garden. Car park.
Directions: Exit 5/M2, turn left and follow main road through Templepatrick. At second roundabout take second exit signed Dunadry. Hotel is one mile on the left. (Map 18, C7)

Shelleven House

61 Princetown Road, Bangor, Co Down BT20 3TA
Telephone: +44(0)2891 271777
shellevenhouse@aol.com
www.shellevenhouse.co.uk

Two large Victorian houses set in landscaped gardens have been converted into a substantial guesthouse that's just five minutes walk from the centre of Bangor. Situated in a leafy conservation area, it has been run for the past four years by the amiable Philip and Mary Weston, who are dab hands at putting the comfort and well being of their guests first. There are eleven simply decorated, tasteful bedrooms. Those located at the front of the house have views of the Irish Sea and all are en-suite with lots of facilities such as Sky TV and telephones. Room four, for example, is large, light and airy with terracotta walls and contrasting floral fabrics and a sea view. Personal touches include pretty prints on the walls, fresh flowers, and a newspaper and magazine ordering service. Substantial breakfasts served in the period dining room include fresh fruit, a choice of soda or wheaten bread, with omelettes, pancakes with golden syrup, lemon and sugar or a traditional Ulster breakfast as the main choice. Dinner is by request. There is private parking in a large car park at the front of the house.

Prices: B&B. Dinner by prior arrangement. Set dinner £20.
Rooms: 11 en suite. Single room from £32, double from £46, family room £62.
Other Points: No-smoking area. Children welcome. Garden. Car park.
Directions: In Bangor turn left at the roundabout info Dufferin Avenue. Continue to the small roundabout and go straight over onto Princetown road. Shelleven House is 100 yards on the left at the end of the terrace set back from the road. (Map 18, C8)

The Old Schoolhouse

100 Ballydrain Road, Comber, Co Down BT23 6EA
Telephone: +44(0)2897 541182
info@theoldschoolhouseinn.com
www.theoldschoolhouseinn.com

Ballydrain Primary School was forced to close in 1985, but it gave Terry and Avril Brown the perfect location for their restaurant with rooms: right next door to Castle Espie (wildlife and wetland centre), and on the shores of Strangford Loch. The ancient fire engine in the front gardens gives an indication of what's inside. All manner of antiques and collectibles, built up over the past eighteen years, fill the two deep burgundy painted rooms. Dinner is served by candlelight, a classic French-influenced repertoire that is built on quality raw materials matched by flavourful sauces, say, roast quail with redcurrant and thyme jus, and fillet steak with peppercorn jus. No attempts are made to keep up with fashion but the food is carefully cooked, with proper attention to flavour and balance. Terry is a friend of Miguel Torres and so many of the famous Torres wines appear on the extensive wine list that is split into old, new, and connoisseur's selections. Each of the twelve clean and simple rooms is named after an American President of Ulster descent. Breakfasts are taken in the small, homely dinning room where large Ulster fry ups are served.

Prices: Set dinner £19.95. House wine from £11.90.
Hours: 19.00-22.00. Monday to Saturday. 12.30-15.00 Sunday.
Rooms: 12 en suite. Double room from £65, single from £45.
Cuisine: French.
Other Points: No-smoking area. Garden. Car park.
Directions: From Comber on the A22 turn left at the Brown sign posts. The Old School House is well signposted; follow the signs for approximately two miles. (Map 18, D8)

ULSTER'S LOUGHS AND LIMESTONE HILLS

From the breathtaking beauty of the Antrim coast to County Fermanagh, a regal landscape of lakes, limestone hills and mountains where the local economy is based on tourism, farming and salmon fishing.
Drive length: 352 miles

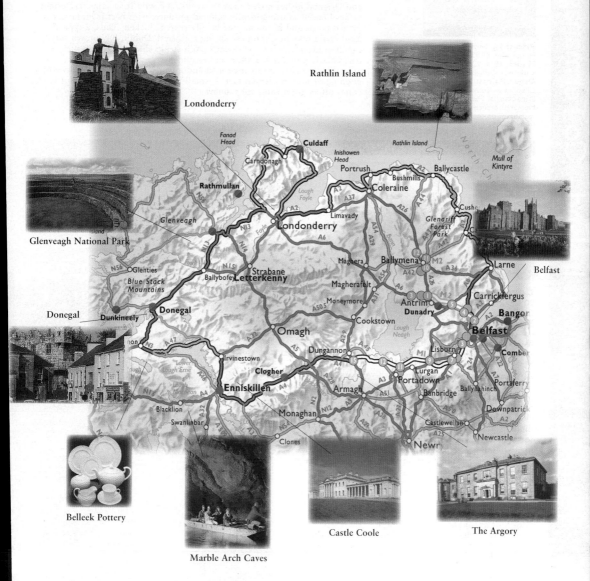

Londonderry

Rathlin Island

Glenveagh National Park

Donegal

Belfast

Belleek Pottery

Marble Arch Caves

Castle Coole

The Argory

● Accommodation/Food

● Accommodation

● Food

🍃 Food Shop

To find the establishments marked here, look up the listing town marked on the map in bold in the town index on page 395

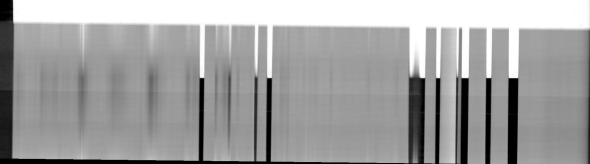

Oscar's Restaurant

29 Belmore Street, Enniskillen, Co Fermanagh BT74 6AA
Telephone: +44(0)28 66327037
www.oscars-restaurant.co.uk

Dermot Magee's art deco-style restaurant reflects the period and flamboyance of local boy Oscar Wilde (educated at Enniskillen's Portora Royal School). Architectural salvage as well as handcrafted furniture have been utilised and the whole place has been painted by a local artist to form a cameo of the life and times of Wilde, including images of the writer and quotations from him and other Irish literary giants. When it comes to food, however, Oscar's Restaurant takes a global view and there certainly is a wide and wonderful choice, with Mexican, Mediterranean and Oriental dishes mixed in with steaks, and wild Irish salmon. Dermot prides himself in using locally sourced produce, with beef from family owned farms and hormone free locally reared chicken. Thus, a typical meal could take in Cantonese spring roll, fresh Dublin Bay prawn salad, Mediterranean chicken, or Oscar's chilli steak; chicken Cordon Bleu is particularly good, and a wide selection of pizzas and pastas is also available. Desserts are own-cooked and might include steamy sticky toffee pudding or luscious lemon tart. A small but well chosen selection of world wines offers good value for money.

Prices: Set dinner £14.99. House wine £9.95.
Hours: 18.00-22.00.
Cuisine: Global.
Other Points: No-smoking area. Children welcome. Car park.
Directions: From the South African War Memorial, branch into Belmore Street; restaurant on the left at the traffic lights. (Map 18, D5)

Corick House

20 Corick Road, Clogher,
Co Tyrone BT76 0BZ
Telephone: +44(0)2885 548216
corickhousehotel@btopenworld.com
www.corickhousehotel.com

Jean Beacom's handsome 17th century William and Mary-style building is surrounded by landscaped gardens. Restoration over the last five years has captured much of the period elegance and the hotel has proved very popular as a wedding venue. Public rooms are filled with stuffed birds in glass cases, longcase clocks, and oriental-style lacquered tables. Of the two dining rooms, the smaller and more intimate is used for breakfast. The large Carleton suite is for more formal dining where the menu offers the traditional (grilled Clogher Valley sirloin steak with brandy cream and peppercorn sauce) and the more adventurous (baked goats' cheese risotto cakes with wintergreens and chilli dressing). A good value set menu is available at the weekend. The wine list, accompanied by a taste guide, is an eclectic mix of old and new world wines with four available by the half bottle. There are a few bedrooms on the ground floor, but the rooms upstairs have the lovely views. Room 202, for example, is decorated in cream tones, has antique furniture and a huge bathroom with striking green tiles and corner bath. Also, visitors have the option of taking a three-bedroom cottage either on a self-catering basis, or as bed and breakfast.

Prices: Set lunch £9.50. Set dinner £16. Main course from £8.95. House wine £9.95.
Hours: 12.30-14.30. 17.00-21.00. Closed Monday and Tuesday.
Rooms: 10 en suite. Double room from £30, single from £45.
Cuisine: Traditional Irish.
Other Points: No-smoking area. Children welcome. Garden. Car park.
Directions: Turn off the main A4 Belfast to Eniskillen road, between the villages of Augher and Clogher on the Corick road turn right. (Map 18, D6)

Bangor, Co Down

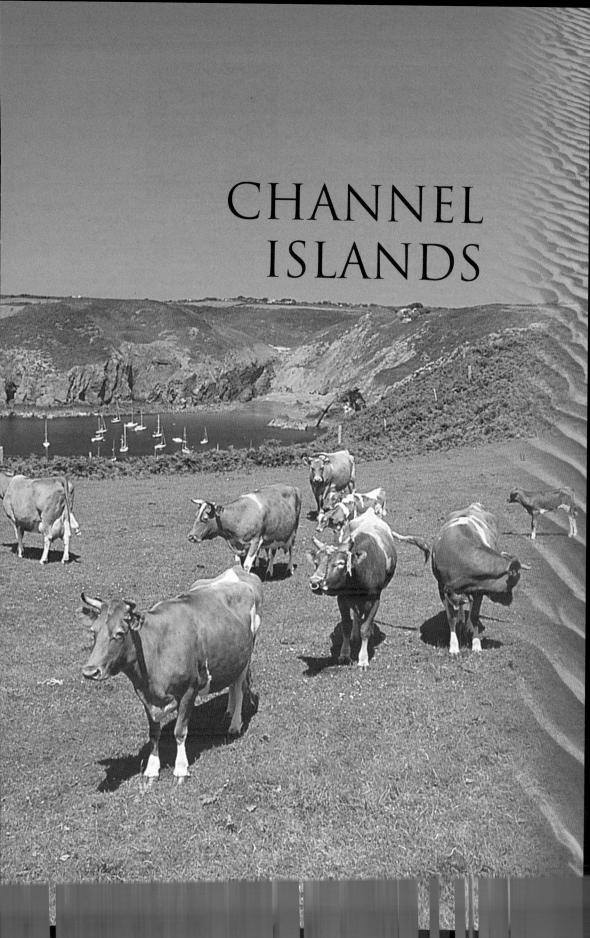

CHANNEL
ISLANDS

White House Hotel

Herm, via Guernsey, Herm GY1 3HR
Telephone: +44(0)1481 722159
hotel@herm-island.com
www.herm-island.com

"Paradise is this close", says the White House's brochure, and indeed at this, the only hotel on the island, there is something for everyone. With no cars on the two kilometres long island, pristine beaches, wonderful walks, birdwatching, a small harbour, pastel cottages, an 11th-century chapel and an inn, it makes an ideal holiday retreat for all the family. The hotel was created from an old house in 1949 by Peter and Jenny Wood and is run today by their daughter and son-in-law. It offers extensive lounges with open fires, a library, games cupboard, solar heated swimming pool, and tennis court. The best bedrooms have sea views and all rooms, by popular demand, have no TV or phones. With oyster beds clearly visible from the dining room windows, local seafood is going to be as fresh as you can get, and local seafood of, say, Guernsey lobsters, crabs or scallops, is available as a supplement to the set evening menu. Or, you could opt for set menu choices of warm pigeon and bacon salad, followed by mains of fillet of beef Rossini. The wine list, mostly pitched below £20, has France to the fore, but finds room for other wine regions of the world.
Prices: Set menu £21.75 (including boat fare). Main course from £6. House wine £9.20.
Hours: The Ship Bar - 09.00-23.00. 12.00-15.00 on Sunday. Closed second week of October to April.
Food served: 12.00-14.00. 19.00-21.00.
Rooms: 40 en suite. £61 per person, half board.
Cuisine: Modern and traditional British and French.
Other Points: No-smoking area. Garden. Children welcome. No cars on Herm Island. Tennis court. Swimming pool. Croquet lawn.
Directions: Fly or take the boat to Guernsey. Regular 20 minute service by boat to Herm Island. (Map 4, E6)

Chateau Valeuse

Rue de la Valeuse, St Brelade's Bay, St Brelade,
Jersey JE3 8EE
Telephone: +44(0)1534 746281
chatval@itl.net
www.user.super.net.uk/~chatval

It really doesn't look like a chateau in the classic French sense, the hotel being more like a splendid Swiss chalet with its large windows and impressive array of balconies and verandas. It is very well situated on the south-facing St Brelade's Bay, set back from the road and surrounded by impeccably maintained gardens. Excellent value bedrooms, some with seaward balconies, are all comfortably furnished, well maintained and have pristine bathrooms. A sun terrace overlooks the garden, and there is a pretty outdoor swimming pool. The restaurant does a very good four-course set menu, perhaps moules marinière, or tiger prawns and mussels in garlic butter, followed by lobster bisque, then chargrilled pork fillets with tarragon and mustard cream or fresh grilled plaice, with pudding chosen from the trolley.
Prices: Set dinner £19 (4 courses). House wine £7.
Hours: 12.30-14.00 (open for bar snacks). 18.30-20.45. Closed to non-residents on Sunday and from November to March.
Rooms: 34 en suite. Rooms from £34 per person including breakfast.
Cuisine: European.
Other Points: No-smoking in restaurant. Children welcome over 5 years. Garden. Car park.
Directions: From the airport take the B4 south towards St Brelade's Bay, then the B6 (La Route de la Baie). Turn left into Rue de la Valeuse; the hotel is on the left. (Map 4, F7)

Best Western Royal Hotel

David Place, St Helier, Jersey JE2 4TD
Telephone: +44(0)1534 726521
royalhot@itl.net
www.royalhoteljersey.com

The Royal Hotel is the oldest established hotel on Jersey (it celebrated its 160th anniversary in 2002) and boasts the largest pillarless ballroom on the Island. Nevertheless, this is a comfortable, centrally located hotel, right in the town centre, within easy walking distance of the business district and shops. Bedrooms have all the expected facilities and public rooms include a stylish bar/brasserie. Here, a set four-course dinner menu offers such dishes as chilled salmon and cod terrine with summer leaves and chilli mayonnaise, apple brandy and tarragon sorbet, braised lamb shank with rosemary mash, confit of cherry tomato and port jus, with raspberry iced parfait with tuille biscuit to finish. The wine list generally keeps prices under £20, perhaps Los Vascos Chardonnay from Chile, or Yalumba Y Series Viognier from Australia. In addition, conference and banqueting facilities are state of the art, amongst the largest available on the Island.

Prices: Main course from £10.50. Main course bar/snack £2.95.
House wine £12.50.
Hours: 11.00-23.00.
Food served: 18.30-21.30.
Rooms: 81 en suite. Double room from £81, single from £50.
Cuisine: English and Continental.
Other Points: Children welcome. Car park.
Directions: From the ferry terminal go along Esplanade, turn left before Grand Hotel, into Rouge Bouillon, Down Midvale Road. (Map 4, F7)

SARK

Prices: Set lunch £19.80. Set dinner
£20.80. House wine £7.50.
Hours: 12.00-14.30. 19.00-21.30.
Closed mid October to Easter.
Rooms: 22 rooms, 12 en suite. Rooms
from £30 to £60 per person.
Cuisine: Modern French.
Other Points: No smoking area. Garden.
Children welcome. Licence for civil
weddings can be arranged.
Directions: Fly to Guernsey and take the
boat to Sark. (Map 4, F6)

La Sablonnerie

Little Sark, Sark GY9 0SD
Telephone: +44 (0)1481 832061

Sark lies a few miles from Guernsey and is reached by boats that run
several times a day. Approximately three-and-a-half miles long and one-
and-a-half miles across at its widest point, there are no cars to disturb the
peace of this stunningly beautiful island. To put visitors inmmediately in
the mood, La Sablonnerie provides a horse-drawn barouche to bring
guests and their luggage from the tiny harbour to Little Sark at the
southernmost tip; it is the ultimate get-away-from-it-all destination.
Owned and run by the Perrée family since 1948, with daughter Elizabeth
firmly at the helm, the heart of the hotel is the low-beamed bar whose
granite walls and massive fireplace hint at the 400-year-old farmhouse
origins. Discreet modernisation has captured the vintage charm, but added
modern comforts to public rooms and individually decorated bedrooms;
surrounded by lovely gardens this is a magical place. It's own farm
ensures that the kitchen is highly self-supporting, supplying meat, fruit,
vegetables and dairy produce, with locally caught lobsters and fish and
shell fish a regular feature on the menu. Dinner begins with canapés in the
bar, followed, perhaps, by baby courgette flowers filled with lobster
mousse with a lemon and thyme jus, then herb soup with Stilton
quenelles, and a lasagne of brill and savoy cabbage filled with ginger
butter on a langoustine sauce, with almond mousse and poached pears

Brighton Seafront, East Sussex

LE CHÂTEAU DE
GRAND-RULLECOURT

Patrice de Saulieu, owner of Les Routiers, France, has opened his restored château as a bed and breakfast with six highly individual bedrooms to choose from. Surrounded by parkland, the Château de Grand-Rullecourt is just 20 minutes away from Arras in the Pas de Calais, or an hour and a half drive from either Paris or Calais by motorway.

Tea or coffee is offered on arrival, reservations can be made for you in good near-by restaurants, and a pre-prandial drink offered before leaving for dinner. Or take advantage of the various lounges to settle down for a game of cards, chess or conversation. If you wish to stay longer hunting, fishing, gliding, golf and tennis are all available 15 minutes from Grand-Rullecourt.

Le Château de Grand-Rullecourt, 62810 Avesnes le Comte, France
Telephone: +33(0)1 221 58 06 37/+33(0)1 41 27 97 37
Fax: +33(0)1 41 27 97 30

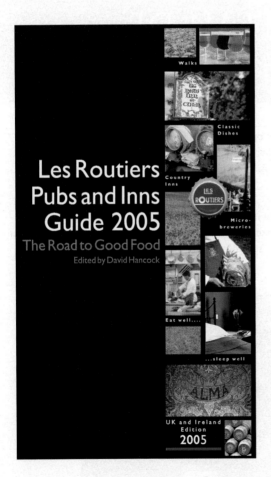

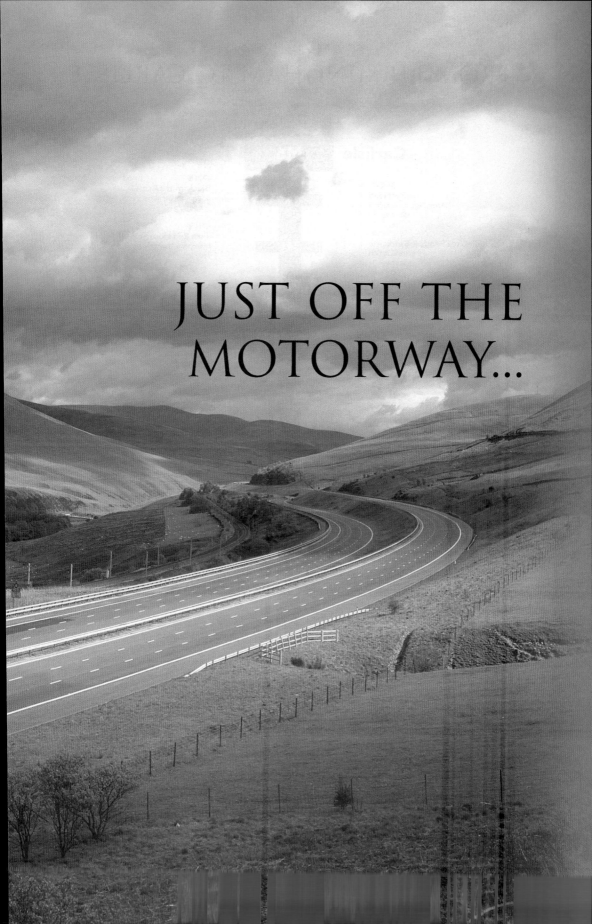

JUST OFF THE MOTORWAY...

idcote Gardens, Gloucestershire

A-Z by Establishment Name

10 Manchester Street, London 23
101 Talbot Restaurant, Dublin City, Co Dublin 328
40a Heriot Row, Edinburgh 255
63 Tay Street Restaurant, Perth, Perth 275
A Room in the Town, Edinburgh 255
A Room in the West End and Teuchters Bar, Edinburgh 257
Abbey Inn, Coxwold, North Yorkshire 224
Abbeyglen Castle, Clifden, Co Galway 332
Adria Hotel, London 37
Aladdin's Indian Brasserie, Tiddington, Warwickshire 211
Alford Arms, Berkhamsted, Hertfordshire 128
Allerston Manor House, Thornton le Dale, North Yorkshire 242
Allt-nan-Ros, Onich, Highland 272
Allt-yr-Ynys Hotel, Walterstone, Herefordshire 127
Alma Tavern, London 32
Almeida Restaurant and Bar, London 29
Altnaharra Hotel, Altnaharra, Highland 266
Ambassador Hotel, Llandudno, Conwy 293
Amsterdam Hotel, London 33
An Sugan Seafood Restaurant, Clonakilty, Co Cork 311
An Tintain Restaurant, Multyfarnham, Co Westmeath 346
Anchor Inn, Barcombe, East Sussex 197
Anchor Inn, Ely, Cambridgeshire 51
Anchorage House Guest Lodge, St Austell, Cornwall 66
Angel, Skipton, North Yorkshire 241
Angel, Hindon, Wiltshire 215
Angel Brasserie, Burford, Oxfordshire 166
Angel Coaching Inn, Warminster, Wiltshire 219
Angel Inn, Stoke-by-Nayland, Suffolk 195
Applecross Inn, Applecross, Highland 268
Appletree Country Inn, Marton, North Yorkshire 233
Ardardan Estate Farm Shop & Nursery, Cardross, Argyll & Bute 251
Ardmore Country House Hotel & Restaurant, Westport, Co Mayo 341
Ariel House, Dublin City, Co Dublin 321
Arlington Lodge Country House Hotel, Waterford City, Co Waterford 344
Art Lovers' Café, Glasgow, Glasgow 263
Ascot House, Harrogate, North Yorkshire 228
Ashlee Lodge, Blarney, Co Cork 311
Assaggi, London 37
Assheton Arms, Downham, Lancashire 139
Auberge Asterisk, St Austell, Cornwall 67
Auchen Castle Hotel and Restaurant, Beattock, Dumfries and Galloway 253
Austwick Traddock, Austwick, North Yorkshire 223
Avoca Cafe, Dublin City, Co Dublin 321
Avoca Cafe, Molls Gap, Co Kerry 338
Avoca Cafe at the Old Mill, Avoca Village, Co Wicklow 349
Avoca Terrace Cafe, Kilmacanogue, Co Wicklow 350
Axis Mundi, Waterford City, Co Waterford 321
Aynsome Manor Hotel, Cartmel, Cumbria 75
Bakers Arms, Thorpe Langton, Leicestershire 144
Bakers Arms, Somerford Keynes, Gloucestershire 114
Balcary Bay Hotel, Castle Douglas, Dumfries and Galloway 253
Baltic, London 32
Banff Springs Hotel, Banff, Aberdeenshire 250
Barleycorn Inn, Marlborough, Wiltshire 216
Barn Yard, Upchurch, Sittingbourne, Kent 137
Barracuda Steak and Seafood Restaurant, Bray, Co Wicklow 349
Barratts Restaurant at Ty'n Rhyl, Rhyl, Denbighshire 294
Barrowville Town House, Carlow Town, Co Carlow 306
Barrtra Seafood Restaurant , Lahinch, Co Clare 310
Bay Hotel, Coverack, Cornwall 62
Beams Restaurant, Carlow Town, Co Carlow 306
Bear Hotel, Crickhowell, Powys 301
Beaufield Mews Restaurant, Gardens and Antiques, Dublin City, Co Dublin 322
Beaufort Arms Coaching Inn and Restaurant, Raglan, Monmouthshire 298
Beaufort Hotel, Chepstow, Monmouthshire 296
Beechwood Hotel, North Walsham, Norfolk 153
Bell, Ramsbury, Wiltshire 217
Bell at Sapperton, Cirencester, Gloucestershire 110
Bell at Skenfrith, Skenfrith, Monmouthshire 298
Bell Inn, Benington, Hertfordshire 127
Bell Inn, East Langton, Leicestershire 142
Bell Inn, Walberswick, Suffolk 195
Bell Inn & Hill House, Horndon-on-the-Hill, Essex 106
Bella Cuba Restaurant, Dublin City, Co Dublin 322
Benleva Hotel, Drumnadrochit, Highland 269
Best Western Royal Hotel, St Helier, Jersey 356
Bewley's Café, Dublin City, Co Dublin 322
Bewley's Oriental Café, Dublin City, Co Dublin 324
Biggin Hall Country House Hotel, Biggin, Derbyshire 91
Bird on the Rock Tearoom, Clungunford, Shropshire 176
Bistro, Barmouth, Gwynedd 294
Black Bear Restaurant and Inn, Betws Newydd, Monmouthshire 294
Black Boy Inn, Hungarton, Leicestershire 143
Black Bull, Coniston, Cumbria 77
Black Bull Inn, Lowick, Northumberland 161
Black Bull Inn, Escrick, North Yorkshire 226
Black Buoy Inn, Wivenhoe, Essex 107
Black Sheep Brewery, Masham, North Yorkshire 233
Blackmore Farm, Cannington, Somerset 180
Blacksmiths Arms, Talkin, Cumbria 74
Blacksmiths Arms, Broughton in Furness, Cumbria 74
Blagdon Manor, Holsworthy, Devon 96
Blairs Inn, Blarney, Co Cork 311
Blue Anchor, Aberthaw, Vale of Glamorgan 302
Blue Lion, Leyburn, North Yorkshire 231
Blue Parrot Cantina, Edinburgh 257
Blue Plate Cafe, Northampton, Northamptonshire 157
Boars Head Hotel, Harrogate, North Yorkshire 228
Boat Inn, Wrexham, Wrexham 303
Bodrugan Barton, St Austell, Cornwall 67
Boot Inn, Lapworth, Warwickshire 210
Botticelli Restaurant, Dublin City, Co Dublin 324
Bowlish House , Shepton Mallet, Somerset 185
Brackenrigg Inn, Ullswater, Cumbria 86
Brae Guest House, Ullapool, Highland 273
Brasserie 10/16, Chester, Cheshire 55
Brewery Bar, Dublin City, Co Dublin 324
Bridge Hotel, Buttermere, Cumbria 75
Bridge House Bar and Dining Room, London 32
Bridge of Cally Hotel, Bridge of Cally, Perth & Kinross 280
Britannia Spice, Edinburgh 257
Brockbushes Fruit Farm, Corbridge, Northumberland 162
Broom Hall Country Hotel, Saham Toney, Norfolk 154
Brough House, Forres, Moray 275
Brown and Forrest Smokery Restaurant, Langport, Somerset 182
Brownlow Arms, Caldwell, North Yorkshire 224
Bryce's, Ockley, Surrey 196
Bull Inn, Charlbury, Oxfordshire 167
Bull's Head and Stables Bistro, London 33
Bunk Inn, Newbury, Berkshire 44
Burlton Inn, Burlton, Shropshire 176
Burnmoor Inn, Eskdale, Cumbria 78
Burnt House Farm, Shepton Mallet, Somerset 185
Bush Inn, Ovington, Hampshire 118
Buskers, Wadebridge, Cornwall 71
Butchers Arms, Painswick, Gloucestershire 113
Byrne's Mal Dua House, Clifden, Co Galway 332
Cabinet Free House and Restaurant, Reed, Hertfordshire 128
Cadgwith Cove Inn, The Lizard, Cornwall 70
Cafe Bagatelle, London 23
Café in the Crypt, London 23
Cafe Paradiso, Cork City, Co Cork 312
Cafe Provencal, Edinburgh 258
Cafe Royal Circle Bar and Oyster Bar Restaurant, Edinburgh 258
Cafe Saffron, Knowle, Warwickshire 209
Café Sol, Kilkenny, Co Kilkenny 338
Caffé Mamma, London 33
Cahernane House Hotel, Killarney, Co Kerry 336
Campions Dining Rooms and Bar, Samlesbury, Lancashire 141
Caragh Lodge, Killorglin, Co Kerry 337
Carpenters Arms, Sherston, Wiltshire 218
Carved Angel, Earls Colne, Essex 105
Carved Angel Cafe, Exeter, Devon 96
Castle Grove Country House, Letterkenny, Co Donegal 320
Castle Murray House Hotel, Dunkineely, Co Donegal 320
Castletown Farm Shop, Rockcliffe, Cumbria 84
Cave, Dublin City, Co Dublin 325
Caviston's Food Emporium, Dun Laoghaire, Co Dublin 329
Centenary Stores, Wexford Town, Co Wexford 348
Charles Bathurst Inn, Arkengarthdale, North Yorkshire 222
Charlotte's Tea House, Truro, Cornwall 70
Chateau Valeuse, St Brelade, Jersey 356
Chatsworth Farm Shop, Pilsley, Bakewell, Derbyshire 92
Chequers, Chipping Norton, Oxfordshire 168
Chequers Inn, Smarden, Kent 136
Chequers Inn, Beaconsfield, Buckinghamshire 47
Cherington Arms, Cherington, Warwickshire 208
Cherry House Restaurant, Werrington, Cambridgeshire 54
Cherry Tree Restaurant, Killaloe, Co Clare 309
Chetwode Arms, Warrington, Cheshire 59
Cholmondeley Arms, Cholmondeley, Cheshire 56
Church Farm Organics, Thurstaston, Wirral, Cheshire 59
City Merchant, Glasgow, Glasgow 263
Claris's Tea Room, Biddenden, Kent 130
Clocktower Tearooms, Sidmouth, Devon 97
Clow Beck House, Darlington, Co Durham 60
Coach House Coffee Shop, Luss, Argyll & Bute 252
Cock Inn, Wishaw, West Midlands 214
Cock Pub and Restaurant, Hemingford Grey, Cambridgeshire 51

Comar Lodge, Cannich, Highland 269
Compasses Inn, Tisbury, Wiltshire 219
Conservatory, Callander, Perth & Kinross 280
Cookhouse, Ludlow, Shropshire 177
Coolclogher House, Killarney, Co Kerry 336
Coopers Arms, London 35
Corick House, Clogher, Co Tyrone 354
Cornucopia, Dublin City, Co Dublin 325
Corporation Arms, Longridge, Lancashire 140
Corse Lawn House Hotel, Tewkesbury, Gloucestershire 115
Cosses Country House, Ballantrae, South Ayrshire 253
Cotswold Lodge Hotel, Oxford, Oxfordshire 172
Cottage Inn, Alnwick, Northumberland 158
Cottage Restaurant, Polperro, Cornwall 65
County, Darlington, Co Durham 60
Court Hotel, Chillcompton, Bath and NE Somerset 42
Courtyard Restaurant, Harrogate, North Yorkshire 229
Crab & Lobster Inn, Benbridge, Isle of Wight 129
Crabmill, Preston Bagot, Warwickshire 210
Craigadam, Castle Douglas, Dumfries and Galloway 254
Craw Inn, Auchencrow, Scottish Borders 284
Cricketers, Clavering, Essex 104
Cridford Inn, Trusham, Devon 99
Crockets on the Quay, Ballina, Co Mayo 340
Crook Inn, Tweedsmuir, Scottish Borders 285
Crooked Billet, Stoke Row, Oxfordshire 173
Crooked Billet, Milton Keynes, Buckinghamshire 49
Croom Mills, Croom, Co Limerick 339
Crown, Great Ouseburn, North Yorkshire 227
Crown, London 27
Crown, Southwold, Suffolk 194
Crown and Castle, Orford, Suffolk 194
Crown and Goose, London 30
Crown and Sandys Arms, Ombersley, Worcestershire 220
Crown and Trumpet Inn, Broadway, Worcestershire 219
Crown at Hopton, Hopton Wafers, Shropshire 177
Crown at Wells and Anton's Bistrot, Wells, Somerset 187
Crown Hotel, Exford, Somerset 182
Cruzzo Restaurant, Malahide, Co Dublin 330
Dalesman Country Inn, Sedbergh, Cumbria 84
Daniel's Bistro, Edinburgh 258
De Greys, Ludlow, Shropshire 177
Dèdés Hotel and Wheel Inn, Ilfracombe, Devon 96
Dering Arms, Pluckley, Kent 136
Devonshire Arms, Beeley, Derbyshire 91
Devonshire Fell, Burnsall, North Yorkshire 224
Dimitris, Hale, Cheshire 56
Dimitris Mediterranean Restaurant and Tapas Bar, Leeds, West Yorkshire 245
Dimitris Tapas Bar and Taverna, Manchester 145
Dog Inn, Over Peover, Cheshire 58
Douglas Hide, Cork City, Co Cork 312
Downcliffe House Hotel, Filey, North Yorkshire 227
Downhill House Hotel, Ballina, Co Mayo 340
Doyles Seafood Restaurant and Townhouse, Dingle, Co Kerry 334
Drapers Arms, London 29
Drapers Café-Bar, St Asaph, Denbighshire 295
Drunken Duck Inn, Ambleside, Cumbria 72
Duck's at le Marche Noir, Edinburgh 259
Duke of Cambridge, London 29
Duke of Cumberland, Midhurst, West Sussex 206
Duke William, Canterbury, Kent 132
Dukes Head, Armathwaite, Cumbria 73
Dunadry Hotel and Country Club, Dunadry, Co Antrim 352
Dundas Arms, Kintbury, Berkshire 43
Dunkerley's of Deal Restaurant, Deal, Kent 134
Dunne and Crescenzi, Dublin City, Co Dublin 325
Dunoon Hotel, Llandudno, Conwy 293
Durham Ox, Warwick, Warwickshire 212
Durham Ox, Crayke, North Yorkshire 226
Durleighmarsh Farm Shop, Durleighmarsh, Petersfield, Hampshire 119
Dusty Miller, Wrenbury, Cheshire 59
Eagle and Child, Stow-on-the-Wold, Gloucestershire 115
Eagle & Child, Staveley, Cumbria 86
Earsham Park Farm, Bungay, Suffolk 192
Earsham Street Café, Bungay, Suffolk 192
Eastern Eye, Bath, Bath and NE Somerset 41
Ebury Wine Bar and Restaurant, London 24
Egan's House, Dublin City, Co Dublin 326
Engineer, London 30
Essington Fruit Farm, Essington, Wolverhampton, Staffordshire 188
Exmoor White Horse Inn, Exford, Somerset 182
Falcon Inn, Oundle, Northamptonshire 158
Falcon Inn, Painswick, Gloucestershire 114
Falkland Arms, Great Tew, Oxfordshire 170
Farmers Arms, Cwmdu, Powys 302
Farmgate Cafe, Cork City, Co Cork 313
Farmgate Restaurant and Country Store, Midleton, Co Cork 317

Fat Lamb Country Inn, Kirkby Stephen, Cumbria 81
Fauhope House, Gattonside, Scottish Borders 284
Feasts, Belfast, Co Antrim 351
Feathers Hotel, Ludlow, Shropshire 178
Feathers Hotel, Woodstock, Oxfordshire 175
Felin Fach Griffin Inn, Brecon, Powys 300
Fighting Cocks, Stottesdon, Shropshire 178
Fish, Abingdon, Oxfordshire 165
Fisherman's Return, Winterton-on-Sea, Norfolk 155
Fishermen's Pier Fish and Chip Van, Tobermory, Argyll & Bute 252
Fitzpatricks Bar & Restaurant, Jenkinstown, Co Louth 340
Five Arrows Hotel, Waddesdon, Buckinghamshire 50
Fleece, Witney, Oxfordshire 174
Floating Bridge Inn, Dartmouth, Devon 95
Flying Horse Inn, Boughton Aluph, Kent 131
Food for Thought, London 24
Forest, Dorridge, West Midlands 213
Fortune's Kippers, Whitby, North Yorkshire 242
Fountain Inn, Tenbury Wells, Worcestershire 221
Fountain Inn and Boxer's Restaurant, Wells, Somerset 187
Fox and Barrel, Tarporley, Cheshire 58
Fox and Goose Inn, Eye, Suffolk 193
Fox and Hounds, Christmas Common, Oxfordshire 168
Fox and Hounds, Pickering, North Yorkshire 234
Fox & Hounds Inn, Great Wolford, Warwickshire 208
Fox Inn, Tangley, Hampshire 124
Fox Inn, Corscombe, Dorset 101
Fox Inn, Lower Oddington, Gloucestershire 113
Foyers Bay House, Loch Ness, Highland 272
Franciscan Well Brew Pub, Cork City, Co Cork 313
Freemasons, Hove, East Sussex 201
Froggies at the Timber Batts, Bodsham, Kent 131
Fruit Garden, Peterston-super-Ely, Cardiff 287
Fung Shing, London 24
Gallery 29 Cafe, Mullingar, Co Westmeath 346
Ganges, Bristol 46
Garden House Hotel, Gretna, Dumfries and Galloway 254
Garrack Hotel & Restaurant, St Ives, Cornwall 69
Garsons Farm, Esher, Surrey 20
Gatchell's Restaurant, Waterford, Co Waterford 345
General Tarleton Inn, Ferrensby, North Yorkshire 227
George, Norton St Philip, Bath and NE Somerset 42
George, Cavendish, Suffolk 193
George and the Dragon, Watton-at-Stone, Hertfordshire 129
George & Dragon, Chichester, West Sussex 202
Georgian Tea Rooms, Bridlington, East Yorkshire 222
Ghyll Manor, Rusper, West Sussex 206
Glangrwyney Court, Crickhowell, Powys 302
Glanrannell Park Country House, Crugybar, Carmarthenshire 287
Gleeson's Townhouse & Restaurant, Roscommon, Co Roscommon 342
Glen Loy Lodge Hotel, Banavie, Highland 268
Glendalough Hotel, Glendalough, Co Wicklow 350
Glenview House, Midleton, Co Cork 317
Golden Grid Fish Restaurant, Scarborough, North Yorkshire 240
Golden Lion, Osmotherley, North Yorkshire 234
Golden Pot, Eversley, Hampshire 117
Gorman's Clifftop House and Restaurant, Dingle Peninsula, Co Kerry 335
Grain Store Restaurant, Edinburgh 259
Grays, Wokingham, Berkshire 46
Great Western Hotel, Newquay, Cornwall 64
Green Dragon, Braintree, Essex 104
Green Dragon, Haddenham, Buckinghamshire 48
Green Man, Cambridge, Cambridgeshire 50
Green Man, Partridge Green, West Sussex 206
Green Welly Stop Restaurant, Tyndrum, Perth & Kinross 282
Greenbank Guest House, Arrochar, Argyll & Bute 250
Greens Restaurant, Witney, Oxfordshire 174
Greyhound, Henley-on-Thames, Oxfordshire 170
Greyhound Inn Hotel, Usk, Monmouthshire 298
Greys, Brighton, East Sussex 198
Griffin Inn, Fletching, East Sussex 201
Griffins Head, Chillenden, Kent 134
Grove Ferry Inn, Canterbury, Kent 132
Gurnards Head Hotel, St Ives, Cornwall 68
Hack & Spade Inn, Richmond, North Yorkshire 239
Hal Pino's, Ennis, Co Clare 308
Half Moon Inn, Kirdford, West Sussex 204
Hampshire Arms, Crondall, Hampshire 116
Hanoi Café, London 27
Harbourmaster Hotel, Aberaeron, Ceredigion 281
Hardwick Inn, Hardwick, Derbyshire 92
Hare and Hounds, Fosse Cross, Gloucestershire 111
Hare and Hounds Freehouse and Inn, Hempstead, Norfolk 151
Harlingford, London 25
Harrow, West Ilsley, Berkshire 45
Hatchet, Lower Chute, Wiltshire 216
Hazeldene Guest House, Aberaeron, Ceredigion 292

Hazelmere Café and Bakery, Grange-over-Sands, Cumbria	78
Heatons House, Dingle, Co Kerry	334
Heavens Above the Sky and the Ground, Wexford Town, Co Wexford	348
Helm, Askrigg, North Yorkshire	222
Henry's Delicatessen, Ennis, Co Clare	309
Hermitage, Shap, Cumbria	84
Heron's Cove, Goleen, Co Cork	316
Highland Drove Inn, Penrith, Cumbria	82
Hillcrest Hotel, Lincoln, Lincolnshire	145
Hive on the Quay, Aberaeron, Ceredigion	292
Hollow Trees Farm Shop, Semur Suffolk	194
Holly Bush, Stafford, Staffordshire	190
Hornacott, Launceston, Cornwall	62
Horns of Boningale, Albrighton, West Midlands	212
Horse & Jockey Inn, Thurles, Co Tipperary	342
Hoste Arms, Burnham Market, Norfolk	147
Hotel Eilean Iarmain, Sleat, Isle of Skye	274
Hotel on the Park, Cheltenham, Gloucestershire	108
Howard Arms, Ilmington, Warwickshire	209
Howard's House Hotel, Teffont Evias, Wiltshire	218
Howbarrow Organic Farm, Cartmel, Cumbria	75
Hudson's Bistro, Navan, Co Meath	341
Hundred House Hotel, Telford, Shropshire	180
Hunters Rest Inn, Bath, Bath and NE Somerset	41
Hush @ Aubars, Limerick City, Co Limerick	339
Hyland's Burren Hotel, Ballyvaughan, Co Clare	307
Inch House Country House & Restaurant, Thurles, Co Tipperary	343
Inn at Lathones, St Andrews, Fife	263
Inn at the Elm Tree, Wentlooge, Newport	299
Inn at Whitewell, Whitewell, Lancashire	142
Inn for All Seasons, Burford, Oxfordshire	166
Inn @ West End, West End, Surrey	197
Inveresk House, Musselburgh, City of Edinburgh	262
Íragh Ti Connor, Ballybunion, Co Kerry	333
Ivy House, Chalfont St Giles, Buckinghamshire	47
Jack in the Green Inn, Rockbeare, Devon	97
Jackdaw Restaurant, Warkworth, Northumberland	163
Jeake's House Hotel, Rye, East Sussex	202
Johnnie Fox's, Glencullen, Co Dublin	229
Jolly Abbot, St Neots, Cambridgeshire	54
Jumble Room, Grasmere, Cumbria	79
Justin James Hotel, London	35
Kama Sutra, Glasgow, Glasgow	264
Kelly's Resort Hotel, Rosslare, Co Wexford	347
Kennedy's Bar and Martha's Vineyard Restaurant, New Ross, Co Wexford	347
Kicking Donkey, Ormskirk, Lancashire	141
Killeen House, Galway, Co Galway	333
King William IV, Heydon, Cambridgeshire	51
Kingfisher, Sherburn-in-Elmet, North Yorkshire	241
Kings Arms, Bradford-on-Avon, Wiltshire	214
Kings Arms Inn, Montacute, Somerset	184
Kings Head, Bawburgh, Norfolk	147
Kings Head, Coltishall, Norfolk	149
King's Head, Stratford-Upon-Avon, Warwickshire	211
Kings Head Inn, Bledington, Oxfordshire	165
Kinmel Arms, St George, Conwy	294
Knock House Hotel, Knock, Co Mayo	341
Kylemore Abbey & Garden, Clifden, Co Galway	332
La Grande Marque, London	25
Lacken House, Kilkenny, Co Kilkenny	338
Lade Inn, Callander, Perth & Kinross	280
Lairbeck Hotel, Keswick, Cumbria	80
Lamb Inn, Burford, Oxfordshire	167
Landseer, London	30
Langar Hall, Langar, Nottinghamshire	164
Langley Castle Hotel, Langley-on-Tyne, Northumberland	161
Langs Hotel, Glasgow, Glasgow	264
Lashbrook Unique Country Pork, Bishopwood, Chard, Somerset	185
Last Wine Bar and Restaurant, Norwich, Norfolk	153
Lastingham Grange, Lastingham, North Yorkshire	231
Laurels, Killarney, Co Kerry	337
Lay & Wheeler on Cornhill, London	25
Lea Gate Inn, Coningsby, Lincolnshire	145
Leatherne Bottel, Goring, Oxfordshire	170
Leathes Head Hotel, Borrowdale, Cumbria	73
Let's Eat, Perth	279
Lewis' Tea Rooms, Dulverton, Somerset	181
Lifeboat Inn, Thornham, Norfolk	154
Linnanes Lobster Bar, New Quay, Co Clare	310
Lion and Lamb, Little Canfield, Essex	107
Lion Hotel & Restaurant, Berriew, Powys	300
Loch Fyne Oyster Bar and Seafood Restaurant, Cairndow, Argyll & Bute	251
Loch Inn, Fort Augustus, Highland	270
Loch Kinord Hotel, Ballater, Aberdeenshire	249
Loch Melfort Hotel, Arduaine, Argyll & Bute	250
Loch Ness Lodge Hotel, Drumnadrochit, Highland	270
Loch Tummel Inn, Pitlochry, Perth & Kinross	281
Locks Restaurant, Dublin City, Co Dublin	326
Lodge, Horton-cum-Studley, Oxfordshire	171
Lodge on Loch Lomond, Luss, Argyll & Bute	252
Loft Restaurant, Blair Atholl, Perth & Kinross	279
London Street Brasserie, Reading, Berkshire	45
Lord Bagenal Inn, Leighlinbridge, Co Carlow	306
Lotamore House, Cork City, Co Cork	313
Lovelady Shield, Alston, Cumbria	71
Lovells Court, Sturminster Newton, Dorset	103
Lovesome Hill Farm, Northallerton, North Yorkshire	234
Lower Bache House, Leominster, Herefordshire	126
Lower Farm, Harpley, Norfolk	151
Madison's Hotel, Belfast, Co Antrim	351
Magpie Café, Whitby, North Yorkshire	243
Maison Bleue, Edinburgh	259
Majestic Hotel, Tramore, Co Waterford	344
Mallard Grange, Ripon, North Yorkshire	240
Mallin House Hotel, Dornoch, Highland	269
Manifesto Restaurant, Athlone, Co Westmeath	345
Manor House, Studland Bay, Dorset	103
Manor House Hotel and Country Club, West Auckland, Co Durham	61
Manor Restaurant, Waddesdon, Buckinghamshire	50
Mansfield House Hotel, Hawick, Scottish Borders	284
Marsham Arms Inn, Hevingham, Norfolk	151
Martins Arms Inn, Colston Bassett, Nottinghamshire	163
Masons Arms, Branscombe, Devon	95
Mayflower Hotel, London	35
McAlpin's Suir Inn, Cheekpoint, Co Waterford	343
McDonagh's Seafood House, Galway City, Co Galway	333
McGrory's of Culdaff, Inishowen Penninsula, Co Donegal	320
McHughs Bar and Restaurant, Belfast, Co Antrim	351
Merchant House, Norwich, Norfolk	153
Merchants, Edinburgh	260
Mike Williams, Caergwrle, Flintshire	295
Mill Park Hotel, Donegal, Co Donegal	319
Mill Race Organic Restaurant, Leeds, West Yorkshire	245
Millbank, Millbank, West Yorkshire	245
Millbrook Inn, South Pool, Devon	98
Millets Farm Centre, Garford, Abingdon, Oxfordshire	165
Minmore House, Glenlivet, Moray	275
Mister Singh's India, Glasgow	264
Molesworth Manor, Padstow, Cornwall	64
Monfin House, Enniscorthy, Co Wexford	347
Monks Bar and Restaurant, Ballyvaughan, Co Clare	308
Monsieurs, Poulton-le-Fylde, Lancashire	141
Moody Cow, Ross-on-Wye, Herefordshire	126
Mortehoe Brasserie, Woolacombe, Devon	99
Mulberry Tree, Wigan, Lancashire	142
Mulberry's, Glasgow	265
Murano, London	36
Museum Inn, Farnham, Dorset	102
Mussel and Crab, Tuxford, Nottinghamshire	164
Nag's Head, London	26
Nags Head Inn, Castle Donington, Derbyshire	92
Nags Head Inn, Pickhill, North Yorkshire	235
Nakon Thai Restaurant, Douglas, Co Cork	316
Nelsons Restaurant, Polperro, Cornwall	65
Netherwood Hotel, Grange-over-Sands, Cumbria	79
New Inn, Shalfleet, Isle of Wight	130
New Inn At Coln, Coln St-Aldwyns, Gloucestershire	111
New Village Tea Rooms, Orton, Cumbria	82
Nineteen, Brighton, West Sussex	198
No 77 Wine Bar, London	31
North Acomb Farm, Stocksfield-on-Tyne, Northumberland	162
Northbeach Cafe, Whitby, North Yorkshire	243
Number 34, Barnard Castle, Co Durham	60
Number 64, Leek, Staffordshire	190
O'Connells in Ballsbridge, Dublin City, Co Dublin	326
O'Neills, Dublin City, Co Dublin	327
Oak Room Restaurant, Cavan Town, Co Cavan	307
Oddfellows Arms, Mellor, Cheshire	57
Old Bank House, Kinsale, Co Cork	317
Old Boat, Lichfield, Staffordshire	190
Old Bridge Hotel, Huntingdon, Cambridgeshire	53
Old Bridge Inn, Ripponden, West Yorkshire	246
Old Count House, St Ives, Cornwall	68
Old Dungeon Ghyll, Ambleside, Cumbria	72
Old Ferryman's House, Boat of Garten, Highland	268
Old Forge, Shaftesbury, Dorset	102
Old Inn, Wincanton, Somerset	187
Old Inn, St Breward, Cornwall	67
Old Laundry, Heydon, Norfolk	152
Old Passage Inn, Arlingham, Gloucestershire	108
Old Presbetery Restaurant, Killarney, Co Kerry	337
Old Rectifying House, Worcester, Worcestershire	221
Old Schoolhouse, Comber, Co Down	352

Old Smokehouse and Truffles, Penrith, Cumbria	83
Old Tollgate Restaurant and Hotel, Steyning, West Sussex	207
Old White Hart Inn, Uppingham, Rutland	176
Olive Branch, Clipsham, Rutland	175
One Elm, Stratford-Upon-Avon, Warwickshire	211
Orange Tree, Chadwick End, West Midlands	213
Organic Farm Shop Cafe, Cirencester, Gloucestershire	110
Osborne Hotel, Torquay, Devon	98
Oscar's Restaurant, Enniskillen, Co Fermanagh	354
Over Farm Market, Over, Gloucestershire	112
Over Kinfauns, Perth	279
Paddy Burkes, Clarinbridge, Co Galway	330
Palio Pasta and Pizza, Inverness, Highland	271
Pamphill Dairy Farm Shop, Pamphill, Wimbourne, Dorset	102
Park House, Lairg, Highland	272
Parmigiana, Glasgow	265
Paskins Town House, Brighton, East Sussex	199
Peacock Inn, Tenbury Wells, Worcestershire	231
Pear Tree, Melksham, Wiltshire	216
Peat Spade Inn, Longstock, Hampshire	117
Peldon Rose Inn, Colchester, Essex	105
Pembridge Court Hotel, London	38
Pend, Dunkeld, Perth & Kinross	281
Penhelig Arms Hotel, Aberdyfi, Gwynedd	295
Penzance Arts Club, Penzance, Cornwall	65
Perch & Pike Inn, South Stoke, Oxfordshire	123
Peter's Cellars, Edinburgh	260
Petit Paris, Edinburgh	260
Pheasant, Cockermouth, Cumbria	76
Pheasant at Ross, Ross-on-Wye, Herefordshire	127
Pheasant Hotel, Helmsley, North Yorkshire	229
Pheasant Inn, Keyston, Cambridgeshire	53
Pheasant Inn, Chester, Cheshire	55
Pheasant Inn, Kielder Water, Northumberland	161
Phelips Arms, Montacute, Somerset	184
Pi Restaurant, Cork City, Co Cork	316
Pilgrim's Restaurant, Battle, East Sussex	197
Plantation, Polperro, Cornwall	66
Plockton Hotel, Plockton, Highland	273
Plough and Flail, Mobberley, Cheshire	58
Plough at Clanfield, Clanfield, Oxfordshire	168
Plough at Eaton, Eaton, Cheshire	56
Plough at Kelmscott, Kelmscott, Gloucestershire	112
Plough Inn, Fadmoor, North Yorkshire	226
Plume of Feathers, Mitchell, Cornwall	64
Polo'D Restaurant, Ballyconnell, Co Cavan	307
Port Gaverne Hotel, Port Gaverne, Cornwall	66
Port Na Craig Restaurant, Pitlochry, Perth & Kinross	382
Port Royal Hotel Russian Tavern, Isle of Bute, Isle of Bute	274
Portobello Gold, London	38
Pot Still, Glasgow	266
Powerscourt Terrace Cafe, Enniskerry, Co Dublin	349
Priory Farm, Nutfield, Surrey	20
Puddleducks, Blairlogie, Stirling	285
Punch Bowl Inn, Kendal, Cumbria	80
Purchases Wine Bar, Chichester, West Sussex	203
QC's Seafood Bar & Restaurant, Cahirciveen, Co Kerry	334
Queen's Head, Bulwick, Northamptonshire	157
Queen's Head, Llandudno, Conwy	294
Queen's Head, Bramfield, Suffolk	191
Queen's Head Hotel, Hawkshead, Cumbria	80
Queens Head, Windermere, Cumbria	90
Quince and Medlar, Cockermouth, Cumbria	76
Quinn Tea Rooms, Abbeyleix, Co Laois	339
Raemoir House Hotel, Banchory, Aberdeenshire	249
Raffles Hotel and Tea Rooms, Blackpool, Lancashire	139
Raglan Lodge, Dublin City, Co Dublin	327
Rainbow Inn, Lewes, East Sussex	202
Rajpoot, Bath, Bath and NE Somerset	41
Ram Jam Inn, Stretton, Rutland	175
Rams Head Inn, Saddleworth, Greater Manchester	146
Ramsons, Ramsbottom, Greater Manchester	146
Ratcatchers Inn, Cawston, Norfolk	149
Rathmullan House, Rathmullan, Co Donegal	321
Rectory Farm, Staunton St John, Oxfordshire	173
Red Bank House and Restaurant, Skerries, Co Dublin	330
Red Cat, St Helens, Merseyside	146
Red House, Nether Broughton, Leicestershire	143
Red House, Marsh Benham, Berkshire	43
Red House Inn, Whitchurch, Hampshire	125
Red Lion, Stodmarsh, Kent	137
Red Lion, Chipping Campden, Gloucestershire	108
Red Lion, London	38
Red Lion, Lacock, Wiltshire	215
Red Lion, Mawdesley, Lancashire	140
Red Lion Inn, Ashbourne, Derbyshire	91
Red Lion Inn, New Radnor, Powys	302
Red Lion Inn, Chalgrove, Oxfordshire	167
Red Lion Inn, Stathern, Leicestershire	144
Regents House Hotel, Edinburgh	261
Restaurant at Wickham Vineyard, Shedfield, Hampshire	119
Revolutions Cafe Bar and Restaurant, Chippenham, Wiltshire	215
Ricci's On the Green, Woodcote, Oxfordshire	174
Richard and Julie Davies, Cromer, Norfolk	150
Riverdale Hall Hotel, Belllingham, Northumberland	160
Riversford Hotel, Bideford, Devon	94
Robin Hood Inn, Elkesley, Nottinghamshire	163
Roebuck Inn, Ludlow, Shropshire	178
Romper, Marple, Cheshire	57
Rose and Crown, Slaithwaite, West Yorkshire	246
Rose and Crown, Snettisham, Norfolk	154
Rose and Crown, Warwick, Warwickshire	212
Rose and Crown at Romaldkirk, Romaldkirk, Co Durham	61
Rose and Thistle, Fordingbridge, Hampshire	117
Rose & Crown, Severn Stoke, Worcestershire	220
Royal Cornwall Museum Café, Truro, Cornwall	71
Royal Hotel, Comrie, Perth & Kinross	281
Royal Oak, Lostwithiel, Cornwall	63
Royal Oak, Cerne Abbas, Dorset	101
Royal Oak, Withypool, Somerset	188
Royal Oak, Marlow, Buckinghamshire	49
Royal Oak, Chichester, West Sussex	204
Royal Oak Inn, Luxborough, Somerset	183
Rusheen Lodge, Ballyvaughan, Co Clare	308
Sablonnerie, Sark	357
Saddleback Foods and Smokerie, Penrith, Cumbria	83
Salusbury, London	31
San Carlo, Birmingham, West Midlands	213
San Carlo Restaurant, Bristol	47
San Carlo Restaurant, Leicester, Leicestershire	143
Sandpiper Inn, Lebyburn, North Yorkshire	231
Sandyford Hotel, Glasgow, Glasgow	266
Sarah Nelson's Grasmere Gingerbread Shop, Grasmere, Cumbria	79
Sawley Arms and Cottages, Sawley, North Yorkshire	240
Scot House Hotel, Kinguisse, Highland	271
Sea Trout Inn, Totnes, Devon	99
Seasons Coffee Shop, Kincardine, Fife	262
Seatoller House, Borrowdale, Cumbria	73
Secretts, Milford, Surrey	21
Selborne Arms, Selborne, Hampshire	119
Seven Stars Inn, Pewsey, Wiltshire	217
Severn & Wye Smokery, Westbury on Severn, Gloucestershire	116
Shanahan's on the Green, Dublin City, Co Dublin	328
Shave Cross Inn, Bridport, Dorset	101
Sheene Mill Restaurant with Rooms, Melbourn, Cambridgeshire	54
Shelleven House, Bangor, Co Down	352
Shepherd's Arms Hotel, Ennerdale, Cumbria	78
Shepherd's Crook, Crowell, Oxfordshire	169
Shepherds Inn, Melmerby, Cumbria	81
Shibden Mill Inn, Shibden, West Yorkshire	246
Shieldaig Bar, Shieldaig, Highland	273
Ship Inn, Owslebury, Hampshire	118
Ship Inn, London	36
Ship Inn, Alnwick, Northumberland	158
Ship Inn, Ipswich, Suffolk	193
Simonstone Hall, Hawes, North Yorkshire	229
Simpson's Restaurant, Kenilworth, Warwickshire	209
Smugglers Cottage of Tolverne, Tolverne, Cornwall	70
Snooty Fox Inn, Faringdon, Oxfordshire	169
Souffle, Maidstone, Kent	135
Spanish Point Restaurant, Ballycotton, Co Cork	310
Spice Box, Boston-Spa, West Yorkshire	244
Spital Hill, Thirsk, North Yorkshire	241
Spotted Dog, Penshurst, Kent	136
Springer Spaniel, Launceston, Cornwall	63
Springwells Bed and Breakfast Hotel, Steyning, West Sussex	207
St Mawes Hotel, St Mawes, Cornwall	69
St Peter's Hall, Bungay, Suffolk	192
Stag, Mentmore, Buckinghamshire	49
Stagg Inn & Restaurant, Kington, Herefordshire	125
Staghunters Hotel, Lynton, Devon	97
Stanshope Hall, Stanshope, Derbyshire	94
Star Country Inn & Restaurant, Weaverthorpe, North Yorkshire	242
Star Inn, Harome, North Yorkshire	228
Star Inn, Waltham-St-Lawrence, Berkshire	45
Station Restaurant, Ballater, Aberdeenshire	249
Steam Packet Hotel, Isle of Whithorn, Dumfries and Galloway	255
Stein Inn, Waternish, Isle of Skye	274
Stephan Langton Inn, Abinger Common, Surrey	196
Stepping Stone Restaurant, Balicanich, Western Isles	285
Stoke Lodge Hotel, Dartmouth, Devon	95
Stone Court Hotel and Chambers Restaurant, Maidstone, Kent	135
Stone Trough Inn, Kirkham Abbey, North Yorkshire	230
Stonor Hotel and Restaurant, Henley-on-Thames, Oxfordshire	171

Stour Bay Café, Manningtree, Essex 107
Strand Inn, Dunmore East, Co Waterford 343
Sun Inn, Swindon, Wiltshire 218
Suruchi Too, Edinburgh 261
Sutton Hall, Macclesfield, Cheshire 57
Swag and Tails, London 26
Swan at the Vineyard, Lamberhurst, Kent 155
Swan Hotel, Stafford, Staffordshire 191
Swan Inn, Barnby, Suffolk 191
Swan Inn, Hungerford, Berkshire 43
Swan Inn, Denham, Buckinghamshire 48
Swan on the Green, West Peckham, Kent 138
Sylvan Cottage, Canterbury, Kent 133
Talbot 15th Century Coaching Inn, Mells, Somerset 183
Talkhouse , Caersws, Powys 301
Tankard Bar & Restaurant, Fenit, Co Kerry 336
Tarn End House Hotel, Talkin, Cumbria 74
Terre a Terre, Brighton, East Sussex 201
Teviotdale House, Edinburgh 261
thecafe at Whalebone House, Cley next the Sea, Norfolk 149
Three Crowns, Brinkworth, Wiltshire 214
Three Hares, Bilbrough, North Yorkshire 223
Three Horseshoes, Madingley, Cambridgeshire 53
Three Horseshoes, Wareham, Norfolk 155
Three Horseshoes, Batcombe, Somerset 180
Three Salmons Hotel, Usk, Monmouthshire 299
Three Tuns, Henley-on-Thames, Oxfordshire 171
Tickell Arms, Whittlesford, Cambridgeshire 55
Tiger Inn, Ashford, Kent 130
Tilley's Bistro, Bath, Bath and NE Somerset 42
Tower Inn, Slapton, Devon 98
Trewithen Restaurant, Lostwithiel, Cornwall 63
Trigony House Hotel, Dumfries, Dumfries and Galloway 254
Troubadour, London 35
Trouble House, Tetbury, Gloucestershire 115
Truc Vert, London 26
Tufton Arms Hotel, Appleby-in-Westmorland, Cumbria 72
Tuggal Hall, Chathill, Northumberland 160
Tulley's Farm, Turners Hill, West Sussex 207
Turmeric Gold, Coventry, Warwickshire 208
Twenty Nevern Square Hotel, London 37
Unicorn Inn, Kincardine, Fife 262
Unicorn Restaurant, Dublin City, Co Dublin 328
Verzons, Ledbury, Herefordshire 126
Victoria at Holkham, Holkham, Norfolk 152
Victoria Hotel, Bamburgh, Northumberland 160
Villa Country House Hotel, Kirkham, Lancashire 140
Village Bakery, Melmerby, Cumbria 81
Villagers Inn, Blackheath, Surrey 196
Vine Tree, Norton, Wiltshire 217
Wallett's Court Country House Hotel and Spa, Dover, Kent 134
Walpole Arms, Itteringham, Norfolk 152
Wasdale Head Inn, Wasdale, Cumbria 86
Water Lily Patisserie & A la Carte Restaurant, Colchester, Essex 104
Waterfall Hotel, Peel, Isle of Man 129
Waterman's Arms, Ashprington, Devon 94
Waterman's Lodge Hotel, Killaloe, Co Clare 309
Watermill, Penrith, Cumbria 83
WatersEdge Hotel, Cobh, Co Cork 312
Weavers Bar - Restaurant, Haworth, West Yorkshire 244
Weavers Shed Restaurant with Rooms, Huddersfield, West Yorkshire 244
Welcome To Town Country Bistro & Bar, Llanrhidian, Swansea 303
Wensleydale Heifer Inn, Leyburn, North Yorkshire 232
Westgate Design, Wexford Town, Co Wexford 348
Whalebone, Colchester, Essex 105
Wheatsheaf Hotel, Milnthorpe, Cumbria 82
Wheatsheaf Inn, Northleach, Gloucestershire 113
Wheelers Oyster Bar, Whitstable, Kent 138
Whistler Restaurant, Tate Britain, London 27
White Hart, Canterbury, Kent 133
White Hart Hotel, St Keverne, Cornwall 69
White Hart Inn, Chalfont St Giles, Buckinghamshire 48
White Hart Inn and Restaurant, Winchcombe, Gloucestershire 116
White Horse, Brancaster Staithe, Norfolk 147
White Horse, Frampton Mansell, Gloucestershire 112
White Horse and Griffin Hotel, Whitby, North Yorkshire 243
White Horse Inn, Chilgrove, West Sussex 204
White Horse Inn, Bridge, Kent 131
White House, Oxford, Oxfordshire 172
White House Hotel, Herm Island, Herm 356
White Lion, Wherwell, Hampshire 124
White Lion Inn, Buckden, North Yorkshire 223
White Lion Pub & Restaurant, Goring, Oxfordshire 169
White Star Tavern & Dining Rooms, Southampton, Hampshire 124
White Swan, Pickering, North Yorkshire 235
White Swan, Harringworth, Northamptonshire 157
White Swan, Leyburn, North Yorkshire 232

Whites Hotel , Minehead, Somerset 183
Wild Duck, Cirencester, Gloucestershire 110
Winder Hall Country House, Cockermouth, Cumbria 76
Windmill at Badby, Badby, Northamptonshire 155
Wineport Lodge, Athlone, Co Westmeath 346
Wodka, London 39
Wolfe Inn, Wolfscastle, Pembrokeshire 299
Wolfscastle Country Hotel, Wolfscastle, Pembrokeshire 300
Wombwell Arms, Helmsley, North Yorkshire 230
Wookey Hole Inn, Wookey Hole, Somerset 188
World Service, Nottingham, Nottinghamshire 164
Wrangham House Hotel, Hunmanby, North Yorkshire 230
Wrightson & Company, Manfield, North Yorkshire 233
Wykeham Arms, Winchester, Hampshire 125
Wyndham Arms Hotel, Clearwell, Gloucestershire 111
Wyvill Arms, Leyburn, North Yorkshire 232
Yorke Arms, Ramsgill, North Yorkshire 235

A-Z by Listing Town

Abbeyleix, Co Laois 339
Aberaeron, Ceredigion 287
Aberdyfi, Gwynedd 295
Aberthaw, Vale of Glamorgan 303
Abingdon, Oxfordshire 165
Abinger Common, Surrey 196
Albrighton, West Midlands 212
Alnwick, Northumberland 158
Alston, Cumbria 71
Altnaharra, Highland 266
Ambleside, Cumbria 72
Appleby-in-Westmorland, Cumbria 72
Applecross, Highland 268
Arduaine, Argyll & Bute 250
Arkengarthdale, North Yorkshire 222
Arlingham, Gloucestershire 108
Armathwaite, Cumbria 73
Arrochar, Argyll & Bute 250
Ashbourne, Derbyshire 91
Ashford, Kent 130
Ashprington, Devon 94
Askrigg, North Yorkshire 222
Athlone, Co Westmeath 345
Auchencrow, Scottish Borders 284
Austwick, North Yorkshire 223
Avoca, Co Wicklow 349
Badby, Northamptonshire 155
Balivanich, Western Isles 285
Ballantrae, South Ayrshire 253
Ballater, Aberdeenshire 249
Ballina, Co Mayo 340
Ballybunion, Co Kerry 333
Ballyconnell, Co Cavan 307
Ballycotton, Co Cork 310
Ballyvaughan, Co Clare 307
Bamburgh, Northumberland 160
Banavie, Highland 268
Banchory, Aberdeenshire 249
Banff, Aberdeenshire 250
Bangor, Co Down 352
Barcombe, East Sussex 197
Barmouth, Gwynedd 296
Barnard Castle, Co Durham 60
Barnby, Suffolk 191
Batcombe, Somerset 180
Bath, Bath and NE Somerset 41
Battle, East Sussex 197
Bawburgh, Norfolk 147
Beaconsfield, Buckinghamshire 47
Beattock, Dumfries and Galloway 253
Beeley, Derbyshire 91
Belfast, Co Antrim 351
Belllingham, Northumberland 160
Bembridge, Isle of Wight 129
Benington, Hertfordshire 127
Berkhamsted, Hertfordshire 128
Berriew, Powys 300
Betws Newydd, Monmouthshire 296
Biddenden, Kent 130
Bideford, Devon 94
Biggin, Derbyshire 91
Bilbrough, North Yorkshire 223
Birmingham, West Midlands 213
Blackheath, Surrey 196
Blackpool, Lancashire 139
Blair Atholl, Perth & Kinross 279
Blairlogie, Stirling 285

Blarney, Co Cork	311
Bledington, Oxfordshire	165
Boat of Garten, Highland	268
Bodsham, Kent	131
Borrowdale, Cumbria	73
Boston-Spa, West Yorkshire	244
Boughton Aluph, Kent	131
Bradford-on-Avon, Wiltshire	214
Braintree, Essex	104
Bramfield, Suffolk	191
Brampton, Cumbria	74
Brancaster Staithe, Norfolk	147
Branscombe, Devon	95
Bray, Co Wicklow	349
Brecon, Powys	300
Bridge, Kent	131
Bridge of Cally, Perth & Kinross	280
Bridlington, East Yorkshire	222
Bridport, Dorset	101
Brighton, East Sussex	198
Brinkworth, Wiltshire	214
Bristol	46
Broadway, Worcestershire	219
Broughton in Furness, Cumbria	74
Buckden, North Yorkshire	223
Bulwick, Northamptonshire	157
Bungay, Suffolk	192
Burford, Oxfordshire	166
Burlton, Shropshire	176
Burnham Market, Norfolk	147
Burnsall, North Yorkshire	224
Buttermere, Cumbria	75
Caergwrle, Flintshire	295
Caersws, Powys	301
Cahirciveen, Co Kerry	334
Cairndow, Argyll & Bute	251
Caldwell, North Yorkshire	224
Callander, Perth & Kinross	280
Cambridge, Cambridgeshire	50
Cannich, Highland	269
Cannington, Somerset	180
Canterbury, Kent	132
Cardross, Argyll & Bute	251
Carlow Town, Co Carlow	306
Cartmel, Cumbria	75
Castle Donington, Derbyshire	92
Castle Douglas, Dumfries and Galloway	253
Cavan Town, Co Cavan	307
Cavendish, Suffolk	193
Cawston, Norfolk	149
Cerne Abbas, Dorset	101
Chadwick End, West Midlands	213
Chalfont St Giles, Buckinghamshire	47
Chalgrove, Oxfordshire	167
Charlbury, Oxfordshire	167
Chathill, Northumberland	160
Cheekpoint, Co Waterford	343
Cheltenham, Gloucestershire	108
Chepstow, Monmouthshire	296
Cherington, Warwickshire	208
Chester, Cheshire	55
Chichester, West Sussex	202
Chilgrove, West Sussex	204
Chillcompton, Bath and NE Somerset	42
Chillenden, Kent	134
Chippenham, Wiltshire	215
Chipping Campden, Gloucestershire	108
Chipping Norton, Oxfordshire	168
Cholmondeley, Cheshire	56
Christmas Common, Oxfordshire	168
Cirencester, Gloucestershire	110
Clanfield, Oxfordshire	168
Clarinbridge, Co Galway	330
Clavering, Essex	104
Clearwell, Gloucestershire	111
Cley next the Sea, Norfolk	149
Clifden, Co Galway	332
Clipsham, Rutland	175
Clogher, Co Tyrone	354
Clonakilty, Co Cork	311
Clungunford, Shropshire	176
Cobh, Co Cork	312
Cockermouth, Cumbria	76
Coggeshall, Essex	104
Colchester, Essex	105
Coln St-Aldwyns, Gloucestershire	111
Colston Bassett, Nottinghamshire	163
Coltishall, Norfolk	149
Comber, Co Down	352
Comrie, Perth & Kinross	281
Coningsby, Lincolnshire	145
Coniston, Cumbria	77
Cork City, Co Cork	312
Corscombe, Dorset	101
Coventry, Warwickshire	208
Coverack, Cornwall	62
Coxwold, North Yorkshire	224
Crayke, North Yorkshire	226
Crickhowell, Powys	301
Cromer, Norfolk	150
Crondall, Hampshire	116
Croom, Co Limerick	339
Crowell, Oxfordshire	169
Crugybar, Carmarthenshire	287
Cwmdu, Powys	302
Darlington, Co Durham	60
Dartmouth, Devon	95
Deal, Kent	134
Denham, Buckinghamshire	48
Dingle, Co Kerry	334
Dingle Peninsula, Co Kerry	335
Donegal, Co Donegal	319
Dornoch, Highland	269
Dorridge, West Midlands	213
Douglas, Co Cork	316
Dover, Kent	134
Downham, Lancashire	139
Drumnadrochit, Highland	269
Dublin City, Co Dublin	321
Dulverton, Somerset	181
Dumfries, Dumfries and Galloway	254
Dun Laoghaire, Co Dublin	329
Dunadry, Co Antrim	352
Dunkeld, Perth & Kinross	281
Dunkineely, Co Donegal	320
Dunmore East, Co Waterford	343
Earls Colne, Essex	105
East Langton, Leicestershire	142
Eaton, Cheshire	56
Edinburgh	255
Elkesley, Nottinghamshire	163
Ely, Cambridgeshire	51
Ennerdale, Cumbria	78
Ennis, Co Clare	308
Enniscorthy, Co Wexford	347
Enniskerry, Co Dublin	329
Enniskillen, Co Fermanagh	354
Escrick, North Yorkshire	226
Eskdale, Cumbria	78
Essington, Staffordshire	188
Eversley, Hampshire	117
Exeter, Devon	96
Exford, Somerset	182
Eye, Suffolk	193
Fadmoor, North Yorkshire	226
Faringdon, Oxfordshire	169
Farnham, Dorset	102
Fenit, Co Kerry	336
Ferrensby, North Yorkshire	227
Filey, North Yorkshire	227
Fletching, East Sussex	201
Fordingbridge, Hampshire	117
Forres, Moray	275
Fort Augustus, Highland	270
Fosse Cross, Gloucestershire	111
Frampton Mansell, Gloucestershire	112
Galway City, Co Galway	333
Gattonside, Scottish Borders	284
Glasgow	263
Glencullen, Co Dublin	329
Glendalough, Co Wicklow	349
Glenlivet, Moray	275
Gloucester, Gloucestershire	112
Goleen, Co Cork	316
Goring, Oxfordshire	169
Grange-over-Sands, Cumbria	78
Grasmere, Cumbria	79
Great Ouseburn, North Yorkshire	227
Great Tew, Oxfordshire	170
Great Wolford, Warwickshire	208
Gretna, Dumfries and Galloway	254
Haddenham, Buckinghamshire	48
Hale, Cheshire	56
Hardwick, Derbyshire	92

Harome, North Yorkshire	228	Longstock, Hampshire	117
Harpley, Norfolk	151	Lostwithiel, Cornwall	63
Harringworth, Northamptonshire	157	Lower Chute, Wiltshire	216
Harrogate, North Yorkshire	228	Lower Oddington, Gloucestershire	113
Hawes, North Yorkshire	229	Lowick, Northumberland	161
Hawick, Scottish Borders	284	Ludlow, Shropshire	177
Hawkshead, Cumbria	80	Luss, Argyll & Bute	252
Haworth, West Yorkshire	244	Luxborough, Somerset	183
Helmsley, North Yorkshire	229	Lynton, Devon	97
Hemingford Grey, Cambridgeshire	51	Macclesfield, Cheshire	57
Hempstead, Norfolk	151	Madingley, Cambridgeshire	53
Henley-on-Thames, Oxfordshire	170	Maidstone, Kent	135
Herm Island, Herm	356	Malahide, Co Dublin	330
Hevingham, Norfolk	151	Manchester	145
Heydon, Cambridgeshire	51	Manfield, North Yorkshire	233
Heydon, Norfolk	152	Manningtree, Essex	107
Hindon, Wiltshire	215	Marlborough, Wiltshire	216
Holkham, Norfolk	152	Marlow, Buckinghamshire	49
Holsworthy, Devon	96	Marple, Cheshire	57
Hopton Wafers, Shropshire	177	Marsh Benham, Berkshire	43
Horndon-on-the-Hill, Essex	106	Marton, North Yorkshire	233
Horton-cum-Studley, Oxfordshire	171	Masham, North Yorkshire	233
Hove, East Sussex	201	Mawdesley, Lancashire	140
Huddersfield, West Yorkshire	244	Melbourn, Cambridgeshire	54
Hungarton, Leicestershire	143	Melksham, Wiltshire	216
Hungerford, Berkshire	43	Mellor, Cheshire	57
Hunmanby, North Yorkshire	230	Mells, Somerset	183
Huntingdon, Cambridgeshire	53	Melmerby, Cumbria	81
Ilfracombe, Devon	96	Mentmore, Buckinghamshire	49
Ilmington, Warwickshire	209	Midhurst, West Sussex	206
Inishowen Penninsula, Co Donegal	320	Midleton, Co Cork	317
Inverness, Highland	271	Millbank, West Yorkshire	245
Ipswich, Suffolk	193	Milnthorpe, Cumbria	82
Isle of Bute	274	Milton Keynes, Buckinghamshire	49
Isle of Whithorn, Dumfries and Galloway	255	Minehead, Somerset	183
Itteringham, Norfolk	152	Mitchell, Cornwall	64
Jenkinstown, Co Louth	340	Mobberley, Cheshire	58
Kelmscott, Gloucestershire	112	Molls Gap, Co Kerry	338
Kendal, Cumbria	80	Montacute, Somerset	184
Kenilworth, Warwickshire	209	Mullingar, Co Westmeath	346
Keswick, Cumbria	80	Multyfarnham, Co Westmeath	346
Keyston, Cambridgeshire	53	Musselburgh, City of Edinburgh	262
Kielder Water, Northumberland	161	Navan, Co Meath	341
Kilkenny, Co Kilkenny	338	Nether Broughton, Leicestershire	143
Killaloe, Co Clare	309	New Quay, Co Clare	310
Killarney, Co Kerry	336	New Radnor, Powys	302
Killorglin, Co Kerry	337	New Ross, Co Wexford	347
Kilmacanogue, Co Wicklow	350	Newbury, Berkshire	44
Kincardine, Fife	262	Newquay, Cornwall	64
Kington, Herefordshire	125	North Walsham, Norfolk	153
Kinguisse, Highland	271	Northallerton, North Yorkshire	234
Kinsale, Co Cork	317	Northampton, Northamptonshire	157
Kintbury, Berkshire	43	Northleach, Gloucestershire	113
Kirdford, West Sussex	204	Norton, Wiltshire	217
Kirkby Stephen, Cumbria	81	Norton St Philip, Bath and NE Somerset	42
Kirkham, Lancashire	140	Norwich, Norfolk	153
Kirkham Abbey, North Yorkshire	230	Nottingham, Nottinghamshire	164
Knock, Co Mayo	341	Ockley, Surrey	196
Knowle, Warwickshire	209	Ombersley, Worcestershire	220
Lacock, Wiltshire	215	Onich, Highland	272
Lahinch, Co Clare	310	Orford, Suffolk	194
Lairg, Highland	272	Ormskirk, Lancashire	141
Lamberhurst, Kent	135	Orton, Cumbria	82
Langar, Nottinghamshire	164	Osmotherley, North Yorkshire	234
Langley-on-Tyne, Northumberland	161	Oundle, Northamptonshire	158
Langport, Somerset	182	Over Peover, Cheshire	58
Lapworth, Warwickshire	210	Ovington, Hampshire	118
Lastingham, North Yorkshire	231	Owslebury, Hampshire	118
Launceston, Cornwall	62	Oxford, Oxfordshire	172
Ledbury, Herefordshire	126	Padstow, Cornwall	64
Leeds, West Yorkshire	245	Painswick, Gloucestershire	113
Leek, Staffordshire	190	Pamphill, Dorset	102
Leicester, Leicestershire	143	Partridge Green, West Sussex	206
Leighlinbridge, Co Carlow	306	Peel, Isle of Man	129
Leominster, Herefordshire	126	Penrith, Cumbria	82
Letterkenny, Co Donegal	320	Penshurst, Kent	136
Lewes, East Sussex	202	Penzance, Cornwall	65
Leyburn, North Yorkshire	231	Perth, Perth	275
Lichfield, Staffordshire	190	Petersfield, Hampshire	119
Limerick City, Co Limerick	339	Peterston-Super-Ely, Cardiff	287
Lincoln, Lincolnshire	145	Pewsey, Wiltshire	217
Little Canfield, Essex	107	Pickering, North Yorkshire	234
Llandudno, Conwy	293	Pickhill, North Yorkshire	235
Llanrhidian, Swansea	303	Pilsley, Derbyshire	92
Loch Ness, Highland	272	Pitlochry, Perth & Kinross	281
London		Plockton, Highland	273
Longridge, Lancashire	140	Pluckley, Kent	136

Polperro, Cornwall	65	Tangley, Hampshire	124
Port Gaverne, Cornwall	66	Tarporley, Cheshire	58
Poulton-le-Fylde, Lancashire	141	Teffont Evias, Wiltshire	218
Preston Bagot, Warwickshire	210	Telford, Shropshire	180
Raglan, Monmouthshire	298	Tenbury Wells, Worcestershire	221
Ramsbottom, Greater Manchester	146	Tetbury, Gloucestershire	115
Ramsbury, Wiltshire	217	Tewkesbury, Gloucestershire	115
Ramsgill, North Yorkshire	235	The Lizard, Cornwall	70
Rathmullan, Co Donegal	321	Thirsk, North Yorkshire	241
Reading, Berkshire	45	Thornham, Norfolk	154
Reed, Hertfordshire	128	Thornton le Dale, North Yorkshire	242
Rhyl, Denbighshire	294	Thorpe Langton, Leicestershire	144
Richmond, North Yorkshire	239	Thurles, Co Tipperary	342
Ripon, North Yorkshire	240	Thurstaston, Cheshire	59
Ripponden, West Yorkshire	246	Tiddington, Warwickshire	211
Rockbeare, Devon	47	Tisbury, Wiltshire	219
Rockliffe, Cumbria	84	Tobermory, Argyll & Bute	252
Romaldkirk, Co Durham	61	Tolverne, Cornwall	70
Roscommon, Co Roscommon	342	Torquay, Devon	98
Ross-on-Wye, Herefordshire	126	Totnes, Devon	99
Rosslare, Co Wexford	347	Tramore, Co Waterford	344
Rusper, West Sussex	206	Truro, Cornwall	70
Rye, East Sussex	202	Trusham, Devon	99
Saddleworth, Greater Manchester	146	Turners Hill, West Sussex	207
Saham Toney, Norfolk	154	Tuxford, Nottinghamshire	164
Samlesbury, Lancashire	141	Tweedsmuir, Scottish Borders	285
Sark	357	Tyndrum, Perth & Kinross	282
Sawley, North Yorkshire	240	Ullapool, Highland	273
Scarborough, North Yorkshire	240	Ullswater, Cumbria	86
Sedbergh, Cumbria	84	Upchurch, Kent	137
Selborne, Hampshire	119	Uppingham, Rutland	176
Semer, Suffolk	194	Usk, Monmouthshire	298
Severn Stoke, Worcestershire	220	Waddesdon, Buckinghamshire	50
Shaftesbury, Dorset	102	Wadebridge, Cornwall	71
Shalfleet, Isle of Wight	130	Walberswick, Suffolk	195
Shap, Cumbria	84	Walterstone, Herefordshire	127
Shedfield, Hampshire	119	Waltham-St-Lawrence, Berkshire	45
Shepton Mallet, Somerset	185	Wareham, Norfolk	155
Sherburn-in-Elmet, North Yorkshire	241	Warkworth, Northumberland	163
Sherston, Wiltshire	218	Warminster, Wiltshire	219
Shibden, West Yorkshire	246	Warrington, Cheshire	59
Shieldaig, Highland	273	Warwick, Warwickshire	212
Sidmouth, Devon	97	Wasdale, Cumbria	86
Skenfrith, Monmouthshire	298	Waterford City, Co Waterford	344
Skerries, Co Dublin	330	Waternish, Isle of Skye	274
Skipton, North Yorkshire	241	Watton-at-Stone, Hertfordshire	129
Slaithwaite, West Yorkshire	246	Weaverthorpe, North Yorkshire	242
Slapton, Devon	98	Wells, Somerset	187
Sleat, Isle of Skye	274	Wentlooge, Newport	299
Smarden, Kent	136	Werrington, Cambridgeshire	54
Snettisham, Norfolk	154	West Auckland, Co Durham	61
Somerford Keynes, Gloucestershire	114	West End, Surrey	197
South Pool, Devon	98	West Ilsley, Berkshire	45
South Stoke, Oxfordshire	173	West Peckham, Kent	138
Southampton, Hampshire	124	Westbury on Severn, Gloucestershire	116
Southwold, Suffolk	194	Westport, Co Mayo	341
St Andrews, Fife	263	Wexford Town, Co Wexford	348
St Asaph, Denbighshire	295	Wherwell, Hampshire	124
St Austell, Cornwall	66	Whitby, North Yorkshire	242
St Brelade, Jersey	356	Whitchurch, Hampshire	125
St Breward, Cornwall	67	Whitewell, Lancashire	142
St George, Conwy	294	Whitstable, Kent	138
St Helens, Merseyside	146	Whittlesford, Cambridgeshire	55
St Helier, Jersey	356	Wigan, Lancashire	142
St Ives, Cornwall	68	Wincanton, Somerset	187
St Keverne, Cornwall	69	Winchcombe, Gloucestershire	116
St Mawes, Cornwall	69	Winchester, Hampshire	125
St Neots, Cambridgeshire	54	Windermere, Cumbria	90
Stafford, Staffordshire	190	Winterton-on-Sea, Norfolk	155
Stanshope, Derbyshire	94	Wishaw, West Midlands	214
Stanton St John, Oxfordshire	173	Withypool, Somerset	188
Stathern, Leicestershire	144	Witney, Oxfordshire	174
Staveley, Cumbria	86	Wivenhoe, Essex	107
Steyning, West Sussex	207	Wolfscastle, Pembrokeshire	299
Stocksfield, Northumberland	162	Wokingham, Berkshire	46
Stocksfield on Tyne, Northumberland	162	Woodcote, Oxfordshire	174
Stodmarsh, Kent	137	Woodstock, Oxfordshire	175
Stoke Row, Oxfordshire	173	Wookey Hole, Somerset	188
Stoke-by-Nayland, Suffolk	195	Woolacombe, Devon	99
Stottesdon, Shropshire	178	Worcester, Worcestershire	221
Stow-on-the-Wold, Gloucestershire	115	Wrenbury, Cheshire	59
Stratford-Upon-Avon, Warwickshire	211	Wrexham	303
Stretton, Rutland	175		
Studland Bay, Dorset	103		
Sturminster Newton, Dorset	103		
Swindon, Wiltshire	218		
Talaton, Somerset	185		

To the Editor, Les Routiers Guide 2005
Report Form

☐ From my personal experience the following establishment should be a member of Les Routiers.

☐ From my personal experience the following establishment should not be a member of Les Routiers.

Establishment ....

PLEASE PRINT IN BLOCK CAPITALS

Address ....

....

....

I had ☐ lunch ☐ dinner ☐ stayed there on (date) ....

Details ....

....

....

....

....

....

....

....

....

....

....

Reports received up to the end of May 2004 will be used in the research of the 2005 edition.

☐ I am not connected in any way with management or proprietors.

Name ....

Address ....

....

....

As a result of your sending Les Routiers this report form, we may send you information on Les Routiers in the future.

If you would prefer not to receive such information, please tick this box ☐

To send your report...
Fax: Complete this form and fax it to 020 7370 4528
Post: Complete this form and mail it to
The Editor, FREEPOST, Les Routiers, 190 Earl's Court Road, London, SW5 9QG
E-mail: info@routiers.co.uk

To the Editor, Les Routiers Guide 2005
Report Form

☐ From my personal experience the following establishment should be a member of Les Routiers.

☐ From my personal experience the following establishment should not be a member of Les Routiers.

Establishment

PLEASE PRINT IN BLOCK CAPITALS

Address

I had ☐ lunch ☐ dinner ☐ stayed there on (date)

Details

Reports received up to the end of May 2004 will be used in the research of the 2005 edition.

☐ I am not connected in any way with management or proprietors.

Name

Address

As a result of your sending Les Routiers this report form, we may send you information on Les Routiers in the future.
If you would prefer not to receive such information, please tick this box ☐

To send your report...
Fax: Complete this form and fax it to 020 7370 4528
Post: Complete this form and mail it to
The Editor, FREEPOST, Les Routiers, 190 Earl's Court Road, London, SW5 9QG
E-mail: info@routiers.co.uk

To the Editor, Les Routiers Guide 2005
Report Form

☐ From my personal experience the following establishment should be a member of Les Routiers.

☐ From my personal experience the following establishment should not be a member of Les Routiers.

Establishment

PLEASE PRINT IN BLOCK CAPITALS

Address

I had ☐ lunch ☐ dinner ☐ stayed there on (date)

Details

Reports received up to the end of May 2004 will be used in the research of the 2005 edition.

☐ I am not connected in any way with management or proprietors.

Name

Address

As a result of your sending Les Routiers this report form, we may send you information on Les Routiers in the future.

If you would prefer not to receive such information, please tick this box ☐

To send your report...
Fax: Complete this form and fax it to 020 7370 4528
Post: Complete this form and mail it to
The Editor, FREEPOST, Les Routiers, 190 Earl's Court Road, London, SW5 9QG
E-mail: info@routiers.co.uk

To the Editor, Les Routiers Guide 2005

Report Form

☐ From my personal experience the following establishment should be a member of Les Routiers.

☐ From my personal experience the following establishment should not be a member of Les Routiers.

Establishment ....

PLEASE PRINT IN BLOCK CAPITALS

Address ....

....

....

I had ☐ lunch ☐ dinner ☐ stayed there on (date) ....

Details ....

....

....

....

....

....

....

....

....

....

....

Reports received up to the end of May 2004 will be used in the research of the 2005 edition.

☐ I am not connected in any way with management or proprietors.

Name ....

Address ....

....

....

As a result of your sending Les Routiers this report form, we may send you information on Les Routiers in the future.
If you would prefer not to receive such information, please tick this box ☐

To send your report...
Fax: Complete this form and fax it to 020 7370 4528
Post: Complete this form and mail it to
The Editor, FREEPOST, Les Routiers, 190 Earl's Court Road, London, SW5 9QG
E-mail: info@routiers.co.uk

To the Editor, Les Routiers Guide 2005
Report Form

☐ From my personal experience the following establishment should be a member of Les Routiers.

☐ From my personal experience the following establishment should not be a member of Les Routiers.

Establishment

Address

PLEASE PRINT IN BLOCK CAPITALS

I had ☐ lunch ☐ dinner ☐ stayed there on (date)

Details

Reports received up to the end of May 2004 will be used in the research of the 2005 edition.

☐ I am not connected in any way with management or proprietors.

Name

Address

As a result of your sending Les Routiers this report form, we may send you information on Les Routiers in the future.
If you would prefer not to receive such information, please tick this box ☐

To send your report...
Fax: Complete this form and fax it to 020 7370 4528
Post: Complete this form and mail it to
The Editor, FREEPOST, Les Routiers, 190 Earl's Court Road, London, SW5 9QG
E-mail: info@routiers.co.uk

To the Editor, Les Routiers Guide 2005
Report Form

☐ From my personal experience the following establishment should be a member of Les Routiers.

☐ From my personal experience the following establishment should not be a member of Les Routiers.

Establishment ....

PLEASE PRINT IN BLOCK CAPITALS

Address ....

....

I had ☐ lunch ☐ dinner ☐ stayed there on (date) ....

Details ....

....

....

....

....

....

....

....

....

....

....

....

Reports received up to the end of May 2004 will be used in the research of the 2005 edition.

☐ I am not connected in any way with management or proprietors.

Name ....

Address ....

....

....

As a result of your sending Les Routiers this report form, we may send you information on Les Routiers in the future.

If you would prefer not to receive such information, please tick this box ☐

To send your report...
Fax: Complete this form and fax it to 020 7370 4528
Post: Complete this form and mail it to
The Editor, FREEPOST, Les Routiers, 190 Earl's Court Road, London, SW5 9QG
E-mail: info@routiers.co.uk

To the Editor, Les Routiers Guide 2005

Report Form

☐ From my personal experience the following establishment should be a member of Les Routiers.

☐ From my personal experience the following establishment should not be a member of Les Routiers.

Establishment ....

PLEASE PRINT IN BLOCK CAPITALS

Address ....

....

....

I had ☐ lunch ☐ dinner ☐ stayed there on (date) ....

Details ....

....

....

....

....

....

....

....

....

....

....

....

Reports received up to the end of May 2004 will be used in the research of the 2005 edition.

☐ I am not connected in any way with management or proprietors.

Name ....

Address ....

....

As a result of your sending Les Routiers this report form, we may send you information on Les Routiers in the future.
If you would prefer not to receive such information, please tick this box ☐

To send your report...
Fax: Complete this form and fax it to 020 7370 4528
Post: Complete this form and mail it to
The Editor, FREEPOST, Les Routiers, 190 Earl's Court Road, London, SW5 9QG
E-mail: info@routiers.co.uk